Acknowledgements

The editor and publishers wish to thank the authors and the following publishers who have kindly given permission for the use of copyright material.

American Economic Association for articles: Jagdish Bhagwati, Arvind Panagariya and T.N. Srinivasan (2004), 'The Muddles over Outsourcing', *Journal of Economic Perspectives*, **18** (4), Fall, 93–114; David Hummels (2007), 'Transportation Costs and International Trade in the Second Era of Globalization', *Journal of Economic Perspectives*, **21** (3), Summer, 131–54.

Blackwell Publishing Ltd for articles: Alan V. Deardorff (2001), 'International Provision of Trade Services, Trade, and Fragmentation', *Review of International Economics*, **9** (2), May, 233–48; Joseph F. Francois and Ian Wooton (2001), 'Trade in International Transport Services: The Role of Competition', *Review of International Economics*, **9** (2), May, 249–61.

Brookings Institution for excerpts: Tony Warren and Christopher Findlay (2000), 'Measuring Impediments to Trade in Services', in Pierre Sauvé and Robert M. Stern (eds), *GATS 2000: New Directions in Services Trade Liberalization*, Chapter 3, 57–84; James R. Markusen (2005), 'Modeling the Offshoring of White-Collar Services: From Comparative Advantage to the New Theories of Trade and Foreign Direct Investment', in S. Collins and L. Bainard (eds), *Offshoring White Collar Work. Brookings Trade Forum, 2005*, 1–23, 32–4; J. Bradford Jensen and Lori G. Kletzer (2005), 'Tradable Services: Understanding the Scope and Impact of Services Offshoring', in S. Collins and L. Bainard (eds), *Offshoring White Collar Work. Brookings Trade Forum 2005*, 75–116, 131–3.

Elsevier Ltd for articles: Joseph Francois and Ian Wooton (2001), 'Market Structure, Trade Liberalization and the GATS', *European Journal of Political Economy*, **17**, 389–402; Stijn Claessens, Asli Demirgüç-Kunt and Harry Huizinga (2001), 'How Does Foreign Entry Affect Domestic Banking Markets?', *Journal of Banking and Finance*, **25**, 891–911; Denise Eby Konan and Keith E. Maskus (2006), 'Quantifying the Impact of Services Liberalization in a Developing Country', *Journal of Development Economics*, **81**, 142–62.

Joseph F. Francois and Kenneth A. Reinert for their own article: (1996), 'The Role of Services in the Structure of Production and Trade: Stylized Facts from a Cross-Country Analysis', *Asia-Pacific Economic Review*, **2** (1), April, 35–43.

Journal of Economic Integration for article: Terrie L. Walmsley and L. Alan Winters (2005), 'Relaxing the Restrictions on the Temporary Movement of Natural Persons: A Simulation Analysis', *Journal of Economic Integration*, **20** (4), December, 688–726.

Service Sector Activity: Data Needs for GATS 2000', in Robert M. Stern (ed.), *Services in the International Economy*, Chapter 4, 83–115.

World Bank via Copyright Clearance Center for excerpts: Richard H. Snape (1990), 'Principles in Trade in Services', in Patrick A. Messerlin and Karl P. Sauvant (eds), *The Uruguay Round: Services in the World Economy*, Chapter 1, 5–11; Brian Hindley (1990), 'Principles in Factor-related Trade in Services', in Patrick A. Messerlin and Karl P. Sauvant (eds), *The Uruguay Round: Services in the World Economy*, Chapter 2, 12–18; James Hodge (2002), 'Liberalization of Trade in Services in Developing Countries', in Bernard Hoekman, Aaditya Mattoo and Philip English (eds), *Development, Trade, and the WTO: A Handbook*, Chapter 24, 221–34, references.

Every effort has been made to trace all the copyright holders but if any have been inadvertently overlooked the publishers will be pleased to make the necessary arrangement at the first opportunity.

In addition the publishers wish to thank the Library at the University of Warwick, UK, and the Library of Indiana University at Bloomington, USA, for their assistance in obtaining these articles.

Introduction*

Bernard Hoekman

One of the stylized facts of economic development is that the share of services in GDP and employment rises as per capita incomes increase. In the lowest-income countries, services generate some 35–40 percent of GDP. This rises to over 70 percent of national income and employment in OECD countries. The expansion in the services-intensity of economies is driven by a number of factors, including income elasticities of demand that exceed 1 and the incentives for firms to spin off activities to specialized providers as the extent of the market expands. The latter is also reflected in greater international transactions, giving rise to processes variously called outsourcing, fragmentation, production sharing, offshoring, and splintering of the value chain. These phenomena reflect a mix of policy and technological changes that is reducing the cost of producing and trading services.

The process of globalization reflects an ever-increasing internationalization of production, consumption and trade in services as well as goods. Given relative labor abundance in many developing countries, modern information technologies are increasingly permitting cross-border, 'disembodied' trade in labor-intensive services. Well-known examples are call centers and back-office processing activities. More important, the competitiveness of goods-producing firms in open economies increasingly depends on access to low-cost and high-quality producer services – telecommunications, transport and distribution services, financial intermediation, and so on.

While the expanding importance of services in the economy has of course not gone unnoticed, services have not figured prominently in the economic growth and development literature, and have only recently been considered in the trade literature. Economic theory postulates that growth is a function of increases in the quantity and productivity of capital and labor inputs. It accords no special role to services.[1] Traditional international economics textbooks tend to assume (assert) that services are largely nontradable. Initially limited to a few path-breaking studies such as those by Baumol (1967), Fuchs (1968), and Hill (1977), starting in the 1980s more attention began to be devoted to services. One reason for increased attention was the emergence of services on the international policy agenda, largely as the result of US proposals to negotiate multilateral rules on policies affecting trade in services.[2] The initial response of most countries to the US initiative, put forward formally at the 1982 GATT Ministerial meeting, was guarded. One result was to mobilize the first contributions to the trade literature. The initial research effort suggested that many countries had a potential interest in liberalizing trade in services,[3] reflected, for example, in many of the poorest developing countries having a 'revealed comparative advantage' (RCA) in services (Hoekman, 1990).[4] This realization helped overcome some of the early resistance by developing countries to launching negotiations on trade in services in the Uruguay Round.[5]

A substantial amount of research has been undertaken since the mid-1980s on trade in services.[6] The papers included in these two volumes focus on the determinants of the internationalization of services, the impacts of policies affecting international services transactions, and international cooperation – the General Agreement on Trade in Services (GATS) and preferential trade agreements (PTAs) covering services. In this Introduction the included papers are briefly summarized and discussed along with other relevant papers and research findings.

Volume I. Part I   Determinants and Patterns of Trade in Services

Francois and Reinert (1996, Chapter I.1) document the role of services in economies at differing levels of development, using input–output tables to analyze the contribution of services activities to user industries and final (consumer) demand.[7] They note that the importance of services in relative terms increases as countries become richer, and that this is also reflected in an increasing variety of market services (product differentiation). They also observe that even if services are not traded directly, they are embodied in the output of both tradable and nontraded activities, and thus are a determinant of overall employment and productivity. The indirect exports of services embodied in a country's exports of goods can be quite large, with services accounting for the majority of the foreign exchange that is earned.

The rise in the share of services in output and employment as countries become richer reflects a number of factors. Common explanations include increasing specialization and exchange of services through the market ('outsourcing'), with an associated increase in variety and quality that may raise the productivity of firms and the welfare of final consumers, in turn increasing demand for purchased services and the fact that the scope for (labor) productivity in the provision of many 'consumer' services is less than in agriculture and manufacturing. The latter implies that over time the (real) costs of these services will rise relative to merchandise, as will the share of employment in services (Baumol, 1967; Fuchs, 1968).

Sapir (1993, Chapter I.2) notes that the growing role of services in domestic economies is the result of both demand and supply factors. On the demand side, the major impetus has come from firms that have shifted from providing services they require 'in-house' to purchasing these services outside the firm. On the supply side, the main factors have been technological change and deregulation. Sapir summarizes a number of distinct dimensions along which services can be differentiated from goods, and provides a methodological framework for analyzing the structure of the market for services. He argues that three essential features distinguish services from other economic activities: the degree of interaction required between providers and consumers; the extent of asymmetric information affecting transactions; and the degree of regulation of production and consumption. One implication is that considerations relating to consumer protection, prudential supervision and regulatory oversight often induce governments to require establishment by foreign providers or to reserve activities for government-owned or controlled entities.

Because services are often not storable, their exchange frequently requires the proximity of supplier and consumer – either providers have to move to the location of the buyer/consumer of a service, or vice versa. The significance of the proximity constraint for service transactions to be feasible means that 'trade' will often involve a mix of cross-border transactions and the local presence of suppliers. Asymmetric information and the resulting need for regulation also implies that regulatory regimes pertaining to temporary movement of people (visa restrictions; economic needs tests) and longer-term establishment (FDI policies) of service suppliers are important determinants of the feasibility of trade in services. All three factors also have important implications for the market structure that is observed in service industries. On the one hand, proximity requirements may imply the absence of scale economies, while on the other they give rise to potentially extensive product differentiation as services are tailored to individual consumers. However, regulation may generate market power as it gives rise to fixed costs. Indeed, such costs may be important across a range of services where regulatory requirements impose high barriers to entry and/or problems of asymmetric information require firms to invest in and maintain a reputation for quality.

An important economic characteristic of many services is their 'facilitating' role: services support ever finer specialization. As argued by Francois (1990, Chapter I.3), the growth of intermediation services is an important determinant of overall economic growth and development. Much of this intermediation activity facilitates transactions through space (transport, telecoms) or time (financial services) (Melvin, 1989). Francois argues that the increasing importance of producer services in modern (growing) economies reflects economies of scale and specialization. As firm size increases and labor specializes, more activity needs to be devoted to coordinating and organizing the core businesses of a company. This additional activity is partly outsourced to external service providers. Producer services therefore are not just differentiated inputs but play an important distinct role in coordinating the production processes needed to generate (differentiated) goods and to realize scale economies. The associated organizational innovations and expansion of 'logistics' (network) services yields productivity gains that in turn should affect economy-wide growth performance by enhancing the efficiency of production in all sectors. The associated cost reductions result in an increase in overall total factor productivity of firms and the economy as a whole.

Such producer services may of course be provided by foreign firms as well as domestic firms. However, because services are intangible and often difficult if not impossible to store they tend to be embodied in goods, information flows or in people. The implications of the need for proximity between providers and demanders for exchange to be feasible is one of the themes of Bhagwati (1984a), who describes the processes through which services are 'disembodied' or 'splintered' from goods or people as 'carriers'. Starting in the 1980s technological changes were increasingly making such processes more feasible. Trade in services may then expand as a result of the incentive to 'splinter' the production chain geographically, not just in terms of tangible inputs but also services.

Bhagwati notes that long-distance, cross-border exchange through telecommunications networks implies that the same forces that drive trade in goods will also apply to trade in those services where such splintering is possible. The same is true if international transactions occur through the physical movement of consumers to the location of service providers (for example, tourism), or via the temporary entry of service providers into the territory of a consumer (for example, consulting). In a statistical sense all the above transactions comprise trade and are registered as such in the balance of payments. They all involve exchanges between the resident of one country and that of another.

Modes of supply

Sampson and Snape (1985) developed a typology of trade in services that was largely taken up by negotiators in the design of the GATS (see Snape, 1990, Chapter I.4), called 'modes' in

GATS-speak. Mode 1, cross-border supply, applies when service suppliers resident in one country provide services in another country without either the supplier or buyer/consumer moving to the physical location of the other. Mode 2, consumption abroad, refers to a consumer resident in one country moving to the location of the supplier(s) to consume a service. Mode 3, commercial presence, refers to legal persons (firms) moving to the location of consumers on a long-term basis to sell services locally through the establishment of a foreign affiliate or branch.[8] Mode 4, presence of natural persons, refers to a process through which individual service suppliers move to the country of the consumer to provide the service.

Many of the early theoretical contributions on services in the trade literature employed the distinction between factor and non-factor services. This suggested that there was nothing special about services on either the analytical or the negotiation front. Trade in non-factor services can be regarded as being embodied in goods – and thus covered by GATT – while factor services (natural and legal persons) are not. The implication was that negotiating attention should center on FDI and the (temporary) movement of service suppliers – that is, international factor movement (Hindley, 1990, Chapter I.5).[9] Over time, however, it became increasingly apparent that the disembodied cross-border trade in services was not just a theoretical curiosity but was rapidly becoming more important as technological advances permitted services to be transformed into digitized bits of data that could be transported internationally through satellite and telecom networks.

A basic question that arises when thinking about trade in services is whether standard concepts and theories explaining the pattern of trade in goods apply given the complications arising from the existence of alternative modes of supply and the associated factor movement that may occur. A number of theorists focused on this starting in the mid-1980s driven by the policy discussion at the time on whether to launch negotiations on services under GATT auspices (see Feketekuty, 1988). They quickly concluded that standard concepts of comparative advantage and theories of the determinants of trade patterns (technology, endowments, the specific factors model) could be applied to services. Early contributions to this literature include Hindley and Smith (1984). Although modes of contesting services markets are more complex and this has implications for the pattern of trade, the fundamental concepts mostly carry over to the services case. Thus, the principle of comparative advantage continues to apply in an 'average' sense if trade in services is allowed (Deardorff, 1985, Chapter I.6).[10] The same applies to the welfare consequences of trade. Insofar as this involves factor movement standard tools and concepts can be applied, with welfare depending on what is assumed (observed) regarding the income accruing to the factors concerned and the nationality of the owners of the factors.

That said, there are also differences. One difference between services and goods is that goods do not fulfill the type of intermediation role many services do or generate the types of network externalities some service industries do – an issue discussed further below.[11] Another difference is that the predictions of the law of one price – that similar, close substitutes will have the same real price in different locations adjusted for transport costs – will not apply for many services. This is because of the characteristics of services – which will often require local factor inputs to be applied in a transaction. Thus, local factor prices will be a determinant of the prices prevailing in different markets. In addition, local regulation may differ across jurisdictions, impacting differentially on local costs. Indeed, the law of one price may not hold for goods either. Horn and Shy (1996) argue that once account is taken of the fact that many services are 'bundled' with goods, and that the associated services-input bundle is nontradable in the sense that it must be provided locally, in direct proximity to the consumer/buyer of the goods – think of maintenance, training, distribution, and so on – liberalization of trade in goods may not result in the integrated market that is often assumed in models and by policymakers. That is, the law of one price may not result for the goods concerned, because of the ancillary services that make up the 'product bundle'.

Much of the recent growth in cross-border services trade reflects so-called business process outsourcing (BPO) services, which occurs mostly through mode 1-type transactions. Mode 1 has become more controversial in policy terms as the absolute value of such trade has grown. Bhagwati, Panagariya and Srinivasan (2004, Chapter I.7) focus explicitly on the basic economics of mode 1, arguing against those claiming that this type of trade invalidates traditional trade theory by pointing out that mode 1 trade in services is analytically equivalent to a technical change that lowers the relative price (wage) of more skilled-intensive labor in the importing country. This will have associated distributional consequences among factors of production in that country, but generate an overall gain for the economy in the absence of significant adverse terms of trade effects.[12] Such adverse effects may be possible, but in itself this is not something that is specific to the trade being in services or occurring via mode 1. More likely is that such trade will raise productivity if it is an input or raise real incomes if it enters final demand. Bhagwati et al. note that to date the numbers of jobs affected by mode 1 trade in services have been small, in part because the share of total services transactions that involve international flows are just a small part of the total market for services that can be provided at arm's-length (in 'disembodied' form). They also note that much of the mode 1 trade that is observed is intra-firm – flows between a parent and affiliate firms – and that what matters is the net effect. Two-way trade in mode 1 services is important, that is, there is both 'insourcing' as well as outsourcing. Moreover, mode 1 imports are often associated with mode 3 'exports', so that the imports of mode 1 services are complemented by an income flow deriving from FDI in services abroad that supports the mode 1 imports.[13]

Boddewyn, Halbrich and Perry (1986, Chapter I.8) is an early paper focusing on mode 3, analyzing whether what has now become the standard paradigm to explain FDI – ownership, location and internalization incentives – carries over to service multinationals. They argue that it does, but also note that certain features of services are likely to have implications for the form that FDI takes. For example, franchising and leasing type arrangements are likely to be more prevalent, as for some services equity control of affiliates is not needed by the multinational.[14] Markusen (2005, Chapter I.9) is a recent exploration and synthesis of the extent to which the so-called 'knowledge-capital model' of FDI applies to services. They note that there are important differences. For services, physical transport costs need not hinge on distance, while conceptually FDI may involve local establishments that do not serve primarily as production nodes or plants, but rather as transit points for sale of home production to foreign markets. Furthermore, distance costs may be linked to problems of coordination when dealing with customers, rather than with problems linked to physical loading and shipping of goods.

Empirical research on the determinants of services FDI has concluded that services FDI tends to be market seeking and is positively correlated with prior FDI in the manufacturing and industry sectors. Both explanatory variables are intuitive in that they reflect the characteristics of services (non-storability in particular). Raff and Ruhr (2007), for example, develop a model of FDI in business services that predicts that FDI in business services should be affected by informational barriers to entry, and that these barriers are easier to overcome in markets in which there is already a significant US business presence. The implication is that the host market should have a larger effect on service FDI the larger the ratio of US FDI to local market size. They test the predictions of their model using panel data on US FDI in 23 host countries from 1976 to 1995 and find that its predictions cannot be rejected.[15]

Measurement issues: trade, productivity and policy

As mentioned, the approach taken in the GATS/WTO has been to define trade in services as comprising not just cross-border transactions (mode 1) and payments associated with the movement of providers and consumers (modes 4 and 2), but also the sales of foreign affiliates that have been established in host countries. The statistical concept of 'Foreign Affiliates Trade in Services' (FATS) statistics was created by statisticians in the late 1990s in the context of developing a new Manual on Statistics of International Trade in Services. The aim of the manual is to lay out agreed methodologies for defining and collecting data on transactions in services while ensuring consistency with existing international statistical standards (Karsenty, 2000). Sales of services by affiliates of foreign-owned firms are not regarded as trade in the national accounts or balance of payments – giving rise to the need to collect such data separately. As discussed by Whichard (2000, Chapter I.10), progress on collecting such statistics is being made, but the extent of available data remains limited. According to the WTO, the global value of cross-border services exports in 2007 was $3.3 trillion, or some 20 percent of world trade in goods and services. However, the share of services rises to almost 50 percent if transactions are measured in terms of direct and indirect value added content – that is, if trade is measured in terms of the value that is added by the processing of imported components into final products for export as opposed to measuring trade flows on the basis of the gross value of goods crossing the border (Escaith, 2008). If we add in the sales of services by foreign affiliates of multinational firms, then the value of trade in services rises further. Data for 15 OECD countries puts the value of such sales at some $1.5 trillion in 2007 (WTO, 2008).

Since the initial papers were written in the mid-1980s exploring what data were available on international transactions in services, a number of researchers have attempted to estimate the value of trade on the basis of concepts that accord with those that underlie the GATS definition of trade. Baldwin and Kimura (1998, Chapter I.11) is a careful attempt to measure transactions on the basis of ownership, as opposed to the location of factors of production, in order to better capture the close relationship between firms' cross-border trading activities and the sales and purchasing activities of their foreign affiliates. They propose supplementary accounting formats that classify cross-border and foreign affiliate activities on an ownership basis. One format combines net cross-border sales by Americans to foreigners, net sales by foreign affiliates of US firms to foreigners, and net sales of US firms to US affiliates of foreign firms to yield a figure that indicates net sales by Americans to foreigners. Another accounting format measures the value-added embodied in cross-border and foreign affiliate activities on an ownership basis.

Another strand in the empirical literature has focused on measuring productivity in the services sector, as this is important for the long-term growth prospects of countries given the rising share of services in GDP as countries become richer. Triplett and Bosworth (2000, Chapter I.12) report measures of labor and multifactor productivity for a range of US service industries. They also discuss the measurement difficulties that afflict productivity measurement for a number of service industries, due to the fact that it is often difficult to define what is the real output of a service sector. Their paper was part of a larger project, the results of which were summarized in a subsequent book (Triplett and Bosworth, 2004). Their conclusion is that productivity growth has been and can be significant for services, suggesting that the worries expressed by Baumol (1967) in his classic article are less relevant in today's world where technological changes are driving innovations in services as much, if not more, than in manufactures. Triplett and Bosworth (2004) note that during the 1990s, 19 million additional jobs were created in US services sectors, while growth was stagnant in the goods-producing sector. They show that productivity growth in distribution and financial services fueled much of the post-1995 expansion in US productivity and document how information technology and managerial innovations – such as outsourcing and specialization, as well as new concepts of retailing such as the 'big box' store format – helped to transform and accelerate productivity in these sectors. Purchased intermediate inputs also made a substantial contribution to labor productivity growth in the US, especially in the services industries that showed the greatest acceleration.

Inklaar, Timmer and van Ark (2007; 2008) and Havik, McMorrow, Röger and Turrini (2008, Chapter I.13) show that differences in aggregate productivity levels and growth rates are largely attributable to service sectors. That is, productivity levels/growth rates in manufacturing are relatively similar across countries compared to intermediate services. Higher services productivity growth in the post-1995 period for countries such as the US, Canada and the UK is only partially explained by information and communications technology investment/use. More important is total factor productivity (TFP) growth. This TFP growth is not observed for the Euro-land countries in their sample. Decomposition by industry suggests that much of the differential is due to variation in business services performance across countries.

An obvious question raised by this finding is what explains the divergence in performance (that is, what determines services productivity), and to what extent policy variables such as regulation, limits on entry into or scaling up of business services, investment restrictions, and so on affect services performance. This raises the question of the magnitude and incidence of policies that affect trade in services, an area in which a significant amount of work has been done in the last ten years

Part II Services Policies, Trade and Welfare

Because services are generally intangible, barriers to trade do not take the form of import tariffs. Instead, trade barriers take the form of prohibitions, quotas, and government regulation. Quotas may limit the quantity or value of imports of specific products for a given time period, or restrict the number or market share of foreign providers of services that are allowed to establish. Such discriminatory measures are often complemented by nondiscriminatory measures applying equally to foreign and domestic providers. These may consist of limitations on the number of firms allowed to contest a market, or on the nature of their operations. Frequently, this involves either a monopoly (telecommunications) or an oligopolistic market structure (insurance, air transport).

The magnitude and quality of available information on policies that restrict international trade in services is limited. In large part this reflects the immense difficulty of identifying and quantifying barriers to services trade, which in turn is a reflection of the historical nontradability of most services. One reason why there are detailed data on goods trade flows is that these flows are taxed – the data are an ancillary product of the application of tariffs on imports imposed at the border. As services are not observed crossing borders – at best factors of production (labor, suppliers) may be observed – governments need to survey economic activity in order to get a picture of trade in services.

Warren and Findlay (2000, Chapter I.14) survey much of the early quantitative literature investigating the effects of policy, including a major research effort undertaken by the Australian Productivity Commission.[16] They discuss many of the efforts to directly measure the extent of policy barriers on a sectoral and cross-country basis and the use of such measures – usually a policy index of some kind – to estimate the price or quantity effects of policies. They suggest that despite limited information, barriers to trade appear to be substantial, especially for modes 3 and 4. Although there are numerous methodological weaknesses associated with the efforts made to quantify the level and effects of services trade and investment policies, given the importance of services as inputs into production and as elements of final consumption, not surprisingly the papers surveyed suggest that barriers to trade and investment come at a high cost. A more recent cross-country effort to quantify barriers to trade in services is Gootiiz and Mattoo (2009; Chapter 4, Volume II,), discussed below.

The approach taken by many analysts seeking to quantify the magnitude of the trade restrictiveness of services policies is to estimate *ad valorem* tariff equivalents. A major problem in this connection, both conceptually and for empirical research, is to distinguish the effects of nondiscriminatory regulation from discriminatory policies. Regulations generally will increase fixed and/or variable costs of production for firms, and may result in a *de facto* or *de jure* exclusion of new entry, thereby increasing prices. Conversely, insofar as regulation is motivated by the characteristics of specific service industries – for example, network externalities, asymmetric information – such price impacts may be appropriate in social welfare terms. Modeling and assessing the effects of regulation – in particular whether and by how much policies raise costs as opposed to create rents (increase mark-ups) – is important from a national welfare perspective.

Dee, Hanslow and Phamduc (2003, Chapter I.15) assess the impacts of the policy barriers discussed by Warren and Findlay. The different policies are mapped into categories, depending on whether they affect entry and/or operations of firms, and are converted into *ad valorem* equivalents. These are then used to obtain estimates of the impacts of removal of the policy barriers. They conclude that the potential gains from liberalization are larger than from the removal of barriers to trade in goods, and that much of the gains would accrue to – and derive from – the services sectors concerned.

Jensen and Kletzer (2005, Chapter I.16) analyze which service activities are potentially 'exposed' to international trade, using the geographic concentration of service activities within the United States to identify which service activities are traded domestically. They find that there are more workers in tradable professional and business service industries than in manufacturing sectors and that workers in tradable sectors have higher skills and significantly higher wages. One result is that displacement rates are higher from tradable service industries than from nontradable: workers displaced from tradable service activities tend to be more educated, with higher earnings, than workers displaced from nontradable activities.

Konan and Maskus (2006, Chapter I.17), use a CGE model to investigate the potential effects of removing barriers to trade services in Tunisia. Increasing international competition on service markets will reduce what Konan and Maskus call the cartel effect – the mark-up of price over marginal cost that incumbents are able to charge due to restricted entry; and an attenuation of what they call the cost inefficiency effect – the fact that in an environment with limited competition the marginal costs of incumbents are likely to be higher than if entry were allowed. The latter is most important as inefficiency imposes a cost on all sectors and households that consume the services involved. They conclude that removing policies that increase costs can have much greater positive effects on national welfare than the removal of merchandise trade barriers – by up to a factor of seven or eight. Instead of the 'standard' 0.5 to 1 percent increase in welfare from goods liberalization, introducing greater competition on services markets that removes cost inefficiencies raises the gains to 6–8 percent. These large effects of services liberalization reflect both the importance of services in the economy and the extent to which they tend to be protected. The Konan/Maskus study, and earlier papers such as Kalirajan et al. (2000), Nguyen-Hong (2000), and Hoekman and Konan (2001), suggest it is important that empirical work focusses on the effects of policies on mark-ups and costs.

Konan and Maskus also note that the adjustment costs associated with service-sector reforms may be lower than that due to goods liberalization, as many services will continue to be produced locally and thus generate demand for labor. While this is intuitive, less so is their finding that comprehensive reforms that span both services and goods trade will generate less need for factors to be reallocated across industries than just goods liberalization alone. Given that in practice the focus of trade reforms has been on goods, not services, an implication is that past reform programs undertaken by many developing countries may have generated excessive adjustment, insofar as subsequent services liberalization will generate factor flows that may go in the opposite direction. Thus, their analysis has important implications for the sequencing of liberalization – it may be best to proceed on a broad front, targeting both goods and services markets.

Rutherford, Tarr and Shepotylo (2005, Chapter I.18) employ a CGE model to assess the impact on Russia of trade policy reforms. Their model includes data on 55,000 households allowing assessments of the impacts on income distribution and poverty as well as real income. Their analysis includes FDI (mode 3) and allows for endogenous productivity effects. They conclude that in the medium term virtually all households would gain from liberalization, with increases in real incomes in the range of 2 to 25 percent of base year household income. Liberalization of FDI in business services sectors and endogenous productivity effects flowing from this drive much of the impact. The gains from FDI liberalization in services alone are 5.3 percent of the value of Russian consumption, and represent more than 70 percent of the total value of the potential gains from reform. Thus, as was found by Konan and Maskus for Tunisia, the most important driver of potential welfare gains from liberalization are removal of barriers against FDI in services sectors. However, they also find that many households may lose in the short term, making it important to put in place effective safety nets to protect the poorest members of society during the transition.

Kox and Lejour (2006, Chapter I.19) analyze the impact of policy heterogeneity across countries in creating trade and investment costs for service firms doing business in other countries. Service providers have to comply with different rules in each foreign market where they operate. Complying with these regulations causes fixed market-entry costs, specific for each export market. The authors develop an indicator for bilateral policy heterogeneity for EU countries – based on the OECD dataset reported in Nicoletti (2001) and Nicoletti and Scarpetta (2003) – which is used as a proxy for the costs of policy heterogeneity. They then explain bilateral services trade and services FDI in the EU using a gravity model augmented with their policy heterogeneity indicator. They find a strong negative impact of policy heterogeneity costs on services trade and FDI. The empirical results are used for assessing the potential impacts of the Services Directive proposed in 2004 (Commission of the European Communities, 2004), which would have reduced policy-related market-entry costs for services providers. Kox and Lejour project that the original 2004 Services Directive might have increased intra-EU services trade by 30 percent to 62 percent and FDI in services by 18 percent to 36 percent. The revised directive that was adopted in 2006 is unlikely to have such effects given that key aspects of the initial proposal – in particular acceptance of home country regulation – were removed.

Many researchers have used CGE methods to assess the likely impacts of services liberalization in part because the panel datasets that are needed for cross-country empirical analysis of the effects of reforms do not exist. As a result, empirical work on the link between policy and economic performance has tended to be limited to cross-section regression analysis. An example is Mattoo, Rathindran and Subramanian (2006), who find that controlling for other determinants of growth, countries with open financial and telecommunications sectors grew, on average, about 1 percentage point faster than other countries. Fully liberalizing both the telecommunications and the financial services sectors was associated with an average growth rate 1.5 percentage points above that of other countries.

Eschenbach and Hoekman (2006, Chapter I.20) utilize three indicators of the extent of policy reform in banking, non-bank financial services and infrastructure, constructed by the EBRD spanning the period 1990–2004 to investigate the impact of changes in services policy on economic performance over this period for a sample of 20 transition economies. The value of the policy indices is set at zero for 1989, so that the 2004 value provides a measure of the progress that has been made by countries in converging to 'best practice' standards. They find that changes in policies towards financial and infrastructure services, including telecommunications, power and transport, are highly correlated with inward FDI. Controlling for regressors commonly used in the growth literature, they conclude that measures of services policy reform are statistically significant explanatory variables for the post-1990 economic performance of the transition economies in the sample. They also note that if instead of the services policy indices measures of the investment climate or governance indicators are used, similar results obtain. They conclude that the investment climate variables used in much of the empirical growth and development literature may be capturing services-related policies. More important, given that services policies can be directly influenced by governments, whereas it is less clear what needs to be done to improve the investment climate or 'governance', greater emphasis on collection of data on services policies could help identify the policy handles that should be targeted by policymakers.

Deardorff (2001, Chapter I.21) illustrates the importance of transport-related costs as a barrier to trade in goods (and services), and the potential welfare gains from actions that lower such costs. These gains may be much larger proportionately than those that can be obtained from merchandise trade policy reforms insofar as the transport costs generate real resource costs as opposed to rents. With tariff liberalization there is redistribution from producers and the government (tariff revenue) to consumers, so that gains are limited to removal of the deadweight losses associated with taxing trade. Lowering trade service (transport) costs also results in the recovery of deadweight losses, but not the redistribution of tariff revenue. Whether the net welfare gains to cost reduction exceed those from an equivalent tariff reduction depends on the size of the reduction in costs. However, insofar as policy requires redundant procedures and duplication of fixed costs the potential gains from liberalization of 'trade services' are likely to be large.

Actions by governments to remove policies restricting competition in transport, and, more importantly, technological change have resulted in a dramatic fall in international transport costs in the post Second World War period. Hummels (2007, Chapter I.22) summarizes some of the estimates of how much different types of transport costs have fallen, and argues that the decline in air freight and the logistics associated with rapid movement of goods in particular has been a critical input into the process of global integration that has occurred in recent decades.

Francois and Wooton (2001, Chapter I.23; 2010), examine the interaction between the different modes of market access liberalization in services – cross-border and establishment – and the prevailing market structure in a domestic services industry. They develop a simple model of a domestic service sector that is imperfectly competitive (acts as a cartel) and in which there are barriers to cross-border competition ('trade costs'). They then investigate the implications of lowering these barriers and giving the foreign firm access to domestic consumers through establishment (FDI or mode 3). They illustrate that in such a setting domestic firms have an incentive to accommodate the entry of a foreign firm by inviting it to establish (FDI) and join the domestic cartel. If trading costs affecting the use of mode 1 remain high enough, the effect of foreign entry through mode 3 will be welfare reducing for the domestic country as it results in part of the rents generated by the cartel going to the foreign firm. This paper illustrates one of the ways in which there are interdependencies across modes of supply and the policies affecting the feasibility (cost) of using alternative modes. In their case, as the costs of mode 1 fall (for whatever reason), the incentive for domestic oligopolistic sectors to accommodate foreign competitors through welfare-reducing establishment rises. The policy implication is that there is a need for active domestic competition law enforcement in such instances.

A necessary but not sufficient condition for free trade in services is the elimination of discrimination between alternative sources of supply. Thus, foreign products/providers should be subject to regulations that are no less favorable than those applied to domestic products/ providers (that is, national treatment), and all foreign products/providers should be subject to the same barriers, if any (that is, nondiscrimination or most-favored-nation (MFN) treatment). Liberalization then refers to actions that reduce discrimination. However, reducing discrimination may not result in a greater volume of international transactions. If government policies support a monopoly, national treatment and MFN will have no effect, as entry is barred to all potential sources, whether foreign or domestic. In such cases greater competition will require a change in domestic regulatory policies. As discussed below, assessing the interaction between domestic (nondiscriminatory) regulation and discriminatory (trade) policies is a major area for further research.

A challenge for the analysis of the effects of policies is to consider the relationships between modes of supply for a specific service and the 'vertical' relationships between margin services or producer service inputs and other parts of the economy. Thus, the potential implications of trade liberalization in services are tied closely to the mode of liberalization (establishment or cross-border trade) and to the underlying market structure. Because many services operate as margin sectors (facilitating exchange, such as banks in the savings–investment market and transport firms in the international goods market), the implications of liberalization are closely tied to gains from trade in other sectors. From the perspective of quantifying trade barriers, much depends on how policies impact on different modes of supply and whether these modes are complements or substitutes. If they are substitutes, a prohibitive policy on one mode may not have much effect if another mode can be used. If the unconstrained mode is the most efficient one, the policy is redundant in terms of its impact on trade. If it is not the first-best mode, the effect of the policy is equivalent to the difference in costs involved in shifting across modes, giving rise to standard deadweight losses. Conversely, if modes are complements, a very liberal policy with respect to one mode may 'hide' the fact that in practice access is highly restricted.

Yet another challenge is to determine whether observed price–cost margins or estimated tariff equivalents reflect real costs (red tape) or rents. This is very important for the estimation of the welfare consequences of policy reform. If the policies generate real costs, removing them may give rise to much greater welfare gains than is the case if the policies generate rents that are captured by domestic agents. In the 'waste' or real costs case, a policy that restricts the most efficient mode will not just generate deadweight losses, but also a social cost equivalent to the amount consumed times the difference in cost entailed by the less efficient mode. In the 'rent' case, policy reforms (liberalization) will mostly involve a redistribution of income across agents. Generally it will involve income being transferred away from producers to consumers, and transfers between factors of production. However, if there are rents there is also the possibility that policy reforms result in international transfers from domestic producers to foreign firms. This can easily arise in instances where liberalization is partial and is associated with entry by a few foreign firms into an imperfectly competitive domestic market. The extreme case is one where a domestic monopoly is transferred to foreign ownership without any change in market structure.

Hodge (2002, Chapter I.24) reviews the theory and evidence on gains from services trade for developing countries, drawing on examples of specific sectors and liberalization episodes. He emphasizes the importance of putting in place appropriate regulatory frameworks and promotion of effective competition through appropriate development of institutions. He also discusses issues relating to adjustment costs and the need for sequencing of reforms so as to reduce such costs.

Whalley (2004) assesses the extant quantitative literature that seeks to evaluate the potential impacts of global services trade liberalization, with a special focus on impacts on developing countries. He argues that a major problem with the literature is that the heterogeneity of service activities is typically ignored in quantitative studies, even though this may have important implications for the effects of services trade liberalization. One of the issues stressed by Whalley is that an implication of the fact that many services are 'margin' or intermediation services is that the welfare impacts from partial liberalization of services trade can be negative. Because liberalization involves a fall in prices of goods and thus greater consumption/trade, the associated increase in aggregate intermediation costs may exceed the efficiency gains derived from lower 'unit' intermediation costs.

The basic message that emerges from these papers is that liberalization of services matters, perhaps much more than trade in goods, but that there is also a lot of uncertainty. Clearly much depends on how well the characteristics and economic functions of different services are captured, the accuracy of estimated or assumed impacts on costs and prices of services, whether policies create rents or simply raise costs, and if there are rents, what share accrues to foreign factors. These are all issues where the current state of knowledge is still quite limited. Improving our knowledge on such matters requires more in-depth, country-specific, time-series analysis as well as sector-specific research. That said, the positive TFP effects suggested by theoretical analyses that incorporate differentiated producer services is observed in the firm-level datasets that have recently become available. For example, in studies of the Czech Republic and Chile, respectively, Arnold, Javorcik and Mattoo (2007) and Fernandes and Paunov (2008) analyze the effects of allowing foreign providers greater access to services industries on the productivity of manufacturing industries relying on services inputs. The results show a positive relationship between FDI in services and the performance of domestic firms in manufacturing.

Sectoral and 'mode of supply' studies

The importance of the financial sector for economic growth has long been documented. The empirical work on finance tends to use financial development indicators such as the size of the banking sector, the degree of private sector involvement in financial services, and cost measures (interest rate spreads, and so on) as independent variables in growth regressions. Trade in financial services has not figured prominently until recently. One of the first papers to focus on the effects of barriers to financial services trade is Claessens, Demirgüç-Kunt and Huizinga (2001, Chapter I.25). They ask whether the entry of foreign banks makes domestic banks more competitive. Using bank-level data for 80 countries for 1988–95, including data on the extent of foreign ownership in national banking markets, they compare net interest margins, overheads, taxes paid, and the profitability of foreign and domestic banks. They note that the comparative functions of foreign banks and domestic banks is very different in developing and industrial countries, possibly because of a different customer base, different bank procedures, and different regulatory and tax regimes. In developing countries foreign banks tend to have greater profits, higher interest margins, and higher tax payments than do domestic banks. In industrial countries it is the domestic banks that have greater profits, higher interest margins, and higher tax payments.[17] Claessens, Demirgüç-Kunt and Huizinga show that increasing the foreign share of bank ownership reduces profitability and overhead expenses in domestically owned banks. The number of foreign entrants matters more than their market share, suggesting that they affect local bank competition more on entry rather than after gaining a substantial market share. These effects hold even when controlling for the fact that foreign banks may be attracted to markets with certain characteristics, such as low banking costs.

The literature on this subject tends to find a positive link between financial sector openness and economic growth performance.[18] Given that developing countries tend to have higher restrictions on foreign competition, this points to a significant potential growth bonus for developing countries who move from closed regimes toward regimes comparable (in terms of openness) to those of the OECD countries. What matters most is to ensure a contestable market – while foreign participation is an important source of new knowledge and products, benefits depend importantly on precluding the creation or maintenance of significant policy-based barriers to entry that create rents for incumbents.

An important intermediation service – especially for international trade in goods – is maritime shipping. This remains an industry characterized by a toleration of imperfect competition, reflected in exemptions from antitrust law for liner conferences, cargo reservation schemes, restrictions on foreign ownership of ports, and bans on foreign participation in cabotage. In assessing the implications of imperfect competition in international shipping for the gains from trade in goods, Francois and Wooton (2001, Chapter I.26) argue that, at the extreme, monopolization of trade routes can lead to up to half the gains from trade liberalization being lost as shippers increase prices to take advantage of increased market power (which follows from tariff reductions). Their simulations involve an assessment of relative gains, given variations in market structure in the shipping sector. In Africa, for example, their experiments suggest that monopoly in shipping implies that, with tariff reductions in export markets, the resulting welfare gains are only 50 percent of those realized if the shipping lines are competitive.

Fink, Mattoo and Neagu (2002, Chapter I.27) is an empirical analysis of the impact of maritime liner arrangements and private restrictive practices, as well as formal government policies that restrict the ability of foreign providers to supply shipping services and barriers to competition in the provision of port services on transport prices for goods shipped to the US from developing countries.[19] They conclude that private anticompetitive practices appear to have a larger effect on prices than government policies that restrict foreign competition, although the latter are also a statistically significant factor affecting prices. Port-related excess costs due to limitations on competition in port services account for one-third of the total potential gain from liberalization.[20]

Cho (1988, Chapter I.28) highlights some policy lessons from the opening of the Korean insurance market in the 1980s. Cho stresses the importance of market structure and policies that restrict competition, analyzing how the existence of limited competition in the Korean insurance market motivated efforts (successful) on the part of US companies to gain access to the market, in the process strengthening the coalition opposing more general (MFN) liberalization. This paper provides some empirical evidence for the theoretical framework developed in Francois and Wooton (2001, Chapter I.23) to analyze the incentives for a domestic cartel confronting foreign pressure to open the market to competition to allow in only a few foreign firms.

The foregoing papers focus on specific services. An alternative approach is to focus instead on specific modes of supply. As most of the attention in the literature has centered on modes 1 and 3 – many of the papers already discussed deal with these two modes – what follows focuses on modes 2 and 4. Trade in health services is an example of mode 2 type transactions insofar as patients move to the location of providers for treatment. While other modes will surely also play a role – for example, providers may want to establish a commercial presence (engage in FDI) or send health providers abroad on a temporary basis – there is great potential for expanding mode 2 trade. A major barrier to such trade is the lack of portability of health insurance in OECD countries. For example, US federal or state government reimbursement of medical expenses is limited to certified facilities in the United States or in a specific US state. This constraint is also significant because it deters elderly persons from retiring abroad. Those who do retire abroad are often forced to return home to obtain affordable medical care. The potential impact of permitting portability could be substantial. Mattoo and Rathindran (2006) find that extending health insurance coverage to overseas care for just fifteen types of tradable treatments could produce savings for the United States of over $1 billion a year even if only one in ten American patients travel abroad. The lower costs of health services abroad offer the opportunity to extend medical benefits to people who currently are not insured.

Perhaps the greatest potential gains from trade are associated with liberalization of mode 4 – temporary movement of service suppliers. Temporary movement offers arguably a partial solution to the dilemma of how international migration is best managed given the substantial political resistance that exists against it in many high-income countries. It could allow the realization of gains from trade while addressing some of the concerns of opponents to migration in host countries, while also attenuating the brain drain costs for poor source countries that can be associated with permanent migration. Walmsley and Winters (2005, Chapter I.29) show that if OECD countries were to expand temporary access to foreign service-providers by the equivalent of 3 percent of their labor force, the global gains would be greater than those associated with full liberalization of merchandise trade. Both developed and developing countries would share in these gains, and they would be largest if both high-skilled mobility and low-skilled mobility were permitted. There are of course large political obstacles that must be overcome for such mode 4 trade expansion to be feasible, but movement towards liberalization may be possible if designed appropriately. This is one area where the GATS could play an important role.[21]

The conclusion suggested by the empirical literature is that the potential gains from services trade and investment liberalization are substantial. While partial reforms may not be welfare-enhancing for reasons discussed previously, both theory and the evidence suggests that in practice benefits are likely to outweigh costs by a large margin especially if accompanied by goods trade liberalization, and that the potential gains from full services liberalization may well be several times that from goods liberalization. Insofar as the markets concerned are not competitive and policies prohibit new entry, opening up to competition (both foreign and domestic) should lead to major welfare improvements.[22] The major qualification to this presumption pertains to ensuring that the regulatory preconditions to ensure both equity and efficiency have been satisfied. As discussed below, this is one of the major concerns of many governments, and is a key factor limiting the use that is being made of the GATS. One important issue here concerns the sequencing of reforms. A case can be made that the weight of empirical evidence implies that domestic regulatory reform needs to be put ahead of removing policies that discriminate against foreign firms in that the former is likely to generate larger welfare payoffs. However, as discussed below, from a negotiating perspective it is easier to focus on discriminatory policies – indeed, that is the traditional domain of trade talks. Insofar as domestic, nondiscriminatory policies matter more for efficiency and growth, there is a risk that the trade negotiating process may divert attention away from the policies that should be addressed on a priority basis at the domestic level.

Volume II. Part I   The GATS: Genesis and State of Play

A major motivation for much of the research that is collected in the volume was the launch of negotiations to liberalize trade in services. Such negotiations were initiated in the GATT in 1986 with the launch of the Uruguay Round. They have also become prominent in the context of regional integration agreements, in particular the EU, but also more recent regional initiatives. The literature on negotiations on services and the GATS is large, and only a few papers are included in this set of readings.[23] Drake and Nicolaïdis (1992, Chapter II.1) discuss the genesis and intellectual foundations of the GATS. They survey much of the early policy-oriented literature, and document both the important role played by industry interest groups in pushing services on the negotiating agenda, and the role of epistemic communities in influencing the thinking and discussions of how to structure an international agreement.

Hoekman (1996, Chapter II.2) assesses the outcome of the Uruguay Round negotiations, briefly summarizes the main features of the GATS and discusses its strengths and weaknesses. He concludes that coverage of sector-specific commitments on national treatment and market access is limited, and that the GATS effectively was limited to partial 'locking in' of policies that had already been implemented by members on a unilateral basis. That is, the Uruguay Round did not deliver any actual liberalization. For many developing countries the coverage of specific commitments was well below 50 percent of all services and modes of supply. Adlung and Roy (2005, Chapter II.3) update Hoekman's assessment of the coverage of commitments, and find that very little progress was made in extending the coverage, including through provisional requests and offers in the six years following the launch of new negotiations on services in 2000. They argue that this lack of progress suggests there is need to reconsider the use of traditional request–offer negotiation modalities.

Gootiiz and Mattoo (2009, Chapter II.4) use a new database on services trade barriers compiled at the World Bank to assess the extent to which GATS commitments lock in applied policies. They conclude that there is a very significant gap between applied and 'bound' policies, and that the offers that were put on the table in the Doha Round at the time of writing did relatively little to reduce the water in the commitments of WTO members. They also document that applied policies in a number of sectors are much more restrictive than in others, with mode 4 being the least open.

The economic fundamentals analyzed in the papers included in this volume and cited in the references suggest that from a development perspective services should be center stage in multilateral negotiations. The WTO can potentially help to improve services performance by inducing countries to liberalize access to markets or to (pre-) commit to doing so, thus increasing competition. An important question is how large the incentives are for countries to use the multilateral process/mechanisms. Hoekman (2008, Chapter II.5) explores a number of hypotheses why the GATS may not be as effective as the GATT was to induce countries to make commitments to bind policies and reduce levels of protection. These include more limited scope in the services context for traditional reciprocity-driven market access negotiations given the importance of regulatory policies and that inefficient service industries will generate costs for all downstream sectors. The latter suggests that unilateral reform incentives may be larger than is true for trade in goods. In practice most reforms that have been implemented by developing countries have been autonomous. Hoekman argues that reciprocity can play less of a role because exporters of services are often not big, so the standard political economy of negotiations breaks down: opposition to reform and liberalization cannot be counterbalanced by export interests seeking better access to foreign services markets. Moreover, the importance of regulation implies that trade negotiators cannot simply employ the tools of their trade to incrementally change regulatory regimes – this can easily be welfare reducing. The prospect of negative outcomes is enhanced if account is taken of the factors analyzed by Cho, Francois and Wooton and others – trading partners may be more interested in sharing the rents created by policy than in pushing for free entry and efficient regulation.

An implication is that the focus of attention should be on strengthening and maintaining a robust capacity for identifying, understanding and designing the domestic regulatory reforms that need to be undertaken in services in order to enhance the efficiency of the economy and bolster economic growth prospects. The strategy pursued by China in the context of its accession to the WTO illustrates how trade negotiations can be used to good national advantage. As documented by Mattoo (2003, Chapter II.6), China's GATS commitments represent the most radical services reform program negotiated in the WTO. China promised to eliminate most restrictions on foreign entry and ownership, as well as most forms of discrimination against foreign firms. Realizing the potential gains from this liberalization will require the implementation of complementary regulatory reform and the appropriate sequencing of reforms. Three issues, in particular, are highlighted by Mattoo: (i) the fact that initial restrictions on the geographical scope of services liberalization could encourage the further agglomeration of economic activity in certain regions in a sub-optimal way, and this may not be reversed completely by subsequent country-wide liberalization; (ii) the remaining restrictions on foreign ownership, even if temporary, may dampen the incentives of foreign investors to improve firm performance; and (iii) improved prudential and pro-competitive regulation is necessary to deliver the benefits of liberalization in key sectors such as financial services, basic telecommunications and other network-based services.

Eschenbach and Hoekman (2006, Chapter II.7) analyze the extent to which the EU-15 and 16 transition economies used the GATS to commit to service sector policy reforms. GATS commitments are compared with the evolution of actual policy stances over time. While there is substantial variance across transition economies on both actual policies and GATS commitments, they find an 'inverse relationship' between the depth of GATS commitments and the 'quality' of actual services policies as assessed by the private sector. In part this can be explained by the fact that the prospect of EU accession made the GATS less relevant as a commitment device for many of the transition countries concerned. However, for many of the non-EU accession candidates the WTO seems to be a weak commitment device. A possible explanation is that the small size of the markets concerned generates weak external enforcement incentives. Their findings suggest greater collective investment by WTO members in monitoring and transparency is needed to increase the benefits of WTO membership to small countries.

Many observers have expressed concerns that the GATS will deprive regulators of the ability to achieve social objectives. This is clearly a factor explaining the reluctance of many countries to make new commitments or expand on existing ones. The challenge is to achieve a balance between improving market access for foreign providers while preserving desirable regulatory freedom. Four chapters discuss various dimensions of the 'access–regulation constraint'. Kirkpatrick and Parker (2005) focus on the law and economics of one of the most sensitive sectors: environmental services, particularly water distribution. Their discussion is motivated by concerns that liberalization of water services under the GATS would severely restrict the ability to regulate and ensure delivery of services in the pursuit of public policy objectives such as universal service, and that increased private provision would result in a concentration of new investment and services delivery on higher-income consumers in urban areas and higher prices. They assess the available evidence relating to the interface between domestic regulation of water services, the experience with liberalization and GATS rules on environmental services, and conclude that liberalization (and thus specific commitments to that effect in the GATS) should be conditioned on having in place an appropriate regulatory framework and the capacity to implement it. They also call for greater ex ante assessments of the likely benefits and costs of policy changes in this sector.

Adlung (2006, Chapter II.8) is an in-depth discussion of what is and what is not subject to GATS rules and disciplines when it comes to the coverage of public services. The scope of GATS disciplines in this area has become the subject of some concern for many NGOs in particular. Governments can and do reserve specific activities for provision by the State – in principle providing a mechanism for precluding private provision of certain services. GATS Art. I:3(b) states that the GATS does not apply to measures affecting trade in services 'supplied in the exercise of governmental authority'. There is some uncertainty what this means and there is little agreement in the relevant literature. Most studies take the view that in practice many 'public' services will fall within the sectoral coverage of the GATS and that the implied constraints on policy remain limited as long as governments do not make market access commitments in the areas concerned. However, as noted by Adlung, since the transparency and predictability effects associated with such commitments may help to attract investment and to expand sector segments that are open to private participation (for example, language training or higher education), the question arises whether and how governments can commit to access conditions in some segments without compromising their ability to exercise their 'governmental authority' in others (for example, primary and secondary education).

Evans (2003, Chapter II.9) and Trolliet and Hegarty (2003, Chapter II.10) focus on two sectors where regulation is prominent – energy services and accountancy. Evans examines the issues and prospects for deepening GATS commitments in energy services. As in other service industries, there has been a shift from government planning and control in the energy sector toward greater competition and private ownership and investment. However, domestic regulations continue to create unnecessary and costly impediments to the supply of energy services on a competitive non-discriminatory basis. Evans argues that the GATS classification system and disciplines needs to be augmented to allow for assurances for third party access to essential facilities, regulatory transparency, competition safeguards, and independent regulation. A precondition for deeper energy services trade commitments is likely to be provisions ensuring the right of governments to pursue environmental protection, energy efficiency, energy security and other public policy objectives.

The accountancy industry, discussed by Trolliet and Hegarty (2003, Chapter II.10), provides another illustration of the tension between regulation and liberalization, as the latter is conditional on governments accepting/recognizing each other's regulatory regimes. An important question is whether the WTO is the appropriate forum to discuss regulatory standards, a subject that is addressed in other international fora. Accountancy was one of the professional services that became the focus of a work program under GATS auspices after the conclusion of the Uruguay Round, which was intended to lead to additional, deeper commitments upon reaching agreement on stronger multilateral disciplines as regards domestic regulation – such as qualification requirements, standards and licensing procedures. Trolliet and Hegarty discuss the experience of the Working Party, which among other things established guidelines for mutual recognition agreements in the accountancy sector in 1998. They conclude that the WTO/ GATS has not been a force for liberalization in this sector, in part because there has not been any focus on defining a positive agenda for reform. A precondition for the GATS to work as a 'lock-in' device is that there is first agreement on a framework of regulatory principles, something that will need to be developed elsewhere.[24]

A major role of the WTO is enforcement of negotiated commitments through dispute settlement. There were two major services disputes during 1995–2010, as well as a number of goods trade disputes that had major services dimensions.[25] Neven and Mavroidis (2006, Chapter II.11) focus on a dispute brought by the US against Mexico. At issue in the case were the conditions under which foreign telecom operators could terminate calls in Mexico. This case, the first to involve only GATS provisions, was also the first to deal with telecommunication services and the rules agreed in the so-called Reference paper on pro-competitive regulatory principles. The US argued that the Mexican regulation of termination charges was not in conformity with the obligations contained in the Reference paper in that, *inter alia*, termination charges were not cost-oriented and that Mexico had set up a cartel of telecom operators. The authors briefly describe the Mexican regulations in dispute and the relevant provisions of the Reference paper, and then go on to analyze whether and how termination charges are covered by the Reference paper. They are critical of the framework of analysis constructed by the panel on this issue, noting that the panel effectively interpreted the GATS agreement as imposing a discipline on exports. They also argue that the interconnection provision of the Reference paper is applied by the panel to a market for which it was not designed (essential facilities); that the criterion used to determine if the termination fees charged by Telmex were cost-oriented – long-run average incremental cost – is open to question; that it is not clear that cartels fall within the scope of the Reference paper; and that the panel's interpretation of what is 'anti-competitive' behavior is not fully consistent with antitrust practice.

Pauwelyn (2005, Chapter II.12) discusses the second GATS dispute, a complaint by Antigua and Barbuda concerning US policies that prohibit foreign suppliers from offering gambling and betting services to US consumers over the Internet. The US had made a mode 1 commitment in the sector that includes gambling services. The question was whether this precluded a Member from banning the provision of the service on a non-discriminatory basis, that is, through domestic regulation. The GATS declare market access restrictions (such as import quotas or limitations on the number of service suppliers) to be, in principle, prohibited if a specific commitment to that effect is made. In contrast, domestic regulations (such as internal taxes, standards, and safety requirements) are only prohibited when discriminatory or more trade restrictive than necessary. Pauwelyn argues that a domestic regulation should not be regarded as a market access restriction simply because it has the effect of banning certain imports. By broadly interpreting the *per se* prohibited market access restrictions exhaustively listed in Article XVI GATS, the Appellate Body in the online gambling case considerably expanded the reach of GATS prohibitions from explicitly numerical, quantitative restrictions to include also substantive, qualitative regulations applied indistinctly to overseas and domestic suppliers. Pauwelyn worries that this may well mean that, with the stroke of a pen, the validity of scores of domestic services regulations, including those that are non-discriminatory, are threatened. The result could be to seriously undermine the regulatory autonomy of WTO members beyond anything imagined by the drafters of the WTO treaty, in effect giving additional cause to NGOs opposing international commitments to argue that the GATS hollows out domestic regulatory autonomy.

What these cases reveal is that it is not necessarily clear what the implications are of existing rules and commitments, and that the rule-making agenda is as important as the market access agenda. Both cases involved the US, the first as the plaintiff, the second as the respondent. Noteworthy is that in the second case the plaintiff was an extremely small country, illustrating the importance of the WTO DSU for such countries – it is very unlikely that Antigua would have been able to get the attention of the US on the matter through bilateral channels. While this is clearly a major positive dimension of the WTO framework, it remains a mercantilist body. One implication of this is that small countries are less likely to be the subject of disputes. As discussed above, this may reduce the value of WTO membership for such nations.

Jara and del Carmen Doménguez (2006, Chapter II.13) and Mattoo (2005, Chapter II.14) discuss the negotiating agenda and process in the Doha Round. A precondition for progress is that negotiators identify a set of broad goals for the services negotiations that make sense from a development perspective, provoke engagement from the business community, and satisfy the overall mercantilist constraint of ensuring a 'balance of concessions'. Mattoo argues that such a balance could be achieved by limiting commitments to measures that discriminate (pre- and post-entry) against foreign providers of services, as opposed to seeking disciplines that also target measures that do not discriminate in any way – that is, generally applicable sectoral regulation. Making national treatment the primary discipline covering all forms of *de jure* and *de facto* discrimination (pre- and post-establishment) would cover the bulk of the most important prevailing restrictions.

Since the entry into force of the GATS, there have been several sectoral negotiations and work programs aimed at further elaboration of specific rules in areas such as e-commerce and domestic regulation, mostly matters on which no agreement was possible during the Uruguay Round. Among such issues three are particularly prominent: disciplines on the use of safeguards, subsidies and government procurement. Little progress was made in these various areas before the launch of the Doha Round in 2001, and in principle all outstanding issues became the subject of negotiation in the Doha Round. The status quo on these subjects, the challenges that confront negotiators and options for moving forward are discussed by Sauvé (2002, Chapter II.15).[26]

A major challenge in negotiating international disciplines on services-related policies is to define meaningful commitments that will be beneficial to the countries that undertake them and be of value from a mercantilist negotiating perspective. A problem here is that not only do the poorest countries have weak export interests in most services, they confront particularly high barriers in the one mode that is of export relevance to them – mode 4. The papers included in these volumes suggest most of the potential gains will come from domestic reforms. However, many developing countries will not be of much export interest to large players in the WTO. Moreover, successful liberalization in these countries will often require substantial strengthening of domestic regulatory institutions and infrastructure.

These considerations suggest mercantilist bargaining may not do much to improve outcomes in many of the poorest countries. Arguably what is needed are additional instruments that focus attention on the policies that are most detrimental. One such instrument is what has come to be called 'aid for trade'. Such aid can help ensure that regulatory preconditions for liberalization to be beneficial are satisfied. By adding an additional instrument – development assistance – to the table, the GATS could become much more relevant as a mechanism to promote not just services liberalization but, more importantly, to bolster and improve domestic reform in services. The WTO has a major potential role to play in assisting governments to address the domestic reform agenda in low-income countries by helping to identify these needs and using its 'commitment and monitoring technologies' to mobilize both liberalization and assistance. Hoekman and Mattoo (2007) argue that if WTO members were to expand the transparency mandate of the organization by making the WTO a focal point for multilateral discussions and assessments of the state of members' service sectors, the institution could do much to help address the needs of its poorer members. It would do so by raising the policy profile of the services agenda in poor countries, helping governments identify where development assistance is needed, and monitoring the delivery and effectiveness of such assistance.

Part II   Services in Regional Integration Agreements

International cooperation on trade in services is of course not limited to the GATS. Regional agreements to liberalize international transactions in services became more prominent starting in the late 1980s. Examples include the Canada–United States Free Trade Agreement, the Australia–New Zealand Closer Economic Relations trade agreement (CER), and the North American Free Trade Agreement (NAFTA). Of course, the deepest regional effort to integrate services markets is the EU. In the 1990s the trend accelerated, and numerous additional trade agreements were negotiated that include services.

Mattoo and Fink (2004, Chapter II.16) ask whether the characteristics that are associated with services and trade in services imply any need to modify the conclusions in the literature regarding the economic implications of RIAs. They examine the implications of unilateral policy choices in a particular services market and identify the circumstances in which a country is more likely to benefit from cooperation in a regional rather than multilateral forum. They conclude that compared to the status quo, a country is likely to gain from preferential liberalization of services trade at a particular point in time, in contrast to the more ambiguous conclusions emerging for goods trade. The main reason is that barriers are often prohibitive and not revenue generating, so there are few costs of trade diversion. Insofar as there is scope for increased competition and exploitation of scale economies, as well as the possibility of inducing knowledge spillovers, the presumption that a country would gain from an RIA in services is strengthened.

Most preferential trade agreements (PTAs) negotiated since the early 1990s include provisions on services. Although many early PTAs did (and do) not go much beyond the GATS, more recent vintage agreements often have a higher level of ambition, although none comes close to the EU. An assessment by Roy, Marchetti and Lim (2007, Chapter II.17) concludes many of the trade agreements reported to the WTO since 2000 have a sectoral coverage that greatly exceeds the commitments the countries involved made in the GATS. This applies both to the existing GATS commitments and the offers that were on the table in the Doha Round as of mid-2006 when the talks were suspended. Roy et al. also conclude, however, that the substantive disciplines (rules) that are included in many of the agreements are similar to those in the GATS, that is, the depth of the associated commitments often does go much beyond what PTA members committed to under the WTO.

A question that motivates much of the ever-expanding literature is whether regional agreements and the multilateral process are complementary or substitute paths to liberalizing services markets. Fink and Jansen (2009, Chapter II.18) and Fink and Molinuevo (2007) review in some depth the extent of services liberalization in PTAs. They find that there is great variance across PTAs in terms of coverage of services and the depth of commitments, with more commitments made in sectors where countries have also made more extensive commitments in the GATS. Sensitive sectors such as health, transport and financial services as well as the movement of service suppliers (mode 4) tend to be subject to the fewest commitments. In areas where there are no WTO disciplines, there tend not to be PTA rules either – for example, safeguards, subsidies, or procurement. The same is true as regards domestic regulation. An important conclusion by Fink and Jansen is that the rules of origin that are contained in the PTAs are mostly liberal, in that PTA benefits extend to non-member firms that are established (have a commercial presence) and substantial business operations in a PTA member. They argue that such liberal rules of origin necessarily mean PTAs on services are multilateralizing in nature – that is, building blocks for multilateralism.

Dee (2007) investigates whether Asian agreements negotiated in the 2000s have tended to target regulatory restrictions that discriminate explicitly against foreigners, and if so, if these are the restrictions that matter most, in an economic sense. She argues that because RIAs covering services insist on being preferential, they liberalize only the trivial services trade barriers. They do not deal with the policies that result in the greatest mark-up of prices over costs (that is, rents) – which tend to be nondiscriminatory regulatory policies.

Marconini (2009, Chapter II.19) reviews in some depth the disciplines on services policies that are embodied in a number of the more recent vintage PTAs. Marconini summarizes the alternative approaches that have been taken to define the coverage of agreements and analyzes the specifics of the disciplines that are imposed both with respect to market access and regulatory issues. As do other authors, Marconini concludes that the PTAs tend to revolve around prevailing policies and do little to liberalize services trade or achieve greater regulatory cooperation.

There is clearly still much scope for further liberalization of trade in services. Langhammer (2005) documents one dimension of this – the EU is still not a customs union when it comes to services policies. Indeed, it is not even a free trade area. Langhammer uses the EU's GATS commitments and the offers the EU put on the table in the Doha Round to assess the extent to which there are still differences between national trade and investment regimes across service sectors. These are found to be significant, although full implementation of the EU offer would move the Community closer towards achievement of the customs union objective.

Conclusion

Compared to the early 1980s, the literature on trade in services has grown enormously. Our understanding of the key questions is now much better than 25 years ago, as is our knowledge of the factors that determine trade and investment flows, the effects of such flows, and the types of policies that affect trade. That said, it is fair to say that the current state of affairs is one that leaves much to be desired. Twenty-five years after the launch of international discussions to liberalize trade in services there is still much uncertainty about the extent to which countries actually restrict trade and what would be the impact of liberalization – the magnitude of potential net gains, the distributional implications of reforms, the size of the associated adjustment costs, and so on.

The papers included in these volumes and the literature that has been surveyed above clearly reveals that services are important for economic growth and development. Services may be an engine of growth for some countries – India may be an example – but more important is that they are a key determinant of the competitiveness of all firms in open economies, no matter what they produce. The services content of goods will keep rising with economic growth – more and more of the value of any product is associated with inputs at the upstream and downstream ends of the production chain, not the manufacturing process *per se* – R&D, finance, design, marketing, distribution, product/brand management, and so on. Even countries with comparative advantage in goods – manufacturing, agriculture – need to ensure that domestic services industries are efficient and that firms have access to foreign services know-how.

The sectoral studies reveal that it makes little sense to speak of 'the service sector'. Different services play different roles in the economy, will have very different market structures, and rely on (require) different modes of supply in contesting foreign markets and as a result be affected by very different types of policies. An implication for analysis of policy is that these idiosyncrasies must be taken into account. While perhaps obvious, in practice much of the trade and growth literature does not do this, even though it is necessary to better understand the interactions between various modes of supply for specific services (modes 3 and 4 in accounting; modes 1 and 3 for off-shoring of back office services, all four modes for health services, and so on). This is also needed to determine in practice which particular policies are a binding barrier to trade and which are redundant. It is also important to identify the appropriate sequencing and design of reforms.

To date the evidence suggests that with the exception of the EU most services policy reform has been unilateral. The contribution of the GATS to services reform has been very limited, and the same can be said for many if not most RIAs. In services markets, access and regulation are closely intertwined. In many markets the key need is to address regulatory policies that impede contestability. Whether this can be facilitated through trade agreements is still very much an open question. Services are activities where there is often a need for some type of regulation to address market failures or achieve social (noneconomic) objectives. Moreover, technological developments have major implications for the design of appropriate regulatory instruments to ensure both efficiency and equity. Many of the 'backbone' services that are critical for the competitiveness of firms in a country – such as transport, energy, and telecommunications – are industries with important network externalities. An implication is that regulation to ensure that markets are contestable needs to focus not only on 'traditional' types of entry barriers – outright bans, licensing, and so on – but on the ability to connect to the network at a reasonable price, apply the relevant technologies, and so on. Designing and enforcing policies to achieve this is anything but trivial, suggesting a cautious approach towards the setting of enforceable international standards in trade agreements.

Notes

*   Some of the material in what follows, draws on Francois and Hoekman (2010). The views expressed are personal and should not be attributed to the World Bank. I am grateful to Kym Anderson, Philippa Dee, Joe Francois, Keith Maskus and Aaditya Mattoo for helpful comments on earlier drafts and discussions along the way.

1.   Although a strand of the growth literature that (implicitly) emphasizes a services dimension stresses the importance of human capital (education) and R&D (a 'service' activity) in generating (endogenous) growth.

2. References to papers included as readings identify first the volume number, followed by the chapter number.
3. In addition to the papers included in this volume, see, for example, Sapir and Lutz (1980, 1981), Bhagwati (1987), Hindley (1988), and Stern and Hoekman (1987). Sapir and Winter (1994) and Stibora and de Vaal (1995) survey the literature through the early 1990s. Griffiths (1975) is an early study documenting barriers to trade in services.
4. The RCA index is the ratio of a country's exports of specific products to its total exports relative to the world average. If the ratio is greater than one the country is said to have a revealed comparative advantage in the product.
5. See Feketekuty (1988) for a comprehensive discussion of how services were put on the agenda of the GATT as well as a contemporary survey of the issues involved.
6. Much of this either focuses on the Uruguay Round talks and/or the GATS or is inspired by it. Books that have been published on the economics of services, services trade and economic development in the last 25 years include Inman (1985), Riddle (1986), Giarini (1987), Giersch (1988), Messerlin and Sauvant (1990), Harker (1996), UNCTAD and World Bank (1994), Stibora and de Vaal (1995), Sauvé and Stern (2000), Stern (2000) and Findlay and Warren (2000).
7. See also Kravis, Heston and Summers (1983), Inman (1985), Blades (1987), Stern and Hoekman (1988), Park (1989), Park and Chan (1989) and Uno (1989).
8. As of the early 1990s, some 50 percent of the global stock of FDI already involved services activities (Sauvant and Zimny, 1987; Hoekman, 1990).
9. Grubel (1987) was a prominent proponent of the argument that all trade was embodied in goods or in factors (people, FDI). Implicitly if not explicitly empirical studies of the factor content of a nation's trade are premised on this view.
10. While Melvin (1989) suggested that standard predictions may not hold, this paper did not really address the issue appropriately in that the focus was on a combination of goods and factor trade, not on services trade as a distinct activity.
11. As discussed below, this is also important because it may imply that the techniques used to assess the impacts of barriers to entry and competition for goods may be inappropriate.
12. Bradford Jensen and Kletzer (2005) assess the impacts of services trade on wages and employment of workers with different skill levels in the US.
13. See Markusen (2005) for a more in-depth analysis of the determinants and effects of offshoring of producer services that comes to similar conclusions regarding the applicability of existing theoretical 'toolkits'. Amiti and Wei (2005, 2006) and van Welsum (2004) discuss the magnitude of services outsourcing and the relationship with in- and outward FDI. Murray and Kotabe (1999) analyze the determinants of domestic vs. international services sourcing decisions of US firms.
14. The role of licensing or franchising as a method of exploiting firm-specific assets in services industries such as hotels or transport raises the question of how to measure international transactions in services. Franchising essentially involves a payment flow for an intangible asset (knowledge, reputation, and so on). Do such payments reflect the value of the services provided? More generally, how should the 'services content' of FDI be measured? In an early paper, Rugman (1987) argues that the inclusion of the financial returns related to all FDI outflows should be included in the definition of trade in services, as a proxy for the non-reported intra-firm trade in intermediate services between parent and affiliates. The trade in such 'headquarter' or 'management' services associated with coordination and running of the firm has become a basic feature of international trade theory that allows for the existence of multinationals and FDI and intra-firm transactions (for example, Helpman and Krugman, 1985; Rivera-Batiz and Rivera-Batiz, 1992; Markusen and Venables, 1998, 2000).
15. Other empirical papers in this vein include Erramilli and Rao (1993), Buch and Lipponer (2007) and Kolstad and Villanger (2004). UNCTAD (2004) is a recent survey of services FDI that references the empirical literature. Sauvant and Zimny (1987) and Rivera-Batiz and Rivera-Batiz (1992) are early papers stressing the importance of FDI as a mode of supplying services in a foreign market.
16. UNCTAD and World Bank (1994) and Hoekman and Primo Braga (1997) are earlier surveys.
17. Berger et al. (2004) study the determinants of entry by foreign financial services providers and conclude that a mix of traditional comparative advantage and firm-specific assets can explain these findings.

18. Other analyses of trade in financial services include Barth et al. (2004), Kalirajan et al. (2000), Murinde and Ryan (2003), Claessens (2004), Dobson and Jacquet (1998) and the contributions to Claessens and Jansen (2000).
19. They focus only on international shipping and thus capture only part of the impact of policies on transport costs. Estimates of the price-increasing effect of the US Jones Act (which restricts maritime cabotage between US ports to US flag vessels) range from 100 to 300 percent of the average world price (Francois et al., 1996).
20. In a subsequent paper, Clark et al. (2004), using the dataset developed by Fink et al. (2001) augmented with survey-based indicators of perceptions of port efficiency, conclude that port inefficiency-related costs account for a larger share of the total costs – and thus the potential gain from reform.
21. Mechanisms that could facilitate agreement to liberalize mode 4 trade are discussed in Mattoo and Carzaniga (2003) and in Mattoo (2005, chapter II.14). The experience of Canada in managing temporary movement is discussed in Blouin (2005); Bhatnagar and Manning (2005) discuss developments in this area in ASEAN.
22. One reason for this was pointed out by Romer (1994) – the economy will get access to products that were not available before, enhancing both consumer utility directly as well as firm productivity through access to more specialized inputs.
23. See, for example, Messerlin and Sauvant (1990) and Sauvé and Stern (2000). Hoekman et al. (2002) contains a number of chapters that summarize the GATS and the state of play in the WTO. Sapir (1999) reviews the first six years of the GATS.
24. See Maijoor et al. (1998) for an analysis and discussion of the European experience in liberalization of audit services.
25. See, for example, Millan-Smitmans (2000).
26. Analyses of these issues can also be found in several of the contributions to Stern and Sauvé (2000) and Hoekman (1993).

References

Amiti, M. and S. Wei (2005), 'Fear of Services Outsourcing: Is it Justified?' *Economic Policy* 20: 308–47.

Amiti, M. and S. Wei (2006), 'Service Offshoring, Productivity and Employment: Evidence from the US', CEPR Discussion Paper 5475.

Arnold, J., B. Javorcik and A. Mattoo (2007), 'The Productivity Effects of Services Liberalization: Evidence from the Czech Republic', World Bank Policy Research Working Paper 4109.

Barth, John, Gerald Caprio and Ross Levine (2004), 'Bank Regulation and Supervision: What Works Best?', *Journal of Financial Intermediation* 13: 205–48.

Baumol, William (1967), 'Macroeconomics of Unbalanced Growth', *American Economic Review* 57: 415–26.

Berger, A., C. Buch, G. DeLong and R. DeYoung (2004), 'Exporting Financial Institutions Management via FDI, Mergers and Acquisitions', *Journal of International Money and Finance* 23: 333–66.

Bhagwati, Jagdish N (1984a),'Splintering and Disembodiment of Services and Developing Nations', *The World Economy* 7: 133–44.

Bhagwati, J. (1984b), 'Why are Services Cheaper in Poor Countries,' *Economic Journal* 94: 279–86.

Bhagwati, Jagdish (1987), 'Trade in Services and the Multilateral Trade Negotiations', *The World Bank Economic Review* 1: 549–69.

Bhatnagar, Pradip and Chris Manning (2005), 'Regional Arrangements for Mode 4 in the Services Trade: Lessons from the ASEAN Experience', *World Trade Review* 4(2): 171–99.

Blades, Derek (1987),'Goods and Services in OECD Countries', *OECD Economic Studies* 8: 159–84.

Blouin, Chantal (2005), 'Liberalizing the Movement of Services Suppliers: Lessons from the Canadian Experience with Temporary Worker Programmes', *Journal of World Trade* 39(5): 881–94.

Bradford, Scott (2005), 'The Welfare Effects of Distribution Regulations in OECD Countries', *Economic Inquiry* 43(4): 795–811.

Bradford Jensen, J. and Lori Kletzer. 2005. 'Tradable Services: Understanding the Scope and Impact of Services Outsourcing,' IIE Working Paper 05-9.

Buch, C. and A. Lipponer (2007), 'FDI vs. Exports: Evidence from German Banks,' *Journal of Banking and Finance* 31(3): 805–26.

Claessens, Stijn (2004), 'Regulatory Reform and Trade Liberalization in Financial Services', in A. Mattoo and P. Sauvé (eds) (2004), *Domestic Regulation and Service Trade Liberalization*. Washington, DC: The World Bank and Oxford University Press.

Claessens, Stijn and M. Jansen (eds) (2000), *The Internationalization of Financial Services*, Kluwer.

Clark, Ximena, David Dollar and Alejandro Micco (2004), 'Port Efficiency, Maritime Transport Costs and Bilateral Trade', *Journal of Development Economics* 75(2): 417–50.

Commission of the European Communities (2004), Proposal for a Directive of the European Parliament and of the Council on Services in the Internal Market, SEC(2004) 21, Brussels.

Dee, Philippa (2005), 'A Compendium of Barriers to Trade in Services', Australian National University, mimeo.

Dee, Philippa (2007), 'East Asian Economic Integration and its Impact on Future Growth', *The World Economy* 30(3): 405–23.

Dobson, W. and P. Jacquet (1998), *Financial Services Liberalization in the WTO*. Washington, DC: Institute for International Economics.

Erramilli, M. and C.P. Rao (1993), 'Services Firms' International Entry Mode Choice: A Modified Transactions Costs Approach', *Journal of Marketing* 57(3): 19–38.

Escaith, Hubert (2008), 'Measuring Trade in Value Added in the New Industrial Economy: Statistical Implications', MPRA Paper 14454, University Library of Munich.

Feketekuty, Geza (1988), *International Trade in Services: An Overview and Blueprint for Negotiations*. Cambridge MA: Ballinger Publications.

Fernandes, A. and C. Paunov (2008), 'FDI in Services and Manufacturing Productivity Growth: Evidence for Chile', World Bank Policy Research Working Paper 4730.

Fink, Carsten and Martin Molinuevo (2007), 'East Asian Free Trade Agreements in Services: Roaring Tigers or Timid Pandas?', East Asian and Pacific Region, Report No. 40175, (The World Bank), available at http://go.worldbank.org/5YZF3TK4EO

Francois, Joseph (1990), 'Trade in Producer Services and Returns Due to Specialization Under Monopolistic Competition', *Canadian Journal of Economics* 23: 109–24.

Francois, J. and B. Hoekman (2010), 'Services Trade and Policy,' *Journal of Economic Literature* 48(3): 642–92.

Francois, Joseph and Ian Wooton (2010), 'Market Structure and Market Access', *The World Economy* 33(7): 873–93.

Francois, Joseph, Hugh Arce, Kenneth Reinert and Joseph Flynn (1996), 'Commercial Policy and the Domestic Carrying Trade; A General Equilibrium Assessment of the Jones Act', *Canadian Journal of Economics* 29(1):181–98.

Fuchs, Victor (1968), *The Service Economy*. New York: Columbia University Press.

Giarini, Orio (ed.) (1987), *The Emerging Service Economy*. New York: Praeger.

Giersch, H. (ed.) (1988), *Services in World Economic Growth*. Tubingen: J. Mohr.

Griffiths, B (1975), *Invisible Barriers to Invisible Trade*. London: MacMillan.

Grubel, H (1987) 'All Traded Services are Embodied in Materials or People', *The World Economy* 10(3): 319–30.

Helpman, Elhanan and Paul Krugman (1985), *Market Structure and International Trade*. Cambridge: MIT Press.

Hill, T.P (1977), 'On Goods and Services', *The Review of Income and Wealth* 23: 315–38.

Hindley, Brian (1988), 'Service Sector Protection: Considerations for Developing Countries', *World Bank Economic Review* 2: 205–24.

Hindley, Brian and Alasdair Smith (1984), 'Comparative Advantage and Trade in Services', *The World Economy* 7: 369–90.

Hoekman, Bernard (1990), 'Services-related Production, Employment, Trade, and Foreign Direct Investment: A Global Perspective', in Patrick Messerlin and Karl Sauvant (eds), *The Uruguay Round: Services in the World Economy*. Washington, DC: The World Bank.

Hoekman, Bernard (1993), 'Safeguard Provisions and International Agreements Involving Trade in Services', *The World Economy* 16: 29–49.

Hoekman, Bernard (2000), 'The Next Round of Services Negotiations: Identifying Priorities and Options', *Federal Reserve Bank of St. Louis Economic Review* July/August: 31–48.

Hoekman, Bernard and Carlos A. Primo Braga (1997), 'Protection and Trade in Services: A Survey', *Open Economies Review* 8(3): 285–308.

Hoekman, Bernard and Denise Konan (2001), 'Deep Integration, Nondiscrimination and Euro-Mediterranean Free Trade', in Jürgen von Hagen and Mika Widgren (eds), *Regionalism in Europe: Geometries and Strategies After 2000*. Kluwer Academic Press.

Hoekman, B. and A. Mattoo (2007), 'Regulatory Cooperation, Aid for Trade and the GATS', *Pacific Economic Review* 12(4): 399–418.

Hoekman, Bernard, Aaditya Mattoo and Philip English (eds) (2002), *Development Trade and the WTO: A Handbook*. Washington, DC: World Bank.

Horn, Henrik and Oz Shy (1996), 'Bundling and International Market Segmentation', *International Economic Review* 37(1): 51–69.

Inklaar, R., M. Timmer and B. van Ark (2007), 'Mind the Gap! International Comparisons of Productivity in Services and Goods Production', *German Economic Review* 8(5): 281–307.

Inklaar, R., M. Timmer and B. van Ark (2008), 'Market Services Productivity across Europe and the US,' *Economic Policy* 23: 141–94.

Inman, Robert P (ed.) (1985), *Managing the Service Economy: Prospects and Problems*. New York: Cambridge University Press.

Kalirajan, K (2000), *Restrictions on Trade in Distribution Services*, Productivity Commission Staff Research Paper, Canberra: Ausinfo.

Kalirajan, K., G. McGuire, D. Nguyen-Hong and M. Schuele (2000), 'The Price Impact of Restrictions on Banking Services', in C. Findlay and T. Warren (eds), *Impediments to Trade in Services: Measurement and Policy Implications*. London: Routledge.

Karsenty, Guy (2000), 'Assessing Trade in Services by Mode of Supply', in P. Sauvé and R.M. Stern (eds), *GATS 2000: New Directions in Services Trade Liberalization*. Washington, DC: Brookings Institution Press, pp. 33–56.

Kirkpatrick, Colin and David Parker (2005), 'Domestic Regulation and the WTO: The Case of Water Services in Developing Countries', *The World Economy* 1491–508.

Konan, Denise and Karl Kim (2004), 'Beyond Border Barriers: The Liberalisation of Services Trade in Tunisia and Egypt', *The World Economy* 27(9), 1429–47.

Kravis, Irving B., Alan W. Heston and Robert Summers (1983), 'The Share of Services in Economic Growth', in F.G. Adams and B. Hickman (eds), *Global Econometrics: Essays in Honor of Lawrence R. Klein*. Cambridge: MIT Press.

Langhammer, Rolf (2005), 'The EU Offer of Service Trade Liberalization in the Doha Round: Evidence of a Not-Yet-Perfect Customs Union', *Journal of Common Market Studies* 43(2): 311–25.

Lejour, Arjan and Jan-Willem de Palva Verheijden (2004), 'Services Trade within Canada and the European Union', CPB Discussion Paper 42.

Maijoor, Steven, Willem Buijink, Roger Meuwissen and Arjen Van Witteloostuijn (1998), 'Towards the Establishment of an Internal Market for Audit Services Within the European Union', *European Accounting Review* 7(4): 655–73.

Markusen, James (1989), 'Trade in Producer Services and in Other Specialized Intermediate Inputs', *American Economic Review* 79: 85–95.

Markusen, James and Anthony Venables (1998), 'Multinational Firms and the New Trade Theory', *Journal of International Economics* 46: 183–203.

Markusen, James and Anthony Venables (2000), 'The Theory of Endowment, Intra-Industry and Multinational Trade', *Journal of International Economics* 52: 209–34.

Mattoo, Aaditya and Antonia Carzaniga (eds) (2003), *Moving People to Deliver Services*. Washington, DC: Oxford University Press and World Bank.

Mattoo, A. and R. Rathindran (2006), 'How Health Insurance Inhibits Trade in Health Care', *Health Affairs* 25(2): 358–68.

Mattoo, Aaditya, Randeep Rathindran and Arvind Subramanian (2006), 'Measuring Services Trade Liberalization and its Impact on Economic Growth: An Illustration', *Journal of Economic Integration* 21: 64–98.

Melvin, James (1989), 'Trade in Producer Services: A Heckscher–Ohlin Approach', *Journal of Political Economy* 97: 1180–96.

Messerlin, Patrick and Karl Sauvant (eds) (1990), *The Uruguay Round: Services in the World Economy.* Washington, DC: The World Bank and UNCTC.

Millan Smitmans, Hector (2000), 'Dispute Settlement in the Services Area Under GATS', in S. Stephenson (ed.), *Services Trade in the Western Hemisphere.* Washington, DC: Brookings and Organization of American States, pp. 105–36.

Murinde, Victor and Cillian Ryan (2003), 'The Implications of WTO and GATS for the Banking Sector in Africa', *The World Economy* 26(2): 181–207.

Murray, Janet and Masaaki Kotabe (1999), 'Sourcing Strategies of US Service Companies: A Modified Transactions Cost Analysis', *Strategic Management Journal* 20(9): 791–809.

Nguyen-Hong, D. (2000), *Restrictions on Trade in Professional Services*, Productivity Commission Staff Research Paper, Canberra: Ausinfo.

Nicoletti, Giuseppe (2001), 'Regulation in Services: OECD Patterns and Economic Implications', OECD Economics Department Working Paper 287.

Nicoletti, Giuseppe and Stefano Scarpetta (2003), 'Regulation, Productivity and Growth', *Economic Policy* 36: 9–72.

Park, Se-Hark (1989), 'Linkages Between Industry and Services and Their Implications for Urban Employment Generation in Developing Countries', *Journal of Development Economics* 30: 359–79.

Park, Se-Hark and Kenneth Chan (1989), 'A Cross-country Input–Output Analysis of Intersectoral Relationships between Manufacturing and Services', *World Development* 17: 199–212.

Raff, H. and M. von der Ruhr (2007), 'FDI in Producer Services: Theory and Empirical Evidence,' *Applied Economics Quarterly* 53(3): 299–321.

Riddle, Dorothy (1986), *Service Led Growth: The Role of the Service Sector in World Development.* New York: Praeger.

Rivera-Batiz, F. and L. Rivera-Batiz (1992), 'Europe 1992 and the Liberalization of Direct Investment flows: Services vs. Manufacturing', *International Economic Journal* 6: 45–58.

Romer, Paul (1994), 'New Goods, Old Theory and the Welfare Cost of Trade Restrictions', *Journal of Development Economics* 43: 5–38.

Rugman, Alan (1987), 'Multinationals and Trade in Services: A Transaction Cost Approach', *Weltwirtschaftliches Archiv* (Review of World Economics) 123: 651–67.

Ryan, C. (1992), 'The Integration of Financial Services and Economic Welfare', in L. Alan Winters (ed.), *Trade Flows and Trade Policy After 1992.* Cambridge: Cambridge University Press, pp. 92–118.

Sampson, Gary and Richard Snape (1985), 'Identifying the Issues in Trade in Services', *The World Economy* 8: 171–81.

Sapir, André (1999), 'GATS 1994–2000', *Journal of World Trade* 33(1): 51–66.

Sapir, André and Ernst Lutz (1980), 'Trade in Non-Factor Services: Past Trends and Current Issues', World Bank Staff Working Paper No. 410, Washington, DC.

Sapir, André and Ernst Lutz (1981), 'Trade in Services: Economic Determinants and Development-Related Issues', World Bank Staff Working Paper No. 480, Washington, DC.

Sapir, André and Chantal Winter (1994), 'Services Trade', in David Greenaway and L. Alan Winters (eds), *Surveys in International Trade.* Oxford: Basil Blackwell.

Sauvant, Karl and Zbigniew Zimny (1987), 'Foreign Direct Investment in Services: The Neglected Dimension in International Service Negotiations', *World Competition* 31(October): 27–55.

Stern, R.M. (ed.) (2000), *Services in the International Economy.* Ann Arbor: University of Michigan Press.

Stern, Robert M. and Bernard Hoekman (1987), 'Analytical Issues and Data Needs for GATT Negotiations on Services', *The World Economy* 10: 39–60.

Stern, Robert and Bernard Hoekman (1988), 'The Service Sector in Economic Structure and in

International Transactions' in Leslie V. Castle and Christopher Findlay (eds), *Pacific Trade in Services*. Sydney: Allen & Unwin.

Stibora, Joachim and Albert de Vaal (1995), *Services and Services Trade: A Theoretical Inquiry*. Rotterdam: Netherlands Economic Institute.

Triplett, Jack E. and Barry P. Bosworth (2004), *Productivity in the US Services Sector: New Sources of Economic Growth*. Washington, DC: Brookings Institution Press.

UNCTAD (2004), *World Investment Report 2004: The Shift Towards Services*. Geneva: United Nations.

UNCTAD and World Bank (1994), *Liberalizing International Transactions in Services: A Handbook*. New York: United Nations.

Uno, K (1989), *Measurement of Services in an Input–Output Framework*. Amsterdam: North Holland.

Van Welsum, Desiree (2004), 'In Search of Offshoring: Evidence from US Imports of Services', Birkbeck Working Paper in Economics and Finance 0402.

Whalley, John (2004), 'Assessing the Benefits to Developing Countries of Liberalization in Services Trade', *The World Economy* 27(8): 1223–53.

WTO (2008), *International Trade Statistics*, Geneva: WTO.

Part I
Determinants and
Patterns of Trade in Services

[1]

The Role of Services in the Structure of Production and Trade:
Stylized Facts from a Cross-Country Analysis *

Joseph F. Francois
World Trade Organization and CEPR

Kenneth A. Reinert
Kalamazoo College

Executive Summary

Services dominate the economic landscape of the post-industrial OECD economies, typically accounting for between 60 and 70 percent of employment and a comparable share of GDP. Growth of the service sector is also recognised to be an important aspect of economic development and is strongly associated with income growth and economic modernisation. Explanations for the importance of services in modern economies, relative both to low-income countries and to historic patterns within OECD countries themselves, have emphasised demand-side factors. Yet, while emphasis in the services literature has been placed on final expenditure patterns and prices, some of the most striking aspects of service sector growth relate instead to the relationship of services to the production structure of economies, and particularly the relationship of the service sector to manufacturing.

In this paper, we explore the role of services in the structure of production and trade. Our basic objective is to develop a set of empirically-based stylised facts. Working with a sample of national income data for 15 countries, we explore upstream and downstream service linkages and their relationship to changes in income levels and the input-output structure of production. The analysis provides five results which we interpret as stylised facts.

(i) Income levels are positively associated with employment shares for intermediate services and with the share of indirect labour in total manufacturing employment.

(ii) The share of value added originating in services, including both private services and trade, transport, and communications services, is also positively linked to the level of development.

(iii) Income levels are strongly linked to demand by firms for intermediate or producer services, particularly in manufacturing.

(iv) While changes in the allocation of non-production (i.e. service) activities between manufacturing and service firms may explain a small share of service sector growth, the basic story seems instead to be one of fundamental changes in the structure of production.

(v) The importance of services for export performance depends on the level of development. As we move from the middle-income to upper-income range of our country sample, private services and trade, transport, and communications services become the most important sectoral elements of exports via interindustry linkages.

The last result relates to the economic structure of the OECD economies. While their exports are concentrated in manufactures, their economies are concentrated in services. At the same time, however, our results serve as a reminder that, in terms of the intermediate structure of production, services are a major aspect of production, even for exportables. Hence, while Japan's exports in material terms are concentrated in transport equipment and other machinery and equipment, the activity composition of Japanese exports is actually concentrated in services, which are almost 50 percent again more important than transport equipment and machinery and equipment on an activity basis. Similar patterns hold for Canada, the European Union, and the United States. Even for middle-income countries such as Korea, the significance of the service sector for overall exports is much greater than the direct trade balance suggests.

This paper represents the opinions of the authors, and is not meant to represent the views of any institution with which they may have ever been affiliated, particularly the WTO and its members. An earlier version has circulated as part of the CEPR research programme on *Market Integration, Regionalism, and the Global Economy* thanks to a grant from the Ford Foundation (no. 920-1265).

Introduction

Services dominate the economic landscape of the post-industrial OECD economies, typically accounting for between 60 and 70 percent of employment and a comparable share of GDP. Growth of the service sector is also an important aspect of economic development and is strongly associated with income growth and economic modernisation. Explanations for the importance of services in modern economies, relative both to low-income countries and to historic patterns within OECD countries themselves, have emphasised demand-side factors. Clark (1940) was the first to note a rising share of services associated with economic growth and attributed this to demand side factors. A related issue emphasised by Clark and later by Kravis, Heston, and Summers (1982) is the correlation between final-expenditure service prices and income levels. The theoretical literature on income-price linkages includes Balassa (1964), Samuelson (1964), Bhagwati (1984a, 1985), and Panagariya (1988). Also in this vein, Baumol *et al.* (1985) relate the pattern of rising service prices to relative productivity differentials.

While emphasis in the services literature has been placed on final expenditure patterns and prices, some of the most striking aspects of service sector growth relate instead to the relationship of services to the production structure of economies, particularly the relationship of the service sector to manufacturing. As discussed in the later sections of this paper, the cross-country pattern of employment and GDP shares for producer services (services employed as intermediates in production) is strongly correlated with income levels. The share of producer services in total intermediate demand by manufacturing firms is also linked to income levels. Katouzian (1970) and Greenfield (1966) have argued that we should expect to find that the demand for producer services grows with development. Both Katouzian and Francois (1990) link this expansion to growth in round-about production and the associated conversion of local markets into national markets. Alternatively, Bhagwati (1984b) has suggested that such producer service growth may simply be related to "splintering", wherein service activities once performed within manufacturing firms are spun off to specialised service providers.

Past empirical evidence on the rise of the service sector was indirectly provided by Chenery and Taylor (1968) through their examination of GNP shares for agriculture and manufacturing. Park (1989), Park and Chan (1989), and Uno (1989) empirically confirmed rising service inputs into manufacturing. The decline in manufacturing employment and the shift to service sector employment in the post-war period has been well documented (e.g. Sachs and Schatz, 1994, Francois, 1990, and Dighe, Francois, and Reinert, 1995).

In this paper, we explore the role of services in the structure of production and trade. Our basic objective is to develop a set of empirically-based stylised facts. Working with a cross-country sample of national income data for 15 countries, organised as a set of social accounting matrices, we explore upstream and downstream service linkages and their relationship to changes in income levels and the input-output structure of production. The analysis provides five results which we interpret as stylised facts. First, the employment shares of services increase with the level of development, and within manufacturing there is an increase in indirect labour (manufacturing labour engaged in non-production activities). Second, both value added in commercial services relative to manufacturing value added and intermediate demand for commercial services relative to intermediate demand for manufacturing rise with per capita income levels. Third, the relative economy-wide importance of services is related to expansion of private-sector intermediate demand for services and particularly to increased demand in the manufacturing sector for service inputs. Fourth, while changes in the allocation of non-production activities between manufacturing and service firms may explain a small share of service sector growth, the basic story seems instead to be one of fundamental changes in the structure of production. Finally, the embodied service component of exports is also linked to the level of development, with the exports of the high income countries including the greatest level of embodied services.

National income data

We work with national income data organised into social accounting matrices (SAMs). The SAM is a form of single-entry national income accounting, where incomes or receipts are shown in the rows of the SAM while expenditures or outlays are shown in the columns.[1] This structure provides a comprehensive and consistent record of national income accounting relationships between different sectors and regions. It is based on a fundamental, general

---

[1] The basic principles of SAMs, with application to trade policy modelling, are summarised in Reinert and Roland-Holst (forthcoming).

equilibrium principle of economics -- every income (receipt) has a corresponding expenditure (outlay). The strength of this framework is that it provides a comprehensive and consistent record of the interrelationships of an economy, including intermediate and final demand linkages. For our purposes, it offers the advantage of linking consumption and external trade patterns explicitly to the inter-industry structure of intermediate demand. This allows for a fuller analysis than is possible when working with input-output tables. The SAMs are supplemented with data on employment from the OECD and ILO and data on purchasing power parity based income levels from the International Comparison Project (ICP) as published in the Penn World Tables (Summers and Heston; 1991, 1994).

The basic dataset includes 27-sector SAMs for 15 countries and regions.[2] Each national SAM is a 37 x 37 matrix of national economic activity, and is a combination of the matrix of inter-sectoral expenditures and additional elements for households, government, investment, and trade. The SAMs are drawn from the Global Trade Analysis Project (GTAP) dataset (Gelhar *et al.*, 1996), and represent 1992 values for production, expenditures, and trade. We will focus in this paper on the SAM sector termed *commercial services*. This sector excludes utilities, construction, trade and transportation, and public services. It includes financial services, insurance, legal services, accounting, data processing, engineering, architectural services, advertising, machinery and equipment rental, and other business services. These services are the focus of much of the literature discussed in the Introduction, and are an important aspect of intermediate demand.

Services and the structure of production

We start with the role of services, particularly commercial services, as intermediates in production, and the manner in which this role changes with the level of development. We examine the role of services in the structure of production from four points of view: employment, demand for services as intermediates, interindustry linkages, and splintering vs. changes in the structure of production.

Employment

The cross-country pattern of service sector employment is illustrated in Figures 1 and 2. Figure 1 presents employment in service sectors that serve primarily as intermediates in production (producer services).

Figure 1: Producer Service Employment and GDP

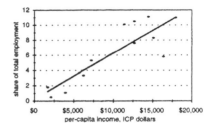

Figure 2 presents indirect or non-production labour as a share of total manufacturing employment. Indirect labour, as defined by the ILO, performs intermediate service activities (accounting, engineering, etc.) within manufacturing firms. The Appendix presents ANOVA results for the underlying data in the figures. These relate to correlation patterns between per-capita income levels measured in ICP dollars (see Summers and Heston; 1991, 1994) on the one hand, and either producer service employment shares or the indirect labour share of manufacturing on the other.

For our sample, changes in the employment share of services (and conversely negative changes in manufacturing

Figure 2: Indirect Labour Shares and GDP

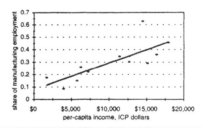

---

[2] The countries/regions are: Australia; Canada; China; the European Union; Indonesia; Japan; South Korea; Malaysia; Mexico; New Zealand; the Philippines; Singapore; Taiwan; Thailand; and the United States. The sectors are: grains; other crops; livestock; forestry; fisheries; primary mining; processed food; textiles; clothing; leather manufactures; wood products; pulp, paper, and printing; petroleum and coal products; chemicals; non-metallic mineral products; primary steel; primary non-ferrous metals; fabricated metal products; transport equipment; machinery and equipment; other manufactures; electricity, water, and gas; construction; trade, transport, and communications; commercial services; public services; ownership of dwellings.

employment) are positively related to income levels. Even within manufacturing, there is an apparent shift from direct production labour towards indirect labour. In other words, the rise in services employment is linked to an associated parallel shift toward service activities within the "manufacturing" labour force itself. This cross-sectional result is consistent, at least in spirit, with the findings of Berman, Bound, and Griliches (1994) on the recent historical experience of the United States. They report, over time, a rising share of skilled non-production labour employment within manufacturing which is also linked to changes in the structure of production. The importance of non-production workers in the United States is strongly linked to R&D spending and labour-saving technological change. As developed further below, the broad employment patterns we have identified here also relate to an increased use (in relative terms) of services as inputs by manufacturing firms.

Demand for producer services

An important feature of service sector growth in the OECD countries has been expansion of the intermediate service sector. Based on our social accounting data, Figures 3 and 4 present the share of the commercial services sector in value added relative to manufacturing, and the share of commercial services in total manufacturing demand for intermediates. Both are plotted relative to per-capita income. Underlying ANOVA results are again presented in the Appendix. There is a strong correlation, within our sample, between per-capita income levels, rising relative demand for services by the manufacturing sector, and a rising share for intermediate services in total value added.

Intermediate linkages

We next turn to intermediate linkages. In an earlier cross-country comparison of input-output structures, Park and Chan (1989) found that services exhibit fewer interindustry linkages overall than manufacturing. At the same time, cross-country studies of the structure of demand point to non-homothetic preferences as an important final demand factor in the growth of the service sector (e.g. Hunter and Markusen 1988, Kravis, Heston, and Summers 1985, and Cornwall and Cornwall 1994). The pattern of non-unitary income elasticities implies a demand-side shift in preferences from agriculture through manufacturing and into services as incomes rise. On net, we therefore expect a shifting pattern of production, driven both by demand and supply side changes, which will also lead to a consequent shift in the pattern of economy-wide, interindustry linkages.

Manufacturing is characterised by particularly strong intermediate linkages to other sectors, relative to both agriculture and services. With development, therefore, an initial shift from agriculture implies increased density of the intermediate use matrix (i.e. an increase in the relative importance of intermediate production linkages). This pattern may be reinforced by increased round-about production and the integration of internal markets (Katouzian 1970). With a further shift from manufacturing and into services, economy-wide density of the intermediate use matrix should fall again.[3]

To examine these production linkages, we begin by denoting a country's n x n social accounting matrix by **S** and a column unit n-vector by **e**. Then **c** = **e'S** is the column-sum vectors of **S**. If a ^ over a vector is used to denote the corresponding n-dimensional diagonal matrix, then

Figure 3: Commercial Services Value Added

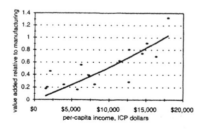

Figure 4: Manufacturing Demand for Services

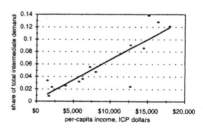

[3] We may also expect density to fall, even within manufacturing, if development is also associated with a process of horizontal integration. We do find some evidence of such a pattern for the manufacturing sector in our data.

$$A = S \hat{c}^{-1} \qquad (1)$$

represents the column-sum normalised SAM. An element A_i is the proportion of sector j's expenditure received by sector i. Working with the column-normalised **A** matrix, we examine correlations between cross-country per capita income levels and the basic density of the intermediate use matrix by formally defining the linkage index D as:

$$D = \frac{\sum_{j \in \lambda} \sum_{i \in \lambda} A_{ij}}{\sum_{j \in \lambda} \sum_{i \in \omega} A_{ij}} \qquad (2)$$

where λ is the set of industry accounts and ω is the set of industry plus value-added accounts. The index D measures the relative importance of intermediate linkages as a share of total sectoral activity.[4] It reflects the importance of backward linkages between sectors, relative to the total level of production activity. The Appendix presents ANOVA results for the relationship between interindustry SAM density and income levels. Data points and the estimated functional form are plotted in Figure 5. While there is a great deal of variability in the data, we do identify a broad pattern of rising economy-wide interindustry density through $12,000 per-capita income, and a falling-off from that point on.

Splintering vs. the structure of production

We next turn briefly to the production factors driving the apparent growth of demand for producer services, particularly with regard to demand from the manufacturing sector. Splintering refers to outsourcing of indirect production activities, and has been emphasised as a

Figure 5: Interindustry Linkages

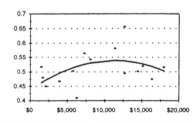

possible explanation for the apparent growth in producer services. (See Bhagwati 1984b). As we noted in the Section I, explanations in the literature have included both (i) real changes related to a basic shift in the structure of production, or alternatively (ii) apparent changes driven instead by the outsourcing of service-type activities by manufacturing firms.

To the extent that the changes can be explained by outsourcing or shifts in the location of service production between firms, we should expect the share of indirect labour within manufacturing firms to fall as the share of services in intermediate demand by manufacturing rises. Alternatively, structural change related to income levels will be reflected in the correlation of demand growth with per-capita income levels. Figure 6 and the Appendix present the results of OLS-based analysis of relative movements between manufacturing demand for private services, on the one hand, and both income levels and indirect manufacturing employment levels, on the other.

The results reported in the Appendix for Figure 6 "explain" roughly 70 percent of the variation in intermediate demand for services (the adjusted R^2 is .71). The estimated relationship is plotted in Figure 6 overleaf for the range of income levels and indirect labour shares covered by our sample. From the figure, it can be seen that, while falling indirect labour shares do "explain" a small rise in intermediate demand, this effect is far outweighed by a much stronger apparent positive relationship between rising income levels and rising intermediate demand for services. This result does not, of course, in any way explain the pattern of changes underlying the positive relationship between producer service growth and income. It does, however, point strongly to real structural change rather than outsourcing as the most promising direction for further research on this data pattern.

Services and the structure of trade

We next turn to the role of services in the structure of trade. We emphasise the importance of commercial services, not only as direct exports, but also as intermediates embodied in manufacturing exports. Formally, we divide the n accounts of a country's SAM into two groups: m endogenous accounts and k exogenous accounts. Following the standard convention in the SAM literature, we define the

---

[4] Technically, the D index measures the activity density of the column-normalised intermediate use matrix.

[5] The matrix **M** is not the standard Leontief multiplier matrix, since a number of institutional accounts are endogenous. For a more detailed discussion of this distinction, see Roland-Holst (1990).

Figure 6: Commercial Services as a Share of Manufacturing Intermediate Demand

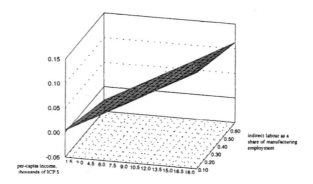

k exogenous accounts as the government, capital, and rest-of-world accounts (see Robinson, 1989). All remaining accounts, including the consumption account, are endogenous. We define the submatrix of **A** consisting of the m endogenous accounts as A_{mm}. The multiplier matrix is then given by

$$M = (I_m - A_{mm})^{-1} \qquad (3)$$

A representative element of the **M** matrix, M_i, gives the direct and indirect effects on sector i income caused by an exogenous unit increase in sector i income.[4]

Following Reinert and Roland-Holst (1994), we derive direct and indirect trade linkages from the individual SAMs based on the **M** matrix and the trade vectors. Defining f_i as the export final demand for commodity i and f as the column vector of these elements, the coefficient

$$\phi_i = f_i / f'e \qquad (4)$$

then gives the share of commodity i in total export demand, while the column vector ϕ contains the full set of these coefficients. This vector simply represents direct export shares. To account for intermediate linkages, further manipulation is required. We therefore also define the column vector

$$\Omega = M\phi \qquad (5)$$

which gives the weighted average direct and indirect effect on activity in sector i of increasing export demand by one dollar while holding its sectoral composition constant.

From the matrix ϕ, we have a measure of the direct sectoral trade pattern. It gives the share of sectoral exports in each dollar of total export demand. In contrast, the matrix Ω gives the sectoral intensity of the overall export pattern. It measures the increase in economic activity (in value terms) that follows from a one dollar increase in total export demand. This includes both direct export demand, and demand for intermediates employed in producing exports from other sectors. What stands out in the data is the relative service intensity of exports in the high income countries, based on Ω. Based on net shares (equation (4)), the exports of the high income countries are concentrated in the upper-end of the manufacturing spectrum. However, on an activity basis (equation (5)), where we account for the full set of economy-wide intermediate linkages, we find that the most important sectors for export performance are the service sectors. This pattern is illustrated in Figure 7, in which we plot the pattern of total export intensity of commercial services against income. The underlying ANOVA results for Figure 7 are presented in the Appendix. The adjusted R^2 for the underlying OLS regression is 0.73.

Figure 7: Commercial Service Exports

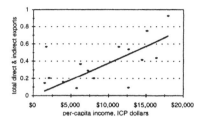

per-capita income. ICP dollars

In terms of income levels, we find middle income countries (defined as up to $10,000 per year in per capita income) concentrated in exports of manufacturing activities. In Korea, for example, the most important sector for both direct and indirect exports in our data is machinery and equipment. Beyond this point, the economies in our sample shift in relative terms from exporting manufacturing activities to exporting service activities. The trade, transport, and communications sector exhibits an overall pattern similar to that for commercial services shown in Figure 7. For Australia, Canada, the European Union, Japan, Mexico, New Zealand, the United States, these two SAM sectors, (i) trade, transport, and communication and (ii) commercial services, are the most important export sectors measured on an activity basis. Hence, while the net composition of exports is concentrated in tangible exports, the leading cost component of these exports is actually service activities in the OECD economies.

Summary
Services are the dominant feature of the post-industrial OECD economies, and growth of the sector is an important feature of economic development. In this paper we work with a cross-country sample of national income data. We examine changes in the structure of production and trade, and the overall relationship of services to these patterns. What emerges is a set of stylised facts that match closely the historical experience of the OECD countries. To summarise:

(i) Income levels are positively associated with employment shares for intermediate services and with the share of indirect labour in total manufacturing employment.

(ii) The share of value added originating in services, including both commercial services and trade, transport, and communications services, is also positively linked to the level of development.

(iii) Income levels are strongly linked to intermediate demand for services, particularly in manufacturing.

(iv) While changes in the allocation of non-production activities between manufacturing and service firms may explain a small share of growth in intermediate demand for services, the basic story seems instead to be one of fundamental changes in the structure of production.

(v) The importance of services for export performance depends on the level of development. As we move from the middle-income to upper-income range of our sample, commercial services and trade, transport, and communications services become the most important sectoral elements of exports via interindustry linkages.

The last result relates to the economic structure of the OECD economies. While their exports are concentrated in manufactures, their economies are concentrated in services. At the same time, however, our results serve as a reminder that, in terms of the intermediate structure of production, services are a major aspect of production, even for exportables. Hence, while Japan's exports in material terms are concentrated in transport equipment and other machinery and equipment, the activity composition of Japanese exports is actually concentrated in services, which are almost 50 percent again more important than transport equipment and machinery and equipment. Similar patterns hold for Canada, the European Union, and the United States. Even for middle-income countries such as Korea, the significance of the service sector for overall exports is much greater than the direct trade balance suggests.

APPENDIX

ANOVA results — services and the structure of production and trade

	sample size	F	Significance of F	Coefficients		t-Statistic
Figure 1: Service Sector Employment						
	13	33.28	0.00012	Intercept	2.4309É-01	0.2080
				y	6.0329E-04	5.7691
Figure 2: Indirect Labour Employment in Manufacturing						
	12	15.27	0.00293	Intercept	8.0563E-02	1.2747
				y	2.1254E-05	3.9072
Figure 3: Value Added in Commercial Services relative to Manufacturing						
	15	15.46	0.00048	Intercept	1.0259E-08	2.0276
				y	4.4660E-05	2.0276
				y*y	7.1751E-10	0.4680
Figure 4: Manufacturing Demand for Commercial Services						
	15	38.26	0.00003	Intercept	2.2549E-03	0.2012
				y	6.5267E-06	6.1857
Figure 5: SAM Density as a Measure of Intermediate Linkages						
	15	1.51	0.26098	Intercept	4.3766E-08	9.5800
				y	1.7997E-04	1.5070
				y*y	-7.9919E-10	-1.2719
Figure 6: Manufacturing Demand for Commercial Services						
	12	14.34	0.00159	Intercept	-3.0275E-03	-0.1758
				y	8.5094E-06	3.8938
				s	-5.7014E-02	-0.7133
Figure 7: Commercial Services as a Share of Total Exports on an Activity Basis						
	15	6.38	0.01293	Intercept	8.3584E-09	1.5788
				y	3.6387E-05	1.5789
				y*y	1.2086E-10	0.0753

note: s :   indirect labour as a share of manufacturing employment
        y :   per-capita income
        y*y :   per-capita income squared

The sample size for various regressions depends on the coincident availability of SAM data, ICP data, and ILO employment data. As a result, sample size varies.

FRANCOIS and REINERT - THE ROLE OF SERVICES IN THE STRUCTURE OF PRODUCTION AND TRADE

References

Balassa, B. (1964), 'The Purchasing Power Parity Doctrine: A Reappraisal', *Journal of Political Economy*, 72, 564–96.

Baumol, W.J., S.A.B. Blackman, and E.N. Wolff (1985), 'Unbalanced Growth Revisited: Asymptotic Stagnancy and New Evidence', *American Economic Review*, 75:4, September, 806–17.

Berman, E., Bound, J. and Grilliches, Z. (1994), 'Changes in the Demand for Skilled Labour within U.S. Manufacturing: Evidence from the Annual Survey of Manufactures', *Quarterly Journal of Economics*, 109, 367–98.

Bhagwati, J.N. (1984a), 'Why Are Services Cheaper in the Poor Countries?', *Economic Journal*, 94, 279–86.

———— (1984b), 'Splintering and Disembodiment of Services and Developing Nations', *World Economy*, 7:2, 133–43.

———— (1985), 'Trade in Services and Developing Countries', London: Tenth Annual Geneva Convention at the London School of Economics.

Chenery, H.B. and L. Taylor (1968), 'Development Patterns Among Countries and Over Time', *Review of Economics and Statistics*, 50:4, November, 391–416.

Clark, C. (1940), *The Conditions of Economic Progress*, Macmillan, London,.

Cornwall, J. and W. Cornwall (1994), 'Growth Theory and Economic Structure', *Economica*, 61:242, May, 237–51.

Dighe, R.S., J.F. Francois, and K.A. Reinert (1995), 'The Role of Services in U.S. Production and Trade: An Analysis of Social Accounting Data for the 1980s', in P.T. Harker (ed.), *The Service Productivity and Quality Challenge*, Kluwer, Boston, 43–80.

Francois, J.F. (1990), 'Producer Services, Scale, and the Division of Labor', *Oxford Economic Papers*, 42:4, October, 715–29.

Gehlhar, M.J., D. Gray, T.W. Hertel, K. Huff, E. Ianchovichina, B.J. MacDonald, R. McDougall, M.E. Tsigas, and R. Wigle (1996), 'Overview of the GTAP Data Base', in T.W. Hertel (ed.), *Global Trade Analysis: Modeling and Applications*, Cambridge University Press, Cambridge.

Greenfield, H.I. (1966), *Manpower and the Growth of Producer Services*, London: Columbia University Press.

Hunter, L. and J.R. Markusen (1988), 'Per-Capita Income as a Determinant of Trade', in R. Feenstra (ed.), *Empirical Methods for International Economics*, MIT Press, Cambridge, Massachusetts, 89–109.

Katouzian, M.A. (1970), 'The Development of the Service Sector: A New Approach', *Oxford Economic Papers*, 22:3, November.

Kravis, I.B., A. Heston, and R. Summers (1982), *World Product and Income: An International Comparison of Real Gross Domestic Product*, Baltimore: Johns Hopkins University Press.

Panagariya, A. (1988), 'A Theoretical Explanation of Some Stylized Facts of Economic Growth', *Quarterly Journal of Economics*, 103, 509–26.

Park, S.-H. (1989), 'Linkages between Industry and Services and their Implications for Urban Employment Generation in Developing Countries', *Journal of Development Economics*, 30, April, 359–79.

Park, S.-H. and K.S. Chan (1989), 'A Cross-Country Input-Output Analysis of Intersectoral Relationships between Manufacturing and Services and their Employment Implications', 17:2, February, 199–212.

Reinert, K.A. and D.W. Roland-Holst (1994), 'Structural Change in the United States: Social Accounting Estimates for 1982–1988', *Empirical Economics*, 19:3, 429–49.

———— (forthcoming), 'Social Accounting Matrices', in J.F. Francois and K.A. Reinert (eds.), *Applied Methods for Trade Policy Analysis: A Handbook*, Cambridge University Press, Cambridge.

Robinson, S. (1989), 'Multisectoral Models', in H.B. Chenery and T.N. Srinivasan (eds.), *Handbook of Development Economics*, North Holland, Amsterdam, 885–947.

Roland-Holst, D.W. (1990), 'Interindustry Analysis with Social Accounting Methods', *Economic Systems Research*, 2:2, 125–45.

Sachs, J.D. and H.J. Schatz (1994), 'Trade and Jobs in U.S. Manufacturing', *Brookings Papers on Economic Activity*, 1, 1–84.

Samuelson, P. (1964), 'Theoretical Notes on Trade Problems', *Review of Economics and Statistics*, 46, 145–54.

Summers, R. and A. Heston (1991), 'The Penn World Table (Mark 5): An Expanded Set of International Comparisons, 1950–1988,' *Quarterly Journal of Economics*, May. (with revisions released as PWT 5.6 through NBER), November 1994.

Uno, K. (1989), *Measurement of Services in an Input-Output Framework*, North Holland, Amsterdam.

[2]

The structure of services in Europe:
A conceptual framework

André Sapir[1]

EC Commission (DG II) and Université Libre de Bruxelles

Contents

---

[1]   I am grateful to Patrick Bolton, Pierre Buigues, Fabienne Ilzkovitz, Alexis Jacquemin, Colin Mayer and Oliver Ruyssen for helpful discussions on an earlier draft.

Tables

1. Introduction

Thirty years ago, when the Treaty of Rome was put into action, agriculture and manufacturing dominated economic activity in the European Community (EC). Today, in every Member State, services account for more production and employment than agriculture and manufacturing combined.[1] The increasing importance of services in the economy is not, however, distinctive of Europe. All other industrial countries have been witnessing similar trends.[2]

The growing role of services in domestic economies is the result of both demand and supply factors. On the demand side, the shift towards services by households reflects rising incomes and changing socio-economic patterns.[3] But the greater increase in demand has come from firms that have shifted from in-house to out-house service provision.[4] On the supply side, the main factors have been technological change and deregulation. Recent developments in information technology and the trend toward deregulation have created new services and transformed nearly every existing service activity. The creation and transformation of business has been particularly important in sectors that provide services to other (manufacturing or service) industries.[5]

As Michael Porter notes in his latest publication, 'Not only has the service landscape changed markedly within national economies, but the foundations have been laid for a new era of international service competition'.[6] Governments, however, impose restrictions that limit international trade and foreign direct investment in services. Such restrictions are one of the major topics of negotiations in the Uruguay Round.

In the EC, transactions among Member States have often remained limited despite 30 years of efforts to abolish 'restrictions on freedom to provide services within the Com-

munity'.[7] The maintenance of internal barriers has generated substantial costs to European countries.[8] In the 1980s, it became clear that the removal of these barriers was essential to increase competition and improve efficiency in the EC. In order to achieve a common market for services, the 1985 White Paper listed proposals for liberalizing financial, telecommunications and transport services as well as for the free movement of labour and the professions.[9] It was later agreed that the single European market should be achieved by 1992.

This paper is part of a study on the impact of 1992 on European service industries. Its purpose is to provide a methodological framework for analysing the structure of the market for services in Europe on the eve of 1992.

Section 2 identifies three essential features that set services apart from other economic activities. These features are used in Section 3 to examine in detail factors that determine the market structure of service industries. Section 4 briefly sketches how these factors can help to characterize the present structure of European services. The conclusion offers conjectures about the future shape of service industries in Europe.

2. Nature and characteristics of services

The first question that arises, when tackling the analysis of the determinants of market structure and competitive advantage in services, is whether services are different from goods in an economically meaningful manner. In other words, do the traditional determinants of market structure and competitive advantage apply equally to goods and services? At first sight, the answer to this question must be an unqualified 'yes'. After all, on the supply side, goods and services use similar factors of production and production processes; equally, on the demand side, both goods and services compete for the consumer's income.[10] Although a common approach to both goods and services is therefore warranted, it appears, none the less, that services exhibit certain characteristics deserving special attention.

---

[1]   In 1987, the share of services in GDP was lowest in Portugal and Ireland (52%) and highest in Belgium, Denmark, France and the Netherlands (66%) (World Bank (1989), Table 3).
[2]   In 1987, services accounted for 68% of GDP in the United States and 57% in Japan (World Bank (1989), Table 3).
[3]   A major factor has been increased women participation rates. The relationship between services and female labour force participation also runs the other way. The growth of services has been an important factor in attracting women to the labour force. This hypothesis is put forward by Fuchs (1985).
[4]   This phenomenon is documented by Green (1985) for the EC.
[5]   Such services are usually called business, intermediate or producer services.
[6]   Porter (1990), pp. 247 and 248.

[7]   Article 59 of the Treaty of Rome. This Article applies to all services, with the exception of financial and transportation services which are dealt with separately in the Treaty.
[8]   See Commission of the European Communities (1988).
[9]   See Ernst and Whinney (1988).
[10] See Kierzkowski and Sapir (1987).

Economists have attempted to provide all-encompassing definitions of services based on a single characteristic. In such attempts, services are defined as activities that produce either an intangible, a non-storable, an invisible or a transient output. Single-dimension definitions, however, fail to make clear-cut distinctions in several instances. Accordingly, many authors prefer to simply list the activities encompassed under the term 'services'. The catalogue of services generally includes the following categories of activities: business and professional services (accounting, advertising, construction and engineering, legal services, medical services, etc.), communications, distribution, financial services, tourism, and transport.

The span and variety of service industries explains the lack of a universal definition of services. Nor is there a generally agreed taxonomy of services. Several authors distinguish services according to their users: individuals and households ('personal services') or businesses and institutions ('producer services'). Although such a taxonomy may be useful, it fails to provide a framework for analysing the determinants of market structure and competitive advantage. Our approach, instead, is based on three parameters which relate directly to such determinants:

(i)   the degree of interaction required between consumers and producers of services;

(ii) the extent of asymmetric information in service markets;

(iii) the degree of regulation of services.

These three factors are the major blocks around which our analysis of the determinants of market structure and competitive advantage will be built. Clearly, none of these factors is unique to services. But although each plays a role in a variety of manufacturing industries, their presence would seem to be more frequent and their intensity more strongly felt in most service industries. A preliminary discussion of the first two factors is provided in the present section. Their role in determining the market structure of services will be analysed in Section 3, which also considers the role of regulation.

2.1. The degree of interaction between consumers and producers

One feature of services which is often emphasized in recent literature and which was first noted by Hill (1977) is that the consumption of a service must generally take place simultaneously with its production. Accordingly, services cannot be stored by producers. For instance, flying on an aeroplane is altogether non-storable by producers: the service must be consumed at the same time as it is produced.

The non-storable nature of services implies that production and consumption tend to occur not only at the same time, but also in the same location. The requirement of physical proximity between users and providers has been extensively explored by Bhagwati (1984) and Sampson and Snape (1985). These authors distinguish between two categories of services: those that require physical proximity and those that do not.

One of the major implications of the need for interaction between consumers and producers of services concerns the type of international (as well as interregional) competition that exists in service industries. Drawing on the work by Bhagwati and Sampson and Snape, Porter (1990) distinguishes three types of international competition in service industries:

Type 1. Mobile users from one nation travel to another nation to have services performed. This type of competition is most frequent in tourism, education, health care, ship repair and airport services.

Type 2. Mobile providers from one nation travel to another nation in order to perform services. Such a situation occurs in certain business services, such as engineering, where frequent or close interaction is not required.

Type 3. Providers from one nation establish a branch in another nation in order to perform services. This is the most common pattern of international service competition, involving frequent and close interaction between buyers and sellers. It is the dominant type in most services, including accounting, advertising, banking, consulting services and distribution.

The first two types of international service transactions fall into the category of international trade; the third one belongs to foreign direct investment.

There are several implications resulting from the distinction between the different types of international service competition. First, given the prevalence of Type 3 competition, foreign direct investment plays a crucial role in international service transactions. A report by the US Office of Technology Assessment (1986) indicates that in activities such as accounting, advertising and insurance, sales by US affiliates abroad far outweigh direct exports by US corporations. Table 1 reproduces the relevant information for a few sectors.[1]

---

[1]   Extracted from McCulloch (1988), Table 13.

Table 1

Foreign revenues of US service firms, 1983

(billions of US dollars)

Activity	Direct exports	Affiliate sales	Total
Accounting	0,2-0,5	3,7-4,0	3,9-4,5
Advertising	0,1-0,5	1,7	1,8-2,2
Data processing	0,1-1,2	2,5-3,7	2,6-4,9
Engineering	1,1-1,6	4,0	5,1-5,6
Insurance	2,7-3,6	10,1-12,1	12,8-15,7
Retailing	0,0	25,4	25,4
Telecommunications	1,3	1,3	2,6
Transportation	17,1	10,9	28,0
Travel	14,1	0,0	14,1

Second, barriers to transactions in services typically involve restrictions regarding establishment (Type 3 competition) or the movement of key personnel (Type 2 competition). Third, the border between the different types of international competition, especially Type 2 and Type 3, is not impermeable. In consulting services, for instance, much of the foreign work is provided by local establishments (Type 3 competition), but key personnel travel from the home office to provide specialized services (Type 2 competition). Finally, the border between the different types of competition is moving. Complementary innovations in data processing and telecommunications have reduced the need for interaction between consumers and producers in several services such as retailing (teleshopping) or banking (telebanking). This has enhanced the tradability of services, partly eroding Type 3 competition in favour of Type 2. Many service industries are also witnessing a greater interaction between international trade and foreign direct investment.

2.2. The extent of asymmetric information in services

The quality of certain goods can be determined by consumers prior to a purchase. For other goods, the quality can only be learned after they are bought and consumed. In yet other cases, the quality is never fully learned, even after consumption. These three categories of goods have been labeled 'search goods', 'experience goods' and 'credence goods'.[1]

---
[1] See Tirole (1988), Chapter 2.

Since services only exist while they are being consumed (i.e. they are intangible), their quality cannot be assessed prior to consumption. Services are, therefore, rarely search goods. Most are experience goods, and a few (such as medical services) are credence goods. Thus, a major issue for services is information.

Although it can be argued that the ultimate quality of certain services depends on the interaction between users and providers ('it takes two to tango' or 'it takes an effort on the part of both consumers and producers to produce quality services' — especially in the case of education and business services such as advertising or legal services), it remains that sellers know more a priori about product quality than buyers. Asymmetric information about product quality between consumers and producers creates two types of problems: moral hazard and adverse selection.[2]

Moral hazard on the producer side arises when consumers have little means of monitoring quality. It implies that sellers have little incentive to provide quality services. The moral-hazard problem is especially acute in one-shot relationships between consumers and producers. This explains why many travellers encounter problems with taxi-cabs, restaurants or other services.

If, as in the case of most services, quality changes over time (i.e. a good service today may not imply a good service tomorrow), repeat purchases can help overcome the moral-hazard problem by inducing suppliers to develop a reputation. There are two necessary conditions for repeat purchases to drive firms to build a reputation and provide quality services: the difficulty for buyers in assessing quality must be relatively low and the frequency of their purchase relatively high. Tirole (1988) notes that 'repeat purchases need not be made by the same consumer at the same outlet or of the same goods in order to have an effect. First, word of mouth between consumers may do the job; one may deal with a real-estate agent or a contractor infrequently, but learn about the quality of their recent services through family or friends. Second, brand names and chains can support the development of reputation when the repeat purchases concern similar but different goods'.[3]

---
[2] See Holmström (1985) for an early discussion of the role of asymmetric information in the context of services.
[3] Tirole (1988), p. 112.

Asymmetric information also generates the so-called adverse-selection or lemons problem.[1] This problem arises when the seller cannot distinguish between different types of buyers, or when the buyer cannot distinguish between different types of sellers. Examples of the former situation include the insurance market and the loan market, where firms are uncertain about the risk attached to different individuals. The latter situation applies to most professional services (such as consulting, legal or medical services), where buyers are confronted with suppliers of various competence. In such instances, 'good' buyers (i.e. low-risk individuals in the insurance or loan markets) or 'good' sellers (i.e. competent consultants, jurists or doctors) will tend to be driven from the market by 'bad' buyers or 'bad' sellers.[2] Adverse selection, therefore, reduces the frequency of market transactions.

The fact that problems of asymmetric information pervade many service industries has several consequences. First, imperfect information is one of the major reasons for the prevalence of regulatory controls in services (see below). Second, the frequent use of reputation to signal quality implies that service markets are often characterized by nonprice competition. Lastly, reputation, like any other intangible asset, creates an incentive to sell in foreign markets in order to maximize the rent that can be gained. Given the need for interaction between consumers and producers, such incentive usually translates into foreign direct investment. Moreover, Sapir (1988) notes that service firms often become multinational in order to follow their customers. Service firms tend to acquire a quasi-contractual relationship with their customers 'based on trust that lowers the cost of contracting and the risks of opportunistic behaviour. If the service firm has such a quasi-contractual relationship with a parent (multinational), it enjoys a transactional advantage for supplying the same service to [its] foreign subsidiaries'.[3]

3. The determinants of market structure in services

In the previous section, the three factors playing a key role in many services are identified. The purpose of this section is to examine how these three parameters interact with other factors in determining the market structure in service industries.

The section is organized in three parts. The first one looks at technology and preferences as determinants of 'natural' industry structure. The second part examines how natural and strategic barriers to entry affect the degree of competition in markets for services. The last part singles out the role of regulation.

3.1. 'Natural' determinants: Technology and preferences

Many economists view the structure of an industry as jointly determined by the optimal firm size and the size of the market.[4] In the traditional paradigm, the optimal firm size is determined by the position of the cost function. For firms producing a single output, the production size is directly related to the degree of scale economies. In the multiproduct case, in addition to economies of scale, firms may enjoy cost savings from the joint production of several outputs. Such economies of scope result from the existence of certain inputs that, because of indivisibilities, are common to several outputs.

Given the cost function, the optimal (or 'natural') number of firms in an industry depends on the size of the market which is determined by the demand curve. A natural monopoly situation will prevail if the level of demand allows only one efficient producer operating at a cost-minimizing scale. If there is room for several producers, there will be a natural oligopoly. If the cost function exhibits no economies of scale or scope, there will be many producers operating in a competitive environment.

Demand conditions play a role not only in determining the optimal number of firms. They also dictate whether products are homogeneous or differentiated. The separation between these two categories depends upon the degree of substitutability, perceived by consumers, among competing products. The more consumers perceive two products to be close substitutes, the more homogeneous they are.

The previous discussion can be summarized by a two-way classification of types of 'natural' market structure based on the optimal number of firms and the nature of the product.[5] This classification is shown in Table 2.

For a given level of demand, the natural market structure, therefore, depends upon two parameters: the extent of scale economies and the degree of product differentiation.

---

[1] See Akerlof (1970) who discusses adverse selection with reference to the American market for second-hand cars, where bad cars are dubbed 'lemons'.
[2] See Inman (1985).
[3] Caves (1982), p. 11.

[4] For a complete exposition of this approach, see Panzar (1989).
[5] This classification is directly inspired by Table 2.1 in Scherer and Ross (1990).

Table 2

Types of 'natural' market structure

Nature of products	Optimal number of firms		
	One	A few	Many
Homogeneous products	Natural monopoly	Natural oligopoly	Pure competition
Differentiated	Natural monopoly	Natural oligopoly	Monopolistic competition

What can be said about these two parameters in service industries and where do these industries belong in the classification?

As far as economies of scale are concerned, service industries fall into three categories:

(i) The first comprises a very small number of sectors where the degree of scale economies (and/or economies of scope) has been traditionally alleged important: telecommunications and railways.[1]

(ii) Most service industries belong to the other extreme of the spectrum, where economies of scale have traditionally been very small or non-existent. This situation stems largely from the proximity requirement between buyers and sellers of most services which has led to the existence of small firms operating in localized markets.[2]

(iii) The third category includes services where economies of scale are present, but remain quite low. Financial services and airlines belong to this category.[3]

Services are differentiated products *par excellence*. The differentiation of services operates along three dimensions. First, services are spatially differentiated in the sense that the location of producers matters to consumers. For instance, to

a client, a bank located around the corner from his residence or place of work is not the same as a bank situated 50 kilometres away, even if it is identical in all other respects. Second, service attributes vary across suppliers. For instance, one airline offers non-stop flights between London and Tokyo, others make a stopover. Third, the service quality differs among producers. For instance, some consultants write better reports than others.

The picture that emerges is one where service industries fall into the three bottom categories of Table 2: a few sectors have been traditionally classified as natural monopolies (telecommunications and railways); others are often viewed as naturally oligopolistic (financial services and airlines); but the majority of services (business and professional services, distribution and tourism) seem to belong to the category of monopolistic competition.

An important implication is that sellers in service industries tend to enjoy some degree of market power, the extent of which depends on the importance of barriers to entry and regulatory controls.

Before closing the discussion on the technological determinants of market structure, it is important to emphasize that neither the cost nor the demand functions are immutable. As technology and demand evolve over time, so does the natural market structure. Changes have occurred recently that greatly affect the structure of many service industries. In certain services traditionally classified as natural monopolies, rapid technological change and demand growth have lowered unit costs, at least in certain segments of the business. For instance, in telecommunications, there has been an increase in the optimal number of firms size which has challenged the traditional natural monopoly view of the industry.

Demand growth and technological change are also responsible for transforming the structure in monopolistically com-

---

[1] For a review of empirical studies on scale economies in telecommunications, see Panzar (1989).
[2] See Porter (1990), Chapter 6.
[3] In the banking sector, most empirical studies find that scale economies are rather modest (see, for instance, Gilibert and Steinherr (1989)). The same applies in the insurance sector (see, for instance, McKinsey (1989) quoted in Commission of the European Communities (1990)). For evidence on the airlines industry, see Caves, Christensen and Tretheway (1984). This study finds no economies of scale but substantial economies of scope in the US airline industry.

The structure of services in Europe: A conceptual framework

petitive service industries where scale economies were traditionally small or non-existent. The rise in demand and the advent of information technology have resulted in the growth of 'multi-unit service firms' that provide relatively standardized services at many locations.[1] Examples include not only hamburger restaurants or pizzerias, but also auto-centres, consulting services and hotels. While information technology can serve to create a network of coordinated units drawing on centralized support functions, it can also help in reducing the number of units when the need for interaction between buyers and sellers of services is diminished. In both instances, the introduction of information technology transforms the structure of service industries by increasing the optimal scale of firms. It creates a new environment where large, usually multi-unit service firms coexist with small, specialized local competitors.[2]

Finally, the use of information technology also seems to increase the optimal scale of operation in certain oligopolistic sectors. In financial services, for instance, several studies report that computer systems add to size advantages.[3]

3.2. Barriers to entry

Although many would agree that, in the long run, the relative positions of the cost and demand functions are ultimately determining industry structure, the recent literature on industrial organization has challenged such narrow technological determinism.[4] Supporters of the new paradigm refute the traditional view that the cost and the demand curves are 'exogenously given constructs'.[5] They argue, instead, that economic agents act upon supply and demand 'in complex games of power and economic domination'.[6]

The central feature that sets apart these two schools lies in their respective views about the importance of private entry barriers (i.e. barriers that are not erected by government actions). Barriers to entry are defined here as factors that

confer an advantage to incumbent firms.[7] In the traditional school, such barriers play a relatively modest role, so that firms are unable to enjoy a significant degree of market power. The potential monopoly rents earned by incumbents are rapidly dissipated by either the actual or the threat of entry by new firms. On the other hand, the new paradigm insists that firms not only base their actions on exogenous or natural barriers, but also erect strategic barriers in order to deter entry by new rivals.[8]

The issue of entry barriers is a crucial one for determining the actual structure of a market. In a market where barriers to entry are negligible, the actual structure may be competitive even though the optimal, technologically-determined number of firms is very small. Conversely, if entry barriers are important, firms may possess strong monopoly power, even though their number is relatively large.

What is the importance of barriers to entry in service industries? What is the role of economies of scale and product differentiation as entry deterrents in such industries?

The existence of important scale economies was generally considered a barrier to entry. It is now recognized, however, that economies of scale, in themselves, are not sufficient to protect incumbent firms from potential competition. Recent attention has focused instead on sunk costs. Sunk costs are defined as fixed costs associated with irreversible investments. An important contribution to the literature on market structure that builds on the notion of sunk costs is the theory of the contestable market presented by Baumol, Panzar and Willig (1982). According to the theory, a market is defined as perfectly contestable when three conditions are met: there are potential entrants with the same cost functions as incumbents; there are no sunk costs; and potential entrants can enter and leave the market before incumbents can react. A perfectly contestable market reproduces the perfectly competitive outcome. Although the optimal number of firms may be extremely small due to economies of scale and scope (there could even be a natural monopoly), prices do not exceed average cost.

As Scherer and Ross (1990) note, 'The key question concerning the contestability theory is not whether the internal logic holds, but whether the conditions required are likely to be found in practice.'[9] The crucial condition is that fixed costs

---

[1]   This concept is used by Porter (1990).
[2]   Such a pattern can be found in retailing, where a few pan-European stores (like Benetton, Ikea or Marks & Spencer) have emerged (*The Economist*, 12 May 1990).
[3]   See Commission of the European Communities (1990).
[4]   For a detailed discussion of the tenets of both the classical and the new industrial organization literature, see Jacquemin (1987).
[5]   Panzar (1989), p. 33.
[6]   Jacquemin (1987), p. 5.

[7]   For a review of various definitions of entry barriers, see Gilbert (1989).
[8]   Strategic barriers are examined by Encaoua, Geroski and Jacquemin (1986).
[9]   Scherer and Ross (1990), p. 376.

are not sunk. There is widespread agreement that investment is at least partially irreversible in most goods-producing industries. On the other hand, there is support for the view that 'capital or resources or both are sufficiently reversibly mobile to make the [contestable] model descriptively useful ... in some of the service industries ... [where] capital can be rented and has multiple uses'.[1]

Clearly, fixed costs are not sunk in service industries such as business and professional services, distribution and financial services, where investment can easily be transferred to other uses at little cost. Sunk costs also seem to be low in transportation industries such as airlines, shipping and trucking. This would suggest that service industries are often contestable.[2]

Although sunk costs may not be important in most service industries, barriers to entry are none the less present in association with the differentiation of services. As the previous discussion has indicated, services are differentiated along three dimensions: location, attributes and quality. In principle, each dimension of differentiation could constitute a barrier to entry.

Given the proximity requirement between buyers and sellers, many service markets tend to be localized. Potential entrants may, therefore, choose to locate in markets hitherto not serviced by existing firms. In order to preserve their dominance, incumbents may be tempted to pre-empt such locations by setting up new branches. The fact that pre-emptive investments are likely to be reversible (i.e. not sunk) for most service industries implies that they may not serve as a credible entry barrier.

In addition, existing firms may attempt to deter entry by offering services covering a wide array of attributes. As in the case of location, the degree of reversibility of pre-emptive investments required to offer services with new attributes may not appear sufficient to constitute a credible barrier to entry.

So far, the analysis of entry barriers in service industries has, at least implicitly, assumed that investment takes place solely in tangible assets (i.e. buildings and equipment). Given the pervasive problem of asymmetric information about the quality of services, firms also tend to invest in reputation. In many service industries, such investment plays a role as large, if not larger, than that of other investments. A crucial

point is that, contrary to most tangible assets used in service industries, reputation is largely a sunk cost.[3]

The fact that services are experience (or perhaps credence) goods creates a barrier to entry in two complementary ways. First, imperfect knowledge by consumers about quality implies, because experimenting is costly, that they treat differently identical services according to whether they have experienced them or not.[4] The presence of such consumer switching costs or consumer inertia helps incumbents to deter entry.[5, 6] Second, the use of reputation mechanisms by firms to ensure quality creates price rigidities and entry barriers.[7] Because of switching costs, new firms on the market may offer price discounts to induce consumers to switch to their services. But price discounts may fail to attract customers if they are interpreted as a signal of low quality. For instance, consumers may be suspicious about new financial institutions that offer deposit rates well above the going rate.

The importance of both information asymmetry about quality and reputation also has implications for the previous discussion on differentiation. It was argued that tangible assets in many service industries may be too easily reversible to constitute a credible barrier to entry. By contrast, extending the scope of reputation, either in new locations or with new service attributes, may help deter entry by potential rivals. In financial services, for instance, established firms have often attempted to pre-empt unfilled niches threatened by potential entrants.

In conclusion, service industries tend to incur fixed costs in two types of assets: tangible (buildings and equipment) and intangible (reputation). The first does not generally involve many sunk costs. On this account, many service markets can be regarded as contestable. The second type of fixed cost,

---

[1]   Spence (1983), p. 987.
[2]   For a discussion of conflicting evidence, see Baumol and Willig (1986) and Scherer and Ross (1990), Chapter 10.

[3]   Clearly, there is a positive correlation between reputation and the degree to which tangible assets are sunk, or at least perceived as such.
[4]   See Tirole (1988), Chapter 7, for a discussion of informational differentiation in the context of experience goods.
[5]   Markets with consumer switching costs have been extensively analysed by Klemperer (1987a and 1987b).
[6]   There is evidence of consumer inertia in many services. In financial services, for instance, 'large banks ... report that the vast majority of the population strikes up a relationship with one bank in early adulthood and stays faithful to it for the rest of their days.' (*Financial Times*, 26 May 1990).
[7]   For a discussion of price rigidities in the context of reputations, see Stiglitz (1989).

The structure of services in Europe: A conceptual framework

however, is much more likely to be irreversible. Unless other mechanisms exist for conveying information about quality (see below), reputation may severely reduce the degree of actual or potential competition in certain services.

3.3. Regulation

In most countries, government agencies intervene to modify the shape of market structure. Instruments of public intervention cover a wide range of control. Public authorities may indirectly control economic activity by taxes and subsidies; they may intervene through regulation; or they may even operate directly nationalized enterprises. Governments also affect market structure through competition policy.

Although other forms of public intervention are also common, regulation plays a dominant role in most service industries. This section examines the rationales for regulating services as well as the reasons for the regulatory reform movement that started in the United States and is now spreading in Europe and Japan.

The traditional rationale for regulation is to remedy market failures and thereby improve efficiency. Three types of failure are usually distinguished: imperfect competition, imperfect information and externalities.[1]

As we have seen earlier, service industries fall into three categories of imperfect competition. First, some industries may be natural monopolies. In this case, regulation may be required to ensure that the efficiency from monopoly is not outweighed by monopolistic abuse. Regulation of railways and segments of telecommunications (so-called basic services) is commonly justified on the basis of this argument. Second, and more frequently, service industries may be oligopolistic. Under certain conditions, this may lead to an unstable equilibrium and produce welfare losses. This so-called excessive or destructive competition argument has been used extensively for regulating certain transportation services (airlines, shipping and trucking) as well as banking. It is generally viewed with great suspicion by economists who prefer policies that promote, rather than limit, competition. The general attitude is that a strong competition policy is desirable in all oligopolistic service industries, unless proved otherwise.[2] Third, service industries that operate under conditions of monopolistic competition do not require regulation, except in cases of imperfect information.

The second type of market failure that prevails in service industries is imperfect information. As we have seen, asymmetric information about the quality of services generates problems of moral hazard and adverse selection. Government intervention in the form of occupational licensing and certification is common in many professions (as for accountants, doctors or lawyers). An alternative mechanism for conveying information about quality, based on the market, is reputation. However, as discussed previously, the use of reputation mechanisms itself introduces a barrier to entry that may require government intervention, for instance by improving market information. Finally, reputation and other market channels may not be sufficient information devices in certain cases. Credence services (such as medical services) are obvious examples.

The third type of market failure is externalities. These occur when actions by economic agents give rise to costs or benefits to other agents. External effects may arise in two ways in service industries. The first situation derives from the problem of asymmetric information about the quality of certain services. The main point is that adverse selection creates a negative externality. As Holström notes, 'Bad lawyers cause an externality ... [because] they cause good lawyers to carry too much risk.'[3] A similar kind of externality is present in financial services, where failure by one institution may cause problems to others. These situations call for regulation through licensing and certification. The second type of external effect found in services is positive network externalities. These arise when the value of a service to a user increases with the number of users of the same service. The typical example is telecommunications services. Such externalities require government intervention to encourage network compatibility and prevent entry deterrence.[4]

Since the early 1970s, the traditional view that regulation improves resource allocation has been under severe attack. The critiques that have been addressed raise two related issues: the motivation and the effectiveness of public regulation.

Starting with the contributions by Stigler (1971), Posner (1974) and Peltzman (1976), economists associated with the 'Chicago School' have emphasized that regulation tends to be captured by interest groups seeking to acquire monopoly rents.[5] According to this view, regulation is motivated by politically organized incumbent firms aiming to limit compe-

---

[1]　See, for instance, Kay and Vickers (1988) or Noll (1989).
[2]　See Kay and Vickers (1988).

[3]　Holmström (1985), p. 195.
[4]　See Gilbert (1989).
[5]　See Noll (1989) for an extensive review of the literature.

tition and raise their income at the expense of politically weak consumers and potential entrants. Regulation, therefore, not only redistributes income, but may also create barriers to entry and inefficiency.

More recently, economists have questioned the basic premise that regulation remedies market failures, or at least that it does so effectively. Their attacks do not support the claim that government intervention is doomed to fail. However, they suggest that alternatives to traditional regulation may be more suited to produce efficient outcomes. The most spectacular, and successful, contribution has been the contestable market theory which provided the intellectual foundations of the deregulation in several US service industries (such as airlines and trucking). The policy implication of the theory is that government intervention should not be based simply on the number of firms in a market (as measured by concentration ratios), but should also take into account the degree of contestability. Other contributions in this vein also propose market-based government interventions as alternatives to regulation. These include the provision of information or the imposition of norms ensuring compatibility among networks.

The main criticism of regulation is that it often tends to limit rather than foster competition. The recent mood among economists is well illustrated in the most popular industrial organization textbook, by Scherer and Ross, which states, 'It has become increasingly clear ... that in many instances the public would be better off relying upon unfettered market processes as a regulator, even though the market functions a good deal less than perfectly.'[1] Such a widely-shared view has contributed immensely to the deregulation movement that started in the United States in the late 1970s,[2] moved to Britain in the early 1980s,[3] and is spreading throughout the rest of Europe in preparation for 1992.[4] This movement covers nearly all service industries, from transportation and telecommunications services to financial and professional ones.

4. The market structure in the EC on the eve of 1992

This section presents two instruments intended to analyse the structure of service industries prevailing today in Europe's Member States. These tools can also be used to examine the likely impact of 1992. They are based closely on the concepts developed in Sections 2 and 3.

The first analytical tool is presented in Table 3. It offers a way to collect and analyse systematically information on individual service industries. Its purpose is to determine the expected structure of service industries in the absence of government intervention.

The information contained in Table 3 does not pertain specifically to the situation in the EC or elsewhere. It seeks, instead, to define a benchmark based on sectoral knowledge about factors such as the degree of economies of scale or the importance of reputation.

The second analytical tool is shown in Table 4. It provides a way to collect and analyse systematically information about the actual market structure of service industries in each Member State. It also supplies information about the type and extent of government intervention.

Table 4 can be used, by itself, to provide a picture of the situation in Europe on the eve of 1992. It can also be utilized in conjunction with Table 3 to infer the impact of the completion of the internal market. The underlying assumption here is that 1992, by eliminating certain government interventions, will modify the structure of European service industries observed in Table 4 in the direction of the expected structure described in Table 3.

Finally, it is important to emphasize that the practical implementation of Tables 3 and 4 requires a careful definition of the relevant service industry and market. A bad definition of either could produce information of little pertinence to the study.

5. Conclusion

This paper has identified three distinctive features of services: proximity between consumers and producers, asymmetric information about quality, and regulation. It has shown that these parameters play a key role in shaping market structure in service industries.

[1]   Scherer and Ross (1990), p. 11.
[2]   See Weiss and Klass (1986).
[3]   See Kay and Vickers (1988).
[4]   See Hindley (1987).

The structure of services in Europe: A conceptual framework

Table 3

Taxonomy of service industries

	Industry A	Industry B	....	Industry Z

Determinants of 'natural' market structure

Economies of scale and scope
Degree of differentiation

Barriers to entry

Sunk costs
Reputation
Proximity requirement

Expected market structure

Table 4

Taxonomy of service markets in Member State X

	Industry A	Industry B	....	Industry Z

Observed market structure

Number of firms
Concentration
Size of firms
Imports
Presence of foreign firms

Government intervention

Regulation
Discrimination
Public enterprises
Competition policy

To conclude, we offer a few conjectures about the impact of 1992 on the future shape of the European common market in services.

First, for most services, the high degree of proximity required between consumers and producers implies that 1992 is not likely to greatly affect the location of production. Ownership of firms, however, could be vastly transformed as local service providers become parts of multinational networks.

This may shift the production of certain activities from the local point of consumption to the headquarters of the multinational network.

Second, for most services, the high degree of imperfect information about quality and the use of reputation mechanisms confers advantages to incumbents. This explains attempts by established firms to pre-empt unfilled niches (i.e. locations or market segments) threatened by potential entrants. Such behaviour, in anticipation of the 1992 liberalization, can be observed in several service industries (such as airlines and banking). It may require a strong competition policy by European authorities to prevent incumbents to deter entry.

Finally, for most service industries, government intervention is likely to remain beyond the 1992 deregulation. Such intervention would require, however, a careful analysis in order to determine the appropriate level of authority (Community, national, regional or local). It is likely that, in several instances, national regulations should be replaced by EC-wide interventions. In addition, whatever the appropriate level of intervention, more room should be made for market-based regulations.

The structure of services in Europe: A conceptual framework

References

Akerlof, G. (1970), 'The market for "lemons": Qualitative uncertainty and the market mechanism', *Quarterly Journal of Economics*, 84, pp. 488-500.

Baumol, W., Panzar, J. and Willig, R. (1982), *Contestable markets and the theory of industry structure*, New York, Harcourt Brace Jovanovich.

Baumol, W. and Willig, R. (1986), 'Contestability: Developments since the book', *Oxford Economic Papers*, 38 (supplement), pp. 9-36.

Bhagwati, J. N. (1984), 'Splintering and disembodiment of services and developing nations', *The World Economy*, June.

Caves, R. E. (1982), *Multinational enterprises and economic analysis*, Cambridge, Cambridge University Press.

Caves, D. W., Christensen, L. R. and Tretheway, M. W. (1984), 'Economies of density versus economies of scale: Why trunk and local service airline costs differ', *Rand Journal of Economics*, 15, pp. 471-489.

Commission of the European Communities (1988), 'The economics of 1992', *European Economy*, No 35.

Commission of the European Communities (1990), 'Developments in the European insurance industry', II/E, mimeo.

Encaoua, D., Geroski, P. and Jacquemin, A. (1986), 'Strategic competition and the persistence of dominant firms: A survey', in Stiglitz, J. E. and Mathewson, G. F. (eds), *New developments in the analysis of market structure*, Cambridge, Mass, MIT Press.

Ernst and Whinney (1988), *A common market for services*, produced for the Commission of the European Communities.

Fuchs, V. R. (1985), 'An agenda for research on the service sector', in Inman, R. P. (ed.), *Managing the service economy*, Cambridge, Cambridge University Press.

Gilbert, R. J. (1989), 'Mobility barriers and the value of incumbency', in Schmalensee, R. and Willig, R. (eds), *Handbook in industrial organization*, Volume 1, Chapter 8, Amsterdam, North Holland.

Gilibert, P. L. and Steinherr, A. (1989), 'The impact of financial market integration on the European banking industry', *EIB papers*, No 8, Luxembourg, European Investment Bank.

Green, M. J. (1985), 'The evolution of market services in the European Community, the United States and Japan', *European Economy*, No 25.

Hill, T. P. (1977), 'On goods and services', *The review of income and wealth*, pp. 315-338.

Hindley, B. (1987), 'Trade in services within the European Community', in Giersch, H. (ed.), *Free trade in the world economy*, Tübingen, J. C. B. Mohr.

Holmström, B. (1985), 'The provision of services in a market economy', in Inman, R. P. (ed.), *Managing the service economy*, Cambridge, Cambridge University Press.

Inman, R. P. (1985), 'Introduction and overview', in Inman, R. P. (ed.), *Managing the service economy*, Cambridge, Cambridge University Press.

Jacquemin, A. (1987), *The new industrial organization*, Oxford, Clarendon Press.

Kay, J. and Vickers, J. (1988), 'Regulatory reform in Britain', *Economic Policy*, 3, pp. 286-351.

Kierzkowski, H. and Sapir, A. (1987), 'International trade in services: Perspectives from the developing countries', paper presented at the World Bank Conference on Developing Countries Interests and International Transactions in Services, Washington, DC, 15 and 16 July.

Klemperer, P. D. (1987a), 'Markets with consumer switching costs', *Quarterly Journal of Economics*, 102.

Klemperer, P. D. (1987b), 'Entry deterrence in markets with consumer switching costs', *Economic Journal*, 97 (conference papers).

McCulloch, R. (1988), 'International competition in services', in Feldstein, M. (ed.), *The United States in the world economy*, Chicago, The University of Chicago Press.

McKinsey (1989), 'Beyond 1992: Winning in the new Europe', Top Management Forum for European Insurance Executives.

Noll, R. G. (1989), 'Economic perspectives on the politics of regulation', in Schmalensee, R. and Willig, R. (eds), *Handbook in industrial organization*, Volume 2, Chapter 22, Amsterdam, North Holland.

Office of Technology Assessment, United States Congress (1986), *Trade in services: Exports and foreign revenues*, Washington, DC, US Government Printing Office.

Panzar, J. C. (1989), 'Technological determinants of firm and industry structure', in Schmalensee, R. and Willig, R. (eds), *Handbook in industrial organization*, Volume 1, Chapter 1, Amsterdam, North Holland.

Peltzman, S. (1976), 'Toward a more general theory of regulation', *Journal of Law and Economics*, 19, pp. 211-240.

Porter, M. E. (1990), *The competitive advantage of nations*, London, MacMillan.

Posner, R. A. (1974), 'Theories of economic regulation', *Bell Journal of Economics and Management Science*, 5, pp. 335-358.

Sampson, G. and Snape, R. (1985), 'Identifying the issues in trade in services', *The World Economy*, 8, pp. 171-182.

Sapir, A. (1988), 'International trade in telecommunications services', in Baldwin, R., Hamilton, C. and Sapir, A. (eds), *Issues in US-EC trade relations*, Chicago, University of Chicago Press.

Scherer, F. M. and Ross, D. (1990), *Industrial market structure and economic performance*, Boston, Houghton Mifflin.

Spence, M. (1983), 'Contestable markets and the theory of industry structure: A review article', *Journal of Economic Literature*, 21, pp. 981-990.

Stigler, G. J. (1971), 'The theory of economic regulation', *Bell Journal of Economics and Management Science*, 2, pp. 3-21.

Stiglitz, J. E. (1989), 'Imperfect information in the product market', in Schmalensee, R. and Willig, R. (eds), *Handbook in industrial organization*, Volume 1, Chapter 13, Amsterdam, North Holland.

Tirole, J. (1988), *The theory of industrial organization*, Cambridge, Mass, MIT Press.

Weiss, L. W. and Klass, M. W. (eds) (1986), *Regulatory reform*, Boston, Little, Brown & Company.

World Bank (1989), *World development report 1986*, New York, Oxford University Press.

[3]

Oxford Economic Papers 42 (1990), 715–729

PRODUCER SERVICES, SCALE, AND THE DIVISION OF LABOR

By JOSEPH F. FRANCOIS*

1. Introduction

IT is generally recognized that the services sector represents an important and growing aspect of employment in industrial economies. Until recently, however, formal analyses of the services sector have tended to emphasize final expenditure services, even though the most dramatic growth in this sector has not been in consumer services, but rather in producer or intermediate services. Reactions to the rise of the service economy have been mixed. It is often met with concern by those who view the services sector as a low wage, stagnant or non-productive sector. This viewpoint suggests that the service economy may bring with it a slowdown in productivity growth. (For example, *see* Baumol *et al.* 1985.) This approach usually places emphasis on consumer services, without giving full consideration to the unique function that services perform in production. An alternative viewpoint, which has not received the same degree of attention in the literature, is that services are an important aspect of production in modern economies.

This paper explores the relationship of producer services to market expansion and integration and the division of labor, highlighting the role of services as a complement rather than a substitute to the manufacturing process. The critical role for services emphasized here stands in sharp contrast to the commonly held view that the services sector is stagnant.[1] In this paper I analyze the implications of the relationship between intermediate services, scale, and specialization, developing a model that incorporates an explicit role for producer services in the linkage, coordination and control of specialized, interdependent operations. This includes consideration of both internal market expansion and changes in the extent of the market due to increased opportunities for trade. I use the model to argue that the post-war expansion of the producer services sector in modern industrial economies may be, in part, a result of both the integration of internal markets and the expanded opportunities for trade that have

---

* Mudge Rose Guthrie Alexander and Ferdon and The University of Maryland (University College). This paper is drawn indirectly from my dissertation research, and thanks are thus due to Arvind Panagariya for much helpful discussion, as well as to Chris Clague and Patricia Succar. The paper was completed while I was with the Research Division of the US International Trade Commission. Thanks are thus also due to Hugh Arce, Bob Feinberg, Seth Kaplan and Jose Mendez, as well as to two anonymous referees.

[1] The view that services are a stagnant or non-productive sector can be traced back at least as far as Adam Smith, who classified labor in the services sector as unproductive. "'Menial servants', government officials, military personnel, as well as 'some of the gravest and most important, and some of the most frivolous professionals', are included in the unproductive category: 'churchmen, lawyers, physicians, men of letters of all kinds; players, buffoons, musicians, opera-singers, opera-dancers, etc.'" (Spiegel 1983, p. 247). The marxist practice of including only material product in measures of national product is also a reflection of this view, which really obscures the importance of producer or intermediate services to the operation of modern industry.

716   PRODUCER SERVICES, SCALE, AND THE DIVISION OF LABOUR

accompanied post-war trade liberalization. This liberalization has resulted in
an ongoing integration of various national markets. Post-war productivity gains
in manufacturing may also be linked, in part, to this growth of producer services
and associated changes in scale.[2]

The recent theoretical literature emphasizing producer services includes
Francois (1988, 1990), Grubel and Walker (1988), Jones and Kierzkowski
(1988), Markusen (1989) and Rivera-Batiz and Rivera-Batiz (1988). Greenfield
(1966) has pointed out that the growing relevance of services to production is
a critical aspect of economic development. He has argued that these services
are important to the coordination and control of specialized operations within
firms. They are the bonds that hold together the diverse elements of a modern,
specialized economy, becoming a more significant aspect of production as scale
increases and production processes become more complex. Katouzian (1970)
has argued that the demand for producer services (which he refers to as
complementary services) can be expected to grow with the growth of round-
about production and the associated conversion of local markets into national
markets. The demand for these services increases with the "range and
complexity of intermediate goods". Gold (1981) observes that, with changes in
scale and the degree of specialization, one often observes a more than
proportional increase in salaried and technical personnel needed "to ensure the
effective planning, servicing, coordination, evaluation and improvement of the
resulting wider array of more specialized and mutually interdependent operations". Similar arguments have been made more recently by Jones and
Kierzkowski and Francois.

While the producer services sector has been informally linked to scale and
specialization, few of these arguments have been formally presented or analyzed,
nor have the implications of this relationship been fully explored. While
Rivera-Batiz and Rivera-Batiz analyze the implications a specialized, nontraded intermediate services sector can have for the gains from foreign
investment, they do not explicitly consider the function of the services sector
discussed here, one of coordinating and linking together specialized operations.
Neither does Markusen. Rather, Markusen emphasizes specialization within
the services sector itself, using a variation of Ethier's (1982) model of international returns to scale.

In contrast, this paper formally examines the role of services suggested by
Gold, Jones and Kierzkowski, and Katouzian. The remainder of the paper is
organized as follows. Section 2 discusses the growth of the producer services
sector. Section 3 develops a one-sector monopolistic competition model which
exhibits increasing returns due to specialization in the production of a
differentiated product. An explicit role for services is assumed in the coordination
of specialized intermediate producers. Section 4 then considers the implications
of the model. It both analyzes the effect a change in the extent of the market

---

[2] For more on growth, trade, and specialization, *see* Ethier (1982), Romer (1987), and Jefferson
(1988).

has on specialization, product differentiation, real income, and the relative employment share of producer services, and examines the effect the integration of markets through liberalization of trade has on the division of labor and on employment in the producer services sector. The paper is summarized and conclusions are made in Section 5.

2. The growth of the producer services sector

The growth of modern industrial economies has been accompanied by dramatic growth in the services sector. Clark (1940) was the first to note a rising share of services in income associated with economic growth. His observation was that the share of labor devoted to the production of services goes up with income. Clark emphasized the role of income levels, arguing that the reasons for the growth of the tertiary sector had to be sought on the demand side. Summers (1985, p. 48 n) has emphasized that Clark's view was concerned with the share of employment devoted to production of services, and was not strictly that consumer services were income inelastic. Because of the changing employment and price patterns observed by Clark and more recently by Kravis, Heston, and Summers (1982), an important issue in the theoretical literature on services has been the correlation between final-expenditure service prices and per-capita income levels. This includes work by Balassa (1964), Samuelson (1964), Bhagwati (1984a, 1985), Clague (1985) and Panagariya (1988). The emphasis of this literature has been on consumer rather than producer services, and on why the price of non-tradable final expenditure services varies systematically with per-capita income levels.

While the share of services in final expenditures increases dramatically with income levels, the most dramatic changes in terms of employment have been for producer or intermediate services. Table 1 presents employment data for

TABLE 1
US Full-time Equivalent Employment Shares by Industry

Industry	1929	1939	1947	1959	1969	1977	1985
Services	55.13	59.94	56.61	61.66	64.91	68.40	70.48
Producer	5.85	5.83	6.06	8.23	10.03	11.96	14.80
Distributive	15.66	12.90	13.54	12.15	10.97	11.36	11.93
Retail	11.93	12.22	12.57	12.70	13.00	14.18	14.28
Government	9.07	17.19	14.16	18.58	20.48	19.57	18.33
Consumer	10.77	9.61	7.67	6.47	5.75	4.99	4.24
Nonprofit	1.85	2.19	2.61	3.52	4.57	6.34	6.94
Agriculture	8.35	6.59	4.31	3.18	1.74	1.90	1.63
Extractive and Transformative	36.52	33.46	39.08	35.16	33.35	29.70	27.89
Manufacturing	29.51	27.75	32.27	28.91	27.66	24.10	21.83

Source: Stanback *et al.* (1977), *Survey of Current Business* (US Department of Commerce), and the *Employment and Earnings Survey* (US Department of Labor).

718   PRODUCER SERVICES, SCALE, AND THE DIVISION OF LABOUR

TABLE 2

Non-Production Workers as a Share of Manufacturing Employment

Country	1949	1959	1964	1969	1974	1979	1984*
United States	18.4†	24.2	26.0	26.8	27.1	28.4	31.4
Canada	—	—	—	—	29.4	29.3	32.6
Japan	—	—	26.0	27.7	32.3	33.7	34.6
Spain	—	—	—	—	20.3		
United Kingdom	—	—	22.8	26.0	26.7	28.6	28.8
Norway	—·	—	19.6	21.0	—	31.1	34.3
Finland	—	—	17.1	20.5	22.6	24.5	26 4
Denmark	—	—	22.5	24.5	26.2	27.2	29.7

* The US data are for 1984, and the data for other countries are for 1983.
† The US figure remained steady at least from 1919 (when data are first available) until the mid 1950s at around 19%.
Source: US data are from the *Employment and Earnings Survey*, while other country data are from the OECD's *Labour Force Statistics 1963–1983* (1985).

the US for select years from 1929 through 1985.[3] The producer services sector, which accounted for 6% of US employment in 1949, accounted for almost 12% of employment and approximately 20% of national product in 1977. By 1985, free-standing producer services accounted for 14.8% of employment. The employment share of consumer services, in contrast, fell from 10.77% in 1929 to 4.24% in 1985.

Bhagwati (1984b) has suggested that producer services appear to be a growing sector in part because firms are externalizing service activities once performed inside the firm. While the "splintering" away of activities once performed inside manufacturing firms may explain part of the shifting pattern of employment in producer services, it does not fully explain the rise of the producer services sector. In fact, producer services also represent an increasingly important share of the remaining activities that are still performed within manufacturing firms. Based on Greenfield's observation that indirect labor is usually involved in producer-service activities, Table 2 presents the relative importance of non-production workers as a share of total manufacturing employment for eight industrial countries. These non-production workers are interpreted as manufacturing employees engaged in producer service activities. It can be seen that non-production workers accounted for 18.4% of manufacturing employment in 1949 in the United States. This figure had increased to 31.4% by 1984. While comparable data are not available for other countries prior to 1964, the rest of the sample has exhibited a similar pattern of shifting employment shares since 1964. This suggests that the importance of services in production is due to other factors in addition to externalization.

[3] The employment figures in Table 1 are from Stanback *et al.* 1981 and from the US Department of Commerce's *Survey of Current Business* and the US Department of Labor's *Employment and Earnings Survey*. The employment categories used by Stanback are based on Singleman (1978).

Greenfield has suggested that the importance of services in production is related to the emphasis placed in modern economies on specialization in production. He has observed that, with economic development, there are important qualitative changes in the input mix of the labor force in expanding firms. Larger plant size implies a larger share of non-production labor in employment. Increased output at the firm level requires the creation of additional departments within the firm and the increased specialization of personnel and equipment. The changing input mix of the labor force is an important qualitative change associated with economic development. "Economic development, as is well known, does not proceed through quantitative increments to plant and equipment, labor force, and other resources" (Greenfield, 1966, p. 116). More recently, Gold has argued that such specialization is at the heart of the realization of returns to scale.

3. The Model

In this section I develop a one-sector model characterized by increasing returns and monopolistic competition. In the production side of the model, there are increasing returns to scale at the firm level. The specification of returns to scale is consistent with Gold's (1981, p. 15) definition of scale as "the level of planned production which determines the extent to which specialization has been applied to the subdivision of the component tasks of a unified operation". An explicit role for services is introduced in the specialization process.

Assume that different firms produce different varieties of a differentiated product x by employing labor L. Production of any variety x_j is subject to increasing returns due to specialization. There are a large number of production techniques available for producing any variety. Different techniques involve different levels of specialization of the production process. Formally, these techniques are assumed to be indexed by v, where $v = 1 \ldots n$ and v is an index of the degree of specialization. v can be thought of as the number of distinct processes or stages into which production has been divided. Different production techniques are all assumed to take the form

$$x_j = \beta_v \prod_{i=1}^{V} D_{ij}^{\alpha_{iv}}, \qquad (3.1)$$

where $\beta_v = v^\delta$, $\delta > 1$, $\alpha_{iv} = 1/v$. D_{ij} represents labor employed in direct production activity i for production of variety j. This is the functional form used by Edwards and Starr (1987) in their discussion of specialization. Any member of the set of available production techniques exhibits constant returns in direct labor costs. However, there are increasing returns to direct labor associated with higher degrees of specialization. Strong symmetries have been imposed on the parameters of equation (3.1) to ensure the tractability of the model. Given our parameter restrictions, direct labor will be allocated equally across all production activities at a given level of specialization. This means that direct

720   PRODUCER SERVICES, SCALE, AND THE DIVISION OF LABOUR

labor demanded by firm j is

$$D_j = \sum_{i=1}^{v} D_{ij} = v^{1-\delta} x_j. \tag{3.2}$$

I also assume that producer services are important to the production process. Producer services coordinate the specialized production members of a complex production process into a unified operation. Labor is hired by the firm to perform these indirect production activities. (In principle, services might be produced internally by the firm, or purchased from free-standing service firms. The distinction is not critical to the results of the model. Because services are needed for the coordination and control of the production process, service costs are assumed to be an increasing function of the complexity of the production process, as measured by v. To express this relationship, I assume that service costs, in terms of labor units, are

$$S_j = \gamma_0 v + \gamma_1 x_j, \tag{3.3}$$

where S_j represents the total quantity of indirect labor employed in producer service activities by firm j. The parameter γ_0 can be interpreted as the overhead cost of management, engineers and other technical personnel responsible for managing and coordinating the activities of an additional, specialized operation within the rest of the firm. Given equations (3.2) and (3.3), any particular production technique exhibits constant marginal costs.

The total cost function can be expressed in terms of x_j, v, and the wage rate w. Since I assume that direct and indirect labor requirements both depend on scale and the degree of specialization, we effectively have a technology where indirect and direct labor are combined in proportions that depend on the degree of specialization. These requirements are consistent with a production function of the form

$$x_j = \min\left[((S_j - \gamma_0 v)/\gamma_1), \left(\beta_v \prod_{i=1}^{v} D_{ij}^{\delta} \right) \right]. \tag{3.4}$$

The cost function $C(x_j)$ associated with equation (3.4) is the sum of direct and indirect labor costs, which are given by equations (3.2) and (3.3).

$$C(x_j) = [v^{1-\delta} x_j + \gamma_0 v + \gamma_1 x_j] w. \tag{3.5}$$

Production function (3.4), and its associated cost function (3.5), allow producers to substitute direct for indirect labor by varying the degree of specialization. For a given level of output, the choice variable for a cost-minimizing producer is thus v. Setting the partial derivative of (3.5) with respect to v equal to zero and solving for v yields

$$v = [((\delta - 1)/\gamma_0) x_j]^{1/\delta}. \tag{3.6}$$

The degree of specialization is an increasing function of x and a decreasing function of the overhead parameter γ_0. Substituting (3.6) into (3.5), we obtain the minimum cost function $C^*(x_j)$:

$$C^*(x_j) = [(\delta - 1)^{1/\delta}\gamma_0^{(\delta-1)/\delta}(\delta/(\delta-1))x_j^{1/\delta} + \gamma_1 x_j]w$$
$$= f(x_j)w, \tag{3.7}$$

where $f' > 0$ and $f'' < 0$. All firms are assumed to produce subject to the cost structure embodied in equation (3.7). The function $f(x_j)$ measures the amount of labor employed by firm j.

To solve for the firm's demand for direct labor as a function of x_j, substitute equation (3.6) into equation (3.2). This yields

$$D_j = ((\delta - 1)/\gamma_0)^{(1-\delta)/\delta}x_j^{1/\delta}. \tag{3.8}$$

Demand for direct labor increases with the scale of production, but at a decreasing rate. Demand for indirect labor can be solved for by substituting equation (3.6) into equation (3.3). This yields

$$S_j = [\gamma_0((\delta - 1)/\gamma_0)^{1/\delta} + \gamma_1 x_j^{(\delta-1)/\delta}]x_j^{1/\delta}. \tag{3.9}$$

Equations (3.8) and (3.9) can be combined to yield the ratio of indirect to direct labor within the firm, $(S/D)_j$.

$$(S/D)_j = (\delta - 1) + \gamma_1 x_j^{(\delta-1)/\delta}((\delta - 1)/\gamma_0)^{(\delta-1)/\delta}. \tag{3.10}$$

This is plotted in Figure 1 as the curve (S/D). Another relationship between employment and output is given by equation (3.7). In equation (3.7), the function $f(x_j)$ measures the quantity of labor employed by a firm producing output x_j as a function of the level of output. This can be inverted to yield x as a function of labor employed, L_j. This is plotted in Figure 1 as the line $x(L)_0$. Finally, equation (3.6), which determines the degree of specialization, is also plotted in Figure 1 as the curve $v(x)$. Together, this system of curves determines the degree of specialization and the relative importance of services and direct labor in the production of variety x_j. The intersection of the $x(L)$ and (S/D) curves determines the relative employment shares of indirect and direct labor, while the intersection of the $x(L)$ and $v(x)$ curves determines the degree of specialization.

Consider the effect of changes in scale. As the scale of production expands, this results in a movement of the $x(L)$ line from $x(L)_0$ to $x(L)_1$. Two other qualitative changes occur in the firm with this change in scale. The degree of specialization increases. In addition, the relative importance of producer services, in terms of employment, increases with the scale of production. As firms grow, we observe an increased degree of specialization and an increasing ratio of indirect to direct labor.[4] The production side of the model thus

---

[4] In the model presented here, the measure of the relative size of the service sector corresponds to the measurement used in Table 1. It is the ratio of indirect to direct labor. In principle, firms may also be hiring some of their service inputs from free-standing firms. In addition, firms may externalize some of the specialized direct production activities that emerge as scale increases. However, this paper is not concerned with externalization.

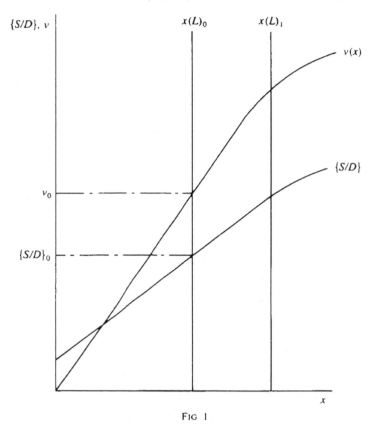

FIG 1

incorporates the assumption that the relative importance of services in production depends on the scale of production and on the degree of specialization in production.

All firms are assumed to produce subject to the costs expressed in equation (3.7). The activities required to produce a given variety are assumed to be unique enough that joint production can be ruled out.[5] Each firm produces only one variety of the differentiated product. All firms price at average cost because of free entry.

---

[5] One could modify the model presented here by assuming that certain types of activities can be produced jointly. The structure of firms, and the number of varieties they produce, would then depend on the scale of production of each variety, the number of stages into which production had been divided, and the opportunity for joint production in some of these different distinct activities. Presumably, opportunities for joint production would then be limited by the scale of the market, as well as by any associated coordination costs. However, economies of scale are beyond the scope of the present paper.

I assume demand is characterized by Lancaster preferences.[6] Different consumers prefer different varieties of the differentiated product. Strong symmetries are imposed on preferences, so that preferences for different varieties are placed with uniform density in product space. This results in an aggregate preference for variety. Helpman and Krugman (1985) demonstrate that with strong symmetries and Lancaster preferences, the elasticity of demand for each available variety will be a function of the total number of varieties available.

Consumers each prefer what they consider to be an ideal variety of the differentiated product. Different consumers consider different varieties of the differentiated product to be ideal. When a consumer's ideal variety is unavailable, he chooses the variety that comes closest to approximating his ideal. To quantify the similarity of different varieties, assume that any product variety x_j can be represented by a reference point on the circumference of a circle. The shortest arc distance between corresponding reference points measures the similarity of different varieties. Formally, the distance between point t_i and any other point t is measured by the function $d(t, t_i)$.

By using the distance function $d(\cdot)$, we can convert any product variety into "ideal variety equivalents". Ideal variety equivalents measure how much of the ideal variety is necessary to give the consumer the same satisfaction as a certain quantity of some other variety. For a consumer whose ideal variety is $\hat{t}$, the ideal variety equivalent $\hat{D}(t_i)$ of $D(t_i)$ units of variety t_i is assumed to be

$$\hat{D}(t_i) = D(t_i)/h[d(t_i, \hat{t})]. \tag{3.11}$$

The $h[d(\cdot)]$ function measures how much a unit of the ideal variety is worth to a consumer in terms of a unit of any other variety. I assume that $h[0] = 1$, h', $h'' > 0$ for $d > 0$, and $h' = 0$ for $d = 0$. Utility, U, is defined in terms of ideal variety equivalents.

$$U = \hat{D}(t_i) = D(t_i)/h[d(t_i, \hat{t})]. \tag{3.12}$$

A consumer will spend all of his income on the product variety which offers the lowest price for ideal variety equivalents $\hat{P}(t_i)$, where $\hat{P}(t_i) = h[d(t_i, \hat{t})]P(t_i)$ and where $P(t_i)$ is the actual price of t_i.

Assume that preferences are distributed with uniform density in product space. Because we have imposed strong symmetries on preferences and on production costs, available varieties will be identically priced and will be located symmetrically in product space in equilibrium. In such an equilibrium, the elasticity of demand for variety j, σ_j, is identical for all varieties and is a function of the number of available varieties, n.

$$\sigma_j = \sigma(n), \sigma' > 0. \tag{3.13}$$

---

[6] Lancaster preferences are more realistic than the Dixit-Stiglitz type of preferences, though they are also less tractable. With the formulation of Dixit-Stiglitz preferences often found in differentiated product models, the scale of individual firms remains fixed. Changes in output result solely from the entry and exit of firms. Since the emphasis of this paper is on the effect of changes in the scale of individual firms, we must sacrifice tractability for realism.

4. The implications of the model

This section uses the model developed above to analyze the role of the producer services sector in growth due to specialization. Changes in the extent of the market, and the resulting change in the size of operations, leads to both an increasing degree of specialization and to a growing share of labor employed in indirect production activities. There is also a secular rise in per-capita income levels. Labor productivity in direct production activities increases as the market expands. This is due to the increased division of labor associated with an expanding market. However, it is producer services that make this increased division of labor possible. The realization of increasing returns due to specialization depends on an expanding service sector. Liberalization of trade leads to similar results.

Because of the symmetries in our model, all available varieties will be produced in identical quantities and will be identically priced in equilibrium. For this reason, the subscript on x_j is dropped. Since equilibrium prices can be expressed in terms of any common unit, I arbitrarily set the price of labor to 1. Because we have increasing returns and free entry, there will be only one firm engaged in the production of a given variety. This firm will be a monopolist, pricing according to the condition

$$P(1 - (1/\sigma(n))) = f'(x). \tag{4.1}$$

In addition, average cost pricing means that the price of each variety will be

$$P = f(x)/x. \tag{4.2}$$

Full employment of the labor force L is assumed. This means that

$$L = \sum_{j=1}^{n} L_j = nf(x). \tag{4.3}$$

Together, equations (3.6), (3.10), (4.1), (4.2) and (4.3) define a system of five equations and five unknowns. The solution to this system can be expressed geometrically. The zero profit condition (equation 4.2) can be combined with the marginal pricing condition (equation 4.1) to obtain the relationship between n and x that is plotted as the ZZ curve in Figure 2.[7] Another relationship between n and x is offered by the full employment condition. This is plotted as the FF curve. Finally, equations (3.6) and (3.10) are plotted in the upper quadrant of Figure 2 as the $v(x)$ and (S/D) curves. Together, this system determines the scale of individual firms, the number of product varieties

---

[7] The ZZ and FF curves represent the well-known conditions for equilibrium in a monopolistically competitive industry that can be found in models like those of Krugman (1979, 1980), Helpman (1981) and Dixit and Norman (1980). (For a more complete discussion, *see* Helpman and Krugman, 1985.) With Dixit-Stigliz preferences, the ZZ curve would be a horizontal line, with the size of individual firms being fixed. With Lancaster preferences, the ZZ curve slopes up when we have fixed marginal costs. Otherwise, its slope depends on the potential for scale economies, as measured by the ratio of marginal to average cost. In a market where the division of labor is limited by the extent of the market, the ZZ curve will slope up as drawn.

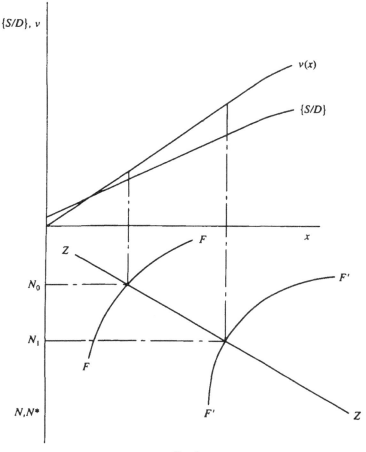

Fig. 2

available, the division of labor, and the relative employment shares of producer services and direct production activities.

Consider a change in the extent of the market resulting from expansion of the labor force. As the economy expands, the FF curve in Figure 2 moves from FF to $F'F'$. The ZZ, (S/D), and $v(x)$ curves are not affected by this change in the supply of labor. The result is that the number of firms increases from n_0 to n_1. The scale of individual firms also expands in terms of employment and output. As firms expand, they split their production activities into more distinct stages of production. This increased division of labor requires employing additional labor in producer service activities. As a result, the share of labor employed in indirect production activities grows. This is because the productivity of direct labor increases with specialization, but only if it is accompanied by an expanding service sector. Prices, in terms of labor, also fall as the market expands. Per-capita incomes rise because prices fall relative to the wage rate. This can be seen by inspection of equation (4.1). As the scale of production increases, average costs in terms of labor decline. The model generates productivity changes consistent with the stylized relationship between growth and productivity known as Verdoorn's Law. It also links the growth of the producer services sector to the realization of these productivity changes.

In the model, expansion of the market is accompanied by increasing per-capita incomes, increased product differentiation, larger firms, an increased division of labor and a growing employment share for services. The increased division of labor is only possible because it is supported by an expanding service sector. Within the model, producer services are a critical part of the realization of returns due to specialization. As firms expand and production is increasingly specialized, the ratio of indirect to direct labor increases. To the extent that services are critical to the coordination and control of specialized, inter-dependent operations, the model suggests that the post-war increase in the relative importance of the producer services sector may be due, in part, to expanded markets.

The integration of markets through trade leads to results in our model similar to those resulting from expansion of the labor force. This can be demonstrated by contrasting a non-trade and a trade equilibrium in a two-country context. While this represents a static analysis of what is really a dynamic process, we are able to contrast equilibrium conditions that would result under the restricted and liberalized trade regimes. The result suggests that with trade liberalization, the effective integration of markets and the resulting change in the extent of the market can also add impetus to the expansion of the producer services sector.

Assume we have two economies, home and foreign, with demand and supply conditions like those described above. Home country values are designated by small letters, and foreign country values by capital letters. With identical technologies, endowments, and preferences, we will have $x = X$ and $l = L$. Equation (4.1) is replaced by

$$P(1 - (1/\sigma(n^*))) = f'(x), \qquad (4.4)$$

where $n^* = (n + N)$. The full employment condition is replaced by

$$l + L = n^* f(x). \qquad (4.5)$$

The rest of our system remains unchanged. With autarky, each country produces subject to its own FF curve like that in Figure 2. However, by introducing trade, the autarky FF curves are replaced by a combined FF curve like $F'F'$ in Figure 2. $F'F'$ is defined by equation (4.5).

Consider the removal of prohibitive restrictions on trade. As markets are integrated, there is a consolidation among existing firms, with the remaining firms being larger than before trade. While consumers have a large number of varieties available to choose from (because they can choose from both home and foreign varieties), the total number of firms actually declines. Integration leads to a decline in $(n + N)$. Because the remaining firms are larger than before trade, they will find it advantageous to apply an increased division of labor to the production process. This means that after firms have consolidated, they will emphasize increasingly specialized methods of production. To facilitate this specialization, more labor will be allocated to indirect production activities. The service sector grows in absolute terms and relative to direct production activities. Expanded opportunities for trade which result in expanded markets imply a growing producer service sector, increased specialization and rising per-capita income levels.

5. Summary and conclusions

Recently, attention has again been focused on the importance of the services sector in modern economies. However, emphasis is usually placed on consumer or final-expenditure services. The focus of this paper, in contrast, is producer services. While the producer services sector has been informally linked in the literature to changes in scale and to the coordination of complex production processes, the implications of this relationship for the changing role of the producer services sector in modern economies have not been explored. This paper develops a model that incorporates this relationship between services and scale, explicitly assuming that producer services are important to the coordination and control of specialized production processes. The model is then used to consider the implications of this role for the relationship of the services sector to the scale and productivity changes that result from changes in the extent of the market. Recent evidence (Jefferson, 1988) has suggested that the observed correlation between labor productivity and output growth can be attributed, in large part, to internal scale economies and to returns from specialization. This paper has argued, in turn, that the growth of the producer services sector may be important to this process.

In the context of the model, producer services are important to the realization of returns to scale. Rather than a drag on productivity, a growing producer service sector is an important, positive aspect of expanding economies because it facilitates an increased division of labor within unified operations and associated productivity changes. The arguments related to services and specialization that I have presented here suggest that the post-war expansion of the producer services sector can be explained, in part, by the expansion and integration of internal markets and by the effective integration of markets that has resulted from trade liberalization. Both of these contribute to changes in the extent of the market and to resulting changes in scale and the importance, of services in production. The model also formalizes an alternative explanation for some of the post-war productivity gains realized by industrial countries. In the model, such gains are related to the growing services sector and to the expansion of markets that is again due, in part, to trade liberalization. Trade liberalization, accompanied by an increase in the scale of individual firms and

728   PRODUCER SERVICES, SCALE, AND THE DIVISION OF LABOUR

a rising employment share for services, results in the realization of returns due to specialization. Services are critical to realizing these returns.

The arguments presented in this paper highlight the importance of services to production in complex, modern economies. The cost and availability of producer services may be a limit to the realization of increasing returns due to specialization. Where services do play the role assumed in the model, the realization of returns to scale and the pace of development is tied to the pace of growth of the producer services sector. The disintegration of production into specialized intermediate stages depends on both scale and on the supply of producer services. This suggests that an expanding producer service sector is an important aspect of growth. Access to producer services through direct trade or through multinationals may help developing countries to take part in this process of specialization. Traded services may facilitate both increased specialization within borders and participation in a process of international specialization in various stages of production, playing a critical role in the realization of "international returns to scale".[8]

REFERENCES

BALASSA, B. (December 1964). "The Purchasing Power Parity Doctrine: A Reappraisal", *Journal of Political Economy*, 72, 564–96.

BAUMOL, W. J., BLACKMAN, S. and WOLFF, E. N. (September 1985). "Unbalanced Growth Revisited: Asymptotic Stagnancy and New Evidence", *The American Economic Review*, 75, 806–17.

BHAGWATI, J. N (1985). "Trade in Services and Developing Countries", London: Tenth Annual Geneva Convention at the London School of Economics.

BHAGWATI, J. N. (June 1984a) "Why Are Services Cheaper in the Developing Countries?", *The Economic Journal*, 94, 279–86.

—— (June 1984b). "Splintering and Disembodiment of Services and Developing Nations", *The World Economy*, 133–44.

CLAGUE, C. K. (1985). "A Model of Real National Price Levels", *Southern Economic Journal*, 51, 998–1017

CLARK, C. (1940). *The Conditions of Economic Progress*. London: Macmillan and Company.

DIXIT, A. and NORMAN, V. (1980). *Theory of International Trade: A Dual, General Equilibrium Approach*. London: Cambridge University Press.

EDWARDS, B. K. and STARR, R. M. (March 1987). "A Note on Indivisibilities, Specialization, and Economies of Scale", *American Economic Review*, 77, 192–94.

ETHIER, W. J. (June 1982). "National and International Returns to Scale in the Modern Theory of International Trade", *American Economic Review*, 72, 389–405.

FRANCOIS, J. F. (1988). "Trade in Producer Services and the Realization of Increasing Returns Due to Specialization". Doctoral dissertation, College Park: The University of Maryland.

—— (February 1990). "Trade in Producer Services and Returns Due to Specialization Under Monopolistic Competition", *Canadian Journal of Economics*, 23, 109–124.

GOLD, B. (March 1981). "On Size, Scale, and Returns: A Survey", *Journal of Economic Literature*, 19, 5–33.

GREENFIELD, H. I. (1966). *Manpower and the Growth of Producer Services*. London: Columbia University Press.

GRUBEL, H. G. and WALKER, M A. (1988). "Modern Service Sector Growth: Causes and Effects" (mimeo).

[8] *See* Francois (1988, 1990) on trade in producer services like those discussed here.

HELPMAN, E. (1981). "International Trade in the Presence of Product Differentiation, Economies of Scale, and Monopolistic Competition", *Journal of International Economics*, 11, 305–40.

HELPMAN, E. and KRUGMAN, P. R. (1985). *Market Structure and Foreign Trade: Increasing Returns, Imperfect Competition, and the International Economy*. Cambridge: The MIT Press.

JEFFERSON, GARY H. (1988). "The Aggregate Production Function and Productivity Growth: Verdoorn's Law Revisited", *Oxford Economic Papers*, 40, 671–91.

JONES, R. W. and KIERZKOWSKI, H. (1988). "The Role of Services in Production and International Trade: A Theoretical Framework". Paper presented at the Spring 1988 Meetings of the Midwest International Economics Conference, University of Minnesota-Minneapolis.

KATOUZIAN, M. A. (1970). "The Development of the Service Sector: A New Approach", *Oxford Economic Papers*, 22, 362–83.

KRAVIS, I. B., HESTON, A. V. and SUMMERS, R. (1982). *World Product and Income: International Comparisons of Real Gross Product*. Baltimore: Johns Hopkins University Press.

KRUGMAN, P. R. (November 1979). "Increasing Returns, Monopolistic Competition, and International Trade", *Journal of International Economics*, 9, 469–80.

—— (June 1980). "Scale Economies, Product Differentiation, and the Pattern of Trade", *American Economic Review*, 70, 950–59.

MARKUSEN, JAMES R. (March 1989). "Trade in Producer Services and in Other Specialized Intermediate Inputs", *American Economic Review*, 79, 85–95.

Organization for Economic Cooperation and Development (1985). *Labour Force Statistics 1963–1983*, Paris.

PANAGARIYA, A. (August 1988). "A Theoretical Explanation of Some Stylized Facts of Growth", *Quarterly Journal of Economics*, 103, 509–26.

RIVERA-BATIZ, F. L. and RIVERA-BATIZ, L. (1988). "The Effects of Direct Foreign Investment in the Presence of Increasing Returns Due to Specialization". Paper presented at the Spring 1988 Meetings of the Midwest International Economics Conference, University of Minnesota-Minneapolis.

ROMER, PAUL M. (May 1987). "Growth Based on Increasing Returns Due to Specialization", *American Economic Review*, 77, 56–62.

SAMUELSON, P. (May 1964). "Theoretical Notes on Trade Problems", *Review of Economics and Statistics*, 46, 145–54.

SINGLEMAN, J. (1978). *From Agriculture to Services*. Beverly Hills: Sage Publishing.

SPIEGEL, H. W. (1983). *The Growth of Economic Thought*. Durham: Duke University Press.

STANBACK, T. M., JR., BEARSE, P. J., NOYELLE, T. J. and KARASEK, R. A. (1981). *Services: The New Economy*. Totowa NJ: Allanheld, Osmun & Co.

SUMMERS, R. (1985). "Services in the International Economy". In *Managing the Service Economy: Prospects and Problems*, Robert Inman (ed.). Cambridge: Cambridge University Press.

[4]

Principles in Trade in Services

Richard H. Snape

Services come in a great variety of forms; perhaps more than goods they are adapted individually to the demander. Indeed, differentiation of goods frequently arises from the services that accompany their sale. With so many forms of services, how is one to approach the question of barriers to their trade? One helpful starting point is to look at the means by which trade takes place in order to find common elements in barriers that may extend across a whole range of traded services. If ways of negotiating these forms of barriers can be identified, it may be possible to develop a general agreement that covers services just as the General Agreement on Tariffs and Trade (GATT) covers trade in all types of goods.[1]

Both goods and services are produced by labor, capital, and other factors of production. International trade in services is the supply by residents of one country to demanders resident in another country of services that are not incorporated in goods (other than in the paper, film, disks, and the like used to record and transfer the service).[2] The receiver of the service may be a person (for, say, a haircut, entertainment, or transport), a legal entity such as a company or government (for insurance or banking, for example), or objects such as airplanes (for repairs or airport services) or merchandise (for transport).

For some services it is necessary that the receiver of the services be in close proximity to the supplier; for others the supplier and the receiver can be at a distance from each other. Examples of services that require proximity are tourist and transport services, surgery, and repairs. Those for which it may not be necessary include architectural and computing services, broadcast entertainment, and anything else that can be communicated through the mail or by electronic means. If service suppliers and receivers must be in physical proximity, physical movement of one or the other will generally be necessary.

The receiver of the service should be distinguished from the demander (that is, the payer). The receiver could be an object (an airplane to be repaired) or a person other than the demander (a child to be educated). An international transaction takes place when the transaction is between a supplier and a demander who are residents of different countries, irrespective of the location of the receiver of the service.

In negotiations concerning services trade, as for all international trade, considerable emphasis is given to the exchange of reductions in barriers to trade, as though the importers of services were imposing a cost on themselves by importing them. This neglects the gains from international trade that are earned by the importing countries as well as the exporters; if there were no importing, there would be little point in exporting. The gains from trade in services are similar to those from trade in goods. Trade enables a country to concentrate production on the products in which it has a comparative advantage; it provides access to new products and technology; and it facilitates the achievement of economies of scale in production. As with trade in goods, economists and others have given a great deal of attention to thinking of situations in which domestic industries should be protected against imports. But cases in which economic logic (in terms of the interests of a country as a whole) supports such protection tend to be rare, both in theory and in practice. There is a strong economic presumption that international trade in services, as in goods, is economically beneficial.

Nevertheless, a wide range of barriers does exist to international trade in services, as in goods. And these barriers do not, in general, exist by accident. Although they may often be the result of economic misperceptions, they are frequently the product of domestic political forces, and invariably they have their defenders. But despite the political costs that may have to be incurred in their reduction—and these costs may explain why trade negotiations are entered into in the form of an exchange of "concessions"—importing as well as exporting countries will generally realize economic gains from reducing barriers to trade in services as well as in goods.

Richard H. Snape

Determinants of Trade in Services

What determines the patterns of international trade in services? Because all production arises from the services of factors of production, the same considerations that affect trade in goods can be expected to affect trade in services. Without barriers to trade, countries with relatively large amounts of unskilled labor will tend to export labor-intensive services as well as labor-intensive goods. Such service exports can be in many forms: the temporary movement of construction crews, the manning of ships, and the simple processing of electronically transmitted data are three examples. Countries with relatively skilled labor will have a comparative advantage in exporting services that require relatively large inputs of such labor—architectural and financial services, the writing of computer software, and the like. Countries that for reasons of geography or history have built up skills in ocean fishing are likely to export shipping services, those that have endowments of beautiful scenery will have a comparative advantage in the export of tourist services, and so on. In other words "factor endowments" are important in determining the pattern of trade in services just as with goods.

Economies of scale and scope are also likely to be important in some service industries, as for some goods. When such economies are particularly important, a large domestic market may help to provide an advantage on world markets. Thus a litigious society is likely to develop specializations in law that, at least in their international dimensions, may be marketed internationally. Financially rich countries will develop expertise in financial institutions and a whole range of interacting financial activities and will tend to export these services.

High-income countries may have an initial comparative advantage in services that are demanded by people with high incomes. But if labor costs are an important component of total costs in such industries, countries with relatively low labor costs but with the required skills may be able to compete successfully over time and take markets from those that were first in the field—international air transport is an example of this, as are data processing and typesetting. Once processes become standardized, production in many areas moves from the innovators to countries with abundant labor that possess the required skills and the necessary complementary capital equipment. Such developments are analogous to those that have occurred in some goods markets.

The availability and quality of the necessary complementary capital equipment can be particularly important. In data processing, for example, protection of a domestic computer industry, because of its effects on the costs and availability of computer hardware and software, may

discourage the export of computing services by countries that would otherwise be well suited for it. Similarly the export by Ethiopian Airlines[3] of aircraft repairs and training to other African countries and elsewhere would not be possible without complementary capital equipment.

Extending the horizon to incorporate international trade in the services of financial capital leads one to consider countries that are net borrowers and lenders. Net lending is the result of an excess of domestic saving over investment; net borrowing is the opposite. Such excesses may be attributable to the choice of individuals between frugality and profligacy, to the state of development of a country, or to the budgetary policies of governments. Comparative advantage in the export of the services of financial capital thus will be linked to these considerations.

Many services that can be provided by employees of firms (that is, within a firm) can also be provided on a contractual basis from outside the firm. A manufacturer may obtain accounting services from employees or from a firm of accountants; cleaning of premises may be undertaken by employees or by contract cleaners; on-the-job training may be supplied by employees or by contractors; and so on. In each case services may be traded on the market or produced within the firm. It has been suggested that more services are being supplied on a contractual basis than in the past. Some possible reasons for this are changing technology (particularly electronic), changing laws regarding the responsibilities and liabilities of firms toward their employees, changing composition of the work force, increasing specialization owing to the growth of knowledge, and increased payroll taxes and workers' compensation insurance premiums. This turn toward contracting-out has been referred to as a splintering of services (Bhagwati 1984). To the extent that this splintering of services from goods occurs, it will lead not only to expanded domestic trade in services but also to expanded international trade. When it occurs because of increasing labor costs, provision of services is likely to move to lower-labor-cost countries—provided, as noted above, that firms in these countries have access to the required complementary equipment.

It is apparent that a whole range of services may be traded internationally purely as services or may be incorporated into traded goods. A country may import automobile design and build the automobiles itself, or it may import automobiles—which, of course, incorporate the design services. Thus among the factors that determine the pattern of trade in services must be counted not only the barriers to trade in services themselves but also the barriers to trade in goods. Barriers to imports of automobiles may lead to imports of automobile design. But we now focus on direct barriers to trade in services rather than on indirect effects through barriers to trade in goods.

Barriers to Trade in Services

Regulation is pervasive in services industries, and this in turn affects international trade. Regulation is explicitly protective of domestic producers only when it discriminates against foreigners; otherwise it will tend to protect some producers against all other producers, domestic and foreign.

Frequently, regulation is designed to protect consumers. Consumer protection in goods often takes the form of the prescription of standards for the goods produced. Such control on output is much more difficult to enforce for many services—can the quality of surgery, education, or insurance be monitored continually? Control is often exercised instead by issuing licenses for producers and by enforcing prudential or other qualifications for entry to the industry (Hindley and Smith 1984). Of course, like other regulations, restrictions on entry to industries can easily develop into protective barriers for those who are already in the industry.

Discrimination against foreign suppliers may be intentional in many cases; in others, the discrimination may be unintended and subtle. For example, if there are prudential asset requirements for entry to an industry and the assets must be held in the country imposing the restrictions, foreigners may be at a disadvantage (Hindley and Smith 1984, p. 381). Or discrimination may be a product of the difficulty of assessing foreign professional qualifications for occupations in which registration is required.

We focus now on barriers to international trade as such and not on regulations that may restrict participation by both nationals and foreigners. Depending on the manner in which services are traded, international trade in services can be discriminated against by barriers to the movement of the suppliers of the service, to the movements of the receivers of services, or to the trade itself.[4] Examples for each category follow.

1. *Barriers to the movement of service suppliers.* Restrictions on the inflow of labor for construction, artistic purposes, and the like; restrictions on the inflow of foreign investment; restrictions on foreign professionals practicing domestically; taxation of landing or port facilities for foreign carriers

2. *Barriers to the movement of service receivers.* Restrictions on residents traveling abroad for education, tourism, and so on; restrictions on equipment moving abroad for servicing or repairs

3. *Barriers to trade itself.* Restrictions on the placement of architectural, computing, accounting, and other contracts abroad; restrictions on the receipt of electronic

transmissions from abroad; restrictions on the placement of banking or insurance business abroad; foreign exchange restrictions; domestic content requirements in radio and television broadcasting, in the cinema or theater, and in shipping.

The restrictions on trade in services that are most comparable to restrictions on trade in goods are those in category 3. Such services have been termed disembodied or separated services (Bhagwati 1984; Sampson and Snape 1985). As with tariff and nontariff barriers to the movement of goods, they are restrictions on the product of factors of production, not on the movement of the means to provide the service (as in category 1) or on the receivers of the services (as in category 2). It is to category 3 that the principles of the GATT are most obviously applicable, but they also apply to the barriers in categories 1 and 2.

Application of GATT Concepts

The GATT comprises a set of trading rules that apply generally across commodities and contracting parties. There are exceptions for both countries (developing countries, in particular) and commodities (agricultural products, in particular). In addition, certain products have been effectively excluded from the general provisions of the agreement for a considerable time with respect to some countries—the two main exceptions in this category are waivers for many developed countries for agricultural imports and special provisions for textile and clothing imports from a growing number of developing countries by most developed countries. But despite these exceptions, which have grown considerably since the GATT was first formulated more than forty years ago, the basic thrust of the General Agreement is toward rules of general application across countries and commodities.

The fundamental principles of GATT are to be found specifically in the main articles but are also implied by the force of the agreement as a whole. These principles include nondiscrimination among contracting parties, transparency and predictability of barriers, liberalization of trade, and equality of treatment of foreign and domestic products once the frontier has been crossed ("national treatment"). It is these principles that are most relevant in considering the extension of the GATT principles to services and, in particular, to those services that are traded without movement of the service providers or receivers. But as noted, they are also relevant to the latter categories.

Most Favored Nation (MFN)

Nondiscrimination in the GATT is expressed in the most favored nation concept in its unconditional form. Article

Richard H. Snape

I of the GATT provides, "With respect to customs duties and charges of any kind imposed on . . . importation or exportation . . . any advantage, favor, privilege, or immunity granted by any contracting party to any product originating in or destined for any other country shall be accorded immediately and unconditionally to the like product originating in or destined for the territories of all other contracting parties." In addition to stating that any "advantage" (and so on) has to be extended to all, it implies that any advantage that is withdrawn from any member has to be withdrawn from all—you cannot do to any what you are not prepared to do to your best friend. Unconditional MFN is a powerful protector of the weak and of those who might be regarded as troublemakers.[5] There are exceptions in the GATT to this rule of nondiscrimination—provisions relating to customs unions and free trade areas were part of the GATT from its inception, and preferences for developing countries were added later. Nevertheless, nondiscrimination is at the heart of GATT.

The requirement of article I that a concession given to one has to be given to all could discourage negotiation of the reduction of barriers. Each country could drag its feet in negotiations knowing that it would get the benefit from reductions in other countries' barriers whether or not it reduced any of its own: it could free-ride on the negotiations of others. Free riding has been curtailed in the successive rounds of negotiations under GATT by negotiating concessions between principal suppliers on narrowly defined products while at the same time covering a wide range of products in the negotiations as a whole (Finger 1979). In the Tokyo Round a formula reduction in barriers (with exceptions) was adopted, and this also helped to curtail free riding.

A standard argument why country A should be prepared to see concessions it has "bought" from country B extended to country C without C's "paying" for them is that country A will in turn benefit, unconditionally, from any concessions exchanged between countries B and C. It appears, however, that unconditional MFN is being eroded in goods trade as many countries focus more on the bilateral than on the multilateral and systemic aspects of trading policies (Snape 1988). In recent years there has been considerable reluctance by the main players in GATT to extend to all members the benefits under new agreements concluded under GATT auspices, even when these agreements have been interpretations of the GATT articles. Many signatories have extended the benefits only to the cosignatories of the particular agreement.[6] With such attitudes prevalent, there is little likelihood that the benefits of agreements on services will be extended to any except the signatories to the relevant agreements.

Be that as it may, the concept—if not the practice—of unconditional MFN is quite easily extended to many forms of services trade. For services in category 3—that is, where the providers and receivers do not have to come together—and for barriers to trade that resemble tariffs, the application of unconditional MFN is easy. Converting some of the barriers to services trade to tariff-like imposts would be helpful, for when trade barriers are in the form of tariffs, the application of nondiscrimination is easy and visible. This "tariffication" could apply, for example, to trade in television, radio, and movie programs, whether received directly from abroad or on tape, film, or disk; professional services that are supplied at a distance; placement of insurance and banking business abroad; and subscriptions to foreign news, educational, and similar services. Nondiscrimination, then, would simply be the application to all trading partners of the same tariff-like impost. With nondiscrimination defined and measured in this way, unconditional MFN follows easily: the same tariff-like charges would be applied to all parties to the agreement, and reductions in the charges imposed on the imports from any source would be granted to all, whether or not they gave any concessions in return.

Even if barriers to trade in these services are not converted to tariff-like levies, nondiscrimination and unconditional MFN can still be applied. For example, if there are domestic content requirements for cinemas, nondiscrimination implies (as it does already in article IV of the GATT) that the importers should have equal access to all foreign suppliers; unconditional MFN implies that access given to any foreign country would be available to all member countries without conditions. Similar provisions could apply to engaging foreign professional services if such engagement is restricted by one means or another. Thus, where entry to an industry is restricted by licensing arrangements, MFN implies equal opportunity for all foreign suppliers when licenses are issued.

When movement of the service provider or receiver is involved, similar principles can be applied, although in practice things may be more difficult in some cases. In transport services bilateral arrangements are common—bilateral reciprocity pervades international air transport, while in shipping the 40-40-20 rule[7] of the UNCTAD Shipping Code is discriminatory on a bilateral basis. In these areas nondiscriminatory tariffs or import quotas would be alternatives to the present arrangements that would allow protection of domestic suppliers while also satisfying the unconditional MFN principle.

When a domestic presence is involved as part of the international trade in a service—that is, when the provider needs labor or capital (financial or physical) in the

Principles in Trade in Services

host country—questions relating to visas, work permits, and foreign investment policy arise. Again, application of an unconditional MFN policy is easily specified in principle: the labor and capital of all parties to an agreement should be treated equally with respect to entry and, for labor, with respect to professional and related qualifications. This does not imply that all types of labor should be treated equally—only that nationality should not be a criterion for differentiation. Similarly, it does not imply that if professional architectural qualifications are a condition for practice in the host country, qualifications obtained in all countries should be treated equally if in fact they are not equal; it is the quality of the training that should be the criterion, not the country in which it is earned. With respect to both labor and capital the application of unconditional rather than conditional MFN requires that equality of treatment be applied to all parties to the agreement—and to all new parties to the agreement—without specific conditions being imposed once the general agreement has been concluded.

As noted earlier, in many services entry is limited for both domestic and foreign firms. Postal and telegraph systems are often government monopolies, and restrictions on entry to banking, insurance, and broadcasting are common even when these areas are not limited to public enterprises. Entry to many professions is also restricted. So long as entry is prohibited to foreigners, the question of MFN does not arise. If entry is allowed, then MFN would imply equal opportunity of access for nationals of all other member countries. Unconditional MFN could imply that no specific conditions regarding reciprocal rights of entry be attached.

National Treatment

National treatment is to be distinguished from MFN; it refers to the treatment of foreign products (or suppliers) not with respect to each other but with respect to national products or suppliers. Article III of the GATT requires that "internal" taxes, regulations, and the like "should not be applied to imported or domestic products so as to afford protection to domestic production."[8] It has sometimes been implied that for some services national treatment means equality of treatment of foreigners and nationals. The word "internal" in article III could suggest that once a product has cleared the port of entry, no discrimination can be applied against foreign products. But what is the port of entry for services that can be traded in a disembodied or separated form—that is, separated from the producer? Perhaps a better way to approach the GATT provision with respect to national treatment is to note that the GATT authorizes or legitimizes certain forms of discrimination against goods produced by foreigners. The

generally authorized form of discrimination according to source is an import tariff, although in some circumstances quantitative restrictions on imports are permitted. National treatment then implies that once the authorized form of discrimination has been imposed on a product, there should be no further discrimination according to national source.

When one views national treatment in this manner, the way in which it could be extended to services is readily apparent. A general agreement on services could include a provision for specifying particular means of discrimination against foreign-produced services. Sector-specific agreements could then identify the particular form or forms of authorized discrimination for the services in that sector, and particular levels of these forms of discrimination could be bound among the parties to that agreement. National treatment would then imply that in all other respects domestic and foreign producers should be treated equally.

The GATT already provides one example of this in services; a local content provision for the screening of cinema films, but article IV provides for equality of treatment in all other ways—that is, for national treatment. The local content provision is not imposed at importation but at the actual screening time. As noted above, a tariff-like impost could be an appropriate form of authorized barrier for many services, including cinema films, if protection of the domestic producer is the objective of policy.

Liberalization, Transparency, and Predictability

Liberalization, transparency, and predictability are considered together because of their interconnections. Although the GATT is not an agreement to secure or even to attempt free trade, containment and reduction of trade barriers are fundamental to it. It sets a framework within which concessions can be negotiated and bound between contracting parties. There are procedures for withdrawing concessions and for raising barriers, but these are seen as temporary deviations from the norm, although in practice many such actions have been far from temporary. The GATT's procedures have provided an effective basis for reducing tariff barriers, and in its first couple of decades nontariff barriers, at least on manufactured goods, were also reduced. More recently, nontariff barriers, often in exotic forms designed to avoid the restrictive provisions of GATT, have proliferated, and attempts to curtail them have had but moderate success.

Experience with the GATT and other trade negotiations shows that reductions in tariffs are easier to negotiate across a broad front than are reductions in nontariff barriers. In general, tariffs are the most easily identified

Richard H. Snape

form of trade barrier and, in comparison with most forms of nontariff barriers, provide relatively little scope for bureaucratic licence and chicanery. Therefore they are relatively transparent and their effects relatively predictable. The GATT itself helps to ensure transparency by emphasizing tariffs as the generally authorized form of trade barrier and by requiring notification and publication of trade barriers.

For services, nontariff barriers, not tariffs, are the norm (Hindley 1988, p. 3). This in itself creates difficulties for liberalization: it is hard to get agreement for exchanges of concessions on a range of products when the forms of barriers are disparate and the levels often unquantifiable. Frequently it is even difficult to verify whether there *are* trade barriers, as has been noted in much of the discussion of Japanese trade policy in recent years. In such circumstances the emphasis tends to be on single products; experience teaches that such an emphasis is less conducive to significant liberalization. Thus "tariffication" of barriers to services, where feasible, could facilitate liberalization.

If this route is not attractive or is not feasible for particular services, the GATT provisions for publication and notification should be easily applicable to other forms of trade barrier. Negotiation, binding, and liberalization would thus be facilitated.

A General Agreement, or Sector by Sector, or Both?

As noted above, the GATT is a *general* agreement that applies generally, although with specific exceptions, to all parties and all goods. Furthermore, it is an open club, accessible to new members on conditions similar to those of foundation membership.

Trade negotiations that have centered on forms of barriers across a range of products have been more liberalizing than negotiations that have focused on specific products. Some examples of the latter are the Multifibre Arrangements, the codes for dairy products and bovine meat negotiated in the Tokyo Round of multilateral trade negotiations, and the UNCTAD Shipping Code. Although all of these agreements tend to organize and restrict rather than liberalize trade, it should be acknowledged that it may be the characteristics of these industries that have led to the forms of negotiations and that the agreements may be liberalizing in comparison with the situation without agreements. The comparison should be made with an alternative scenario for the product in question, not with other products. Further, extraction of, for example, textiles and clothing from coverage by the general rules of the GATT may have been the price of maintaining liberalizing coverage by the GATT on other products.

This said, and if trade liberalization is the objective, it seems wise to approach negotiations on a broad front, identifying characteristics that extend across many products, rather than product by product. Costs can then be offset by benefits within a country to a much greater extent than will normally be possible when a narrowly defined class of products is being considered. If sensitive products are involved, however, there is a tradeoff between the extent of coverage and the firmness of the liberalizing thrust of an agreement. Inclusion of sensitive products in a broad agreement can lead to ambiguous and soft wording, leaving unresolved different interpretations by different parties.

International movements of persons and capital have frequently raised sensitivities of a different nature from the international movement of goods. Just as with trade in goods, there are some services that are more sensitive than others—including some services that do not involve the international movement of service providers or receivers (category 3); clothing and textiles have their parallels in the area of services. So it may not be possible to have the same set of rules cover even all the services that fall into category 3, and, just as with goods, there will be a tradeoff between the extent of product coverage by an agreed set of rules and the liberalizing thrust and enforceability of these rules. In any case, to try to force into the same mold as category 3 the services that fall within categories 1 and 2 would appear unwise, as it would detract from what could be achieved in category 3.

These considerations have led to the proposal for a two-level set of agreements for services: a framework agreement specifying a set of principles applicable to a broad range of services and a subsidiary set of agreements (or annotations) that would apply these principles to specific service sectors. This is the manner in which the Uruguay Round negotiations on services has been proceeding. In the midterm review ministers agreed that negotiations for a multilateral agreement should continue and that a framework agreement should incorporate provisions on transparency, progressive liberalization, national treatment, most favored nation treatment and nondiscrimination, market access, increasing participation for developing countries, safeguards and exceptions, and "regulatory situation," the last item "recognizing" the right of developing countries to introduce new regulations for services, consistent with commitments under the framework. Work is now under way in the Group of Negotiations on Services to explore the application of these principles to particular service sectors.

The two-level concept still leaves open the question of the breadth of coverage of the framework and the sector agreements. The GATT covers all goods unless (as for agriculture) there are specific provisions for particular

Principles in Trade in Services

goods: it is, after all, a general agreement. The agreements for services could be structured on the same all-encompassing principle, or they could embrace only the services that are specifically identified. The contrast is between a positive list that includes only those services named and a negative list that includes all services except those specifically excluded.

Two recent bilateral free trade agreements take opposite positions on this question with respect to services. The Canada–U.S. Free Trade Agreement adopts the positive list approach; a recent extension of the Closer Economic Relationship Agreement between Australia and New Zealand provides for free trade in all services unless they are specifically exempted. For a multilateral agreement, and in particular one that does not provide for free trade, it may be more difficult to adopt the negative list approach, although experience with respect to quantitative trade barriers to goods shows that the negative list approach is more liberalizing. Thus, in the context of the Uruguay Round one of the "sector" agreements could apply to all services except those for which there are specific provisions.

Conclusion

Although it is likely that countries gain economically from trading services, as from trading goods, international negotiations in services, as for goods, tend to focus on the opportunities for exporters and not on the opportunities for gains from importing. Expressed in general form, the principles of comparative advantage apply to services trade much as they do to goods, although some services trade requires the movement of the service provider or receiver. Developed countries tend to export services that are dependent on high levels of human, physical, or financial capital; developing countries have considerable opportunities to export labor-intensive services. Many of the latter services require temporary movement of labor, and others require that complementary capital equipment be available. Barriers to trade in this equipment, often erected for the protection of domestic industries, can prevent the development of exports of these services.

Breadth of coverage appears to be an important ingredient in achieving an international agreement on services that is truly liberalizing; product-specific agreements have a history of encouraging organized and restricted trade. The main GATT principles of nondiscrimination, national treatment, liberalization, transparency, and predictability can be applied to trade in services, and the conversion of many of the regulatory barriers to services trade to forms analogous to import tariffs would facilitate the building of a GATT-like, liberalizing, agreement. But

movements of labor and capital raise particular problems, and special provisions will be necessary for them in any services agreement—although GATT principles could still be applied.

Notes

Grateful acknowledgment is made of comments by Geza Feketekuty, Max Kreinin, Roger Mauldon, and Patrick Messerlin.

1. Discussion of many of the points covered may be found in Feketekuty (1988).

2. The distinction between goods and services can become rather blurred when such "services" as architectural drawings, computer programs, and musical recordings are transported in a physical form.

3. "Flying in the Face of Marxist Dogma," *Financial Times*, June 22, 1989.

4. This classification is based on that of Sampson and Snape (1985).

5. The provisions in GATT for safeguarding industries on a temporary basis from "fair" trade do not allow for discrimination, although there was considerable pressure from some developed countries for such selectivity in the Tokyo Round of multilateral negotiations (see Sampson 1987; Winham 1986), and this pressure has continued in the Uruguay Round. Such discrimination would be mainly against developing countries and has been resisted by them. Trade remedies can be applied on a selective basis against members if they cause injury to the industries of other members by means of export-promoting subsidies or by dumping—practices that are frequently described as unfair trade.

6. There is a tendency for some countries to adopt a unilateral approach toward determining whether others have satisfied the conditions of new agreements and thus toward extending to others the benefits under the agreements. This applies in particular to the Subsidies Code concluded in the Tokyo Round of multilateral trade negotiations.

7. That is, 40 percent for the carriers of country A, 40 percent for those of country B, and 20 percent for all others, for carriage of the trade between A and B.

8. Article III explicitly permits subsidies on domestic production.

References

Bhagwati, Jagdish N. 1984. "Splintering and Disembodiment of Services and Developing Nations." *World Economy* 7, no. 2 (June):133-43.

Feketekuty, Geza. 1988. *International Trade in Services: An Overview and Blueprint for Negotiations.* Cambridge Mass.: American Enterprise Institute and Ballinger.

Finger, J. Michael. 1979. "Trade Liberalization: a Public Choice Perspective." In Ryan C. Amarcher, Gottfried Haberler, and Thomas Willett, eds., *Challenges to a Liberal International Order.* Washington D.C.: American Enterprise Institute.

Hindley, Brian. 1988. "Introducing Services into the GATT: A Progress Report on the MTN." World Bank, Washington, D.C. Processed.

Hindley, Brian, and Alasdair Smith. 1984. "Comparative Advantage and Trade in Services." *World Economy* 7, no. 4 (December):369-89.

Sampson, Gary P. "Safeguards." 1987. In J. Michael Finger and Andrzej Olechowski, eds., *The Uruguay Round: A Handbook on the Multilateral Trade Negotiations.* Washington, D.C.: World Bank.

Sampson, Gary P., and Richard H. Snape. 1985. "Identifying the Issues in Trade in Services." *World Economy* 8, no. 2 (June):171-81.

Snape, Richard H. 1988. "Is Non-Discrimination Really Dead?" *World Economy* 11, no. 1 (March):1-17.

Winham, Gilbert R. 1986. *International Trade and the Tokyo Round Negotiations.* Princeton, N.J.: Princeton University Press.

[5]

Principles in Factor-related Trade in Services

Brian Hindley

Services and goods differ in a number of ways. But in discussing international transactions, the difference of dominant importance is that whereas goods are tangible and, with more or less trouble or cost, can be transported from one place to another, services, which are a change in the condition of a thing or a person (Hill 1977), are not tangible and cannot be shifted from place to place.

The outcome of a service—the person or thing changed by the service—can be transported. So can the signifiers of property rights generated by a service (for example, a bank statement or an insurance policy). And, of central importance, the means of providing a service—people or goods—can be moved.

The nontransportability of services is often expressed by saying that the provision of a service requires proximity of the provider of the service and the good or the person receiving it. For this reason, international transactions in services are much more likely to require some form of international factor movement than are international transactions in goods. This does not necessarily mean that the factors of production involved in providing the service have to move to the country of the receiver of the service (Sampson and Snape 1985), but that is what it often means in practice.

This simple fact affects basic economic concepts. Consider, for example, the notion of an integrated world market. For a good, the concept is reasonably clear; it implies that the price of the good is the same in each national market when costs of transport and differences in national taxes are taken into account. If the price of a good is higher in one market than in another, shipments of the good will be diverted from the low-price to the high-price market. Hence, to produce an integrated world market in a good, obstacles to flows of the good have to be removed.

An integrated world market for a service involves different considerations. Arbitrage in goods can occur without any change in the location of the producers of the goods, but this is not true of services. Often, the means of providing the service must be to some degree located in the market of the receiver of the service. If a service is overpriced in one market in relation to another, correction of the disequilibrium requires a flow of factors.

If profits on the route from A to B are higher than those on the route from C to D, it is necessary to move ships, aircraft, or trucks—and perhaps crews—from the CD to the AB route. If the earnings of lawyers and doctors in A are higher than those in B, equalization of earnings by an arbitrage-like process will require the movement of lawyers and doctors from B to A. An integrated market for a service requires something much more akin to the process by which economists imagine that profits are equalized among different industries or wages among different occupations than to the process by which they imagine that the prices of goods are equalized among different national markets.

Even if arbitrage is unimpeded, however, it is unlikely to lead to a situation in which a service is priced the same in different national markets. One reason is that provision of a service in a locality almost inevitably entails the use of local as well as imported factors of production. Possibly more important, establishment in B is likely to require conformity with B's regulatory system, and the regulatory system in effect is likely to affect the producers' costs. Hence there is no reason to suppose that service providers from country A can exactly reproduce in country B the price-quality combinations that they can provide in A.[1]

The term "regulatory system," moreover, must be interpreted broadly in this context. A national regulatory system is usually taken to consist of rules for specific service industries, such as requirements for minimum levels of reserves or for minimum years of training at approved institutions. But an integrated world market for a service entails international factor flows, and the term "national regulatory system" must therefore be interpreted to include, for example, laws on immigration, laws regarding the establishment of foreign firms or subsidiaries or branches of foreign firms, and conditions imposed on employment generally, such as minimum wage laws and contributions to social security.

A construction company from a developing country, using labor from that country and paying its workers on that country's terms, may be capable of constructing a highway or an airport of a given quality in Europe more cheaply than could a European company using European labor. But a company from a developing country will have great legal difficulty in getting labor from the developing country into Europe. Even if it could do so, it might not be able to produce more cheaply were that labor, once in Europe, subject to European employment laws.

Not all international transactions in services call for proximity in the immediate geographic sense of labor employed to construct an airport or highway. "Tradable services"—or, in the terminology of Bhagwati (1984), long-distance services—do exist. These are services that can be provided by a supplier in country A to a user in country B without relocation by either of them, such as conducting banking business by computer terminal. Any service transaction that takes place within a country entirely by mail, fax, or phone, without direct personal contact, can also be traded internationally. This class of services is growing rapidly and may be expected to grow even faster in the future, but it is not yet large in relation to the service sector as a whole.

The scope of tradable services can be extended somewhat by adding to the category services that require only brief periods of relocation rather than permanent or semi-permanent residence. An architect or consulting engineer, for example, may be able to function effectively with a few brief visits to the site of a project. By contrast, a bank is likely to need a permanent presence in a country if it is to successfully provide a full range of banking services.

Another possible exception occurs when potential users of the service can move to the location of foreign suppliers of the service (or when both are able to meet in some third location). Even if service suppliers are not free to locate in the national market, temporary relocation of users of a service might produce many of the consequences of a national market that is integrated with the world market. That this is more likely to be true the lower the cost of transport services suggests that it is more likely to apply to Luxembourg than to New Zealand.

These exceptions do not appear to constitute a major breach in the general rule that factor flows are required to produce an integrated world market in a service. The idea of permitting factor flows, however, is not popular anywhere.

Why this should be so is an interesting question. Suppose that a construction firm from the Republic of Korea,

if allowed to locate Korean labor in Europe temporarily, can construct a road or an airport in Europe more cheaply than any European firm supplying a similar quality of output. If the output were a product manufactured in Korea and sent to Europe, like motor cars or television sets, most economists would reject the notion that the relative cheapness of Korean labor constituted a valid reason for resisting the import of those goods. European airports, however, cannot be built in Korea and shipped to Europe; they have to be built in Europe. But despite this difference, the logic of comparative cost that applied to cars and television sets seems to apply to airports. And that logic suggests that if the airport can be built at a lower cost by Koreans, they should build it. That in turn implies that they should be allowed to locate temporarily in Europe for that purpose.

That an idea is consistent with the logic of comparative advantage is not at all the same thing as its being politically feasible. It is as well to understand, however, that the fundamental difficulty with the idea of shifting factors of production to a location when the output of the factors cannot be shifted is political rather than economic.[2]

Developing countries, symmetrically, often reject local establishment by foreign providers of services, even when the services cannot be provided otherwise. They take this position although the terms of the rejection often concede, implicitly or explicitly, that foreign providers are more efficient than their local counterparts.

Factor Movements to Provide Services and the Uruguay Round

The United States opened the discussion of including services in the GATT with the proposal that negotiations be restricted to nonfactor services. Thus it suggested that the emphasis should be on services that can be traded in the conventional sense—a person or firm in one country sells something to a person or firm located in another country without relocation of either buyer or seller.

One motive for this suggestion was to avoid too great an affront to institutional conservatism. The GATT has in the past dealt with trade in goods, not with foreign investment. Focusing on tradable services seemed more consonant with GATT tradition.

The suggested restriction on the scope of the negotiation had the additional advantage of avoiding the difficult and contentious issues of foreign direct investment and rights of establishment. It also avoided the at least equally contentious issues that would be raised if developing countries made a counterclaim regarding a right of labor to temporarily reside in a foreign country for the purpose of supplying services.

Brian Hindley

This attempt to avoid one set of problems created others. One appeared in the form of a conflict within the United States on its negotiating position. Whatever the tactical advantages of focusing on traded nonfactor services in GATT negotiations, many U.S. service suppliers perceive their main international problem to be the lack of a right of establishment in foreign markets. They were therefore skeptical of the value of negotiations that did not include discussion of rights of establishment.

The emphasis on tradable services raised different problems for developing countries, which were not convinced that the issue of foreign direct investment could be avoided. Developing countries perceive that the logic of liberalization in the service sector requires a right of service providers to locate in the proximity of service receivers. They are typically suspicious of foreign direct investment, however, and many are hostile to the notion of introducing a GATT right of foreign service suppliers to locate in their territories—a point on which some developed countries are also likely to have doubts.

That the issue appeared as a problem of foreign investment, however, was a consequence of the way in which it had been posed. Analytically, the need of service industries that make intensive use of capital or skilled labor to locate those factors in potential markets is symmetrical with the need of providers of labor-intensive services to locate unskilled and semiskilled labor in potential markets.

Another problem that the emphasis on tradable services raised for developing countries was that whereas service suppliers based in developed countries might find it easier to use local establishments, almost all of the services for which trade without establishment is possible are those in which developed countries currently appear to possess a comparative advantage (for example, banking and financial services and informatics). Any successful liberalization in this restricted range of services would therefore probably mean an increase in developing country imports of services from developed countries without any compensating increase in their exports of services.

In GATT terms, this raises a significant problem. GATT negotiations center on exchanges of "concessions," where a concession is defined as a reduction in restrictions on imports and where concessions from other countries are won at the "cost" of relaxations in one's own import regime. Economists often scoff at the language of GATT negotiations. Ricardo's demonstration of the principle of comparative advantage, they say, destroyed once and for all the possibility of regarding increased openness to imports as a cost. That is true. It is also true, however, that economic analysis offers no solution to the

political problem that the GATT process addresses through concessions.

The structure of protection in a particular country at a particular time must be taken to represent the outcome of some process of political equilibrium. To change the protective structure, therefore, the factors that support the underlying political equilibrium must be changed. An exchange of concessions offers one means of achieving this. By altering the opportunities available to actors in the domestic political process—by providing exporters with a direct connection between the barriers they face in foreign markets and the level of their own country's protection against imports—the offer of concessions alters the economic interests involved and makes possible new domestic coalitions. Hence the offer of an exchange of concessions is likely to help a government that wishes to liberalize but faces domestic opposition and may also put pressure on a government that is not persuaded of the case for liberalization.

The U.S. suggestion that the GATT negotiations be restricted to tradable nonfactor services, however, defined services in such a way that comparative advantage lay predominantly with developed countries. Hence the great bulk of potential GATT concessions in services would come from the developing countries, and this seemed to preclude the possibility of an equal exchange of concessions between developed and developing countries within the service sector.

One response to this problem has been to point to the economic gains available to developing countries as a result of liberalization in their service sectors. That such gains exist seems very likely (Hindley 1988), but their existence does not solve the dilemma for the multilateral trade negotiations. The economic gains that developing countries can obtain by liberalizing their service sectors can for the most part be obtained through unilateral action. But gains that can be obtained unilaterally are unlikely to be enough to persuade a government to join a multilateral liberalization—especially if the government has already rejected unilateral liberalization, as have the governments of most developing countries.

Bhagwati (1987) has suggested a single solution to these two problems—the desire of U.S. service suppliers to obtain some kind of establishment in foreign markets and the lack of concessions of interest to developing countries. His proposal is to introduce rights of establishment into the GATT talks but to define them to include a right to locate labor in a country temporarily for the purpose of supplying a service.

Half of this potential solution has been broached. Early in the negotiations the United States abandoned its insistence on confining the negotiations to tradable services.

For example, its first submission to the Group of Negotiations on Services (United States 1987, p. 3) states:

> The framework should apply to cross-border move-
> ment of services *as well as to the establishment of
> foreign branches and subsidiaries for the purposes of
> producing and delivering the service within the host
> country* (emphasis added) .

The notion of a right of location for labor that is supplying services has been mentioned by a number of developing countries. So far, however, it has been less sharply
crystallized.

The Statement of the Trade Negotiating Committee
Meeting at Ministerial Level, issued after the midterm
review held in Montreal in December 1988, deals with
the question in terms of definition:

> Work on definition [of services] should proceed on
> the basis that the multilateral framework may include
> trade in services involving cross-border movement of
> services, cross-border movement of consumers, and
> cross-border movement of factors of production
> where such movement is essential to suppliers.

A later paragraph, under the heading of market access,
states:

> When market access is made available to signatories
> it should be on the basis that consistent with the other
> provisions of the multilateral framework and in accor-
> dance with the definition of trade in services, foreign
> services may be supplied according to the preferred
> mode of delivery.

These words clearly do not commit anybody to anything
much. Nevertheless, the possibility that the negotiation
will attempt to liberalize international factor movements
for the purpose of supplying services is open. The question of the legal and institutional forms available for the
purpose is therefore relevant.

Rights of Establishment, Access, and Presence

The concept of a right of establishment is fairly clear. For
example, chapter 2 (articles 52-58) of the EEC Treaty,
which is the legal basis of the European Economic Community, is entitled "Rights of Establishment." Article 52
states:

> . . . restrictions on the freedom of establishment of
> nationals of a Member State shall be abolished by
> progressive stages. . . . Such progressive abolition

> shall also apply to restrictions on the setting up of
> agencies, branches or subsidiaries by nationals of any
> Member State established in the territory of any Mem-
> ber State.
> Freedom of establishment shall include the right to
> take up and pursue activities as self–employed per-
> sons and to set up and manage undertakings, in par-
> ticular companies or firms . . . under the conditions
> laid down for its own nationals by the law of the
> country where such establishment is effected.

The last sentence of this passage adds to the right of
establishment a requirement of national treatment: a
government shall not use differences in nationality as a
basis for differences in legal treatment. Thus the treaty
gives to a Greek national who wishes to set up a bank or
an insurance company in France or Germany a legal right
to do so, subject to the condition that an otherwise similar
French or German national would be legally entitled to do so.
A right of establishment as such is very extensive.
Application of the principle of national treatment can
significantly limit the exercise of that right. For example,
the two conditions taken together do not prevent a government from banning the establishment of new banks,
although they do prevent acts or regulations that discriminate between the government's own nationals and those
of other countries. Their combined effect is to provide
that a government cannot prevent a foreigner from establishing a bank if it would have allowed a similarly
qualified national to do so. A government can, however,
subject the foreign-owned bank to any conditions that
would apply to a bank owned by its own nationals.[3]
Many governments—some governments of developed
countries among them—are likely to resist the notion of
granting through a multilateral agreement a right of
establishment to foreign providers of services. And even
governments that might support the notion in principle
would be likely to experience difficulties in practice. The
United States, for example, does not permit foreign ownership of U.S. television stations or airlines.
Partly to deal with this difficulty, two new concepts
have developed: the idea of a right of access and the idea
of a right of commercial presence. The third principle of
the Declaration on Trade in Services annexed to the
Agreement on the Establishment of a Free Trade Area
between the United States and Israel illustrates both:

> Each party will endeavor to provide that a supplier of
> a service produced within the other nation is able to
> market and distribute that service under the same
> conditions as a like service produced within the first
> nation, including situations where a commercial pres-
> ence within the nation is necessary to facilitate the

Brian Hindley

export of a service from the other nation or is required by that Party.

The idea of a right of access—the ability to market and distribute the service product—is intended to parallel GATT provisions on goods. Article III of the GATT requires national treatment for goods once duties have been applied at the border. In other words, it requires that tariffs (or other border measures, when authorized) should be the only means of discrimination between foreign and national suppliers. When applied to services, this idea can raise problems. For many services border measures such as tariffs are an impractical means of discrimination, and when the GATT version of national treatment is interpreted as authorizing only border measures, advocacy of national treatment tends to merge with advocacy of free trade in services.

Nevertheless, the basic perception that there is little point in attempting to negotiate a liberalization of particular barriers to international transactions if foreign products can be blocked by other barriers, such as denial of access to distribution networks, is as valid for goods as for services. Thus any sensible GATT (or other) agreement on liberalizing international transactions in services will attempt to guarantee that service products which have cleared the hurdles authorized by the GATT will receive national treatment with respect to local distribution networks—that is, right of access.

Commercial presence is a related but different concept. A footnote to the passage quoted above notes:

> . . . in the area of commercial banking, the concept of a commercial presence refers to the activities of representative offices, but not to agencies, branches or subsidiaries of commercial banks.

"Commercial presence" therefore encompasses establishments that are necessary to facilitate cross-border trade in services. It falls far short of a right of establishment. A right of establishment would allow a foreign bank to establish "agencies, branches, or subsidiaries."

Rights of establishment, access, or presence pertain to organizations (which may be small—for example, firms of lawyers or architects or the "self-employed persons" referred to in article 58 of the EEC Treaty). Establishment of a foreign-owned enterprise may mean that foreigners associated with the enterprise are admitted to the country of establishment on privileged terms to perform work there. But it does not necessarily mean that. Immigration issues—the question of which persons will be admitted to a country—are in principle separate from establishment issues—the question of which organizations will be allowed to provide services in the country.

The International Movement of Labor to Provide Services

The general question of the freedom of labor to locate in a foreign jurisdiction to provide services has numerous subdivisions. "Labor" is a broad term, and the period during which it is necessary to "locate" in order to effectively provide a service may vary from hours to years or decades.

The needs of one form of labor—that involved in the supply of professional services—has received considerable attention (see, for example, University of Chicago Legal Forum 1986). This discussion is relevant to the interests of developing countries in the multilateral trade negotiations, since these countries have considerable potential for exporting professional services.

The problems of liberalizing international transactions in professional services and those of liberalizing international transactions in labor–intensive services have elements in common, but they are not identical. Liberalization of labor-intensive services may provide a focus for developing countries' interest in supplying services for foreign markets, should the associated problems prove to be soluble and negotiable.

As noted above, the problems with making operational a temporary right of abode for the provision of services (TRAPS) are primarily political, not economic. Nevertheless it seems useful to identify some points on which decisions are essential and to sketch the consequences of the choices that might be made.

Suppose that in country H labor engaged in supplying a certain service earns $1 an hour, whereas in country F the same labor, similarly employed, is worth $5 an hour. It seems fair to assume that even if a TRAPS is negotiated in the Uruguay Round, the number of TRAPS visas issued will not be enough to bring about equalization of the occupational wage rate in H and F. But if the wage rates are not equalized, the question arises: who obtains the difference between the wage at which H labor would be willing to work in F (say, for simplicity, $1 an hour) and the value of H labor when employed in F? The answer is that the difference will accrue to those who receive the TRAPS visa rights.

The right to employ persons under the TRAPS scheme could be issued to, say, providers in country F of the service that employs this particular kind of labor. Those F employers would have a right to hire in country H at $1 an hour labor that in F is valued at $5 an hour. This allocation of TRAPS rights implies that providers of the service in F receive the difference.

At the other extreme, the rights could be issued to workers in country H (on a first-come-first-served basis, say, since there are likely to be more H workers willing

Principles in Factor-related Trade in Services

to work in F for $1 an hour than there are TRAPS visas). The outcome for the post-TRAPS distribution of income would then be quite different. Assuming competition among F employers willing to pay $5 an hour, allocation of TRAPS rights to H workers would mean that those H workers fortunate enough to receive the rights would be paid $5 an hour by employers in F. In this case the fortunate H workers would receive the difference between the $1 an hour at which they are willing to work in F and the $5 an hour that their labor is worth to F employers.

An alternative and perhaps more plausible way of distributing TRAPS visa rights to H residents would be to allocate the rights to H firms that wish to supply the associated service in F. The consequence of that distribution would be that H firms willing to make the attempt would receive the $4 an hour difference—in effect, a substantial subsidy to their export of the service.

An issue that is likely to be central to political discussion of a TRAPS is the application of F employment laws to H workers entering F under a TRAPS visa. But the answer arrived at is not crucial from the standpoint of the economics of the scheme. In the first place, the displacement from employment of competing F workers will be controlled by the assumed limit on the number of H workers admitted to F, not by the wages they receive in F. In the second place, H workers willing to work in F for $1 an hour but not allowed to work for less than, say, $4 an hour by F law or union rules will be prepared to pay $3 an hour for the right to work at the official rate in F. Such a payment can be made in many ways. To determine whether it actually has been made is therefore likely to be difficult or impossible.

Another issue that is likely to be central in political discussions has more economic relevance: whether the limit on the number of TRAPS visas should be for the service sector as a whole or should be subdivided among service industries. The latter course seems more politically feasible, as it would avoid the possibility that workers in any one industry would bear the full brunt of the employment consequences of a TRAPS scheme. It might also have the advantage, especially when combined with the allocation of TRAPS visas to foreign service-providing firms, of increasing the variety of services that such firms have an incentive to export.

Concluding Comment

There is no doubt that improving the ability of service-providing factors of production to move internationally could lead to significant economic gains for both developed and developing countries. The difficulties in achieving that result are primarily political. Service industries in which international transactions require international factor mobility are often unused to foreign competition, and they do not all welcome the prospect. In developing countries resistance acquires additional political force because industries that feel threatened often have a central economic position and substantial financial resources (examples are banks and insurance companies). In developed countries the industries in which employment might be threatened are those that employ low–wage domestic labor, which, as experience with international trading arrangements in the textiles and garment and footwear industries has made clear, can also command a great deal of political support. Nevertheless, the potential economic gains are there, and many of them would accrue to developing countries—which, by and large, have shown the greatest resistance to the attempt in the multilateral trade negotiations to introduce services into the GATT.

Of course, even if something like a temporary right of abode to provide services were offered in the Uruguay Round, developing countries might not regard it as a satisfactory quid pro quo for the rights of presence or establishment called for by developed countries. But unless the negotiation is to proceed on the basis of threats, either a quid pro quo must be found or the possibility must be faced that the bulk of developing countries will not join any eventual agreement—or will join it only on terms that make the agreement vacuous, at least as far as they are concerned.

Notes

1. This is also true of goods at the retail level. The equality of price to be expected in an integrated world market for a good is the net-of-transport-cost price at the dock, before any local services have been applied to it. An essential difference between goods and services is that for many services there is no equivalent of the dock—no point, short of delivery to the ultimate user of the service, at which it makes any sense to talk about the price of the service.

2. The *Financial Times* of July 12, 1988, however, reports John Reed, chairman of Citicorp and of the Services Policy Advisory Committee (which advises the U.S. administration), as saying that "U.S. business wanted a global agreement on services with as broad a participation as possible by developing countries. The Reagan administration should be prepared to trade off freer movement of Third World labor to U.S. projects in return for greater access for U.S. service companies to developing markets." Reed's remarks were made as he arrived in Geneva with U.S. Special Trade Representative Clayton Yeutter and fourteen members of the committee "to push for swifter progress on services in GATT's trade-liberalizing Uruguay Round."

3. The United States (1987, p. 6) noted this difficulty:

In some cases in the past, regulators have effectively cartelized a given services sector by denying the issuance of new licenses for decades. National treatment obviously has no value in these instances from the standpoint of trade liberalization. While in a few instances regulators have established a legitimate need to limit the number of participants, a framework agreement should provide for a degree of foreign participation if such restricted circumstances recur.

Brian Hindley

4. This is not equivalent to the proposition that F residents who are members of the occupation receive $5 an hour. It is not necessary to the argument that H and F labor be of the same quality.

References

Bhagwati, Jagdish. 1984. "Splintering and Disembodiment of Services and Developing Nations." *World Economy* 7, no. 2 (June):133–44.

———. 1987. "International Trade in Services and Its Relevance to Economic Development." In Orio Giarini, ed., *The Emerging Service Economy*. Oxford: Pergamon Press for the Services World Forum.

GATT Secretariat. 1988. *Statement of the Trade Negotiating Committee Meeting at Ministerial Level.* Montreal.

Hill, T. P. 1977. "On Goods and Services." *Review of Income and Wealth* 23, no. 4 (December):315–38.

Hindley, Brian. 1988. "Service Sector Protection: Considerations for Developing Countries." *World Bank Economic Review* 2, no. 2 (May):205–24.

Sampson, Gary, and Richard Snape. 1985. "Identifying the Issues in Trade in Services." *World Economy* 8, no. 2 (June):171–81.

University of Chicago Legal Forum. 1986. *Barriers to International Trade in Professional Services.* Chicago, Ill.: University of Chicago Law School.

United States. 1987. *Concepts for a Framework Agreement in Services.* MTN.GNS/W/24, October 27. Geneva: GATT Secretariat.

[6]

Comparative advantage and international trade and investment in services

Alan V. Deardorff
University of Michigan

My purpose in this paper is to evaluate the theoretical validity of the principle of comparative advantage as it applies to international trade in services. I will focus only on the positive issue of whether trade, if undistorted by policy, will conform to a pattern that is explainable by comparative advantage, and I will not treat, except tangentially, the welfare effects of such trade. Even so, as I will explain in a moment, it is probably impossible to provide a conclusive answer to the question of whether services trade follows comparative advantage. Instead, I will confine my attention to two distinctive characteristics of trade in services, and use these as the basis for theoretical models. Within these models I will show that, while there exist ways of defining comparative advantage and trade such that the principle of comparative advantage holds quite nicely, there is nonetheless at least one case in which trade will appear to violate the principle. Thus it is not clear that comparative advantage is necessarily the most useful criterion for explaining international trade in services.

The difficulty that arises in evaluating trade in services - and this applies to the problem in both its positive and normative aspects - is the lack of consensus as to what constitute services. Most can agree on a list of real-world activities that are services, and with some exceptions there is no difficulty in distinguishing the items on the list from goods. But it is harder to identify what it is economically that distinguishes all goods from all services, and then to use this difference as the basis for theoretical analysis.

At one extreme, economists are accustomed to lumping all goods and services together, assuming implicitly that there are no economically meaningful differences between them. It then follows of course that what is said of goods applies equally well to services, and in particular that the principle of comparative advantage is as valid for services as for goods. But this follows from the failure to distinguish between them in the first place, and it proves nothing. The opportunity remains for someone to point out a difference between goods and services and to object that this difference has not been taken into account. Without explicitly considering models of all possible characteristics that might distinguish goods and services, as well as all possible combinations thereof, one cannot claim to have proved one's case conclusively. Since there is no end to the list of characteristics that might be advanced as distinguishing at least some goods and services, I conclude that the issue of this paper is one that can never be resolved once and for all.

On the other hand, just as we often know intuitively which things are goods and which are services, we also know intuitively that some of the differences between goods and services are unimportant for the issue of comparative advantage. Hindley and Smith (1984) illustrate this in the following comment on the view that services have been ignored in theories of comparative advantage:

> The underlying premise is that services are different from goods, which may indeed be so. But a bunch of flowers and a ton of coal and a jet airliner are very different things also. It may be true that no economist has discussed international trade in brussels sprouts or used that vegetable to illustrate comparative advantage. That surely does not raise any substantial question as to whether the conceptual and theoretical apparatus of comparative cost theory is applicable to brussels sprouts.

Even this, of course, presumes our agreement that the brussels sprout is just another vegetable. Were it known, instead, that brussels sprouts are addictive, or that their production fouls the environment, or that they are valued primarily as collectables, then we might recognize that some of the postulates that are normally assumed in proving comparative advantage are violated by brussels sprouts, and we would not be so sanguine.

40

Thus the only way to proceed on an issue like this, I believe, is piecemeal. Select, one at a time, various characteristics that distinguish services from goods, characteristics that intuition suggests *may* have a bearing on trade and comparative advantage. Build a model that can capture these characteristics and examine its implications. Finally, base one's conclusion, first, on a judgement as to the empirical relevance of those characteristics, if any, that do seem to undermine comparative advantage, and second, on the comprehensiveness of the list of characteristics that do not. In all, one must keep an open mind: there always remains the possibility that some other characteristic, so far unexamined, will be found to overturn the results.

In subsequent sections, then, I will follow this approach, examining in theoretical terms three separate characteristics that seem important for at least a portion of the international trade in services. The sections are largely independent, since different techniques turn out to be useful in each. I will try only at the end to tie them together in some fashion.

The first characteristic that I will consider is also the least general: the fact that traded services often arise as a byproduct of trade in goods. While trade services, such as transportation, cargo insurance, and trade financing, are not the only kind of services that are traded, there is reason to think that they fail to satisfy one of the standard assumptions of trade theory, and thus may make a re-examination of comparative advantage worthwhile. It turns out that comparative advantage continues to work quite well to explain such trade, but the exercise is nonetheless fruitful in providing other insights.

In the next section, I turn to another characteristic that is often regarded as more general, and also more likely to transcend comparative advantage. This is the fact that trade in services frequently requires, or is at least accompanied by, international direct investment. If comparative advantage explains only trade in goods, and if trade in services is really a form of trade in the factors of production, then one might question the relevance of comparative advantage for explaining trade in services. It turns out, however, that international factor movements are just as much the creatures of comparative advantage as is trade in goods. This is implicit in some of the theoretical writings on comparative advantage, and can be made explicit quite easily. Thus if services trade were really just a

41

disguised form of international factor movement, it would still be determined by the principle of comparative advantage.

However, it is my view that the characterization of services trade as factor trade is overly simple and perhaps misleading. In the last section, therefore, I will suggest an alternative interpretation in which services are distinct from goods in terms of the location requirements of production. Loosely following Hill (1977), I will assume that while goods can be produced elsewhere from where they are consumed, services cannot. In contrast, however, and to make trade in services (as distinct from factors) possible in these circumstances, I will also assume that production of services is possible even though some of the factors of production from which they are produced are not present but instead make their contribution from a distance, perhaps even from a different country.

To formalize this concept, I look at a simple 2x2x2 model in which one of the sectors is identified as producing a service. The labour in this sector can produce only for domestic demand, but the second input – call it management – can be provided from abroad.[1] If we think of the ownership of the firm as abiding with management, then it is natural to think of the firm as exporting the service, even though the actual production takes place within the importing country using local labour. Since management itself does not move, one would not observe international investment occurring here, except perhaps if one were to infer such investment from the repatriation of earnings that are necessary to pay the managers at home. Furthermore, it turns out that, depending on the factor intensities of production in the two sectors, one can easily get a case in which the service is exported from a country in which it would have been relatively expensive in autarky, thus violating comparative advantage.

Before beginning, I should mention one characteristic of some services trade that I will not consider. I will not look at any models of imperfect competition, and even in the last section, where I model what might be viewed as multinational corporations, I continue to assume that these corporations behave competitively. My reason for this is twofold. First, I wish to give comparative advantage a fair chance of working, and existing models of trade, even in goods, have not established that comparative advantage is descriptively correct for all of the possible imperfectly competitive market structures. Presumably, if comparative advantage has difficulty in my

42

competitive model, as it does in the last section, then it would have no
less difficulty in a model of imperfect competition.

Second, while it is true that many of the multinationals that deal in
services are too large to be regarded as competitive, this is equally
true of those that deal in goods. Thus it is hard to see that imperfect
competition is an identifying characteristic of trade in services per se.
With that in mind, I prefer to look at the simplest models that do
incorporate such identifying characteristics, and for this the
competitive framework seems appropriate.

TRADE IN TRADE SERVICES

Not all services are rendered directly to consumers. Many services are
intermediate inputs to production, and some are inputs to other
activities such as trade. Indeed, trade in goods inevitably requires
that goods be moved from one country to another, and the provision of
that transportation is a service. In the modern world, other services
too are used by traders, such as cargo insurance, trade financing, and
legal help in dealing with different countries' regulations. Thus one
can say that trade in goods constitutes a source of demand for a
variety of services that I will call trade services.[2]

Now these trade services are not themselves inevitably traded.
Exporters and importers could, if they wished, deal only with
transporters, insurers, banks, and lawyers from their home countries.
But it is also natural for traders to be aware of the availability of these
services from other countries, and thus one might expect trade in
trade services to arise earlier in history than trade in services of other
kinds and for other uses. Thus trade in trade services, if it is distinct
at all from other forms of service trade, seems worthy of examination.

Furthermore, trade in trade services does have one very special
property that distinguishes it from other forms of trade: the demand
for it arises solely from other trade. Why is this important for our
discussion of comparative advantage?

A first reason is that comparative advantage is customarily
measured in terms of autarky prices. Yet trade services by definition
are not demanded in autarky, and therefore their autarky prices do
not exist. Thus we must look elsewhere for an indicator of
comparative advantage in trade services, and this alone makes them
of some interest. One possibility, if the services are produced using
factors of production that have well-defined autarky prices, would be

to measure comparative advantage in terms of their minimum costs of production at autarky factor prices.[3] Yet even this may be suspect, since the autarky factor prices in no way reflect the demands for them that may arise when they are used to produce trade services.

A second reason is that trade services violate an assumption that is often made in trade theory, and to the extent that demonstrations of comparative advantage rest on that assumption, they need at least to be reconsidered.   The assumption in question is that demand conditions are identical across countries; that is, that faced with identical prices consumers in different countries will demand goods in identical proportions. This assumption is sometimes used in proofs of the Heckscher-Ohlin theorem, and when it is not, differences in demand are incorporated in comparisons of relative autarky prices. But as just noted, autarky prices are not obviously available in the case of trade services.

There is a final problem that would seem on the face of it to cause problems: trade in trade services itself is not well defined. We are not accustomed in trade theory to worrying about where, in the process of trade in a good, the ownership of that good changes hands. But in defining trade in trade services this may make a difference. Consider, for example, the case of a good that is sold by a domestic exporter to a foreign importer, and that must be transported from one to the other. Suppose further that the transportation service is provided by a firm based in the importing country.[4] If that transportation is purchased by the importing firm, then the transaction involves no trade in transportation services. But if it is purchased by the exporting firm, our country will be regarded as importing these services. The actual production that takes place, including the production of the transportation service, is the same in both cases, but the recording of how much trade has occurred is quite different. Clearly there are similar problems whenever a trade service is provided, since there are always two parties to the goods-trade transaction and either may be the demander of the service.

What difference could all of this make for comparative advantage? A couple of interesting possibilities suggest themselves.

Consider, for example, a country with a cost advantage in providing transportation services. By the usual argument of comparative costs, this country should become a net provider of these services to the world, once trade is allowed. Suppose however that the country is very remote from world markets, and that as a result it is also an unusually great demander of transportation services, once it enters into trade. We may then find it being an importer of transportation, in spite of its comparative cost advantage. Note too that the country's distance from world markets will not be reflected in its autarky costs of transportation, as would be the case if it had an unusual demand for a good or factor instead, since in autarky its demand for transportation is not revealed to any market.

A second difficulty that might be expected to arise from trade services has to do with the effect that restrictions on trade in services may have on patterns of trade in goods. Suppose, for example, that a country has a comparative advantage in a particular good that happens to require a large dose of some trade service, say insurance, if it is to be traded. This in itself need not interfere with its exporting the good, so long as all countries pay the same price for trade insurance. But suppose instead that trade in insurance is not permitted and that the country has a strong comparative disadvantage in providing this service. Then the cost to it of exporting, should it be required to insure its trade itself, could be prohibitive of its exporting the good at all. Thus it appears that acknowledging the existence of trade services in a model of trade in goods may alter what we can say even about the latter.

In fact, however, trade in trade services does not make as much difference for comparative advantage as all of this suggests. To see this, I introduce the following formal model.

Consider a world of n countries and m goods and let there be also s services that will be useful only if there is trade in goods In vectors of appropriate lengths, and omitting implicit country superscripts, let X be a particular country's outputs of goods, C its final demands for these goods, and thus $T = X - C$ its net exports of goods. Similarly, let S be the trade services it produces, U the trade services that it uses in the course of trade, and $V = S - U$ its net exports of trade services.

In order to characterize the technology of production and trade, I must first define the physical meaning of trade, and as I have done before in Deardorff (1980) I will make use of the convenient fiction of a single world port. That is, suppose that there exists a single point on the globe through which all trade must pass. Further, to resolve the ambiguity mentioned above in the definition of trade in trade services, I will assume that each country's own traders are responsible for getting its goods to and from the world port, so that if a foreigner provides trade services between a country and the port, this will be regarded as imports of those services.[5] These assumptions are not as restrictive as they seem, as I argued in the appendix to Deardorff (1980).

Technology can now be defined quite simply. For production, let $F = \{(X,S)\}$ be the set of all feasible outputs of goods and services that can be produced by a country given its technology and factor endowments. It is a production possibility set of the usual sort, and it admits negative values for elements of X, representing the net use of goods as intermediate inputs. Only non-negative values of S are in the set, however, since the services here are useful in trade only, and not in domestic production. The manner in which they may be used is described by another set, $G = \{(T,U)\}$, the set of all possible vectors of net trade in goods and (non-negative) vectors of trade services used. If a particular service, U_1, were required in fixed proportion to the amount of trade in a particular good, T_1, for example, then a cross-section of the set G would be as indicated in Figure 1. That is, U_1 must be at least as great as the appropriate constant times the absolute value of T_1. In general, of course, more complicated shapes are possible, and I assume only sufficient boundedness on the technology to make the relevant maximization problems possess solutions. These sets, F and G, may differ in general from country to country.

I turn now to characterization of equilibria, making such assumptions, familiar in trade theory, as perfect competition, the weak axiom of revealed preference, profit maximization, and balanced trade. I will consider only three types of equilibrium: autarky, in which there is no trade in either goods or services; free trade, in both goods and services; and what I will call semi-autarky, in which there is free trade in goods but no trade at all in services, so that, for example, each country's own transportation firms must move its exports to the port and its imports from the port. More general cases of nonprohibitive tariffs and other restrictions on the two kinds of trade could easily be allowed with additional notation.

An autarky equilibrium consists of vectors of prices of goods, p^a, prices of services, q^a, and outputs of goods, X^a, which are feasible to

46

FIGURE 1

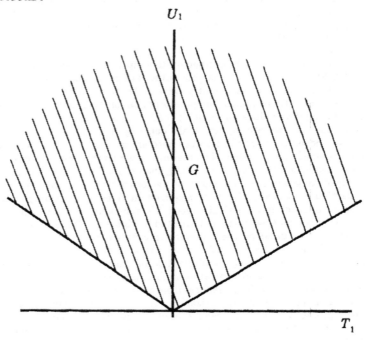

produce, are demanded by consumers facing these prices, and maximize the value of the country's output:

$$p^a X^a \geq p^a X + q^a S \text{ for all } (X,S) \, \varepsilon \, F. \tag{1}$$

Note that, while the output of trade services is zero in autarky equilibrium, we can still speak of equilibrium prices for these services as long as these are prices at which profit-maximizing producers of services would be content not to produce. However, since negative values of S are excluded from F, this is likely to mean that these prices

47

are not unique. Indeed, for any equilibrium that satisfies (1), any other prices of services not greater than q^a will also be an autarky equilibrium.

A free-trade equilibrium is somewhat more involved. It consists, for a given country, of both domestic and world prices, p^d and p^w, the latter being the prices of goods at the international port, together with world prices of services, q^w, as well. In addition, there are quantities of goods produced and consumed, X^f and C^f respectively, and quantities of services produced and used, S^f and U^f. To be an equilibrium, all of these quantities must be feasible, the goods consumed must be willingly demanded at the prices p^d, and production and trade must yield as great a value as any other available opportunity. Thus

$$p^d X^f + q^w S^f \geq p^d X + q^w S \text{ for all } (X,S) \, \epsilon \, F. \tag{2}$$

and

$$(p^w - p^d)T^f - q^w U^f \geq (p^w - p^d)T - q^w U \text{ for all } (T,U) \, \epsilon \, G. \tag{3}$$

Finally, I require balanced trade:

$$p^w T^f + q^w V^f = 0. \tag{4}$$

To complete the specification of the free-trade equilibrium, I would need the requirement that world markets clear for both goods and services. I would also note that world prices of goods and services are the same for all countries, while domestic prices need not be.

A semi-autarky equilibrium, as described above, requires essentially the same conditions as (2), (3), and (4), though in this case the quantities of services produced and used, call them S^s and U^s, must be the same, and the prices of services, p^s, can vary across countries. I will not bother to write down the analogous conditions.

I am now in a position to examine the role of comparative advantage in these equilibria. As in Deardorff (1980), the crucial relationship involves the value of trade at autarky prices. Since this value is the inner product of the vector of net trade with the vector of autarky prices, its sign turns out to give us various correlations between autarky prices and trade. And it is easy to show, much as in Deardorff (1980), that

$$P^a T^f + q^a V^f \leq 0. \qquad (5)$$

To see this, first note that

$$
\begin{aligned}
p^d C^a &= && p^d X^a && (6)\\
&\leq && p^d X^f + q^w S^f \\
&\leq && p^d X^f + q^w S^f + [(p^w - p^d)T^f - q^w U^f] \\
&= && p^d C^f + p^w T^f + q^w V^f \\
&= && p^d Cf
\end{aligned}
$$

where the first inequality follows from (2), the second inequality follows from (3) using $T = U = 0$ on the right-hand side of (3), and the last two equalities use the definitions, $T = X - C$ and $V = S - U$, and equation (4). Relation (6) says that free-trade consumption is revealed preferred to autarky consumption, and thus the weak axiom of revealed preference implies that

$$p^a C^a \leq p^a C'. \qquad (7)$$

Finally, the autarky value of trade can be evaluated as follows:

$$
\begin{aligned}
p^a T^f + q^a V^f &= && p^a X^f + q^a S^f - p^a C^f - q^a U' && (8)\\
&\leq && p^a X^a - p^a C^f - q^a U^f \\
&= && p^a C^a - p^a C^f - q^a U^f \\
&\leq && - q^a U^f \\
&\leq && 0
\end{aligned}
$$

where the first inequality follows from (1), the second from (7), and the last from the fact that both q and U must be non-negative vectors. This completes the proof of (5).

The inequality in (5), then, establishes that the principle of comparative advantage holds in this model of trade in both goods and trade services. That is, it must be true on average that the goods and services a country exports must be worth less to it in autarky than the goods and services it imports. Of course, this average relationship permits individual goods and services to be traded in ways that seem contrary to comparative advantage, and thus some examples such as those I discussed above are possible. But there is nothing special about services in this respect: similar examples can be found also for trade in goods alone, as I showed in Deardorff (1979). Thus it seems that this particular characteristic of trade in services – the fact that much of it is demanded only as a byproduct of trade in goods – does not after all undermine the usual result of comparative advantage.

There is, however, more that one can say in this particular model. First, recall that the autarky prices of services that appear in (5) are to a large extent arbitrary. Given any prices for which (2) holds, (2) will also hold if these prices are replaced by prices of services that are closer to zero, and even if they are replaced by zero itself. Thus it follows as a corollary to (5) that

$$p^a T^f \leq 0 . \tag{9}$$

This looks exactly like the traditional result from a model without services, but it applies to this model in which the trade in goods that is included in T is only a part of the trade that is going on. Thus the principle of comparative advantage, it turns out, applies to trade in goods alone, even when trade services are also being traded.

There is yet another corollary that follows in turn from (9). It is possible in general for a country to exchange goods for services and vice versa. But in a model like this, in which all services are trade services, it is impossible for there to be net trade in just one good in exchange for services. For if there were, then $p^a T^f$ would be positive for the country that exports the good, thus violating (9).

Finally, consider what would happen in a semi-autarky equilibrium in which there is trade in goods but not in services. All of the conditions used above still apply, with the superscript 'f' replaced by 's'. Thus the result in (5) continues to hold in a semi-autarky equilibrium, and

$$p^a T^s \leq 0 \tag{10}$$

since V^s is zero by definition. Thus comparative advantage continues to explain trade in goods, even if trade in traded services is not permitted. Evidently, my example above, showing how prohibition of trade in services might undermine a country's comparative advantage in a good that it finds expensive to trade, indicates only how trade can be reduced or eliminated by this phenomenon, but not that its pattern can be reversed.[6]

To conclude this section, then, allowing for trade in trade services leads to some interesting possibilities as far as the trade in particular goods and services may be concerned, but it does not in any way undermine the principle of comparative advantage as the general indicator of the patterns of trade that can take place. On the contrary, the principle is strengthened in a sense, for it now applies even to the subcategory of trade in goods alone, as well as to trade in goods and services together.

SERVICES TRADE AS INTERNATIONAL FACTOR MOVEMENTS

A notable feature of much of the trade in services is that it may require a *presence*, on the part of the exporting firm, within the importing country. This means that some employees of the exporting firm may have to be present to administer, market, or oversee the service. Or it may mean the need to establish a physical plant in which or from which the service can be provided in the importing country. Either way, this suggests the need for labour, capital, or both to move from the exporting country to the importing country in order to provide the service. I will argue in the next section that such factor movements are not in fact an inevitable feature of trade in services, but they certainly can occur in conjunction with it and have been identified by many as a crucial aspect of services trade. Therefore, it seems sensible at this point to ask if factor movements do give reason to doubt the validity of comparative advantage as it applies to services.

The answer, fortunately, is easily found. Quite independently of whether they involve services or not, international factor movements fit neatly into the theory of comparative advantage. It is true, of course, that factor movements can reduce - even to zero - the amount of trade in goods that occurs in response to comparative advantage. But it is also true that trade in goods and factors together conforms to the principle of comparative advantage in the usual sense that those goods and factors that are exported will, on average, have been cheaper in autarky than those that are imported.

It is unnecessary to prove this result here since it has appeared elsewhere. In my own article (1980), this result was implicit, since the

51

goods in that model were defined to include 'all final goods, intermediate goods, and services of primary factors of production', any or all of which could be traded or nontraded. The result has also been made explicit by Ethier and Svensson (1983) as one of many theorems of trade theory that they extend to a model with factor mobility.

Thus, to observe that trade in services often involves international direct investment, for example, in no way suggests that it should therefore fail to conform to comparative advantage. On the contrary, if the export of certain services requires the export of capital, then one would expect the countries that export these services to be also those in which capital is relatively cheap. Similarly, if other services require the movement of certain types of labour in order for them to be traded, then those countries where this labour is readily available will be the most likely to export them.

As always in general discussions of trade patterns, one can find cases in which particular goods, services, or factors appear to be traded perversely. This is usually either a result of the greater importance of some other determinant of relative costs, or the result of some form of complementarity with another good or service. For example, suppose that a service relies heavily on both skilled and unskilled labour, and is relatively expensive in the United States because the scarcity of the latter outweighs the abundance of the former. If trade in the service requires that only skilled labour move internationally, the necessary unskilled labour being taken from the local labour market in the importing country, then one could easily find the service being exported by the United States in spite of its relatively high autarky cost here. In this example, the trade in the service alone appears to run counter to comparative advantage, but the trade in goods and services together, including the trade in skilled labour, would not. A proper evaluation of comparative advantage requires only that we succeed in taking into account all of the trade that is actually taking place.

On the other hand, this example is very similar to the situation that I will describe in the next section. For suppose that the skilled labour just mentioned could make its contribution to production without actually moving to the country to which the service is being exported. Trade in the service would continue to occur but trade in skilled labour would not. Since the trade in the service is what appeared perverse, we would then be left with an apparent violation of comparative advantage without any offsetting trade in factors. Thus it may not be movement of factors internationally, but rather the possibility that they need not move in order to make a contribution, that causes the greatest difficulty for the principle of comparative advantage as it applies to services. This is what I will examine more formally in the next section.

SERVICE TRADE WITH ABSENT FACTORS

I noted above the tendency for service trade to require the presence of the service exporting firm in the importing country. This is a general property of services trade, especially if one follows Hill (1977) in defining services as marketable activities in which production must take place in the presence of the demander. Hill argues that services in general cause a change in either the person or the property of the consumer of the service. If the change is in a person, then obviously that person must be present during production, but even if the change is in some good owned by the consumer, the need to maintain that ownership intact during whatever transformation occurs makes it unlikely that production can take place too far removed from the consumer. In any case, I will from now on let this property be one of the defining characteristics of a service: that its production must take place in the same location (or at least the same country) as is occupied by the person or firm that purchases it.

In the previous section, this characteristic led to the association of services trade with international factor movements, on the assumption that a firm can produce in a foreign country only if it also moves some of its factors of production there. But this is not a good assumption, as recent observation of the behaviour of multinational corporations makes clear. To produce in a foreign country, a firm needs to employ factors of production there. But these need not be factors that it brought from its home country; they can be hired on local factor markets. Indeed for many years trade theorists felt that we had covered the subject of multinational enterprises implicitly in our studies of international capital movements, and only recently have we explicitly recognized that such enterprises typically organize much of their financial and other activities locally, in the same countries where they produce. Furthermore, even when they do raise funds on international capital markets, their decisions are truly international, and have little to do with where their home offices are located.

Thus a firm that wishes to export a service may do so by setting up a branch in a foreign country, hiring local labour, and financing any necessary local capital expenditures within the local market of the foreign country as well. If it does all of this, one may then wonder what it is that is actually being exported. The answer in general is that there is some other factor that contributes to the profitability of the firm. This may be a unique method of management, a proprietary product or brand name, or a technique of production to which only it has access. In any case, if the export of the service is truly an export at all, there must be something that is provided by the home office of the firm that contributes to its profitability. Otherwise, it would pay its entire revenue to local factors, and no international transactions would take place at all.

To capture this idea I will follow Markusen (1984) and Helpman (1984) in their models of multinational corporations, and assume that production of services requires inputs of at least some factors that need not be physically present at the same location where production takes place. These 'absent factors' can encompass all of the contributions described above that a multinational can make to its subsidiaries, but for ease of reference I will, from now on, simply call them management.

Markusen and Helpman both go well beyond what I want to do here, in their pursuit of explanations for multinationals. For one thing, they make no distinction between goods and services, and their multinationals may implicitly produce both. In addition, they assume that what I am calling absent factors are also, in a sense, public goods within the firm, which is able to provide services to additional numbers of subsidiaries without additional effort in the home office. This in turn leads them also to assume that multinationals are large and noncompetitive. I will make neither of these assumptions, since I do not view imperfect competition as more likely for services than for goods, and I want therefore to remain in an environment where small competitive firms are possible. Thus my factor, management, is just like any other factor in a neoclassical production function, except that it need not be located where production of services takes place.

Notice, then, the dichotomy that I am assuming in the technologies of goods and services. Production of goods, I assume, requires the simultaneous presence of all factors of production, but does not require the presence of those who will consume or otherwise use the goods once they are produced. Services, on the other hand, do require the presence of consumers, but do not require the presence of all factors of production. Naturally, real-world activities are not so clearly separated. There are services in which there is no absent factor contribution, but these can be dispensed with as unable to enter international trade. There are also goods that can make use of absent factors, and this could complicate the analysis a bit since their location of production might then be indeterminant. But it will be convenient here to consider only the two extremes.

In fact, what seems to be crucial for the results that follow is not that some factors can be absent, but rather that some factors must be present, and that for services this presence must be in the same location as the consumer of the service. Since goods can be transported, it is hard to think of examples of exports of goods for which some factor of production must be present in the importing country.[7]

To show what this view of goods and services can imply for comparative advantage, I turn now to a very simple model of international trade that incorporates this view. The model is like the standard textbook Heckscher-Ohlin (H-O) trade model of two goods, two factors, and two countries. However, in this case I make one of the goods a service, and require that it be produced where it is consumed. Further, as just explained, I call one of the two factors of production management, and let it contribute to services production *in absentia*. Otherwise, the assumptions of the model are exactly those of the H-O model.

In autarky this model looks exactly like the H-O model. Since autarky constrains all factors, production, and consumption to locate within the same closed country, the special location requirements of services are unimportant. Thus, for example, the autarky relative price of the service will depend on demand for the service relative to the good, the endowments of the two factors, labour and management, and the intensities with which these two factors are required in production of the good and the service. In particular, comparing two countries, A and B, I will assume that the autarky relative price of the service is lower in Country A than in Country B. With identical homothetic demands and identical technologies, this could either mean that services are management-intensive and that Country A has a relative abundance of management, or that services are labour-intensive and A is well endowed with labour. Alternatively, the price difference could result from differences in technology. In any case, Country A has a comparative advantage in services by the usual criterion of relative autarky prices, and we wish to see if this advantage is reflected in its trade, once trade is allowed.

In the H-O model, free trade equates the prices of traded goods across countries. This in turn equates factor prices across countries as well, if the other assumptions of the factor-price-equalization theorem are satisfied, in particular if technologies are identical and if both goods are produced in both countries. In the model here, things are different but the outcome may be the same.

Free trade directly equates the price, across countries, of only the good, not the service. If the producer of a service were to observe a higher price abroad than at home, that in itself would not induce it to export, since to serve the foreign market it must produce there and must employ at least some local factors. The fact that it can produce more cheaply at home using domestic factors is of no help, since those factors cannot in general be used for production abroad.

On the other hand, I assume that one of the domestic factors, management, *can* be used for production abroad, since it is not required to be present where production takes place. Under what circumstances, then, will a service firm be able to compete successfully abroad? Obviously the answer depends on technology and the price of management in the two countries, not on the price of the service itself. If management is cheaper in Country A than in Country B, and if technologies are everywhere the same, then producers from A will be able to undercut the prices charged by producers in B, since they will have access to the same labour market in B, but will be able to use cheaper management. In fact, the same would be true for producers in B, were we to permit them to hire managers from A, but I will assume that the identity of the firm lies with its managers and exclude this possibility.

Continue to assume, for the time being, identical, constant-returns technologies. Clearly, then, trade in services will take place, if it is permitted, whenever the price of management differs between the countries. This could lead to specialization of various sorts, for example, all of the services in Country B being provided by Country

A's firms. But if it does not, then such trade will equate the prices of
management in the two countries, just as trade in a good equates the
price of the good. Further, once the price of the one good and the price
of the one factor, management, are equated across countries, then the
logic of the factor-price-equalization theorem will work to equate the
remaining prices; those of the other factor, labour, and of the service.
Thus free trade will tend to equate the price of services in the two
countries, but not because of arbitrage in the markets for services
themselves. The requirement that services be produced where they
are consumed prevents such arbitrage. Instead the prices of services
are equated indirectly, just as factor prices are equated in the H-O
model.

Formally, let the countries produce a good, X, and a service, S,
using factors of production labour, L, and management, M. Prices of
the good, p, and of the service, q, will equal the minimum unit costs of
whatever firms produce them, and these costs are functions of the
wage of labour, w, and the salary of management, s:

$$p = c_X(w,s); q = c_S(w,s) \tag{11}$$

where each of the four prices should bear appropriate superscirpts to
indicate which country's good, service, and factors are being described.
With free trade in the good, we must have $p^A = p^B$, and thus, if the
good is produced in both countries,

$$p^A = c_X(w^A, s^A) = c_X(w^B, s^B) = p^B \tag{12}$$

With free trade in the service industry, Country A's producers will
expand their operations in B's market whenever $c_S(w^B, s^A) < q^B$, since
they can use their own managers and B's workers. If in equilibrium
producers from both countries continue to serve B's market, this
relationship must hold with equality, and thus

$$c_S(w^B, s^A) = c_S(w^B, s^B), \tag{13}$$

which, given the nature of the unit cost functions, will be true only if

$$s^A = s^B \tag{14}$$

Similar reasoning implies (14) if service producers from both countries share *A*'s market, so that it is only if a single country's producers take over the provision of services in both countries that salaries will fail to be equalized.

Furthermore, once salaries are equalized, it follows from (12) that wages will be equalized as well, and then from (11) that prices of services will be equalized. Thus, with incomplete specialization, free trade in this model implies complete factor price and service price equalization, much as in the H-O model.

In order to examine further the nature of the free-trade equilibrium, it is helpful to use diagrams. In Figure 2, I show the two countries' transformation curves between X and S as they would appear if both countries were to use their labour and management only in domestic production. These are conventional transformation curves, and I have drawn them to reflect my assumption that Country *A* has an apparent comparative advantage in services. Thus if services could be traded directly, a world relative price of services, q^f, would prevail in both countries.[8] Production and consumption would take place at points H and C respectively, and Country A would export S to Country B in exchange for X.

In the present model, such direct trade in services is not possible, but if there is factor price equalization as just described, the same price, q^f, will clear the market. To make this possible, some of the management in one of the countries will be withdrawn from production of domestic services, and put into use instead as an absent factor in production of services abroad. While the factor does not actually move internationally, the production possibilities in the two countries will be affected exactly as if it did.

Which country's management will do this? To determine this, one could either look at the autarky prices and the incentives they provide, or look at the changes in output that take place as production possibilities shift and see if they take us toward or away from equilibrium. Fortunately, both approaches yield the same result, as the reader can verify. But the result does depend on relative factor intensities, and so I now consider two cases. A third case, with unequal technologies, will follow.

FIGURE 2

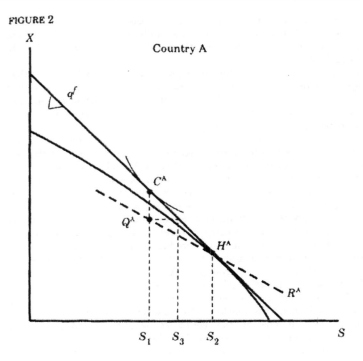

FIGURE 2

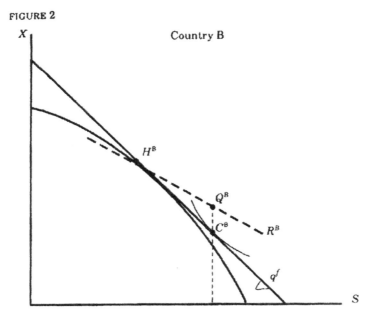

Case I: Services are management intensive

In this case, for Country A to have the assumed comparative advantage in services, it must also have a relative abundance of the factor, management. Thus in autarky, the salary of managers in A would be less than those in B, and there would be an incentive, as described above, for A's service producers to export services: they will set up operations in B and provide services using labour that they hire there, while continuing to use managers located within A. These managers, while they remain physically in A, are no longer contributing to production there, and A's production possibilities contract exactly as though the managers had moved abroad. As a result, A's transformation curve shifts inward in Rybczynski fashion. At the constant relative price, q^f, Country A's production point in Figure 2 will move to the left and upward, following the Rybczynski line R^A. Likewise, as these managers begin to contribute to production in Country B, that country's production possibilities will expand and its production point will follow the parallel Rybczynski line, R^B, down and to the right.

When will this process end? Since services must be produced where they are consumed, it will end when the outputs of services in both countries exactly equal what the countries' own consumers demand. Thus the equilibrium is found in A and B along the Rybczynski lines vertically below and above, respectively, the consumption points, C^A and C^B.

In this equilibrium, Country A imports good X, paying for it with what it earns from the provision of services in Country B's market. These services, which amount physically to the quantity $S_2 - S_1$ in Figure 2, are worth a good deal more than the imports of X that Country A gets in return. The difference, of course, is paid to labour in Country B.

It is a bit unclear how one should measure what is going on here. It seems clear that Country A is exporting services, but what is the quantity of services that is being exported? If we measure it as the total produced abroad, $S_2 - S_1$, then we either appear to have unbalanced trade or we must say in addition that service firms in A are *importing* labour from B. The latter is peculiar, since B's workers are neither moving to A, nor providing input to production there. Alternatively, one could measure the export of services by the amount that the service firms repatriate, and which they use in turn to pay their managers. This, in units of services, is $S_3 - S_1$ in Figure 2 and is equal in value to the imports of X, but it gives the appearance of measuring an input rather than an output. Finally, one could give up trying to measure trade in services at all, on the grounds that services cannot, strictly speaking, be traded, and measure instead the export of factor services – management in this case – that is taking place implicitly within the service firms. This would give the same value as the second alternative.

In any case, whatever its amount, if there is trade in services here at all, it is clearly Country A that is doing the exporting. This is not surprising, since I assumed at the outset that A had a comparative advantage in services. But in fact comparative advantage has nothing to do with this result, as the next case I consider will make clear.

Case II: Services are labour intensive

If services are labour intensive, then Country A's assumed low relative price must be the result of an abundance of labour. This case is shown in Figure 3, where the transformation curves and free-trade price lines are the same as in Figure 2. What is different is the incentive for trade in services.

As a result of its abundance of labour, it is the wage, not the salary, that must be relatively lowest in Country A in autarky. Attempts therefore by A's service producers to penetrate B's market will be frustrated, since they will find themselves employing B's more expensive labour as well as their own more expensive managers, the worst of both worlds. Instead, it is B's producers of services that will have the incentive to trade, and they will begin to use their managers together with Country A's labour to produce services in A.

This causes A's production possibility curve this time to shift outward, and B's to shift inward, their production points as before moving along Rybczynski lines until markets are cleared. But this time, since services are now labour-intensive, these Rybczynski lines are steeper than the transformation curves rather than flatter, and the equilibria in Figure 3 are found above C in Country A and and below C in Country B. This is as it should be, since A is now importing services, paying for them in part with its own labour, and in part with its exports of the good, X.

62

FIGURE 3

Country A

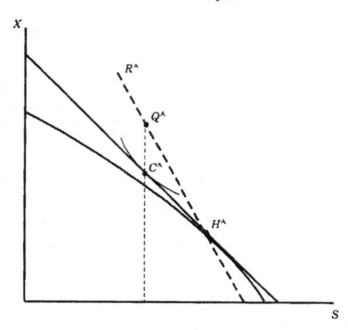

FIGURE 3

Country B

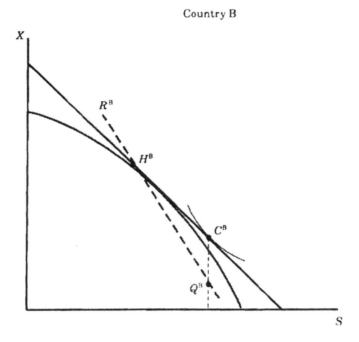

Thus, we have a case in which trade in services appears to run counter to comparative advantage. Labour-scarce Country B exports labour-intensive services in spite of the fact that these services cost more in B than in Country A in autarky. The reason for this result is that direct competition in the service industry is ruled out by the need to produce in the presence of consumers, together with the inability to move labour internationally. Instead, the only thing that matters for this kind of trade is the price of the only factor whose services can, in a sense, be traded: the factor I have called management whose productive services can operate from a distance. Since management is the abundant factor in B, this pattern of trade makes sense.

Whether this pattern of trade should in fact be thought of as violating the principle of comparative advantage is another question, however. It turns out that by carefully reinterpreting what we mean by the principle, we can assure that it remains valid even in this model.

One possibility, in line with the third method of measuring trade mentioned above, would be to say that services are not being traded at all, and that what is being traded is the productive contribution of the factor, management. Since in both cases I and II considered above, services are exported by the country in which management has the lower relative autarky salary, trade then follows comparative advantage.

Another possibility, more in line with modern interpretations of the generalized Heckscher-Ohlin model, is to focus not on trade itself but on the factor content of that trade. In that case, since the activity of producing the service abroad incorporates a contribution from only one domestic factor, management, the factor content of that trade is exclusively management. It follows again that each country tends to export, in factor content terms, its abundant factors.

Unfortunately, neither of these interpretations is particularly useful when it comes to explaining what is commonly meant by trade in services. For that, the model of this section has to suggest that the principle of comparative advantage is of little use, largely because in this model trade in services is not trade in the conventional sense.

Case III: Differences in technology

A final case should be briefly considered, since it casts doubt on even the successful interpretations of comparative advantage mentioned above. Suppose that factor endowments are the same in the two countries and that autarky prices differ instead because Country A has a different technology for producing services than does Country B. There are many ways that technologies could differ, and the nature of the difference can be important, as is well known even in the conventional H-O model.[9] I will assume simply that A has a Hicks-neutral technological advantage in the industry. It is also important, in this model, whether the superior technology continues to be available to a firm if it produces abroad. There are some interesting possibilities here, but I will assume that a country's managers know their technology, so that its use abroad is possible.[10]

Consider first how the autarky equilibria in the two countries will compare. If the two countries were to face the same price, A would clearly produce more services and less goods than B. If demands are identical, it follows that the autarky price of services in A must be lower than in B, and thus that the relative amount of services that is produced and consumed in A will be greater than in B. What this means for factor prices depends both on the degree of substitution between goods and services in demand and on the relative factor intensities of the two industries.[11] It is enough to consider one possibility. It may be that the salary of management in A, measured in units of X, is higher than in B, but by less than the full extent of A's technological advantage.

If that is the case, then when trade is permitted, A will clearly export services to B. For A's producers have a superior technology, and their managers, though paid more than managers in B, are not paid enough to offset their firms' competitive edge.

Now this is as far as we need to go to see the implications of this example for comparative advantage. On the one hand, comparative advantage in the usual sense now seems to be working quite well: A is exporting services, which it produced more cheaply than B in autarky. On the other hand, consider the alternative interpretations of comparative advantage that were used above to reconcile case II with comparative advantage. In this case the autarky price of management is higher in A than in B, but with trade Country A nonetheless appears to export the services of management. Thus the suggestion above that this model really involves trade in management, not services, and that this trade is in accord with

66

comparative advantage, fails to work once differences in technology are introduced.

Summary of the cases

Note, then, what these three cases together suggest about the validity of various versions of the principle of comparative advantage:

Version 1 *Countries tend to export those goods and services for which their relative autarky prices are lowest.* This version is false in case II above, where services make intensive use of the factor that must be employed locally where the service is provided. The reason is that a low autarky price in this case primarily reflects the cheapness of this factor at home, and this is of no use in exporting the service.

Version 2 *Countries cannot trade service outputs, since these must be produced where they are consumed, but can only trade those inputs to the production of services whose contribution can be made internationally. Thus countries tend to export those goods and those international service inputs for which their relative autarky prices are lowest.* This version is true in both case I and case II above, where countries share identical technologies. But if technologies differ, as in case II, then this version is no longer necessarily true. Service inputs such as management may be highly paid as a result of a technological advantage, and may nonetheless, because of that advantage, be able to compete in producing services abroad.

Version 3 *In terms of the factor content of trade, countries tend to export those factors (embodied in both goods and services) for which their relative autarky prices are lowest.* This version, like version 2, is true in both case I and case II, but may be false in case III.

Thus, no version of the principle of comparative advantage that I have been able to find is valid in all three cases. It is interesting that version 3 is a form of what is usually regarded as the Heckscher-Ohlin theorem, rather than the principle of comparative advantage. Since we have always known that the H-O theorem is valid only with identical technologies, one can say that it is made no less valid by introducing services. On the other hand, the conventional principle of comparative advantage, which version 1 probably comes closest to expressing, has been presumed to be much more generally true than

67

the H-O theorem.[12] Thus it seems that allowing for services in the manner done here has much more serious implications for comparative advantage than it does for the factor proportions theory as embodied in the H-O theorem.[13]

CONCLUSION

I have looked in this paper at three different characteristics of trade in services, to see in each case what they suggest for the validity of the principle of comparative advantage. These characteristics were, first, that traded services often are demanded as a byproduct of trade in goods; second, that trade in services often goes hand in hand with international movement of factors; and third, that services may be provided internationally by transnational firms, some of whose factors of production make their contributions from a distance. The first two of these characteristics, I argued, do not in any way undermine the usefulness of comparative advantage in explaining trade, but the effect of the third is more troublesome. While it may be possible to reconcile trade with comparative advantage in this case, to do so requires a reinterpretation of trade in a way that interferes considerably with the usefulness of comparative advantage as a guide to empirical reality. Furthermore, when comparative advantage results from differences in technology rather than differences in factor endowments, then the reinterpretation actually makes matters worse. I am left with the uneasy feeling that the principle of comparative advantage may not be as robust as many, including myself, have thought.

The question remains as to whether the model of the last section, which led to this conclusion, has any validity itself. That many corporations transcend national boundaries is clear, and that activities in the home office might contribute to the productivity of subsidiaries seems to me to be eminently reasonable. The particular form assumed for this contribution in the model is of course far too simple, but as an illustration of how this phenomenon might matter for trade, I feel it is appropriate. In any case, I look forward to the impressions of others as to the usefulness of the approach taken here.

I do find the troublesome case II especially interesting because of the way it seems in one sense to correspond to reality. It has been observed that services tend to be relatively expensive in the United States relative to the world at large.[14] Nonetheless, as is evident from the US concern with trade liberalization in services, many regard the United States as at least a potentially important exporter in these industries.   Now admittedly, this apparent contradiction of comparative advantage may result entirely from an aggregation problem: the particular services that we are likely to export are quite different from the bulk of very labour-intensive servies that even the United States would be more than content to see remain largely nontraded or restricted. But it is interesting that Country B in the case II example was also a labour-scarce Country and that it nonetheless could profit from exporting services that were, in comparison with goods, labour-intensive.

A final remark is in order regarding the welfare implications of what I have said about trade in services. Nothing that I have done here should be regarded as casting doubt on the potential for countries to gain from free trade, in services as well as goods. Even in the case II example, where trade might be said to run counter to comparative advantage, there is still a very clear gain from trade for both the countries involved.

NOTES

1   One might be uncomfortable with the idea that managers never set foot in the country where production takes place. Presumably, the presence of managers when a subsidiary is first established may be necessary, even if the subsidiary can function without them present later on.

2   These are services that Stern (1985) calls complementary to goods.

3   Another possibility, in some cases, would be to use the autarky prices of similar services that are used within the domestic market even in autarky. This may be misleading, however, since the requirements of international trade are often different from those of domestic trade.

4   Similar problems arise if transportation is provided by the exporting country or even by a third country.

5   A more realistic but more cumbersome specification would be to define all trade services produced as exported and all trade services used as imported, since trade statistics typically measure a country's trade from its own border. Obviously the results here, which relate to net trade, would not be affected by this specification.

6   Note that (10) is consistent with $T^s = 0$. That is, even though trade in goods is permitted in semi-autarky, it may be that none will occur, if the costs of domestically produced trade services turn out to be prohibitive.

7   On the other hand, Bob Staiger has pointed out to me that local content legislation has precisely this effect. It is interesting to speculate on whether, given the findings below, such legislation can undermine comparative advantage even in goods.

8   I am now taking the price of the good as numeraire, $p^A = p^B = 1$.

9   See Findlay and Grubert (1959), for example.

10 With this in mind one might prefer to think of the technology as embodied in the managers, so that it would be factor-augmenting instead of Hicks neutral. I do not believe that alternative specifications of the technological advantage would make much difference for the point that I wish to make here.

11 If preferences were Cobb-Douglas, for example, A and B, with their identical factor endowments, would produce the same amount of the good, X, in autarky and factor prices would be the same in the two countries in units of X. If the elasticity of substitution in demand is other than one, on the other hand, demand for X will be either larger or smaller in A than in B, and factor prices will differ also, in accordance with the relative factor intensity of X.

12 Compare the treatments in Deardorff (1980) and Deardorff (1982).

13 In his comment below, Ron Jones suggests that something like version 2 of comparative advantage can be salvaged even in the case of nonidentical technologies if one either allows managers in the two countries to be viewed as different factors, or regards managers in one country as embodying more units of management services than managers in the other. I am attracted by this interpretation, but I am also uneasy with it for a number of reasons. First, since the technological advantage need not, in the technical sense, be factor-augmenting (as in general the Hicks-neutral advantage assumed above is not), the difference between the management factors in the two countries may not be well defined. Second, in the case III example, the technological advantage exists only in the service industry, and the management factor is the same in the two countries when employed in the goods industry. Thus it is not the case that one

70

country's managers unambiguously embody more units of management services than the others, but only if employed in a particular industry. And third, I am generally leery of attempts to rescue comparative advantage by defining goods traded by different countries as different goods, and my reservations extend to doing the same thing with factors. This practice, it seems to me, comes close to making the principle of comparative advantage tautological.

14 See, for example, Stern's (1985) contribution to this conference.

REFERENCES

Deardorff, Alan V. (1979) 'Weak links in the chain of comparative advantage'. *Journal of International Economics* 9, 197-209 (May)
– (1980) 'The general validity of the law of comparative advantage'. *Journal of Political Economy* 88, 941-57 (October)
– (1982) 'The general validity of the Heckscher-Ohlin theorem'. *American Economic Review* 72, 683-94 (September)
Ethier, Wilfred J. and Lars E.O. Svensson (1983) 'The theorems of international trade with factor mobility'. Working Paper No. 1115, National Bureau of Economics Research (May)
Findlay, R. and H. Grubert (1959) 'Factor intensities, technological progress and the terms of trade'. *Oxford Economic Papers* 11, 111-21
Helpman, Elhanan (1984) 'A simple theory of international trade with multinational corporations'. *Journal of Political Economy* 92
Helpman, Elhanan and Paul R. Krugman (1984) *Increasing Returns, Imperfect Competition, and International Trade*. In process (May)
Hill, T.P. (1977) 'On goods and services'. *Review of Income and Wealth* 23, 315-38 (December)
Hindley, Brian and Alasdair Smith (1984) 'Comparative advantage and trade in services'. Presented at a Conference on Restrictions on Transactions in the International Market for Services, Wiston House, West Sussex, England, 30 May – 2 June
Markusen, James R. (1984) 'Multinational, multi-plant economies, and the gains from trade'. *Journal of International Economics* 16
Stern, Robert M. (1985) 'Global dimensions and determinants of international trade and investment in services'

[7]

Journal of Economic Perspectives—Volume 18, Number 4—Fall 2004—Pages 93–114

The Muddles over Outsourcing

Jagdish Bhagwati, Arvind Panagariya and
T.N. Srinivasan

I n the early 1980s, "outsourcing" typically referred to the situation when firms expanded their purchases of manufactured physical inputs, like car companies that purchased window cranks and seat fabrics from outside the firm rather than making them inside. But in 2004, outsourcing took on a different meaning. It referred now to a specific segment of the growing international trade in services. This segment consists of arm's-length, or what Bhagwati (1984) called "long-distance," purchase of services abroad, principally, but not necessarily, via electronic mediums such as the telephone, fax and the Internet. Outsourcing can happen both though transactions by firms, like phone call centers staffed in Bangalore to serve customers in New York and x-rays transmitted digitally from Boston to be read in Bombay, or with direct consumption purchases by individuals, like when someone hires an offshore firm to provide plans for redesigning or redecorating a living room.

Thus, in February 2004, the members of President Bush's Council of Economic Advisers stated the following: "Outsourcing of professional services is a prominent example of a new type of trade" (Mankiw, Forbes and Rosen, 2004). The chair of the CEA, Gregory Mankiw, made a similar point in a press interview (Andrews, 2004): "I think outsourcing is a growing phenomenon, but it's something that we should realize is probably a plus for the economy in the long run. We're very used to goods being produced abroad and being shipped here on ships or planes. What we are not used to is services being produced abroad and being sent here over the

■ *Jagdish Bhagwati is University Professor, Columbia University, and Senior Fellow in International Economics, Council on Foreign Relations, both in New York, New York. Arvind Panagariya is a Professor of Economics and the Jagdish Bhagwati Professor of Indian Political Economy, Columbia University, New York, New York. T.N. Srinivasan is Samuel Park Jr. Professor of Economics, Yale University, New Haven, Connecticut.*

Internet or telephone wires. But does it matter from an economic standpoint whether values of items produced abroad come on planes and ships or over fiber-optic cables? Well, no, the economics is basically the same."

Mankiw's comments caused a considerable stir, with critics complaining that he had endorsed a reduction in U.S. jobs. Journalists jumped on the bandwagon, with Lou Dobbs of CNN going so far as to list on his program U.S. companies that "ship jobs abroad." Many Americans had similar concerns; for example, an Associated Press-Ipsos poll in May 2004 found that 69 percent of Americans thought that "outsourcing" hurts the U.S. economy, against only 17 percent who think it helps (reported at ⟨http://www.pollingreport.com/trade.htm⟩).

The resulting public debate over outsourcing has been marred by two sets of serious muddles. The first set of muddles relates to what is meant by outsourcing. When many politicians, journalists and even some economists start discussing "outsourcing," they soon leap beyond purchases of offshore arm's-length services to include, without analytical clarity, phenomena such as offshore purchases of manufactured components and even direct foreign investment by firms. Thus, we begin by discussing how outsourcing, properly defined as the offshore trade in arm's-length services, is addressed in the World Trade Organization in its General Agreement on Trade in Services. Based on this definition, we then discuss recent estimates of the extent of outsourcing.

The second set of muddles is more subtle: even some economists who use the appropriate definition of outsourcing sometimes worry about whether arm's-length trade in services should be treated with the same analytical tools as trade in goods, or whether it presents different issues. We present some models to illustrate the effects of outsourcing, and we use the models to consider how trade in offshore purchase of such arm's-length services might affect national output, wages and distribution of income. We argue that outsourcing is fundamentally just a trade phenomenon; that is, subject to the usual theoretical *caveats* and practical responses, outsourcing leads to gains from trade, and its effects on jobs and wages are not qualitatively different from those of conventional trade in goods. We also distinguish between outsourcing issues arising in two alternative ways: first, because of new technological possibilities that convert previously nontraded services into traded arm's-length services (at any given skills and factor endowments of countries) and, second, as skills accumulate in countries such as India and China in information technology activities that can augment internationally traded arm's-length services (at any given technology for trading such services).

Muddles over the Definition of Outsourcing

The economics literature on trade in services has long made distinctions based on the different ways in which the provider and the user could transact. For example, Bhagwati (1984) distinguished between "long-distance" arm's-length ser-

Jagdish Bhagwati, Arvind Panagariya and T.N. Srinivasan   95

vices and those requiring the provider and the user to get together.[1] Sampson and Snape (1985) offered further distinctions in the latter group. The language of the World Trade Organization (WTO), under its General Agreement on Trade in Services (GATS), categorizes four different ways in which services can be traded.

In Mode 1 of the WTO terminology, trade in services involves arm's-length supply of services, with the supplier and buyer remaining in their respective locations. Although Mode 1 purchases have come into prominence because of the advances in electronic information and communications technology that allow rapid flow of voluminous data across international boundaries, such transactions also take place through conventional communications; for example, accounting work for a firm in New York can be done in Bangalore with records going back and forth by snail-mail. Mode 1 trade in services is generally distinguished from goods trade in that it cannot be readily subjected to customs inspection. Both individuals and firms can provide Mode 1 services. In the former category, we have independent designers, architects and consultants who sell their services electronically to manufacturers and consumers around the world. In the latter, we have large firms that manage call centers, back offices and software programmers.

Mode 2 services are provided by moving the service recipient to the location of the service provider. Travel by foreign residents including tourists is the dominant form of Mode 2 exports and contributed $64.5 billion to the U.S. services exports in 2003, according to the U.S. Bureau of Economic Analysis (⟨http://www.bea.gov/bea/di/home/bop.htm⟩). Other examples of Mode 2 exports include medical care rendered to foreign patients and education provided to foreign students. The latter generated as much as $13.4 billion in export revenues for the United States in 2003.

In Mode 3, the service provider establishes a commercial presence in another country, requiring an element of direct foreign investment. The direct investment involved is assumed to be minuscule, existing only to facilitate sales and purchases. The most prominent examples of Mode 3 services are banking and insurance. Mode 3 is therefore held to entail only the "right to establish," to distinguish it from full-scale direct investment.

In Mode 4, the service seller moves to the location of the service buyer. Construction and consulting services are often provided through this mode. Also included in this category are medical and educational services provided by moving doctors and teachers to the location of the recipient. Thus, Mode 4 implies temporary migration, which can shade over into permanent migration, since the experience with the guestworker (*gastarbeiter*) program in western Europe has shown that it can be enormously difficult to return temporary workers to their countries of origin. As the Swiss novelist Max Frisch remarked movingly when the German authorities could not bring themselves to return guestworkers to their

---

[1] Bhagwati (1984) also initiated the analysis of what he called "splintering" of services from manufacturing. Splintering occurs when part of the manufacturing value added, such as, say, painting a car, is done by contracting it out to a separate painting firm, and the painting value added then becomes part of the service sector, with little change in the overall real situation. Some economists now call this the "fragmentation" phenomenon.

96   Journal of Economic Perspectives

countries of origin in the distressed economic times of the 1970s, "We imported workers and got men instead."

Trade in Mode 1 services is what most economists have meant when they discuss "outsourcing." Moreover, international trade in tourism (Mode 2), banking and insurance (Mode 3) and programs of temporary or permanent migration (Mode 4) present distinctive issues of their own, so that Mode 1 trade in services is the primary focus of this article. But it is worth noting the historical irony that when trade in services was brought into the fold of international trade rules via the General Agreement on Trade in Services (GATS), concluded as a part of the Uruguay Round Agreements that created the World Trade Organization (WTO) in 1995, trade in Mode 1 services was the least controversial, while Modes 3 and 4 were the most controversial. The developed countries demanded the expansion of the right to commercial presence abroad (Mode 3) and opposed the inward movement of people (Mode 4). Developing countries, on the other hand, resisted liberalization in Mode 3 services and pushed for the liberalization of Mode 4 services, which offers their unskilled populations the possibility of offering services in developed countries. Neither side showed much resistance to the Mode 1 cross-border trade in services, perhaps because by definition, it did not involve accepting a foreign presence on one's soil. Indeed, the bulk of the liberalization commitments made as a part of the GATS negotiations under the Uruguay Round were under Mode 1. In the years immediately following the creation of the WTO in 1995, the United States aggressively pushed the idea that the WTO members commit to zero duty on Internet trade.

In the public controversy over outsourcing and its effects on American prosperity, jobs and wages, at least two phenomena have been muddled up with the purchase of long-distance services à la Mode 1 of WTO, making the discussion of the outsourcing phenomenon opaque and misleading, to say the least.

First, the public outcry often slides over into imports of all services, not just Mode 1 services. Sometimes the critics of outsourcing appear to include even the imports by firms of manufacturing components, as under the early-1980s definition of "outsourcing." In fact, such enlargement of the scope of the phenomenon of outsourcing should include imports of products for final consumption as well: after all, there is no difference in principle between an American factory owner importing French brie and Burgundy for his supper, instead of consuming Milwaukee beer and Kraft cheese, and his importing a Japanese lathe rather than one manufactured in Ohio for his factory in Youngstown. Second, the phenomenon of direct foreign investment is often added indiscriminately to the discussion of outsourcing of Mode 1 services, as when a firm closes its plant in Boston and invests in production in Bombay, or when a firm simply opens up a factory in Nairobi instead of in Nantucket.[2] This confuses the phenomenon of trade in services with direct foreign investment.

---

[2] For a prominent recent example of expanding the definition of "outsourcing" to include other forms of trade, see Dobbs (2004), the jacket of whose book, *Exporting America*, condemns that "Employment in the auto industry has dropped by 200,000 jobs over the past four years, while imports of Chinese auto

But direct foreign investment is *not* the same as offshore outsourcing, even though sometimes both phenomena are tied together as, for example, when Dell invests in an outsourcing facility for call answering in Bangalore. The two phenomena are both empirically and analytically distinct. The pros and cons of direct foreign investment are much discussed in the massive academic literature on the subject. It would be fair to say that today direct foreign investment is considered to be desirable, even if the gains from it to the recipient and to the sending countries need not always be substantial and occasionally a downside can occur.[3] Regardless, we will ignore this question, concentrating instead on analyzing outsourcing of Mode 1 services, as defined and distinguished above.

How Many U.S. Jobs Have Been Outsourced?

Despite the heated level of rhetoric over outsourcing, the magnitude of jobs affected by outsourcing of Mode 1 services in the U.S. economy appears quite modest. The smallness of the number emerges whether we look at the buyer's side of the transaction or that of the seller.

On the buyer's side, perhaps the most frequently cited estimate is due to a 2002 report from Forrester Research, Inc., authored by McCarthy (2002), according to which the total number of U.S. jobs outsourced will reach 3.3 million—recently revised to 3.4 million in McCarthy (2004)—by 2015. Forrester does not explain whether the prediction is that the U.S. economy will have 3.3 million fewer jobs in 2015 than it would otherwise have had because of outsourcing, which seems implausible given the common belief among economists that the number of jobs in the long run is determined by the natural rate of unemployment, or whether the prediction is that outsourcing will cause 3.3 million U.S. workers to shift from jobs that they might otherwise have had into different jobs, which is a more plausible claim. Nor does this report focus on just Mode 1 services, so in that sense the estimate for outsourcing is likely to be overstated.

---

parts have doubled." Similarly, Dobbs complains on the flap of his book jacket: "Carrier, maker of air-conditioning and heating units, closes its Syracuse, New York, plants—and most of its 1,200 jobs go to Singapore and Malaysia." Politicians on all sides make similar conceptual errors. For example, John Kerry's website advocates "Close Loopholes In International Tax Law That Encourage Outsourcing," and the surrounding discussion makes clear that "outsourcing" covers any company with a foreign subsidiary (<http://www.johnkerry.com/issues/economy/jobs.html>, accessed September 2, 2004). Matching this confusion, Republicans like U.S. Senate Majority Leader Bill Frist have struck back at the critics of outsourcing by highlighting the number of major foreign companies like Nissan who "insource," that is, build manufacturing plants in the United States (for examples, see <http://www.ofii.org/facts_figures/>). Whatever the merits of such arguments about foreign subsidiaries and the location of manufacturing, it is conceptually quite different from Mode 1 trade in services.

[3] The voluminous literature has been reviewed by many, including Richard Caves (1996), a principal researcher in this area. A review and assessment from the perspectives of civil-society complaints about direct foreign investment, including whether multinationals exploit foreign workers in poor countries, can be found in Bhagwati (2004).

But even accepting these estimates at face value, Forrester is suggesting an average annual outflow of jobs of at most 300,000 (without any offset for the inflow of jobs due to outsourcing by other nations from the United States). The Forrester report associates this outflow with nine occupational categories—for example, management, architecture and engineering and computer and mathematical operation—identified as especially subject to outsourcing. The estimated number of jobs affected turns out to be a minuscule 0.53 percent of the 56.7 million jobs in 2002 in these nine occupational categories.[4] Alternatively, considering that the U.S. economy destroyed as many as 30 million jobs in 2003 and created approximately as many of them, according to the Business Employment Dynamics survey of the Bureau of Labor statistics at ⟨http://www.bls.gov/bdm/home.htm⟩, the Forrester estimate of job outflows is about 1 percent of the number of jobs destroyed and created annually currently.

Evidence on job losses from yet other sources reinforces the conclusion that the aggregate effect of outsourcing has so far been negligible. Companies that lay off 50 workers or more are asked by the U.S. Department of Labor to explain the reason. Only 2 percent of the layoffs in the past five years are reported to have come from companies reallocating operations overseas or from import-competition pressure. Evidently, Mode 1 outsourcing of services must be only a small part of these 2 percent of the total layoffs.

Likewise, Mann (2003) calculates that once we cut through the dotcom boom and bust, adjust for the business cycle downturn and compare more meaningfully therefore the employment in the information technology-related industries during end-1999 to October 2003, employment in architecture and engineering occupations is stable, in computer and mathematical occupations is 6 percent higher and in business and financial occupations is 9 percent higher. These figures do not directly measure the extent of outsourcing, but insofar as the occupational categories they represent are the ones subject to outsourcing, a stable or rising employment trend in them suggests relatively little impact of outsourcing on employment.

The number of outsourced jobs can also be measured from the seller's side. India is by far the largest provider to date of offshore Mode 1 services. According to India's National Association of Software and Service Companies (NASSCOM), employment of workers such as software developers and call center operators serving clients outside India increased by 353,000 between March 2000 and March 2004, reaching 505,000. Of the increase, 70 percent or 247,000 workers went into serving clients in the United States. This works out to 61,750 jobs per year. In the Philippines, the increase in the number of workers doing back-office work for

---

[4] Kirkegaard (2003) offers a detailed and careful analysis of the job losses in the nine occupational categories between 2000 and 2002. Though manufacturing accounted for less than 10 percent of employment in these categories, it accounted for the vast majority of the job losses in them. Services experienced a net gain in jobs in the categories. Among the nine occupational categories, management accounted for 60 percent of the job losses.

non-Philippine companies between 2002 and 2003 was 14,500.[5] Adding up these numbers and accounting for some missing countries and categories, it is unlikely that the number of workers engaged in providing offshore services to the United States companies could have averaged more than 90,000 to 100,000 per year.

Moreover, even if outsourcing sometimes reduces jobs proximately at certain firms or in certain sectors, in other cases it can help to create new U.S. jobs. This happens when the availability of the cheaper lower-end skilled workers abroad makes an activity that also uses higher-end skilled workers in the United States financially feasible. For example, the Information Management Consultants (IMC) of Reston, Virginia, several years ago considered producing software that would allow biotech companies to exploit better the new human genome research. The project seemed financially nonviable if undertaken entirely in the United States. But having its Indian subsidiary do the bulk of the coding work made the project viable. The outcome was a thriving line of business in bio-informatics for IMC and employment at six-figure salaries in the United States. For each engineer in India, the firm now employs six engineers in the United States (Pearlstein, 2004).

Moreover, any proximate job losses due to outsourcing from the United States must be set against the proximate job gains due to others outsourcing to the United States. The United States is a substantial exporter of services in fields as diverse as legal, medical and accounting services. These include outsourcing of Mode 1 services, of course. We analyze more fully below the consequences of outsourcing for jobs in the United States, but we may remark here that while linking sectoral trade balances to aggregate jobs is inappropriate on theoretical grounds, if we were to disregard this *caveat* and join the policy debate on whether we proximately export more service jobs than we import, the large U.S. trade surplus in services— $51.1 billion in 2003 according to the U.S. Bureau of Economic Analysis—surely has to favor outsourcing. Since the U.S. economy offers high-value Mode 1 services while importing low-value ones instead, the net trade balance in Mode 1 services is also almost certainly in America's favor, just as it is on services more generally.

Given then the meager evidence that outsourcing has been or will be quantitatively important in U.S. labor markets, why has the issue risen to such prominence? One answer is that stagnant job growth since the recession of 2001 has led to a search for possible causes. This attempt to draw a connection between international trade in services and slow U.S. job growth in the early 2000s is surely linked to the crude and incorrect view often used by protectionists that all imports, whether of goods or services, cause a "loss of jobs" for Americans. These complaints reduce to the conventional witticism: Trade is good but imports are bad. This fallacy is, of course, all too pervasive; but it has regained popularity at a time when trade deficits are large and job generation has been slow. Another reason for the

---

[5] We take the numbers cited in this paragraph so far from the Hilsenrath (2004) story in the *Wall Street Journal*. He also says that, in Ireland, the number of jobs created by U.S. multinationals between 2002 and 2003 was only 1,139 per year; but these numbers relate to direct foreign investment rather than outsourcing.

furor over outsourcing is that the technological advances in computing, communications and information technology have made the outsourcing of services a practical possibility in a way that was not possible in the past, creating fear of job loss among white-collared workers. A presidential election campaign in 2004 added intensity to this volatile mix of ingredients.

Analyzing Outsourcing

Some economists have expressed a concern that outsourcing may be less likely than other forms of international trade to be beneficial to overall prosperity and more likely to harm the workforce. Conventional analysis of trade policy distinguishes three issues: how does trade affect aggregate economic welfare; what is its effect on the level of employment; and how does it affect income distribution, especially the real wages of workers? The popular textbook models of trade, like the two-country, two-factor, two-country model (Bhagwati, Panagariya and Srinivasan, 1998, chapters 5, 6 and 10) used extensively by international trade theorists and associated with Paul Samuelson's classic stripped-down version of the Heckscher-Ohlin model, typically answer these questions along these lines. First, free trade in this model raises the overall income of each nation over what it will have under autarky; it enlarges the size of the pie available to each country in the process. Second, this model focuses on long-run analysis and therefore assumes full employment, which means it *assumes* that trade has no effect on the aggregate number of jobs. Third, the model allows factor prices to adjust to maintain full employment, and therefore, trade can *cause* changes in income distribution.

In particular, imagine a country that is relatively abundant in skilled labor, like the United States, and that begins to trade with a country that is relatively abundant in unskilled labor, like India. In such a case, trade may increase the real income of skilled labor in the United States and lower that of unskilled labor. The need for the reallocation of resources may also cause workers to experience dislocation—that is, the loss of a job, followed by a period of unemployment, followed perhaps by finding that the available jobs pay less than the ones held earlier. In models with flexible real wages, unskilled workers can experience a decline in their real wages.

Nothing changes in this conventional analysis of trade policy when we consider outsourcing. To illustrate this conclusion, we consider three alternative models that capture different aspects of trade in services according to Mode 1. The first model uses one (aggregate) final good and two factors of production. With only one final good, there is no basis for trade initially. But the introduction of outsourcing opens the possibility of trading labor services for the final good. This outsourcing leads unambiguously to welfare gains, with the usual distributive effects between the two factors. The second model contains two goods and three factors. This model allows for conventional trade in goods at fixed world prices initially and then introduces outsourcing. It shows that the country still gains overall from outsourcing, albeit with the income-distribution effects just as in the first model. The third model has three goods and two factors, and it shifts the nature of outsourcing to one where, with two traded goods, the third non-traded good becomes tradable online. In this model, allowing the nontraded good to be imported at a lower price, thanks to offshore trading becoming feasible, leads to welfare gain and to both factors becoming better off, thus refuting the presumption that outsourcing will necessarily harm the real wages of particular factors of production. The overall message of these models is that offshore outsourcing is generally beneficial to an economy (with conventional caveats, and also the distributional effects are not necessarily divisive).

Model 1: Gains from Outsourcing in a One-Good Model

Let's start with a model that has only one good, which is produced with two factors of production, labor and capital. Assume diminishing returns to the factors, and let the MP_L curve in Figure 1 represent the marginal product of labor, given the fixed endowment of capital in the economy. Letting L^0 be the endowment of labor, the wage in terms of the final good is represented by W^0. The wage bill is the area formed by the rectangle $OW^0E^0L^0$. The return to capital is the area under the MP_L curve and above the horizontal line W^0E^0.

Given only one good, this model offers no scope for conventional international trade. Suppose, however, that an innovation allows the economy to buy the services of labor abroad electronically at the fixed wage W'. The economy continues to hire the same endowment of domestic labor, but now paying the lower wage. In this case, the economy buys L^0L' labor abroad paying the rectangle $L^0L'E'R$ for it. Domestic labor receives OL^0RW' and capital the area under the MP_L curve and above the horizontal line $W'E'$.

The following economic effects obtain. The country's total income rises by the triangular area E^0RE', which is the net gain from outsourcing. The income of labor, the "import-competing" factor, declines by area W^0E^0RW' and is redistributed to capital. Thus, capital owners make a gain of $W^0E^0E'W'$.

This model captures much of the popular rhetoric that expresses doubts about outsourcing. That is, the model shows that outsourcing may benefit society as a whole. But in the absence of a method for some of the social benefits received by capital to be transferred to workers, firms or owners of capital receive more than 100 percent of the social benefits from outsourcing, while workers experience losses.

Model 2: Gains from Outsourcing in the Presence of Trade

Now consider a two-good, three-factor model in which the country already trades in the world markets and a technological innovation makes outsourcing possible. Following Samuelson (1971) and Jones (1971), let there be two final goods, each produced using a sector-specific factor and another factor that is common to both goods. For concreteness, say that the import-competing good uses unskilled labor as its specific factor, while the exportable good uses capital as its specific factor, with the common factor to producing both goods being skilled

Figure 1
Economics of Outsourcing

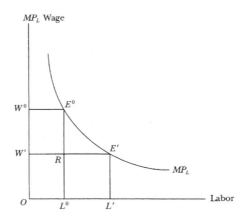

labor. Now imagine that a technological change makes it possible for skilled labor
to be outsourced.

Taking the world prices as given for the moment, Figure 2 shows the initial
trading equilibrium in the absence of outsourcing. Axis $O_1 O_2$ represents the total
endowment of skilled labor in the economy. We measure skilled labor employed in
sector 1 of import competing goods to the right from O_1 and that in sector 2 of
exportable goods to the left from O_2. Thus, any point on $O_1 O_2$ represents an
allocation of skilled labor between the two sectors. The $VMPL_1$ and $VMPL_2$ denote
the value-of-marginal-product curves for skilled labor in sectors 1 and 2, respectively. The equilibrium allocation of skilled labor between the two sectors is given
by S^0, where the skilled wage offered by the two sectors is the same, R^0. The GDP
can be then measured by the sum of the areas under the two curves up to the point
indicating the employment of skilled labor, S^0, which will show the total production of both goods.

Suppose now that an innovation allows the country to purchase the services of
skilled labor abroad at a lower wage shown by R'. At this wage, there is excess
demand for the services of skilled labor equaling GE'. This demand is satisfied
through outsourcing, which expands the skilled-labor supply by $O_2 O_2'$ such that
$O_2 O_2' = GE'$.

To locate the new equilibrium, we shift the $VMPL_2$ curve horizontally to the
right by $O_2 O_2' = GE'$ as shown by $VMPL_2'$ (alternatively, we could shift the $VMPL_1$
curve to the left by the same amount). Because the size of this horizontal shift to the
right is the same at every point, $E^0 A = GE'$ by construction, sector 1 employs $S^0 S'$
of the outsourced supply and sector 2 employs $S' S''$. The quantity of outsourced
labor is $O_2 O_2'$, and it is paid the wage R'.

The arrival of outsourcing increases national income. To see this on the

Figure 2

Outsourcing with Pre-Existing Trade in Goods

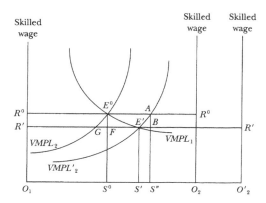

diagram, first consider sector 1 and then sector 2. Before outsourcing, the original total value of output of sector 1 at the original wage R was given by the area under the $VMPL_1$ curve, up to the quantity of skilled labor input O_1S^0. After outsourcing, the value of output is the area under the $VMPL_1$ curve up to the quantity of skilled labor input O_1S'. However, the extra rectangle $S^0FE'S'$ represents wages that need to be paid to the workers who provided the outsourced services, so the output value gain in sector 1 is the triangle E^0FE'. Now consider sector 2, where in graphical terms, the addition of outsourced labor has "pulled" both the right-hand axis and the $VMPL_2$ curve to the right. Because of this horizontal shift, the original value of output of sector 2, which was the area under $VMPL_2$ given the skilled labor input O_2S^0 (measuring from right to left), is exactly equal to the area under $VMPL'_2$ given the input of skilled labor from O'_2 to S''. However, sector 2 can also increase output by making use of outsourced labor from S'' to S'. The rectangle $S'E'BS''$ must be paid to foreign workers in sector 2, but the triangle ABE' represents a social gain. Thus, the increase in output for the home country consists the sum of the two triangles E^0FE' and ABE'.

The distributional issues become more complex in this setting. However, assuming diminishing returns to all factors of production, the increase in quantity used of skilled labor and a decline in the skilled wage will cause the unskilled wage and the rental on capital to rise.

As long as we assume that the country is small so that the terms of trade are fixed and there are no other distortions in the form of prior tariffs or distortionary taxes, outsourcing remains beneficial in this setting. However, if we assume that the country is large, the introduction of outsourcing will not necessarily lead to a welfare gain, because the opening to outsourcing can shift the terms of trade in the final goods. There are two alternative ways to understand this result.

First, imagine that at the initial prices, outsourcing expands the output of the exportable good more than the demand for it, which raises the possibility that the terms of trade in the goods market deteriorate (that is, it will cost a nation more in terms of exports to purchase a fixed quantity of imports). This deterioration may more than offset the direct benefits from outsourcing. Alternatively, if outsourcing largely expands the output of the import competing good, the demand for imports declines, which lowers the price of the imported good and improves the terms of trade. In this case, the direct gain from outsourcing is reinforced by the improvement in the terms of trade.

A second way to understand how outsourcing can lead to welfare losses draws on the generalized theory of immiserizing growth, developed in Bhagwati (1968). Bhagwati demonstrated that a nation's own growth in the presence of distortions could be immiserizing to the nation itself when it occurred in the presence of an uncorrected distortion. The secondary loss from the distortion can be accentuated by the growth, outweighing the primary gain from the growth. When trade opportunity increases such as that resulting from the information technology that converts the hitherto nontradable service into a Mode 1 service, this is analytically the equivalent of growth. But when a large country is following a free trade policy instead of exploiting its monopoly power in trade by adopting an optimal tariff, the free trade policy itself is a kind of distortion—and the enhanced trade opportunity may accentuate the loss from such a policy (Bhagwati, Panagariya and Srinivasan, 1998, chapter 29).

In thinking about the welfare consequences of Mode 1 services in this model, it is worth stressing that there really are three scenarios: autarky, free trade before outsourcing and free trade after outsourcing. Either of the trade outcomes will be preferable to autarky in welfare terms. However, while free trade with outsourcing will be preferable to free trade without outsourcing in an economy with fixed terms of trade and no other distortions, this conclusion can, but need not, be overturned if those assumptions change.

Model 3: Both Factors Gain

In the previous model, outsourcing leads to an adverse impact on the real income of the factor of production imported online. But this outcome is not inevitable. Consider a three-good, two-factor model such that goods 1 and 2 are traded, while good 3 is initially a nontraded service. Assume, as before, that the country is small and produces both traded goods. Perfect competition ensures that the average cost of each trade good, which is a function of the two-factor prices, equals the exogenously given goods price. The two average-cost-pricing equations then ensure that the factor prices themselves are fixed as long as the traded good prices are fixed. Given these fixed factor prices, the average cost of good 3 is fixed as well, implying that its supply curve is horizontal with its equilibrium quantity determined entirely by demand.[6]

---

[6] This is the well-known Komiya (1967) model that has been generalized to a dynamic context by Findlay (1970).

Suppose now that due to an innovation, the formerly nontraded service becomes tradable and is available from abroad at a lower price than the one at which it is supplied at home. It then follows that the domestic supply of the service will disappear altogether, with the resources released by it absorbed by production of goods 1 and 2. As long as both of these goods continue to be produced, the factor prices measured in terms of those goods will be unchanged. But since the price of the service, good 3, has declined, the buying power of the two factors in terms of that good rises. Thus, outsourcing ends up making the owners of both factors better off.

These models underline the fact that trade in outsourced services is just another kind of trade, subject to the same principles that the theorists of commercial policy have developed in the postwar period (and are set out in Bhagwati, 2002). With trade in either goods or services, the precise manner in which the benefits of outsourcing filter through the economy depends on the structure of the economy. Thus, if outsourcing principally takes the form of an intermediate input into the production of other goods, it will act like input-saving technical change, augmenting productivity. An example would be customized software or designs supplied at lower costs through outsourcing to the firms producing, say, automobiles in the United States. On the other hand, if outsourcing takes the form of a new product or an old product supplied at a lower price to the final consumers, it will directly add to real income.

These three models can be thought of as describing several possible outcomes of a technological change that leads to increased outsourcing. In the first model, outsourcing benefits society, but the benefits arrive in a combination of higher returns to capital and lower wages. In the second model, with multiple factors of production and fixed goods prices, outsourcing again provides aggregate benefits, but some workers gain while others lose. In the final model, outsourcing provides benefits in a way that, at least after workers make a transition to other industries, leads to higher real incomes for all workers.

Accumulation of Skills Abroad

So far, we have analyzed outsourcing as involving technical change that entails converting a nontradable service, initially requiring proximity of provider and user, into a Mode 1 traded service. The phenomenon is analytically analogous to a reduction in transport costs that turns some initially nontraded goods into traded goods. It therefore has effects on the United States similar to those of conventional freeing of trade, holding the factor endowments including skill levels constant.

But offshore outsourcing may also be augmented, holding the technology of outsourcing constant, when skills levels increase abroad in countries like India and China. Some of the recent outsourcing fears have arisen from this analytically distinct possibility. For example, Craig Barrett, the chief executive officer of Intel, has argued that India and China will soon have 300 million high-skilled workers and that this situation poses a danger to the U.S. prosperity and to skilled workers in the U.S. economy (Sickinger, 2004; "Q & A: Intel CEO Craig Barrett," 2003).

Fears have been aroused that the acquisition by foreign workers of the information technology related, medical and other skills would lead to losses both for the U.S. economy in the aggregate and for the skilled American workers.

While we will later question the empirical relevance of these fears, we focus here on the analytic issue they raise. Taking the outsourcing technology as given, what is the effect of an increase in the number of skilled workers abroad on U.S. prosperity and on U.S. skilled workers? The three models we have outlined above readily permit the analysis of this question.

The effect of the expansion of skilled labor force abroad feeds directly into the U.S. economy through the wage paid to the workers providing outsourcing services in Models 1 and 2 and indirectly through the price of good 3 in Model 3. In Models 1 and 2, the increased supply of skilled labor in the foreign economy leads to a decline in the skilled wage there. In consequence, in Model 1, the augmented skill levels abroad will increase aggregate U.S. welfare but will also reduce the real wages of the skilled workers in the United States.

In Model 2, the same results should follow, but there is a complication because of trade in goods. If the United States were a "small country" in the sense that it cannot affect the goods terms of trade, the storyline is the same as with Model 1: overall gain, loss for skilled workers. But if the terms of trade can shift, we must take a possible induced (secondary) effect into account. If terms of trade deteriorate for the United States, this secondary loss can outweigh the primary gain from the lower wage of skilled offshore services, resulting in a net loss of U.S. welfare.

In Model 3, where the skill accumulation abroad can only work its trade effects indirectly through the goods markets, the expansion of skills abroad will manifest itself in a decline in the price of good 3, with beneficial effect for the United States. Moreover, under the small-country assumption, since the two factor prices continue to be determined by the average-cost-pricing conditions in the goods market, the real returns will be unchanged in terms of the traded goods but will rise in terms of good 3: both factors will therefore benefit.

Evidently, therefore, the message again is much like that from analysis in conventional trade models. That skills accumulation abroad, or for that matter any exogenous change abroad, will harm or help the United States, depending on what happens to the terms of trade, is a message that is in fact pretty well understood in the analytical literature that goes back over half a century. Thus, when the U.S. economy was growing more briskly than the European economy in the 1950s, and there was a celebrated "dollar shortage," Europeans were concerned that U.S. growth injured their standard of living. When Japan was growing rapidly in the 1960s and 1970s, many Americans, fearful of Japan becoming the premier world economy, were equally concerned that Japanese growth would harm the United States. The same argument is now surfacing again in the context of China and India, spurred by the loss of a few jobs to offshore outsourcing.[7]

---

[7] In the 1930s, fear of cheap Japanese exports of textiles, lamps, hurricane lanterns and other labor-intensive products led to talk of the "yellow peril." The most feared product that made it into popular

The answer that all depends on the induced terms of trade change, if any, can be traced back to the literature inspired by the European fears of U.S. productivity growth in the 1950s. In one of several pioneering contributions, Harry Johnson (1954) constructed a two-country, two-good model in which each country specialized entirely in one good. When the U.S. economy grew, the production of its export good increased and, provided the import good was not inferior in U.S. consumption, the effect was to increase U.S. exports of its own good, lower the price of U.S. exports and help Europe. Johnson (1955) then generalized the analysis by allowing the production of both goods by each country: this allowed the consumption effect of growth to be offset by the production effect of the growth, so that (consistent with market stability) the terms of trade could either rise or fall, leaving the effect on European welfare ambiguous.[8]

Whether the change abroad is significant enough, in terms of its net effects on excess demands and supplies of goods at existing terms of trade, and whether it makes sense to worry about sufficiently large "national monopoly power" in international trade such that large terms of trade changes may follow from modest changes in excess demands and supplies, are empirical questions where our presumptions (addressed in part below) are to discount and dismiss the possibility of significant terms of trade changes following skills accumulation abroad.

Implications for Outsourcing and the U.S. Economy: Welfare, Jobs, Wages and Dislocation

Let us now turn to a consideration of the implications of outsourcing for the U.S. economy. There are four issues to consider: overall welfare; the total number of jobs; the quality of jobs; and dislocation.

Overall Welfare

Our theoretical analysis leads us to conclude that there is a strong presumption that outsourcing that turns previously nontraded services into Mode 1 tradable

---

consciousness was the "one-dollar blouse." Recent years have seen revived fears of the "yellow peril," involving either exports from Asian "tiger" economies like South Korea, Thailand and Indonesia and also from China. The offshore "outsourcing" of services might be called the "brown peril," since the foreign country most prominently involved in media reports is India.

[8] In a theoretical contribution in this journal, Paul Samuelson (2004) has constructed a Ricardian model where the effect of productivity change abroad is to make the autarkic price ratios between goods identical between the trading countries so that the gains from trade disappear for each of the trading countries. This means, of course, that the country that has not experienced any change is immiserized: the external change has eliminated the gains from trade while the country has no primary gain of its own to set against that loss. It is like being hit by a cyclone that arrives exogenously to one's actions. Panagariya (2004) shows, however, that the Samuelson analysis does not capture the essence of the offshore outsourcing phenomenon. The recent work of Gomory and Baumol (2001, chapter 2) is understood in a similar way: it shows some countries gaining and some losing from changes in productivity coefficients in a Ricardian economy.

services is beneficial to the United States. We have also shown that taking the phenomenon of outsourcing as given, the expansion of skills abroad that we already import is also beneficial for the U.S. economy, since it makes the imported services even cheaper. The main qualification results from the possibility of the deterioration of the terms of trade in other goods—specifically, that the primary beneficial impact of the introduction of outsourcing or expansion of skills abroad may give rise to a sufficiently strong adverse secondary terms of trade effect in the traded goods to offset the former.

This may happen, for example, because the U.S. exports goods that are more intensive in information technology services and imports goods that are less intensive in information technology. Taking outsourcing as given, foreign (say, Indian and Chinese) growth then makes the outsourced information technology services cheaper to the United States, which is beneficial, but it also has the harmful effect that it expands the world supply of the information technology intensive good that the U.S. economy exports and, thus, worsens the U.S. terms of trade.

There are good reasons to believe that this last possibility does not capture the reality of outsourcing, however. For one thing, growth in China and India in the near future is likely to remain concentrated in low-end information technology services that they are already exporting to the United States. The notion that India and China will quickly educate 300 million of their citizens to acquire sophisticated and complex skills at stake borders on the ludicrous. The educational sectors in these countries face enormous difficulties. The students enrolled in colleges and universities in India account for only 6 percent of the population in their age group (18–24 years). Of those that do enroll in college, only a tiny fraction have the minimal English language skills that would enable them to function even moderately well in occupations such as call answering. Moreover, with the exception of a handful of institutions such as the Indian Institutes of Technology and Indian Institutes of Management, the higher education system in India is in a dire state and starved of resources. Adding 300 million to the pool of the skilled workers in India and China will take some decades.

Even if we were to grant the possibility of substantial expansion of complex skills in China and India, the conventional Johnson-type model (1955) that predicts losses due to the deterioration of the terms of trade becomes less relevant. When the revival of Europe and Japan brought their skill levels closer to those of the United States, the gains from trade induced by "factor endowment differences" were increasingly replaced by gains from "intraindustry" trade; for example, the United States now specializes in high-end chips such as Pentium, while leaving more standard semiconductor chips to foreign producers. Similarly, we can confidently expect "intraservice" and "intraindustry" trade to grow between the United States on the one hand and China and India on the other as the latter acquire more skills. Models such as those of Johnson in the 1950s do not give a particularly helpful handle on the analysis that is called for today.

One final source of gains from outsourcing is the gain in productivity that lower-priced services used as intermediate inputs can bring. Mann (2003), drawing on Mann and Kirkegaard (2003), points to very substantial productivity gains for the United States from the globalization of information technology hardware production. She reports that globalized production and trade made information technology hardware 10 to 30 percent cheaper than it would have been otherwise. Taking the mid-point of these estimates, she calculates that the price decrease translated into higher productivity growth and a faster real GDP growth of 0.3 percent per year from 1995 to 2002 in the United States. She hypothesizes that globally integrated production of information technology software and services will follow a similar pattern, reduce the prices of these products and promote further diffusion of information technology throughout the U.S. economy. In turn, this would give further boost to productivity growth.

The Total Number of Jobs

Economists typically argue, with plausibility for the current U.S. economy, that macroeconomic policy determines the total number of jobs, whereas trade policy affects the composition of jobs.[9] Thus, Brainard and Litan (2004) note in their recent analysis of outsourcing that the number of jobs has flexibly adjusted to the growth in the labor force in the United States. Despite declining barriers to trade, rapid expansion of the volume of imports and the innovation of what appear to be job displacing technologies, the U.S. economy has added 30 million workers to its payrolls since 1985—including the 2001 recession and the relatively slow growth in jobs during the recovery. Moreover, the growth in jobs has been attended by a rise in the median family income by 20 percent during the last two decades.

Those who contend that all or most service jobs will be outsourced to India and China are both empirically and theoretically mistaken. The empirical mistake is that not all service jobs can be outsourced. About 70 percent of the jobs in the United States are in service industries such as retailing, catering, restaurants and hotels, tourism and personal care that require the consumer and producer to be present in the same place and, therefore, cannot be outsourced (Agrawal and Farrell, 2003). The theoretical mistake is that the possibility that all jobs, in both manufactures and services, will go to China and India, whether through outsourcing or other trade, because of low labor costs, comes perilously close to confusing absolute and comparative advantage.

---

[9] In certain situations, trade policy can affect the total number of jobs. For example, in a Keynesian economy, tariffs can shift a given expenditure toward home goods, yielding an expansionary effect on output and employment. Or in a situation of sticky real wages with associated unemployment, trade policy can affect total employment, as analyzed in pioneering articles by Brecher (1974a, b). But neither possibility applies in a significant manner to the U.S. economy currently. This view seems implicit also in the writings of labor economists like Alan Krueger who say that the number of jobs in the United States is determined by the supply of workers: a view that is inconsistent with Keynesian unemployment or inflexible real wage neoclassical models.

Finally, not all outsourcing results in direct displacement of the U.S. workers. In some cases, it may create services not previously available, which is like opening an economy to the imports of products not produced in the country. For example, getting telephone numbers through 411 and 555-1212 had become very expensive, and as a U.S.-based service, it would have been virtually eliminated. Instead, the availability of call centers abroad has made it possible to retain this service. In other cases, outsourcing may replace capital rather than workers in the United States. Outsourcing allows some human operators abroad to answer the phone for many billing and business inquiries, rather than having such tasks replaced by fully automated electronic response systems. Likewise, outsourcing may lead to a return to manual inputting of checks into the computer system instead of using expensive imaging software.[10]

But even if outsourcing and trade are unlikely to reduce *total* employment, *specific* types of jobs can certainly be lost, like jobs in telephone call centers or in routine tax preparation. The interesting question is whether the new jobs that workers displaced by outsourcing will find are going to be "better" jobs that pay more or "worse" jobs that pay less. Are computer programmers earning $60,000 going to be bumped down into $15,000 jobs stocking shelves and bagging groceries at Wal-Mart?

Will Other High-Value Jobs Arise?

There are several reasons to expect that other high-value jobs will arise for any workers displaced by outsourcing, so that outsourcing is unlikely to lower overall wage level of the displaced U.S. workers.

First, outsourcing from the U.S. economy is generally for low-value jobs, like back-office operations, phone centers and data entry. There are admittedly some exceptions—R&D laboratories have been set up in India, for instance—but this process seems unlikely to go very far in intermediate run, since the labs often have to be close to home where new products tend to be developed. This effect of outsourcing is like the first stage of what Raymond Vernon (1966) famously called the "product cycle," where innovating firms introduce and debug the product in the domestic market, and once the product matures and is standardized, they shift its production to countries where it is cheapest to produce, with the home country eventually becoming an importer of the product. On the other hand, insourcing to the United States—where others buy American-produced legal, medical, educational and other services online—leads to higher-value jobs. Thus, outsourcing means that the U.S. economy loses low-wage call centers, but gains high-wage jobs in medical, legal and other services. On balance, therefore, the outsourcing phenomenon, or the expansion of trade in Mode 1 services, seems likely to offer America a transition to higher-value jobs.

---

[10] The example here has been drawn from Agrawal, Farrell and Reemes (2003), who cite several others.

The claim that outsourcing will lead to a reduction in information technology jobs in the U.S. economy seems especially far-fetched. The *Occupation Outlook Handbook* (*OOH*) of the Bureau of Labor statistics, as discussed in Mann (2003), projects that three of the ten largest numerical increases in job categories will be computer-related occupations: computer support specialists, computer software applications engineers and computer software systems engineers. The *OOH* also predicts that 13 percent of the total number of jobs created in the economy up till 2010 will be related to information technology. The growth in these occupations will be 43 percent, compared with an economy-wide job growth rate of 13 percent. Although the precise growth rates in the *OOH* predictions should not be taken too seriously, the general direction of the trends seems clear.

The general point is that the dynamic U.S. economy grows by a continuous infusion of new products and processes, which in turn offers a stream of new jobs. Even if some computer support technicians start answering phone questions from overseas, an increased number of service firms will provide technicians to set up, repair and manage computer and infrastructure services here in the United States. These "electronic plumbers" of the future, like the water-oriented plumbers of old, will earn more money than many professors. Similarly, even if some jobs for medical technicians, like reading x-ray charts, migrate overseas, surely no one expects that the U.S. health care industry as a whole will diminish its number of jobs with an aging population and an obesity epidemic. As long as the U.S. economy continues to raise its levels of technology, human capital and physical capital and to run an economy not too far from full employment, then the dynamic twists and turns of that economy will produce higher-wage jobs.

Job Dislocation

Popular economic models of trade, at least the basic ones used in this paper, typically assume that workers who lose one job can readily find another (although the wage may change, and not necessarily for the worse). But in the real world, workers may suffer through a period of joblessness and displacement.

One of the most influential studies of the costs of trade displacement, by Lori Kletzer (2001), divides manufacturing industries into low, medium and high import competing, based on the change in the import share during 1979–1994. For example, the import-competing group includes the usual labor-intensive industries such as apparel, footwear, knitting mills, leather products, textiles, blast furnaces, radio and television and toys and sporting goods and accounts for 6.5 million, or 38 percent, of the total jobs displaced in manufacturing during 1979–1999. Across all three groups of industries, about two-thirds of those displaced are reemployed within two years, with about half of that group ending up with job that paid roughly as much or more than their previous job and the other half experiencing a wage cut of 15 percent or more. Thus, the rate of reemployment and wage changes for workers that Kletzer characterizes as trade displaced are quite similar to those for other workers. In other words, a common factor, most likely technological change, is behind the displacement in all categories.[11]

The issue of how society should deal with displaced workers will arise in any dynamic market-oriented economy. For example, the United States has unemployment assistance that applies regardless of whether a worker loses a job because of poor management, poor personal performance, a shift in demand, a shift in the technology of production, a shift in many of the domestic policies, domestic competition, foreign competition or outsourcing. The United States has also had specific assistance programs for the manufacturing-sector employees displaced by imports competition for over four decades (Baicker and Rehavi, 2004) and international economists have vigorously analyzed adjustment assistance as far back as the 1980s (Bhagwati, 1982). Trade adjustment assistance of this type seems a prudent public policy if openness to international trade is to be maintained. Such trade adjustment assistance should be extended to workers who are displaced by outsourcing. More broadly, wage insurance schemes for all dislocated workers, such as the one proposed by Kletzer and Litan (2001) and experimentally built into the Trade Promotion Authority legislation of 2003, are also an important innovative idea.

Concluding Remarks

A productive public debate about outsourcing might usefully begin by restricting the "outsourcing" phraseology to services traded internationally at arm's length and principally on-line: what the WTO calls Mode 1 services. Next, it would help to admit that outsourcing is a relatively small phenomenon in the U.S. labor market. Finally, it would be useful to discuss outsourcing as a trade phenomenon, with effects that are not qualitatively different from those of conventional trade in goods. Thus, outsourcing leads to gains from trade and increases in national income, with the caveats that are standard in this literature. For example, at a theoretical level one must recognize, as trade theorists have long done, the complexity introduced by induced deterioration in the terms in trade if the country has monopoly power in trade. At a policy level, one needs to be concerned about workers who are displaced from certain sectors. But outsourcing is not a small step that will take a preponderance of U.S. workers off the edge of an abyss into prolonged unemployment and re-employment only at low wages. Over time, high-value jobs can be expected to arise and expand.

We hope that our analysis will dispel some of the fear of outsourcing. But fear,

---

[11] One can raise methodological questions about this study, like how the industries are categorized. Also, the study focuses on manufacturing rather than services or outsourcing, and job-specific or industry-specific skills are likely more important in manufacturing firms while service-oriented skills like accounting or payroll may transfer across firms and industries more easily. But these kinds of concerns seem unlikely to overturn the main result.

as the Russian proverb says, has big eyes. It also can have deaf ears. However, we remain optimistic.

■ *We acknowledge helpful conversations with Ralph Gomory, Koichi Hamada and Paul Craig Roberts, valuable comments from Alan Deardorff, Douglas Irwin, Murray Kemp, Lori Kletzer, Catherine Mann, Paul Samuelson and John Williamson and excellent editorial assistance from James Hines, Andrei Shleifer, Michael Waldman and, above all, Timothy Taylor.*

References

Agrawal, Vivek and Diana Farrell. 2003. "Who Wins in Offshoring." *McKinsey Quarterly.* Special Edition: Global Directions, pp. 37–41.

Agrawal, Vivek, Diana Farrell and Jaana K. Remes. 2003. "Offshoring and Beyond." *McKinsey Quarterly.* Special Edition: Global Directions, pp. 25–35.

Andrews, Edmund L. 2004. "Democrats Criticize Bush Over Job Exports." *New York Times.* February 11, p. A26.

Baicker, Katherine and M. Marit Rehavi. 2004. "Policy Watch: Trade Adjustment Assistance." *Journal of Economic Perspectives.* Spring, 18:2, pp. 239–55.

Bhagwati, Jagdish. 1968. "Distortions and Immiserizing Growth: A Generalization." *Review of Economic Studies.* 35:104, pp. 481–85.

Bhagwati, Jagdish, ed. 1982. *Import Competition and Response.* Chicago: University of Chicago Press.

Bhagwati, Jagdish. 1984. "Splintering and Disembodiment of Services and Developing Nations." *World Economy.* 7:2, pp. 133–44.

Bhagwati, Jagdish. 2002. *Free Trade Today.* Princeton, N.J.: Princeton University Press.

Bhagwati, Jagdish. 2004. *In Defense of Globalization.* New York: Oxford University Press.

Bhagwati, Jagdish, Arvind Panagariya and T.N. Srinivasan. 1998. *Lectures in Trade Theory.* Cambridge, Mass.: MIT Press.

Brainard, Lael and Robert E. Litan. 2004. "'Offshoring' Service Jobs: Bane or Boon and What to Do?" Policy Brief No. 132, Washington, D.C., Brookings Institution.

Brecher, Richard. 1974a. "Minimum Wage Rates and the Pure Theory of International Trade." *Quarterly Journal of Economics.* 88:1, pp. 98–116.

Brecher, Richard. 1974b. "Optimal Commercial Policy for a Minimum Wage Economy." *Journal of International Economics.* 4:2, pp. 139–49.

Caves, Richard E. 1996. *Multinational Enterprise and Economic Analysis, Second Edition.* Cambridge: Cambridge University Press.

Findlay, Ronald. 1970. "Factor Proportions and Comparative Advantage in the Long Run." *Journal of Political Economy.* 78:1, pp. 27–34.

Gomory, Ralph and William Baumol. 2001. *Global Trade and Conflicting National Interests.* Cambridge, Mass.: MIT Press.

Hilsenrath, Jon E. 2004. "Behind Outsourcing Debate: Surprisingly Few Hard Numbers." *Wall Street Journal.* April 12, p. A1.

Johnson, Harry. 1954. "Increasing Productivity, Income-Price Trends and Trade Balance." *Economic Journal.* 64, pp. 462–85.

Johnson, Harry. 1955. "Economic Expansion and International Trade." *Manchester School of Economic and Social Studies.* May, 23, pp. 95–112.

Jones, Ronald W. 1971. "A Three-Factor Model in Theory, Trade and History," in *Trade, Balance of Payments and Growth.* J. Bhagwati et al., eds. Amsterdam: North Holland, pp. 3–21.

Kletzer, Lori. 2001. *Job Loss from Imports: Measuring the Costs.* Washington, D.C.: Institute for International Economics.

Kletzer, Lori and Robert Litan. 2001. "A Prescription to Relieve Worker Anxiety." Policy Brief 01-2, Washington D.C., Institute for International Economics.

Komiya, Ryutaro. 1967. "Non-Traded Goods

and the Pure Theory of International Trade." *International Economic Review* 8:2, pp. 132–52.

Mankiw, N. Gregory, Kristin J. Forbes and Harvey S. Rosen. 2004. "Testimony before the Joint Economic Committee, U.S. Congress: 'The Economic Report of the President.'" February 10; Available at ⟨http://www.whitehouse.gov/cea/economic_report_20040210.html⟩.

Mann, Catherine. 2003. "Globalization of IT Services: and White Collar Jobs." Policy Brief PBO 3-11, Washington, D.C., Institute for International Economics.

Mann, Catherine L. and Jacob Kirkegaard. 2003. "Globalization of Information Technology Firms and the Impact on Economic Performance." Mimeo, Institute for International Economics, May 2.

McCarthy, John. 2002. "3.3 Million US Jobs to Go Offshore." Cambridge, Mass., Forrester Research, Inc., November 11.

McCarthy, John. 2004. " Near-Term Growth of Offshoring Accelerating: Resizing US Services Jobs Going Offshore." Cambridge, Mass., Forrester Research, Inc., May 14.

Panagariya, Arvind. 2004. "Why the Recent Samuelson Article in NOT about Offshore Outsourcing." Available at ⟨http://www.Columbia.edu/~ap2231/⟩.

Pearlstein, Steven. 2004. "Still Short of the Offshoring Ideal." *Washington Post.* March 12, p. E1.

"Q & A: INTEL CEO Craig Barrett." 2003. *Mercury News.* December 27.

Sampson, Gary P. and Richard H. Snape. 1985. "Identifying the Issues in Trade in Services." *World Economy.* June, 8, pp. 171–81.

Samuelson, Paul. 1971. "An Exact Hume-Ricardo-Marshall Model of International Trade." *Journal of International Economics.* 19:1, pp. 1–18.

Samuelson, Paul. 2004. "Where Ricardo and Mill Rebut and Confirm Arguments of Mainstream Economists Supporting Globalization." *Journal of Economic Perspectives.* Summer, 18:3, pp. 135–46.

Sickinger, Ted. 2004. "'Outsourcing' Not Bad, Intel Chief Says." *Oregonian.* May 12; Available at ⟨http://www.oregonlive.com/business/oregonian/index.ssf?/base/business/108436374459910.xml⟩.

Vernon, Raymond. 1966. "International Investment and International Trade in the Product Cycle." *Quarterly Journal of Economics.* May, 80, pp. 190–207.

[8]

SERVICE MULTINATIONALS:
CONCEPTUALIZATION, MEASUREMENT AND THEORY

J.J. Boddewyn*
Baruch College

Marsha Baldwin Halbrich**
Baruch College

and

A.C. Perry***
The American University

Abstract. The application of MNE definitions, measurements and theories to international services is still in its infancy, despite the considerable size and growth of this sector. There are problems in defining, classifying, measuring, comparing and explaining service MNEs, but they do not require special definitions and theories. Still, research to date suggests: (1) delinking the concepts of multinational enterprise and foreign direct investment under certain conditions, and (2) qualifying the nature of ownership, internalization and location advantages in FDI theory, as far as service MNEs are concerned.

*J.J. Boddewyn is Professor of International Business at the Baruch College of the City University of New York, and a Fellow of the Academy of International Business.

**Marsha Baldwin Halbrich (MBA, Baruch College) is a consultant with Susan Horowitz & Associates and with Ibero-American Productions, both in New York City.

***A.C. Perry is an Assistant Professor of International Business at The American University in Washington, DC. An appendix reviewing the domestic literature on the nature of services can be obtained by writing to either Professor Boddewyn or Perry.

This is a revised version of a paper presented at the Annual Meeting of the Academy of International Business, Cleveland Ohio, October 1984. Helpful comments and suggestions were provided by J.N. Behrman (North Carolina), P.J. Buckley (Bradford), Mark Casson (Reading), Kang Rae Cho (Pennsylvania State), H. Peter Gray (Rutgers), Robert Grosse (Miami), B. Herman (Netherlands Economic Institute), Howard Perlmutter (Wharton), C.P. Kindleberger (MIT, Brandeis), A.M. Rugman (Dalhousie), Kenneth Simmonds (London Business School), Helmut Soldner (Augsburg), J.M. Stopford (London Business School), Raymond Vernon (Harvard), A.F. Weinstein (Massachusetts at Boston), L.T. Wells (Harvard) and Mira Wilkins (Florida International) as well as by three anonymous reviewers. Betty Appelbaum and Thomas Quinlan (Baruch College) extended valuable copy-editing help.

Received: January 1985; Revised: May, August & December 1985; Accepted: January 1986.

42   JOURNAL OF INTERNATIONAL BUSINESS STUDIES, FALL 1986

Many international service firms are already household words around the world: American Express, McDonald's, Avis, Thomas Cook, Merrill Lynch, Citibank, Club Med, Pan Am, McKinsey, Arthur Andersen, Barclay's, Dun & Bradstreet and Hilton, among others.[1] Yet, conceptual and theoretical analysis has not kept pace with the size and growth of this sector.[2]

Therefore, this critical essay integrates recently available definitions and theories to answer the following questions: (1) when is a firm in "international services;" (2) what problems are encountered in locating, measuring and comparing international service firms; (3) do the criteria used to categorize an international company as a "multinational enterprise" (MNE) apply to those dealing in services; and (4) are the prevalent theories of foreign direct investment (FDI) relevant to understanding them? It will be argued that newer MNE/FDI definitions and theories are applicable to such firms, provided important characteristics of international services and their providers are kept in mind when researching them.

THE NATURE OF INTERNATIONAL SERVICES

In the general literature on services, many criteria are used to define them: intangibility (a telephone call), perishability (a plane ride), customization (an engineering plan for a factory), simultaneity of production and consumption (a bank loan), consumer participation in production (remote computer data-processing), and use without ownership (a car rental). Actually, every one of these criteria *by itself* has been found lacking in fully differentiating a "service" from a "non-service." In this analysis, emphasis is placed on those services satisfying at least one of two criteria, namely, intangibility and/or dependence on a customer's participation or input (his person or assets) in the service's production.

When services cross borders, they can be classified in a threefold manner.[3] The *foreign-tradeable service* generates a product that is separable from the production process itself as well as transportable across national boundaries from the site of production to the location of consumer receipt or use — for example, financial loans. On the other hand, a *location-bound service* is tied to the service's production location because its production's time and space constraints are shared by producer and consumer, as in hotel accommodations.[4]

In *combination services*, part of the production process is location-bound and another part is capable of producing a foreign-tradeable product. Thus, in remote computer data-processing, the customer's participation in production can take place at a national site different from the producer's location. The foreign-tradeable elements between these two locations are the semi-processed information from the customer's terminal and the final information from the producer's mainframe, but a location-bound quality is also present because the site of the customer's final use or receipt of the product is tied to his production participation when he provides and receives information on line at his terminal or printer.

This classification is not an idle exercise in typology but has serious research implications. For example, a comparison of exporting vs. foreign direct investment is not appropriate in the cases of location-bound and combination services - as could be surmised from the international-product-lifecycle theory [Vernon 1966] which implies a possible choice between exporting and foreign direct investment, and a progressive evolution from the former toward the latter under certain conditions. In fact, some services require foreign direct investment or alternative non-equity forms of international product *from the very beginning*, when part of the production-delivery-use chain must be performed abroad (see below for further elaboration of these implications).

LOCATING, MEASURING AND COMPARING INTERNATIONAL SERVICES

Additional problems are encountered in locating, measuring and comparing international service firms.

Center-periphery Allocation

Determining the existence and magnitude of international services is more problematic than may be assumed, particularly when service investments and revenues are spread over several countries. For example, how should investments in communication links between mainframe and user locations — land lines, microwave relay paths, underwater cables, satellite links and communication computers — that are necessary for data transmission within a global system be assigned between one country and another? A similar question arises in apportioning assets in the air-transport industry where capital equipment in airplanes far outweighs sales and support-operations equipment. This industry offers a core service that is produced and consumed largely across national borders and even over international waters so that these assets cannot simply be attributed to the home-country parent organization that made the investment. Besides, revenue allocation between home and abroad is difficult, thereby complicating the determination of the foreign component of a service firm [Herman and van Holst 1984].

Difficult Comparisons

Most studies have dealt with only a single service industry and are not comparative in nature, but further research is bound to extend to more industries and involve comparisons.[5] One major comparative problem centers on *size*. Thus, the *Fortune's* "Service 500" directory [1985] divides its firms into seven categories, each with a primary ranking criterion for measuring that category's relative size and growth: (1) different types of assets are used for ordering diversified-financial, commercial-banking, life insurance and utilities firms; (2) diversified services and retailing are ranked by sales, and (3) transportation companies are compared in terms of operating revenues. These rankings also rest on different types of income: sales, fees, commissions, interest charges, etc.

44   JOURNAL OF INTERNATIONAL BUSINESS STUDIES, FALL 1986

Consequently, it is difficult to compare one group of service MNEs with another as well as service with non-service firms in terms of size. For instance, contrasting the revenues and assets of a manufacturer and a bank is unrealistic. The latter's income is composed of net interest receipts, fees, commissions and other revenues that cannot be compared to those received by the manufacturer in the form of sales; while its assets include huge deposits at interest, which bear little resemblance to the manufacturer's assets. Yet, a ranking of the 100 largest U.S. multinationals in terms of "foreign revenue" mixes both service and non-service firms [Curtis 1984]. While this problem is also encountered outside of service MNEs, it is certainly magnified in the latter's case.

Cut-off Points

MNE definitions use some minimum amount of international involvement as a cutoff point — for example, in terms of number of host countries, size and percentage of worldwide revenues, assets, production and personnel related to foreign operations [e.g., Stopford 1982, p. xii]. However, service operations run the gamut from "equipment-based" (e.g., airlines) to "people-based" (e.g., management consulting) firms [Thomas 1978]; and service production is being "industrialized" through hard, soft and hybrid technologies [Levitt 1976]. Therefore, using a standard formula (e.g., X percent of foreign revenues or assets) across service industries to select a sample of service MNEs will prove as arbitrary as in the case of non-service firms, if not more so.

DEFINING SERVICE MULTINATIONALS

Various problems have been encountered in applying older MNE definitions to services. On the other hand, new conceptualizations of the multinational enterprise raise intriguing questions about what types of international service firms belong to the MNE category.

Can Service Firms Be MNEs?

Most conceptualizations of the multinational enterprise have dealt only with industrial and extractive firms, or they have been presented as applying to all types of enterprises, including services, without further differentiation. On the other hand, a few scholars (e.g., Behrman) have excluded services producers from the ranks of MNEs as defined in their models.

Building on Perlmutter's [1969] distinction between the ethnocentric, polycentric and geocentric orientations of international firms, Behrman [1974] has formulated a definition of MNEs that effectively excludes international service organizations. According to him, there are three types of international firms. The "classical investor" invests overseas to secure export markets for home-country production or to supply home-country facilities and markets from abroad. An "international holding company" (IHC), on the other hand, produces in each country in a polycentric manner to supply that specific market only; and production efforts are duplicated in each country-market location because they are highly independent of the parent organization and other subsidiaries. Finally, Behrman's geocentric-like "multinational enterprise" is intended to supply the world market through integration and coordination of its production facilities in a number of countries. True MNE production is characterized by flexibility in siting subsidiaries; each subsidiary's contribution to the global system is capable of change, and the MNE produces highly standardized products under conditions of least-cost efficiency.

Services are largely absent from Behrman's MNE category. He states that "services industries are, by nature, highly locally-oriented (p. 5)," and he confines them to illustrations of the polycentric IHC (e.g., hotels) and, in the case of trade-facilitating services (e.g., international trading companies), to the ethnocentric classical-investment type.

Behrman is correct in stressing that many services are significantly location-oriented, but some services also require that the consumer participate to varying degrees in the production process. In other words, they are also location-bound, as was seen above. This location-*boundedness* in the case of services, however, does not imply a solely or even significantly local *orientation* since such services can also be provided to non-residents. Thus, a consumer service that is not foreign tradeable (such as a hotel accommodation) must be produced and ultimately delivered within a particular geographic area even though the original sale of that service may have taken place in another country where the consumer purchased his reservation.

If the international hotel chain that Behrman lists in his IHC category provides a fairly standardized service, the parent organization must have more control over its foreign hotels than would be expected from Behrman's characterization of the IHC. Yet, such hotel chains cannot enter Behrman's MNE category because hotel-service production is unavoidably location-bound and inflexible in its ability to alter its contribution to the global production system.

How does Behrman's classification accommodate a high-technology service such as remote data-processing? Unlike computer manufacturing, this service demands customer locations that are bound to the latter's participation in the product's production and in its receipt and use. Let us assume that one mainframe location serving a great number of foreign user locations is the most efficient arrangement, and that user input into the system is controlled and standardized to an extent that ensures acceptance by the mainframe operation. In such a case, these remote-processing operations cannot be considered polycentric because: (1) part of the multistage production process is located outside the user country, and (2) each user-country production component is under the control of the parent organization which has established a fairly standardized form of user participation.

Can remote data-processing operations then be considered as a form of

46   JOURNAL OF INTERNATIONAL BUSINESS STUDIES, FALL 1986

ethnocentric/classical investment? Raw data from abroad feed the main-frame operations that yield the final product (that is, ordered information) at home. This final product is transported back through the system to the data-originating market. Is this process comparable to the export of wood in one direction and the import of furniture using that wood in the other direction? No, because in the case of data-processing, the service customer's use-location is bound to his production-participation location. As defined by Behrman, such production operations are therefore neither polycentric/IHC nor ethnocentric/classical; and they are not MNE production operations either because the customer production component is necessarily duplicative and inflexible in its country location-boundedness and in its contribution to the entire production system.

Consequently, Behrman's classification cannot accommodate the location-bound service (e.g., hotels) nor the combination service (e.g., remote data-processing), despite its usefulness for other purpose.

When Are International Service Firms MNEs?

Answering this question requires a review of older and newer MNE definitions. Although no definite agreement exists or is likely, there has been a fairly general consensus that: (1) a multinational enterprise is involved in foreign direct investment, and (2) foreign direct investment means (a) the transfer or formation overseas of all or some of the necessary factors of production (the "ownership" or "equity" dimension), and (b) some element of "control" over their use abroad.[6] If these conditions are not met, a firm will simply be called something like an "international company" engaging either in portfolio investment or in foreign trade.

New MNE Definitions. It is interesting to observe the evolution at the United Nations which first defined the multinational corporation (MNC) as covering "all enterprises which *control* assets — factories, mines, sales offices and the like — in two or more countries [1973, p. 5]." A more recent U.N. exercise defines a transnational corporation (its new term for MNC) as "an enterprise (a) comprising entities in two or more countries, regardless of the legal form and fields of activity of those entities, (b) which operates under a system of decision-making permitting coherent policies and a common strategy through one or more decision-making centers, (c) in which the entities are so linked, *by ownership or otherwise*, that one or more of them may be able to exercise a *significant influence* over the activities of the others, and, in particular, to share knowledge, resources and responsibilities with others" [1984, p. 2]. Observe that the word "control" has disappeared from the second definition which also does not require equity ("by ownership or otherwise"). The definitions by Buckley [1983a], Casson [1982] and Dunning and McQueen [1982] have evolved in the same direction of ignoring equity as a criterion (see below).

Some international service companies clearly fit the more traditional definitions. For example, a bank with retail-banking branches in many countries as well as a Japanese trading company with parent-owned offices in major centers around the world would indisputably be termed a "multinational enterprise." On the other hand, no one would care to apply the label "multinational" to mere exporters selling services to many countries but with no offices overseas. However, "new forms of international investment" [Oman 1984] such as licensing and management contracts present problems in applying older definitions to international service firms while the newer definitions encompass such forms much more readily.

Problems Associated with Licensing and Management Contracts. A major definition problem arises when licensing, franchising[7] and/or management-contracting are involved. In their pure forms, they do not involve any equity since only technology or management skills are sold to another party [Buckley 1983b]. Besides, they use the "external market" rather than "internalization" within the international firm as a mode of transfer [Buckley and Casson 1985, p. 51]. Therefore, *they cannot be considered forms of foreign direct investment.*

In particular, international licensing must be considered service *trade* rather than investment because the actual use of the factors transferred overseas is *controlled by the licensee.* The fact that a licensing agreement contains restrictions and obligations applying to the licensee does not mean that the latter is "controlled" in the common meaning used to differentiate "foreign direct investment" from "foreign portfolio investment." After all, even foreign trade in tangible goods (e.g., computers) may involve restrictions and obligations (e.g., not to resell the computers to certain countries) but the latter are not sufficient to transform "trade" into "investment" which requires ownership in any case.

For the same reasons, entering into a management contract with a foreign firm to administer the latter's assets is also a form of service *trade.* A service (that is, management) has been sold, but this factor of production is not "controlled," in the FDI sense, by a parent company located in some home country; and no equity investment is necessary on the part of the contract's seller. It is the buyer of the management contract who ultimately owns and "controls" the use of that factor of production, just as he owns and controls his land, labor and capital, while the management-contract's seller "controls" operations only in a delegated manner (see note 10).

A further relevant touchstone is that foreign direct investment normally involves the earning of *profits* on some foreign-based equity whereas trade is associated only with collecting sales, commissions, fees, interest charges, etc. In the cases of international licensing and management-contracting, it is such gross revenues[8] that apply, rather than return on foreign-based equity — a criterion that demonstrates again that one is dealing with trade rather than investment.

The key question then becomes: Can an international service firm based in one country, that only collects licensing and management-contract

48   JOURNAL OF INTERNATIONAL BUSINESS STUDIES, FALL 1986

revenues from other countries but does not own or control assets overseas, still be considered a multinational enterprise even though it is not engaged in foreign direct investment? The answer has to be affirmative if one accepts the following syllogism developed by adding to the above discussion what some researchers (particularly Dunning, McQueen, Buckley and Casson) have advanced:

1. An international firm does not need foreign equity tobecome a multinational enterprise, but can do sothrough licensing and management contracts (see belowfor support of this assertion).

2. "Non-equity" licensing and management-contracting areforms of trade involving the market as a mode of entry(see above).

3. Therefore, international trade firms using only licensing and management contracts are multinational enterprises (assuming that the other criteria regarding size have been satisfied).

On the first point, Dunning and McQueen [1982, p.98] state, "It is our reading of the situation in the hotel sector that, in general, [equity-based] control is not necessary to advance the benefits of global integration and to ensure that the best interests of the parent company are promoted" — the very purposes of "control."[9] Casson confirms this view: "The MNE does not need to be a foreign direct investor since all resources (except possibly inventories) in the foreign location can be hired rather than owned outright. This reflects the fact that the definition employs an income or value-added concept of production rather than a capital or asset concept, as do some other definitions" [1982, p. 36].[10]

Let us assume that, after extrapolating recent developments to a plausible ending, Exxon Corporation has finally relinquished all ownership in foreign oil wells, refineries and gas stations and has come to use other companies to transport, refine and retail the oil products it bought overseas. Should one then say that Exxon is no longer a multinational corporation? The answer would have to be affirmative if Exxon buys foreign oil only to resell it abroad and at home (where it may have kept its refineries and gas stations), but it would have to be negative if Exxon retains licensing and management-contract arrangements with foreigners.

Let us take another limit case where the relaxation of U.S. banking regulations and the improvement of telecommunications have allowed Citicorp to conduct all of its international borrowing and lending from its International Banking Facility unit in New York City, after closing its offshore centers, but with its international-banking officers "jetting" and "telexing" around the world to close such deals. We would then have to say that Citicorp is no longer a multinational enterprise because it no longer has foreign equity, and because licensing and management contracts are not used in this kind of business services [Dunning and Norman 1983].[11]

Altogether, the new definitions of the multinational enterprise dictate that some forms of pure foreign trade (that is, licensing, franchising and management contracting), which do not involve foreign equity or control as conventionally defined in the literature, be brought into the MNE category.

APPLYING FDI-MNE THEORY TO SERVICES

Mainstream theories of foreign direct investment and the multinational enterprise have recently been extended to several international service industries, mainly hostelry, banking, and a range of business services. A brief review of these theories is appropriate, prior to introducing necessary qualifications as far as international services are concerned.[12]

Mainstream Theories

Buckley and Casson [1976 and 1985] have conceptualized the MNE as an enterprise responding to imperfect intermediate-product markets by developing "internal markets" across national boundaries. Their views have widened the focus of international activities from the production of final services and goods to include such intermediate products as semi-processed materials, knowledge and expertise, managerial and marketing skills, and technology. Because intermediate-product markets are difficult to organize due to various imperfections, there is an incentive to bypass them and to bring the activities of producing and marketing *within* the organization's ownership and control, that is, to "internalize" them.

Casson [1982] has added to this theory of internalization by demonstrating that buyer uncertainty is a significant transaction cost, especially in consumer goods and services. This cost creates a sufficient condition for the MNE to internalize its ownership advantage(s) when quality control is crucial and when international communication between buyer and producer is best achieved under control of the enterprise (see below).

While also emphasizing "internalization," Rugman [1981] views a (monopolistic) firm-specific advantage in "knowledge" (p. 61) as the key characteristic of the MNE. This advantage, which leads to foreign direct investment when there are imperfect good or factor markets, replaces or complements the country-specific advantages that support trade; and it prompts the creation of an internal market to retain control over firm-specific advantages [Rugman 1981, p. 39].

Dunning's [1980] "eclectic model" of international production (foreign production based on FDI) integrates these and other views. It rests on three simultaneous conditions: ownership-specific, internalization-specific and location-specific advantages. If the enterprise possesses only the first two advantages, it will export domestic production. On the other hand, the MNE must find it profitable to combine its assets with factor endowments located in foreign countries for international production to take place.

Corroboration of Mainstream Theories

The above theories have been able to accommodate several international service industries. International banking, in particular, has lent itself well

50   JOURNAL OF INTERNATIONAL BUSINESS STUDIES, FALL 1986

to explanation by both the internalization and eclectic theories. Thus, Rugman [1981] has concluded that: "In the same way that the multi-national enterprise creates an internal market to overcome imperfect world good and factor markets, so does the multinational bank use internalization to overcome imperfections in international financial markets" (p. 89). Similarly, Yannopoulos has reasoned that Dunning's eclectic theory of international production can successfully explain the growth of transnational banking [1983, p. 251]. Gray and Gray [1981],[13] Cho [1983], Grubel [1977], Pecchioli [1983] and Wells [1983] have reached fairly identical conclusions.

Necessary Qualifications and Elaborations of Mainstream Theories

Still, studies of other service industries (particularly of the international hotel industry and of foreign branches of business service companies) suggest some qualifications and/or elaborations regarding the nature of ownership, internalization and location advantages.

Ownership Advantages. Dunning, Norman, McQueen and Casson have identified some *intangible* advantages associated with international service firms, that compare with the more tangible ones of non-service firms. Thus, Dunning and Norman [1983] illustrate these intangible advantages for foreign branches providing a variety of *business* services:

> If the possession of product, process or materialtechnology is one of the foundations of ownershipadvantages in manufacturing industry, then that ofinformation and management, organizational and marketingtechnology, is the key to success in the provision ofbusiness services. Comparable to the exclusive orprivileged access to raw materials in resource-processingindustries is access to information in the office sector; comparable to the market provided by parent companies to their manufacturing affiliates, auditing, accounting andother business-service affiliates may find a ready-made market for their output from firms that normally deal with parent companies at home; comparable to the spreading of fixed capital and research-and-development overheads that enable large firms in high-technology industries to export such benefits to their affiliates at low marginal costs, so in office activities the tremendous reservoir of organizational and manager-ial expertise that has been built up over the years can provide branch offices with information at a cost very much lower than a de novo indigenous firm would have to incur; comparable to trademarks which explain why some firms in the tobacco, confectionery, toilet preparations and detergent industries have advantages over others, so there is an identifiable image perceived by purchasers of the services supplied by enterprises like McKinsey's, Foster Wheeler, Peat Marwick, Arthur Andersen, Chase Manhattan Bank, etc., that give these enterprises an important advantage over their lesser-known competitors (pp. 678-679).

In Dunning and McQueen's [1982] study of a *consumer* service, the hotel product is described as: (1) on-premises "room" services; (2) the provision or arrangement of "before, at-the-time or after off-premises services" such as transportation to and from the hotel, tours and reservations at restaurants and other hotels, and (3) a "trademark of guarantee" that the consumer will receive the services contracted. The hotel chain's ownership advantages include experience in serving the market (primarily international business travelers) in other locations, product differentiation, and brand-image marketing of the hotel "experience" good. Training is likened to manufacturing R&D in its contribution to maintaining a brand image (p. 103). Again, these are all intangible advantages.

Casson interprets Dunning and McQueen's hotel study as demonstrating that international hotel chains address quality-conscious markets, do not necessarily depend on product-differentiation advantages, serve mostly international travelers rather than local customers, utilize brand names and, by using international reservations systems, integrate producer and consumer markets [1982, p. 39]. There is "something of value" that allows such international hotel chains to distinguish themselves from their host-country competitors — what Casson calls "quality" [1982, p.38].

This discussion stresses that the analysis of the ownership advantages of service MNEs must be focussed on the intangibility of their offerings even though one can raise the intriguing question of whether service and non-service firms differ at all conceptually in this respect. As Raymond Vernon put it in a private communication: "Inasmuch as the transmission of knowledge can usually be substituted for the transmission of goods, a serious discussion of manufacturing MNEs entails exploring some of the same considerations [as with service MNEs]." In other words, if ownership advantages can be reduced to "knowledge" of various kinds (hard or soft, patentable or not, externally diffusible or not, etc.), one can postulate that *all MNEs are service MNEs.*

Such a view is compatible with Buckley's recent definition of the multinational enterprise as "a firm which adds value by producing in more than one national economy" [1983a, pp. 34-35]. Since all economic activity is about "adding value," and since to add value is to provide a "service," everything that happens in firms — extractive, industrial, commercial, financial, etc. — is essentially a "service." Therefore, all firms are "service" firms and all MNEs are ultimately "service MNEs" in some respects.

While this is an extreme view, it suggests that *we examine carefully, on a case-by-case basis, the ownership advantages proper to each service and non-service industry, rather than assume significant differences between the two types a priori.*

Internalization Advantages. Two issues arise here: (1) explaining internalization in service industries that are typically not R&D-intensive and thus rely mostly on "low technology" as the basis for their firm-specific advantages, and (2) accounting for "non-equity FDI" in services — a topic already broached above.

52   JOURNAL OF INTERNATIONAL BUSINESS STUDIES, FALL 1986

Regarding the first problem, Casson [1982, pp. 24-25] suggests that the non-R&D-intensive MNE is best explained by extending the scope of internalization theory. This can be done by taking account of additional sources of market imperfections that generate "transaction costs" incurred to overcome these obstacles through "market-making activities" (p. 25). He stresses that buyer uncertainty is a significant transaction cost, especially in *consumer* goods and services. The incidence of this cost creates a sufficient condition for the existence of an MNE, even one with low or soft technology which includes a wide range of marketing skills. The recent strategic literature on MNEs adds weight to this argument by emphasizing more intangible advantages such as global distribution networks and brands rather than "high" or "hard" technology advantages considered to be fleeting and more readily copiable and displaceable [Hamel and Prahalad 1985; Ohmae 1985].

Casson illustrates his transaction-cost theory with the banana and hotel industries, demonstrating that the consumer-product MNE comes into existence when quality control is crucial. It can integrate backward to control production; it can reduce international buyers' transaction costs by offering its services in multiple locations, and t can produce some parts of the market-making service (contact-making, specification and negotiation) elsewhere, thereby reducing buyer risks in international communication. It can also generate and transmit market-making skills via the enterprise's internal market.

Four reasons for market-making production to occur in many different country markets are identified by Casson: (1) major production economies of scale exist so that it is efficient to supply and integrate several country markets from one production location; (2) internationally mobile consumers encourage the replication of market-making production in different country markets; (3) consumers want to place orders in one country location for supply in a different one, and/or (4) the enterprise has an internationally transferable absolute advantage in market-making production. [1982, pp. 36-38].

Casson's first category is illustrated by the banana industry, but this class can also accommodate the linkages between many location-bound data-production sites and a mainframe computer-service facility located in the home or some third production country. One mainframe facility serves many integrated consumer production and use locations, and thus offers major economies of scale in the production of the ordered-information product.

Casson's second and third categories are represented by the location-bound international hotel chain and its reservation system but these two categories can also be applied to non-location-bound (i.e., foreign-tradeable) services such as some types of international banking services. For example, banks provide financial information across national borders to other MNEs, and they intermediate in transactions involving parties located in different countries — all non-R&D-intensive activities. Regarding this fourth category of absolute advantage, Casson acknowledges that it fits in with "the orthodox theory of the MNE" and, as such, does not raise any special problem of applicability to service MNEs of all types. *Therefore, no major problem is encountered in applying the central MNE concept of internalization to "low-technology" service firms.*

Regarding the second issue associated with internalization, several studies have explained the existence of "non-equity" FDI in both business and consumer services. On the one hand, equity-based FDI is common in the case of *business* services such as accountancy, finance, consulting and advertising because quality control is difficult to achieve through the licensing or franchising of such services [Dunning and Norman 1983]. Besides, foreign direct investment in offices generally requires lower initial outlays (for example, in real-estate property) than are needed to buy or build a hotel of international standard, so that internalization is the preferred mode for exploiting ownership advantages in such business services (p. 680).

On the other hand, the quality-control problem is more surmountable in *consumer* services where franchising is common (e.g., fast foods). Thus, the high frequency of management contracts in the international hotel industry has been well explained by Dunning and McQueen on the basis of what they call "contract-based control" [1982, p. 91]:

> The owners of the hotel may have little knowledge of hotel operations and employ a professional management company to operate the hotel. The management company in turn will only become involved if they can protect their ownership advantage, and in practice this may require a large degree of control of the assets. The hotel-management company, however, may be unwilling to invest in the ownership of the hotel either because it regards itself as having little expertise in property development, or because it regards ownership as a high-risk venture, or because expansion would be reduced by the need to borrow large sums of capital. We therefore often find that it is to the mutual advantage of both parties for de jure control to be with the hotel owners but de facto control to be established through contracts. These contracts are more easily arranged because of the characteristics of the industry, in the sense that unlike manufacturing, there is no need for a policy of market sharing by the affiliates to maximize the global profits of the MNE, nor is there any production specialization, while there exist ample opportunities to appropriate the economic rent from the MNE's activities (pp. 104-105).

Similarly, Buckley points out, "It is through the use of internal markets in capital, labor management, technology and intermediate goods that effective control of foreign subsidiaries is exercised, rather than through equity ownership"[1983b, p. 202], and, "it is not necessary to own a production process to control it" [1983a, p. 41]. *Therefore, international services can readily be accommodated by internalization theory even in the absence of equity investment although this accommodation applies only in the case of consumer services.*

Location Advantages. The matter of where the services are provided has already been discussed. Foreign-tradeable services obviously exhibit great mobility. On the other hand, location-bound services present problems: "As in the case of some primary products, the location of hotels is country-specific since they have to be situated where the tourists want to be" [Dunning and McQueen 1982, p. 88]. If the hotel product is to be consumed in Paris, it must be produced there even if Lyon or Marseille were more efficient locations.

Beyond that, common variables such as size of the market, quality of local resources, government policies and political climate affect location choices as in any other type of foreign trade or investment (see Dunning and McQueen [1982] and Dunning and Norman [1983] for further elaboration of these factors).[14] *Therefore, international services encounter no special problems in terms of the locational requirements of FDI/MNE theory, except in the case of location-bound services* since the choice of host countries is dictated by consumer requirements in the latter's case.

CONCLUSION

The applicability of FDI/MNE definitions, measurements and theories to international service firms is finally receiving some well-deserved attention although not in proportion to services' fast-growing share of international business nor in relation to their long history which predates that of industrial and extractive foreign direct investment [Kindleberger 1983].

Comparisons will always be difficult on account of the variety of size measurements that must be applied to various types of service firms, and also when comparing the latter to industrial firms. Therefore, specific analyses of each service subsector should prove more fruitful than the creation of a general category of "service MNEs" in view of the heterogeneity of this group.

Besides, no special FDI-MNE theories for international service firms are necessary. The existing ones can be readily accommodated through relatively simple qualifications and elaborations while we wait for the initiation and results of more international service studies. Such research is very much needed in view of the reasonable anticipation that, by the year 2000, more than half of the world's multinational enterprises will be in services.

NOTES

1. *Fortune* has published an annual list of the U.S. "Service 500" since 1983 [1985]; and a similar compendium of foreign service companies is included in *Fortune* and *Forbes* lists of large overseas firms [The International 500, 1985; Curtis 1984].

2. The size and growth of international services and the multinationalization of service enterprises are not considered here. Furthermore, it is assumed that service producers "go international" and become MNEs for the same reasons that producers of tangible goods do. Some corroboration for this assumption is provided by Weinstein's study of multinational advertising agencies [1977]. He demonstrated that their services, whose production alternatives include production for export, foreign direct investment and contractual arrangements, are motivated by offensive, defensive, client-service, and executive-interest considerations significantly similar to those identified for manufacturing

I sketch the outlines of a number of candidate "template" models, each of which captures some aspect of the problem. From analytical insights and numerical simulations of these models, I am then able to answer questions about the effects and consequences of technological or institutional innovations that permit offshoring to arise. These include effects on the national income of each country, effects on the relative and real prices of skilled and unskilled labor in each country, and effects on the volume of trade in goods (for example, are trade in goods and trade in services complements or substitutes?).

Before proceeding, I wish to emphasize that my goal here is to suggest *ways of thinking about the issues* in formal models. I was distressed following my presentation at the Brookings conference to find many people focusing on the *results* of some simulations, particularly with respect to "northern" welfare (read as U.S. welfare). All readers should understand that no theory says that a move from partial liberalization to full liberalization makes everyone better off. To push the point further, I am confident that I can concoct a model to generate any result desired by a reader with a deep pocketbook. I have tried hard to stick to reasonable and relevant structures and assumptions, but even so, qualitative results sometimes depend on specific parameter values, as we shall see.

In the following section, I provide a brief overview of some of our theory portfolio and then identify some of the crucial aspects of offshoring we wish to capture. Finally I present a series of template models.

Our Theory Portfolio

We can usefully draw from existing theories and models of trade in order to make progress on offshoring. I do not claim that the list is exhaustive or that alternative taxonomies might not be more useful; I just believe that these particular elements will prove useful.

—*Comparative advantage theories of trade in goods.* Our traditional trade theory tends to focus on differences among countries as the primary motive for trade. The Ricardian model of trade, in which countries possess different technologies, is usually listed first. Second, the workhorse model of trade is factor-proportions or Heckscher-Ohlin theory, in which differences in factor intensities among goods intersect with differences in factor endowments among countries to determine a pattern of comparative advantage and trade. This ever-popular approach not only gives an intuitive explanation for the direction of trade, but permits a detailed analysis of the distributional consequences of trade within countries and of aggregate gains from trade. Other country characteristics that fit here include differences in market distortions among countries and country (internal market) size.

   —Non-comparative-advantage theories of trade. This category is largely the domain of the "new trade theory," a term I dislike: "industrial organization approach" to trade is more apt (and avoids the awkward problem of what to call the theory that comes after the new theory). The principal motives for trade are scale economies, imperfect competition, and product differentiation.

   A subcategory of this branch of theory involves the existence of firm-specific assets, an especially useful approach to the theory of the multinational firm. These range from managerial and technology assets to brand names and trademarks. This approach has resurfaced more recently in heterogeneous firm models, in which (potential) firms get productivity "draws" from some distribution that make some firms more productive than others (Melitz 2003; Helpman, Melitz, and Yeaple 2004). Productivity in turn determines whether firms enter foreign markets and if so whether by exports or foreign production.

   —Trade in factors. While trade in goods has drawn the most attention in both theory and empirical analysis, the topic of trade in factors has always lurked in the background. Generalization of theoretical findings is difficult, but the loose consensus among trade economists is that trade in goods and trade in factors tend to be substitutes in comparative-advantage models. Indeed, Mundell's (1957) early demonstration of this might explain the lack of interest in trade in factors. An elegant treatment of this substitutability is found in Jones, Coelho, and Easton (1986). Later it was shown that trade in goods and trade in factors tend to be complements for virtually any other causes of trade other than factor proportions (Markusen 1983) and even in some versions of factor-proportions models (Neary 1995).

   —Theories of foreign direct investment and arm's-length trade in firm-specific assets. I think it is fair to say that, until the mid-1980s, FDI was just viewed as part of the theory of capital movements in a factor-proportions world. Eventually a huge amount of empirical evidence, most notably that most foreign direct investment (FDI) not only comes from but goes to other high-income capital-rich countries, led to new approaches to what we are now calling offshoring.

   Theory split into two branches. One could be called the vertical or resource-seeking approach, an early example of which is described by Helpman (1984). This is in fact a natural extension of factor-proportions comparative-advantage models in which activities differ in factor intensities and countries differ in factor proportions. The alternative is the horizontal or market-seeking approach, in which firms exploit firm-specific assets in multiple markets, an early example of which is described by Markusen (1984). The latter is more a part of non-comparative-advantage theory and, while both approaches are important, does the job of explaining the large volume of intra-industry FDI among the high-income countries. I believe it is accurate to say that the overwhelming weight of empirical evidence, beginning with Brainard (1997), is more consistent with the horizontal approach.

Intertwined with this literature on FDI is a long-standing literature on "internalization," now being called by its inverse name, "outsourcing." Both terms address whether firms keep certain activities internal to the firm or use arm's-length contractors to supply intermediates or to provide assembly, services, distribution, and so forth. Early analyses include that by Dunning (1977). Some more recent authors seem unaware of this large literature, but it is still a pertinent antecedent, and changing the name from internalization to outsourcing does not change that fact. This literature argues that the choice between internal and arm's-length modes depends on issues such as moral hazard, adverse selection, hold-up, contract enforcement, and intellectual property protection.

—Trade in business services (non-factor, non-trade-mediating services). There was an earlier wave of interest in trade in business services in the late 1980s, in Canada in particular. In my view (and I was a participant) the theory that came out of this was not very successful. Several authors got bogged down in trying to define services, an elusive goal, as Daniel Trefler (this volume) has so nicely indicated with a quote from Justice Potter Stewart. One traditional view of business services is that they are hard to trade, requiring the spatial and temporal proximity of supplier and customer. Herbert Grubel (1987) went so far as to argue that all trade in services is embodied in goods or persons. It is very clear from the topics we are considering today that this view is at best badly outdated.

One area where progress has been made is in the theory of the multinational. The modern view is that parent firms are exporters of the services of knowledge-based assets to foreign subsidiaries (although goods and intermediates are often traded as well) (Markusen 1995, 2002).

—Liberalization: trade expansion at the extensive margin. Much traditional trade theory involves liberalization expanding the volume of trade in existing traded goods. We could call this expansion at the intensive margin. But these models do not seem appropriate to the current discussion, in which we are looking at new things being traded. Some existing theory bears on this. In comparative-advantage models, liberalization expands trade at the intensive margin, but some "middle" goods can become traded as trade costs fall, as in the Dornbusch-Fischer-Samuelson (1977) Ricardian continuum model. Yi (2003) has a neat Ricardian model in which goods are produced in distinct stages of production

that can be geographically fragmented. Other valuable empirical evidence is found in Hummels, Ishii, and Yi (2001).

In the theory of the horizontal multinational, investment liberalization allows intrafirm trade in the services of knowledge-based assets, so more things are traded. For vertical multinationals and arm's-length offshoring, innovations in technology, liberalization, or institutions (intellectual property protection) allow fragmentation of the production chain so that more things are traded: capital-intensive intermediates go out, labor-intensive assembly takes place abroad in labor-abundant countries, with much of the final output shipped back to the parent country. In all of these models, trade expands at the extensive margin.

Empirical Characteristics of Offshoring of White-Collar Services to Capture in Theory Models

Here is a wish list of characteristics for theoretical models of offshoring of white-collar services.

—*Expansion of trade at the extensive margin: new things traded due to innovations in communications and technology.* This poses a number of challenges to theory, especially the fact that we are talking about nonmarginal changes and discrete movements of something being nontraded to potentially lots of trade. Traditional comparative-statics analysis is of little use: it focuses on marginal changes in activities that are already in use in the benchmark.

—*Vertical fragmentation of production: the new traded services tend to be intermediates, and they may be upstream, downstream, or not part of a sequence.* Traded white-collar services often have important characteristics that cannot be captured in the simplest off-the-shelf models, which assume a set of final goods. One is that they may be firm-specific rather than bought and sold in arm's-length markets. Another is that they may form part of a particular production sequence, such as a well-defined upstream (design) or downstream (after-sales service) component of overall production. A third is that there may be crucial complementarities among different elements of the production chain, such as between skilled labor and telecommunications equipment and infrastructure.

—*Offshoring of medium-skilled or even highly skilled services to skilled-labor-scarce countries. Is this at odds with factor-proportions theories?* The simplest off-the-shelf 2 x 2 Heckscher-Ohlin model is not going to offer insights into why relatively skilled-labor-intensive services are being offshored to very skilled-labor-scarce countries. One of the most important tasks of theory, in my

6

opinion, is to develop richer but empirically plausible models of why this is taking place. Yet the factor-proportions approach to trade does not necessarily have to be abandoned; but it must be enriched to include multiple goods or factors, or both, so that fragmentation and the complementarities just discussed can be analyzed.

—*Reversal in the direction of trade from existing multinationals models. New offshoring is exporting services back to high-income-country firms (intrafirm back to parents or via arm's-length contracting).* Trade in white-collar services is not new. The modern theory of the multinational has emphasized that parents are exporters of white-collar services, including management and engineering consulting, marketing, finance, and others, to their subsidiaries. One thing that is relatively new and that has generated much of the current interest is the reversal in the direction of trade that we are seeing. In some ways this is closely related to the previous point.

—*Firms, or specifically owners of knowledge-based assets, may offshore skilled-labor-intensive activities that are complements to these assets.* A plausible worry is that skilled workers in the high-income countries are being hurt while their companies profit from offshoring. This cannot be dismissed and requires investigation. To me, it calls for at least a three-factor model, in which firms possess specific factors or other assets that are complements to skilled labor. One example is software engineers as complements to telecommunications equipment and network infrastructure, in which the third factor is physical capital. Or it could be that software engineers are complementary to managerial sophistication, organization infrastructure, and marketing channels. The complementary input is knowledge-based assets.

Without services trade, you can train an engineer in India, but there will be no demand for his or her skills if there is nothing useful to do. The implication is that, in the absence of offshoring, these skilled workers are cheap even though they are relatively scarce in comparison with the availability of skilled workers in the country with the complementary factors. Offshoring that allows trade in the third factor causes that factor (or its services) to move to the skilled-labor-scarce country to combine with cheap skilled labor there. This setup obviously has the elements of a story in which skilled labor is harmed in the high-income country, while owners of the complementary physical or knowledge-based assets benefit.

This phenomenon is relatively easily modeled either in a competitive multi-factor model or using Markusen's knowledge-capital approach to the multinational. The latter approach has also proved a useful starting point for looking at the internalization versus outsourcing decision in relation to the offshoring decision. The idea is that transacting in knowledge-based assets creates special problems for the owner (the multinational firm). For example, there are several labor-turnover models in which workers in the host country absorb or learn the substance of the knowledge-based assets and can defect to start rival firms. Other issues that have been considered in the theory literature involve asymmetric information, reputations, and hold-up.

The next few sections of the paper construct and analyze some simple template models that incorporate these features. All of the models presented have been coded into numerical simulation models using GAMS. Code for these models is available from the author. An appendix to the paper lays out the structure of model 1.

Models

Model 1: A 3 x 2 x 2 Heckscher-Ohlin Model with Fragmentation

Suppose we begin with a simple two-final-good, two-factor, two-country Heckscher-Ohlin model and then allow one good to fragment into two separate production activities, giving three in total. If we assume free trade, just considering free versus prohibitive fragmentation costs, we do not need to specify which is the upstream and which is the downstream activity. For a much more comprehensive treatment of this case, see Markusen and Venables (2005). For a more general approach, see Deardorff (2001, 2005a, 2005b). Here are the principal features of the model.

(A) Two factors of production: skilled (H) and unskilled (U) labor
(B) Two final goods, three production activities
    Y: unskilled-labor-intensive
    X: skilled-labor-intensive
    X: can fragment into high-tech manufacturing (M) and services (S)
      M: more skilled-labor-intensive than X
      S: middle skill intensity: less than X, more than Y
(C) Two competitive, constant returns economies
    North: high-skilled-abundant
    South: low-skilled-abundant

The service component of good X is thus chosen to have a middle factor intensity between integrated X and good Y; specifically, the complete ranking from most to least skill intensity is: $M > X > S > Y$. This choice definitely matters for the results. We are thinking here of things like business process outsourcing or call centers, which are less skill intensive than the overall industry, but more than a developing economy's traditional sector of comparative advantage.[2]

I will report and analyze the qualitative results of numerical simulations. Begin with fragmentation banned; that is, M and S used for X must be produced in the same location. For this case, I calibrated the model so that the two countries are initially specialized in X (North) and Y (South) in free trade: factor endowments have a bigger spread than factor intensities.

Now allow for the geographic fragmentation of X production. This results in some or all of the middle-skill-intensive service activity switching from North to South, with services exported back to North or M exported to South to be combined with S. This does not really matter with free trade, except that measured changes in trade volume will depend on which is which. For our purposes, it is perhaps better to think of the services as exported back to North, where they are combined with M to produce the completed good.[3]

There is a *fundamental tension* that arises in general equilibrium when the ability to fragment manufacturing and services is introduced.

1. Services, which are middle-skill intensive, shift from North to South, increasing the relative demand for skilled labor in both countries. This is an idea familiar from Feenstra and Hanson (1996a, 1996b, 1997) and also arises in multinationals models (Zhang and Markusen 1999). North sheds an activity that is unskilled-labor-intensive from its point of view, but South gains an activity that is skilled-labor-intensive from its point of view. Thus we expect the real and relative price of skilled labor to rise in both countries.

2. However, general equilibrium is bedeviled by terms-of-trade (TOT) effects: North moves from integrated X production to exporting M and importing S. A fall in the relative price of M harms North, possibly outweighing efficiency gains for North. The ability to fragment X production has an effect loosely related to a technical improvement. South can produce S more cheaply than integrated

2. In his comments on this paper, Douglas Irwin quite properly wonders about the robustness of results based on one particular ranking of factor intensities, yet also wants to avoid sliding down the "slippery slope" into taxonomy. I agree with both thoughts. My decision is to concentrate on a central case that I find the most empirically plausible: the offshored service has a middle intensity between Y and integrated X production.

3. Furthermore, allowing the service to be provided by southern workers is close to the same thing as moving foreign workers to North. If allowing the service to move results in factor-price equalization, they are exactly the same (provided the welfare of each country is that of its original residents).

North, and North can produce M more cheaply. But as the countries begin to specialize, *their relative size* will do a lot to determine the *relative price* of M versus S. The equilibrium relative price of M to S is *higher* the *smaller* North is. When North is large, an adverse terms-of-trade change can make it worse off than before fragmentation despite the efficiency gain. When North is not large, efficiency gains outweigh the terms-of-trade shift and both countries benefit.[4]

Closely related to this are two results that emerge from the simulations. First, my results indicated that while skilled labor is the *relative* gainer in North, both factors could suffer an *absolute* loss of real income when North is large. This occurs with a low equilibrium relative price for M as just mentioned. Second, results indicate that skilled labor is an absolute gainer in South, but that it might be a relative loser when South is large. South shifts its output to a more skilled-labor-intensive sector, but that sector (services) suffers a price fall relative to the no-fragmentation case. The latter effect is large when South is large: skilled labor gains absolutely but loses relatively. Results from my simulations over a range of parameter values can be summarized as:

MODEL 1 RESULTS

1. South gains, North loses if North is large; both countries gain if South is large.[5]

2. Skilled labor is the relative gainer in North (*but* a real-income loser if South is small: TOT effect dominates).

3. Skilled labor is a real-income gainer in South (*but* gains relatively less if South is large: TOT effect dominates).

4. Unskilled labor is a real-income gainer in South, a loser in North.

5. Volume of trade in goods increases: goods and services trade are complements (*but* can fall if South is small: South is self-sufficient in S, does not export).

4. An alternative intuition about the terms-of-trade effect is as follows. North has a factor endowment that is well suited to integrated X production. When fragmentation is allowed, the equilibrium price of X falls, harming North, which specializes in X. The question is whether shifting to specialization in M more than recoups this loss. The answer is yes if North is not large. Perhaps this intuition also shows why South always gains: this terms-of-trade effect against X must benefit South.

5. A finding that North can lose is not new. Gomory and Baumol (2004) note this in a model with increasing returns. Samuelson (2004) shows a case with constant returns and perfect competition. Many other such cases occur in models with multinationals (Markusen 2002). Note that some results "guaranteeing" gains from trade *compare autarky to free trade* with fragmentation (Deardorff 2005a). To me this is irrelevant: the relevant question is comparing free trade in goods to free trade in goods and services.

Despite having done countless runs of this model, I cannot guarantee that there are no other possibilities, and of course, reordering the factor intensities will change the results. What I can say is that it is easy to find ranges of parameters that generate these results, but we should all regard them as suggestive and not definitive.

Model 2: A 3 x 3 x 2 Missing Input Model with Fragmentation

My second model is designed to capture the idea that skilled labor can be cheap where it is scarce. It again has three production activities and two countries, but three factors.

(A) Three factors of production: skilled (H) and unskilled (U) labor and know-how (K). K could be high-tech physical capital, such as telecommunications equipment and networks, or knowledge capital (managerial techniques, organization infrastructure, marketing channels).

(B) Two final goods, three production activities

Y: unskilled-labor-intensive

X: skilled-labor- and know-how-intensive

X: can fragment into high-tech manufacturing (M) and services (S)

M: more skilled-labor-intensive than X

S: skilled-labor- and know-how-intensive

(C) Skilled labor and know-how are *complements* in the production of S

(D) Two competitive, constant returns economies:

North: high-skill- and know-how-abundant:

South: low-skill-abundant, very know-how-scarce

The complementarity between skilled labor and know-how in producing S is crucial. Specifically, this is modeled as a very low elasticity of substitution between H and K in producing S. When a country is very know-how-scarce, there is little for its skilled workers to do. You can train engineers, but there are no jobs for them.

Assume initially that K (or its services) and skilled workers cannot move between countries. K is used with skilled workers largely in the North, which exports integrated X. The *fundamental tension* caused by introducing trade in K and S is now going to occur between northern and southern skilled workers.

1. Skilled labor is initially cheap in South (even though scarce) owing to a lack of K to work with.

2. Skilled labor in North and in South compete directly, introduction of trade in K moves K to South, shifting relative demand for skilled labor to South.

The introduction of the third factor, complementary to skilled labor, makes it straightforward to create a situation where skilled labor is initially cheap where it is scarce. In addition, the model is less sensitive to country-size issues, at least with respect to factor prices. But as in the previous model, there is a terms-of-trade issue for North. The ability of the owners of K to move their factor to South to work with cheap skilled labor there erodes not only the return to skilled labor in North, but also North's implicit monopoly power over good X. The result in all of my simulations was that welfare decreases in North when trade in K and S is permitted and North is large. As in the previous model, both countries gain when North is not large. Here are my results for permitting trade in K and S.

MODEL 2 RESULTS

1. South gains, North loses when North is large; both gain when North is not large.

2. Skilled labor is real-income loser in North, absolute gainer in South.

3. Real return to know-how rises in North, falls in South.

3. Unskilled labor is real-income gainer in North, loser in South.

4. Volume of trade in goods increases (*complements* services).

Losses to North and northern skilled labor in particular are two of the things that analysts have worried about with respect to the offshoring of white-collar services. This model potentially validates the worry that northern business owners or owners of particular physical capital and knowledge-based assets will benefit considerably at the expense of northern skilled workers. Of course, the model is in part deliberately designed to do that, so this is hardly a coincidence. On the one hand, I cannot say with confidence that a thorough search would not lead to alternative models with quite different results. On the other hand, I would not have put this model forward if I did not find it empirically plausible and relevant.

Model 3: A 3 x 2 x 2 Knowledge-Capital Model of Multinationals

Now I would like to return to something close to model 1, but add in multinational firms following the knowledge-capital model of the multinational that I developed some time ago. This version of the model is based on Zhang and Markusen (1999). Markusen (2002) is the best source for the complete development of the theory, and this section is based on Chapter 9.

(A) Two factors of production: skilled (H) and unskilled (U) labor

(B) Two final goods, three production activities

   Y: unskilled-labor-intensive, constant returns, perfect competition

X: skilled-labor-intensive, increasing returns at the firm level: firm and establishment-level fixed costs, constant marginal cost

X: can fragment into high-tech manufacturing (M) and services (S)

M: more skilled-labor-intensive than X. By assumption, *only North can produce* M.

S: middle skill intensity: less than X, more than Y

(C) Cournot output competition by X firms, free entry and exit in two firm types

National firms: produce M and S in North, export X to South

Multinational firms: produce M in North, which is exported to South, where S is produced, or vice versa

(D) Two economies

North: high-skill-abundant

South: low-skill-abundant

The reader will see that this resembles model 1 insofar as X can fragment into a skilled-labor-intensive phase and a medium-skilled-labor intensive phase. I have modeled the S phase as largely unskilled-labor-intensive in marginal costs, but establishment fixed costs as having a sizable skilled-labor component. I do not think that this affects the results.

A nice feature of this model, aside from its probable empirical relevance, is that it avoids the "curse of Stolper-Samuelson"[6] and the terms-of-trade effects that are so important in the competitive, constant-returns models. Because of procompetitive effects leading to increased firm scale and lower markups, it is entirely possible that both countries and all factors gain following a liberalization.[7]

The way this works in the present model is straightforward. Again, begin in a situation where trade in disembodied S is not allowed: S and M must be produced together. This is equivalent here to not allowing multinationals to enter. Having to use North's factor endowment for both M and S is a binding constraint on the world economy and limits the number of firms in free-entry equilibrium, which in turn leads to a high markup and a low output per firm (high average cost). When this constraint is relaxed by allowing firms to fragment X, much, perhaps all, of service production moves to South. This again tends to have the Feenstra-Hanson effect of raising the relative demand for skilled labor

6. I didn't invent this phrase, though I wish I had. I think I heard it first from Ron Jones.

7. Alternatively, we could model the final goods or intermediate services as differentiated, using the now well-known large-group monopolistic-competition framework. As far as welfare is concerned, there is a benefit from increased variety analogous to the procompetitive effect of the oligopoly model that tends to generate large welfare gains. See Ethier (1982) and extensions by Markusen (1989).

in both countries. But now this also increases the profitability of the existing firms, which leads to entry, which in turn leads to lower markups and higher output per firm (lower average costs).

There are, however, a lot of possibilities depending on relative endowments and intensities and again on country size. Chapters 8 and 9 of Markusen (2002) show that many outcomes are possible. I can say that it is easy to find parameter values for which allowing fragmentation leads to welfare increases for both countries and gains for skilled labor in both countries. I have to admit that I did not find a set of parameters for which the real prices of all four factors increase, however. I tended to find that the real return to unskilled labor in North fell following fragmentation and trade in services. Here are some typical, but not robust, results for the effects of allowing multinationals to enter, equivalent here to allowing trade in services.

MODEL 3 RESULTS (for a range of parameterizations)

1. South gains, North gains.
2. Skilled labor is a relative and an absolute gainer in North and South.
3. Unskilled labor loses in North and gains in South.
4. Procompetitive effects lead to more firms, lower markups, higher output per firm.

Model 4: A 3 x 3 x 2 Model That Combines the Knowledge-Capital Model with the Missing Factor Model

Our fourth template combines the knowledge-capital model with the missing factor model. I take the skilled labor in North and assume that some portion of it is factor K, which is complementary to skilled labor in producing establishment fixed costs. In fact, I coded up this model first and then moved to model 3 by simply allowing the substitution between K and H in producing establishment fixed costs to move to infinity. Otherwise, the models are the same.

In the initial equilibrium, trade in K (or the services of K) is not permitted; alternatively, multinational firms are not permitted to enter. These results are then compared with allowing trade in K, or equivalently allowing multinationals to enter. Again, a range of outcomes is possible. But for the same parameterization that model 3 just indicated, the liberalization here generates a stronger adverse terms-of-trade effect for North. North's welfare declines if North is large. As with model 2, now the skilled labor in North competes directly with skilled labor in South. The introduction of multinationals moves K from North to work with initially cheaper skilled labor in South. This lowers the real return to skilled labor in North with the big beneficiary being owners of the factor K.

MODEL 4 RESULTS

1. South gains, North loses if North is big; both gain if South is big.
2. Skilled labor is relative and a real-income loser in North, a gainer in South.
3. Large gain in North for the owners of know-how.
4. Unskilled labor gains in both countries.
5. Procompetitive effects lead to more firms, lower markups, higher output per firm.

The Offshoring–Outsourcing (Location–Mode Choice) Relationship

Internalization or its inverse, outsourcing, is a decision about the boundaries of the firm and what activities to keep inside or internal to the firm's ownership structure and which to contract to arm's-length firms. Multinationals offshore but do not outsource, keeping their foreign activities within owned foreign affiliates. Firms that contract or license in some way to foreign firms are engaging in both offshoring and outsourcing.

As I indicated earlier, the internalization decision, also known as mode choice, has a long history of analysis, particularly in the international business literature. Its rediscovery under the name outsourcing has coincided with many researchers overlooking this long tradition. In any case, the traditional focus of the internalization/outsourcing decision has been on the various transactions costs, particularly when offshoring, of doing business at arm's length rather than internal to the firm.

It is important to keep offshoring and outsourcing decisions distinct: they are *location* choice and *mode* choice decisions, respectively. A factor that encourages outsourcing might at the same time discourage offshoring in favor of exporting from the home country or choosing a third country. There are in fact a number of factors associated with producing abroad that do precisely this: they encourage outsourcing but discourage offshoring. Some of these are:

—restrictions on foreign investment

—restrictions on the right of establishment

—restrictions on immigration (generally temporary) of foreign business personnel

—lack of intellectual property protection

—lack of contract enforcement

The first three in this list generally follow from the fact that offshoring requires setting up a foreign subsidiary, which in turn requires foreign investment and the use of home-country personnel in the host country for some period of time.

Thus, problems in any of these three areas would encourage a firm to outsource to a local firm, but they also discourage offshoring relative to other outside alternatives. The last two points involve various aspects of moral hazard and hold-up when firms make investments, both sunk physical capital and investments in training local workers, in connection with establishing a subsidiary. Again, they tend to encourage outsourcing but discourage offshoring. The problem of transferring knowledge and skills probably exists for both modes of offshoring, about which I will say more shortly.

Two formal approaches found in the theory literature may be useful. The first I will call the "labor-learning model." Variations of this are set forth by Ethier and Markusen (1996), Fosfuri, Motta, and Rønde (2001), Markusen (2001), and Glass and Saggi (2002). All of these papers discuss multinationals that make a foreign investment that is profitable owing to knowledge-based assets of the firm. However, workers in the host country acquire this knowledge themselves and can later defect to start a rival firm. If binding contracts cannot be written, then the firm will have to pay these workers a premium in subsequent periods to hold them in the firm. Thus, the multinational must share rents with local employees if contracts cannot be written or enforced.

A second promising line of research involves the Grossman and Hart (1986) hold-up model, which has been developed in a series of papers by Antràs (Antràs 2003, 2005; Antràs and Helpman 2004). Here the idea is that the multinational firm and a local agent must each make sunk, relationship-specific investments in a project. In the absence of complete contracts or contract enforcement, this creates a bilateral ex post hold-up problem. The optimal mode of entry is generally that ownership, defined as residual rights in assets if bargaining breaks down, should go to the party with the larger sunk investment. As in the labor-learning model, this approach requires the multinational to share rents with a local agent whether or not that agent is the manager of an owned subsidiary or the owner of an arm's-length contractor.

Alternative assumptions can produce alternative correlations between offshoring and outsourcing. Suppose that a firm wishes to supply a product X in South. If the fixed costs of setting up a foreign plant are not too large but large relative to the sunk investments of the local partner, then the firm will tend to choose both offshoring (in preference to exporting) and internalization: a negative correlation between offshoring and outsourcing.

A difference between the labor-learning model and the hold-up model is that, in the latter, both the multinational and the local manager make ex ante sunk investments that generate bilateral hold-up. In the labor-learning model, workers acquire bargaining power ex post as they learn. I think that both approaches have something to contribute to the offshoring of white-collar services. There is no question that there are a lot of training costs for the foreign workers. Information technology (IT) and business process outsourcing (BPO) activities are often learned on the job by workers who already possess good general skills. It is my understanding that many call-center workers are trained by independent firms before landing a call-center job.

Here is my suggestion for one approach that combines the labor-learning approach and the sunk-cost hold-up approach. Think of this as, perhaps, a model of business process outsourcing or call centers.

Model 5: Template for an Integrated Outsourcing-Offshoring Approach

(A) Begin with the "missing input model," two time periods.

(B) Interpret this as firm-specific knowledge capital à la Markusen's knowledge-capital model: skilled workers in the host country are cheap because they lack crucial physical or knowledge-based inputs.

(C) With appropriate technological and institutional conditions, this asset can be "exported" by a firm (used abroad) in combination with local skilled workers.

(D) However, local workers "absorb" the relevant knowledge and are able to "defect" to start rival firms on their own in the second period.

(E) Also assume a capital investment in land, structures, and telecommunications is needed. Whoever owns this *defines* whether the project is a subsidiary (internalized) or an arm's-length relationship (outsourced). The cost must be borne by the multinational.

I suppose that many researchers in the international business field would conjecture that given complete and enforceable contracting, the firm would prefer outsourcing on a simple cost basis, so let us make that assumption.

MODEL 5 RESULTS (conjecture! this paper has not been written!)

1. Given complete and enforceable contracts, outsourcing is preferred (by assumption).

2. If contracts are not enforced, then the multinational will want to own the physical capital—that is, internalization is chosen by the Grossman-Hart-Antràs argument.

3. However, even if it is possible to contract for physical capital (local firm contracts to pay a mortgage), the firm may still want to own it if it is not possible to contract for the intellectual capital (skills) that is transferred to local workers, in order to reduce the ex post hold-up problem of skilled workers threatening to leave.

4. On the other hand, if the learned skills of the foreign manager are relationship-specific—that is, they are only useful to the contracting multinational—then there is limited hold-up from the workers and outsourcing would be preferred. Indeed, in this case it seems as though the firm would have ex post hold-up power, and so the manager would want to own the capital.

Again, this is conjecture. I am working on this project, but not yet certain of the results. As a final point, recall again that the agency costs and rent-sharing costs to the firm, whether they be less in the internal or the outsourcing mode, also affect the firm's offshoring choice. For a firm seeking to serve the local host market, these costs may lead the firm to choose exports rather than offshoring. For a firm seeking to serve its own home market, these costs may lead it to choose domestic outsourcing or search for a third supplier.

Summary and Conclusions

I have argued in this paper that we can make good progress in understanding the offshoring of white-collar services at the theory level from our existing portfolio of models. Many important features of offshoring white-collar services can be modeled from a recipe that mixes and matches elements from the existing inventory. Useful elements from our portfolio include:
  —vertical fragmentation of production
  —expansion of trade at the extensive margin
  —fragments that differ in factor intensities, countries that differ in endowments
  —knowledge stocks of countries or firms that are complementary to skilled labor; these create missing inputs for countries otherwise well suited to skill-intensive fragments
  —knowledge-based assets that create particular contractual and agency issues for firms engaging in international business. Existing models of labor-learning and hold-up are useful places to start in considering the outsourcing (mode) choice in relation to the offshoring (location) choice.

These features allow us to construct relatively simple and tractable general-equilibrium models that predict changes induced by fragmentation on aggregate welfare, factor prices (income distribution), the location of production activities, and the direction and volume of trade.

While I view this paper as listing a number of plausible and empirically relevant ways of modeling the offshoring of white-collar services, it was clear at the conference that many people were much more interested in specific results from these models. Unfortunately, it is hard to offer robust conclusions, especially about the aggregate welfare of countries. Trade theorists are well aware of the underlying problem: any move from partial liberalization to more liberalization (allowing more things to be traded in our case) often does not result in Pareto improvements for the trading partners. It would be intellectually dishonest for me to report only cases in which everyone is better off.

Overall, my simulation models suggest a clear gain for world welfare and for South in particular, but North *may* lose if it is large. This result is very familiar to all trade theorists in different contexts; for example, a large country may well prefer a Nash equilibrium in tariff rates to free trade with a small country. Stephen Magee and Kwang-Yeol Yoo (2005) have argued persuasively that the *United States is not a large country* in the sense of my models, which might give us some comfort.

Results on factor-price changes are interesting and consistent with a range of existing literature. In the two-factor models, skilled labor is the relative and (usually) absolute gainer in both regions, as activities that are not skill intensive from North's point of view are transferred to South, where they are. Results for unskilled labor are more mixed.

I have been asked to indicate which model may fit reality the best, and I have to say that I think that the three-factor "missing input" model is my favorite, preferably with multinationals. I have called the third factor "know-how": it could be knowledge capital, high-tech physical capital, or highly skilled knowledge workers, including management. I started working with this model in connection with Central and Eastern Europe, where the productivity of workers with excellent skills in math, science, and engineering was very low: they were missing the crucial organizational, managerial, quality control, and marketing skills needed to complement their other skills. Many case studies I have read about East Asia suggest that the same circumstances prevail. You can educate scientists or engineers, but if there is nothing for them to do they will not be productive.

I capture this by making North rich in know-how as distinct from general skilled labor, and by making know-how a strong complement to general skilled labor. The result is that skilled labor is cheap in South where it is scarce, a principal stylized fact that has generated much of the white-collar offshoring. This model sets up a tension between the general northern skilled labor and the southern skilled labor; perhaps routine programmers and routine business-process workers are examples. Allowing fragmentation moves know-how, or rather the services of the know-how, to South, generating big gains from the owners of the know-how and losses for general skilled labor in North. We should keep in mind, however, that much of the know-how is surely embodied in the human capital of highly skilled tech workers, managers, marketers, and so forth, and this may suggest that second-level white-collar workers are the ones who are most at risk.

I will close with another caveat about theory. Strong and robust findings about welfare gains from fragmentation are not forthcoming from a general approach to theory. Alternatively, it is usually possible to find some strange model that generates whatever result a client wants. I have tried to construct models that I feel are plausible and relevant, but some residual ambiguity remains. I hope I have at least left us with some sense of why this ambiguity exists.

Appendix

Example of the Simulation Models Used in the Paper

The models in the paper seem simple enough. The first model begins with the classic 2 x 2 x 2 workhorse model of trade theory. All students of economics learn the analytics of this model, many of these as undergraduates. Any economist can reasonably conjecture that introducing the ability to geographically fragment some activities should still permit analytical solutions.

Unfortunately, it is not nearly that simple. Let us take model 1 as an example, our simplest model. We go from two to four production activities: Y, M, S, and final X instead of just Y and X. The number of possible production specialization patterns for a country goes from three to fifteen (this assumes that you have to produce some of something). In addition, there are a great many more possible trade patterns, the number going from two to fourteen. In other words, the dimensionality of the model increases greatly, making the simple analytical methods we are used to much less useful.

Second, the entire model must now be formulated in terms of inequalities, not equations. We do not know which of these will hold for a particular set of parameters (for example, which production activities and which trade activities are slack), and, indeed, the set that holds with equality will typically change a lot when parameters are changed. Allowing fragmentation can, for example, reverse the direction of trade in X or Y, or both. The models are termed nonlinear complementarity problems in math programming language: each weak inequality is associated with a non-negative complementary variable. If an inequality holds as a strict equality in the solution, the complementary variable is positive; if it holds as a strict inequality (for example, marginal cost exceeds price), the complementary variable (quantity in this case), is zero. Traditional comparative-statics techniques used on sets of equalities are of no use. If you read some of the existing literature on production fragmentation, you will then understand why almost none of it actually solves for a world general equilibrium.

Thus, I have chosen to approach the template models using simulations. I use software from GAMS, which has the only powerful and robust nonlinear complementarity solver in the business. All models consist of three sets of inequalities and complementary variables. First, there are *zero-profit inequalities* for each production and trade activity: marginal cost is greater than or equal to price. The complementary variable is the output or "activity level" of that activity. A *quantity* variable is complementary to the *price* inequality.

Second, there are *market-clearing inequalities*: the supply of a commodity (good, factor, import, or other) is greater than or equal to its demand. The complementary variable is the price of that commodity. A *price* variable is complementary to a *quantity* equation. Finally there is an *income balance equation* for each country.

In this appendix, I give the set of inequalities for model 1. There are thirty-four production and trade activities, twenty-four "commodities" (final goods, intermediate goods, imports and exports, and utility, which is treated as a good produced from inputs of X and Y in the code), and two income levels. Walras's Law makes one equation redundant: I fix the world price of Y at 1 and drop the world market-clearing equation for Y. Thus the entire model consists of fifty-nine weak inequalities, each with an associated non-negative variable.

In the body of the paper, I introduced only the notation needed to describe the models in basic economic terms. Here are the definitions of additional notation needed for the formal model.

p_{ki} producer price (that is, marginal cost) of good k in country i
              ($k = Y, X, M, S$; i = North, South)
p_{cki} consumer/import price of good k in country i
p_k world price of good k
w_{ji} price of primary factor j in country i ($j = U, H$)
$c_k(...)$ unit cost of producing good k (includes "cost" of producing utility:
              the unit expenditure function)
EK_i exports of good k by country i
IK_i imports of good k by country i
W_i welfare of country i
I_i income of country i

Other:

James R. Markusen   21

(1) market-clearing inequalities make extensive use of Shepard's lemma, in which the unit demand for a good or factor is the derivative of the unit cost function with respect to the price of that good or factor.

(2) very small trade costs, 0.05 percent, are used to prevent "ties" or, more formally, model degeneracy. This prevents, for example, its being equally profitable to both import and export a good, which would lead to indeterminacy of gross trade flows and possibly a failure to solve (infinitely many solutions differing in gross trade flows).

(3) solutions without fragmentation permitted are computed by constraining import and export activities for S and M to be zero.

(4) all production activities using more than one input are Cobb-Douglas, with shares as follows:

Y	-	U: 0.70	H: 0.30
M	-	U: 0.17	H: 0.83
S	-	U: 0.60	H: 0.40
X	-	M: 0.70	S: 0.30

implied shares of primary factors in X produced from domestic M and S are the inverse of share for Y.

X	-	U: 0.30	H: 0.70

(5) factor endowment ratios for North and South are symmetric:

North	-	H: 0.90	U: 0.10
South	-	H: 0.10	U: 0.90

The model is thus symmetric between North and South and between X and Y without fragmentation. Endowment ratios have a bigger spread (9/1) than intensities (7/3). If countries are the same size, then the no-fragmentation equilibrium is symmetric with both countries specialized, a goods terms of trade of one, factor-price ratios that are inverses in the two countries, and equal welfare across countries.

22   *Brookings Trade Forum: 2005*

Inequalities	Complementary variable	
zero profit inequalities	activity levels	description (no. of inequalities)
$c_y(w_{ui}, w_{hi}) \geq p_{yi}$	Y_i	production of Y in i (2)
$c_m(w_{ui}, w_{hi}) \geq p_{mi}$	M_i	production of M in i (2)
$c_s(w_{ui}, w_{hi}) \geq p_{si}$	S_i	production of S in i (2)
$c_x(p_{mi}, p_{si}) \geq p_{xi}$	X_{di}	production of X_i from S_i, M_i (2)
$c_x(p_{mi}, p_{csi}) \geq p_{xi}$	X_{si}	production of X_i from S_j, M_i (2)
$c_x(p_{cmi}, p_{si}) \geq p_{xi}$	X_{mi}	production of X_i from S_i, M_j (2)
$c_x(p_{cmi}, p_{csi}) \geq p_{xi}$	X_{ni}	production of X_i from S_j, M_j (2)
$p_{mi} \geq p_m$	EM_i	exports of M by i (2)
$p_m \geq p_{cmi}$	IM_i	imports of M by i (2)
$p_{si} \geq p_s$	ES_i	exports of S by i (2)
$p_s \geq p_{csi}$	IS_i	imports of S by i (2)
$p_{xi} \geq p_x$	EX_i	exports of X by i (2)
$p_x \geq p_{xi}$	IX_i	imports of X by i (2)
$p_{yi} \geq p_y$	EY_i	exports of Y by i (2)
$p_y \geq p_{cyi}$	IY_i	imports of Y by i (2)
$p_{cyi} \geq p_{yi}$	YY_i	home supply of Y_i to i (2)
$c_w(p_{xi}, p_{cyi}) \geq p_{wi}$	W_i	production of welfare in i (2)
$Y_i \geq YY_i + EY_i$	p_{yi}	supply - demand of Y prod (2)
$YY_i + IY_i \geq \dfrac{\partial c_{wi}}{\partial p_{cyi}} W_i$	p_{cyi}	supply - demand of Y cons (2)
$M_i \geq \dfrac{\partial c_x}{\partial p_{mi}} X_{di} + \dfrac{\partial c_x}{\partial p_{mi}} X_{si} + EX_i$	p_{mi}	supply - demand for M_i (2)
$IM_i \geq \dfrac{\partial c_x}{\partial p_{cmi}} X_{mi} + \dfrac{\partial c_x}{\partial p_{cmi}} X_{ni}$	p_{cmi}	supply - demand for imported M (2)

James R. Markusen   23

market clearing inequalities	prices	description (no. of inequalities)
$S_i \geq \dfrac{\partial c_x}{\partial p_{si}} X_{di} + \dfrac{\partial c_x}{\partial p_{si}} X_{mi} + ES_i$	p_{si}	supply - demand for S_i (2)
$IS_i \geq \dfrac{\partial c_x}{\partial p_{csi}} X_{si} + \dfrac{\partial c_x}{\partial p_{csi}} X_{ni}$	p_{csi}	supply - demand for imported S (2)
$X_{di} + X_{mi} + X_{si} + X_{ni} + IX_i \geq \dfrac{\partial c_{wi}}{\partial p_{xi}} W_i + EX_i$	p_{xi}	supply - demand for X_i (2)
$\sum_i EY_i \geq \sum_i IY_i$	p_y	world market and price for Y (1)
$\sum_i EM_i \geq \sum_i IM_i$	p_m	world market and price for M (1)
$\sum_i ES_i \geq \sum_i IS_i$	p_s	world market and price for S (1)
$\sum_i EX_i \geq \sum_i IX_i$	p_x	world market and price for X (1)
$W_i \geq I_i/p_{wi}$	p_{wi}	supply - demand for utility (2)
$U_i \geq \dfrac{\partial c_{yi}}{\partial w_{ui}} Y_i + \dfrac{\partial c_{mi}}{\partial w_{ui}} M_i + \dfrac{\partial c_{si}}{\partial w_{ui}} S_i$	w_{ui}	market for unskilled labor in i (2)
$H_i \geq \dfrac{\partial c_{yi}}{\partial w_{hi}} Y_i + \dfrac{\partial c_{mi}}{\partial w_{hi}} M_i + \dfrac{\partial c_{si}}{\partial w_{hi}} S_i$	w_{hi}	market for skilled labor in i (2)

Income balance inequalities	incomes	description (no. of inequalities)
$I_i = w_{ui} U_i + w_{hi} H_i$	I_{ij}	income balance in country i (2)

References

Antràs, Pol. 2003. "Firms, Contracts, and Trade Structure." *Quarterly Journal of Economics* 118 (4): 1375–1418.

———. 2005. "Incomplete Contracts and the Product Cycle." *American Economic Review* (September): 1054–73.

Antràs, Pol, and Elhanan Helpman. 2004. "Global Sourcing." *Journal of Political Economy* 112 (3): 552–580.

Bhagwati, Jagdish, Arvind Panagariya, and T. N. Srinivasan. 2004. "The Muddles over Outsourcing." *Journal of Economic Perspectives* 18 (Fall): 93–114.

Brainard, S. Lael. 1997. "An Empirical Assessment of the Proximity-Concentration Tradeoff between Multinational Sales and Trade." *American Economic Review* 87 (4): 520–44.

Deardorff, Alan V. 2001. "Fragmentation in Simple Trade Models." *North American Journal of Economics and Finance* 12 (2): 121–37.

———. 2005a. "Ricardian Comparative Advantage with Intermediate Inputs." *North American Journal of Economics and Finance* 16 (1): 11–34.

———. 2005b. "A Trade Theorist's Take on Skilled-Labor Outsourcing." *International Review of Economics and Finance* 14 (3): 259–71.

Dornbusch, Rudiger, Stanley Fischer, and Paul A. Samuelson. 1977. "Comparative Advantage, Trade, and Payments in a Ricardian Model with a Continuum of Goods." *American Economic Review* 67 (5): 823–39.

Dunning, John H. 1977. "Trade, Location of Economic Activity and the Multinational Enterprise: A Search for an Eclectic Approach." In *The International Allocation of Economic Activity*, edited by B. Ohlin, P. O. Hesselborn, and P. M. Wijkman, pp. 395–418. New York: Macmillan.

Ethier, Wilfred. 1982. "National and International Returns to Scale in the Modern Theory of International Trade." *American Economic Review* 72 (3): 389–405.

Ethier, Wilfred, and James R. Markusen. 1996. "Multinational Firms, Technology Diffusion and Trade." *Journal of International Economics* 41 (1): 1–28.

Feenstra, Robert C., and Gordon H. Hanson. 1996a. "Foreign Investment, Outsourcing, and Relative Wages." In *The Political Economy of Trade Policy: Papers in Honor of Jagdish Bhagwati*, edited by R. C. Feenstra, G. M. Grossman, and D. A. Irwin, pp. 89–127. MIT Press.

———. 1996b. "Globalization, Outsourcing, and Wage Inequality." *American Economic Review* 86 (2): 240–45.

———. 1997. "Foreign Direct Investment and Relative Wages: Evidence from Mexico's Maquiladoras." *Journal of International Economics* 42 (3): 371–93.

Fosfuri, Andrea, Massimo Motta, and Thomas Rønde. 2001. "Foreign Direct Investment and Spillovers through Workers' Mobility." *Journal of International Economics* 53 (1): 205–22.

Glass, Amy Joyce, and Kamal Saggi. 2002. "Multinational Firms and Technology Transfer." *Scandinavian Journal of Economics* 104 (4): 495–513.

Gomory, Ralph E., And William J. Baumol. 2004. "Globalization: Prospects, Promise, and Problems." *Journal of Policy Modeling* 26 (4): 425–38.

Grossman, Stanford J., and Oliver D. Hart. 1986. "The Costs and Benefits of Ownership: A Theory of Vertical and Lateral Integration." *Journal of Political Economy* 94 (4): 691–719.

Grubel, Herbert. 1987. "All Traded Services Are Embodied in Materials or People." *World Economy* 10 (3): 319–30.

Helpman, Elhanan.1984. "A Simple Theory of Trade with Multinational Corporations." *Journal of Political Economy* 92 (3): 451–71.

Helpman, Elhanan, Mark J. Melitz, and Stephen R. Yeaple. 2004. "Exports versus FDI with Heterogeneous Firms." *American Economic Review* 94 (1): 300–16.

Hummels, David, Jun Ishii, and Kie-Mu Yi. 2001. "The Nature and Growth of Vertical Specialization in World Trade." *Journal of International Economics* 54 (1): 75–96.

Jones, Ronald W., I. Coelho, and Stephen T. Easton.1986. "The Theory of International Factor Flows: The Basic Model." *Journal of International Economics* 20 (3–4): 313–27.

Koopmans, Tjalling. 1957. *Three Essays on the State of Economic Science.* New York: McGraw-Hill.

Landes, David. 1998. *The Wealth and Poverty of Nations: Why Some Are So Rich and Some Are So Poor.* New York: W. W. Norton.

Magee, Stephen P., and Kwang-Yeol Yoo. 2005. "The United States Is a Small Country in World Trade: Further Evidence and Implications for Globalization." Working Paper. University of Texas.

Markusen, James R. 1983. "Factor Movements and Commodity Trade as Complements." *Journal of International Economics* 14 (3–4): 341–56.

———. 1984. "Multinationals, Multi-Plant Economies, and the Gains from Trade." *Journal of International Economics* 16 (3–4): 205–26.

———. 1989. "Trade in Producer Services and in Other Specialized Intermediate Inputs." *American Economic Review* 79 (1): 85–95.

———. 1995. "The Boundaries of Multinational Firms and the Theory of International Trade." *Journal of Economic Perspectives* 9 (2): 169–89.

———. 2001. "Contracts, Intellectual Property Rights, and Multinational Investment in Developing Countries." *Journal of International Economics* 53 (1): 189–204.

———. 2002. *Multinational Firms and the Theory of International Trade.* MIT Press.

Markusen, James R., and Anthony J. Venables. 2005. "A Multi-country Approach to Factors Proportions Trade and Trade Costs." Working Paper 11051. Cambridge, Mass.: National Bureau of Economic Research.

Melitz, Mark J. 2003. "The Impact of Trade on Intra-Industry Reallocations and Aggregate Industry Productivity." *Econometrica* 71 (6): 1695–1725.

Moggeridge, Donald, ed. 1983. *The Collected Writings of John Maynard Keynes.* Cambridge, Eng.: Macmillan.

Mundell, Robert A. 1957. "International Trade and Factor Mobility." *American Economic Review* 47 (3): 321–35.

Neary, J. Peter. 1995. "Factor Mobility and International Trade." *Canadian Journal of Economics* 28: S4–S23.

Samuelson, Paul A. 2004. "Where Ricardo and Mill Rebut and Confirm Arguments of Mainstream Economists Supporting Globalization." *Journal of Economic Perspectives* 18 (3): 135–46.

Yi, Kei-Mu. 2003. "Can Vertical Specialization Explain the Growth of World Trade." *Journal of Political Economy* 111 (1): 52–102.

Zhang, Kevin Honglin, and James R. Markusen. 1999. "Vertical Multinational and Host Country Characteristics." *Journal of Development Economics* 59 (2): 233–52.

[10]

Measurement and Classification of Service Sector Activity: Data Needs for GATS 2000

Obie G. Whichard

I. Introduction

Over roughly the last 15 years, growth in trade in services and the advent of trade negotiations and agreements covering services have made it increasingly important that measurement of services trade be as comprehensive, detailed, accurate, and internationally comparable as possible. International organizations and national statistical offices have responded by issuing new methodological guidelines and classifications, improving the coverage of transactions, and reporting services trade in greater detail. In addition, a number of countries have begun to develop data on services delivered to international markets through locally established foreign affiliates. Overall, a remarkable amount of progress has been achieved. Yet the area still is not one most people would consider highly developed. Available data tend to be highly aggregated, particularly in comparison with those on trade in goods, often do not separately identify prices and quantities for specific services, do not indicate the mode through which the service was supplied, and may classify cross-border trade and (if data on them are available at all) sales by foreign affiliates on fundamentally different bases—all limitations that help to define the wish lists of data users.

This paper will examine needs for statistics on trade in services, indicate in general terms what data are now available, describe the existing international body of methodological guidance for statistical compilation, attempt to provide some insight into what is involved in improving trade-in-services statistics (using as an illustration the efforts of the United States, with which the author has been involved), and identify some of the needs that remain unmet and some of the difficulties and special situations involved in data collection.

Because it is likely that many of its readers are most interested in services statistics as a tool for supporting trade negotiations, the paper devotes special attention to identifying areas where negotiators have adopted definitions that differ from those found in guidelines for statistical compilation. For these readers, it may help motivate the discussion that follows to point out a reason why statistics on the trade subject to negotiation may be even more critical for services than for goods—namely, the greater need for indirect tools for gauging impediments. Barriers to services trade are almost exclusively non-tariff barriers and thus difficult to quantify, and impossible to quantify precisely.[1] However, sufficiently detailed and accurate trade statistics might allow levels of protection to be gauged indirectly, through comparisons between actual trade flows and flows predicted by economic models.

II. Data Needs

Data on trade in services are used for a variety of purposes, and it is with these purposes in mind that needs must be considered. The most longstanding purpose is for general economic measurement and accounting. Trade in services is recorded in balance of payments accounts, which provide a statistical record of economic transactions between the residents of a nation and those of other countries; these accounts, in turn, feed into the national income and product accounts used for gauging overall economic activity. Another purpose—and one that has provided much of the impetus for data improvement—is for use in connection with trade policy, including the support of negotiations and the resulting agreements. Finally, the data may be used by businesses in assessing market opportunities and by researchers in conducting economic analysis.

Needs for data on trade in services may be approached from different perspectives. The one that comes most readily to mind is that of the *types* of information needed, and this is the principal concern addressed below. However, no less important are issues related to the *quality* and the *comparability* of the data. For users to feel they can depend upon them, the data must be accurate and timely. For the data to be as useful as possible analytically, it must be possible to compare them from country to country and to relate them to statistics on the domestic economy.

The types of information required to meet the needs of economic accountants, negotiators and policy officials, business analysts, and researchers can be stated rather straightforwardly. Putting aside for the time being questions of what is feasible or cost effective, four basic types of needs can be identified; these are discussed below under the headings of *values*, *prices*, *modes of supply*, and *foreign-affiliate activities*.

Values.—The most basic need is simply for data on the values of services exports and imports, both in the aggregate and for specific services. These should be available in some degree of detail, preferably classified according to an internationally agreed system that allows comparisons among countries and, for a given country, with data on domestic production and consumption of those same services.

Prices.—Information on the prices governing the transactions is needed to allow estimates of trade flows in real terms to be developed, to address terms-of-trade issues, and to assist in efforts to estimate and analyze supply and demand for traded services.

Modes of supply.—A relatively new need is for a breakdown of statistics on the basis of the "modes of supply" through which services are delivered. While analysts had for some time recognized that services transactions may be differentiated based on the location of the producer and consumer of the service at the time of the transaction, the discussion was mostly couched in theoretical terms.[2] It was only with the General Agreement on Trade in Services (GATS), under which commitments may be restricted to services supplied via particular modes, that mode of supply became identified as a significant statistical need.[3]

Foreign-affiliate activities.—Related to the need for mode-of-supply information is the need for data on the sales and other activities of foreign affiliates. Though important for both goods and services, supply through foreign affiliates may be particularly important for services, due to the need for close and continuing contact between producers and consumers and, in many cases, the impracticality—or even impossibility—of supplying the market through any other mode. Although given impetus by trade agreements, data on foreign affiliates' activities also are needed in connection with the study of globalization phenomena and, in particular, of the ways multinational firms organize their international operations and of the effects of these operations on home- and host-country economies.

III. Data Availability

A good overall impression of the availability of data on trade in services may be obtained by examining publications of international organizations that recompile data supplied by their member countries. Data for the largest number of countries are those found in the International Monetary Fund's *Balance of Payments Statistics Yearbook* (IMF, 1998). In it, data on services trade (and other international transactions) are broken down according to the standard components recommended by the Fund's *Balance of Payments Manual* (5th edition, often referred to as "BPM5"), which provides guidelines for balance of payments compilers (IMF, 1993). (These guidelines will be discussed in the next section.) The 1998 edition of the *Yearbook* contains data for 159 countries and covers the years 1990-97. Of the 159 countries, data on total services trade are provided for both 1990 and either 1996 or 1997 for 110 countries.[4] Table 1 shows how many of these countries reported data for each of the various services components for 1990 and for the latest year reported (1997, in all but a few cases).

86   Services in the International Economy

Table 1. Number of IMF Member Countries Providing Services Data

	Exports		Imports	
	1990	1996 or 1997	1990	1996 or 1997
Total services	110	110	110	110
Transportation	105	106	108	109
Travel	105	106	104	107
Other services	109	109	109	109
Communications	30	66	32	67
Construction	16	34	16	40
Insurance	83	86	97	98
Financial services	16	41	17	43
Computer and information services	8	34	8	33
Royalties and license fees	34	46	52	66
Other business services	102	102	105	108
Personal, cultural, and recreational services	11	31	20	36
Government, n.i.e.	95	102	99	104

Note—This table covers the 110 countries for which data on total services are shown for both 1990 and either 1996 or 1997 in the 1998 edition of the *Balance of Payments Yearbook.*

As can be seen, almost all of the countries reported data for the three major categories—transportation, travel, and "other" Within "other," however, a category encompassing a very wide variety of services, the picture is not so bright. Most countries reported on insurance, "other business services," and government services, but for several other services, only a minority of countries reported. For construction, financial services, computer and information services, and personal, cultural and recreational services, a minority— generally around 30-40 percent in the latest year—reported for both exports and imports. For royalties and license fees—basically, transactions related to intellectual property—a minority reported exports (receipts), perhaps reflecting to some extent a genuine absence of such exports by a number of mainly less-developed countries, but around 60 percent of the countries reported imports (payments). Considering that this is a highly aggregated list to begin with—only 11 categories altogether, excluding subtotals—these results probably are not very encouraging to trade negotiators. (The Services Sectoral Classification List (often referred to as the "W120 list") used in connection with the GATS, for example, lists about 150 separate services.[5])

Despite the rather low numbers of countries reporting on several of the services, it is encouraging that these numbers are growing. For construction, financial services, computer and information services, and personal, cultural and recreational services, the numbers of countries reporting more than doubled from 1990 to 1996-97 for both exports and imports. This would seem to indicate that countries are beginning to devote increased attention and resources to providing more detailed and comprehensive data on services trade, even if the available detail remains rather limited. Of course, during this developmental period, the changing number of countries reporting various services itself greatly complicates the analysis of global trends in services trade, and this factor must be kept in mind in interpreting the available data. A related complication stems from the fact that newly reported services may in some cases have been included previously in higher-level groupings, making it difficult to know the extent to which discontinuities for individual services carry over to groups of services or services as a whole.

While the IMF data are the most comprehensive in terms of country coverage, the aggregated nature of the standard components does not allow analysis of data availability for very many specific types of services. However, it is likely that most of the countries that have more detail are developed countries (one would expect this *a priori*, and their reporting of the IMF standard components tends to be the most complete), and many of these countries report detailed data on services trade to the Organization for Economic Co-Operation and Development. Table 2 indicates the number of countries, from among the 27 covered by a recent OECD statistical publication on trade in services, reporting data for different types of services, including several that are not broken out separately in the IMF *Yearbook*.

The general impression obtained from the table is one of good coverage of the major broad categories, with lesser but still significant coverage of most individual services. Several countries do not provide separate information on most or all of the services within the "business, professional, and technical" group, but a significant number do. Reporting for exports and imports is very similar, with there being just a few instances of trade reported in only one direction.

All the data described above show values only and do not distinguish between movements attributable to price change and movements attributable to changes in quantities. Nor do they distinguish among the different modes of supply. To the best of the author's knowledge, comparable cross-country estimates breaking down values for specific services into price and quantity components or allocating those values on the basis of mode of supply simply do not exist.[6]

Concerning sales of services by foreign affiliates and other related information on the operations of direct investment enterprises that might relate to the commercial presence mode of supply, the data availability situation is difficult to assess. For most countries, this is a relatively new area of data collection; only a few have actually begun it. International guidelines are still evolving, and systematic recompilation by international organizations has not yet

88   Services in the International Economy

Table 2. Number of OECD Countries Providing Statistics on Trade in Different Types of Services, 1996

	Exports	Imports
Total services	27	27
Transportation	27	27
Travel	27	27
Communications	25	24
Construction	23	23
Insurance	27	27
Financial services	25	26
Computer and information services	22	22
Royalties and license fees	25	25
Other business services	27	27
Merchanting and other trade-related	23	22
Operational leasing	23	24
Misc. business, professional and technical services	26	26
Legal, accounting, management, and public relations services	20	20
Advertising, market research, and public opinion polling	20	20
Research and development services	20	19
Architectural, engineering, and other technical consultancy	17	17
Agricultural, mining, and on-site processing	16	16
Other business, professional and technical services	20	20
Services between affiliated enterprises, n.i.e.	14	14
Personal, cultural, and recreational services	26	26
Audio-visual and related services	18	18
Other personal, cultural, and recreational services	18	17
Government services, n.i.e.	27	27
Other services	25	25

Source: OECD, 1999; derived from tables B.1 - B.28

begun. Among the countries that have collected data on sales by foreign affiliates for some time are the United States, Japan, and Sweden. These data are classified by the primary industry of the affiliate rather than by type of service, and only the United States data break down sales by affiliates in each industry as between sales of goods and sales of services.

In 1997, the Statistical Office of the European Communities (Eurostat) issued a *FATS Task Force Report*, reporting on the work of a task force established to investigate statistical issues related to activities by foreign affiliates—which the report termed "foreign affiliates' trade."[7] Included in the report was a prototype survey, later implemented jointly with the OECD, requesting information disaggregated by industry of affiliate on five key operating statistics—turnover (sales), employment, value added, exports, and imports. About a dozen responses were received, most of them providing information on only some of the items requested and only for foreign-owned firms in the domestic economy (inward direct investment). Additional countries can be expected to make progress in this area in the coming years, at least with respect to inward investment, though there is no indication that the availability of data is likely to become truly widespread any time soon.[8]

IV. The International Methodological Infrastructure for Trade-in-Services Statistics

International organizations have influenced the available statistics on trade in services not only by republishing member-country data, but also by providing definitions and methodological guidelines for compilation, generally through internationally coordinated consultative processes involving member-country statistical offices. The organizations most directly involved in these activities have been the IMF, the OECD, and the UN, all of which have major statistical functions as integral parts of their work programs. These organizations, together with the World Trade Organization and Eurostat, are jointly endeavoring to integrate and expand the body of international guidance on trade-in-services statistics through a Task Force on Statistics of International Trade in Services, whose activities are described below along with those of the primary statistical organizations.

International Monetary Fund (IMF)

Of the numerous steps international organizations have taken to promote better data on services trade, perhaps the most fundamental ones are those reflected in the 5th edition of the IMF's *Balance of Payments Manual*. Published in 1993, BPM5 was the first edition of the *Manual* to provide a statistical definition of trade in services, together with a single heading within the current account under which services trade would be separately recorded. It gave definitions of what to include under this heading and what to exclude, and it specifically addressed a number of borderline cases. In recommending that the total be distributed among a number of "standard components," it provided a broad international classification for trade in services.

Because of its centrality in determining how trade in services is statistically recorded and because agreements such as the GATS may use definitions that differ from the statistical definitions, it will be useful to review some of BPM5's main features relating to trade in services, to describe how it handles certain borderline cases, and to call attention to its treatment of a few services that present unique definitional issues.

90   Services in the International Economy

Residency.—BPM5 defines international transactions in terms of residency. Specifically, a transaction is considered "international" if it is between residents and nonresidents of the compiling economy. In most cases, an individual must remain in a country for a period of a year or more to be considered a resident of that country. Exceptions are provided for students, medical patients, and government employees, such as diplomats and military personnel, all of whom are considered residents of their country of origin even if they remain in another country for a year or more. For a business enterprise, a foreign operation is considered to constitute a foreign affiliate, resident in its country of location, if it maintains a production establishment in that country and plans to do so "indefinitely or over a long period of time" (para. 73). In addition, it must qualify as a bona fide business enterprise in the host country, such as by maintaining its own accounts, receiving funds for its own account for work that it does, having a physical presence in the country of location (e.g., plant and equipment and employees), and paying local income taxes.

To give a concrete example of how these definitions would work in the context of services, if an individual stayed abroad as a service provider for a period of six months, then the fees charged by the individual to residents of the foreign country for performing the service would be recorded as an international transaction—specifically, as an export by the individual's permanent country of residence and as an import by the country in which the services were performed. However, if the individual remained in the latter country for, say, 18 months, then for statistical purposes the individual would be deemed a resident of that country and the fees would be regarded, not as international transactions, but as transactions occurring wholly within the country where the services were performed.

Trade negotiations and agreements might not differentiate between these two cases, or they might do so in a way different from that adopted for statistical purposes. In the GATS, for example, a natural person (i.e., an individual) is regarded as a "natural person of another Member" if the person is, under the law of that Member, a "national" (or the equivalent, in certain special cases).[9] This is more of a legal definition than one geared to economic measurement and accounting, and it could result in situations where service providers working outside their country of nationality are considered for statistical purposes as resident in the country where they work, but for purposes of the GATS remain persons of their country of nationality. Their fees for providing services would be relevant to the agreement, yet they would not be recorded statistically as international transactions. While the practical importance of the variance from the statistical definition may not be great in most cases, the potential for differences exists, and users of the data need to be aware of how definitions differ, to have reflected upon how the differences may affect the usefulness of the data for their particular purposes, and possibly to determine whether any supplemental information may be required.

Similar definitional issues may arise with respect to enterprises. For example, a construction project abroad may be accounted for statistically either as a services export by the home country of the construction firm that carries it out or as an operation of that firm's foreign affiliate in the country of the project, depending on its duration and other characteristics, following the guidelines outlined above. In the former case, the transaction would be included in the balance of payments accounts as an international transaction, whereas in the latter, the transaction would be wholly within the country of the project and thus would (apart from the related capital and income flows) be excluded. (However, it *would* be included in statistics covering the activities of foreign affiliates, provided the countries involved maintained them.)

It is worth noting that these statistical definitions differentiate only between transactions that are between residents of the same country and transactions that are between residents of different countries. No distinctions are drawn based on the location of the provider and the consumer of the service at the time the service is performed—the key criteria for determining the mode of supply. However, the treatment of foreign affiliates as residents of their countries of location (rather than of their owners' countries) does—by resulting in the exclusion of sales by these entities from the balance of payments accounts—help to isolate transactions effected through commercial presence from transactions effected through the other modes of supply.

Definition of services.—BPM5 does not provide a conceptual definition of services, but it is, with only a few noted exceptions, harmonized with the *System of National Accounts 1993* (SNA), which states that "services are heterogeneous outputs produced to order and typically consist of changes in the conditions of the consuming units realized by the activities of producers at the demand of the consumers."[10] In any event, there are relatively few economic outputs that might be treated as services by some definitions but not by others, and BPM5 takes note of some of these and provides conventions for treating them statistically. However, because some of the conventions are at variance with the way outputs have been categorized by negotiators, it is useful to highlight these cases.

Among the borderline cases specifically addressed by BPM5 are transactions involving repair, processing, goods procured in ports by transportation carriers, merchanting, and intellectual property. These will be discussed in turn below, both to illustrate the issues involved and to indicate their resolution. It is not, strictly speaking, possible to say how closely these definitions are aligned with the GATS, because the GATS does not itself define "services" for purposes of the agreement (other than to exclude services supplied in exercise of governmental authority). However, sectoral classification lists or other information can sometimes be used as the basis for inferences.

BPM5 calls for transactions in *repair* to be recorded under trade in goods. Although often thought of as a service in a domestic context, repair in an international context often involves such activities as major overhauls of vessels or aircraft—activities that may take place in factory-type settings and may have more in common with manufacturing activities than with services operations. In meetings of balance of payments compilers held in connection with

92   Services in the International Economy

BPM5, consideration was given to drawing a distinction between repairs to investment goods and repairs to other goods, and including the latter in services (a treatment followed in the SNA), but a decision not to attempt this was made on practical grounds, taking into consideration the apparent predominance of repair to investment goods in international transactions. Although recorded statistically as trade in goods, for purposes trade agreements, repair may be among the activities considered as services. For example, the W120 list includes an entry for "maintenance and repair of equipment."

Processing presents another borderline case. Processing occurs when goods are imported, have value added to them, and then are re-exported without a change in ownership having occurred. In the fourth edition of the *Balance of Payments Manual*, processing was recorded on a net basis as a service; that is, the goods themselves were excluded from exports and imports of goods and the processor's fee recorded as a service. In BPM5, in contrast, the goods before and after processing are to be recorded on a gross basis, as separately identifiable components of exports and imports of goods. This treatment presumably is more closely aligned with the needs of negotiators than the treatment of the fourth *Manual*, inasmuch as the activities involved, such as petroleum refining or factory-type assembly work done under contract, are seldom discussed in connection with services.[11]

In another change from the fourth *Manual*, *goods procured in ports by transportation carriers* is included by BPM5 in trade in goods, rather than as a part of transportation services. While this helps sharpen the distinction between services and goods, this item may be considered to provide additional information pertinent to agreements on air and maritime transport, and special note of this treatment is therefore taken here.

Merchanting refers to cases where goods are bought and subsequently resold by a resident of a country, without the goods physically entering or leaving that country. If both the purchase and sale occur in the same period, the difference between the acquisition cost and sale proceeds is to be recorded as a service in the balance of payments of the country of the merchant.[12] However, from the standpoint of trade agreements, the transaction presumably would be governed by provisions applicable to trade in goods between the country where the goods were acquired and (if different) the country where they were resold.

As a final illustration of borderline cases, *royalties and license fees*—payments for use of such items of intellectual property as patents, trademarks, copyrights, and proprietary industrial processes—are included by BPM5 in trade in services, even though, as returns on existing assets, consideration had been given to regarding them as payments of income, to be grouped with investment income and compensation of employees. Here, the issue for negotiators relates to the way negotiations have been structured and, in particular, to the fact that multilateral negotiations and agreements related to intellectual property rights have been handled separately, outside the GATS.

Special definitions.—By and large, trade in tangible goods is measured the same way for all goods. Trade in most services is likewise measured uniformly, in terms of the total values of the receipts and payments that flow between buyer and seller. There are a few instances, however, in which special definitions have been adopted to provide an economically more meaningful measure of the trade, or in which special definitions might have been appropriate conceptually but have not been implemented for practical reasons. These concern transportation, insurance, financial services, travel, and government services. The issues involved and the treatment recommended by BPM5 are outlined below.

For *transportation* services, the value of the actual payments between residents and nonresidents for transportation of freight is not the measure recorded as international transactions. Were it to be, an inconsistency in the valuation of merchandise would exist, inasmuch as merchandise values would sometimes include and sometimes exclude transportation charges, depending on whether the buyer or the seller was responsible for paying the freight. To provide for uniform valuation of merchandise, as well as to simplify data collection and reporting, a convention has been adopted under which all freight charges are deemed to be paid by the importer. Thus, for a given country, freight exports are defined as domestic carriers' receipts for carriage of the country's exports (as well as any receipts for carrying freight between foreign countries), and freight imports are defined as domestic residents' payments to foreign carriers for carriage of the country's imports. Figures computed on this basis provide the information needed for compiling the balance of payments. However, because confusion may arise if information from industry sources gives a different picture (perhaps because of the inclusion of data covering transportation that is "international" in the sense of involving movement of freight from one country to another but that does not fall within the scope of the above definitions), it is important that data users be familiar with the definitions underlying the published statistics.

For *insurance* services, the value of trade is measured in BPM5, not by total premiums, but by "service charges included in total premiums" (para. 257). Different methods of estimating the insurance service charge are given for different types of insurance, but the basic concept underlying all of them is that of intermediation, in which a portion—ordinarily a large one—of premiums simply represents transfers between all policyholders and those policyholders to whom claims are paid, with a smaller amount representing the value of the services provided by insurance companies.[13] For other purposes, however, knowledge of the gross financial flows involving insurance is needed, and in this regard it can be noted that the OECD and Eurostat have developed an expanded list of components, consistent with the BPM5 components but with added detail, in which gross premiums and claims are requested as memorandum items. (This list is described below.)

Financial services are sometimes provided without an explicit charge, with the cost of services being implicitly covered by the difference between

94   Services in the International Economy

the rates of interest financial institutions charge to borrowers and the rates they pay to depositors, or by bid-asked spreads on traded financial assets. For this reason, an imputed amount—"financial intermediation services indirectly measured" (FISIM)—is provided in the SNA as a measure of such services. For practical reasons, BPM5 does not require the estimation of FISIM in the measurement of international transactions in financial services. However, negotiators and other users of the data should be aware of this omission, and of the fact that it tends to result in an understatement of the relative importance of financial services in international trade. They may wish to examine data on international income flows in conjunction with data on explicit charges for financial services, to obtain an idea of the international borrowing and lending activity that might have been subject to FISIM, and thus to gauge the order of magnitude of the understatement.

Travel is regarded by BPM5 as a service, and in fact is one of the largest services in international trade. Strictly speaking, however, travel is not a *type* of service, but rather a category for recording all of the expenditures of non-resident individuals, including expenditures for goods as well as for services. *Government services, n.i.e.* likewise is a transactor-based category and may include expenditures for goods as well as services.

Organization for Economic Cooperation and Development (OECD)

Some of the earliest international discussions on services statistics were those held in the OECD. In the early 1980's, statistical issues began to arise from time to time in the Trade Committee, a group normally concerned with trade policy. In 1983, the Working Party of the Committee met for the first time in a "statistical mode" to discuss services statistics, with representatives of statistical offices joining the trade policy officials that usually attended these meetings. Subsequently, regular meetings dealing solely with statistics began to be held, and a work program was developed, housed within the regular statistical part of the organization. The major elements of the program have been the development of a classification of trade in services and the compilation of member country data on services trade.

Recognizing that the need for data was immediate, whereas it would take considerable time to agree to a classification and even longer for widespread implementation to occur, work on both elements was pursued in tandem, rather than postponing the compilation efforts until a classification had been agreed upon and reflected in data collection. The initial compilations followed the then-current (i.e., the fourth) edition of the IMF *Manual* as far as the major categories were concerned, but with whatever additional detail countries could provide within those categories. Because there was then no agreed international classification for trade in services, there was considerable heterogeneity among countries in both the amount of detail and how it was grouped and presented. While the compilation was a unique resource, analysis of the data was hampered by the country-to-country inconsistencies in classification.

The OECD-Eurostat Trade in Services Classification was designed with a view to promoting international consistency in classification, at least among OECD members. Preliminary versions of this classification were available during the period when BPM5 was being developed, and as the result of close cooperation between the organizations involved and efforts to avoid inconsistencies, the OECD-Eurostat Classification can be characterized as an "extended subsystem" of the BPM5 standard components for services. That is, it contains all of the standard components, but with further breakdowns provided for a number of services. While the OECD-Eurostat classification provides for more detail by type of service than BPM5, its extensions are relatively modest. Its aim was for a level of detail that most OECD member countries could be expected to provide, not for separate enumeration of every possible traded service.

The OECD-Eurostat Classification is given in the annex at the end of this paper. In it, BPM5 standard components and "services sub-items" (items suggested to be provided as supplementary information) are labeled with an asterisk (*), so that the table can be used to display the BPM5 classification as well. This classification, or one very much like it, is likely to be the primary basis for compilation of data on services trade (except via commercial presence) worldwide for some time to come. It is, with minor modifications (mainly involving additional memorandum items needed in connection with the GATS), to be the basis recommended in an international manual on trade-in-services statistics that is currently being prepared. In 1998, for the first time, the OECD and Eurostat requested that submissions of trade-in-services data be reported on the basis of this classification, and the data were presented in this format in the data publication released in 1999 (OECD, 1999).

In a separate exercise conducted within a working group of the Industry Committee, the OECD also has also done work that should help in the development of international guidelines for compilation of data on the activities of foreign affiliates. It is through this group that a manual of globalization indicators is being prepared, and this manual and the above mentioned manual on trade-in-services statistics are to be harmonized, insofar as possible. This work is still in progress, and the details of the statistical recommendations are still in flux. However, it appears likely that the recommendations will be for these statistics to be applied to foreign affiliates that are majority-owned by direct investors, for the principal basis of attribution to be an industry classification rather than a product (i.e., type of good or service) classification, and for a variety of indicators of affiliate activity—such as sales, value added, employment, exports, and imports—to be covered.

Finally, although its recommendations have now been incorporated in the SNA and in BPM5, the OECD is the originator of the currently accepted international guidelines for compiling statistics on foreign direct investment (OECD, 1996). While the relationship of this to trade in services may seem tangential, its significance becomes more apparent in light of the fact that relatively few countries (and hardly any developing countries) now maintain the

96   Services in the International Economy

kinds of statistics on foreign-affiliate activities that are needed for monitoring the commercial presence mode of supply. Though they are not exactly what is needed, statistics on foreign direct investment do provide an alternative indicator of commercial presence. In addition, they may contribute to the development of the statistics that *are* needed, by providing a readily available register of firms that are foreign-owned.

United Nations (UN)

The United Nations has influenced statistics on trade in services in a number of ways. The UN is of course among the international organizations responsible for the SNA, whose external account for goods and services is almost completely harmonized with BPM5 and which therefore provides a somewhat parallel source of guidance with respect to trade in services, but without some of the details covered by BPM5 and presented in the larger context of the overall national accounts. However, it is perhaps with respect to classification that the UN has had the largest effect on trade-in-services statistics, for it is both the originator and the custodian of the major international systems for classifying economic outputs by product and by industrial activity.[14]

The Central Product Classification (CPC) is the only international product classification covering both goods and services. It began to be developed during the mid-to-late 1970s and was published as a provisional classification in 1991. In 1997, the UN Statistical Commission approved a revised version to be released as version 1.0, which was published the following year (United Nations, 1998). Inasmuch as an international product classification already existed for goods (the Harmonized System, with which the goods portion of the CPC corresponds very closely), the principal contribution of the CPC can be said to lie in its classification of services. While the CPC was not designed specifically as a trade classification, it has played a prominent role in such classifications. For example, the CPC was used in drawing up the above mentioned W120 list used in connection with the GATS. In addition, BPM5 contains an appendix (Appendix III) that relates its classification of services to the CPC, and the OECD/Eurostat classification also has been concorded to the CPC.[15] The forthcoming international statistical manual on trade-in-services statistics likewise will relate its classification of services trade to the CPC. Because concordance with the CPC is a common element in each of these trade-related classifications, the CPC thus provides a tool through which the classifications can be related to one another.[16]

While the CPC has thus played a significant role in international classifications of trade in services, it has served more as a dictionary, used to describe the content of the various services categories, than as a guide to aggregation structure or even as a guide to the boundary between goods and services. As would be expected, the trade classifications are designed to show the greatest detail for the services that figure most prominently in international trade. In addition, the trade classifications include two categories—travel and government services—that are transactor-based rather than product-based.[17] Finally, while the CPC has not been represented as a guide to distinguishing goods from services, its groupings and nomenclature suggest different dividing lines in some cases from those reflected in the classifications for international trade. Among the more significant differences are the classifications for repair and processing, both of which are among the borderline cases discussed above. Repair, treated by BPM5 as a part of trade in goods, is included in the CPC division for "maintenance and repair services." Processing, called for by BPM5 to be recorded on a gross basis in exports and imports of goods, is covered by the CPC division for "production services, on a fee or contract basis."

With respect to industry classification, the UN is responsible for the International Standard Industrial Classification of All Economic Activities (ISIC), which promises to figure prominently in statistics on the activities of foreign affiliates (United Nations, 1990). Now in its third revision, the ISIC is recommended as a basis for industry classification in the SNA and in the *OECD Benchmark Definition of Foreign Direct Investment*. Pilot surveys on foreign-affiliate activities conducted by the OECD have requested reporting on the basis of a selected subset of ISIC categories, and a similar ISIC-based classification is being proposed for the forthcoming statistical manual on trade-in-services statistics. Many national and regional industry classification systems follow the ISIC, in whole or in part. For example, the NACE system used within the European Union is very closely related to the ISIC, and the recently introduced North American Industry Classification System used by Canada, Mexico, and the United States is designed to be consistent with the ISIC at the 2-digit level.

Task Force on Statistics of International Trade in Services

In 1994, the UN Statistical Commission established the Interagency Task Force on Services Statistics. In recognition of the fact that all of its work involved *trade* statistics, it was subsequently redesignated as the Task Force on Statistics of International Trade in Services. Apart from facilitating communication among the international organizations represented and thus helping to rationalize work on trade-in-services statistics and avoid duplication of effort, the main project of the Task Force has been the preparation of a manual on trade-in-services statistics. This manual—the *Manual on Statistics of International Trade in Services*—will take account of a broad spectrum of statistical needs, specifically including those of the GATS. It will do this by building upon, rather than by attempting to replace, existing standards for compilation.

The manual will be consistent with existing international guidelines for statistical compilation—specifically including BPM5—but it will provide for the added dimensions called for by needs such as those of the GATS. Thus, for example, in addition to the core BPM5 rules for recording trade between residents and nonresidents will be recommendations for disaggregating this trade on the basis of mode of supply or as between intrafirm trade and trade between

98   Services in the International Economy

unrelated parties. Also provided will be guidelines for compiling data on the activities of foreign affiliates—to be termed "foreign affiliates trade in services," or FATS (a usage which has been adopted for the remaining sections of this paper). Recognizing that the totality of the recommendations to be provided generally lies beyond the capability of most, if not all, countries to implement in the short term, the manual will also indicate priorities for implementation. The priorities should be particularly useful for developing countries, which will tend to have the most work ahead of them and the least resources available for doing it.

V. The Step-by-Step Approach to Data Improvement

From the standpoint of developing statistics, one of the key distinctions between trade in services and trade in goods is the fact that services lack a central registration point that can be exploited as a data collection vehicle. While there may be numerous and varied impediments to services trade, customs declarations, specifying the type of service and its value, are not required for services. Add to this lack of administrative records the above-discussed special definitions and conventions and the requirement for data on commercial presence, and it becomes obvious that improving trade-in-services statistics is a multidimensional exercise, more likely to involve many small steps than a few large ones. Whether this makes statistics *harder* to improve for trade in services than for trade in goods is difficult to say. On the one hand, the sheer number of steps that must be taken can be daunting. On the other hand, there are likely to be many opportunities, varied in terms of difficulty of implementation, to make improvements, and at any given time there usually will be at least *some* opportunity that is within reach. Furthermore, the improvements do not have to be made all at once, but may be implemented incrementally over time.

While the steps taken to improve data on trade in services in any given country will depend on the particulars of the needs, the available resources, and the institutional framework for data collection, in many cases the improvements will involve one or more of three broad elements— methodological realignment, new or expanded surveys, and indirect estimation. Each of these may, in turn, involve multiple steps. What each of these may involve will be discussed momentarily, illustrated by the experience of the United States, with whose statistics the author has been involved.[18] Before any significant improvements can be made, however, a country must know the dimensions of the task and also must have a sense of priorities—what is most important. In addition, the responsible statistical office must have the legal authority to collect the necessary data. This preparatory work, though not a data improvement in itself, is nonetheless essential and can be considered as a fourth typical element in a data improvement program. It is termed here "setting the stage" and is discussed first.

Setting the stage.—Because of the lack of a central registration point and the diverse sources of information and methodologies that typically must be used in developing estimates, data on trade in services cannot be collected through a single all-inclusive instrument, such as a survey. For example, travel transactions, which involve individuals, require a different instrument from transactions between businesses, such as those in advertising, accounting, or legal services. Furthermore, the specific categories for which data are desired generally must be enumerated in surveys, inasmuch as residual, "all other" categories can be confusing to respondents in a system based on multiple instruments. (It is difficult to enforce exclusion from a given residual of those items for which data are collected using other instruments.) To sort out these issues, actual collection of additional data may need to be preceded by a period of study, in which the national statistical office attempts to make a precise determination of the largest or most important data gaps, and to develop a strategy for filling them.

In the United States, a number of studies were conducted to review and evaluate data on trade in services and to recommend improvements. As early as 1984, the Bureau of Economic Analysis, which compiles the balance of payments accounts and also provides statistics describing the operations of multinational companies, issued a staff paper that described the then available data on U.S. trade and investment in services, identified gaps in the data, and made a number of suggestions for improvement (Whichard, 1984). Two years later, a report by the Congressional Office of Technology Assessment addressed some of these same issues (U.S. Congress, 1986). In 1992, after a number of data improvements had already been made, a study panel organized by the National Research Council issued a report in which the improvement efforts were evaluated and a number of suggestions for further improvements were made (National Research Council, 1992). Finally, although it did not issue any comprehensive reports, an important part of the process of sorting out data needs and of reaching a consensus within the U.S. Government on the approach to data improvement was through the work of an Interagency Task Force on Services Trade Data. Established in 1982, it was chaired by the Office of the U.S. Trade Representative and was charged with reviewing existing statistics, examining the specific needs of data users, recommending data improvements, and generally coordinating the interagency aspects of work in this area.

An outcome of the study phase of an improvement program should be not only the identification of gaps and other data inadequacies, but also the setting of priorities for improvements. In the not unlikely event that more needs are identified than can be met in the near term, plans for sequencing improvements must be developed. Although not formally structured as such, this exercise is akin in spirit to a cost-benefit analysis, in which answers are sought to the questions "What improvements are most important?" and "How do the improvements rank from the standpoint of cost and feasibility of implementation?" This process of sorting out priorities could be particularly important for

100   Services in the International Economy

developing countries, which, as mentioned, are likely to have numerous needs, but only limited resources that can be devoted to meeting them.

Because the initial U.S. studies predated the publication of BPM5, methodological issues did not play a major role in their recommendations. Rather, the recommendations dealt for the most part with the identification of gaps in coverage. One major need for improvement that was identified was in the areas of business, professional, and technical services—services that may not have been important in international trade in the past but that appeared to be increasing in significance as cheaper and better means of international travel and communication made them more tradable and as increasingly globalized markets for goods and capital stimulated their demand.[19] Needs also were identified for information on services delivered through foreign affiliates. As described later, major improvements were made in both of these areas.

Judging from the information on data availability presented earlier, these same types of needs seem likely to be the ones most often identified in other countries as well. A typical pattern for many countries is to provide data on travel and transportation, but to have at least some gaps—often major ones— in the area of business services. Data on services supplied through foreign affiliates tend to be even more fragmentary. Thus, as a working hypothesis, it is not unrealistic to suppose that the needs most often identified will be in these two areas—conventional resident/nonresident trade in business services and services sold through foreign affiliates. In any event, this pattern is probably sufficiently prevalent that it is a useful stereotype for illustrating approaches to developing priorities.

For a country that has major gaps in both areas—as is likely to be true of many developing countries—top priority probably should be given to improving the data on trade in business services, for these are needed not only to support trade policy, but also for entry in the basic economic accounts needed in the conduct of monetary and fiscal policy. Furthermore, in the absence of direct measures of services supplied through foreign affiliates, data on stocks and flows of direct investment may provide acceptable, if somewhat indirect, interim indicators of commercial presence.

For a country with some data on business services—perhaps limited in detail—but no data on foreign-affiliate activities—a pattern still prevalent among many middle-to-high-income countries—the choice is less clear-cut. A strategy observed in a number of OECD countries has been to attempt to make some progress on both fronts, while limiting resource commitments by relying on least-cost approaches to developing the information on affiliate activities. Typically this has meant developing information on affiliate activities only with respect to inward investment, using links between statistics on inward direct investment and domestic enterprise statistics, which may allow statistics to be derived for the foreign-owned subset of enterprises with little or no new data collection.

To promote international co-ordination in the sequencing of improvements, the forthcoming *Manual on Statistics of International Trade in Services* will—as mentioned earlier—suggest priorities for implementing its recommendations. As reflected in the draft circulating at the time of this writing, a very high priority will be assigned to providing the basic statistics on resident/nonresident trade recommended by BPM5, with intermediate priority given to providing additional details on the specific types of services traded and to providing basic measures of services supplied through foreign affiliates, and lower priority given to nuances such as disaggregating trade flows by mode of supply or on the basis of whether the trade is within multinational firms or between unrelated parties.[20]

Not only study, but also legal authority and financial resources are essential precursors of a data improvement program for trade in services. To the extent that surveys are involved in the improvements, mandatory authority is generally necessary to ensure complete reporting. Businesses on the whole benefit from statistical improvements, particularly in a case such as trade in services, where the data may be used in support of efforts to create a more open and liberalized trading environment. However, responding to surveys is not without cost, and it may be difficult to connect the benefits to one's own individual response. Thus, it is better if reporting is mandatory, both from the standpoint of the resulting statistics and from that of the individual respondent, who can devote efforts to recordkeeping and responding in the knowledge that competitors are having to do the same. In the United States, new survey work for trade in services did not begin until legal authority was secured for collecting the data on a mandatory basis. At about the same time, additional funding was obtained to finance increased survey work and other data improvements.

Methodological realignment.—What is meant here by "methodological realignment" is simply the reconfiguration of definitions and classifications to conform to current international standards. Countries cannot, of course, be compelled to follow these standards, but they generally see the benefits from conformity, the chief one being that it facilitates comparisons with statistics compiled by other countries. Because the standards themselves have recently changed or, in the case of statistics on the activities of foreign affiliates, are still evolving, realignment is likely to be a part of the data improvement program of almost every country.

For the United States, a fairly large number of steps toward realignment have been taken. Given the magnitude of the task, as well as the fact that some steps had to await the development of new source data or were not identified as needs until some time after the initial studies were conducted, the steps have tended to be spread out over time rather than being implemented all at once. While an all-at-once approach might have been better from the standpoint of minimizing the number of disruptions imposed on data users, the incremental approach was, realistically, the only option feasible. The steps taken have ranged from very broad changes in the structure of the accounts—perhaps the broadest being the creation of a separate subtotal for services within the current account—to very specific issues involving classification of individual types of transactions.

Expanded surveying activity.—While there may be some countries that have no need for additional data collection on trade in services, they are likely to be few and far between. Trade in services has only recently become a central concern of balance of payments compilers, and relatively few countries maintain statistics on the services activities of foreign affiliates in their countries of location. Furthermore, trade in services not only is growing, but it also is coming to encompass new and different types of services. Finally, information on mode of supply has been identified as a new need, but little or no data are now being collected on that basis.

In the United States, two new "families" of surveys have proved necessary to achieve satisfactory coverage of trade in services, along with a number of improvements to pre-existing surveys. One family—consisting of a benchmark survey conducted every 5 years and a more limited annual survey conducted in nonbenchmark years—currently collects data on about 30 different types of mainly business, professional, and technical services.[21] The second family— also consisting of benchmark and annual surveys—collects data on financial services. In addition to these new surveys, existing surveys have been expanded, both to improve coverage and to increase the possibilities for subdividing the data by type of service. One of the more important changes to existing surveys involved the surveys on the operations of multinational companies. In those surveys, questions on the sales of foreign affiliates of U.S. companies and of U.S. affiliates of foreign companies were expanded to require reporting of sales of services separately from sales of goods. In this way, an economical means was found for measuring services delivered to foreign markets by U.S. firms, and in the U.S. market by foreign firms, through affiliates, thus providing information relevant to the GATS commercial presence mode of supply.

Indirect estimates.—While surveys may provide the most obvious source of information on services trade, they can be costly for governments to conduct, and they impose burdens on the respondents who must complete them. Fortunately, it is sometimes possible to develop information without surveying the universe of transactors. One example of this is when benchmark and annual surveys are conducted. An effort is made to capture essentially the entire universe of transactions only in the benchmark survey. Higher reporting thresholds are used in the annual surveys, with the unreported part of the universe being extrapolated forward from the benchmark year, based on movements in the transactions reported by firms that report in both types of surveys. This is done in the United States, for example, for the services covered by the two new surveys discussed above.

Estimation may also be used where a price or unit value is available from a sample of transactions and a universe measure or indicator of the volume of transactions is available from another source. For example, average expenditures of travelers to foreign countries may be estimated based on surveys given to a sample of travelers; this average may then be multiplied by the total number of travelers, obtained from the immigration authorities, to obtain an estimate of total expenditures by all travelers. As another example, transportation charges per unit of freight hauled may be estimated using a sample; this average can then be multiplied by the total volume of freight, obtained from customs documents, to produce an estimate of the total value of transportation charges. Similarly, expenditures of students studying abroad may be estimated by multiplying average charges for tuition and other expenses, which may be obtained from educational institutions or associations, by the numbers of students, which may be obtained either from these same sources or from visa information.

In the United States, a number of data improvements have taken the form of such indirect estimates, which not only help to minimize reporting burdens on the businesses or individuals involved in the transactions, but also do a great deal to economize on scarce statistical agency resources. These have involved the services mentioned above, as well as a few others.

VI. Issues in Data Collection

While considerable progress in improving data on trade in services has been made already, and while further improvements are underway, there are a number of difficult issues in data collection and estimation that should be acknowledged, with the aim of informing the data user, stimulating thinking about possible solutions, and—to face a hard fact—recognizing the existence of a few difficulties that simply tend to defy resolution. What follows is a discussion of what the author views as some of the more difficult or important problem areas. Four areas are discussed—services sold to individuals, price data, mode-of-supply information, and data on affiliate activities related to outward direct investment (sometimes termed "outward FATS statistics").

Services sold to individuals.—Except for questionnaires distributed to travelers, surveys of international trade in services are almost exclusively surveys of businesses, not of individuals. While international travelers are not hard to identify—they can be found at airports and customs checkpoints—the same cannot be said of individuals in general. The percentage of individuals involved in international trade in services other than as travelers is very small, yet collectively their transactions could be significant—becoming more so as developments in electronic commerce and the international use of credit cards make it increasingly easy and convenient for individuals to purchase services directly from abroad.[22] In almost all cases, the individuals in question are dealing, not with other individuals, but with businesses. Thus, problems in capturing services sold to individuals tend mainly to be those of compilers in the importing country. How can these transactions be identified? The answers, it must be said, are far from obvious.

As a concrete example, consider telecommunications callback services. These services may lower the cost of international calls by shifting their origin to a country that has lower rates than the country of the customer. Traditionally, telecommunications services are tracked statistically through the use of data on settlements payments between telecommunications common carriers. With callback services, however, funds also flow between individual customers and the callback service providers, typically through charges to credit cards. While data can be collected from the providers, the country of the customer would have only the individual customers from whom to collect data. However, it would have little way of identifying them, and—inasmuch as it may be illegal, or at least a gray area of the law, to bypass the national telephone monopoly in this way—the customers, even if aware of the need for reporting, might be reluctant to reveal themselves. Faced with such a situation, how is the importing country to obtain these data? In some cases, data exchanges with exporting countries might offer a solution, though the exporting countries typically would have no reason to track callback receipts as a separate item. In others, information obtained from credit card companies might be explored, though privacy concerns might preclude this alternative in many countries. A final possibility is for compilers simply to make their own rough estimates, based on industry sources or other information. Such estimates can be useful in eliminating downward biases in broad aggregates, but they cannot be regarded as providing precise information on trade in particular types of services.

Prices.—Almost all discussions of statistics on trade in services are about statistics on the values of the trade. Perhaps this is simply out of a sense of realism as to what is, or could be expected to become, available. It could not be for a lack of need for separate information on prices and quantities, for these are among the most basic variables in all of economics; indeed, supply and demand are defined in terms of them. Nor could it be because the information is altogether lacking. After all, exports and imports enter into the computation of GDP, an aggregate for which almost all countries provide estimates in real terms as well as in terms of current-period prices. Rather, what tends to be missing is service-by-service deflators, developed on the basis of a sampling of prices applicable to traded services alone.

One might think the law of one price would allow domestic prices to proxy for international prices. However, the validity of this method for purposes of analyzing trade in specific services tends to be limited by the aggregated nature of the categories for which value data are collected, together with the likelihood that the composition of international transactions within these categories differs significantly from that of domestic transactions and the fact that there may be added costs (which would be reflected in prices) of conducting business across national boundaries. Furthermore, in some cases the output itself—consulting or legal services provided in connection with a large international merger, for example—is almost uniquely defined, with the result that it is difficult even to state the units of output to which the prices apply. While hedonic techniques—through which what might be called "virtual products" are constructed in terms of their underlying characteristics—have been used to good effect to estimate prices of goods that have varied and rapidly changing characteristics (e.g., computers), it stretches the imagination to suppose that data on traded services will be collected in sufficient detail to permit an analogous approach to be used for services anytime soon.

Probably the best that can be expected is for price indexes specific to international transactions to be developed for selected services for which prices can be related to outputs readily and in a manner that can be followed consistently over time. In the United States, for example, the International Price Program of the Bureau of Labor Statistics provides price indexes for international transportation, including passenger transportation. Before expansion of the program was limited due to resource constraints, communication was being considered as an area for future work.

Modes of supply.—Many statisticians must have wondered why it was necessary for the GATS to add such a requirement as mode of supply to a data improvement agenda that was already rather formidable. However, it would have been hard for the GATS to ignore this dimension of services trade, for it is not simply a basis for making commitments under the agreement, but a factor that was reflected in existing barriers. To take medical services as an example, access to a country's local market through movement of natural persons or commercial presence might be effectively restricted through board-certification requirements or the existence of a national health care system, yet the country's own nationals might be free to seek care abroad (consumption abroad mode of supply), and local practitioners might be free to utilize remote diagnostic services (cross-border supply). With policies differentiated in this manner, it was almost a necessity that a mode-of-supply perspective be reflected in the agreement, calling in turn for the establishment of a new statistical domain.

While the need is thus clear, the means of supplying it is not. Although data on transactions between residents and nonresidents will naturally be separated from data on services supplied through foreign affiliates, and mode of supply will occasionally be identifiable as a result of differences in the types of transactors involved (see the next paragraph), the author knows of no data on resident/nonresident trade that are actually collected with a particular view to allocating the transactions by mode of supply. The prospects for this dimension to be reflected in collection efforts are clouded by both practical and conceptual difficulties. Not only would statistical agencies require added resources to collect data by mode of supply, but the companies that must supply the data would face an increase in reporting burden; considering that mode-of-supply is not a dimension ordinarily tracked by corporate accounting systems, the increase could be significant. A further difficulty stems from the fact that transactions involving multiple modes of supply probably are not uncommon.[23]

Considerations such as these suggest that the straightforward addition of a mode-of-supply dimension to statistical questionnaires on trade in services probably is not going to happen in the near or medium term, and perhaps not even in the long term. A more likely, and promising, course is that through study and analysis, the range of uncertainty concerning mode of supply can be

106   Services in the International Economy

narrowed. First steps in this direction are reflected in the above-cited work of Karsenty (2000). Case studies of particular service industries might provide further insights. Finally, a few services may be naturally differentiated along mode-of-supply lines, because of differences in the identity of the participants to the transactions. For example, with respect to educational or medical services, there should be no problem in determining the portion of the total that represents consumption-abroad transactions, inasmuch as these reflect the activities of readily identifiable classes of individuals.

Outward FATS statistics.—As mentioned earlier, a number of countries are beginning to develop statistics on the activities of foreign-owned enterprises in the domestic economy (inward FATS), but only a very small number have collected data on the activities of their own residents' foreign affiliates (outward FATS). Why is this? I believe it is for two basic reasons, both of which may be rooted as much in perceptions as in reality. The first is related to the difficulty in collecting the data; the second, to relative differences in the need for the data. While these factors, individually or in combination, may reasonably lead a country to compile FATS statistics only with respect to inward investment, a case can be made for greater efforts to cover outward investment as well.

First, the issue of difficulty. Unlike statistics on inward FATS, which can often be tabulated simply by identifying the foreign-owned portion of the universe of firms covered by domestic enterprise statistics, developing statistics on outward FATS will invariably entail additional data collection, with attendant increases in the resource requirements of statistical agencies and in the reporting burdens imposed on companies. An added obstacle to data collection that is often cited is the fact that the firms covered by the statistics are located, not in the compiling economy, but abroad. While this should be recognized as an obstacle, regarding it as an overwhelming one probably is not justified. As generally implemented, only majority-owned affiliates are covered by FATS statistics, and basic information on the operations of such affiliates would be needed by the parent company, both to prepare consolidated financial statements for the worldwide enterprise and to manage that enterprise effectively. In addition, a few countries have actually collected outward FATS statistics, thus providing an empirical demonstration of feasibility.

Even if it can be accepted that the development of outward FATS statistics is within the realm of possibility, a country must ask itself if the effort is justified. Here, a reasonable case can be made that inward FATS statistics should be given the higher priority. Under the GATS, countries make commitments with respect to the supply of services in their own economies, not services they supply abroad. Thus, for services supplied via the commercial presence mode, the most directly related data may be those on the activities of foreign-owned firms in the domestic economy. Nonetheless, the reason countries make commitments presumably is to improve their ability to supply services abroad.[24] For commercial presence, this supply is tracked by data on outward FATS, which therefore also must be considered to be relevant.

Whatever the arguments related to needs or practicalities, the reality is that in the near to medium term, far more countries are likely to develop FATS statistics for inward investment than for outward investment. However, because one country's inward FATS statistics are another country's outward FATS statistics, there is the potential for data exchanges to provide countries with information on the overseas activities of their multinational corporations, even if it is through data compiled by partner countries rather than by themselves.[25] The importance of standardized definitions and methodologies in assembling such data is obvious, and in this regard the international organizations can play an important role. In addition, by republishing member-country data, these organizations can, in effect, serve as clearinghouses for the information. The value of such clearinghouses can be considerable, inasmuch as they can help to achieve a kind of consistency in presentation and can reduce the number of contacts required to assemble the data.

VII. Conclusion

As this paper has attempted to demonstrate, considerable progress has been made in improving data on trade in services, yet unmet needs remain. While further progress can be expected, the new requirements for data flowing from the GATS are considerable, and some of them are likely to be met only over an extended period of time or will have to be satisfied through such expediencies as indirect indicators, proxy measures, or data exchanges among partner countries. There is work to do both for national statistical offices, which must collect and compile additional data, and for international organizations, which must assist in developing internationally agreed standards for compilation and which can play an important role in facilitating data exchanges and in disseminating member country data in consistent formats.

Notes

[*] Bureau of Economic Analysis, U.S. Department of Commerce. I would like to thank Bernard Hoekman for providing useful comments on an earlier draft. The views expressed in this paper are those of the author and do not necessarily represent those of the U.S. Department of Commerce.

[1] Despite the difficulties, some efforts to quantify these barriers have been made. For a discussion of the work in this area, see Warren and Findlay, 2000.

[2] See, for example, Stern and Hoekman, 1987.

[3] As many readers are no doubt already aware, the GATS identifies four modes of supply. Three of them subdivide the bulk of the services transactions between residents and nonresidents that are recorded in balance of payments accounts: Cross-border supply (service is transmitted from a producer in one country to a consumer in another country), consumption abroad (purchaser consumes the service in the country of the producer), and presence of natural persons (producer performs the service in the country of the consumer). A fourth mode—commercial presence—covers services supplied

through foreign affiliates or through short-term commercial operations that do not qualify as direct investment (e.g., some construction projects).

[4] Most of the remaining countries did not exist in the same form throughout the period (e.g., Soviet republics that became separate countries) or began reporting during the period.

[5] The IMF Yearbook contains additional detail that is not shown in table 4.1, but all of it is within travel and transportation, many countries did not supply some or all of it, and its addition would in any event still leave the list far more aggregated than the W120 list. The W120 list was originally published in GATT, 1991; a more generally accessible source is United Nations Conference on Trade and Development and the World Bank, 1994, pp. 169-72. For a discussion of linkages between the W120 list and the statistical classifications used by balance of payments compilers, see Henderson, 1997.

[6] Notwithstanding the statement in the text, Karsenty has found it possible to make order-of-magnitude assessments of the relative importance of the different modes of supply, by making assumptions about the various categories of transactions recorded in balance of payments accounts and by examining the available data on activities of foreign affiliates (Karsenty, 2000).

[7] Statistical Office of the European Communities, 1997. In this publication, "FATS" stands for "foreign affiliates trade statistics." In the draft Manual of Statistics of International Trade in Services—described in the next section—the same acronym is used to represent "foreign affiliates trade in services." These terms have largely replaced the term "establishment trade," which for many years was used in trade policy circles as a shorthand way of referring to activities falling under the commercial presence mode of supply.

[8] The greater availability of data for inward investment than for outward investment is likely to be a continuing feature of data on foreign-affiliate operations. For inward investment, it may be possible to develop estimates by linking data on direct investment, which can help to identify the firms in the domestic economy that are foreign-owned, with domestic enterprise statistics. In this way, estimates can often be developed without any actual new data collection being required. For outward investment, in contrast, no such linking opportunities are available, and so new surveys or expansion of existing surveys generally would be required to develop the data. Some of the implications of this situation are considered in the last section of the paper.

[9] See GATS, Article XVIII, Section k.

[10] Commission of the European Communities, International Monetary Fund, Organisation for Economic Co-operation and Development, United Nations, and World Bank, 1993, paragraph 6.3. This definition derives from Hill, 1977, p. 318.

[11] It has been argued, however, that a services aspect may be present in some such cases. Feketekuty has put forth the view that "[t]he globalization of production, which results in the unbundling and distribution of different steps in the production process to different countries gives manufacturing many of the same characteristics as the production of services. . . [I]t can be argued that partial processing of manufactured goods is more effectively treated as the production of a value-added service rather than as the manufacturing of a good" (Feketekuty, 2000).

[12] If the purchase and resale occur in different periods, the purchase is recorded as an import of goods, and the subsequent resale is recorded as a deduction from such imports (i.e., as a negative goods import).

[13] In the SNA, an additional element, represented by income on technical reserves, is included in the insurance service charge for domestic transactions. However, both the SNA and BPM5 indicate that, for practical reasons, this element is to be ignored in the measurement of international trade in insurance. This omission may result in some understatement (similar to the case of "financial intermediation services indirectly measured," discussed below with respect to financial services), though the types of insurance for which income on technical reserves is most important probably are not the ones most important in international trade.

[14] The assistance provided to the UN by the group of country experts known as the Voorburg Group in connection with these classification systems should be acknowledged. This group met for the first time in 1986 (in Voorburg, the site of the Statistics Netherlands headquarters offices), primarily to provide a means through which representatives of national statistical offices could assist the UN Statistical Office with the parts of the classifications dealing with services. Over time, it has evolved into an annual forum for the exchange of views and information on a wide variety of statistical issues pertaining to services.

[15] The existing concordances are with the provisional CPC. Work is underway to create concordances with CPC ver. 1.0.

[16] The CPC is used in this way in the previously cited work of Henderson, relating the W120 list to balance of payments classifications (Henderson, 1997).

[17] It is true, as some have pointed out, that what is recorded under these categories consists of specific goods and services, all of which have a place in the CPC. However, for practical reasons the trade classifications do not call for these to be separately enumerated, either by CPC category or by any other product classification.

[18] For a more detailed account of the U.S. data improvements than will be provided here, see Ascher and Whichard, 1991. Improvements subsequent to this paper are described in various issues of the *Survey of Current Business*, where both the U.S. balance of payments accounts and the U.S. data on foreign affiliate activities are published.

[19] As is well known, a significant share of the demand for traded services is a derived demand, stemming from international trade in goods and flows of capital. For example, a firm in one country may engage an accounting or consulting firm in another country for help in connection with an acquisition of a firm in that other country, or a firm may provide after-sale service and support abroad for its products that are sold in foreign countries.

[20] For more information on the draft manual, see Arkell (1999).

[21] When this survey was instituted in 1986, it collected data for 18 types of services; new services have been added in connection with each subsequent benchmark survey.

[22] Consonant with the topic of this paper, services alone are mentioned in the text; however, these developments obviously also create new potentials for gaps in statistics on trade in goods.

110   Services in the International Economy

[23] As an illustration of a multi-mode transaction, a consultant might go abroad to study a situation on behalf of the client (presence of natural persons mode of supply), then return home to prepare a report, which is then transmitted to the client via a postal or telecommunications link (cross-border supply).

[24] There may be efficiency gains from having more services supplied from abroad, but these could be achieved through unilateral liberalization.

[25] While this approach offers promise as a means of overcoming resource constraints or concerns about reporting burden, one drawback is that it may tend to leave countries, such as many developing countries, that cannot compile statistics for inward investment out in the cold, inasmuch as it deprives them of what might otherwise be a promising source of information on the operations of foreign-owned firms in their own economies (namely, partner countries' statistics for outward investment).

References

Arkell, Julian. 1999. "Manual on Statistics of International Trade in Services," paper prepared for World Services Congress, Atlanta, GA, November.

Ascher, Bernard, and Obie G. Whichard. 1991. Developing a Data System for International Sales of Services: Progress, Problems, and Prospects. In Peter Hooper and J. David Richardson (eds.), *International Economic Transactions: Issues in Measurement and Empirical Research*. Chicago: University of Chicago Press: 203-34.

Commission of the European Communities, International Monetary Fund, Organisation for Economic Co-operation and Development, United Nations, and World Bank. 1993. *System of National Accounts, 1993*. Brussels/Luxembourg, New York, Paris, Washington.

Feketekuty, Geza. 2000. "Assessing the WTO General Agreement on Trade in Services and Improving the GATS Architecture," in Pierre Sauvé and Robert M. Stern (eds.), *Services 2000: New Directions in Services Trade Liberalization*. Washington, D.C.: Brookings Institution.

GATT Secretariat. 1991. *Services Sectoral Classification List*. Document MTN.GNS/W/120. Geneva.

Henderson, Hugh. 1997. "On Building Bridges: A Canadian Perspective on Linking Services Categories of the World Trade Organization and Balance of Payments Compilers," paper presented at Tenth Meeting of IMF Committee on Balance of Payments Statistics. Washington, DC, October.

Hill, T.P. 1977. "On Goods and Services," *Review of Income and Wealth* 23 (December): 315-38.

International Monetary Fund. 1993. *Balance of Payments Manual*, 5th ed. Washington, DC.

International Monetary Fund. 1998. *Balance of Payments Statistics Yearbook*. Washington, DC.

Karsenty, Guy. 2000. "Just How Big Are the Stakes? An Assessment of Trade in Services by Mode of Supply," In Pierre Sauvé and Robert M. Stern (eds.), *Ser-*

vices 2000—New Directions in Services Trade Liberalization. Washington, D.C.: Brookings Institution.

National Research Council, Panel on Foreign Trade Statistics. 1992. *Behind the Numbers*, Anne Y. Kester, ed. Washington, DC: National Academy Press.

Organisation for Economic Co-Operation and Development. 1996. *OECD Benchmark Definition of Foreign Direct Investment*, 3rd edition. Paris.

Organisation for Economic Co-Operation and Development. 1999. *Services: Statistics on International Transactions, 1987-96*. Paris.

Statistical Office of the European Communities (Directorate B, Unit B-5). 1997. *Fats Task Force Report*, January.

Stern, Robert M., and Bernard M. Hoekman. 1987. "Issues and Data Needs for GATT Negotiations on Services," *World Economy* 10 (March): 39-60.

United Nations Conference on Trade and Development and the World Bank. 1994. *Liberalizing International Transactions in Services: A Handbook*. New York and Geneva.

United Nations, Department of Economic and Social Affairs, Statistics Division. 1998. *Central Product Classification (CPC)*, version 1.0 (United Nations, Statistical Papers, Series M, No. 77, Ver. 1.0).

United Nations. 1990. *International Standard Industrial Classification of All Economic Activities*, Statistical Papers, Series M, No. 4, Rev. 3. New York.

U.S. Congress, Office of Technology Assessment. 1986. *Trade in Services: Exports and Foreign Revenues—Special Report*, OTA-ITE-316. Washington, DC: U.S. Government Printing Office, September.

Warren, Tony, and Christopher Findlay. 2000. "How Significant are the Barriers? Measuring Impediments to Trade in Services," in Pierre Sauvé and Robert M. Stern (eds.), *Services 2000: New Directions in Services Trade Liberalization*. Washington, D.C.: Brookings Institution.

Whichard, Obie G. 1984. "U.S. International Trade and Investment in Services: Data Needs and Availability," U.S. Department of Commerce, Bureau of Economic Analysis, Staff Paper 41.

112   Services in the International Economy

Annex—Joint OECD-Eurostat Trade In Services Classification

*1. Transportation

    *1.1 Sea transport
      *1.1.1 Passenger
      *1.1.2 Freight
      *1.1.3 Other

    *1.2 Air transport
      *1.2.1 Passenger
      *1.2.2 Freight
      *1.2.3 Other

    1.3 Other transport
      1.3.1 Passenger
      1.3.2 Freight
      1.3.3 Other

Extended classification of other transport (1.3)
1.4 Space transport
1.5 Rail transport
    1.5.1 Passenger
    1.5.2 Freight
    1.5.3 Other

1.6 Road transport
    1.6.1 Passenger
    1.6.2 Freight
    1.6.3 Other

1.7 Internal waterway transport
    1.7.1 Passenger
    1.7.2 Freight
    1.7.3 Other

1.8 Pipeline transport

1.9 Other supporting and auxiliary transport services

Memorandum items
Freight transportation on the basis of an ex works valuation of mer

chandise:
Sea freight
Air freight
Road freight
Other freight

*2. Travel*2.1 Business
        2.1.1 Expenditure by seasonal and border workers
        2.1.2 Other

    *2.2 Personal
        *2.2.1 Health-related
        *2.2.2 Education-related
        *2.2.3 Other

Memorandum items:
        Tourists
        Goods purchased in the frontier area by travelers
        Hotel and restaurant services

*3. Communications services
        3.1 Postal and courier services
        3.2 Telecommunication services

    Memorandum items
    Postal services
    Courier services

    *4. Construction services
        4.1 Construction abroad
        4.2 Construction in the compiling economy

    *5. Insurance services
        5.1 Life insurance and pension funding
        5.2 Freight insurance
        5.3 Other direct insurance
        5.4 Reinsurance
        5.5 Auxiliary services

        Memorandum item
        Gross insurance premiums
        Gross insurance claims

*6. Financial services

114   Services in the International Economy

*7. Computer and information services
    7.1 Computer services
    7.2 Information services

*8. Royalties and license fees

*9. Other business services

      *9.1 Merchanting and other trade-related services
        9.1.1 Merchanting
        9.1.2 Other
      *9.2 Operational leasing services

     *9.3 Miscellaneous business, professional, and technical services
       *9.3.1 Legal, accounting, management consulting, and public relations
         9.3.1.1 Legal services
         9.3.1.2 Accounting, auditing, book-keeping and tax consulting services
         9.3.1.3 Business and management consultancy and public relations services
       *9.3.2 Advertising, market research, and public opinion polling
       *9.3.3 Research and development
       *9.3.4 Architectural, engineering and other technical services
       *9.3.5 Agricultural, mining and on-site processing services
         9.3.5.1 Waste treatment and depollution
         9.3.5.2 Other
     9.3.6 Other
     9.3.7 Services between affiliated enterprises, n.i.e.

     Memorandum items
      Merchanting gross flows
      Agricultural services
      Mining services

*10. Personal, cultural, and recreational services
    *10.1 Audiovisual and related services
    *10.2 Other personal, cultural and recreational services

*11. Government services, n.i.e.
    11.1 Embassies and consulates
    11.2 Military units and agencies
    11.3 Other

Note.—Items marked with an asterisk (*) are listed in BPM5 as standard components or "services sub-items" (items suggested to be provided as supplementary information).

Source: OECD. 1999.

[11]
Measuring U.S. International Goods and Services Transactions

Robert E. Baldwin and Fukunari Kimura

1.1 Introduction

One of the roles of economists concerned with organizing national and international economic data into meaningful accounting formats is to ask periodically whether existing sets of accounts adequately describe important economic trends and are as useful to public and private policymakers as possible. The Panel on Foreign Trade Statistics established under the auspices of the National Academy of Sciences (NAS) in 1989 (which Baldwin chaired) considered addressing this question to be an important part of its task. In particular, it focused on whether existing ways of presenting data on firms' cross-border trading activities and the sales and purchasing activities of their foreign affiliates adequately captured the close relationship between these two types of international economic transactions.

The panel concluded that the present system of economic accounting could be improved in this regard and recommended that cross-border sales (exports) and purchases (imports) of goods and services as well as net sales of foreign affiliates of U.S. firms (FAUSFs) and net sales to U.S. affiliates of foreign firms (USAFFs) be presented on an ownership basis to supplement the residency approach followed in the balance-of-payments accounts (National Research Council 1992).[1] In the net sales calculations, the selling and purchasing activities of firms are measured as those undertaken by the firms' capital own-

Robert E. Baldwin is professor emeritus of economics at the University of Wisconsin–Madison and a research associate of the National Bureau of Economic Research. Fukunari Kimura is associate professor of economics at Keio University.

The authors gratefully acknowledge financial support from the Ford Foundation and Keio University. They also thank especially Robert E. Lipsey and J. David Richardson for helpful comments.

1. It should be emphasized that the panel did not propose that the existing framework for the balance of payments be changed but rather that additional information on international transactions be presented in supplementary accounting formats.

10   Robert E. Baldwin and Fukunari Kimura

ers and employees, that is, by the productive factors used directly to create value added by the firm. Thus, net sales of foreign affiliates are defined as sales less purchases of intermediate goods and services.[2] This suggested supplemental framework combines net cross-border sales of Americans to foreigners, net sales by FAUSFs to foreigners, and net sales of U.S. firms to USAFFs to yield a figure that shows net sales of Americans to foreigners. The panel report also estimated value added on this basis, and we believe that measuring cross-border and foreign affiliate activities on a value-added basis is also a useful accounting format for representing international transactions. However, fundamentally, the usefulness of these as well as existing or other formats depends on the purpose for which the information is utilized.

The outline of the paper is as follows. Section 1.2 discusses the need for a supplementary framework and its benefits to both private and public officials. Section 1.3 considers various conceptual and practical issues that arise in measuring cross-border and foreign affiliate activities on a net sales basis and also discusses some of the key relationships brought out in the tables measuring international transactions on an ownership basis over the period 1987–92. Measurements of cross-border and direct investment activities on a value-added basis for this period are presented in section 1.4, and important relationships based on this approach are discussed. Section 1.5 presents net sales figures on an industry basis and includes an analysis of the international structure and relative competitiveness of American industries that these figures reveal. Section 1.6 briefly summarizes the main argument of the paper.

1.2   The Need for a Supplementary Framework

A key aspect of the increasing internationalization of economic activities is that firms have found they can profitably exploit their unique technological and managerial knowledge by establishing production units in foreign countries as well as by exporting to or importing from foreign firms or permitting foreign firms to use their specialized knowledge. Thus, when supplying goods and services to foreign markets, business decision makers consider the alternatives of producing the goods and services domestically and exporting them or undertaking direct foreign investment and producing them in their facilities abroad. If they do choose to produce abroad, firms must also decide on the extent to which they will export components for further processing in their overseas facilities or purchase the needed intermediate inputs abroad. To compare the economic importance of these alternative means of serving foreign markets, it is necessary to have comparable data with respect to these different activities.

---

2. Consequently, purchases from foreigners by FAUSFs, e.g., include purchases by the firms of intermediate goods and services from foreign-owned firms located abroad but do not include the cost of foreign labor hired directly by the affiliates of U.S. firms.

11   Measuring U.S. International Goods and Services Transactions

The current set of accounts documenting the international activities of U.S. and foreign firms does not provide such comparability. The balance of payments summarizes international transactions between residents of one country and residents of other countries. Total merchandise and service exports and imports of firms residing in the United States and in other countries are recorded, but no information is provided concerning whether the exports are shipped from U.S.-owned firms to FAUSFs or USAFFs to their foreign parents. Imports also are not distinguished on an ownership basis. Furthermore, since total exports include imported inputs, one is not able to compare properly the relative importance of value added through export activities with value added through affiliate activities or with total value added (GDP).

More important, the only measure of the level of activity of FAUSFs or USAFFs in the balance of payments is the income earned on U.S. direct investment abroad and on foreign direct investment in the United States. Comparing these income receipts and cross-border merchandise and service trade leads to an apples-and-oranges adding problem. The balance-of-payments framework measures the participation of U.S.-owned firms located in the United States in cross-border activities by their sales but measures their participation in direct investment activities abroad by the income earned on these direct investment activities. Since exports and direct investment income are not comparable (the first is a sales figure, while the second represents factor income), one does not get an adequate picture of the nature of firms' international activities from the balance of payments.

Economic data on sales and purchases of foreign affiliates of domestic firms and domestic affiliates of foreign firms are available for the United States and Japan, but these are presented in other sets of accounts constructed by these governments.[3] The U.S. government, for example, annually publishes data on the operations of U.S. parent companies and their foreign affiliates and the operations of USAFFs. These reports provide information on the cross-border trade between parent firms and their foreign affiliates as well as on the foreign sales and purchases of foreign affiliates. However, prior to the work of DeAnne Julius (1990, 1991) and an earlier study by Evelyn Lederer, Walter Lederer, and Robert Sammons (1982), no effort apparently had been made to integrate information in both sets of accounts as a means of better understanding the nature of the increasing globalization of economic activities.

Not only are supplementary statistical summaries of cross-border and foreign-based transactions of firms needed to improve our understanding of the evolving international economy, but such accounting frameworks would be helpful to government officials in reaching policy decisions. As the various papers in this conference volume indicate, ownership as well as geography matters for economic behavior. For example, the domestic content of foreign-

---

3. Purchases by FAUSFs can only be estimated indirectly.

owned firms in the United States, though high, is substantially lower than that
of domestic U.S.-owned firms. Similarly, plants owned by foreign multinational companies are more capital intensive, more technology intensive, and
more productive and pay higher wages than the average U.S. plant. Moreover,
the output of these firms is generally growing at a different (sometime faster,
sometime slower) pace than is output of domestically owned firms. National
tax rules also affect the way in which foreign-owned firms report taxable income, price their products, and locate their production activities in a manner
that differs from the behavior of domestic firms. Furthermore, foreign affiliates
may respond differently to domestic monetary policies than domestically
owned firms do because their access to international capital markets is likely
to be better. Since these various differences are important for a variety of macroeconomic and microeconomic policy decisions by governments, it is useful
to have an accounting framework that facilitates the comparison and interpretation of the differences. However, quite aside from the various differences in
economic behavior between domestically owned and foreign-owned firms, it
seems prudent on national security grounds to measure the cross-border and
affiliate activities of U.S.-owned and foreign-owned firms on a comparable
basis.

Expressing cross-border and affiliate activities in comparable terms can also
be helpful to trade negotiators. Increasingly, it is the objective of governments
not only to reduce the restrictive effects of traditional border measures but to
reduce the discriminatory effects of various rules and regulations imposed by
other governments that restrict the selling and buying activities of foreign affiliates within foreign markets. To determine the extent to which a country's
negotiators have achieved both objectives, it is necessary to assess the liberalization achieved in both areas in a comparable manner, a goal that is not attained by only utilizing the information available in the balance of payments.
Furthermore, the proposed accounting frameworks are helpful in informing
the ongoing debate on American competitiveness in the world economy. By
providing data on the extent to which U.S. firms compete against foreign firms
through sales and purchases from their foreign-based operations as well as
through their cross-border sales and purchases, government officials can better
inform the public on this issue.[4]

Of course, for most public policy and research issues, the relevant relationships are the level of domestic activity, regardless of whether it is undertaken
by domestically owned or foreign-owned firms, and the income accruing to
U.S.-owned firms from their foreign investment activities rather than the level
of activities of their foreign affiliates. The traditional residency approach followed in the balance of payments remains the appropriate accounting framework to utilize under these circumstances.

---

4. However, as Guy Stevens points out in his comment on this paper, no simple accounting
measure can accurately measure the many different meanings of international competitiveness.

13   Measuring U.S. International Goods and Services Transactions

1.3   Measuring Cross-Border and Direct Investment Activities on a Net Sales Basis

1.3.1   Some Conceptual Issues

The first issue that arises in estimating net sales of goods and services by Americans to foreigners is how to define U.S.-owned and foreign-owned firms. For balance-of-payments purposes, the Bureau of Economic Analysis (BEA) regards a business located abroad (in the United States) as representing U.S. (foreign) direct investment if one U.S. (foreign) person, in the legal sense that includes a firm, controls 10 percent or more of the voting securities of the business. Under such a practice, two or more countries can treat the same firm as a foreign affiliate. This will lead to double counting of total sales and purchases for the world if an affiliate is assigned to each country. One way of avoiding this problem would be to allocate the sales and purchases of affiliates in proportion to the ownership interests of the different countries. Another would be to include only those affiliates that are majority owned, that is, affiliates in which the combined ownership of those persons individually owning 10 percent or more of the voting stock from a particular country exceeds 50 percent. One could assign all sales and purchases of affiliates to countries with majority ownership interests or only the proportions equal to the ownership interests.

The procedure followed here is to treat only majority-owned affiliates as U.S.-owned or foreign-owned firms and assign all the sales and purchases to either the United States or foreigners, depending on who has the majority ownership interest. Unfortunately, while data on the sales and purchases of goods and services are available for majority-owned FAUSFs, data on majority-owned USAFFs, although collected, are not published. In the tables included in this paper, figures on these affiliates cover firms in which the ownership interest is only 10 percent or more.[5]

Another problem in identifying U.S.-owned and foreign-owned firms is that some FAUSFs may belong to U.S. firms that are themselves USAFFs, and some USAFFs may belong to foreign firms that are themselves FAUSFs. Unfortunately, the data for identifying such firms and properly classifying them as foreign-owned and domestically owned firms are not available. Still another issue in estimating net sales of Americans to foreigners is the lack of data on sales and purchases of U.S. citizens living abroad and households of foreign citizens living in the United States. Because of this problem, it is necessary to classify households on a country-of-residence basis, as in the balance-of-payments statistics. That is, the household of a private foreign citizen in the United States (not employed by a foreign government) is combined with house-

---

5. An exception is service data from DiLullo and Whichard (1990) and Sondheimer and Bargas (1992, 1993, 1994), which cover majority-owned USAFFs.

14   Robert E. Baldwin and Fukunari Kimura

holds of U.S. citizens living in the United States and the U.S. government and regarded as an American unit. Similarly, the household of a private U.S. citizen living abroad (not employed by the U.S. government) is combined with households of foreign citizens living abroad and foreign governments and regarded as a foreign unit.

The focus is on identifying the selling and purchasing activities of FAUSFs and USAFFs. Thus, the term "Americans," as used here, refers to U.S.-owned firms in the United States and abroad, households of U.S. and private foreign citizens residing in the United States (U.S.-resident households), and U.S. government units. Similarly, the term "foreigners" refers to foreign-owned firms in the United States and abroad, households of foreign and U.S. citizens residing abroad (foreign-resident households), and foreign governments.

In comparing the net sales of Americans to foreigners over time, it is, of course, necessary to deflate the value figures by appropriate price indexes. Cross-border sales should be deflated by U.S. export and import price series, while the appropriate deflator for net sales to USAFFs is an index of U.S. producer prices. Net sales of FAUSFs should be deflated by a weighted average of foreign producer prices, where the weights reflect the relative importance of the sales of FAUSFs across the countries.[6]

1.3.2 Estimates of Net Sales of Americans to Foreigners

Estimates of the net balance of sales by Americans to foreigners for 1987–92 are presented in table 1.1. The net sales figure is the sum of three parts: (1) cross-border sales to and purchases from foreigners by Americans, (2) sales to and purchases from foreigners by FAUSFs, and (3) sales to and purchases from USAFFs by Americans. Panel I of the table indicates cross-border sales (exports) to and purchases (imports) from foreigners only. Cross-border sales to foreigners are obtained by subtracting from total exports of goods and services both U.S. exports to FAUSFs and U.S. exports shipped by USAFFs.[7] Since the first export figure represents sales by U.S.-owned firms and U.S. private residents to U.S.-owned firms located abroad and the second represents sales of foreign-owned firms to foreigners abroad, both must be excluded in estimating sales by U.S.-owned domestic firms and U.S. private residents in the United States to foreigners abroad. In 1987 exports of U.S. firms to their foreign affiliates equaled 25 percent of total exports, while exports of U.S. affiliates of foreign firms amounted to another 15 percent. In 1991 these figures

---

6. A problem of growing importance with regard to measuring cross-border trade is that many goods and services now pass across borders with no transactions taking place. Consequently, cross-border flows are increasingly imputations, akin to those for the services of owner-occupied housing. Moreover, for many internationally traded goods and services, there are no markets comparable to the rental market for homes from which to draw prices in imputing the value of trade.

7. These subtractions exclude both intrafirm exports and exports to FAUSFs by nonaffiliated U.S.-owned firms and by USAFFs to nonaffiliated foreigners. The BEA surveys on U.S. investment abroad collect the data needed to divide exports into these different categories, if such a breakdown is desired.

15   Measuring U.S. International Goods and Services Transactions

were 23 and 18 percent, respectively. The estimate of cross-border sales (exports) to foreigners by Americans in 1991 is $344,725 million. (Data for 1991 rather than 1992 are cited in the text, since the figures for 1992 are preliminary.)

The $344,725 million figure is only an approximate estimate for several reasons.[8] For example, since exports by USAFFs to FAUSFs are included in both U.S. exports to FAUSFs and in U.S. exports shipped by USAFFs, this amount is subtracted twice from total exports of goods and services. Also, data on U.S. exports of services to FAUSFs, which should be subtracted from total exports of services, are not available except for the sales of some services by U.S. parent companies to their foreign affiliates. These divergences between the desired and actual figures are not likely to be large, however.

Cross-border purchases (imports) of goods and services from foreigners are estimated in a manner similar to cross-border sales. U.S. imports from FAUSFs and U.S. imports shipped to USAFFs are both subtracted from total imports of goods and services in order to obtain just the trade between Americans and foreigners.[9] In 1987 U.S. imports from FAUSFs amounted to 15 percent of total imports, while imports shipped to USAFFs were equal to 29 percent of total imports. By 1991 the first ratio had risen to 17 percent and the second to 31 percent. As before, the $320,364 million estimate of purchases by Americans from foreigners for 1991 is only approximate because of the double subtraction of U.S. imports from FAUSFs going to USAFFs and the absence of data on service imports shipped to USAFFs, except for some services obtained by USAFFs from their foreign parent companies.

A more serious problem concerns the subtraction of merchandise imports going not just to USAFFs where the ownership interest is 50 percent or more but to USAFFs with an ownership interest of 10 percent or more. This causes the import figure of $320,364 million to be too small compared to the export figure and thus the estimate of the surplus in net cross-border sales, namely, $24,361 million, to be too large.

Estimates of sales and purchases by FAUSFs are presented in panel II of table 1.1. To obtain net sales of these firms to foreigners, it is necessary to subtract both sales among themselves and sales to the United States from their total sales. This yields sales to foreigners of $898,046 million. This figure also is only an approximation of the desired number, since it improperly excludes the sales of FAUSFs to USAFFs. But, again, this exclusion is likely to be comparatively small.

No direct data are available on the purchases of intermediate goods and services by FAUSFs, let alone their purchases of these goods and services from foreigners. A rough estimate of purchases of goods from foreigners by

---

8. For a detailed discussion of the differences between the estimate of net sales by Americans to foreigners and the conceptually correct measure, see National Research Council (1992, app. A).

9. The same point about intrafirm and arm's-length transactions made in n. 7 also applies here.

Table 1.1   Net Sales of Goods and Services by Americans and Foreigners, 1987–92 (in millions of dollars)

Transaction	1987	1988	1989	1990	1991	1992
I. Cross-border sales to and purchases from foreigners by Americans						
Exports to foreigners						
+ U.S. exports of merchandise and services	348,024	430,216	488,955	537,605	581,197	619,848
− U.S. exports to FAUSFs	87,647	106,036	117,218	122,631	132,352	139,587
− U.S. exports shipped by USAFFs	51,843	73,520	92,024	99,185	104,120	108,166
Total	208,534	250,660	279,713	315,789	344,725	372,095
Imports from foreigners						
+ U.S. imports of merchandise and services	500,005	545,040	579,300	615,986	609,117	659,575
− U.S. imports from FAUSFs	75,986	86,053	94,703	100,721	102,879	110,939
− U.S. imports shipped to USAFFs	146,985	159,400	176,607	188,687	185,874	189,849
Total	277,034	299,587	307,990	326,578	320,364	358,787
Net cross-border sales by Americans to foreigners	−68,500	−48,927	−28,277	−10,789	24,361	13,308
II. Sales to and purchases from foreigners by FAUSFs						
Sales by FAUSFs						
+ Sales by FAUSFs	815,541	927,886	999,506	1,184,823	1,213,719	1,266,717
− Sales among FAUSFs	125,107	144,401	150,392	186,427	194,133	215,797
− Sales to the United States by FAUSFs	88,923	101,444	111,106	120,437	121,540	126,378
Total	601,511	682,041	738,008	877,959	898,046	924,542
Purchases abroad from foreigners by FAUSFs	358,715	395,973	431,885	541,755	559,050	575,265
Net sales to foreigners by FAUSFs	242,796	286,068	306,123	336,204	338,996	349,277
III. U.S. sales to and purchases from USAFFs						
U.S. sales to USAFFs	425,915	523,318	646,596	727,988	735,018	757,244
U.S. purchases from USAFFs						
+ Sales by USAFFs	723,956	860,037	1,022,163	1,139,792	1,142,903	1,181,633
− Sales among USAFFs	n.a.	n.a.	n.a.	n.a.	n.a.	n.a.

– U.S. exports shipped by USAFFs	51,843	73,520	92,024	99,185	104,120	108,166
Total	672,113	786,517	930,139	1,040,607	1,038,783	1,073,467
Net sales to USAFFs	–246,198	–263,199	–283,543	–312,619	–303,765	–316,223
IV. *Net sales by Americans to foreigners*	–71,902	–26,058	–5,697	12,796	59,592	46,362
Reference						
Cross-border merchandise trade balance	–159,557	–126,959	–115,249	–109,033	–73,802	–96,138
Cross-border trade balance of merchandise and services	–151,981	–114,824	–90,345	–78,381	–27,920	–39,727

Estimation Procedure and Data Sources: Cross-border trade data are on a calendar-year basis, while data on FAUSFs and USAFFs are on a financial-year basis. Data on FAUSFs are for majority-owned nonbank affiliates, while data on USAFFs are for nonbank affiliates with an ownership of 10 percent or more, except for data from DiLullo and Whichard (1990) and Sondheimer and Bargas (1992, 1993, 1994). In the following, figures in parentheses are for 1987, 1988, 1989, 1990, 1991, and 1992, respectively.

U.S. exports of merchandise and services: U.S. merchandise exports (250,208; 320,230; 362,116; 389,303; 416,937; 440,138) and U.S. service exports (97,816; 109,986; 126,839; 148,302; 164,260; 179,710) are from Murad (1993, 71, table 1).

U.S. exports to FAUSFs: U.S. exports of goods to FAUSFs (74,907; 90,780; 97,488; 100,232; 108,839; 114,139) are from FAUSF87, 88 (table 51), 89, 90, 91, 92 (table III.H.2). U.S. exports of services to FAUSFs are not directly available; royalties and license fees (7,400; 8,893; 10,613; 12,867; 13,819; 15,226) and other private services (5,340; 6,363; 9,117; 9,532; 9,694; 10,222) received by U.S. parent companies from their foreign affiliates, obtained from Sondheimer and Bargas (1992, tables 4.2, 4.3, 6.1, 6.2) for 1987 and 1988 data; Sondheimer and Bargas (1993, tables 4.1, 6.1) for 1989 data; and Sondheimer and Bargas (1994, tables 4.1, 4.2, 4.3, 6.1, 6.2) for 1990, 1991, and 1992 data.

U.S. exports shipped by USAFFs: U.S. exports of goods shipped by USAFFs (48,091; 69,541; 86,316; 92,308; 96,933; 100,615) are from USAFF87, 88, 89, 90, 91, 92 (table G-1). U.S. exports of services shipped by USAFFs (3,752; 3,979; 5,708; 6,877; 7,187; 7,551) are from DiLullo and Whichard (1990, table 11) for 1987 and 1988 data; Sondheimer and Bargas (1992, table 10) for 1989 data; Sondheimer and Bargas (1993, table 10) for 1990 data; and Sondheimer and Bargas (1994, table 10) for 1991 and 1992 data.

U.S. imports of merchandise and services: U.S. merchandise imports (409,765; 447,189; 477,365; 498,336; 490,739; 536,276) and U.S. service imports (90,240; 97,851; 101,935; 117,650; 118,378; 123,299) are from Murad (1993, 71, table 1).

U.S. imports from FAUSFs: U.S. merchandise imports from FAUSFs (65,542; 75,578; 84,298; 88,641; 90,512; 98,850) and U.S. service imports (10,444; 10,475; 10,405; 12,080; 12,367; 12,089) are from FAUSF87, 88 (tables 51, 42), 89, 90, 91, 92 (tables III.H.2, F.18).

U.S. imports shipped to USAFFs: U.S. merchandise imports to USAFFs (143,537; 155,533; 171,847; 182,936; 178,702; 182,152) are from USAFF87, 88, 89, 90, 91, 92 (table G-1). U.S. service imports are not directly available; royalties and license fees (1,141; 1,285; 1,632; 1,967; 2,830; 3,069) and other private services (2,307; 2,582; 3,128; 3,784; 4,342; 4,628) paid by USAFFs to their foreign parents, obtained from Sondheimer and Bargas (1992, tables 4.2, 4.3, 6.1, 6.2) for 1987 and 1988 data; Sondheimer and Bargas (1993, tables 4.1, 6.1) for 1989 data; and Sondheimer and Bargas (1994, tables 4.1, 4.2, 4.3, 6.1, 6.2) for 1990, 91, 92 data.

(continued)

Table 1.1   (continued)

Sales by FAUSFs: Sales of goods by FAUSFs (718,086; 816,597; 889,875; 1,051,484; 1,069,729; 1,113,043) and sales of services by FAUSFs (97,455; 111,289; 109,631; 133,339; 143,990; 153,674) are from FAUSF87, 88 (tables 40, 42), 89, 90, 91, 92 (tables III.F.14, F.18).

Sales among FAUSFs: Sales of goods by FAUSFs to other foreign affiliates (110,606; 128,425; 137,587; 173,671; 181,112; 200,761) and sales of services by FAUSFs to other foreign affiliates (14,501; 15,976; 12,805; 12,756; 13,021; 15,036) are from FAUSF87, 88 (tables 40, 42), 89, 90, 91, 92 (tables III.F.14, F.18).

Sales to the Unites States by FAUSFs: Sales of goods by FAUSFs to the United States (78,479; 90,969; 100,701; 108,357; 109,173; 114,289) and sales of services by FAUSFs to the United States (10,444; 10,475; 10,405; 12,080; 12,367; 12,089) are from FAUSF87, 88 (tables 40, 42), 89, 90, 91, 92 (tables III.F.14, F.18).

Purchases abroad from foreigners by FAUSFs: Purchases of goods abroad from foreigners by FAUSFs (309,137; 705,845; 779,024; 934,474; 970,398; 1,021,043: FAUSF87 [table 28], 88 [table 33]—see below for calculation of 1989, 1990, 1991, and 1992 figures) employee compensation (105,452; 117,418; 132,565; 151,051; 160,082; 169,623: FAUSF87, 88 [table 49], 89 [table III.G.2], 90, 91, 92 [table III.G.7]), depreciation, depletion, [and like charges] (24,847; 26,245; 29,191; 33,190; 33,542; 37,095: FAUSF87 [table 28], 88 [table 33], 89 [table III.D.2], 90, 91, 92 [table III.E.2]), production royalty payments (3,384; 2,677; 3,285; 3,424; 3,551; 3,542: FAUSF87 [table 28], 88 [table 33], 89 [table III.J.2], 90, 91, 92 [table III.E.2]), purchases from other FAUSFs (equal to sales among FAUSFs; see above for data sources), and U.S. exports shipped to FAUSF (74,907; 90,780; 97,488; 100,232; 108,839; 114,139: see above for data sources).

For 1989, 1990, 1991, and 1992, first sum up "cost of goods sold and selling, general, and administrative expenses" (913,308; 1,080,482; 1,126,092; 1,183,876: FAUSF89, 90, 91, 92 [table III.E.2]) and "other costs and expenses" (41,317; 64,634; 63,046; 67,322: FAUSF89, 90, 91, 92 [table III.E.2] and multiply it by the 1988 ratio of "cost of goods sold" (705,845; FAUSF88) to the sum of "cost of goods sold" and "other costs and expenses" (705,845 + 159,106: FAUSF88) to obtain cost of goods sold in 1989, 1990, and 1991 (779,024; 934,474; 970,398; 1,021,043). Then follow the same procedure as for 1987 and 1988.

Purchases of services abroad from foreigners by FAUSFs (48,774; 55,573; 52,977; 68,849; 75,778; 79,382) are estimated as follows: major sectors for service sales are finance, insurance, and services. Thus, estimate purchases/sales ratio of 0.78 from the sales and purchases data of these sectors of USAFFs from Lowe (1990, table 6). Then multiply total sales of services by FAUSFs (97,455; 111,289; 109,631; 133,339; 143,990; 153,674: see above for data sources) by 0.78 to obtain total purchases of services (76,015; 86,805; 85,512; 104,004; 112,312; 119,866). Subtract U.S. exports of services to FAUSF (7,400 + 5,340; 8,893 + 6,363; 10,613 + 9,117; 12,867 + 9,532; 13,819 + 9,694; 15,226 + 10,222: see above for data sources) and sales of services by FAUSFs to other foreign affiliates (14,501; 15,976; 12,805; 12,756; 13,021; 15,036: see above for data sources) from total purchases of services (76,015; 86,805; 85,512; 104,004; 112,312; 119,866).

The sum of local purchases of goods abroad by FAUSFs (309,941; 340,400; 378,908; 472,906; 483,272; 495,883) and those of services (48,774; 55,573; 52,977; 68,849; 75,778; 79,382) is local purchases abroad by FAUSFs (358,715; 395,973; 431,885; 541,755; 559,050; 575,265).

U.S. sales to USAFFs: U.S. sales of goods to USAFFs or local purchases of goods by USAFFs (356,963; 434,310; 533,167; 604,544; 602,465; 622,597) are estimated as follows: subtract from cost of goods sold (616,310; 733,908; 877,203; 984,080; 993,949; 1,024,825: USAFF87 [table E-1]—see below for 1988–91), employee compensation (96,009; 119,588; 144,158; 163,592; 175,969; 181,709: USAFF87, 88, 89, 90, 91, 92 [table F-1]), depletion and depreciation (19,801; 24,477; 28,031; 33,008; 36,813; 38,367: USAFF87, 88, 89, 90, 91, 92 [table D-8]), and U.S. merchandise imports shipped to USAFFs (143,537; 155,533; 171,847; 182,936; 178,702; 182,152: see above for data sources).

For 1988–91, first multiply "cost of goods sold and selling, general, and administrative expenses" (859,963; 1,027,871; 1,153,105; 1,164,669; 1,200,848: USAFF88, 89, 90, 91, 92 [table E-1]) by the 1987 ratio of "cost of goods sold" (616,310: USAFF87 [table E-1]) to the sum of "cost of goods sold" and "selling, general, and administrative expenses" (616,310 + 105,857: USAFF87 [table E-1]) to obtain cost of goods sold in 1988–91 (733,908; 877,203; 984,080; 993,949; 1,024,825). Then follow the same procedure as for 1987.

U.S. sales of services to USAFFs or local purchases of services by USAFFs (68,952; 89,008; 113,429; 123,444; 132,553; 134,647) are estimated as follows: major sectors for service sales are finance, insurance, and services. Thus, use again the estimate of purchases/sales ratio of 0.78 calculated above. Multiply total sales of services by USAFFs (92,820; 119,071; 151,524; 165,634; 179,135; 182,492: USAFF87, 88, 89, 90, 91, 92 [table E-12]) by 0.78 to obtain total purchases of services (72,400; 92,875; 118,189; 129,195; 139,725; 142,344). Subtract U.S. imports of services shipped to USAFFs (1,141 + 2,307; 1,285 + 2,582; 1,632 + 3,128; 1,967 + 3,784; 2,830 + 4,342; 3,069 + 4,628: see above for data sources) from total purchases of services (72,400; 92,875; 118,189; 129,195; 139,725; 142,344).

The sum of U.S. sales of goods to USAFFs (356,963; 434,310; 533,167; 604,544; 602,465; 622,597) and those of services (68,952; 89,008; 113,429; 123,444; 132,553; 134,647) is U.S. sales to USAFFs (425,915; 523,318; 646,596; 727,988; 735,018; 757,244).

Sales by USAFFs: Sales of goods by USAFFs (631,136; 740,966; 870,639; 974,158; 963,768; 999,141) and sales of services by USAFFs (92,820; 119,071; 151,524; 165,634; 179,135; 182,492) are from USAFF87, 88, 89, 90, 91, 92 (table E-12).

Sales among USAFFs: Not available.

Cross-border merchandise trade balance: From Murad (1993, 71).

Cross-border trade balance of merchandise and services: From Murad (1993, 71).

Note: FAUSFs: foreign affiliates of U.S. firms abroad; USAFFs: U.S. affiliates of foreign firms in the United States.

FAUSFs is obtained by subtracting employee compensation, depreciation, depletion, and other charges, production royalty payments, purchases from other FAUSFs, and U.S. exports shipped to FAUSFs from the cost of goods sold. Purchases of services from foreigners are estimated by applying the ratio of total purchases of USAFFs by the finance, insurance, and service sectors to the total sales of these sectors, namely, 0.78 (as calculated from Lowe 1990), to the total sales of services by FAUSFs to yield a total purchases estimate. A part of imports of services from the United States and purchases from other FAUSFs are then subtracted from the total purchases figure to yield the estimate of local purchases of services from foreigners. Adding this to the sum for goods yields a total of $559,050 million for local purchases for goods and services by FAUSFs. Since these calculations only approximate the purchases of intermediate goods and services, the figure of net sales to foreigners by FAUSFs ($338,996 million) must be interpreted carefully.

Panel III of table 1.1 presents the estimates of net sales by Americans to USAFFs. Again, the data on U.S. sales of goods and services to USAFFs, or, in other words, local purchases of intermediate goods and services by USAFFs, are not available directly. The estimate of U.S. sales of goods to USAFFs is obtained by a procedure similar to the one used in estimating local purchases by FAUSFs, except that there are no data on production royalty payments and purchases from other USAFFs. U.S. sales of services to USAFFs are also estimated in a manner similar to local purchases of services by FAUSFs. The sum of U.S. sales of goods and services is $735,018 million. U.S. purchases of goods and services from USAFFs, or, in other words, sales to Americans by USAFFs, are estimated by subtracting U.S. exports shipped by USAFFs from total sales by USAFFs. The 1991 estimate of this figure is $1,038,783 million. Data on sales among USAFFs are not available. Thus, the estimate of net U.S. sales of goods and services to USAFFs is −$303,765 million.

By summing up the three components, we obtain an estimate of net sales of goods and services by Americans to foreigners in 1991 of $59,592 million (panel IV of table 1.1). The conventional cross-border trade balance in 1991 was −$27,920 million, as shown at the bottom of the table. The estimates of net sales by Americans to foreigners for 1987, 1988, 1989, 1990, and 1992 are −$71,902, −$26,058, −$5,697, $12,796, and $46,362 million, respectively. These net sales figures have not been deflated but, instead, are expressed in current dollars.

As the table shows, in 1987 net sales to foreigners by FAUSFs were about 16 percent greater than export sales by Americans to foreigners. However, this margin gradually declined between 1987 and 1991 so that by the latter year, net sales to foreigners by FAUSFs were 2 percent less than exports by Americans to foreigners. Cross-border purchases by Americans from foreigners in 1987 were about 13 percent greater than net purchases by Americans from USAFFs. In 1991 this margin was 5 percent.

21   Measuring U.S. International Goods and Services Transactions

1.4   Measuring Cross-Border and Direct Investment Activities on a Value-Added Basis

Although the volume of firms' sales is widely used to compare the relative importance of their different economic activities, a comparison more closely related to national accounting procedures is based on the value added by the primary productive factors involved in these economic activities. By rearranging the data presented in table 1.1, the value added by FAUSFs and by USAFFs can easily be estimated. These estimates are presented in table 1.2. The value added by FAUSFs ($328,184 million in 1991, e.g.) is calculated by subtracting from sales of goods and services by FAUSFs the sum of local purchases abroad by FAUSFs, imported goods and services by FAUSFs, and purchases from other locally located FAUSFs.[10] The value added of USAFFs ($222,011 million in 1991) is derived in the same manner.[11]

To help readers understand the economic significance of affiliates, ratios of value added by FAUSFs to value added by all U.S.-owned firms (the latter being defined as U.S. GDP minus value added by USAFFs plus value added by FAUSFs) are also presented in table 1.2, as well as ratios of value added by USAFFs to the GDP of the United States. The former ratios indicate that in 1991 5.6 percent of the value-adding activities of U.S.-owned firms were performed by their foreign affiliates, whereas 3.9 percent of the country's GDP was contributed by USAFFs.

Another relationship brought out in the table is the lower ratio of value added to total sales for USAFFs (19 percent in 1991) than for FAUSFs (27 percent in 1991). This asymmetry could be due to several factors. One may simply be that foreign firms in the United States choose to produce products with a low value-added component. However, another may be the existence of low profits for USAFFs (see Lipsey 1993). Profits for these firms may be low because foreign firms are forced to move their production sites to the United States by the threat of formal or informal American protectionism, even if these operations are not very profitable. Or the relatively recent rapid increase in foreign direct investment in the United States may simply mean that many production plants of USAFFs are in their initial stages of activity and have not been able to earn significant profits thus far. Other possibilities are the existence of pervasive transfer pricing practices to avoid U.S. taxation and the greater concentration of USAFFs compared to FAUSFs in trading activities as opposed to manufacturing.

---

10. Inventory changes should be included in the calculation of value added by FAUSFs, but information on these changes is not available. However, this information is available for USAFFs in 1987 and is taken into account in estimating value added by these firms.

11. In the absence of any change in inventories, value added by USAFFs will exceed (fall short of) net sales of USAFFs to Americans by the amount by which imports of intermediate goods and services falls short of (exceeds) sales of goods and services by USAFFs to foreigners.

Table 1.2   Value Added by FAUSFs and USAFFs, 1987–92 (in millions of dollars)

Transaction	1987	1988	1989	1990	1991	1992
I. *Value added by FAUSFs*						
+ Sales by FAUSFs	815,541	927,886	999,506	1,184,823	1,213,719	1,266,717
− Purchases abroad from foreigners by FAUSFs	358,715	395,973	431,885	541,755	559,050	575,265
− U.S. goods and services imported by FAUSFs	87,647	106,036	117,218	122,631	132,352	139,587
− Purchases from other FAUSFS	125,107	144,401	150,392	186,427	194,133	215,797
Total	244,072	281,476	300,011	334,010	328,184	336,068
In goods and services sold to						
Americans	64,054	74,578	78,491	86,507	85,357	90,781
Foreigners	180,018	206,898	221,520	247,503	242,827	245,287
Received by						
Americans	n.a.	n.a.	n.a.	n.a.	50,820	n.a.
Foreigners	n.a.	n.a.	n.a.	n.a.	277,364	n.a.
Value added/sales ratio (%)	29.93	30.34	30.02	28.19	27.04	26.53
II. *U.S. value added in exports of U.S.-owned firms*[a]	278,410	335,294	373,115	412,115	448,452	480,981
In exports to FAUSFs	82,388	99,674	110,185	115,273	124,411	131,212
In exports to foreigners	196,022	235,620	262,930	296,842	324,042	349,769
III. *Value added by USAFFs*						
+ Sales by FAUSFs	723,956	860,037	1,022,163	1,139,792	1,142,903	1,181,633
− Purchases within the United States by USAFFs	425,915	523,318	646,596	727,988	735,018	757,244
− Imported goods and services by USAFFs	146,985	159,400	176,607	188,687	185,874	189,849
− Purchases from other USAFFs	n.a.	n.a.	n.a.	n.a.	n.a.	n.a.
+ Inventory changes by USAFFs	4,671	n.a.	n.a.	n.a.	n.a.	n.a.
Total	155,727	177,319	198,960	223,117	222,011	234,540

In goods and services sold to					
Americans	144,575	162,161	181,048	203,701	201,785	213,070
Foreigners	11,152	15,158	17,912	19,416	20,226	21,470
Received by					
Americans	n.a.	n.a.	n.a.	n.a.	223,461	n.a.
Foreigners	n.a.	n.a.	n.a.	n.a.	−1,450	n.a.
Value added/sales ratio (%)	21.51	20.62	19.46	19.58	19.43	19.85
IV. Value added in exporting country by foreign-owned firms[a]	398,578	431,448	455,521	484,349	475,864	515,718
In exports to Americans	260,412	281,612	289,511	306,983	301,142	337,260
In exports to USAFFs	138,166	149,836	166,011	177,366	174,722	178,458
Reference					
GDP of the United States	4,539,900	4,900,400	5,250,800	5,546,100	5,724,800	6,020,200
Ratio of value added of FAUSFs to that of U.S.-owned firms (%)	5.27	5.62	5.61	5.90	5.63	5.49
Ratio of value added of USAFFs to U.S. GDP (%)	3.43	3.62	3.79	4.02	3.88	3.90

Data Sources: Inventory changes by USAFFs, Lowe (1990, 51, table 6). GDP of the United States, ERP95 (274, table B-1). See table 1.1 for the other figures.

Note: "Gross product" of FAUSFs in *Survey of Current Business* 74 (February 1994): 42–63: 319,994 (1989), 356,033 (1990), and 356,069 (1991). "Gross product" of USAFFs in *Survey of Current Business* 72 (November, 1992): 47–54: 157,869 (1987), 191,728 (1988), 226,031 (1989), and 241,182 (1990).

[a]Figures in panels II and IV are estimated using the share of imported outputs in exports (6 percent). See the text for details.

Since value added is a more fundamental measure of economic activity than net sales, an alternative approach for measuring the international activities of a country's firms is to measure both cross-border and affiliate activities on a value-added basis.[12] This approach involves combining the value added abroad by FAUSFs ($328,184 million in 1991) and the U.S. value added by U.S.-owned firms embodied in their cross-border sales (exports) to obtain a measure of the international activities of American firms. The export figure can be calculated by subtracting exports of USAFFs from total cross-border exports and then subtracting the import component in the remaining exports. (One would also have to estimate the U.S. affiliate component in these exports to avoid double counting.) Unfortunately, good data on the use of imports as intermediate inputs do not exist, but a rough estimate can be made by utilizing information in the U.S. input-output table. A special unpublished BEA study (Planting 1990) of the use of imports as intermediate goods indicates that the share of imported inputs in U.S. exports in 1977 was about 6 percent. Using this import ratio, the estimate of the U.S. value added in exporting by U.S.-owned firms is $448,452 million for 1991, as reported in table 1.2. Thus, the estimated value added by U.S.-owned firms through their export and foreign affiliate activities is $776,636 for 1991.

In calculating the foreign value-added component in the exports of foreign-owned firms of goods and services to the United States, input-output tables of these countries should be used to net out the imported input component in these exports. Unfortunately, the lack of such tables for many countries makes it impossible to measure adequately the imported input component in the exports of foreign countries to the United States. The 6 percent share of imported inputs in U.S. exports is probably smaller than the figure for most other countries because of the large size of the United States. However, for lack of an adequate estimate for foreign countries, the U.S. figure is used to obtain an estimate of the net value added abroad through the exports of foreign-owned firms to the United States. This net value-added figure was $475,864 million in 1991. Combining this with the 1991 value added by USAFFs ($222,011 million) yields a figure of $697,875 for the 1991 total value added by foreign-owned firms in exporting to the United States and in undertaking affiliate activities in this country.

The value-added approach can also be used in focusing on transactions between Americans and foreigners, as under the net sales approach. The value added by FAUSFs can be divided into the value-added components in the goods and services sold by FAUSFs to foreigners and in the goods and services sold by these firms to Americans by assuming that the value-added share in the sales to the United States by FAUSFs is the same as in total sales. The 1991 breakdown of value added on this basis yields figures of $242,827 and $85,357

---

12. As Lois Stekler (1993) has pointed out, except for net changes in inventories, net sales of Americans to foreigners are equal to the trade balance plus the value added by FAUSFs minus the value added by USAFFs.

25   Measuring U.S. International Goods and Services Transactions

million, respectively. Similarly, the U.S. value-added component in the exports
of U.S.-owned domestic firms can be divided into the value-added components
in their exports to FAUSFs and in their exports to foreigners by assuming the
same fraction of imported inputs in these exports. In 1991, the value-added
components in these two types of exports were $124,411 and $324,042 million, respectively.

The breakdown of value added in the goods and services sold by USAFFs
both to Americans and to foreigners as well as the value added in goods and
services imported both by Americans and by USAFFs from foreign-owned
firms located abroad can be estimated in a similar fashion. For 1991, the estimates for the first breakdown are $201,785 and $20,226 million, respectively,
and for the second $301,142 and $174,722 million, respectively. The value-
added component in the net sales of Americans to foreigners is the sum of the
value-added components in the net cross-border trade (exports less imports)
between Americans and foreigners ($22,900 million for 1991), in the net sales
of FAUSFs to foreigners ($242,827 million in 1991), and in the net sales of
Americans to USAFFs (−$201,785 million in 1991), or $63,942 million in
1991. As indicated in table 1.1, under the net sales approach the net sales figure
for 1991 is $59,592 million.

The value-added approach indicates that in 1991 the economic activity (as
measured by value added) embodied in the goods and services purchased by
foreigners located abroad and produced by U.S.-owned firms in the United
States ($324,042 million) exceeded the value added embodied in goods and
services purchased by foreigners located abroad and produced by U.S. firms
abroad ($242,827 million) by 33 percent. With regard to purchases by Ameri-
cans from foreigners, the value-added approach indicates that the value added
embodied in goods and services produced by foreign firms abroad ($301,142
million) exceeded the value added in goods and services produced by foreign
firms in the United States ($201,785 million) by 49 percent.

The value-added data can also be arranged to show the contribution of foreign affiliates and domestic firms engaged in international trade to a nation's
output and the income of its citizens. The value added in exporting by domestic
U.S.-owned firms plus the value added by USAFFs ($448,452 million plus
$222,011 million, or a total of $670,463 million, in 1991) measures the contribution of these activities to the GDP of the United States. Similarly, the importing and foreign affiliate activities of Americans contributed $804,048 mil-
lion to the GDP of foreign countries. Furthermore, combining the portion of
the value added by FAUSFs that represents the net receipts of the U.S. owners
of these affiliates ($50,820 million in 1991; see Landefeld, Whichard, and
Lowe 1993, table 4), the value added by USAFFs less the net receipts of the
foreign owners of these firms ($222,011 million minus −$1,450 million, or
$223,461, in 1991; Landefeld et al. 1993, table 4), and the value added in the
United States by the export activities of U.S.-owned firms ($448,452 million in
1991) yields the income earned by Americans in these international activities,

namely, $722,733 million in 1991. These relationships bring out the point that exporting activities by American firms are still twice as important as a source of income for Americans than the activities of USAFFs and that the income earned by Americans from FAUSFs is only about 11 percent of the income earned through exporting.

The sum of the income earned by foreigners from the activities of FAUSFs ($277,364 million in 1991), from the earnings of USAFFs ($-$1,450 million in 1991), and from exporting to the United States ($475,864 million in 1991) amounted to $751,778 in 1991. Thus, although international activities between the United States and foreign firms contributed 20 percent more to the GDP of foreign countries than to the GDP of the United States in 1991, the division of the total value added from these activities into income shares yields a figure for foreigners only 4 percent higher than the income earned by Americans.

One argument often made in support of using only the balance-of-payments accounts to depict international economic transactions is that this accounting framework is integrated with the broader national accounts. The current account balance (exports minus imports) taken from the balance of payments (with minor adjustments) is added to the expenditures on goods and services by consumers, business, and the government, that is, $C + I + G$, to yield GDP. Exports minus imports (rather than just exports) are added to the other three components because these expenditures are measured inclusive of imports. In other words, in calculating GDP, the current account balance is used mainly to correct the other three expenditure components. The only items in the balance of payments that are direct measures of domestic or national product are the net receipts of FAUSFs and of USAFFs. In contrast, calculating trading and direct investment activities in value-added terms measures both types of international transactions in terms of standard national accounts concepts. By separating value added by firms engaged in international transactions on a nationality and geography basis, the value-added approach supplements the traditional national accounts framework under which the GDP accounts divide aggregate production activities on the basis of geography and the GNP accounts allocate value added by primary factors on the basis of nationality. The value-added approach can easily be presented in a form that yields the current account balance needed for estimating aggregate domestic and national product. Consequently, this advantage of the balance-of-payments approach could be incorporated into the value-added accounting framework.

1.5   A Sectoral Approach

1.5.1   Sectoral Net Sales

Net sales balances by nationality can be measured for individual industrial sectors as well as for the entire economy. These net sales figures provide a rough idea of the relative international performance of American and foreign

27   Measuring U.S. International Goods and Services Transactions

firms by industry. If technological know-how and managerial ability are major determinants of firms' competitiveness in international markets, these data may be more appropriate for analyzing international activities by nationality than cross-border trade balances alone.

Nationality-adjusted sales for individual sectors are calculated by subtracting U.S. exports shipped by USAFFs, U.S. exports to FAUSFs, sales to the United States by FAUSFs, and sales to other FAUSFs by FAUSFs from the sum of U.S. cross-border exports and sales by FAUSFs. Nationality-adjusted purchases are estimated by subtracting U.S. imports from FAUSFs, U.S. imports shipped to USAFFs, U.S. exports shipped by USAFFs, and sales to other USAFFs by USAFFs from the sum of U.S. cross-border imports and sales of USAFFs. Data on sales among USAFFs or between FAUSFs and USAFFs are unfortunately not available.

A major difficulty in estimating nationality-adjusted net sales balances by industry arises in trying to estimate purchases of FAUSFs and USAFFs. Sectoral intermediate input purchases by industry origin are not available. One possible way to estimate such purchases would be to use input-output tables and assume identical input-output structures for U.S.-owned firms in the United States, FAUSFs, and USAFFs. Instead, it is assumed here that each industry purchases intermediate inputs only from its own industry. Such an assumption greatly simplifies the derivation of nationality-adjusted net sales by sector: nationality-adjusted net sales are simply cross-border net sales (net exports) plus value added by FAUSFs minus value added by USAFFs.

Another problem is that the value-added estimates for FAUSFs are classified by industry, while those for USAFFs are disaggregated on an establishment basis. As Lipsey (1993) points out, this could generate biases in the estimation procedure. In addition, the U.S. cross-border exports and imports only include merchandise trade, while value added by FAUSFs and USAFFs contains both merchandise and service transactions. However, this is unlikely to cause serious measurement errors, since the machinery industry (except electrical) is the only manufacturing sector that has large service sales (about 10 percent of total sales).

Table 1.3 shows both net cross-border sales (net exports) and estimated nationality-adjusted net cross-border plus affiliate sales for individual manufacturing sectors from 1988 through 1991. The ratios of net cross-border sales to total sales in the United States and nationality-adjusted net cross-border sales to total sales of U.S.-owned firms are also presented as indicators of firms' "revealed" international competitiveness. To discuss comparative advantage across industries, it would be necessary to adjust the net export data for macroeconomic trade balances by using some method such as the one in Bowen and Sveikauskas (1992). Table 1.3, however, presents unadjusted figures only.

Despite significant problems with the estimation process, the figures provide a number of useful insights about the competitiveness of U.S. industries. For the total manufacturing sector, the ratios of nationality-adjusted net cross-

Table 1.3   Cross-Border and Nationality-Adjusted Sales by Manufacturing Sector

SIC Code and Sector		Cross-Border Net Sales (Net Exports)ª				Nationality-Adjusted Net Salesª			
		1988	1989	1990	1991	1988	1989	1990	1991
	Manufacturing total	-147,002	-132,163	-100,833	-69,246	-312,073	-81,733	-89,922	-68,153
22	Food and kindred products	-3,989	-3,613	-3,750	-1,754	-18,178	-9,550	-7,887	-4,311
21	Tobacco products	2,918	3,646	5,045	4,588	3,758	5,736	7,534	7,600
22+23	Textile products and apparel	-23,986	-26,446	-26,293	-26,305	-24,079	-27,094	-27,310	-27,658
24+25	Lumber and furniture	-5,570	-5,257	-4,505	-3,596	-5,369	-4,999	-4,091	-3,302
26	Paper and allied products	-4,831	-4,649	-3,896	-2,338	-5,022	-2,361	-482	-316
27	Printing and publishing	268	1,085	1,535	1,921	-6,192	-6,988	-7,469	-7,135
28	Chemicals and allied products	7,463	10,601	10,569	11,650	-28,453	-1,896	-2,454	-1,626
29	Petroleum and coal products	-10,169	-10,850	-12,318	-8,046	-67,246	36,771	-8,263	-3,764
30	Rubber and plastics products	1,326	596	2,283	4,281	2,648	-1,121	-446	1,443
32	Stone, clay, and glass products	-7,397	-7,084	-5,844	-5,364	-9,837	-14,717	-10,454	-9,865
33	Primary metal industries	-16,868	-14,203	-11,888	-8,217	-24,213	-21,163	-20,544	-16,612
34	Fabricated metal products	-5,711	-4,868	-3,488	-2,817	-2,514	-5,314	-3,758	-4,283
35	Industrial machinery and equipment	-2,158	-2,155	4,357	10,087	-16,870	18,407	29,654	31,026
36	Electronic and other electric equipment	-23,775	-21,889	-16,088	-14,847	-29,323	-25,607	-18,269	-19,032
37	Transportation equipment	-33,998	-29,156	-19,676	-11,414	-41,262	-3,143	5,661	11,993
38	Instruments and related products	744	2,765	3,224	3,617	-16,483	1,980	2,968	3,201
31+39	Other manufacturing industries	-21,268	-20,685	-20,099	-20,689	-21,385	-21,745	-20,880	-21,344

SIC Code and Sector		Cross-Border Net Sales/Total Sales of Firms in the U.S. (%)				Nationality-Adjusted Net Sales/Total Sales of U.S.-Owned Firms (%)			
		1988	1989	1990	1991	1988	1989	1990	1991
	Manufacturing total	-5.48	-4.75	-3.51	-2.45	-10.76	-2.73	-2.88	-2.21
20	Food and kindred products	-1.13	-0.94	-0.98	-0.45	-5.00	-2.44	-1.98	-1.06
21	Tobacco products	12.24	14.13	16.86	14.32	12.71	15.85	17.90	16.60
22+23	Textile products and apparel	-18.48	-21.91	-20.17	-20.07	-18.57	-22.60	-21.14	-21.48
24+25	Lumber and furniture	-5.01	-4.55	-3.88	-3.25	-4.81	-4.30	-3.50	-2.95
26	Paper and allied products	-3.94	-3.54	-2.96	-1.81	-3.95	-1.70	-0.34	-0.23
27	Printing and publishing	0.19	0.72	0.98	1.23	-4.53	-5.05	-5.15	-4.91
28	Chemicals and allied products	2.87	3.81	3.67	3.99	-10.01	-0.64	-0.80	-0.51
29	Petroleum and coal products	-7.74	-7.55	-7.14	-5.09	-42.50	20.32	-3.96	-1.87
30	Rubber and plastics products	1.41	0.67	2.25	4.25	2.71	-1.25	-0.44	1.45
32	Stone, clay, and glass products	-11.73	-11.13	-9.21	-9.00	-17.09	-27.29	-18.62	-18.50
33	Primary metal industries	-11.31	-9.29	-8.14	-6.19	-18.36	-16.44	-17.07	-15.32
34	Fabricated metal products	-3.60	-3.20	-2.14	-1.79	-1.55	-3.44	-2.26	-2.71
35	Industrial machinery and equipment	-0.89	-0.85	1.70	4.14	-5.50	5.70	8.73	9.54
36	Electronic and other electric equipment	-12.72	-11.36	-8.26	-7.50	-15.11	-12.88	-8.87	-9.22
37	Transportation equipment	-9.60	-7.97	-5.34	-3.14	-9.27	-0.69	1.22	2.62
38	Instruments and related products	0.65	2.33	2.60	2.84	-13.38	1.57	2.23	2.34
31+39	Other manufacturing industries	-47.76	-45.27	-42.68	-44.71	-47.59	-47.84	-43.57	-45.18

Data Sources: FAUSF88 (tables 33, 40, 42, 49), 89 (tables III.D.2, E.2, E.3, F.14, F.18, G.2, J.2), 90, 91 (tables III.E.2, E.3, F.14, F.18, G.7); UN90, 92; USEST88, 89, 90, 91 (table 1.1).

Notes: Nationality-adjusted net sales = cross-border net exports + value added by FAUSFs − value added by USAFFs.
We are assuming that purchases by an industry are all from own industry since by-origin purchases data are not available.

[a] In millions of dollars.

border and affiliate sales are larger than the ratios for cross-border trade alone from 1989 through 1991.[13] This suggests that U.S. industries have a greater "revealed" comparative advantage than indicated by the cross-border trade balance alone.[14] Industries where the total ratios are larger than those for trade alone include industrial machinery and transportation equipment. Thus, considering only cross-border import penetration for these industries may be misleading in appraising their international competitiveness. Industries where the combined ratio is lower than the trade ratio are stone, clay, and glass and primary metal products. In particular, cross-border net exports indicate that the chemical industry is a leading export industry of the United States, while nationality-adjusted total net sales are negative.

1.5.2 Sectoral Significance of FAUSFs and USAFFs

Ratios of value added by FAUSFs and USAFFs relative to value added for the U.S. economy as a whole are given in table 1.2. Since the activities of FAUSFs and USAFFs are concentrated in the manufacturing industries and the wholesale trade sector, the impact of multinational enterprises on those sectors is generally more significant than at the macroeconomic level.

Table 1.4 indicates for the various manufacturing sectors the share of sales of FAUSFs in total sales of U.S.-owned firms and the share of sales by USAFFs in total sales of firms in the United States from 1988 through 1991.[15] In addition, comparable shares in employment terms are shown in the table. Note that the data for USAFFs and firms in the United States are on an establishment basis, while those for FAUSFs are on an industry basis.[16] Also note that the data for USAFFs are again for affiliates in which the foreign ownership interest is 10 percent or more. The sales, value added, and employment ratios of FAUSFs to U.S.-owned firms in the total manufacturing sector in 1991 were 22, 14, and 17 percent, respectively. Considering the size of the whole U.S. manufacturing sector, the magnitude of the activities of FAUSFs was surprisingly large. The sales, value added, and employment ratios of USAFFs to firms in the United States in total manufacturing were also significant, namely, 15, 14, and 11 percent, respectively, for 1991. Thus, more than 10 percent of manufacturing activity in the United States was accounted for by foreign companies.

It is in the chemicals, petroleum and coal, industrial machinery, electronics

---

13. Nationality-adjusted net sales in 1988 are much smaller than those in other years because the estimated value added earned by FAUSFs is small. In 1988, sales of FAUSFs were smaller than usual, while purchases were larger.

14. Kravis and Lipsey (1987) agree with the view that taking the activities of FAUSFs into consideration is useful in appraising the international competitiveness of U.S. firms.

15. Lipsey (1993) examines the shares of USAFFs in all U.S. firms in terms of assets, employment, and plant and equipment expenditures.

16. The definition of value added in the establishment data is also slightly different from the one used here, although the difference does not seem to cause large estimation errors. See the detailed note in U.S. Department of Commerce, Economics and Statistics Administration (1994b, M-6).

Table 1.4   Sales, Value Added, and Employment Shares of FAUSFS and USAFFS (percent)

SIC Code and Sector	Share of FAUSF in U.S.-Owned Firms				Share of USAFF in Firms in the U.S.			
	1988	1989	1990	1991	1988	1989	1990	1991
	Sales							
Manufacturing total	17.95	19.44	21.25	22.04	11.31	13.36	14.53	14.97
20 Food and kindred products	13.42	12.91	15.36	16.66	10.44	11.17	12.20	12.29
21 Tobacco products	19.37	28.70	28.89	30.04	0.00	0.00	0.00	0.00
22+23 Textile products and apparel	3.21	4.28	4.82	4.14	3.29	4.94	5.69	5.79
24+25 Lumber and furniture	1.71	2.26	2.89	3.20	1.46	1.63	1.99	2.09
26 Paper and allied products	11.49	12.69	15.34	14.99	8.16	7.84	8.67	9.03
27 Printing and publishing	2.27	2.77	3.08	3.38	7.08	10.18	10.51	10.36
28 Chemicals and allied products	31.43	32.17	35.01	35.93	24.97	28.24	30.42	30.70
29 Petroleum and coal products	36.52	40.58	39.56	41.90	23.57	25.18	26.87	26.07
30 Rubber and plastics products	16.73	17.43	17.35	16.92	13.53	16.34	17.55	17.73
32 Stone, clay, and glass products	10.72	8.13	16.17	15.70	18.50	22.16	25.85	24.59
33 Primary metal industries	4.77	4.43	5.13	5.44	15.77	19.58	21.84	22.82
34 Fabricated metal products	9.51	9.93	10.36	10.27	7.70	8.64	8.57	9.76
35 Industrial machinery and equipment	27.34	30.88	33.64	34.65	8.46	11.93	12.10	12.69
36 Electronic and other electric equipment	17.41	19.96	22.16	23.02	14.27	17.41	17.76	19.71
37 Transportation equipment	24.55	25.02	26.73	27.82	5.16	6.35	7.84	9.09
38 Instruments and related products	16.45	17.34	18.85	19.05	10.09	11.78	12.80	12.76
31+39 Other manufacturing industries	8.61	8.13	10.41	11.10	7.79	8.62	8.84	9.24

(continued)

(continued overleaf)

Table 1.4   (continued)

SIC Code and Sector	Share of FAUSF in U.S.-Owned Firms				Share of USAFF in Firms in the U.S.			
	1988	1989	1990	1991	1988	1989	1990	1991
	Value Added							
Manufacturing total	−3.03	15.63	14.08	14.04	10.44	12.38	13.37	13.97
20 Food and kindred products	0.71	9.45	11.23	12.55	11.65	13.52	13.83	14.08
21 Tobacco products	4.67	9.95	9.94	10.95	0.00	0.00	0.00	0.00
22+23 Textile products and apparel	2.87	3.12	3.61	3.43	3.02	4.17	5.26	5.60
24+25 Lumber and furniture	1.80	1.99	2.48	2.29	1.40	1.50	1.68	1.69
26 Paper and allied products	7.35	10.54	12.85	11.29	7.66	7.19	7.87	8.22
27 Printing and publishing	−0.53	1.39	1.49	1.54	6.37	9.53	10.09	10.13
28 Chemicals and allied products	−0.98	23.53	25.58	25.85	25.32	30.08	31.91	32.21
29 Petroleum and coal products	163.73	71.27	26.10	30.35	19.84	18.74	15.09	17.94
30 Rubber and plastics products	15.65	11.25	12.78	12.89	13.26	14.44	17.55	17.80
32 Stone, clay, and glass products	11.81	−0.13	13.01	11.37	18.10	22.05	24.75	23.90
33 Primary metal industries	−0.22	3.29	3.67	3.61	12.81	15.41	19.30	20.97
34 Fabricated metal products	10.26	7.30	7.63	7.58	6.67	7.81	7.94	9.35
35 Industrial machinery and equipment	−4.03	21.98	24.68	24.12	7.80	10.04	10.26	11.33
36 Electronic and other electric equipment	7.28	12.54	13.86	14.11	12.25	15.60	15.61	17.48
37 Transportation equipment	−1.89	17.67	18.87	18.02	3.27	3.74	4.88	5.40
38 Instruments and related products	−16.87	10.02	11.63	11.40	9.59	10.92	11.90	11.85
31+39 Other manufacturing industries	7.60	4.42	6.00	6.38	8.06	8.60	8.98	8.90

Employment

Manufacturing total	15.25	16.29	16.95	17.28	8.06	9.53	10.64	11.10
20 Food and kindred products	18.46	18.99	20.01	20.83	8.44	10.09	10.84	10.63
21 Tobacco products	44.19	48.44	51.88	52.95	0.00	0.00	0.00	0.00
22+23 Textile products and apparel	3.95	4.82	5.02	5.41	2.50	3.40	4.33	4.43
24+25 Lumber and furniture	1.48	3.04	3.82	3.74	1.08	1.21	1.44	1.51
26 Paper and allied products	15.67	18.08	19.57	18.66	7.57	7.47	7.74	7.98
27 Printing and publishing	2.07	2.25	1.97	2.00	5.08	6.22	6.76	6.76
28 Chemicals and allied products	42.68	42.81	44.50	44.94	22.58	25.27	28.41	27.49
29 Petroleum and coal products	53.73	54.14	40.37	38.86	18.83	20.69	22.91	22.51
30 Rubber and plastics products	15.29	14.93	15.59	14.90	10.22	11.32	13.90	14.09
32 Stone, clay, and glass products	12.44	13.31	13.71	13.56	15.47	18.44	20.74	20.16
33 Primary metal industries	5.19	5.08	6.78	6.69	11.16	13.44	16.73	17.83
34 Fabricated metal products	9.28	9.53	9.50	9.29	5.33	6.17	6.49	7.49
35 Industrial machinery and equipment	19.43	22.77	23.36	23.08	7.57	9.96	10.20	10.86
36 Electronic and other electric equipment	24.40	25.64	28.21	28.90	12.21	14.96	15.24	16.49
37 Transportation equipment	24.44	25.69	26.36	27.93	3.60	4.40	5.87	6.54
38 Instruments and related products	14.67	15.73	16.81	17.44	9.86	11.16	12.81	12.50
31+39 Other manufacturing industries	8.43	8.55	10.13	10.11	5.87	6.62	6.44	6.81

Data Sources: FAUSF88 (tables 33, 40, 42, 47, 49), FAUSF89 (tables III.D.2, E.2, F.3, F.14, F.18, G.2, G.7, J.2), FAUSF90, 91 (tables III.E.2, F.3, F.14, F.18, G.4, G.7); USEST88, 89, 90, 91 (table 1.1).

and electrical equipment, and transportation equipment sectors that the sales, value added, and employment shares for FAUSFs are particularly high. The presence of USAFFs is large in chemicals, petroleum and coal, rubber and plastics, stone, clay, and glass, primary metal, and electronics and electrical equipment. The chemical industry looks special in that its shares are very large for both FAUSFs and USAFFs.

1.6 Conclusions

This paper has argued that the increasing internationalization of firms' economic activities has brought about the need for supplementary accounting formats to document these activities better. In particular, because of the close relationship between firms' international trade and international investment decisions, the paper argues for sets of accounts that provide comparable data on both the cross-border trading activities of firms and the selling and purchasing activities of their foreign affiliates. In providing such comparability, the net sales and value-added approaches set forth provide information about the nature of the economic globalization process that can assist government officials in reaching decisions on a variety of international economic policy issues. Fortunately, much of the data required for constructing such accounts already exists, although certain relationships must be investigated more carefully before the figures in the accounts presented here can be regarded as more than rough estimates.[17]

References

Bowen, Harry P., and Leo Sveikauskas. 1992. Judging factor abundance. *Quarterly Journal of Economics* 107 (2): 599–620.

DiLullo, Anthony J., and Obie G. Whichard. 1990. U.S. international sales and purchases of services. *Survey of Current Business* 70 (9): 37–72.

Economic report of the president. 1995. Washington, D.C.: Government Printing Office, February. [ERP95]

Julius, DeAnne. 1990. *Global companies and public policy: The growing challenge of foreign direct investment.* New York: Council on Foreign Relations Press.

———. 1991. Foreign direct investment: The neglected twin of trade. Occasional Paper no. 33. Washington, D.C.: Group of Thirty.

Kravis, Irving, and Robert E. Lipsey. 1987. The competitiveness and comparative advantage of U.S. multinationals, 1957–1984. *Banca Nazionale del Lavoro Quarterly Review,* no. 161 (June): 147–65.

Landefeld, J. Steven, Obie G. Whichard, and Jeffrey H. Lowe. 1993. Alternative frame-

---

17. In particular, there is a need for sales and purchases data for FAUSFs and USAFFs on the same basis in terms of the degree of domestic ownership and for better estimates of the share of imported inputs in exports.

35   Measuring U.S. International Goods and Services Transactions

works for U.S. international transactions. *Survey of Current Business* 73 (December): 50–61.

Lederer, Evelyn Parrish, Walter Lederer, and Robert L. Sammons. 1982. *International services transactions of the United States: Proposals for improvement in data collection.* Paper prepared for the Departments of State and Commerce and the Office of the U.S. Trade Representative, January. Mimeograph.

Lipsey, Robert E. 1993. Foreign direct investment in the United States: Changes over three decades. In *Foreign direct investment,* ed. Kenneth A. Froot, 113–72. Chicago: University of Chicago Press.

Lowe, Jeffrey H. 1990. Gross product of U.S. affiliates of foreign companies, 1977–87. *Survey of Current Business* 70 (6): 45–53. Updated figures are reported in Gross product of U.S. affiliates of foreign direct investors, 1987–90. *Survey of Current Business* 72, no. 11 (1992): 47–54.

Murad, Howard. 1993. U.S. international transactions, first quarter 1993. *Survey of Current Business* 73 (6): 63–101.

National Research Council. Panel on Foreign Trade Statistics. 1992. *Behind the numbers: U.S. trade in the world economy,* ed. Anne Y. Kester. Washington, D.C.: National Academy Press.

Planting, Mark A. 1990. Estimating the use of imports by industries. Washington, D.C.: U.S. Department of Commerce, Bureau of Economic Analysis, March. Mimeograph.

Sondheimer, John A., and Sylvia E. Bargas. 1992. U.S. international sales and purchases of private services. *Survey of Current Business* 72 (9): 82–132.

———. 1993. U.S. international sales and purchases of private services. *Survey of Current Business* 73 (9): 120–56.

———. 1994. U.S. international sales and purchases of private services. *Survey of Current Business* 74 (9): 98–138.

Stekler, Lois E. 1993. Book review of *Behind the numbers: U.S. trade in the world economy. Journal of Economic Literature* 26 (3): 1460–62.

United Nations. 1992. *1990 International trade statistics yearbook.* Vol. 1, *Trade by country.* New York: United Nations. [UN90]

———. 1993. *1992 International trade statistics yearbook.* Vol. 1, *Trade by country.* New York: United Nations. [UN92]

U.S. Department of Commerce. Bureau of Economic Analysis. 1990a. *Foreign direct investment in the United States: 1987 Benchmark survey, final results.* Washington, D.C.: Government Printing Office. [USAFF87]

———. 1990b. *U.S. direct investment abroad: Operations of U.S. parent companies and their foreign affiliates. Revised 1987 estimates.* Washington, D.C.: Government Printing Office. [FAUSF87]

———. 1991a. *Foreign direct investment in the United States: Operations of U.S. affiliates of foreign companies. Revised 1988 estimates.* Washington, D.C.: Government Printing Office. [USAFF88]

———. 1991b. *U.S. direct investment abroad: Operations of U.S. parent companies and their foreign affiliates. Revised 1988 estimates.* Washington, D.C.: Government Printing Office. [FAUSF88]

———. 1992a. *Foreign direct investment in the United States: Operations of U.S. affiliates of foreign companies. Revised 1989 estimates.* Washington, D.C.: Government Printing Office. [USAFF89]

———. 1992b. *U.S. direct investment abroad: 1989 Benchmark survey, final results.* Washington, D.C.: Government Printing Office. [FAUSF89]

———. 1993a. *Foreign direct investment in the United States: Operations of U.S. affiliates of foreign countries Revised 1990 estimates.* Washington, D.C.: Government Printing Office. [USAFF90]

————. 1993b. *U.S. direct investment abroad: Operations of U.S. parent companies and their foreign affiliates. Revised 1990 estimates.* Washington, D.C.: Government Printing Office. [FAUSF90]

————. 1994a. *Foreign direct investment in the United States: 1992 Benchmark survey, preliminary results.* Washington, D.C.: Government Printing Office. [USAFF92]

————. 1994b. *Foreign direct investment in the United States: Operations of U.S. affiliates of foreign countries. Revised 1991 estimates.* Washington, D.C.: Government Printing Office. [USAFF91]

————. 1994c. *U.S. direct investment abroad: Operations of U.S. parent companies and their foreign affiliates. Preliminary 1992 estimates.* Washington, D.C.: Government Printing Office. [FAUSF92]

————. 1994d. *U.S. direct investment abroad: Operations of U.S. parent companies and their foreign affiliates. Revised 1991 estimates.* Washington, D.C.: Government Printing Office. [FAUSF91]

————. Economics and Statistics Administration. 1993a. *Foreign direct investment in the United States: Establishment data for manufacturing, 1989.* Washington, D.C.: Government Printing Office. [USEST89]

————. 1993b. *Foreign direct investment in the United States: Establishment data for manufacturing, 1990.* Washington, D.C.: Government Printing Office. [USEST90]

————. 1994a. *Foreign direct investment in the United States: Establishment data for manufacturing, 1988.* Washington, D.C.: Government Printing Office. [USEST88]

————. 1994b. *Foreign direct investment in the United States: Establishment data for manufacturing, 1991.* Washington, D.C.: Government Printing Office. [USEST91]

[12]

Productivity in the Services Sector

Jack E. Triplett and Barry P. Bosworth

I. Overview and Introduction

From 1949 to 1973, the Bureau of Labor Statistics (BLS) estimates that U.S. non-farm multifactor productivity grew at 1.9% per year. After 1973, multifactor productivity grew only 0.2% per year (table 1). Despite a 20-year intensive research effort to find the cause, no convincing explanation of the post-1973 productivity slowdown exists.

Whatever the ultimate cause, circumstantial evidence suggests that services industries play some important role in the slowdown. In the first place, the aggregate numbers indicate that the productivity slowdown is greater in the non-goods producing portions of the economy. While no official estimate of productivity in services is published by the BLS, non-farm multifactor productivity slowed by 1.7 percentage points (from 1.9% per year to 0.2%), and manufacturing productivity fell by 0.6 percentage points (from 1.5% per year to 0.9%). Because manufacturing accounts for about 22% of non-farm business, this implies a 2 percentage point slowdown in the non-manufacturing sector.[1]

If the data are right, one might infer, as did Baumol (1967) many years ago, that productivity improvements in services are harder to achieve than in goods-producing industries. If so, the shift of the economy toward a larger share of services implies a reduction in the national rate of productivity improvement.

But this view of manufacturing and services is undoubtedly too simple. Substantial disparities exist among productivity growth rates within the manufacturing sector and also within the non-manufacturing sector. It simply is not true that all individual services industries have productivity growth rates that are lower than all individual manufacturing industries, or even below the average for manufacturing industries.

But more importantly, perhaps, the data may not be right. One popular hypothesis about the productivity slowdown is that it is a product of mismea-

24   Services in the International Economy

Table 1. U.S. Labor and Multifactor Productivity, Average Annual Rates of Change, 1949-96 and Selected Subperiods

	Non-Farm Business	Manufacturing	Estimated Non-Manufacturing
Output per Hour			
1949-73	2.8	2.6	3.0
1973-96	1.5^r	2.7	1.0^r
1973-79	1.3^r	2.1	1.0^r
1979-96	1.5^r	2.9	1.1^r
Multifactor Productivity			
1949-73	1.9	1.5	2.1
1973-96	0.2	0.8	0.0
1973-79	0.4	- 0.6	0.8
1979-96	0.1	1.3	- 0.3

^{r} indicates that numbers incorporate the revised October 1999 GDP data.
Sources: output per hour: U.S. Department of Labor, Bureau of Labor Statistics, 1999a; multifactor productivity: U.S. Department of Labor, Bureau of Labor Statistics, 1999b

surement. According to this hypothesis, the mismeasurement of output contributes to the productivity slowdown because an increasing portion of output is not captured in the basic statistics.

Again, circumstantial evidence points to the services industries. Griliches (1994) pointed out that some of the services industries whose productivity growth rates in the 1947-1973 era were as high or higher than productivity growth in manufacturing industries had, since 1973, much lower productivity improvements. Additionally, the productivity slowdown has been particularly intense in services industries where output is hard to measure—health services, for example, have the greatest labor productivity slowdown of any industry in table 2, and both banking and health services have large multifactor productivity slowdowns (see table 3). This points again to possible mismeasurement.

Another puzzle involves computers. The 1992 capital-flow table shows the purchases, by industry, of computer equipment (Bonds and Aylor, 1998). The five industries that are the largest purchases of computers are all services—in order, financial services, wholesale trade, business services, insurance, and communications. Those five services industries account for more than 50% of US investment in computers. Within these industries computers have created new forms of service output that may not be fully captured in the statistics. An example is the growth of ATM machines in banks that reduce the time spent waiting in line for teller transactions, make the transactions available on weekends, and have, with computer-assisted verification systems for credit card purchases, virtually eliminated the need to carry traveler's checks on foreign travel to many countries. Prior to the 1999 revisions to GDP, ATM usage was not reflected in the measure of banking output in the national accounts.

In all of these services industries, conceptual and empirical problems in measuring output and prices are notorious. For example, an economic consulting firm is part of the business services industry. How do we measure the output of an economic consulting firm? How would we construct a price index for economic consulting? And how would we compute the productivity of economists? The science of economics is no closer to developing methods for measuring the output of economists' own activities than it is for measuring the output of banks, law firms, and insurance agents. All of these services pose difficult problems for constructing price indexes and real output measures and therefore for measuring productivity.

This paper gives a progress report of a project we are conducting, with collaborators, on service sector output and productivity. Its major message is that there is no central theme to the problem of services measurement. Each industry we have examined contains unique problems. If quality change is, as Shapiro and Wilcox (1996) put it, the "house-to-house fighting" of price indexes, measuring service output requires, at least, a hedgerow-by-hedgerow assault.

In the next section, we present some measures of the growth in labor and multifactor productivity within the services industries in a form that is consistent with the published measures for the aggregate economy. This allows us to document the wide dispersion of productivity growth rates across industries and the pervasiveness of the post-1973 slowdown. Section III summarizes recent research on individual sectors that have been subjects of Brookings Institution workshops on measurement issues in services industries.

II. Available Data

Reviewing trends in service-sector productivity and measurement issues requires a decision between two alternative databases that can be used for productivity analysis. Other researchers in this field face the same choice.

On the one hand are the aggregate, sector, and industry estimates published by BLS, which cover both labor productivity and multifactor productivity. As a general statement, we believe that the BLS productivity figures, where available, are the best current sources of U.S. productivity trend information. However, the BLS industry labor-productivity estimates do not cover all industries at present, although an expansion is underway that will eliminate most of the lacunae. An aggregate services sector productivity number—which we need for this review—is not available from BLS, though it is possible to infer one (see table 1). It is difficult to combine published manufacturing and non-manufacturing-industry productivity estimates to reach the

Table 2. Labor Productivity by Industry, 1960-97 Annual Percentage Rate of Change

Industry	Percentage		Growth Rate			Change
	Share (1992)	1992 Level	1960-73	1973-97	1987-97	(4)-(2)
	(1)	(2)	(3)	(4)	(5)	(6)
			Thousands			
Nonfarm business – hours	87		3.0	1.1	1.0	-2.0
Nonfarm business – persons	87		2.6	0.9	1.1	-1.5
Total Private - A (Aggregates)	100.0		2.7	0.9	1.1	-1.7
Total Private Sector	100.0	56	2.5	0.9	1.1	-1.4
Agriculture	2.1	37	3.9	3.8	2.2	-1.7
Mining	1.7	142	3.6	1.2	4.4	0.7
Construction	4.3	39	-2.1	-0.7	-0.1	2.0
Manufacturing	19.8	59	3.3	2.7	2.9	-0.4
Durables (ex elect.)	7.8	53	3.7	2.4	2.5	-1.2
Electronics	2.8	63	0.2	5.8	8.7	8.6
Nondurables	9.1	64	3.6	2.1	1.3	-2.2
Services	71.3	57	2.2	0.4	0.7	-1.5
Transportation	3.6	54	3.2	0.9	0.8	-2.4
Communications	3.0	138	5.0	3.9	2.9	-2.1
Public Utilities	3.3	184	4.8	1.5	3.8	-0.9
Wholesale Trade	7.6	65	3.2	2.9	4.0	0.7
Retail Trade	10.1	31	2.0	0.8	1.6	-0.3
Finance	21.4	164	1.3	0.5	1.6	0.4
Other Services	22.4	39	1.3	-0.5	-0.7	-2.0

Finance, Insurance and Real Estate	21.4	164	1.3	0.5	1.6	0.4
Depository and Nondepository Inst.	4.3	95	0.2	-0.3	-0.3	-0.4
Security and Commodity Brokers	0.9	97	0.0	4.0	8.8	8.9
Insurance Carriers	1.6	57	1.9	-0.1	4.6	2.6
Insurance Agents	0.7	48	0.2	-0.8	-0.3	-0.5
Real estate	13.7					
Nonfarm housing	10.3					
Other	3.4	116	1.0	0.5	1.5	0.5
Holding and Investment Offices	0.2	53	0.1	-0.3	0.0	-0.1
Finance less nonfarm housing	*11.1*	*85*	*1.0*	*0.5*	*1.9*	*0.9*
Other Services	22.4	39	1.3	-0.5	-0.7	-2.0
Hotels and other lodging	0.9	34	0.7	0.0	2.9	2.2
Personal services	0.2	24	1.7	-0.9	-0.3	-2.0
Business and professional	0.8	44	-0.2	-0.4	0.0	0.2
Auto repair	1.0	40	2.9	-0.8	0.1	-2.8
Miscellaneous repair	0.3	32	0.0	-1.6	-3.0	-3.0
Motion pictures	0.4	43	0.7	1.0	-1.0	-1.7
Amusement and recreation	0.9	44	-0.8	0.2	-0.8	0.0
Health services	6.9	45	0.6	-1.5	-2.2	-2.8
Legal services	1.7	79	0.9	-2.5	-0.8	-1.7
Educational services	0.9	26	0.0	-0.5	-0.9	-0.8
Social services and membership org.	1.4	19	0.1	-0.3	-0.5	-0.8
Private Households	0.2	12	..	..	..	-0.6

Source: Bureau of Economic Analysis data. Pre-1977 output data are estimated using the 1982-base industry data as extrapolators, except for those sectors whose output can be derived from other tables of the revised national accounts.
Gross product is gross output minus intermediate inputs, and the aggregates are constructed as Fisher aggregates of component industries.
Persons engaged in production are defined as full-time equivalents plus the self-employed (Table 6.8).
The productivity slowdown is measured as the difference in the growth rate between 1987-97 and 1960-73.

Table 3. Multifactor Productivity by Industry, 1960-97 Annual Percentage Rate of Change

Industry	Percentage Share (1992) (1)	Growth Rate 1960-73 (2)	Growth Rate 1973-97 (3)	Growth Rate 1987-97 (4)	Change (4)-(2) (5)
TOTAL PRIVATE SECTOR	100.0	1.7	0.5	0.9	-0.8
Agriculture	2.1	0.4	3.5	2.7	2.2
Mining	1.7	1.4	-0.2	4.0	2.5
Construction	4.3	-2.4	-0.5	0.1	2.5
Manufacturing	19.8	2.5	2.0	2.4	-0.1
Durables (ex elect.)	7.8	3.1	2.0	2.4	-0.6
Electronics	2.8	-0.9	4.6	7.3	8.2
Nondurables	9.1	2.6	1.2	0.5	-2.0
Services	71.3	1.6	0.2	0.5	-1.1
Transportation	3.6	3.3	1.3	1.4	-1.9
Communications	3.0	2.7	1.8	1.4	-1.3
Public Utilities	3.3	3.1	0.4	2.4	-0.7
Wholesale Trade	7.6	0.4	1.0	2.7	2.3
Retail Trade	10.1	1.2	0.4	1.0	-0.2
Finance	21.4	-0.6	-0.9	-0.5	0.1
Other Services	22.4	0.3	-0.6	-0.8	-1.2
Finance, Insurance and Real Estate	21.4	-0.6	-0.9	-0.5	0.1
Depository and Nondepository Inst.	4.3	-1.4	-3.2	-3.7	-2.3
Security and Commodity Brokers	0.9	-0.6	3.6	9.0	9.5
Insurance Carriers	1.6	0.6	-2.3	2.1	1.5
Insurance Agents	0.7	-0.9	-0.7	0.0	0.9
Real estate	13.7	..	..	..	..
Nonfarm housing	10.3	..	..	..	..
Other	3.4	-0.7	0.1	0.4	1.1
Holding and Investment Offices	0.2	-3.5	-0.9	2.2	5.6
Finance less non-farm housing	*11.1*	-0.9	-0.9	-0.3	0.6
Other Services	22.4	0.3	-0.6	-0.8	-1.2
Hotels and other lodging	0.9	0.3	-0.1	2.6	2.3
Personal services	0.2	0.7	-0.8	-0.4	-1.1
Business and professional	0.8	-1.3	0.0	-0.2	1.1
Auto repair	1.0	1.5	-1.3	-1.0	-2.6
Miscellaneous repair	0.3	-0.1	-1.7	-3.2	-3.1
Motion pictures	0.4	-0.2	0.5	-1.6	-1.4
Amusement and recreation	0.9	-0.7	0.9	0.0	0.7
Health services	6.9	-0.3	-1.8	-2.6	-2.3
Legal services	1.7	0.5	-2.6	-1.0	-1.5
Educational services	0.9	0.0	-0.4	-0.9	-0.9
Social services and membership org.	1.4	0.1	-0.3	-0.6	-0.8
Private Households	0.2	..	..	..	..

Source: table 2 plus capital stock data of the Bureau of Economic Analysis and authors' estimates as described in the text

published aggregates, such as the non-farm-business, labor-productivity number (Gullickson and Harper, 1999, show aggregation with "Domar" weights). These are liabilities if one's objective is to compare industry labor and multifactor productivity trends with aggregate and sector labor and multifactor productivity trends.

A second alternative is to make use of the data on gross product originating (GPO) by industry published by the Bureau of Economic Analysis (BEA). The GPO data are consistent with national accounts and with the estimate of non-farm business output. Using BEA gross product data to compute productivity yields estimates that are consistent across industries, can be aggregated to sector and economywide totals, and are consistent between labor productivity and multifactor productivity concepts.

Set against these advantages, however, is the fact that GPO and other BEA data are not exactly what we want for computing industry productivity measures.[2] For its productivity measures, BLS starts from gross output per industry and adjusts for intraindustry sales. GPO is value added and value added deducts, additionally, inputs purchased from other industries. (Value added is used in national accounts in order to obtain an unduplicated total for GDP.) The BLS output measure is preferable for industry-productivity purposes. The BEA series on full-time equivalent employees by industry, which we use, is converted into employment hours by BLS, and nonemployee hours are added; then, an adjustment is made for labor quality. Because these adjustments are larger for the earlier post-war period than for the last decade, our measure of labor input produces a larger productivity slowdown than the BLS labor-input measure (see the first two lines of table 2). Finally, the BLS produces capital input by industry by following the Jorgenson (1989) principles for producing capital services and capital rental prices. The BLS capital-input measure is conceptually superior to the use of BEA net capital stock by industry, which we employ in the calculations for table 3.

In table 4 we calculate the effect of the alternative output concepts, which turns out to matter more for some of the services industries we discuss than for manufacturing. In subsequent work, we will carry out similar comparisons for labor-input and capital-input choices.

Thus, the choice is between comprehensive and consistently compiled industry data from BEA or data that are more fragmentary and less consistent, but more appropriate for productivity analysis, from BLS. Ultimately, our decision to use GPO data and BEA capital and labor measures was motivated by the desire to have a comprehensive data set for all industries, one for which consistent labor and multifactor productivity measures could be derived. We also needed a dataset from which we could split trends at the 1973 onset of the productivity slowdown. A complimentary study of the productivity slowdown that begins with BLS data is Gullickson and Harper (1999). Their study covers

Table 4. Output Versus Product and the Proportion of Output Directed to Final Demand

Industry	Gross Product Percentage Share (1992) (1)	Output/Product Ratio Annual Percentage Change (2)	Final Demand Share (percent) (3)	Methodology (4)
Total Private Sector	100.0	..	..	..
Agriculture	2.1	-2.1	21.0	dd
Mining	1.7	-1.5	4.2	dd
Construction	4.3	-0.6	76.5	dd
Manufacturing	19.8	-0.4	51.4	dd
Durables (ex elect.)	7.8	-0.2	51.6	dd
Electronics	2.8	0.0	58.9	dd
Nondurables	9.1	-0.5	49.2	dd
Services	71.3	..	63.9	..
Transportation	3.6	..	43.9	dd
Communications	3.0	..	54.0	dd
Public Utilities	3.3	0.6	45.2	dd
Wholesale Trade	7.6	-2.8	49.0	dd
Retail Trade	10.1	-1.0	89.9	dd
Finance	21.4	0.0	64.4	..
Other Services	22.4	..	64.7	..
Finance, Insurance and Real Estate	21.4	..	64.4	
Depository and Nondepository Inst.	4.3	..	63.0	x
Security and Commodity Brokers	0.9	2.3	41.7	dd
Insurance Carriers	1.6	1.4	83.7	dd
Insurance Agents	0.7	-0.5	0.4	dd
Real estate	13.7	..	..	
Nonfarm housing	10.3	..	..	
Other	3.4	..	41.0	dd
Holding and Investment Offices	0.2	..	41.7	x
Finance less non-farm housing	*11.1*	..	50.6	
Other Services	22.4	..	64.7	
Hotels and other lodging	0.9	0.9	53.7	dd
Personal services	0.2	0.9	74.4	dd

Industry	Gross Product Percentage Share (1992)	Output/Product Ratio Annual Percentage Change	Final Demand Share (percent)	Methodology
	(1)	(2)	(3)	(4)
Business and professional	0.8	..	20.7	x
Auto repair	1.0	1.0	57.4	dd
Miscellaneous repair	0.3	3.0	74.4	dd
Motion pictures	0.4	1.5	66.0	dd
Amusement and recreation	0.9	..	66.0	dd
Health services	6.9	1.9	97.6	dd
Legal services	1.7	1.1	29.3	dd
Educational services	0.9	..	92.8	dd
Social services and membership org.	1.4	..	92.8	x
Private Households	0.2	..	92.4	dd

Note: For the methodology, dd represents double-deflation, and x represents extrapolation with employment or wage deflation

1947-77, and 1977-92. These are not optimal years for analyzing the productivity slowdown, which began in 1973, not 1977.

Data on Gross Product Originating (GPO) by industry as published by the BEA provide a means of examining the role of the service industries within a framework that is in principle consistent with the aggregate economy-wide productivity estimates for non-farm business. The data are published at the level of 65 private-sector industries; and with the 1996 revisions (Yuskavage, 1996), estimates are available for gross output (shipments), gross product (value-added) and its components, and intermediate inputs beginning in 1977.[3] Because the estimates are tied into the 5-year benchmark input-output tables, they are consistent with the national accounts aggregates. The measures of real gross output and real gross product (value added) incorporate the chain Fisher indexes used for the national accounts. For most industries, real product is derived by separately deflating inputs and outputs, 'double deflation'.

However, the GPO series have not yet incorporated the revisions to GDP that were released by BEA in October 1999. Some of these revisions are substantial. For example, when BLS incorporated them into revised estimates of non-farm labor productivity, the post-1973 growth rate was raised by 0.4 percentage points per year (from 1.1 percent to 1.5 percent—see table 2). When these GDP revisions are eventually incorporated into the GPO series,

32   Services in the International Economy

they will also cause revisions to the industry multifactor productivity rates. The data in this paper reflect pre-October data for GDP, except where noted.

We have used an older data set to extend the estimates for the real value of gross product back to 1960 in order to have a rough perspective on the contribution of the service industries to the post-1973 productivity slowdown.

Labor Productivity

Estimates of gross product per worker are constructed using BEA data on persons engaged in production.[4] We did not incorporate hours worked into the analysis, but variations in hours appear to be significant only in the 1960s. The resulting measures of labor productivity are summarized in table 2.

The level of output per worker, shown in column 2, varies widely by industry, but the average for the broad definition of services is nearly identical to that for manufacturing ($57,000 and $59,000, respectively). Labor productivity is particularly high in the capital-intensive sectors of communications, public utilities and FIRE (finance, insurance, and real estate—but the real estate number is affected by the inclusion of owner-occupied housing, which has no labor input). The notion of low productivity service-sector jobs is accurate only for retail trade and the miscellaneous collection of other services.

Growth rates of labor productivity are reported in columns (3)-(6), where we distinguish between the pre- and post-1973 experiences. We also show the average growth of the last decade. For a number of industries, post-1987 productivity growth is considerably faster than shown in the 1973-97 data.

For comparison purposes, the first two rows of table 2 show the aggregate series for the non-farm business sector. The first row shows the non-farm productivity rate previously published by the Bureau of Labor Statistics (BLS).[5] For the pre-1977 period, the rates are the published version, from the major sector detail of the national accounts (version A) and Fisher indexes of gross product for the private-sector aggregate from our constructed estimates of the underlying industry detail (version B). The discrepancy of 0.2 percentage points over the 1960-73 period is indicative of the error introduced by our use of the old data to extend the output estimates back before 1977.

The industry detail reveals a very pervasive pattern of slowing productivity growth after 1973 (column 3 versus column 4). Within the goods-producing industries, the rate of growth in labor productivity continues to be quite rapid for agriculture and there has been a strong recovery in mining over the 1987-97 period. Although labor-productivity change in construction is negative over the full 37 years, the post-1973 experience actually represents an improvement over the prior period. While the slowdown is often said to have come to an end for manufacturing, the recovery is largely the result of a rapidly expanding electronics industry.[6] Excluding electronics, durable and nondurable manufacturing both still show a deceleration of productivity gains.

It is particularly large for nondurables and it has continued to deteriorate in the most recent period.

The productivity slowdown is more pronounced in the broadly-defined service sector which includes a very heterogeneous mix of industries. For the service sector as a whole, the post-1973 labor slowdown is 1.8 percentage points, measured from the whole period (2.2 minus 0.4), and 1.5 percentage points, using only the last decade's data.[7]

Within the transportation industries, deregulation was followed by substantial productivity gains for railroads, as was anticipated; but the gains from deregulation seem small or nonexistent for trucking and airlines. The high reported rate of productivity improvement for communications (2.9% for 1987-97) actually represents a slowing relative to the 1960-73 period; but there are questions about the extent to which the price indexes incorporate new technologies.

Wholesale trade is an exception in showing an acceleration of productivity growth in the last decade. It is also one of those industries that has made an extensive investment in computers. However, the quality of the data is affected by a blurring of the distinction between manufacturer's distribution activities and wholesalers and the backward integration of retailers into wholesaling. Moreover, the old U.S. SIC system contained a definition of wholesale trade that caused many retailing establishments in office supplies, hardware, and other retailing activities to be classified as wholesalers, which complicates the interpretation of the wholesale trade productivity numbers.

The retail trade sector is reported to have a modest slowdown. But the statistical methodology may not fully capture the effects of continuing changes in store formats. and, as noted, the old SIC system caused many of the most technically dynamic retailers incorrectly to be included in the data for wholesale trade.

Finance, insurance and real estate (FIRE) and the category "other services" include many of the industries where the problems of defining and measuring real output are most severe. For several of these industries, annual rates of change in labor productivity are actually negative.[8] In industries representing about 13 percent of GDP, the estimates of real output growth are based on changes in employment. Recent research also has suggested that there are major problems with the price indexes used to derive output of medical care.[9] Productivity growth has accelerated substantially within finance, but that is primarily due to the large output gains recorded for security brokers during the recent stock market boom. The conceptual basis of the output measures for banking and insurance continues to be an area of substantial debate. Labor productivity is recorded as declining in large portions of other services, including health services.

In summary, the distribution of labor-productivity gains by industry and the pattern of the post-1973 slowdown is consistent only in broad terms with a focus on mismeasurement of output in the service industries. The slowdown

34   Services in the International Economy

has not disappeared in the manufacturing sector, though that sector is of sharply diminished importance in a service-dominated economy. The decline in productivity growth in the early 1970s also seems too abrupt to attribute to a deterioration in the quality of the data.

Within services, the patterns of change are quite disparate and different industries raise different types of potential problems. Furthermore, evidence of a slowdown in productivity growth is quite pervasive across industries, rather than being focused exclusively on industries with difficult measurement problems. For example, it is not clear why auto repair, with negative post-1973 productivity, should be mismeasured (Levy, 1999). Yet, while some of the negative values for productivity change might be explained as the consequence of shifts in the composition of output, their frequency in the service sectors is suggestive of an understatement of real output growth.

Multifactor Productivity

BEA publishes estimates of the stock of plant and equipment by industry which we have used to compute crude measures of multifactor productivity (MFP) at the level of individual industries.[10] Those estimates are shown in table 3.

Since the capital inputs generally grow faster than employment, the growth of MFP is usually less than that for labor productivity. Further, because the growth of capital slowed sharply relative to labor inputs after 1973, the post-1973 slowdown in private-sector MFP is only about half as large as that for labor productivity. At the level of the total private sector, the MFP growth rate slowed by 0.8 percentage points between 1987-97 and 1960-73, compared to 1.5 points for labor productivity. The contribution of increased capital per worker is particularly large in communications, wholesale trade, and financial institutions. After deducting the contribution of increased capital per worker, nearly half of the industries had negative rates of change in MFP over the 1973-97 period, and most of those are in finance and other services. The gains in labor productivity are larger than those for MFP only in transportation, business services, entertainment, and social services.

The estimates of MFP shown in table 3 use gross product (equivalent to value added) as the measure of output. The BLS studies of productivity generally focus on gross output at the industry level, and define multi-factor productivity within a framework that allows for three inputs: capital, labor and inputs purchased from other industries. A recent study by Gullickson and Harper (1999) used that framework to examine the trends in industry productivity over the 1947-92 period.[11] While they use a more refined methodology and focus on different subperiods, the results are broadly similar in finding negative productivity trends for construction, finance and many of the industries included in other services.

The BEA data set includes measures of gross output only for the 1977-97 period; as shown in column 2 of table 4, the distinction between gross output and gross product is important for several industries—particularly public utilities, insurance, and health services. While the choice of the output concept has a large effect on labor productivity, it is less significant for MFP because purchased materials are included as an input in the calculation. If the analysis is limited to those industries for which both output concepts are available, the aggregate growth of gross output exceeds that of gross product by about 0.1 percentage points. But reliance on the gross output concept would significantly raise the growth of labor productivity in the service sector and lower it for the goods-producing industries.

Our use of BEA net capital stocks by industry introduces potential problems among services-industry productivity estimates, especially those industries that are heavy users of computers (which have short service lives). We will explore the implications of this step in later research.

Intermediate Products and Aggregate Productivity

Finally, it is important to note that conclusions about potential bias in the estimates of industry productivity may not carry through to the aggregate economy. The output of some industries is largely consumed as an input by others. Thus, an understatement of productivity growth in one industry may be offset by an overstatement for those industries that use its output.

For example, the real output of business and other services is extrapolated on the basis of employment, producing an assumed zero rate of growth in labor productivity. Yet, as shown in column (3) of table 4, 80 percent of the industry's output is delivered to other industries. Thus, any errors in measuring business services output lead to compensating effects on the inputs and productivity of industries that use business services. Improved measures of real output for business services would have only a minor impact on the estimates of economy-wide productivity growth.

On the other hand, employment is also used to project the output of the banking industry, but nearly two-thirds of its output goes to final demand. The recent revision to the measure of banking in GDP will have an effect on economy-wide GDP. An even more extreme example is provided by medical-care services where nearly all of the output is directed to final demand.

Gullickson and Harper used input-output analysis to adjust for the proportion of an industry's output that is an input to others for those industries with negative productivity trends.[12] They concluded that the inter-industry effects would reduce the economy-wide impact of a change in the industry productivity by about one-third.

III. Individual Services Sectors

As noted in the introduction, there is no overall theme to measurement problems in services industries. Each appears to be a special case, with specific measurement problems unique to the characteristics of services

36   Services in the International Economy

industry output. Each industry problem requires a specific solution, an attack designed uniquely for the special problems posed by the nature of the industry's output. This section reviews some of the problems and the state of the statistics in topics that have been addressed in the series of Brookings Institution Workshops on Measuring Prices and Output of Services Industries.[13]

Business Services

Business services include a diverse set of activities, such as professional and consulting services (other than legal and financial), advertising, data processing and building maintenance. As noted above, about 80 percent of the output of the business services industry is purchased by other domestic firms. The 20 percent that goes to final demand is sold to government and overseas.

The gross product originating (GPO) of the business services sector has more than doubled as a share of GDP over the past quarter century to about 5 percent. It is also one of the fastest-growing export sectors. Yet until recently we had no measures of real output of the industry, or of real exports, and GPO is projected on the basis of employment data (Yuskavage, 1996).

In many cases, measuring the output of business services involves an effort to determine who should receive credit for the productivity gains recorded by the users of business services. When the output of business services is projected on the basis of employment or the use of other inputs, all productivity gains are assigned to the purchaser of the service. If the provider of the service is credited with some productivity gain, it comes at the expense of measured productivity gains in the purchasing industry. Thus, to the extent that business services are intermediate products, they have no implication for the measurement of economy-wide productivity, only its distribution. On the other hand, understanding why the economy is making more use of business services, and why they contribute so strongly to U.S. export performance, demands better measures of output, so improving the measurement of business services is important for other reasons, even if not for measuring aggregate productivity growth.

Since 1995, the BLS has expanded the Producer Price Index to measure the prices or fees for some components of business services. It now publishes indexes for accounting, legal, advertising agency, and engineering services. In each of these cases, the BLS asks respondents to re-price at periodic intervals a bundle of services that was observed in the period where pricing was initiated. This is an application of what is known, internationally, as "model" pricing, a methodology that was first developed by Statistics Canada for pricing construction. The BLS methods and results were described in Gerduk (1999) and Swick (1999).

Model pricing amounts to collecting a hypothetical price for a defined bundle of services. The BLS does ask respondents to take account of market conditions, and they make some adjustments for quality change. However, respondents may simply mark up the individual inputs that go into the bundle of services. The new PPI indexes appear similar to the pattern of change in average hourly earnings.

The problems are even more severe in other areas of business services, such as business consultants, because it is difficult to define the firms' activities in a way that leads to clear measures of their output. A few attempts have been made to collect from business services providers information about what they contribute to the output of their customers. Examples are Nachum (1999), who surveyed a group of European management consulting firms, and Gordon (1999b), who collected information from U.S. consultants. The results are interesting, but have not so far yielded any breakthroughs on the most difficult of the problems. In some cases, management consultants are used to validate decisions already made by management, as a tool to assure broader employee cooperation in a major corporate change, for example; even if this use of the consultant improves the productivity of the purchasing firm, extracting an estimate of the consultant's effect from surveys—either of the seller or the buyer of the service—is not a promising approach.

Because business services are so diverse, measuring them requires an industry-by-industry approach, and painstaking resolutions of unique problems that are found in individual industries.

Retail Trade

For effective measurement of real output and thus productivity in the retail trade sector, several conceptual problems must be resolved. Much of the industry's innovation is reflected in shifts in the distribution of sales among stores with different formats and changes among product lines within stores. Yet, these shifts are explicitly ruled out in the construction of the major price indexes that focus on a specific product in a specific store. The shift of sales from department stores to lower-priced discount outlets, for example, is treated as a reduction in quality (and therefore output), not a reduction in price. Nor is there any estimate of the value of increased product variety. Additionally, the old SIC system may be one of the mismeasurement culprits, because some retail establishments with high productivity may be incorrectly classified in the wholesale trade industry, as noted in a previous section.

At present, two statistical agency programs provide measures of real output in retailing. The BLS produces indexes of output and output per labor hour at the level of three and four-digit SIC codes. BEA publishes a measure of Gross Product Originating (GPO) at the level of total retail trade and measures of gross output for more detailed sub-groups within the retail category. The BLS employs a consistent methodology for all of its industry productivity work of using a concept of *gross output* that is equivalent to shipments or sales, not value added; and the indexes are Tornqvist aggregations of output at the lowest available level of detail.[14] The BEA, on the other hand, uses a measure of the gross margin—sales minus cost of goods sold—as its basic concept of gross output in the retail sector. The two estimates are more nearly similar than might be expected, however, because BEA assumes that the margin is a fixed percentage of sales at the lowest level of detail.

Generally, the output measure for an industry is what the industry sells. A shoe store sells shoes, which is the way the BLS measures retail output. The problems with the BLS approach are well represented by the example of computers. Because of manufacturers' improvements in computational speed and capacity, the real value of computer-store sales has grown spectacularly, over 25 percent per year since the mid 1980s. Much of that growth is in the increased quality per machine. The computer stores, however, are basically selling boxes; and while the number sold has increased, it has not grown at anywhere near the increase in the output of computer manufactures. An index that combines the increase in computer quality with growth in the number of machines bears little relationship to the actual activities of the computer store (even though it is the appropriate way to measure the output of the computer producer).

There are several suggested lines of research to deal with these problems. One option would involve the construction of input price indexes, as for manufacturing, so that a measure of the real value of the gross margin could be obtained by double deflation. However, many analysts doubt that indexes of sufficient accuracy could be developed to obtain, in effect, the real value of the margin as the residual of changes in two large numbers.

Alternatively, it might be possible to develop price indexes that could be used to deflate the gross margin directly. For example, one approach would identify characteristics of stores that account for variation in the gross margins, and construct an hedonic index based on changes in those characteristics or their prices. The BLS is currently conducting a research program that asks individual retailers for the replacement cost of goods sold as well as the retail price. At the same time, they propose to obtain information on the store characteristics, such as number of SKUs, square footage, storage area, and whether the store is a discount, gourmet, warehouse, or combination outlet. This will provide a data set that will allow for the exploration of the sources of variation in retail margins.

Output and productivity in retail trade have been greatly affected in the past by cost-shifting from the store to the customer—self-service retail trade, for example. The evidence is overwhelming that the changes are positively perceived by consumers. But part of the cost shifting ought to be deducted from retail productivity, and increasing services to customers should be added (Oi, 1992; 1998).

E-commerce

One widely cited estimate (Whinston et al, 1999) puts the volume of e-commerce at $301 billion, with a growth rate of 173% per year. What are the issues for measuring productivity that come out of the growth of e-commerce?

First, it helps to understand what are not issues for measuring productivity. The estimate of $301 billion cannot be interpreted as the net contribution of e-commerce to GDP. Only about $101 billion of the total represents final e-commerce sales (Whinston et al, 1999). The other two-thirds represent high-tech investment by e-commerce firms and purchases of other inputs, such as software and web site hosting services. These inputs would be netted out of any GDP estimate, so the $301 billion double counts in the traditional national accounting sense. Although it is of some use to know the total volume of transactions that is associated with e-commerce, the total volume of transactions does not give a measure of unduplicated output, which traditionally is calculated by value added.

Even some of the $101 billion of e-commerce sales are not net additions to GDP. In the case of computers and software (by far the largest category of e-commerce sales at present), only the e-commerce *margin* properly is included in GDP, not the total e-commerce transaction, because manufacturers' sales of computers and software are counted in the manufacturing industries.

Although the growth rates of e-commerce are impressive, its size is still miniscule, even compared to catalog sales. There is no evidence that GDP or aggregate productivity is currently missing very much because of e-commerce. Moreover, unlike the situation with service sector statistics in the past, the Census Bureau has already mounted survey activity to determine how many retail sales take place over the Internet (Mesenbourg, 1999). It appears likely that e-commerce sales will be smoothly integrated into existing retail sales information before they get very large. Accordingly, the macro implications of e-commerce are not very important, and, actually, not very interesting.

The more important questions are: What does e-commerce do to the productivity of firms that adopt it? How does it affect internal business processes, and therefore productivity? What are the effects of displacement on other, competing, industries? And what does it do to competition and the structure of existing industries? Unfortunately, data to study those questions will be harder to obtain.

Some of those questions concern inputs to production. The U.S. statistical system has historically been weak in providing information about detailed input usage, and this is especially true for inputs of high-tech equipment, software, and services. That means there is little benchmark information to determine the changes that will be wrought by e-commerce. Essentially, there is no good picture of business processes and input usage in U.S. statistics before the advent of e-commerce.

40   Services in the International Economy

Many final sales over the Internet, and many business-to-business Internet sales as well, are substitutions for more traditional kinds of retailing, not only against traditional "brick and mortar" stores, but more specifically mail-order catalogs. How readily do people substitute Internet transactions for older types of transactions?

Papers by Brynjolfsson, Smith, and Bailey (1999) and by Goolsbee (1999) suggest that Internet buyers are, first, quite sensitive to price differences, but quite sensitive as well to various nonprice elements, such as advertising, trust, delivery times, and so forth. Indeed, there seem to be two competing forces, which have been described as an "arms war" between business and consumers. On the one hand, it has often been suggested that the Internet makes it easier for consumers to search for prices, which should reduce the amount of price dispersion in markets. On the other hand, businesses use the Internet to increase product differentiation and tailor products to individual buyers, thereby increasing the amount of price dispersion. Studies (Brynjolfsson et al, 1999) have found that when consumers learn about nonprice aspects of the transaction, they turn out to be more sensitive to the nonprice aspects than to the price dispersion. The studies also find a large amount of price dispersion on the Internet, which is consistent with the finding that nonprice aspects of the transaction, including advertising, are very important to Internet sales. The widely-publicized notion of a frictionless Internet economy, with no advantages with respect to seller's size, is not supported by current research.

As another issue, some of the changes wrought by e-commerce cross the traditional "production boundary" used in national accounts. For example, a book bought from a conventional bookstore implies that the consumer incurs travel costs and time costs to go to the bookstore to make the purchase. Those costs are not now counted in the acquisition price of the book. A book purchased over the Internet, however, incurs handling and shipping costs that are included in the price of the book. Conversely, some people like shopping or like to browse in bookstores, which cannot be done over the Internet. Looked at this way, these services are part of the value created by traditional retailing, and the Internet provides fewer retailing services. If our statistics simply compare the price of the book in the two settings we will omit the value of retailing services (which are not explicitly priced) to the ultimate buyer, and miscount as well costs to the buyer that are non-market in the one case (travel costs to the store) but are explicit and charged for in the other (shipping and handling for e-commerce sales).

These problems are no different from other kinds of retailing shifts. There is serious concern that we already mismeasure output in the retailing sector because implicitly-priced store services are not directly accounted for (see the section on retail trade). So in this sense, e-commerce does not raise new issues, but it may raise them in new and particularly intractable forms.

Finally, there are interactions between e-commerce and other economic changes. Declines in communication costs, and perhaps to a lesser degree, in transportation costs, are a major force behind the growth in e-commerce. We may not be measuring the decline in the costs of communication well. The growth of e-commerce may just be a response to other economic innovations that are more fundamental, and e-commerce may not be the major technological change in itself.

A closely related matter is the decline in prices for Internet service providers. Work is underway on this in both the United States (in a Brookings sponsored project) and Canada. But because Internet service contracts are increasingly being bundled into the purchase price for computers, or else Internet service is being paid for by advertising, obtaining price indexes and real output measures for Internet service providers is likely to pose difficulties that have not yet been addressed.

Insurance

Labor productivity for insurance carriers dropped precipitously after 1973, and turned negative, as did multifactor productivity. (The 1973-97 productivity growth rates are –0.1 for labor productivity and –2.3 for multifactor productivity—see tables 1 and 2). Negative productivity growth rates are always suspect, but they are especially so in the case of insurance, because this industry is among the largest purchasers of computer equipment. The use of computers for claims and premium processing is obvious.

After 1987, however, the insurance-carriers industry shows very rapid rates of productivity growth, 4.6% for labor productivity and 2.1% for multifactor productivity, perhaps because investment in IT equipment has borne fruit. As a result, recent productivity growth in the insurance carriers industry exceed its pre-1973 rates.[15]

Despite the insurance industry's recent impressive productivity growth, there are reasons to believe that its output may still be mismeasured, and that the industry's true productivity growth may be stronger than the available current data show. We conclude that a major unresolved problem in measuring the output of insurance is the measurement and valuation of risk. The management of risk is what insurance companies sell. Anecdotal evidence suggests that insurance companies have greatly improved their ability to manage and control for risk. Because there is no explicit adjustment for risk in present price and real output measures, we suspect that output levels and output growth are both understated.

A major difficulty in focusing on what seems to us the real question—that is, measuring and valuing risk—is that insurance has been the topic of one of those long-standing national accounts disputes that seemingly are never resolved. There are a number of interlocking issues, partly real issues and partly, we feel, confusions, which were discussed extensively in the April, 1998 Brookings workshop on measuring insurance.

Two major issues are: (1) Should the current price measure of insurance output be the insurance company's revenue from premiums or, instead, its premiums minus claims paid out? (2) However the first question is resolved, should the insurance company be treated as operating in two lines of business, namely, (a) selling insurance and (b) investing reserves? 16

(1) *The current price (nominal) output measure—premiums versus premiums minus claims.* This output definition controversy corresponds to two different conceptual models about the insurance company's production process. The premiums minus claims view is equivalent to a risk-pooling model where the insurance company is merely a facilitator and administrator. The policyholders create a pool for sharing risk, essentially operating as a cooperative, and the members of the cooperative pay a service fee to the insurance company for administering the pooling scheme. The price of insurance in this model is the service fee for administering the plan. The rationale for this approach to insurance is presented by Hill (1998), and it is the view that is incorporated into the Systems of National Accounts, or SNA (Commission of the European Communities et al, 1993).

In the risk-pooling model of insurance, the insurance company's productivity could rise if it becomes more efficient at processing premiums and claims. But if the premium falls because the insurance company finds ways to identify more risky business (and either rejects it, or prices it to match its greater risk) or if it finds ways to eliminate inflated or fraudulent claims, the effects would be eliminated from the insurance margin, and hence from the insurance industry productivity measure.

In the alternative view, the insurance company assumes the risk. The policyholder buys the service of protection of assets or income from loss. The output is the insurance premium times the quantity of risk assumed. The price charged for assuming risk is $p = P/R$, where p is the price of insurance, P is the premium charged, and R is a measure of risk assumed (Bradford and Logue, 1998). Under this model, the price of insurance reflects both efficiencies in processing premiums and claims and efficiencies in matching and administering risk, so both sets of factors influence insurance industry productivity.

A major implementation problem with the risk-pooling insurance model (the national accounts convention for insurance) arises out of the fact that the insurance business does not function the way this model suggests. Although there are insurance companies with the word mutual in their names, there is very little evidence that they act as cooperatives on behalf of the policyholders. In the April 1998 Brookings workshop, one participant remarked that he had sat on the board of directors for a major insurance company, but nothing he ever heard there suggested that the company thought it was acting on behalf of the policyholders. One of us had a similar conversation with an executive in a large European insurance company. Because insurance companies do not operate as if they were providing administrative services to policyholders, no price or fee corresponding to the risk-pooling model of insurance can be found. Eurostat, in work leading up to its Harmonized Indexes of Consumer Prices (HICP), found that insurance companies could not provide a price that corresponded to the risk-pooling concept (Astin, 1999). Thus, even if a risk-pooling model of insurance were the only one that was compatible with national accounting conventions, it cannot be implemented, in terms of estimating real output from consistently defined measures of current-price output and of prices.

The risk-assuming model of insurance, which yields the gross insurance premium as a measure of current dollar output of insurance, yields a much larger gross output for the insurance industry than does the premiums minus claims view. Sherwood (1999) in his table 2, shows that the smaller definition runs from one-third to one-fifth of the larger one (data are for casualty insurance). This must have implications for international comparisons of productivity. However, it is not exactly clear whether the two concepts of insurance yield different rates of productivity growth in the U.S. economy. Although Sherwood (1999) calculates that the effect of the alternatives on total non-farm business sector output is small, he does not explicitly calculate the effect on insurance industry productivity and does not reach definitive conclusions.

(2) *Insurance company investment earnings.* There is a growing consensus that the investment earnings of insurance companies should be added into their industry output. Because of moral hazard, insurance companies collect premiums in advance of claims liabilities. The surpluses are invested. Evidence strongly suggests that competition among insurance companies leads to the distribution of insurance industry investment earnings back to the policyholders in the form of reduced premiums, and it is commonly observed that casualty insurance companies do not cover the full cost of their claims from their premiums earnings. Treating an insurance company as producing a joint product (insurance policies and investment activity) is not a conceptual step very far beyond the current treatment of other industries that have jointly-produced products. Whether national accountants should also treat the insurance policyholder as earning the insurance company's investment income in the form of more insurance (the treatment prescribed in the SNA) is not central to the question of computing industry productivity measures. (For the record, we do not think this national accounts approach yields a sensible measure of real consumption or of the price of insurance in the CPI.)

If the insurance industry has used computers merely to process premiums, premium notices, and claims services more efficiently, the effects are probably captured in the existing productivity numbers. This use of computers implies substitution of capital for labor and the existing insurance-productivity numbers (4.6% increase in labor productivity and 2.1% increase in multifactor productivity since 1987) are consistent with substantial capital-labor substitution in this industry. On the other hand, if computers combined with innovations in risk management make it possible for insurance companies to be more efficient in assessing and valuing risk, then it is not at all certain that these technological improvements are incorporated into existing statistics.

44   Services in the International Economy

The BLS, in its producer-price index and productivity-measurement programs, has begun to measure the output of the insurance industry with a gross-premiums-plus-investment-income approach (Sherwood, 1999; Dohm and Eggleston, 1998). This is a step forward. Incorporating more explicit measures of risk, and valuation of improvements in insurance companies' ability to manage risk, is the next step toward improving the output measurement of insurance. [17]

Banking

Like insurance, the measurement of banking output in national accounts has been the subject of a long-standing controversy that impedes progress. In the NIPA, as in the SNA, current-price banking output is defined as the spread between borrowers' and depositors' interest rates, plus fees for services that are explicitly priced. The issues in measuring banking output were the subject of a Brookings workshop in November 1998.

Subsequently, BEA introduced a change in its extrapolator for real banking output in the October 1999 GDP revisions. This extrapolator is effectively the measure of banking output that has long been used by the BLS for its banking labor-productivity measures. It includes counts of various banking processes, such as checks cashed and number of ATM transactions. Because we have not yet been able to examine the effects of the BEA change on banking industry output growth, we will address discussion of banking productivity at a later time.

For the record, we think the BEA change is an improvement, but that more work on banking output measurement, both conceptual and empirical, is needed.

Medical Care

It has become commonplace that medical care inflation outstrips the overall inflation rate. For example, between 1985 and 1995, the medical care component of the CPI rose 6.5% per year, when the overall CPI rose only 3.6%.

Until fairly recently, deflators for medical-care output have been based almost exclusively on the medical-care components of the CPI. Many economists believe that the CPI medical-price indexes overstated inflation in medical care. [18] If so, productivity growth in medical care is understated. Significantly, measured productivity in the health-care industry has been negative. From 1973-97, health-care industry productivity declined by 2.6 % per year, and from 1987-97 by 1.8 % per year.

In 1992, BLS introduced new price indexes for health care in its Producer Price Index (PPI) program. These new indexes introduced a new methodology for measuring the price of medical care. Rather than pricing the cost of a day in the hospital, as did the historical CPI, the BLS now draws a probability sample of treatments for medical conditions. For example, for the PPI price index for mental-health-care treatment in a hospital, the probability selection might be "major depression." The BLS then collects the monthly change in costs for treating that identical medical condition (see Berndt et al., 1998, and Catron and Murphy, 1996, for more information on BLS procedures). The new medical-care PPI indexes are great improvements on the previously-available CPI medical-price information (see the assessment in Berndt et al., 1998). Overall, the new PPI indexes present a picture of lower medical care inflation, compared to CPI measures, for the period where the two overlap (Catron and Murphy, 1996).

BLS subsequently introduced similar methodology into the CPI (Cardenas, 1996). However, even with the new PPI methodology, it has been difficult for BLS to find data to adjust for changes in the efficacy of treatment. Although there is some controversy on how far statistical agencies should go in building measures of treatment efficacy into price and output measures, we doubt if anyone seriously disagrees that the price index should be "adjusted" or corrected *in some fashion* for improvements in medical efficacy. Because medical economists generally believe that progress has been made in medical technology—better prognoses, less time spent in the hospital for any given condition, less painful and onerous conditions during treatment, and so forth— they believe that inadequate adjustment for changes in medical technology creates upward biases in price indexes for medical care.

There is less universal agreement, however, on the basis for adjustment. In the PPI, the BLS looks for information on the change in costs that are associated with improvements in medical efficacy. Some economists would go considerably further and ask for information about the medical outcome and the value to the patient of changes in medical outcomes. Research on cataract surgery by Shapiro and Wilcox (1996) serves to illustrate the issues.

At one time, cataract surgery involved a lengthy hospital stay, a week or ten days in intensive care. Now, it is mostly an outpatient procedure, often performed in a doctor's office or clinic. Put another way, the number of days in the hospital has dropped from 10 or more to zero. If one were to ask, in the usual "cost-based" formulation, how much more costly was the improved procedure, the answer is negative. If the price index were based, as the CPI was formerly, on the cost of a day in the hospital, there is no reasonable way to "adjust" the price index for the value of an improvement that reduced the number of days to zero.

But from the patient's point of view, the modern operation is surely better. The operation once required that the patient be immobilized for a lengthy period. Given the choice between immobilization and the far less unpleasant recovery period associated with the modern operation, patients would undoubtedly be willing to pay more for the modern operation. Not only is it less costly *in terms of what is paid for* (hospital care, for example), it is also far less unpleasant for the patient. The operation also has fewer adverse side-

46   Services in the International Economy

effects, does not require wearing thick corrective lenses, and is in many other ways improved from the patient's point of view.

A medical outcome measure would take into account all the ways in which the improvement in cataract surgery was beneficial to the patient. But some of those improvements discussed in the previous paragraph go outside the traditional "market boundary" of national accounts. The patient might well be *willing* to pay for the improved technology, but in fact the technology comes to him (or to his insurance company) for less monetary cost or expenditure of market resources than the old treatment cost.

But should these improvements be credited to the productivity of the medical care industry, or to its output in national accounts? Or should improvements that are not explicitly paid for, and for which the value of a transaction cannot be directly inferred, be ruled out of national accounts (or out of national health accounts) on the grounds that they fall outside the market boundary that has been traditional for measuring GDP?

For example, the time spent in recovery from cataract surgery is part of the cost to the patient—even leaving aside the disutility of immobilization—but this time cost is not traditionally considered in national accounts, nor is the value of the reduction in time in recovery from surgery, or the reduced disutility of reduced time spent immobilized, directly valued. The time cost of the patient, the greater utility to the patient of less unpleasant treatments, and the value to the patient of reductions in unwanted side effects are all elements that would go into a measure of medical outcomes (see Gold et al., 1996). But should they go into an economic accounting for medical care? That remains somewhat controversial among economists.[19] Many of these issues were discussed in the conference papers contained in Triplett (1999a).

Stating the problem this way underscores the difficulties that statistical agencies face in producing price indexes for medical care. Calculating the change in costs for treating an episode of an illness requires not only the traditional statistical agency skills in gathering prices, but also a great deal of medical knowledge about changes in the efficacy of medical treatments (knowledge which, in many cases, is scientifically uncertain, or in contention). It also requires knowledge about patient valuations of changes in treatments, particularly when treatments change in dimensions that involve the patient's time, tolerance for pain, and valuation of the disutility of side effects, or of the onerous implications of treatments (such as, for example, a frequent treatment regimen for a pharmaceutical).

Additionally, some changes in medical treatment cause shifts in expenditures among PPI index categories; the PPI methodology contains no obvious way to take these cost savings into account. As an example, consider increased use of drugs that permit treatment of mental conditions on an outpatient basis, rather than in a mental hospital. Substitution of drugs (and clinical visits) for hospital care will reduce the cost of treatment, but this cost reduction will be reflected inadequately in the PPI because the PPI holds the weights for the various expenditure categories (hospitals, doctors offices, pharmaceuticals, and so forth) constant.

New research price indexes for medical treatments that adjust for changes in the effectiveness of medical treatments include: Cutler et al. (1996, 1999); Frank, Berndt and Busch (1998; forthcoming); and, as already noted, Shapiro and Wilcox (1996). These new price indexes confirm that the historical CPI medical care component was upward biased as a deflator for medical-care-industry output, as does comparison of the new PPI indexes with movements of the CPI. How much do medical care productivity measures that use the historical CPI as output deflators understate the amount of productivity growth in medical care?

To provide an evaluation of the bias in existing measures, Triplett (1999b) "backcasts" an estimate for a mental-health-care-price index. One part of the backcast is an estimate formed by matching, for the period following 1992, PPI and CPI components and using the differences in trends as an adjustment factor for the CPI for the earlier period. He weights these indexes according to costs for treatment of mental health and makes an additional correction based on the research of Frank, Berndt, and Busch (forthcoming). The adjusted mental-health-care-price index shows essentially no medical inflation during the 1985-95 interval (table 5).

He then uses the adjusted price index to estimate the growth in the quantity of per capita mental-health-care services (or real expenditure growth).[20] For the 1985-95 period, the unadjusted real output growth rate is negative, at about -1.5% per year, which is very roughly consistent with the negative 1987-97 productivity trend for health care, shown in table 3, of -2.6% annually. Adjusted, real output growth is substantially positive, at about 6.6% for 1985-95, or nearly 8 percentage points higher than the unadjusted estimates (table 5). The implications for medical care productivity are obvious.

Table 5. Growth Rates, Expenditures and Prices, Mental Health Treatments, 1972-95

	Annual Expenditure Growth Rates	Price Indexes (percent increase)		Real Expenditure Growth	
		Unadjusted	Adjusted	Unadjusted	Adjusted
1985-90	7.06	8.78	-1.11	-1.54	8.31
1990-95	4.94	6.47	-0.04	-1.37	5.02
1985-95	6.00	7.62	-0.58	-1.46	6.66

Source: Triplett, 1999b

48   Services in the International Economy

Mental health may not be representative of the rest of medical care. Improved price indexes for other diseases might not make so much difference to output trends as in the case of mental health. However, the heart-attack price index of Cutler et al. (1996), or the cataract surgery price index in Shapiro and Wilcox (1996) suggest that revisions to real expenditure trends for these disease categories might be similar to the revisions for mental health.

As an exercise, however, Triplett (1999b) assumes that the correction applied to the mental-health price and output measures applies to the entire medical care sector. This would raise medical care productivity from -2.6% per year in table 3 to 5.6% per year. This is clearly a major impact.

It is important to emphasize limitations of this backcast. It is unlikely that the backcast is exactly valid, but neither is the historical CPI. Improvement of productivity in medical care seems more likely than the deterioration that present measures of medical care output show.

Notes

[1] The non-farm multifactor productivity numbers are due for revision in the near future, to incorporate the revisions to GDP that were released in October 1999. This will undoubtedly raise the non-goods estimate but not the manufacturing productivity estimate, because the productivity numbers published by the BLS for the non-farm and manufacturing sectors are based on different data and underlying output concepts.

[2] We should note that BEA does not explicitly produce productivity data, and so the following remarks are not meant as criticism of BEA statistics for their own purposes.

[3] The data on gross product and its components in current prices extend back to 1947.

[4] Person engaged in production are defined as full-time equivalent employees plus the self-employed. Employees on part-time schedules are included as a fraction of a full-time employee on the basis of weekly hours. Unpaid family workers are excluded.

[5] As shown in table 1, the 1.1 previously published BLS labor productivity rate in table 2 has now been revised to 1.5. Additionally, the estimate of 0.9 in table 2 shows the effect of using employment, instead of hours.

[6] The importance of computer manufacture in the post-1994 improvement in productivity growth is emphasized by Gordon (1999a). Because of data limitations, his definition of electronics is a broad one that includes all of SIC 36 and 38 machinery manufacturing industries. This aggregate's productivity growth for the pre-1973 period is not properly interpreted as electronics productivity, partly because much more of it was non-electronic in those days, and partly because the part that was electronic was not as well measured.

[7] This 1.8 point slowdown, calculated directly from the industry data, can be compared with the estimated slowdown (by backing off the manufacturing estimate from the total) of 2.0 percentage points, in table 1.

[8] Banking, insurance agents (and carriers before 1987), personal services, business services (before 1987), and repair, health, legal, and educational services. The negative

rates of growth in labor productivity for many service industries were emphasized in Sliffman and Corrado (1996).

[9] The methodology used to compute gross output and product by industry is reported in Yuskavage (1996), and an overview of the problems with medical care prices is provided in Berndt et al. (1998).

[10] Thus, we are using the net stock of fixed capital as a proxy for the index of capital inputs. The theoretically appropriate measure is the productive stock, which yields the flow of capital services, as emphasized by Jorgenson (1989). The distinction between the net, or wealth, capital stock and the productive capital stock is discussed in Triplett (1996). Capital and labor are combined with a Tornqvist index using the share of labor compensation in GDP after adjusting for the self-employed.

[11] The BLS definition of gross output differs from that of the BEA by excluding intra-industry shipments. In addition, the Gullickson-Harper estimates of multi-factor productivity use a more elaborate measure of capital input that includes land and inventories, and the labor input is based on hours worked, with an adjustment for labor quality.

[12] Gullickson and Harper (1999), pp. 58-59.

[13] Agendas for the workshops, and some of the papers, are accessible at: www.brook.edu\es\research\rs7.htm.

[14] Kunze and Jablonski (1998).

[15] The gains are not shared by the insurance agents industry. This industry will not be considered further in the present discussion.

[16] A third issue is also debated: If the answer to question (2) is positive, should the investment part of the insurance company's output be imputed back to insurance purchasers in the form of imputed increases in the quantity of insurance? The latter question amounts to asking whether there is a difference between insurance *company* output in industry productivity measures and insurance *product* information in, for example, the consumer price index. Because this last issue is important for measuring CPIs and for measuring real consumption, but not for industry productivity measures, it is not included in the present discussion.

[17] Some additional national accounting concerns are present. First, problems arise because the BEA does not have a separate capital account. The insurance premium, and not premiums minus claims, is the cost to current production for keeping the capital stock whole against unforeseen losses. Second, double-counting is of concern to BEA because it wants to use the output of the car repair industry, minus a more or less arbitrary adjustment for repairs to business cars, as a measure in Personal Consumption Expenditures. Finally, insurance claims are not always spent to replace the item of capital equipment that was lost (emphasized by Hill, 1998).

[18] A comprehensive discussion of price indexes for medical care is Berndt et al. (1998). See also Triplett and Berndt, 1999.

[19] We leave aside here problems with measuring medical outcomes, which are formidable. The question is what one wants to do with medical-outcomes measures, if perfected or improved.

50   Services in the International Economy

[20] Treatments for mental disorders account for over eight per cent of total U.S. health care expenditures, about a tenth (9.5%) of all allocable U.S. personal health care expenditures and just over one per cent of gross domestic product (GDP).

References

Astin, John. 1999. Presentation to the Brookings Workshop on Measuring the Price and Output of Insurance, April, 1998.

Baumol, William J. 1967. "Macroeconomics of Unbalanced Growth: The Anatomy of Urban Crises." *American Economic Review* 57: 415-26, June.

Berndt, Ernst R., David M. Cutler, Richard G. Frank, Zvi Griliches, Joseph P. Newhouse, and Jack E. Triplett. 1998. "Price Indexes for Medical Care Goods and Services: An Overview of Measurement Issues." *National Bureau of Economics Working Paper* W6817, November.

Bonds, Belinda and Tim Aylor. 1998. "Investment in New Structures and Equipment in 1992 by Using Industries." *Survey of Current Business* 78 (12), December.

Bradford, David F. and Kyle D. Logue. 1998. "The Effects of Tax Changes on Property-Casualty Insurance Prices." In David F. Bradford (ed.), *The Economics of Property-Casualty Insurance*. Chicago: University of Chicago Press.

Brynjolfsson, Eric, Michael D. Smith, and Joseph Bailey. 1999. "Understanding Digital Markets: Review and Assessment." Paper presented at the Brookings Workshop on E-Commerce, September 24.

Cardenas, Elaine M. 1996. "Revision of the CPI Hospital Services Component." *Monthly Labor Review* 119(12): 40-48, December.

Catron, Brian and Bonnie Murphy. 1996. "Hospital Price Inflation: What Does the New PPI Tell Us?" *Monthly Labor Review* 120(7): 24-31, July.

Commission of the European Communities, International Monetary Fund, Organisation for Economic Co-operation and Development, United Nations, and World Bank. 1993. *System of National Accounts 1993*. Office for Official Publications of the European Communities Catalogue number CA-81-93-002-EN-C, International Monetary Fund Publication Stock No. SNA-EA, Organisation for Economic Co-operation and Development OECD Code 30 94 01 1, United Nations publication Sales No. E.94.XVII.4, World Bank Stock Number 31512.

Cutler, David M., Mark B. McClellan, Joseph P. Newhouse, and Dahlia Remler. 1996. "Are Medical Prices Declining? Evidence from Heart Attack Treatments." *Quarterly Journal of Economics* 113(4): 991-1024, November.

Cutler, David M., Mark B. McClellan, and Joseph P. Newhouse. 1999. "The Costs and Benefits of Intensive Treatment for Cardiovascular Disease." In Jack E. Triplett (ed.), *Measuring the Prices of Medical Treatments*. Washington D.C.: The Brookings Institution Press.

Dohm, Arlene, and Deanna Eggleston. 1998. "Producer Price Indexes for Property/Casualty and Life Insurance." Paper presented to the Brookings Workshop on Measuring the Price and Output of Insurance, April.

Frank, Richard G., Ernst Berndt, and Susan H. Busch. 1998. "Price Indexes for Acute Phase Treatment of Depression." *National Bureau of Economic Research Working Paper* 6799 (November).

Frank, Richard G., Ernst R. Berndt, and Susan Busch. Forthcoming. "Price Indexes for the Treatment of Depression." In Ernst Berndt and David Cutler (eds.), *Medical Care Output and Productivity*. National Bureau of Economic Research, Studies in Income and Wealth 59: Chicago: University of Chicago Press.

Gerduk, Irwin. 1999. "New PPI Indexes for Accounting, Legal, and Advertising Services." Paper presented at Brookings Workshop on Measuring the Output of Business Services, May 14.

Gold, Marthe R., Joanna E. Siegel, Louise B. Russell, and Milton C. Weinstein. 1996. *Cost-Effectiveness in Health and Medicine*. New York: Oxford University Press.

Goolsbee, Austan. 1999. "In a World without Borders: The Impact of Taxes on Internet Commerce." Paper presented at the Brookings Workshop on Measuring the Output of Business Services, May 14.

Gordon, Robert. 1999a. "Has the New Economy Rendered the Productivity Slowdown Obsolete?" Presentation at CBO Panel of Economic Advisors, June 2, 1992 (revised, 14/6/99)

Gordon, Robert. 1999b. "Management Consulting Firms: Some Approaches to Output Measurement." Paper presented at the Brookings Workshop on Measuring the Output of Business Services, May 14.

Griliches, Zvi. 1994. "Productivity, R&D, and the Data Constraint." *American Economic Review* 84(1): 1-23, March.

Gullickson, William and Michael Harper. 1999. "Possible Measurement Bias in Aggregate Productivity Growth," *Monthly Labor Review* (February), pp. 47-67.

Hill, Peter. 1998. "Insurance in the SNA." Paper presented at the Brookings Workshop on Measuring the Price and Output of Insurance, April.

Jorgenson, Dale W. 1989. "Capital as a Factor of Production." In Dale W. Jorgenson and Ralph Landau (eds.), *Technology and Capital Formation*. Cambridge, Mass. The MIT Press.

Kunze, Kent and Mary Jablonski. 1998. "Productivity in Service-Producing Industries." Paper presented at the Brookings Workshop on New Government Datasets, June.

Levy, Frank. 1999. "Some Initial Results on Productivity in Car Dealerships and Auto Repair." Paper presented at the Brookings Workshop on Measuring the Output of Business Services, May 14.

Mesenbourg, Thomas. 1999. "Measuring Electronic Business." Paper presented at the Brookings Workshop on Measuring the Output of Business Services, May 14.

Nachum, Lilac. 1999. "Measurement of Productivity in Swedish Management Consulting Firms." Paper presented at the Brookings Workshop on Measuring the Output of Business Services, May 14.

Oi, Walter. 1992. "Productivity in the Distributive Trades: The Shopper and the Economies of Massed Reserves." In Zvi Griliches (ed.), *Output Measurement*

52   Services in the International Economy

in the Service Sectors. University of Chicago Press for the National Bureau of Economic Research.

Oi, Walter. 1998. "Adapting the Retail Format to a Changing Economy." Paper presented at the Brookings Workshop on Measuring the Output of Retail Trade, September 18.

Shapiro, Matthew P. and David W. Wilcox. 1996. "Mismeasurement in the Consumer Price Index: An Evaluation." *NBER Macroeconomics Annual* 11: 93-142.

Sherwood, Mark K. 1999. "Output of the Property and Casualty Insurance Industry." Paper presented at the Brookings Workshop on Measuring the Price and Output of Insurance, April 1998. Now published in: *Canadian Journal of Economics* 32(2), April.

Sliffman, Larry and Carol Corrado. 1996. "Decomposition of Productivity and Unit Costs," Occasional Staff Studies, OSS-1, Washington DC: Board of Governors of the Federal Reserve.

Swick, Roslyn. 1999. Paper presented at the Brookings Workshop on Measuring the Output of Business Services, May 14.

Triplett, Jack E. (ed.) 1999a. *Measuring the Prices of Medical Treatments.* Washington D.C.: The Brookings Institution Press.

Triplett, Jack E. 1999b. "What's Different about Health: Human Repair and Car Repair in National Accounts and in National Health Accounts." The Brookings Institution. Forthcoming in Ernst Berndt and David Cutler (eds.), *Medical Care Output and Productivity.* National Bureau of Economic Research, Studies in Income and Wealth 59. Chicago: University of Chicago Press.

Triplett, Jack E. 1996. "Depreciation in Production Analysis and in Income and Wealth Accounts: Resolution of an Old Debate." *Economic Inquiry* 34: 93-115.

U.S. Department of Labor, Bureau of Labor Statistics. 1999a. Major sector productivity and costs index, http://146.142.4.24/cgi-bin/dsrv?pr. Accessed November 23, 1999.

U.S. Department of Labor, Bureau of Labor Statistics. 1999b. Major sector multifactor productivity index, http://146.142.4.24/cgi-bin/dsrv?mp. Accessed November 23, 1999.

Whinston, Andrew, Anitesh Barua, Jon Pinnell, and Jay Shutter. 1999. "Measuring the Internet Economy." Paper presented at the Brookings Workshop on Measuring the Output of Business Services, May 14.

Yuskavage, Robert E. 1996. "Improved Estimates of Gross Product by Industry, 1959-94," *Survey of Current Business* (August) pp. 133-55.

[13]

The EU-US total factor productivity gap: An industry perspective

Karel Havik, Kieran Mc Morrow, Werner Röger
and Alessandro Turrini

European Commission

April 2008

Abstract

This paper uses the EU KLEMS industry growth accounting database to explore the determinants of the EU-US total factor productivity (TFP) growth gap which started to emerge in the mid-1990s. The bulk of this TFP gap is explained by a handful of market service industries (notably retail & wholesale; financial; and business services) and ICT-manufacturing, whilst the EU exhibits a considerably stronger performance with respect to the network utilities. Our analysis of the determinants of TFP growth across countries and industries shows that, as found in previous analyses (e.g., Nicoletti and Scarpetta (2003), Griffith, Redding, and Van Reenen (2004), Inklaar, Timmer and Van Ark (2008)), TFP growth appears to be driven by catching-up phenomena associated with the gradual adoption of new-vintage technologies. Compared with previous analyses, it appears that TFP growth is also significantly driven by developments taking place at the "technological frontier", and that these "frontier" effects are becoming stronger since the mid-1990's compared with the catching-up drivers of TFP. Industries with higher R&D expenditure and higher adoption rates for ICT-intensive technologies appear to exhibit higher TFP growth rates, other things being equal. R&D in particular is a crucial determinant of TFP growth in ICT-producing manufacturing. Anti-competitive financial market regulations hamper the ability of countries to share in the TFP developments taking place at the frontier. Product market regulations also appear to be related to reduced TFP growth but only in market services, notably in the network utilities. In the retail & wholesale trade industry, cyclical consumption dynamics which permit a better exploitation of scale economies are a highly significant determinant of TFP growth.

Keywords: growth determinants, total factor productivity, European Union

JEL Classification: D24, O47, O52.

<u>Acknowledgements</u>: The authors would like to thank C. Denis, K. Pichelmann, M. Thiel, I. Szekely and M. Buti for valuable comments and drafting suggestions regarding earlier drafts of this paper. The opinions contained in this paper are those of the authors and should not be attributed to the European Commission.

1

1. Introductory Remarks

The present paper examines the EU's productivity performance relative to the US over recent decades. One of the key aims of the paper is to examine the role played by total factor productivity (TFP) in explaining the productivity patterns which have emerged, since TFP is the main driver of long run productivity growth. An important feature of the analysis is the exploitation of the EU KLEMS industry level database to help identify those policy areas which could potentially have the greatest impact in narrowing the existing TFP gaps.

This issue of TFP divergences must also be seen in the wider context of Europe's overall growth performance since the mid-1990's which has been relatively disappointing. Whilst many EU countries managed to improve their labour market positions, this unfortunately was accompanied by a slowdown on the productivity side in a significant number of Member States, driven both by a deterioration in capital deepening as well as in TFP. This experience was in sharp contrast to many other developed economies around the world, in particular the US. For the US, the secular downward movement in productivity growth rates experienced since the 1970's was spectacularly reversed around the mid-1990's, aided by a strong performance in both the production and diffusion of information and communication technologies (ICT).

These growing divergences in the productivity performances of many developed world economies, and especially the size of the divergences presently being experienced between some of the EU's Member States, has provoked an ongoing debate in the EU regarding the implications of recent trends for future economic prospects :

- The "pessimistic view", largely supported by the Sapir report[1] / van Ark analyses[2], suggests that the EU might be unable to achieve a shift in its resources to sectors with high productivity growth prospects and will continue with production in areas where it has traditionally held a global comparative advantage, namely medium-technology manufacturing industries. This overall strategy appears increasingly threatened with firstly, the emergence of a number of strong competitors around the world in these manufacturing industries (most notably from China and India) and secondly, the potentially negative impact on Europe's ability to compete in the, increasingly more tradeable, global services market.

- The "more optimistic view", as enunciated by Blanchard amongst others[3], is that part of the explanation for Europe's poor productivity performance could be measurement problems / adjustment lags, with perhaps the basis for a future pick-up already firmly established due to the labour, capital and product market reforms which have been progressively introduced since the early 1990's. Under this view the EU may now simply be in a transition phase whereby some of the negative effects of those reforms (e.g. a temporary decrease in productivity due to labour market changes) are visible, whilst the gains to be reaped in the future are not.

---

[1] See Sapir et al. (2003)

[2] See Van Ark, Inklaar and Mc Guckian (2003)

[3] See Blanchard (2004)

2

Most observers, "optimists" and "pessimists" alike, would agree that regulation-induced restrictions concerning labour and product markets; lack of openness to trade and/or foreign direct investments; as well as barriers in terms of access to / generation of new technologies and the diffusion of existing innovations are amongst the key determinants of a country's productivity performance. International comparisons reveal sizeable disparities in investments with regard to physical capital (especially in terms of ICT capital spending), human capital as well as R&D and other forms of intangible investments. The present study will examine those countries and industries where the differences are most acute and assess the extent to which the differences can be linked with overall growth divergences.

Whilst such an analysis at the macro level has been possible for some time, a detailed cross-country examination at the industry level has been more problematic due to the fact that long runs of official industry level data were only available for a relatively small number of countries, industries and variables. This situation has significantly improved with the March 2007 release of the EU KLEMS datasets. The provision in EU KLEMS of detailed industry level series on economic growth, productivity, employment creation, capital formation and technological change for a large range of manufacturing and service industries is particularly noteworthy. A degree of caution is warranted however since the overall quality of the datasets has yet to be thoroughly evaluated by the national statistical institutes and Eurostat. In addition, according to EU KLEMS, the EU-US productivity differences are heavily concentrated in the market services sector where the conceptual and empirical problems in accurately measuring output and price developments have been well documented.

Despite these ongoing difficulties, the EU KLEMS project undoubtedly represents a unique collective effort on behalf of academics, statisticians and policy makers to provide fundamental policy insights into the changes which have occurred at the industry level in Europe, the US and Japan over recent decades. The value added of EU KLEMS is underlined by the provision of detailed industry level capital and labour accounts (and intermediates in the case of gross output) which have been assembled at the national level by the EU KLEMS consortium partners :

- Firstly, industry level investment series have been collected for 7 different types of capital and for 31 industries (A31 level breakdown). These national accounts sourced series are aggregated on the basis of the user cost of capital (i.e. the rental price of employing each asset type for a particular period of time) to produce capital service flows which take into account the widely different marginal productivities of the different components of a country's capital stock.

- Secondly, unlike standard measures of labour input, such as numbers employed or hours worked, the database provides, industry level, measures which take account of the wide differences in the productivity of various types of labour over time (i.e. labour services). Labour force heterogeneity is an integral part of these labour services calculations, with the overall growth contribution of labour being calculated on the basis of the services provided by different groups of employed workers.

These industry level labour and capital accounts are crucial in making a more accurate assessment of the contribution of capital and labour to productivity and value added growth in the different economies. They are particularly pertinent at the present time given the unprecedented deepening in global trade and capital market integration since the early 1990's, allied to the cost-induced and ICT-enabled acceleration in the worldwide relocation of production processes over this period. These globalisation-related processes have dramatically changed the economics of specific industries. Changes have occurred in terms of scale economies, technological spillovers (i.e. diffusion of best technologies / practices); the degree of import competition; and the productivity effects from the reallocation of resources amongst the different market players. Many of these globalisation related transmission mechanisms are having direct knock-on effects in terms of the specialisation patterns of individual countries, with the result that the post-1995 period has been marked by significant, industry-driven, divergences in the productivity and GDP per capita growth trends of specific countries and regions around the world.

Given the above, it is clear that EU KLEMS offers the research community an important additional source of information with which to deepen its existing analyses of productivity developments. The potential of this new dataset has already been exploited for a detailed analysis of sectoral and industry level productivity trends in chapter 2 of "The EU Economy 2007 Review" which concluded that cross-country differences in labour productivity growth predominantly reflect differences in TFP performances, although ICT investment patterns also played a role in a number of specific industries, especially over the second half of the 1990's. Since TFP is normally regarded as constituting the structural component of labour productivity, the present paper examines in more detail the possible sources of these industry level divergences in TFP performance. Using EU KLEMS and a wide range of pertinent datasets for the explanatory variables, panel regressions are employed to assess the degree of statistical support which exists for the major hypotheses explaining TFP divergences over time[4]– i.e. the role played by the regulatory environment (product, labour and financial markets)[5]; by the degree of openness of economies[6]; by demographics[7]; and finally by the efficiency of knowledge production (R&D, education and complementary, ICT-related, investments)[8]. The concluding remarks section looks at the implications of the analysis for the overall direction and sectoral focus of economic policy in the EU over the coming years.

2. Understanding the determinants of TFP growth: What can we learn from EU KLEMS ?

The EU KLEMS analysis in the "EU Economy 2007 Review" showed that the bulk of the EU-US productivity growth differential since 1995 stemmed from diverging trends with respect to total factor productivity (TFP) – a measure of the efficiency with which all factor inputs, including labour, ICT capital and conventional capital (non-ICT equipment and structures), are utilised. Differences between the EU and the US with respect to the growth of capital per worker played much less of a role in shaping the productivity gap, although a further breakdown of the contribution of capital services showed that a shift from conventional to ICT-related capital can be observed in the United States, especially in the private services sector, whereas a similar trend is not discernible to the same degree in

---

[4] See Barro (1990), Barro and Sala-i-Martin (1995), and Mendoza et al (1997).

[5] See Soskice (1997), Nickell et al. (1997), Eichengreen and Iversen (1999), Nickell and Layard (1999), Nicoletti et al (2001), Scarpetta and Tressel (2002), Scarpetta et al (2002), and IMF (2003).

[6] See Sachs and Warner (1995), Alesina et al (1997), Frankel and Romer (1999), and Ben-David and Kimhi (2000).

[7] See EU Review (2002) and Jones (2002).

[8] See Lucas (1988), Romer (1990), Grossman and Helpman (1991), Coe and Helpman (1995), and Aghion and Howitt (1998).

4

Europe. With respect to TFP, almost all of the EU-US TFP growth differential is attributable to developments in only a handful of industries in the manufacturing and private services sectors, including electrical and optical equipment (which includes semiconductors, the main ICT producing industry); wholesale and retail trade; real estate and other business services; and to a lesser extent financial services. Consequently, in the following analysis there will be an attempt to identify the determinants of TFP growth in several of these key industries where the EU-US TFP growth gap is concentrated. By isolating those factors which are critical in explaining differences in the evolution of TFP, the analysis tries to identify those policies which could potentially have the strongest impact in those areas of the economy where the TFP gaps are largest.

2.1 Conceptual framework

A better understanding of the key determinants of TFP growth has been high on the research agenda of international organisations and the academic community over the past decade. For a long period of time growth theory was not endowed with an appropriate paradigm to explain the determinants of TFP growth. In the standard neoclassical growth framework, TFP is exogenous and corresponds to the "Solow residual". In the early wave of endogenous growth models (the so-called "AK models") TFP growth is often the result of capital accumulation, which is assumed not to be subject to decreasing returns to scale, with the implication that growth-friendly policies should be focussed on promoting savings and investment. The predictions of these models do not appear to be consistent with recent stylised facts regarding the EU's growth performance with, for example, investment rates in the second half of the 1990s being higher in Europe than in the US, whilst TFP growth stagnated in the former group of countries and was sustained in the latter.

There is a growing consensus in the literature that recent growth theories, based on "Schumpeterian" creative destruction mechanisms, seem better equipped to interpret recent developments in the EU's growth performance (see, for example, Aghion and Howitt (2005))[9]. This theory focuses on innovation as the key driver of growth in economies at, or close to, the "technology frontier"[10]. Innovators, by introducing superior product varieties and technologies, have the effect of both displacing existing firms and of inducing the adoption of new products and techniques at the wider industry level. At the aggregate level, the innovation rate depends on the resources devoted to the innovation effort (i.e. R&D and human capital) and on the stock of existing knowledge (knowledge spillovers). The growth rate of the economy will depend not only on the rate of innovation but also on the rate at which "state-of-the-art" technologies are adopted / diffused throughout the wider economy. Countries that are close to the technology frontier will mainly grow thanks to the introduction of new technologies, whilst the "follower" grouping of countries will derive the largest share of their TFP growth from the adoption of better, but already existing, technologies which are available "at the frontier".

In this "Schumpeterian" world, institutions and policies play a key role in determining the relative position of countries in the global innovation race. These framework conditions directly impact on the relative ability of countries to innovate at the frontier or to adopt existing, leading-edge, technologies. Whilst follower countries would gain from institutions and policies favouring the cost efficient adoption of existing technologies, countries operating

---

[9] For earlier analyses, see also Nelson and Phelps (1966), Abramowitz (1986) and Benhabib and Spiegel (1994).

[10] Hence, the focus is on TFP growth as the engine of growth.

at the frontier would, on the other hand, profit from policies that promote excellence in higher education and R&D; financial markets that reward risky projects; and regulations that do not put an excessively heavy burden on either incumbent firms nor on potential entrants.

These latter views were reflected in the Sapir report (Sapir, et al. 2003), which was commissioned by the European Commission Presidency to identify policy priorities to re-launch economic growth in the EU. The report concluded that the EU's disappointing growth performance since the mid-1990 was due to institutions which were not sufficiently supportive of an innovation-based economy. High growth in the post-WWII era was driven by high levels of industrial production, economies of scale and imitation of US technological advances. As the EU approached the technological frontier, growth became increasingly dependent on innovation. The report suggests that the EU should focus on reforming their education systems; promoting higher levels of better targeted R&D; ensuring better regulation to facilitate the entry and exit of firms (instead of focussing on competition between existing players); providing more adequate infrastructure to facilitate the free movement of people, goods and ideas; stimulating innovation via financial and tax incentives; and promoting more labour market flexibility, notably through a lower tax burden on workers.

2.2. Existing empirical work

A number of papers in the literature have already analysed the determinants of TFP in a Schumpeterian framework. Most of the existing analyses use panel data information, pooling together data on TFP levels and growth rates over several years and countries. Some papers also use information at the sectoral / industry levels, with the datasets usually obtained from the OECD's STAN database[11]. The available empirical specifications normally reflect a reduced form of the basic innovation-imitation model, with most of them regressing TFP growth on two key explanatory variables:

- a measure of the technology gap (i.e. the distance between the TFP of the country analysed and that of the country with the highest level of efficiency); and

- an estimate of the growth rate of TFP at the frontier (i.e. the TFP growth rate of the most efficient country).

The first variable captures the extent to which TFP growth in a specific country can be explained by the adoption of more efficient existing technologies. The assumption here is simply that the larger the technology gap, the higher the potential gains from adopting more efficient, internationally available, technologies and consequently the faster the rate of TFP growth. The second variable aims at capturing the link between TFP growth in the "catching-up" country with the extent of innovation and knowledge spillovers which are taking place in the technologically most advanced country.

In addition to the above basic explanatory variables, most papers also control for a series of policy and institutional factors that may affect the rate of TFP growth independently or may interact with the "technology gap" and "technology spillovers" variables to have an impact on TFP. Nicoletti and Scarpetta (2003) analyse sectoral TFP growth in a panel of OECD countries and find some support for the view that entry liberalisation and privatisation have a positive impact on TFP. Moreover, this impact appears to be stronger the further away are

---

[11] See, for example, Nicoletti and Scarpetta (2003) and (2005); Griffith, Redding, and Van Reenen (2004), Conway et al. (2006).

countries from the technology frontier. The interpretation is that entry regulation and public ownership prevents the adoption of existing up-to-date technologies, so that the impact is greater away from the frontier, where TFP growth is more strongly based on adoption rather than on innovation. This result contrasts with the findings in Aghion, Bloom, Blundell, Griffith and Howitt (2003) who analyse the patenting activity of UK firms at the US patenting office. They find that when firms are close to the national technological frontier that product market competition has a stronger positive impact for innovation. This conclusion can be explained by the observation that being far from the frontier reduced the incentives to innovate by reducing innovators' rents more strongly. A similar result is obtained in Aghion, Blundell, Griffith, Howitt and Prantl (2006) who analyse patenting activity and TFP growth at the firm and establishment levels in the UK.

In Nicoletti and Scarpetta (2003), it is also found that a human capital variable has a positive impact on TFP growth, although not always significant. Vandenbussche, Aghion and Méghir (2005) analyse aggregate TFP determinants in a panel of OECD countries and show that high-skilled human capital has a positive effect on TFP growth, an effect which is stronger the closer a country is to the technology frontier.

Griffith, Redding and Van Reenen (2004) study TFP determinants across sectors in a panel of OECD countries and show that R&D has both a direct impact on TFP growth and a role in facilitating the cross-country convergence of TFP levels. The result is interpreted as providing support for the two "faces" of R&D in promoting productivity growth: on the one hand, R&D enhances a firm's innovative potential (thus increasing directly the rate of TFP growth); on the other hand, it improves the absorptive capacity of firms and industries, thus facilitating the adoption of existing technologies and spurring TFP convergence.

Most of the existing analyses at a sectoral level are limited to manufacturing industries. However, we learned earlier that TFP growth rates in Europe and the US have been diverging, in recent times, especially in market services. Hence, a better understanding of the TFP growth determinants in these industries is crucial in assessing the factors which are driving the EU's widening productivity gap with the US. With a view to addressing such questions, Inklaar, Timmer and Van Ark (2008) analyse the determinants of TFP growth in market services using the EU KLEMS database. Their analysis shows that although ICT investments were a main driver of labour productivity growth in the service sectors of both the EU and the US, the adoption of ICT-intensive technologies does not appear to be associated with higher growth rates of TFP. Additionally, human capital intensity has no significant explanatory power for TFP growth and entry regulations mattered only in telecommunications, but not in other market service industries.

2.3. Empirical strategy

The aim of the following analysis is to take a step forward compared with existing work by capitalising on the recent release of the EU KLEMS datasets and specifically on the increased availability of TFP data series and of substantially enhanced industry level detail. Compared with Inklaar, Timmer, and Van Ark (2008), we will not limit the analysis to market services. Additionally, there will be an attempt to identify the determinants of TFP growth in a number of specific industry groupings that contributed most to the EU-US TFP growth gap, namely ICT- producing manufacturing industries and retail services, and for those industries where EU countires exhibited a stronger performance, i.e. public utilities. Compared with existing

7

analyses, there will also be an attempt to control for a potentially large number of policy and institutional variables.

The analysis concerns 9 EU countries plus the US over the 1980-2004 period and covers a total of 28 industries[12]. The baseline specification is similar to that found in existing analyses (e.g., Nicoletti and Scarpetta (2003)). TFP growth rates are regressed over a measure of innovation / technology spillovers (i.e. the TFP growth rate of the leader country) and of a technology gap term (i.e. the lagged logarithm of the difference between TFP in a specific country and TFP at the frontier, with the frontier being determined by the country exhibiting the highest TFP level in that particular industry, in that particular year). Country, sector and year fixed effects control for factors that independently may affect TFP growth rates.

The TFP growth rates used in the analysis are those computed using the established "ex-post" capital services method in the EU KLEMS database. With regard to the measurement of the technology gap variable, we make use of the PPP-adjusted TFP levels dataset provided for the 10 countries in Inklaar, Timmer and Van Ark (2007)[13]. As a countercheck, TFP data obtained using an "ex-ante" approach, and "raw" TFP measures that do not distinguish between labour with different skill levels and between ICT and non-ICT capital, are also used[14].

The baseline specification has subsequently been augmented in such a way as to control for the impact of ICT and human capital, R&D, regulations, and other framework conditions. In the following section, only the specifications exhibiting the strongest explanatory power are displayed. A long list of country-level variables, capturing overall macroeconomic conditions; the presence of those economy-wide infrastructures which are most closely associated with the development of new technologies; demographic factors; barriers to entry; and competition, turned-out to be not significant[15].

---

[12] The 9 EU countries are Denmark, Germany, Spain, France, Italy, the Netherlands, Austria, Finland and the UK. The 28 industries are taken from the NACE A31 industry breakdown. Data is only available for a total of 28 industries since some of the smaller headings have been merged with other NACE codes.

[13] The TFP levels data in Inklaar, Timmer and Van Ark (2007) refer to the year 1997. TFP levels for other years are derived from TFP growth rates computed ex-ante. R. Inklaar is gratefully acknowledged for providing the TFP levels data produced in Inklaar, Timmer and Van Ark (2007).

[14] The difference between the ex-post and the ex-ante method for computing TFP is that the latter is based on an exogenous value for the rate of return whereas the ex-post approach estimates the internal rate of return as a residual given the value of capital compensation from the national accounts and estimates for depreciation and capital gains.

[15] The data sources for these variables are as follows : European Commission DG ECFIN's AMECO database for macroeconomic conditions (output gap, relative contribution of consumption to GDP growth, relative contribution of investment to GDP growth); Barro and Lee data on economy-wide education indicators; World Bank Development Indicators for infrastructure (number of internet users, computer diffusion, share of population with tertiary degree, public spending on education, public spending on R&D, number of patent applications) and for the age structure of the population; OECD for economy-wide indicators of product market regulation and barriers to competition (public ownership of firms, public involvement in business operations, regulatory and administrative opacity, administrative burden on start ups, barriers to competition, explicit barriers to foreign trade and investment, other barriers to foreign trade and investment).

2.4. Regression results

2.4.1. Baseline specification: Table 1 presents the results for the baseline specification[16]. Across the whole sample (column (1)), the results suggest that TFP growth is higher when there is stronger TFP growth in the frontier economy (reflecting the impact of innovation and technology spillovers) and when the technology gap is larger (which reflects TFP convergence via the adoption of existing superior technologies).

In comparison with previous similar analyses, whilst a significantly negative relationship between TFP growth and the gap in technology is generally found, the impact of TFP growth at the frontier is not always significant (e.g., Nicoletti and Scarpetta (2003)). Given that our results are strongly significant for "frontier" growth effects, as a robustness check, column (2) in Table 1 also reports the same specification as in column (1) but using "ex-ante" calculated TFP growth rates. It is comforting to note that the results are broadly similar in terms of the coefficient estimate and its significance level. What appears to matter instead for the result is the distinction between labour skills and ICT and non-ICT capital when constructing the TFP variable. Indeed, by repeating the baseline regressions using a "raw" measure of TFP that does not distinguish between labour with different skills and that does not differentiate the marginal productivity of ICT capital, TFP growth taking place at the frontier does not appear to significantly affect TFP growth rates (column (3)). This result suggests that the possibility of taking into account labour and capital inputs of different quality (as is possible with the EU KLEMS database) permits one to get closer to a measure of TFP growth which reflects innovation dynamics and the introduction of new technologies to a greater extent than "cruder" TFP measures. On the basis of the more "sophisticated" TFP measures in EU KLEMS, TFP improvements appear to be more strongly affected by developments taking place at the frontier.

Table 1 : Basic specification

	All industries and years	All industries ("ex-ante" TFP)	All industries ("raw" TFP)	Only manu-facturing sector	Only market services	Only ICT-related sectors	Only years after 1995
	(1)	(2)	(3)	(4)	(5)	(6)	(7)
TFP growth at the frontier	0.159**	0.113**	0.060	0.164**	0.135**	0.138***	0.158*
	(2.98)	(2.61)	(0.54)	(2.38)	(3.39)	(4.70)	(2.08)
Technological gap	-0.046***	-0.038***	-0.036***	-0.060***	-0.029***	-0.027***	-0.046
	(4.48)	(5.12)	(-4.96)	(3.81)	(4.14)	(4.85)	(1.20)
N. obs.	6619	6059	6677	3058	2133	2371	2796
R^2	0.13	0.12	0.10	0.16	0.10	0.50	0.12

Notes: Estimation method: panel OLS regressions; fixed effects included for countries, sectors, and years; standard errors robust with respect to heteroschedasticity and possible correlation within countries. Absolute value of t tests reported in parenthesis. ***, **, * denote, respectively, statistical significance at 1, 5, and 10 per cent level.
TFP growth at the frontier: TFP growth of the country with the highest TFP level in sector s, year t (leader country).
Technological gap: lagged log(TFP level −TFP level of the leader country).

---

[16] Since the explanatory variables are likely to be exogenous, OLS estimation methods are used. Standard errors are robust with respect to heteroschedasticity and the possible autocorrelation of the residuals within countries.

Table 1 also reports results for the basic specification based on different sectoral breakdowns and time periods. Column (4) reports the results when the sample is restricted to the manufacturing sector, whilst columns (5) and (6) do the same for, respectively, private services and ICT-related sectors (the latter comprises both ICT producing manufacturing sectors and all sectors of the economy that use ICT goods intensively). Column (7) reports results for all sectors but in years after 1995 only. A number of results stand out. Firstly, innovation and knowledge spillovers have a broadly similar effect on the TFP growth performance of the manufacturing, private services and ICT-related sectors, as indicated by a similar value for the coefficient of TFP growth at the frontier. Secondly, regarding the technology gap term, TFP growth in the manufacturing sector is relatively more driven by the adoption of superior existing technologies, compared with the private services and ICT related sectors. Finally, in restricting the analysis to the last decade of the sample (i.e. 1995-2004), TFP growth appears to be mostly driven by growth at the frontier, with a non-significant impact from the technology gap variable. This finding is consistent with the view that across Europe, growth is increasingly being driven by innovation activity and less by the adoption of existing up-to date technologies. Given these emerging patterns, these results could be interpreted somewhat negatively given that they appear to indicate that the extent of catching-up across countries is weakening over time.

2.4.2. The role of human capital, ICT capital, and R&D : Table 2 reports the results for the basic specification augmented to take into account the role of human capital, ICT capital, and R&D in affecting TFP growth. On top of the determinants included in the basic specification, the share of skilled labour compensation, the share of R&D expenditure, and the share of ICT capital and non-ICT capital are added to control for, respectively, the role of human capital, R&D, and ICT technologies. All variables vary across countries and sectors and over time. [17]

These additional variables, when introduced in the baseline specification (whilst keeping country, sector, and year fixed effects) appear not to have significant explanatory power. [18] A possible explanation for this poor performance for factors commonly regarded as relevant for TFP dynamics could be that the sample period is not sufficiently long for the impact of these variables to become manifest, or that such effects unfold only gradually and with long lags. The presence of country and fixed effects imply that the impact of the explanatory variables on TFP growth is captured mostly along the time dimension. In order to allow the cross-country dimension to play a role, in column (2) we repeat the same regression as in column (1) but eliminating the country fixed effects. It turns out, allowing for a cross-country dimension, that human capital and R&D play a clearly positive role and have a stronger statistical significance, whilst ICT is still largely insignificant. Column (3) repeats the regression excluding the sector fixed effects. It appears that it is the variation across sectors that permits one to identify a largely significant role for R&D and ICT intensity. In sum, while it seems, other things being equal, that sectors characterised by higher R&D and ICT intensity tend to exhibit higher growth rates of TFP, an across the board increase in R&D and ICT intensity does not appear to translate into higher TFP growth. This result helps to qualify those previously obtained in Inklaar, Timmer, and van Ark (2008) regarding the role of ICT

---

[17] More traditional measures of human capital, like educational attainment levels in the whole economy (Barro and Lee source) were tested but produced only small and insignificant effects.

[18] An exception is the ICT variable when restricting the sample to manufacturing only (column (7)). In this case, the coefficient appears to be significantly negative. A possible explanation is that the introduction of ICT technologies require a re-adaptation of production methods and organization, which could have a temporary negative impact on TFP (see, for example, Basu and Fernald (2007)). The results suggest that such temporary negative TFP effects from ICT are mostly felt in manufacturing.

in market services. Even if their ICT variable differs from ours (being defined as the share of ICT capital returns on total costs), their regressions also include fixed effects for countries, sectors, and years.

A further check on the above results is provided in columns (4) and (5), where regression results without, respectively, country and sector effects are displayed when the TFP measure used is "raw" i.e. it does not take into account labour and capital composition effects. With this measure of TFP, a role for human capital is found for the specification excluding country fixed effects. Countries where the skill intensity of production technologies is higher tend to exhibit higher TFP growth rates, other things being equal. The fact that this result holds only with a "raw" TFP measure suggests that part of the explanation for the role of human capital is related to the fact that TFP growth also captures labour productivity improvements associated with the secular rise in the skill levels of the workforce in general, and that these improvements are stronger in the countries exhibiting higher skill levels on average over the sample period.

As shown in previous analyses, the impact of human capital and R&D may depend on the degree of technological advancement of countries, as captured by distance from the frontier. In order to capture this effect, we add as an explanatory variable our human capital and R&D measures interacted with the "technological gap" variable. In addition, we also interact human capital and R&D with the "TFP growth at the frontier" variable. The idea in this case is that R&D and human capital could be factors facilitating innovation and the absorption of technological spillovers emanating from the technological frontier. To our knowledge this interaction was not performed in previous analyses. A reason could be the weak explanatory power of TFP growth at the frontier as a regressor when using TFP data which fails to appropriately take into account the change in the quality composition of labour and capital, which is not the case with the EU KLEMS data.

Furthermore, since the human capital and R&D variables are standardised in such a way as to have zero mean and unit standard deviation, and since both variables (subject to interaction) are included independently in the empirical specification, the interpretation of the interacted variables is easy. The value of the coefficient of, say, human capital interacted with the technological gap term, represents the change in the technological gap variable associated with a one-standard-deviation increase in the share of skilled labour compensation in total labour compensation. Thus, a positive (negative) coefficient means that more human capital is associated with slower (faster) TFP convergence. The regression coefficient of the non-interacted "technology at the frontier" and technological gap variable represents their impact keeping the value of human capital at zero, i.e., at sample mean. An alternative interpretation is that the change in the coefficient of the human capital variable is associated with a one per cent reduction in the technological gap (i.e. the percentage distance between the TFP in a given country, sector and year and the highest TFP value found across countries in the same sector in that year). Thus, a positive (negative) coefficient means that being closer to (further away from) the frontier raises the impact of human capital. Analogous interpretations are given for the remaining interacted variables.

Column (6) reports the results across the whole sample of sectors. Columns (7), (8), and (9) repeat the same regression limiting the sample to manufacturing, market services, and ICT-related industries respectively. It appears that, across all sectors, human capital has a positive and almost statistically significant coefficient when interacted with both the technological gap variable and TFP growth at the frontier. Hence, consistent with Vandenbussche, Aghion and

11

Méghir (2005), we also find that the positive impact of human capital is stronger the smaller is the technological gap. Moreover, human capital also permits one to share in the TFP improvements taking place at the frontier, either because analogous innovations to those put in place at the frontier become more likely also "at the periphery", or because the capacity to absorb technological spillovers increases with human capital. This role of human capital as facilitator of frontier-type innovation and technological spillovers is highly visible especially when restricting the analysis to market services. In this case, the coefficient of the human capital variable interacted with TFP growth at the frontier is highly significant. R&D also appears to have a positive effect on the ability of a country to share in the TFP improvements taking place at the frontier, as revealed by the positive coefficient of the R&D variable interacted with TFP growth at the frontier, and this effect is stronger in market services.

Table 2: The role of human capital, ICT capital, and R&D

	All industries	All industries	All industries	All industries ("raw" TFP)	All industries ("raw" TFP)	All industries	Only manufacturing sector	Only market services	Only ICT-related sectors
	(1)	(2)	(3)	(4)	(5)	(6)	(7)	(8)	(9)
TFP growth at the frontier	0.186*	0.186*	0.192*	0.025	0.008	0.178**	0.175**	0.397***	0.161**
	(2.18)	(2.20)	(2.27)	(0.13)	(0.05)	(2.84)	(2.41)	(3.19)	(3.94)
Technological gap	0.091**	-0.092**	-0.085**	-0.075***	-0.062**	-0.088***	-0.106**	-0.031	-0.024***
	(3.15)	(3.25)	(3.25)	(-3.65)	(-3.10)	(3.24)	(2.85)	(1.10)	(3.50)
Human capital	-0.003	0.004	0.002	0.007***	0.000	0.003	-0.015	0.008	0.002
	(-0.65)	(1.08)	(0.50)	(3.92)	(0.19)	(0.31)	(0.68)	(1.88)	(0.36)
R&D	0.002	0.004	0.004***	0.006**	0.006**	0.004	0.005	0.037	0.004
	(0.67)	(1.25)	(4.98)	(2.23)	(3.18)	(0.36)	(0.38)	(1.57)	(0.73)
ICT/ non ICT real capital stock ratio	0.002	-0.000	0.006***	0.000	0.009***	0.002	-0.038**	0.001	-0.000
	(0.74)	(0.21)	(3.70)	(0.20)	(4.76)	(0.61)	(3.41)	(0.46)	(0.64)
Interaction TFP growth at the frontier with human capital						0.184	0.213	0.189***	0.133
						(1.46)	(1.42)	(5.59)	(1.43)
Interaction TFP growth at the frontier with R&D						0.011	0.028	0.349	0.048
						(0.31)	(0.76)	(1.17)	(0.99)
Interaction technological gap with human capital						0.028	0.017	0.011	0.009
						(1.48)	(0.48)	(1.38)	(0.59)
Interaction technological gap with R&D						0.010	0.016	0.006	-0.002
						(0.47)	(0.54)	(0.13)	(0.16)
Country fixed effects	Yes	No	Yes	No	Yes	Yes	Yes	Yes	Yes
Sector fixed effects	Yes	Yes	No	Yes	No	Yes	Yes	Yes	Yes
Year fixed effects	Yes	Yes	Yes	Yes	Yes	Yes	Yes	Yes	Yes
N. obs.	2251	2251	2251	2242	2242	2251	1535	574	786
R^2	0.20	0.19	0.19	0.12	0.12	0.22	0.23	0.21	0.32

Notes:
Estimation method: panel OLS regressions; standard errors robust with respect to heteroschedasticity and possible correlation within countries. Absolute value of t tests reported in parenthesis. ***, **, * denote, respectively, statistical significance at 1, 5, and 10 per cent level.
TFP growth at the frontier: TFP growth of the country with the highest TFP level in sector s, year t (leader country). Source EU KLEMS.
Technological gap: lagged log (TFP level –log(TFP level of the leader country). Source: EU KLEMS.
Human capital: share of high skill labour compensation in total labour compensation. Standardised variable. Source: EU KLEMS.
R&D: R&D expenditure/gross output. Standardized variable. Source: OECD STAN.
ICT/non ICT real capital stock ratio. Source: EU KLEMS.

In summary, ICT, human capital, and R&D appear to play some role in TFP growth. However, results seem sensitive to the specification and in particular to the inclusion of sector and country effects and to the approach for measuring TFP. R&D and ICT intensive technologies have a positive impact on TFP only if sector effects are not included, which implies that the relationship is mostly found across sectors. Human capital plays a role in facilitating innovation and spillovers, as indicated by its positive interaction with the "TFP growth at the frontier" variable, which is highly significant especially when the analysis is limited to market services. The impact of human capital also appears stronger the closer is the economy to the technological frontier, a result which confirms the findings of existing analyses.

2.4.3. The role of regulations : The next series of TFP determinants analysed are regulations in product and factor markets. Recent research carried out in international organisations has emphasised the role of regulations in driving efficiency gains (e.g., OECD (2003), IMF (2003)). In addition, the literature which is more closely focused on assessing TFP growth determinants also tends to find some impact of regulations on the growth of TFP (see section 2.2.). In our analysis we have considered regulations in product markets and labour and financial markets separately. Product market regulations are captured by the "Regimpact" indicator developed by the OECD (Conway and Nicoletti (2006)), which measures the "knock-on" effect in each sector of the economy arising from anti-competitive regulations in non-manufacturing sectors. Labour market and financial market regulations are summarised by the "freedom indicators" constructed by the Fraser institute. The indicators quantify the degree of absence of anti-competitive regulations in, respectively, the labour and financial markets. We consider the impact of these indicators taken with a minus sign, to capture instead the effect associated with regulations becoming heavier. All indicators vary across countries and sectors and over time.

Table 3 displays the results. While regulations do not appear to play a significant role when directly added to the list of explanatory variables (and keeping all sectors in the sample (column (1)), their impact is found to be significant when distinguishing sub-groups of industries. Moreover, their interaction with TFP growth at the frontier and the technology gap variable reveals some significant effects.

The results displayed in column (2) suggest that, across all industries, anti-competitive financial market regulations appear to reduce TFP growth directly, and the more so the closer is the economy to the technological frontier. Moreover, heavier financial market regulations reduce the extent to which the economy can share in TFP improvements taking place at the frontier. The same regression shows that more regulated labour markets, although reducing TFP growth directly, have a significant impact on the extent to which TFP growth benefits from developments at the frontier. This evidence highlights the ambiguous role that may be played by labour market regulations on TFP growth (see, e.g, Bassanini and Ernst -2002- for a discussion of the alternative channels highlighted in the theoretical literature). On the one hand, stricter labour market regulations, notably employment protection legislation, by limiting the room for re-adjusting the labour force in the case of redundancies, may hinder the incentives of firms to engage in risky innovation projects, thus reducing TFP growth at the frontier. On the other hand, stronger protection of employment may increase job-tenure and investment in job-specific skills, which may be complementary to TFP growth (Acemoglu and Shimer (2000)) The impact of product market regulation appears to be largely insignificant.

13

Column (3) repeats the same specification as in column (2) but restricted to manufacturing. Unexpectedly, product market regulations appear to play a positive impact on TFP growth both directly and via increased benefits from developments at the frontier. The role of financial market regulations in limiting such benefits is strengthened compared with the case in which the analysis comprises all sectors. By limiting the sample to market services, the impact of product market regulations turns negative, and appears to play an effect both directly and indirectly. In particular, product market regulations appear to reduce TFP growth more strongly when the economy is closer to the frontier. Financial market regulations, conversely, result in having a significantly stronger negative impact the further away is the economy from the technological frontier. The regressions for ICT-related industries are analogous to those for manufacturing for what concerns the role of product market regulations, and to that for market services regarding labour and financial market regulations.

Table 3 : The role of regulations

	All Industries	All Industries	Only manufacturing sector	Only market services	Only ICT-related sectors
	(1)	(2)	(3)	(4)	(5)
TFP growth at the frontier	0.171***	0.175***	0.398***	0.138***	0.153***
	(3.39)	(5.82)	(4.02)	(3.97)	(7.07)
Technological gap	-0.049***	-0.047***	-0.042*	-0.026***	-0.030***
	(5.09)	(5.20)	(2.26)	(5.13)	(6.95)
Product market regulation	-0.002	-0.000	0.126***	-0.008	0.008**
	(0.96)	(0.01)	(3.41)	(1.65)	(2.81)
Labour market regulation	0.008	-0.004	-0.009	0.002	0.006
	(1.45)	(0.79)	(1.46)	(0.36)	(0.95)
Financial market regulation	0.005	-0.007	-0.004	0.009	0.009*
	(1.31)	(1.43)	(0.36)	(1.73)	(2.01)
Interaction TFP growth at the frontier with product market regulation		0.016	0.416**	-0.005	-0.040
		(0.41)	(2.73)	(0.23)	(0.98)
Interaction TFP growth at the frontier with labour market regulation		0.090**	0.080**	0.069*	0.014
		(2.43)	(2.12)	(1.85)	(0.35)
Interaction TFP growth at the frontier with financial market regulation		-0.078	-0.127**	-0.063**	-0.081**
		(1.62)	(2.80)	(2.55)	(2.57)
Interaction technological gap with product market regulation		-0.007	0.064	-0.013*	0.002
		(0.90)	(1.17)	(2.07)	(0.38)
Interaction technological gap with labour market regulation		-0.004	-0.007	-0.005	0.001
		(0.48)	(0.47)	(0.81)	(0.16)
Interaction technological gap with financial market regulation		-0.003	-0.014	0.016**	0.007*
		(0.34)	(0.97)	(2.34)	(1.89)
N. obs.	6340	6340	2929	2043	2271
R^2	0.13	0.14	0.18	0.11	0.22

Notes: Estimation method: panel OLS regressions; fixed effects included for countries, sectors, and years; standard errors robust with respect to heteroschedasticity and possible correlation within countries. Absolute value of t tests reported in parenthesis. ***, **, * denote, respectively, statistical significance at 1, 5, and 10 per cent level.
TFP growth at the frontier: TFP growth of the country with the highest TFP level in sector s, year t (leader country). Source: EU KLEMS.
Technological gap: lagged log(TFP level)–log(TFP level of the leader country). Source: EU KLEMS.
Product market regulation: indicator of the "knock on" sectoral impact of regulations in non-manufacturing sectors. Standardised variable. Source: OECD "Regimpact" indicator.
Labour market regulation: indicator of anti-competitive regulations in the labour market. Standardised variable. Source: Fraser institute freedom indicators (taken with negative sign).
Financial market regulation: indicator of anti-competitive regulations in the labour market. Standardised variable. Source: Fraser institute freedom indicators (taken with negative sign).

Overall, the role of regulations appears to be highly sector-specific. Results suffer from robustness checks with respect to the specification chosen and the sample definition. Additionally, the limited time-variation of the sample used in the regressions makes it difficult to disentangle the short term transitional effects of labour market reforms, introduced by many EU countries since the early 1990's, from the long run impact of those reforms on TFP growth rates. In spite of these caveats and limitations, some results of interest stand up. As expected product market regulations appear to play a negative role for TFP growth in market services. Financial market regulations seem to play a negative role especially concerning the ability of countries to share in TFP improvements taking place at the frontier.

2.4.4. Industry-specific specifications: Part of the problems experienced with the regulatory regressions may be linked to the need to use a lower level of disaggregation than the broad sectoral aggregates which were used for the analysis in Table 3. This highlights the necessity of adapting the empirical model of TFP growth determinants to the different specificities of industries. In the following, our aim is to identify empirical models specific to those industries that gave a large contribution to the EU-US TFP growth gap as well as for those industries where the EU performance was comparatively satisfactory.

As shown earlier, the EU-US TFP gap is concentrated in the ICT producing manufacturing industry (i.e. electrical and optical equipment which includes semi-conductors) and a number of private service industries. In addition to showing where the EU is underperforming, graph 1 also shows that there is a small group of industries where the EU has outperformed the US over the past decade i.e. the "network" industries.

Graph 1 : EU + US – Trend Contributions from TFP in the "Network Industries" to the Value Added Growth Rate of the EU and US economies over the period 1981-2004 (Annual % Change)

Source : EU KLEMS, Commission services

Table 4 presents the results for those TFP determinants which have been selected for ICT-manufacturing industries and retail services as representatives of those sectors accounting for a large share of the EU-US productivity gap, and for utilities, as an example of a sector where the EU has a relatively strong performance. Since the aim is to identify TFP determinants that are distinctive for the sectors under analysis, the table also reports results when the selected variables are used to explain TFP growth in all of the remaining sectors.

Column (1) shows that for the ICT producing industry (i.e. electrical and optical equipment), the basic variables behave somewhat differently to prior expectations. The frontier and technology gap variables are non-significant, with the latter indicating that TFP growth rather than converging is diverging across countries in this particular industry. This result is consistent with the existing evidence which suggests that labour productivity in the "high tech" sectors is not converging across countries, in contrast with what is observed for most other sectors (see, for example, Scarpetta and Tressel (2002)). Interestingly, the results change drastically when the same specification is tested on "total industries" excluding the ICT-producing manufacturing industry itself (column (2)).

15

Regarding retail and wholesale trade services (column (3)), the results indicate a significant role for cyclical factors in providing a direct explanation for observed differences in TFP growth between the US and the EU's Member States (as suggested by the strongly significant positive coefficient for the relative contribution of private consumption to GDP growth).[19] Due to its construction as a residual term, TFP growth also captures productivity improvements associated with the better exploitation of scale economies, which are likely to be a relevant factor in explaining productivity dynamics in this group of service industries. It is worth noting that a similar positive impact of cyclical factors is not observed in the remaining sectors (column (4)).

Table 4: Industry-specific models

	ICT producing manufacturing		Retail and affiliated industries		Utilities	
	Only ICT producing manufacturing	Only remaining industries	Only retail and affiliated industries	Only remaining industries	Only utilities	Only remaining industries
	(1)	(2)	(3)	(4)	(5)	(6)
TFP growth at the frontier	0.007	0.168**	0.152**	0.194**	0.086	0.190***
	(0.05)	(2.34)	(2.61)	(2.37)	(0.47)	(4.08)
Technological gap	0.010	-0.082**	-0.034***	-0.0544***	-0.022	-0.048***
	(0.67)	(3.28)	(4.26)	(4.03)	(0.84)	(4.92)
Interaction TFP growth at the frontier with R&D	0.130***	0.016				
	(3.50)	(0.38)				
Relative contribution of private consumption to GDP growth			0.004***	0.001		
			(5.08)	(1.80)		
Product market regulation					-0.010*	0.004
					(2.00)	(0.063)
Interaction TFP growth at the frontier with product market regulation					0.032	0.043
					(0.33)	(1.32)
Interaction technological gap with product market regulation					-0.115	0.005
					(1.06)	(0.90)
Country fixed effects	Yes	Yes	Yes	Yes	Yes	Yes
Sector fixed effects	No	Yes	Yes	Yes	Yes	Yes
Year fixed effects	No	Yes	Yes	Yes	Yes	Yes
N. obs.	141	2497	836	5030	684	5656
R^2	0.56	0.18	0.17	0.14	0.22	0.13

Notes: Estimation method: panel OLS regressions; fixed effects included for countries, sectors, and years; standard errors robust with respect to heteroschedasticity and possible correlation within countries. Absolute value of t tests reported in parenthesis. ***, **, * denote, respectively, statistical significance at 1, 5, and 10 per cent level.
TFP growth at the frontier : TFP growth of the country with the highest TFP level in sector *s*, year *t* (leader country). Source: EU KLEMS.
Technological gap : lagged log (TFP level)–log(TFP level of the leader country). Source: EU KLEMS.
R&D : R&D expenditure/gross output. Standardized variable. Source: OECD STAN.
Human capital: share of high skill labour compensation in total labour compensation. Standardised variable. Source: EU KLEMS.
Relative contribution of private consumption to GDP growth: GDP growth due to private consumption/GDP growth. Source AMECO.
Product market regulation: indicator of the "knock on" sectoral impact of regulations in non-manufacturing sectors. Standardised variable. Source: OECD "Regimpact" indicator.
Financial market regulation: indicator of anti-competitive regulations in the labour market. Standardised variable. Source: Fraser institute freedom indicators (taken with negative sign).
ICT-producing manufactures: electrical and optical equipment (30t33).
Retail and affiliated industries : Retail sale, maintenance and repair of motor vehicles and motor cycles (50) + wholesale trade and commission trade except motor vehicles and motor cycles (51) + Repair of household goods and retail trade except of motor vehicles and motor cycles (52) + hotels and restaurants (H).
Utilities : energy (E)+transport and storage (60t63)+post and telecommunications (64).

---

[19] A role for cyclical factors is suggested also by the positive and significant coefficient of the output gap as an alternative explanatory variable.

16

Finally, regarding the "network" industries, product market regulations are shown to have a significant negative impact on this grouping of industries but not on the rest of the economy (for which the coefficient has instead an unexpected positive sign - see column (6)). This regulatory impact appears to reflect the "knock-on" effects of regulations in this specific industry grouping on all other sectors of the economy. Its influence is likely to be particularly high, given the amount of regulations which have tended, in the past at least, to be imposed on a number of individual network industries, including electricity, gas and water, as well as on transport and communications. The direct impact exercised should however be interpreted mostly in terms of the better exploitation of scale economies and reduced "X inefficiencies" rather than to any dynamic TFP gains.

2.5. Summary of the main policy-relevant results: Whilst bearing in mind the need for caution in interpreting results that inevitably suffer, to some extent, from the imperfect measurement of TFP and from a number of robustness issues in the econometric specification, some potentially relevant findings stand out from our analysis.

- Firstly, compared with previous analogous studies, the use of the EU KLEMS database permits us to identify a statistically significant role of "TFP growth at the frontier" as an explanatory variable for TFP growth across the whole sample. Therefore, in addition to a significant TFP convergence phenomenon associated with the adoption of existing up-to-date technologies which is generally found in econometric work aimed at assessing TFP determinants with sectoral data, TFP growth also appears to be determined significantly by the capacity of countries to share in developments taking place at the frontier, either because of independently participating in the same innovation trajectories or because of technological spillovers.

- Secondly, whilst there is a generalised tendency towards catching-up across countries in terms of TFP growth, such a tendency seems to be weakening over time, especially in the post-1995 period. Moreover, for the ICT-producing manufacturing sector this process of catching-up is particularly weak. TFP growth appears increasingly associated with innovation and technological spillovers from countries positioned "at the frontier".

- Thirdly, ICT, human capital, and R&D appear to play some role in TFP growth. However, results seem sensitive to the specification and in particular to the inclusion of sector and country effects and to the approach for measuring TFP. R&D and ICT intensive technologies have a significantly positive impact on TFP only if sector effects are not included. The relationship therefore holds mostly across sectors : sectors spending more on R&D and using more ICT-intensive technologies tend to exhibit higher growth rates of total factor productivity. However, there is no significant evidence that an across-the-board increase in R&D expenditures or in the use of ICT-intensive technologies translates into higher TFP growth. The implication for policy is that what matters for aggregate TFP growth is an expansion of the R&D and ICT-intensive industries rather than policies aimed at raising R&D and ICT technologies in all industries. Human capital plays a role in facilitating innovation and spillovers, as indicated by its positive interaction with the "TFP growth at the frontier" variable, which is highly significant especially when the analysis is limited to market services. The impact of human capital also appears

17

stronger the closer is the economy to the technological frontier, a result that confirms the findings of existing analyses.

- Fourthly, the role of regulations appears to be highly sector-specific. Results suffer from robustness checks with respect to the specification chosen and the sample definition and from the limited time-variation of the sample. Notwithstanding these caveats and limitations, some results of interest stand up. As expected, product market regulations appear to play a negative role for TFP growth in market services. Financial market regulations seem to play a negative role especially for what concerns the ability of countries to share in TFP improvements taking place at the frontier.

- Finally, the determinants of TFP growth appear to be largely industry-specific. Against this background, we attempted to identify the TFP growth determinants in those industries that explain the bulk of the EU-US TFP growth gap and in those where the EU's performance is relatively strong. Differences in the ICT-producing manufacturing industry appear to be firmly related to the role played by R&D in allowing countries to share in the TFP growth improvements taking place at the frontier. In the retail and wholesale trade industry, the evidence suggests a possible role for cyclical factors driving consumption dynamics: stronger consumption growth could be the source of TFP growth associated with a better exploitation of scale economies. Finally, TFP growth in the network industries appears to be driven in a comparatively strong fashion by product market regulations. In this respect, the satisfactory TFP growth performance in the EU in this set of industries could be related to the deregulation drive which characterised the behaviour of most EU countries towards these industries over the last two decades, and to the resultant more pro-competitive environment.

3. Concluding Remarks

Over the last decade many EU15 Member States have experienced a slowdown in their productivity performances relative both to previous time periods and to other developed economies across the OECD, most notably the US. The detailed analysis of the EU KLEMS datasets contained in the "EU Economy 2007 Review" showed that most of the EU-US productivity differences were not to be found in investment patterns (although the US was shown to have a much greater focus on ICT related investments) but were mainly driven by developments in TFP, the structural component of productivity.

Whilst the essentially growth accounting approach used in the "2007 Review" was helpful in isolating those industries / sectors where the EU-US TFP differences lay, such an analytical approach has little to say concerning the underlying driving factors behind the divergences which emerged. Using a panel regression approach, the present paper statistically assessed the relative importance of those TFP determinants which have been consistently highlighted in the literature as playing a role. Given the sample of countries used in the analysis, it is clear that the focus was on assessing the drivers of TFP growth at the frontier rather than on analysing catching-up effects (e.g., learning-by-doing and imitation effects), with the role of R&D, human capital and a wide range of regulatory indicators being of specific interest. One relatively clear finding, of a general nature, to emerge from the regression analysis was that

TFP growth is increasingly associated, especially over the post-1995 period, with innovation and technological spillovers from countries positioned "at the frontier".

With respect to understanding the TFP trends in those specific industries where EU-US differences are concentrated, the regression analysis suggests that a relatively wide spectrum of factors is implicated. Whereas R&D intensity factors are linked with the relative under-performance of the EU's ICT producing manufacturing industry (mainly semiconductors), cyclical factors and the better exploitation of scale economies are a feature of the divergences in the retail and wholesale trade industries. Finally, with regard to the EU's out-performance in the network industries, there is evidence to suggest that these are mainly linked to one-off static efficiency gains associated with the sustained deregulation drive which occurred in these industries in many EU Member States over the last two decades.

Whilst the main policy-relevant conclusions from the regression analysis, given in section 2.5, are undoubtedly tentative[20] in nature, they are nevertheless in accordance with the emerging view in the literature that the TFP growth slowdown experienced by a large number of advanced European economies in recent years could be linked to a generalised failure in Europe to sufficiently adapt its policies and institutions from its post world war II phase of development. Over the bulk of the post-war period, Europe drove its relatively successful catching-up process using an economic policy approach which in essence was focussed on imitating US technological advances. As convergence increasingly gave way to a phase in which EU countries joined, and in some cases extended, the global technology frontier, a large number of countries faced growing difficulties in replicating the TFP successes of earlier decades, with these successes in fact increasing their reluctance to acquiesce to the need for change.

The analysis in the present study supports the view that being at, or close to, the technology frontier, demands a re-focussing of policies and institutions more towards an innovation-based economic model, with less emphasis on the imitation of available, leading-edge, technologies and practices and more on sustained improvements in the EU's innovation capacity[21]. The hallmarks of an open-economy, innovation driven, developmental model are world class educational establishments; higher levels of, excellence driven and better targeted, R&D; more market based financing systems; and more flexible regulatory and institutional frameworks delivering a dynamic and competitive business environment. Whilst many aspects of this approach have been introduced in recent years in individual EU countries, the "mindset" shift needed to make an overall success of the process has unfortunately not yet occurred on a sufficiently large scale at the European level, despite the fact that "Lisbon" provides an effective vehicle for managing this essential transition process.

---

[20] While the regression results are thought provoking, it must be made clear that we are still far from a complete understanding of the determinants of TFP growth. Whilst a large number of explanatory variables were tested in the regressions, only a small number of them turned out to be significant, with the high number of insignificant variables suggesting that TFP is still very much a "black box". A degree of caution is also warranted given firstly that the EU KLEMS datasets are still in the "research" rather than the "official" statistics phase and secondly the need to be mindful of the conceptual and empirical problems in accurately measuring output and price developments in some of the market service industries where the greatest EU-US TFP differences have been found.

[21] The shift from an imitative (i.e. catching-up) to an innovation driven economic model has significant implications for EU institutions and policies with, for example, less emphasis to be placed on vocational education and more on third level; more stress on channelling resources to new start-ups rather than on large incumbent firms; more reallocation of scarce labour and capital resources across firms and innovation systems rather than within firms; and a movement away from an innovation system which was traditionally incremental in nature to one focussed on more fundamental breakthroughs.

19

References

Abramowitz, M (1986), 'Catching up, forging ahead and falling behind', *Journal of Economic History*, 46 (2), pp. 385-406.

Abramovitz, M., (1993), "The search for the sources of growth : areas of ignorance, old and new", Journal of Economic History, 53, 217-243.

Acemoglu, D. and R. Shimer, (2000), 'Productivity gains from unemployment insurance', *European Economic Review,* Volume 44, pp. 1195-1224.

Acemoglu, D., Aghion, P. and F. Zilibotti, (2002), "Distance to Frontier, Selection and Economic Growth", NBER working paper 9066.

Aghion, P. and P. Howitt, (1992), "A model of growth through creative destruction", Econometrica, 60, 323-351.

Aghion, P. and P. Howitt (1998), "Endogenous Growth Theory", MIT Press.

Aghion P., Bloom, N., Blundell R., Griffith, R. and P. Howitt, (2003), "Competition and Innovation, an inverted U Relationship", NBER working paper 9269.

Aghion P., Howitt, P. and D. Mayer-Foulkes (2005), 'The effect of financial development on convergence : theory and evidence', Quarterly Journal of Economics, Vol. 120, pp. 173–222.

Aghion, P. and P. Howitt (2005), 'Appropriate growth policies: A unifying framework', *Journal of the European Economic Association*, Vol. 3, Issue 2–3.

Aghion, P. and P. Howitt (2006), "Joseph Schumpeter Lecture: Appropriate Growth Policy: A Unifying Framework" Journal of the European Economic Association, 4(2-3), pp. 269-314.

Aghion P., R. Blundell, R. Griffith, P. Howitt and S. Prantl (2006), 'The effects of entry on incumbent innovation and productivity', *NBER Working Papers*, No 12027.

Alesina, A., E. Solaore and R. Wacziarg (1997) "Economic integration and political disintegration", American Economic Review No 90, pp.1276-96.

Baldwin, R. and W. Gu (2006), 'Plant turnover and productivity growth in Canadian manufacturing', *Industrial and Corporate Change*, Vol. 15, No 3, p. 417–465.

Barro, R.J. (1990), "Government Spending in a Simple Model of Endogenous Growth", Journal of Political Economy, Vol. 98, No 5.

Barro, R.J. and X. Sala-i-martin (1995), "Economic Growth", McGraw Hill, New York.

Bartelsman, E. and M. Doon (2000), 'Understanding productivity: lessons from longitudinal microdata', *Journal of Economic Literature*, Vol. 38, pp. 569–595.

Bartelsmann, E., J. Haltiwanger and S. Scarpetta (2004), 'Microeconomic evidence of creative destruction in industrial and developing countries', *IZA Discussion Papers*, No 1374.

Bassanini, A, and E. Ernst, (2002), "Labour Market Institutions, Product Market Regulation, and Innovation", OECD Economics Department Working Papers No. 316.

Basu, S. and J. Fernald (2007), "Information and Communications Technology as a General-Purpose Technology : Evidence from US Industry Data", German Economic Review, vol 8.

Baumol, W. (1967), "Macroeconomics of Unbalanced Growth: The Anatomy of Urban Crisis", *The American Economic Review*, 57(3), pp. 415-426.

Bellone, F, P. Musso, L. Nesta and M. Quéré (2006), 'Productivity and market selection of French manufacturing firms in the nineties', *OEFC Document de Travail 2006–04*.

Ben-David, D. and A. Kimhi (2000), "Trade and the Rate of Convergence", NBER Working Paper No 7642.

Benhabib, J. and M. Spiegel (1994), 'The role of human capital in economic development : Evidence from aggregate cross-country data', *Journal of Monetary Economics,*, 34, 143-173.

Blanchard, O., (2004), "The Economic Future of Europe", NBER Working Paper 10310.

Bloom, N., R. Griffith, and J. Van Reenen (2002), 'Do R & D tax credits work? Evidence from a panel of countries, 1979–97', *Journal of Public Economics*, Vol. 1, pp. 1–31.

Bloom, N. and J. Van Reenen (2006), 'Measuring and explaining management practices across firms and countries', *CEP Discussion Papers*, No 716.

Bloom, N., R. Sadun and J. Van Reenen (2007), 'Americans Do I.T. Better: US multinationals and the productivity miracle', *CEP Discussion Papers*, No 788.

Blundell, R., R. Griffith and J. Van Reenen (1999), 'Market share, market value and innovation in a panel of British manufacturing firms', *Review of Economic Studies*, Vol. 66, pp. 529–554.

Bottazzi L. and G. Peri (2007), 'The international dynamics of R & D and innovation in the short and in the long run', *Economic Journal*, Vol. 117, pp. 486–511.

Brynjolfsson, E., L.M. Hitt and S. Yang (2002), "Intangible assets : computers and organizational capital" *Brookings Papers on Economic Activity*, Volume 1, pp. 138-199.

Brynjolfsson, E. and L.M. Hitt (2003), "Computing productivity : firm-level evidence" *Review of Economics and Statistics*, 85(4), pp. 793-808.

Cantner, U. and J. Kruger (2005), 'Micro heterogeneity and aggregate productivity development in the German manufacturing sector', Friedrich-Schiller University, Jena.

Cincera, M. and O. Galgau (2005), 'Impact of market entry and exit on EU productivity and growth performance, *European Economy — Economic Papers*, No 222.

Clements, B (2002), 'How efficient is education spending in Europe?' *European Review of Economics and Finance*, Vol. 1, p. 3ff.

21

Coe, D. and E. Helpman (1995), "International R&D spillovers", European Economic Review, No 39, pp. 859-887.

Cohen, W. & D. Levinthal, (1989), "Innovation and learning : the two faces of R&D", Economic Journal, 99, 569-596.

Conway, P. and G. Nicoletti (2006), "Product Market Regulation in the Non-Manufacturing Sectors of OECD Countries : Measurement and Highlights" OECD Economics Department Working Paper, no. 530.

Corrado, C., Hulten, C. and D. Sichel (2006), "Intangible Capital and Economic Growth" *NBER Working Paper*, no. 11948.

Crafts, N. (2006), "Regulation and Productivity Performance", *Oxford Review of Economic Policy*, 22(2), pp.186-202.

Crafts, N. (2008), "What creates multi-factor productivity", paper presented at the conference on "The creation of economic and corporate wealth in a dynamic economy", jointly organised by the ECB, Banque de France and The Conference Board.

Dearden, L., H. Reed and J. Van Reenen (2006), 'The impact of training on productivity and wages : evidence from British panel data', *Oxford Bulletin of Economics and Statistics*, Vol. 68, p. 397.

De la Fuente, A. and M. Ciccione (2003), 'Human capital in a global and knowledge-based economy', *Final Report for European Commission*, Brussels.

Eichengreen, B. and T. Iversen (1999), "Institutions and Economic Performance : Evidence from the Labour Market", Oxford Review of Economic Policy, Vol. 15.

European Commission (2002), "The EU Economy : 2002 Review", European Economy No 73.

European Commission (2003), "The EU Economy : 2002 Review", European Economy No 6.

European Commission (2004), "The EU Economy : 2004 Review", European Economy, No 6.

European Commission (2006), 'Employment in Europe".

Farinas, J. and S. Ruano (2005), 'The dynamics of productivity: a decomposition approach using distribution functions', *Small Business Economics*, Vol. 22, No 3–4, pp. 237–251.

Foster, L., J. C. Haltiwanger and C. J. Krizan (1998), 'Aggregate productivity growth, evidence from microeconomic evidence', *NBER Working Papers*, No 6803.

Foster, L., J. C. Haltiwanger and C. Syverson (2005), 'Reallocation, firm turnover, and efficiency : selection on productivity or profitability?', *IZA Discussion Papers*, No 1705.

22

Foster, L., J. Haltiwanger and C.J. Krizan (2006), "Market Selection, Reallocation, and Restructuring in the U.S. Retail Trade Sector in the 1990s" *Review of Economics and Statistics*, 88(4), pp. 748-758.

Frankel, J. and D. Romer (1999), "Does Trade Cause Growth?", American Economic Review.

Gonard, F (2007), 'The impact of growth on higher efficiency of public spending on schools', *OECD Economics Department Working Papers*, No 547.

Griffith, R., Redding, S., and Van Reenen, J, (2004), 'Mapping the two faces of R&D : Productivity growth in a panel of OECD industries', *The Review of Economics and Statistics"*, No 86 (4), pp. 883-895.

Griffith, R and H. Harmgart (2005), "Retail Productivity", *The International Review of Retail, Distribution and Consumer Research*, Vol. 15, No. 3, 281 – 290, July 2005.

Griffith, R., R. Harrison and H. Simpson (2006), 'The link between product market reform, innovation and EU macroeconomic performance', *European Economy — Economic Papers*, No 243.

Griffith, R., R. Harrison and H. Simpson (2006), "Product Market Reform and Innovation in the EU" *CEPR Discussion Paper*, no. 5849.

Grossman, G.M. and E. Helpman (1991), "Innovation and Growth in the Global Economy", MIT Press.

Grossman, G. and E. Helpman, (1999), Innovation and growth in the global economy, MIT Press, Cambridge MA.

Guellec, D. and B. Van Pottelsberghe (2000), 'The impact of public R & D expenditure on business R & D', *OECD STI Working Papers*, No 4.

Gust, C. and J.Marquez (2004), "International comparisons of productivity growth: The role of information technology and regulatory practices", *Labour Economics*, 11(1), pp.33-58 .

Haltiwanger, J. C., S. Scarpetta and H. Schweiger (2006), 'Assessing job flows across countries : the role of industry, firm size, and regulations', *IZA Discussion Papers*, No 2450, and *World Bank Policy Research Working Papers,* No 4070.

IMF (2003), "Do Institutions Drive Growth ?", World Economic Outlook, April.

IMF (2004), 'Fostering structural reforms in industrial countries', *World Economic Outlook*, Spring, Washington D.C.

Inklaar, R., M. O'Mahony and M. Timmer (2003), 'ICT and Europe's productivity performance: industry level growth account comparisons with the US', *Research Memorandum*, GD-68, Groningen Growth and Development Centre.

Inklaar, R., M. Timmer and B van Ark (2007), "Mind the Gap : International Comparisons of Productivity in Services and Goods Production", German Economic Review, Volume 8, May 2007.

Inklaar, R, M. Timmer and B. van Ark (2008), "Market services productivity across Europe and the US", *Economic Policy*, pp.139-194.

Jones, C. I. (2002), "Sources of US economic growth in a world of ideas", American Economic Review, Vol. 92, pp. 220-239.

Jerzmanowski, M. (2007), "Total factor productivity differences : appropriate technology vs efficiency", European Economic Review, 51, pp. 2080-2110.

Lucas, R., (1988), "On the mechanics of economic development", Journal of Monetary Economics, 22, 3-42.

Mankiw, N. Romer, D. and D. Weil, (1992), "A contribution to the empirics of economic growth", Quarterly Journal of Economics, 107, 407-437.

Mariani M., D. Harhoff et al. (2007), 'Everything you always wanted to know about inventors (but never asked) : evidence from the Patval-EU survey', *CEPR Discussion Papers*, No 5752.

Marrano M. G., J. Haskel and G. Wallis (2007), "What happened to the knowledge economy ? ICT, intangible investment and Britain's productivity record revisited", Queen Mary University of London Working Paper No. 603.

Mendoza, E., G. Milesi-Ferretti and P. Asea (1997) "On the effectiveness of Tax Policy in altering Long-Run Growth", Journal of Public Economics, Vol. 66.

Metcalfe, S. and I. Miles (2007), 'Investigation and comparison of methods for productivity measurement', Part I in *Service Productivity in Europe*, a PriceWaterhouseCoopers study for the European Commission.

Nadiri, M. I. (1993), 'Innovations and technological spillover', *NBER Working Papers*, No 4423.

Nelson, R. and E. Phelps, E (1966), 'Investment in humans, technological diffusion and economic growth', *American Economic Review,* 94(3).

Nickell, S., D. Nicolitsas and N. Dryden (1997), "What makes Firms Perform Well?", European Economic Review, Vol. 41.

Nickell, S. and R. Layard (1999), "Labour market Institutions and Economic Performance", Handbook of Labor Economics.

Nicoletti, G., A. Bassanini, E. Ernst, S. Jean, P. Santiago and P. Swaim (2001), "Product and Labour Market Interactions in OECD countries", OECD Economics Department Working papers, No 312.

24

Nicoletti, G. and S. Scarpetta (2003), "Regulation, Productivity and Growth: OECD Evidence", Economic Policy, 36, pp. 9-72, April.

Nordhaus, W. D. (2004), 'Schumpeterian profits in the American economy : theory and measurement', *NBER Working Papers*, No 10433.

Nordhaus, W. D. (2006), 'Baumol's Disease : a Macroeconomic Perspective', *NBER Working Papers*, No 12218.

Nordhaus, W. D. (2007), 'Two centuries of productivity growth in computing', *Journal of Economic History*, 67, pp 128-159.

OECD (2003), "The Sources of Economic Growth in OECD countries".

OECD (2004), "Understanding Economic Growth".

Romer, P. (1990), "Endogenous technological change", Journal of Political Economy, Vol. 98, pp. S71-S102.

Sachs F. and A. Warner (1995), "Economic Reform and the Process of Global Integration", Brookings Papers on Economic Activity, Vol. 1.

Sapir, A. et al. (2003), "An agenda for a growing Europe : Making the EU system deliver", Report of an Independent High Level Group established on the initiative of the President of the European Commission.

Scarpetta S. and T. Tressel (2002), "Productivity and Convergence in a Panel of OECD industries : Do Regulations and Institutions Matter?", OECD Economics Department Working Papers, No 342.

Scarpetta S., P. Hemmings, T. Tressel and J. Woo (2002), "The Role of Policy and Institutions for Productivity and Firm Dynamics : Evidence from Micro and Industry Data", OECD Economics Department Working Papers, No 329.

Solow, R. (1956), "A contribution to the theory of economic growth", Quarterly Journal of Economics, pp. 65-94.

Soskice, D. (1997), "German Technology Policy, Innovation and National Institutional Frameworks", Industry and Innovation, Vol. 4.

Stiroh, K., (2001), "What drives productivity growth?", Federal Reserve Bank of New York, Economic Policy Review, 7, 37-59.

Stiroh, K. (2004), "Reassessing the Impact of IT in the Production Function : A Meta-Analysis and Sensitivity Tests" forthcoming in *Annales d'Economie et de Statistique*.

Swan, T., (1956), Economic Growth and capital accumulation, Economic Record, 32, 334-361.

Timmer, M,, M. O'Mahony and B. van Ark (2007), "EU KLEMS Growth and Productivity Accounts : An Overview", International Productivity Monitor, Number 14, Spring 2007.

Van Ark, B., Inklaar, R. and R. Mc Guckian, (2003), "Changing gear : productivity, ICT and Service Industries in Europe and the US", in J. Christensen & P. Maskell, eds, The industrial dynamics of the new digital economy, Edward Elgar, 56-99.

Van Ark, B., O'Mahony, M. and M. Timmer, (2008), "The productivity gap between Europe and the United States : Trends and causes", Journal of Economic Perspectives, Volume 22, Number 1 – Winter 2008, pp. 25-44.

Vandenbussche, J., P. Aghion and C. Meghir (2006), "Growth, Distance to the Frontier and Composition of Human Capital", Journal of Economic Growth, 11, pp. 97-127.

Wacziarg R. and K. H. Welch (2003), 'Trade liberalization and growth : new evidence', *NBER Working Papers*, No 10152.

Wagner, J. (2007), 'Entry, exit and productivity : empirical results for German manufacturing industries', *IZA Discussion Papers*, No 2667.

Woesmann, L. and G. Schuetz (2006), 'Efficiency and equity in European education and training systems', analytical Report for the European Commission prepared by the European Expert Network on the Economics of Education (EENEE).

Part II
Services Policies, Trade and Welfare

[14]

Measuring Impediments to Trade in Services

TONY WARREN *and*
CHRISTOPHER FINDLAY

A N IMPORTANT QUESTION for economic research today is how to characterize, assess, and measure the economic impact of policy affecting services trade. Without such details, it is difficult to mobilize the key interests against protectionism in domestic economies, forge coalitions for reform, and improve the confidence of decisionmakers in the strategies, design, transparency, and implementation of national trade policies. Yet little attention has been given to the services sector, and barriers to trade in services remain opaque, given the nature of the transactions involved.

Moreover, where information on such barriers is available, it is often in qualitative form and needs to be culled from a wide range of sources. This chapter shows how this sort of information can be combined into robust assessments of policy that can help explain market outcomes. This in turn opens up new opportunities to use such measures in the design of reform programs and in the international negotiations associated with their implementation.

The next section reviews the nature of trade in services and the impediments involved. The following sections spell out a case for greater

The authors would like to thank Philippa Dee, Greg McGuire, Pierre Sauvé, and Robert Stern for their comments on this paper, and the Australian Research Council for its support.

57

transparency, a method for achieving that transparency in a variety of sectors, related modeling issues, and implications for the negotiating process. The methodologies described should make the scope of the General Agreement on Trade in Services (GATS) less of an impediment to its implementation.

What Are the Barriers to Trade in Services?

A service may be defined as an economic activity that adds value to another economic unit, either directly or indirectly, through a good belonging to another economic unit.[1] Consequently, a defining feature of services is that they require direct interaction between producers and consumers (or at least a consumer's assets) before the service can be rendered.[2]

Service Transactions

The fact that producers and consumers must interact before a service can be rendered influences the manner in which international transactions in services are conducted. If a service producer in one economy is capable of rendering the desired services, then a consumer residing in another country must somehow interact with the producer to acquire those services. GATS has developed a four-part typology of how such capabilities can be accessed internationally: through cross-border communications in which neither the producer nor the consumer moves physically, interacting instead through a postal or a telecommunications network; through the movement of a consumer to a supplier's country of residence; through the movement of a commercial organization to the consumer's country of residence; or through the movement of an individual service supplier to the consumer's country of residence.[3] Consequently, the concept of international services transactions encompasses foreign direct investment and the movement of labor, as well as traditional cross-border transactions. In this discussion, any policy that impedes service producers and consumers interacting through any of these channels (or modes of supply) is considered an impediment to international service transactions.

1. This definition is derived from the classic definition of services first proposed by Hill (1977, p. 317).
2. Hirsch (1989, pp. 45–60).
3. See GATS, Article I. See also Bhagwati (1984); Sampson and Snape (1985).

Categories of Impediments

Impediments to trade in services may be divided into two main categories: market access restrictions and derogations from national treatment.[4] Part III of GATS explicitly introduces the concepts of market access and national treatment into the architecture of international services trade. Surprisingly, GATS does not specifically define market access. Article XVI(1) simply obliges members to grant market access to scheduled industry subsectors, while Article XVI(2):(a)–(f) contains a list of measures considered to be limitations on market access. Article XVII(1) defines national treatment as treatment no less favorable than that accorded to like domestic services and service providers, subject to the limitations and conditions set out in the country's schedule of commitments.

Part III implies that market access and national treatment are broader in scope than the corresponding market access and national treatment provisions in GATT.[5] To begin with, the GATS provision on national treatment does not draw a distinction between frontier and internal constraints but embraces all policies that might discriminate between domestic and foreign suppliers. In contrast, national treatment in GATT extends to matters of internal taxation and regulation only. In effect, the GATS article on national treatment encompasses both national treatment and market access as normally defined.

More important, the GATS article on market access extends beyond traditional concerns of access for foreign service suppliers to all policies that restrict access to a market. This is a major extension of multilateral trade disciplines into the realm of domestic policy, particularly competition policy. It has therefore been suggested that "GATT is almost entirely concerned with relations between 'us' and 'them'; these provisions of GATS are not concerned with 'us' and 'them' but [with] 'some of us' on the one hand and 'the rest of us and them' on the other."[6]

Following this suggestion, we propose to operationalize the distinction between market access and national treatment by focusing on the concept of discrimination as follows:

—Market access means nondiscrimination between incumbents in a particular market and possible entrants (be they domestic or foreign). Hence, a legislated monopoly is considered a market access limitation.

4. For an early example of this kind of distinction in services, see UNCTAD (1994, chaps. 4–7).
5. See Hoekman (1995); Snape (1998).
6. Snape (1998, p. 284).

—National treatment means nondiscrimination between domestic and foreign service suppliers. Hence a policy limiting foreign investment is considered a breach of national treatment.

Why Measure Barriers to Trade in Services?

Owing to the nature of service trade, impediments to such trade tend to come in the form of nontariff barriers (NTBs), reflecting the difficulties inherent in imposing tariffs directly on either the service consumer or the service supplier as they interact across borders. NTBs are notoriously difficult to identify and measure. There have been few systematic attempts to collect information on barriers to entry beyond the periodic trade reviews conducted by national trade negotiators.[7] No equivalent of the United Nations Conference on Trade and Development (UNCTAD) database on NTBs yet exists for the services sector.[8] As a consequence, few studies have attempted to identify the barriers that do exist or to assess the impact of these barriers on economic outcomes. This is a matter of concern on several different levels.

At a policy development level, the lack of information on the extent and impact of impediments to trade in services undermines the liberalization process. Evidence is available to suggest that services industries remain protected for many of the standard political economy reasons: protection is primarily afforded to uncompetitive service industries with significant political muscle.[9] For those involved in multilateral and regional negotiations, this evidence tends to confirm what many already suspect. Negotiations on services encounter the same barriers to progress that are so familiar in negotiations on merchandise and agriculture. Powerful domestic interests limit the extent to which commitments to liberalization will be made. If anything, the barriers to progress in services are even greater because of the relatively widespread involvement of the public sector in service provision and of the private sector in service regulation.

---

7. The problem with these reports, or so-called black books, is that they are seldom comprehensive, simply reflect the interests of exporters, and are usually based on uncollaborated assertions from interested parties. Among the more widely distributed examples are the reports produced by the Office of the U.S. Trade Representative, the European Commission, the Japanese Ministry of International Trade and Industry, and the Canadian Department of Foreign Affairs and International Trade.

8. Although UNCTAD is currently developing its Measures Affecting Services Trade (MAST) database.

9. See Warren (1996, 1997, 1998).

Overcoming the forces of protection is no trivial task and the solution far from simple.[10] In the domestic political process, however, it is generally considered useful to make the costs of protection as transparent as possible. Not only does this help build coalitions of interest for liberalization, it allows policymakers to have greater confidence in the implications of any decisions they may make.[11] Without information on impediments to trade and investment in services and their consequent impact on the economy, policy reformers have fewer tools with which to push for liberalization.

At a negotiating level, the desire for reciprocity has played a major part in determining the pattern of specific commitments made under the auspices of GATS, as it has in other areas of multilateral trade negotiations.[12] Such a negotiating framework appears to lead multiproduct negotiations (whereby concessions in one industry are traded for concessions in another) to more liberal outcomes by extending the set of industries over which concessions can be traded:[13]

> The across-the-board approach has clearly enjoyed the most success. It establishes politically salient overall goals early in negotiation while permitting great flexibility in subsequent negotiations to deal with individual products, sectors, barriers, or framework and institutional issues. By contrast, the product and sector approaches are, taken alone, unlikely to generate enough political interest and momentum to move negotiations forward at an early stage.[14]

When dealing with NTBs, multiproduct negotiations become more difficult technically, because of the issues surrounding the comparability of concessions.[15] During the Uruguay Round, the problem of NTBs affecting agriculture was confronted directly with the development of the Aggregate Measure of Support (AMS) and attempts (subsequently watered down) to have this measure encompass all NTBs (and tariffs) affecting agriculture.[16] Service negotiators had no equivalent to the AMS, or even usable industry-level measures of impediments. During the Uruguay Round this may

---

10. See the various contributions on this point in Williamson (1994).

11. On the usefulness of such information in reform, see Corden (1994); Garnaut (1994); Destler (1995, pp. 304–05).

12. See Hoekman (1995); Warren (1996).

13. One of the major problems with the various post-round negotiations in services was that the sector-specific nature of the discussions limited the scope for successful bargaining.

14. Nau (1987, p. 76).

15. See Olechowski (1987, p. 126); Hoekman and Kostecki (1995, p. 68).

16. See Croome (1995, pp. 113–14).

not have been too significant a problem, as negotiations seemed to have focused on developing the necessary architecture, and the specific commitments made by members appear overwhelmingly to have been examples of binding the status quo. As the next round of services negotiations approaches, however, the lack of information on service impediments will undermine the potential for negotiated liberalization.

How to Measure Barriers to Trade in Services?

A research project initiated in 1997 under the auspices of the Australian Research Council has developed a method to help provide more information about services sectors impediments. This method consists of three steps:

—First, available qualitative evidence that compares the way nations discriminate against potential entrants in various service industries is collected. This evidence is then transformed into a frequency-type index, with every attempt made to weigh discriminatory policies by their economic significance.

—Second, the impact of the policies as measured by the frequency indices is assessed against cross-national differences in domestic prices or domestic quantities. The effect of other factors explaining cross-national differences is explicitly taken into account.

—Third, the measured impact of the frequency indices (the coefficient) on prices or quantities is incorporated into a general equilibrium model to assess the economy-wide impacts of the policies under consideration. Where possible, partial equilibrium modeling is also undertaken to provide insight into the specific impacts of liberalization.

The details of these steps are discussed next, with examples of some of the preliminary results, where appropriate.[17]

Step 1: Frequency Indices

As just mentioned, frequency-type measures of NTBs that affect services received little attention for many years because of the lack of suitable data on impediments. This problem was partly overcome thanks to the GATS requirement that countries agreeing to be bound by the multilateral

17. A full set of results from steps one and two can be found in Findlay and Warren (1999). The modeling results are to be published in early 2000.

trade disciplines would list in their individual GATS schedules those sectors in which they were prepared to make commitments and any specific barriers they wished to retain.

Quantification of the GATS schedules began with Bernard Hoekman's pioneering development of a three-category weighting method.[18] He examined all GATS schedules and for quantification purposes allocated a number to each possible schedule entry (that is, each possible market access or national treatment commitment in each mode in each industry subsector). Specifically, where a member has agreed to be bound without any caveats, a weight of 1 is allocated. A weight of 1 is also allocated in circumstances where a member declares that a particular mode of supply is "unbound due to lack of technical feasibility," if other modes of supply are unrestricted. A common example of this situation is the cross-border supply of construction and related engineering services. Where a member has agreed to be bound, but specific restrictions remain, a 0.5 weight is allocated. If a mode of supply is bound but specific reference is made to the horizontal commitments, a 0.5 weight is also allocated. This is commonly the case for commitments on the movement of natural persons, where immigration constraints continue to apply. Where a member has explicitly exempted that particular entry from the operation of GATS by recording an entry of "unbound" or by simply failing to make any commitments at all, a weight of 0 is allocated.

Hoekman used these measures to quantify the extent of commitments (the greater the number, the more commitments made). Other researchers have inverted the analysis and examined the number of commitments that have not been made (the greater the number the more illiberal the economy). We adopt the latter approach (and report results accordingly) because impediments to trade in services are the central concern here, rather than the extent of GATS coverage.

The Hoekman methodology has several drawbacks.[19] To begin with, it does not distinguish between barriers in terms of their impact on the economy, and minor impediments receive the same weighting as an almost complete refusal of access. Another is the coverage of the GATS schedules, many of which do not give an accurate picture of the actual barriers that are in place. This is particularly the case for developing economies, which have had difficulty providing the details required to meet the complexities of the agreement's scheduling process. There is also some suggestion that

18. Hoekman (1995).
19. Most of these problems are detailed by Hoekman (1995). But see also PECC (1995, chap. 5).

nations with liberal policies left some services unbound so as to maintain a retaliatory capability in future market access negotiations. Therefore some industries that are recorded in the Hoekman indices as impeded may be open, at least to suppliers from some economies.[20]

Various studies, including those produced as part of the Australian services project, have attempted to develop a more complex weighting system at a sectoral and mode of delivery level than that used by Hoekman, seeking to quantify differences in the effect of different partial commitments. More extensive databases have also been drawn upon to overcome some of the informational limitations with the GATS schedules. Brief summaries of these studies are provided next.

Cross-Sectoral Indices

At a cross-sectoral level, Alexis Hardin and Leanne Holmes made a comprehensive attempt to incorporate the relative economic impact of different policies into frequency data on the types of barriers affecting investment.[21] They identified five types of barriers to foreign investment, then developed weights within each of these categories on the basis of the perceived economic impact of each policy category. For example, they give a much greater weight to a policy that completely excludes foreign equity than to a policy that allows more than 50 percent but less than 100 percent foreign equity. Policies that limit investment in existing firms but allow greenfields investment are given a lower weight than those that limit all investment.

Moving beyond the GATS schedules, Hardin and Holmes included in their analysis the information contained in the individual action plans (IAPs) produced by members of the Asia-Pacific Economic Cooperation process.[22] These documents have the advantage of being closer to a negative rather than a positive list of barriers to services trade, although they are still far from an exhaustive description of impediments.

Applying their methodology to fifteen economies of the Asia-Pacific Economic Cooperation (APEC), Hardin and Holmes found that communications and financial services tended to be subject to the most stringent FDI controls (see table 3-1). Scores were particularly high for the communi-

---

20. However, a threat of future retaliation could itself be considered an impediment, in which case the data may not be too misleading.

21. Hardin and Holmes (1997).

22. See the APEC website at www.apecsec.org.sg.

Table 3-1. *FDI Restrictiveness Indices for Selected APEC Economies and Selected Sectors*
Percent

Economy	Business	Communications	Distribution	Education	Financial	Transport
Australia	18	44	18	18	45	20
Canada	23	51	20	20	38	24
China	36	82	28	53	45	46
Hong Kong, China	2	35	5	0	23	9
Indonesia	56	64	53	53	55	53
Japan	6	35	5	20	36	11
Korea, Republic of	57	69	63	55	88	57
Malaysia	32	42	8	8	61	12
Mexico	29	74	33	45	55	28
New Zealand	9	43	8	8	20	13
Papua New Guinea	30	48	30	30	30	30
Philippines	48	76	48	48	95	98
Singapore	26	52	25	25	38	25
Thailand	78	84	78	78	88	78
United States	1	35	0	0	20	3

Source: Hardin and Holmes (1997), App. A.2.
Note: The higher the score, the greater the degree to which an industry is restricted. The maximum score is 100 percent.

cations sector because many economies imposed ownership limits on telecommunications and broadcasting and completely closed postal services to
foreign entry. The least restricted sectors were found to include business and
distribution services.

Financial Services

Several frequency indices of impediments to trade and investment in
financial services reflect the preeminent position of this industry in the
world economy. Such indices can be found in the analysis of Aaditya
Mattoo, who has examined the market access commitments on financial
services made by developing and transition economies as part of the
post-round Agreement on Financial Services concluded in December
1997.[23] Mattoo attempts to unpack the partial commitments whereby
countries accept the GATS disciplines but to list policies that will continue
to limit market access. In particular, he distinguishes between limits on the
number of suppliers allowed in a market and limits on foreign equity in
existing suppliers. He concludes that there has been less emphasis on
introducing competition by allowing new entry than on allowing foreign
equity participation and protecting the position of incumbents.

Table 3-2 provides the GDP-weighted regional averages from the
Mattoo analysis, in a format that reflects the restrictiveness of each region.
Regions with higher scores have made fewer commitments. Of the regions
examined, Latin America appears to be the most restricted in direct insurance and Asia the most restricted in banking services.

The limitations of using information derived from international agreements such as GATS and the APEC individual action plans are graphically
demonstrated in Greg McGuire's detailed analysis of the Australian financial services policy regime (both state and federal).[24] Where applicable, he
includes prudential regulations in the definition of market access and
national treatment restrictions. A host of barriers are uncovered in this
manner, including government monopolies over the provision of certain
types of financial services, prudential regulation, restrictions on direct
foreign investment in banking and insurance, discriminatory government
licensing requirements, and government guarantees to selected financial

---

23. See Mattoo (1998). Mattoo focuses only on direct insurance, both life and non-life, and the acceptance of deposits and lending services. He also excludes the presence of natural persons from his analysis.
24. McGuire (1998).

Table 3-2. *GDP-Weighted Regional Restrictiveness Averages in Direct Insurance and Banking*[a]

Percent

	Direct insurance		Banking	
Region	Life insurance	Non–life insurance	Acceptance of deposits	Lending
Africa	44	48	32	43
Asia	59	58	72	67
Eastern Europe	47	49	40	39
Latin America	78	74	62	66

Source: Mattoo (1998, annex 1).

a. Figures are calculated as 1 – GDP-weighted average of the value of the most restrictive measure applied by a country to each mode in the sector. The higher the score, the greater the degree to which an industry is restricted. The maximum score is 100 percent.

service providers. Some 165 impediments are identified, compared with 38 financial service impediments listed in Australia's GATS schedule.

McGuire then applies the weighting methodology developed by Stijn Claessens and Tom Glaessner and finds that the Australian financial services market is fairly open compared with the eight Asian economies they analyzed (see table 3-3).[25] McGuire's results parallel Mattoo's findings in that banking services are more open than insurance services. Of the three financial service industries, the securities industry appears to be the most impeded. However, it is difficult to place too much weight on the scores for the Asian economies as they are based primarily on the GATS schedules and as such may understate the extent of the impediments in place. It would be informative to have McGuire's detailed data collection undertaken in other jurisdictions.

Building on this earlier research, McGuire and Michael Schuele constructed a set of indices of impediments to trade in banking services from a variety of sources, including the World Trade Organization (WTO) trade policy reviews, APEC IAPs, the International Monetary Fund, the office of the U.S. Trade Representative, and various commercial organizations.[26] McGuire and Schuele differentiated between impediments affecting commercial presence and those affecting operations (such as raising funds), and they differentiated between impediments affecting foreign banks and those

25. See Claessens and Glaessner (1998).
26. McGuire and Schuele (1999).

Table 3-3. *Restrictiveness Indices to Trade in Financial Services for Selected Economies*[a]

Economy	Banking	Securities	Insurance
Hong Kong, China	0.25·	0.60	1.00
Australia	0.80	1.00	1.50
Indonesia	1.80	2.00	2.40
Korea, Republic of	3.30	2.90	2.40
Malaysia	2.60	2.50	2.90
Philippines	1.65	2.60	2.20
Singapore	2.50	2.30	.90
Thailand	2.15	3.00	2.20
India	2.75	2.90	4.00
Average	*1.98*	*2.20*	*2.17*

Source: McGuire (1998, table 4.2).

a. The higher the score, the more closed the financial services market. Scores range from 1 to 5.

affecting all banks. Each of the inputs into the indices were weighted to reflect the degree to which they are perceived to restrict access to the market. Figure 3-1 plots the index measuring impediments to foreign banks (the greater the score, the more restricted the market) against national income. The negative relationship between GNP per capita and financial market restrictions is immediately apparent.

Professional Services

Beyond financial services, the potential scope for frequency weighting systems is most clearly demonstrated by a pilot study of the Organization for Economic Cooperation and Development (OECD) on assessing barriers to trade in professional services.[27] Here a number of questions are asked within a flowchart format and scores allotted to the answers. The approach is designed to mimic the set of questions a service provider might ask when seeking access to a foreign market. For example: Can I gain physical access to the market (market access)? If I can gain access to the market, am I allowed to practice and to what extent (rights of practice)? Can I provide services as an independent firm (rights of establishment)? If I am required to practice in partnership with a local entity, what limitations does this place on me?

After scores are attributed to each answer, a detailed weighting system

27. OECD (1997).

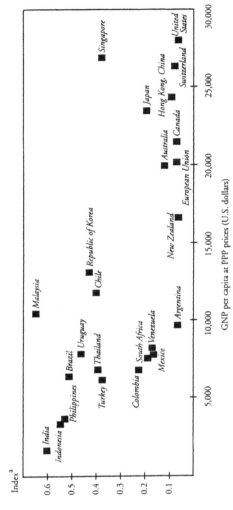

Figure 3-1. *Foreign Restrictiveness Index in Banking and GNP per Capita at PPP Prices (1996)*

Source: McGuire and Schuele (1999).

a. The higher the score, the greater the level of impediment. Purchasing power parity (PPP) prices based on World Bank surveys undertaken since 1993. GNP per capita at PPP prices are used. GNP per capita using official exchange rates tends to undervalue low and middle income economies with relatively low prices.

Figure 3-2. *Restrictiveness Indices to Trade in Telecommunications Services for Top Twenty Service Trading Nations, 1997*

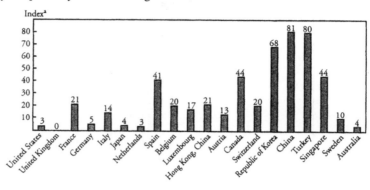

Source: Warren (1999a).
a. The higher the score, the greater the degree to which an industry is restricted. The maximum score is 100 percent.

is proposed. This method was used to examine accountancy services in Australia, Britain, France, and the United States. The United Kingdom was found to be the most liberal of the four countries, the United States to have the highest barriers.

Telecommunications

With the conclusion in February 1997 of the Agreement on Basic Tele-communications, the telecommunications component of the GATS sched-ule in many countries has changed drastically. Mary Marko has updated the Hoekman-type frequency indices on telecommunications to reflect the im-pact of the 1997 agreement for the sixty-nine member nations.[28] She finds that 58 percent of the basic telecommunications services market for all of these countries is now covered by either partial or full GATS commitments.

Moving beyond the GATS schedules, Tony Warren has used a 1997 survey by the International Telecommunications Union (ITU) to construct a set of policy indices for 136 countries.[29] These data have the distinct advantage of being drawn from a survey of actual policies, rather than inferring these policies from commitments made in trade negotiations.

28. Marko (1998).
29. Warren (1999a).

Five indices have been constructed, corresponding to the more important distinctions drawn in the GATS context, namely the differences between market access and national treatment and between trade and investment. Because data are limited, a distinction is made between access to mobile and fixed telecommunications markets only in relation to the market access restrictions on foreign investment.

In constructing these indices, Warren sought to incorporate economic and legal inputs by including a count of the number of firms actually competing in a market, as well as the formal policies. Figure 3-2 provides the unweighted average score across the five indices for the top twenty service trading nations. A high degree of variation is apparent, reflecting the continuing resistance among many countries to the liberalization of their telecommunications markets.

Transport

In the transport sector, McGuire, Schuele, and Tim Smith have developed a technique for assessing impediments to trade in maritime services.[30] The data on policy came from a variety of sources, including a questionnaire developed by the WTO's Negotiating Group on Maritime Services, GATS schedules, WTO Trade Policy Reviews, information from the office of the U.S. Trade Representative, OECD material, and APEC IAPs. In this case, separate indices were constructed to quantify restrictions on foreign maritime service suppliers and all maritime service suppliers.[31] The gap between the scores for these two types of entrants indicates the extent to which a country discriminates against foreign suppliers. The results for thirty-five economies in the Asia Pacific, America, and Europe reveal a large range in the degree of restrictiveness.[32] Chile, the Philippines, Thailand, Turkey, and the United States appear to treat foreign-service suppliers significantly less favorably than domestic firms.

A similar technique is currently being used to develop indices of restrictiveness in air transport services. We discuss that case in more detail in our review of the application of modeling methods.

30. McGuire, Schuele, and Smith (1999).

31. Restrictions are grouped into two broad categories of those imposed on commercial presence and "others." The former includes rules on forms of presence, investment in onshore service suppliers, and permanent movement of people. The latter includes cabotage, port services, the UN Liner Code, treatment of conferences, and temporary movement of people.

32. Brazil, Chile, India, Indonesia, the Republic of Korea, Malaysia, the Philippines, Thailand, and the United States are among the most restricted markets.

72   WARREN AND FINDLAY

Step 2: Partial Impact Measures

Having identified and systematized the various cross-national differences in policy, one is able to estimate the impact of these differences on core economic outcomes (such as prices and consumption) in some industries. The available research on the measurement of NTBs affecting trade in goods provides a useful starting point. Two broad methods of quantifying the economic impact of NTBs have been identified: *price-impact measures,* which examine the impact of NTBs on domestic prices by comparing them with world prices; and *quantity-impact measures,* which compare an estimate of trade volumes in the absence of NTBs with actual trade volumes.[33]

These types of price and quantity-impact measures have been considered impossible to replicate in relation to service industries because of the lack of data. A world price for many service industries is indeterminate. Similarly, the lack of data on systematic bilateral services trade and the highly aggregated nature of the current account data limit the potential for traditional quantity-impact models.[34]

As a consequence of these data concerns, it is necessary to identify alternative benchmarks against which to compare actual prices and quantities. Here the market power analysis associated with competition or antitrust regulation is instructive. The aim of such analysis is to compare actual market outcomes with those that would be expected to prevail if the market were competitive.[35]

Price-Impact Measures

Work being undertaken as a part of the Australian services research project is seeking to assess price impacts for the banking, telecommunications, and transport industries.[36] The theory underlying the approach is that if the market had no impediments to entry, then it would be competitive and prices would be expected to approach a firm's long-run marginal cost, defined as the cost of keeping a particular facility alive and well in the long run.[37] If impediments are present, however, there will be a wedge between price and marginal cost, which might affect not only the margin over costs

---

33. See Deardorff and Stern (1985).
34. See Ascher and Whichard (1991).
35. Areeda, Hovenkamp, and Solow (1995).
36. See also Bosworth and others (1997).
37. The excess of price over marginal cost as a proportion of price is known as the Lerner index. See Lerner (1934).

but also costs themselves. Costs might be higher because low-cost suppliers are excluded from the market or because protected firms are not operating at their lowest possible cost levels. For all these reasons—the margin effect, the cost-difference effect, and the cost-reduction effect—prices observed in the presence of impediments may exceed those in their absence.

As a first step in estimating the impact that impediments to trade in services might have on prices, Kaleeswaran Kalirajan and others examined the price-cost margins (or the "net interest margins") of 694 national and state commercial banks in twenty-seven economies.[38] Using a two-stage econometric technique, they were able to isolate the specific impact that the trade restrictiveness indices developed by McGuire and Schuele had on this margin while correcting for the factors that influence the size of the buffer banks need to manage their cash flow. Table 3-4 provides preliminary estimates of the price effect nonprudential impediments to foreign banks have on the margins for all banks in each of the economies, ranked from the largest effect to smallest. The estimated impacts for Malaysia, Indonesia, and the Philippines are the highest among the twenty-seven economies. The net interest margins are estimated to be at least 45 percent higher than they would be in the absence of restrictions on trade in banking services. For the more developed countries, the restrictions result in smaller margin increases, owing to their greater liberality.

The impact of policy variables on prices in maritime services is also being assessed. An estimate of shipping expenses (derived from comparisons of values at the point of export and the values at the point of import) in bilateral trades in each direction is the proxy for price variables. Statistical methods are being used to test for the significance of the policy measures for variations in prices, after allowing for the impact of other variables that will affect those charges, including the distance between them, the scale of the trade, indicators of the composition of the bilateral trade, the extent of imbalances in the trade flows, and the degree to which the routes are isolated from substitutes. The data set includes 506 observations. Under the method used, policy must be included separately in both partner economies. The results will help researchers determine whether a high degree of restrictiveness is necessary in both economies in order to drive up shipping charges, or whether a high degree in one partner alone is sufficient.

One disadvantage of analyzing margins of prices over costs in order to draw implications for prices is that protected firms tend to extract monop-

38. Kalirajan and others (1999).

Table 3-4. *The Impact of Liberalization on Net Interest Margins (NIMs)*
for Selected Economies
Percent

Economy	Effect of impediments to foreign banks on NIMs
Malaysia	60.61
Indonesia	49.32
Philippines	47.36
Korea, Republic of	36.72
Chile	34.00
Thailand	33.06
Singapore	31.45
Colombia	18.35
Japan	15.26
Australia	9.30
Hong Kong, China	6.91
Switzerland	5.95
Argentina	5.34
Canada	5.34
European Union[a]	5.32
United States	4.75

Source: Kalirajan and others (1999).
a. The European Union excludes Finland, Ireland, and Luxembourg.

oly rents in the form of inflated costs rather than excess margins. In some
industries, international data are available to deflate costs by producing a
world's best-practice (technically and allocatively efficient) cost function
using various statistical techniques, notably in markets for air transport and
for telecommunications, as discussed shortly. With these frontier cost
functions, it is possible to estimate the costs that the world's most efficient
firm would incur if allowed into a country (facing that country's factor
costs and market characteristics). A comparison of this adjusted cost measure with actual prices has the potential to give a more precise measure of
the rents being created by impediments to trade and investment in services.

Quantity-Impact Measures

An alternative approach is to examine output, since price and output
are simultaneously determined in a market. In particular, the demand for
various services is likely to be greater the more competitive its supply,
because the lower relative prices and higher service quality arising from

competition will increase demand, while rivalry in investment will push out supply.

Several recent studies have sought to examine the impact of barriers to entry by focusing on the quantity of mobile telecommunications services consumed within an economy—rather than the quantity traded—and by comparing this with international benchmarks.[39] Their aim is to quantify the comparative impact on telecommunications consumption of limits on competition, controlling for other explanatory variables. Restrictions on competition are modeled directly by a count of the number of mobile operators in each country at each period.[40]

Another analysis included fixed network services, measured in terms of the number of mainlines per hundred persons, and expanded the policy variable beyond a simple count of the number of operators (fixed and mobile) to the ITU-derived indices of telecommunications policies discussed earlier.[41] Two sets of simulations were run. The first investigated the impact of restrictive policies on the number of main telecommunications lines per hundred persons in a country, controlling for other key variables explaining cross-national differences: GDP per capita, housing density, quality, and unmet demand. The second set of simulations undertook the same type of analysis except that it focused on the number of mobile/cellular handsets per hundred persons. Across the 130 or more countries that were examined, policy was found to have a statistically significant impact on the extent of the network.[42]

As a consequence of these insights, it is possible to simulate the impact on network penetration of full liberalization. If these predicted increases are calculated as a percentage of actual network penetration, then in combination with an estimate of the elasticity of demand, one can derive a tariff equivalent estimate. Figure 3-3 details the percentage increase in mainlines per hundred persons that the available international data would indicate likely if the top twenty service trading economies completely

39. See Ralph and Ludwig (1997); Ergas, Ralph, and Small (1998).

40. Ralph and Ludwig (1997) found that the presence of three or more mobile operators substantially increased market penetration in the 150 countries they examined. Movement from one to two operators had minimal impact. Ergas, Ralph, and Small (1998) found that mobile penetration in Australia is high by international standards (about twice the expected level), even when all other variables that affect penetration, including the number of suppliers, are taken into account. Interestingly, Australia has been above the predicted level of penetration only since it liberalized in the early 1990s. From 1987 to 1991 it was consistently below the forecast level.

41. See Warren (1999b).

42. Warren (1999b).

Figure 3-3. *Predicted Quantity Impact and Tariff Equivalents of Restrictions on Entry into the Market for the Supply of Telecommunications Fixed Networks, 1997*[a]

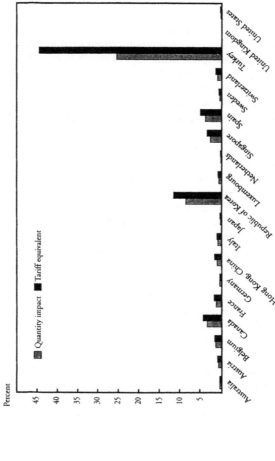

Source: Warren (1999

a. The quantity impact is defined as the predicted quantity with free trade less the predicted quantity with current policies as a proportion of the latter. The tariff equivalent is defined as the predicted price with current policies less the predicted price with free trade as a proportion of the latter.

76

liberalized their telecommunications markets.[43] These percentage changes in quantities can be converted into tariff equivalents using estimates of elasticities of demand. For example, with an elasticity value of -1.2, the tariff equivalents also detailed in figure 3-3 can be generated.[44] For some countries, the tariff equivalents are quite small because of their highly liberal policy environment. For others, a significant increase in the actual number of mainlines and decrease in price could reasonably be expected if liberalization were to occur.

Step 3: Modeling

The price and quantity-impact estimates just outlined have three main drawbacks. First, the nature of the predicted reductions in price or increases in quantity remains a black box. Does liberalization affect economic outcomes through competition effects (reduced market power), cost reduction effects (increased efficiency), and cost differential effects (reduced input prices)? Second, such estimates fail to give a picture of the implications of reform for consumer and producer welfare. Third, even these techniques obviously fail to capture important intersectoral effects. What impact does liberalization of a particular service industry have on the economy as a whole? To overcome these limitations, it is necessary to undertake further economic modeling.

Partial Equilibrium Methods

Air transport markets illustrate the scope for using partial equilibrium modeling methods in the analysis of liberalization effects. Policymakers have various options at their disposal to reform international air transport where market access is often severely curtailed by a series of bilateral agreements.[45] Possible reform strategies include liberalization that permits the entry of further domestic suppliers without changing conditions of

43. China is excluded from figure 3-3 for reasons of scale, but the calculated quantity impact is 70.9 percent, which is consistent with the rates recorded by most developing economies.

44. The elasticity figure of -1.2 is the lower bound of various estimates on the price elasticity of international calls. See Warren, Hardin, and Bosworth (1997, p. 25). This figure is considered inappropriate for developing economies, where the price elasticity of demand is significantly lower.

45. For more details of the regulatory regime in international air transport markets, see Warren, Tamms, and Findlay (1999).

access for foreign suppliers, liberalization that permits commercial establishment by foreign carriers, and liberalization that permits the further entry by foreign carriers (for example, by allowing those currently excluded or restricted under the terms of the bilateral agreements to serve the route).

As noted earlier, liberalization can have an impact on prices and quantities as a consequence of three different effects:[46]

—*Competition effects.* These refer to the reduction in market power that occurs because of the removal of barriers to entry and the increase in the number of suppliers. Markups over costs are expected to be reduced because of this effect.

—*Cost-reducing effects.* These effects come from two sources in air transport markets. First, the greater intensity of competition in the markets affected leads suppliers to operate closer to the frontier levels of costs. Second, the relaxation of constraints otherwise imposed by the bilateral system facilitates the creation of networks, including new hubs. With greater freedom than before, and therefore more choice, airlines could be expected to achieve further cost reductions. This second set of effects therefore finds airlines moving closer to the minimum attainable levels of costs, given the input prices they pay.

—*Cost difference effects.* These arise because airlines based in different locations face different input prices. Airlines from different countries can deliver services to a particular market at varying costs. In other words, some countries are likely to have a comparative advantage in the provision of these services.

It is possible to identify these effects specifically by building on estimates of cost functions for air transport services. Using data from fifty airlines from twenty-seven countries over the period 1982–95, for example, Vanessa Tamms estimated a short-run variable cost equation. She also estimated a frontier function that can be used to assess the extent to which an airline lies off its frontier. These results can in turn be applied in partial equilibrium modeling to identify the effects of reform discussed earlier.[47] These models concentrate on supply and demand in air transport markets alone, but they include a series of markets over which airlines are likely to

---

46. See Elek and others (1999).

47. The cost estimates referred to in this paragraph are reported in Tamms (1999). Australia's Productivity Commission has undertaken modeling that captures these effects for air transport. The results will become available once the Australian government releases the commission's final report on international air services.

construct networks. In addition, they capture networking choices explicitly and incorporate forms of imperfect competition that make explicit the determination of markups over costs.[48]

The second major limitation of price or quantity impact measures is that they are unable to quantify the impact of liberalization on consumer and producer welfare. Airlines and consumers will be affected by reform, but in different ways. The impact of reform on consumers is relatively simple to describe: they gain from all three sorts of effects identified in this chapter. The impact on airlines is more complex. The competition effects reduce airline profits, but the degree of reduction is offset by cost reductions. The major airline beneficiaries of reform are likely to include those carriers with a comparative advantage in the provision of the service. In a market in which airlines provide differentiated services, however, even airlines that are relatively high-cost suppliers may see substantial gains from the scope to redesign their networks. Partial equilibrium modeling can be used to estimate the relative size of these effects on consumers and producers and also the scale of the net benefits, that is, the difference between consumer gains and airline gains or losses.

In summary, partial equilibrium modeling can be used to deal with the first two limitations of price and quantity-impact assessments of the impact of reform, namely the unpacking of the origins of the effects identified and their impacts on consumer and producer welfare in relevant markets. But by definition, the partial equilibrium methods fail to capture the intersectoral effects.

General Equilibrium Issues

The impact of liberalization on the wider economy can only be captured if the measures are incorporated into a general equilibrium model, such as a modified GTAP (global trade analysis project) model capturing the structure of service industries.[49] This will allow policymakers to quantify the costs of maintaining policies designed to exclude potential domestic and foreign entrants from their service markets.

Since services are an input into the production of most industries, an inefficient service sector can be very costly to the economy as a

---

48. For recent estimates of the frontier cost function for a set of telecommunications carriers, see Trewin (1999).

49. See Hertel (1997).

whole.[50] If a country reformed its tariff structure—even reducing rates to zero—but did not include the service sector in the liberalization process, then distortions would still remain and resource allocation would be affected. This point has usually been ignored in modeling work.

Modeling has been constrained, however, by the lack of data on the impact of policies that restrict services trade and investment. Some attempts have been made to convert frequency measures into tariff equivalents and then simulate the effects of reductions in barriers. According to one such study, the welfare gains from Uruguay Round cuts in industrial tariffs would have been three times higher if services barriers had also been cut by 25 percent.[51] Previous efforts at CGE (computable general equilibrium) modeling suggest that the various measures outlined here can be converted into tax equivalents for use in general equilibrium modeling.[52] They also indicate the importance of distinguishing between services supplied by substitute modes (that is, by local firms), by foreign-owned firms operating from a local base, and by foreign firms operating from home base (these are the same three modes of entry that we used as illustrations of reform in our discussion of the application of modeling methods to the air transport market).

It is equally important to determine how impediments affect restrictions on ongoing operations and those on establishment (both of which may apply to local and foreign-owned firms, and may apply differentially to foreign-owned firms, depending on how they want to access the market). Two other essential exercises are to determine the distribution of any rents created between local and foreign interests and to capture the possibility of perverse welfare effects from liberalization. The latter could occur when a form of service is subject to a tax in the initial equilibrium and its output falls as a result of liberalization, for example, as a consequence of the removal of tax on close substitute forms of delivery. The existence of these perverse effects supports the case for a broad program of reform in terms of sectoral coverage as well as modes of delivery.

Preliminary results showing how these features can be incorporated into a general equilibrium model are expected early in 2000. These will, for the first time, allow for a complete assessment of the economy-wide

---

50. See Hoekman and Primo Braga (1997). The intensity of production is an important factor to consider. The inefficiency of services supplied by arm's-length transactions could lead firms to provide a higher percentage of such services in-house.

51. Brown and others (1996).

52. For a review of these efforts, see Dee, Hardin, and Holmes (1999).

impacts of services liberalization and conversely will highlight the ongoing costs to economies of maintaining protection.

Conclusion

This chapter has demonstrated that weighting schemes can be developed for use in measuring policies affecting international services transactions. These schemes reflect some expectation of the economic significance of the restrictions involved. Over time, as the empirical work expands, the weights themselves may be determined endogenously.

Policy measures constructed in this way are also powerful explanators of market outcomes, although at this stage the assessments based on quantity impacts tend to work better than those based on price impacts (possibly because representative price data on services are difficult to obtain). This is especially the case where data on GATS policy can be supplemented by data from industry sources. If market data are available, the significance of the policy measures can be tested in terms of their impact on market outcomes. Where market data are not available, outcomes can be inferred from the policy measures, given the confidence in this methodology based on its applications in other markets.

More explicit modeling in either a partial or general equilibrium framework is always desirable, though sometimes costly. These modeling methods can be used to make explicit the mechanisms by which policy choices affect market outcomes. That information is hidden in the single-equation reduced-form calculations that are generally used in price or quantity-impact approaches. Modeling can also be used to derive other impact measures, including welfare effects and redistributive effects.

Because of their increased sophistication, the techniques discussed in this chapter are providing the first sound measures of impediments to trade in services that can be used in negotiations or in the documentation and comparative assessment of liberalization commitments. This has a number of major implications for international negotiations: information will be available to help set priorities at the national level; commitments in global (and regional) talks can be more easily codified, to the benefit of cross-sectoral negotiations; the constraint on the lack of incremental change—an inhibitor to reform because of the apparent all-or-nothing choices faced by negotiators—will be removed, since partial reform or sequencing will be more easily documented; and it will be easier to document commitments through a negative list approach because more information will be disclosed with these techniques. Negative lists in turn adduce greater pressure for liberalization as the schedules show what remains to be done in sectoral terms. By contrast, the current approach merely documents restrictive measures in sectors in which commitments to reform have been made. Above all, the information produced will enable economies to characterize their policy regimes and therefore participate meaningfully in the negotiations.

References

Areeda, Philip, Herbert Hovenkamp, and John Solow. 1995. *Antitrust Law: An Analysis of Antitrust Principles and Their Application*. Boston: Little, Brown.

Ascher, Bernard, and Obie Whichard. 1991. "Developing a Data System for International Sales of Services: Progress, Problems and Prospects." In *International Economic Transactions: Issues in Measurement and Empirical Research,* edited by P. Hooper and J. Richardson, 203–34. University of Chicago Press.

Bhagwati, Jagdish. 1984. "Splintering and Disembodiment of Services and Developing Countries." *World Economy* 7(2): 133–44.

Bosworth, Malcolm, Christopher Findlay, Ray Trewin, and Tony Warren. 1997. *Measuring Trade Impediments to Services within APEC: The Economic Implications of Liberalizing APEC Tariff and Nontariff Barriers to Trade*. USITC Publication 3101. Washington D.C.: U.S. International Trade Commission.

Brown, Drusilla, Alan Deardorff, Alan Fox, and Robert Stern. 1996. "Computational Analysis of Goods and Services Liberalization in the Uruguay Round." In *The Uruguay Round and Developing Economies,* edited by W. Martin and A.Winters. Cambridge University Press.

Claessens, Stijn, and Thomas Glaessner. 1998. "Internationalization of Financial Services in East Asia." Washington, D.C.: World Bank.

Corden, W. M. 1994. "Comment" in *The Political Economy of Policy Reform,* edited by J. Williamson, 111–13. Washington, D.C.: Institute for International Economics.

Croome, John. 1995. *Reshaping the World Trading System: A History of the Uruguay Round.* Geneva: World Trade Organization.

Deardorff, Alan, and Robert Stern. 1985. *Methods of Measurement of Non-Tariff Barriers.* Geneva: United Nations Conference on Trade and Development.

Dee, Philippa, Alexis Hardin, and Leanne Holmes. 1999. "Issues in the Application of CGE Models to Services Trade Liberalization." In *Identifying the Roadblocks to International Services Business,* edited by Christopher Findlay and Tony Warren. Sydney: Routledge (forthcoming).

Destler, I. M. 1995. *American Trade Politics.* 3d ed. Washington, D.C.: Institute for International Economics.

Elek, Andrew, Christopher Findlay, Paul Hooper, and Tony Warren. 1999. "Open Skies or Open Clubs? New Issues for Asia-Pacific Economic Cooperation." *Journal of Air Transport Management,* June.

Ergas, Henry, Eric Ralph, and John Small. 1998. "Declaration of GSM Roaming: An Economic Analysis." Mimeo submission to the Australian Competition and Consumer Commission.

Findlay, Christopher, and Tony Warren. 1999. *Identifying the Roadblocks to International Services Business.* Sydney: Routledge (forthcoming).

Garnaut, Ross. 1994. "Australia." In *The Political Economy of Policy Reform,* edited by J. Williamson, 51–72. Washington, D.C.: Institute for International Economics.

Hardin, Alexis, and Leanne Holmes. 1997. "Services Trade and Direct Foreign Investment." Staff Research Paper. Canberra: Industry Commission.

Hertel, T., ed. 1997. *Global Trade Analysis: Modeling and Applications.* Cambridge University Press.

Hill, T. P. 1977. "On Goods and Services." *Review of Income and Wealth* 24 (4): 315–38.

Hirsch, Seev. 1989. "Services and Service Intensity in International Trade." *Weltwirtschaftliches Archiv* 125: 45–60.

Hoekman, Bernard M. 1995. "Tentative First Steps: An Assessment of the Uruguay Round Agreement on Services." World Bank Policy Research Working Paper 1455. Washington, D.C. (May).

Hoekman, Bernard M., and Carlos Primo Braga. 1997. "Protection and Trade in Services: A Survey." CEPR Discussion Paper 1705. London: Centre for Economic Policy Research (September).

Hoekman, Bernard M., and Michel Kostecki. 1995. *The Political Economy of the World Trading System: From GATT to the WTO.* Oxford University Press.

Kalirajan, Kaleeswaran, Greg McGuire, Duc Nguyen-Hong, and Michael Schuele. 1999. "The Price Impact of Restrictions on Banking Services." In *Identifying the Roadblocks to International Services Business,* edited by Christopher Findlay and Tony Warren. Sydney: Routledge (forthcoming).

Lerner, A. 1934. "The Concept of Monopoly and the Measurement of Monopoly Power." *Review of Economic Studies* 1: 157.

Marko, Mary. 1998. "An Evaluation of the Basic Telecommunications Services Agreement." Centre for International Economic Studies Policy Discussion Paper 98/09. University of Adelaide.

Mattoo, Aaditya. 1998. "Financial Services and the WTO: Liberalization in the Developing and Transition Economies." Paper presented at the Measuring Impediments to Trade in Services Workshop, Productivity Commission, Canberra (April 30–May 1).

McGuire, Greg. 1998. "Australia's Restrictions on Trade in Financial Services." Staff Research Paper. Canberra: Productivity Commission.

McGuire, Greg, and Michael Schuele. 1999. "Restrictiveness of International Trade in Banking Services." In *Identifying the Roadblocks to International Services Business,* edited by Christopher Findlay and Tony Warren. Sydney: Routledge (forthcoming).

McGuire, Greg, Michael Schuele, and Tina Smith. 1999. "Restrictiveness of International Trade in Maritime Services." In *Identifying the Roadblocks to International Services Business,* edited by Christopher Findlay and Tony Warren. Sydney: Routledge (forthcoming).

Nau, H. 1987. "Bargaining in the Uruguay Round." In *The Uruguay Round: A Handbook for the Multilateral Trade Negotiations,* edited by J. Michael Finger and Andrzej Olechowski, 75–80. Washington, D.C.: World Bank.

Olechowski, Andrzej. 1987. "Nontariff Barriers to Trade." In *The Uruguay Round: A*

Handbook for the Multilateral Trade Negotiations, edited by J. Michael Finger and Andrzej Olechowski, 121–26. Washington, D.C.: World Bank.

Organization for Economic Cooperation and Development (OECD). 1997. "Assessing Barriers to Trade in Services: A Pilot Study on Accountancy Services." TD/TC/WP(97)26. Paris: Working Party of the Trade Committee.

Pacific Economic Cooperation Council (PEEC). 1995. *Survey of Impediments to Trade and Investment in the APEC Region.* Singapore: Asia-Pacific Economic Cooperation Secretariat.

Ralph, Eric, and J. Ludwig. 1997. "Competition and Telephone Penetration: An International Statistical Comparison." Paper presented to the Telecommunications Policy Research Center, Alexandria, Va., September 27–29.

Sampson, Gary, and Richard Snape. 1985. "Identifying Issues in Trade in Services." *World Economy* 8(2): 171–82.

Snape, Richard. 1998. "Reaching Effective Agreements Covering Services." In *The WTO as an International Organization,* edited by Anne O. Krueger, 279–85. University of Chicago Press.

Tamms, Vanessa. 1999. "Frontier Cost Estimates of the Impact of Restrictions on Trade in Air Transport Services." In *Identifying the Roadblocks to International Services Business,* edited by Christopher Findlay and Tony Warren. Sydney: Routledge (forthcoming).

Trewin, Ray. 1999. "Regulation and the Pricing of Telecommunications." In *Identifying the Roadblocks to International Services Business,* edited by Christopher Findlay and Tony Warren. Sydney: Routledge (forthcoming).

United Nations Conference on Trade and Development (UNCTAD). 1994. *Liberalizing International Transactions in Services: A Handbook.* New York: United Nations.

Warren, Tony. 1996. "The Political Economy of Services Trade and Investment Policy: Australia, Japan and the United States." Ph.D. diss., Research School of Pacific and Asian Studies, Australian National University.

———. 1997. "The Political Economy of Reform of Japanese Service Industries." *Pacific Economic Papers* 270. Canberra: Australian National University.

———. 1998. "The Political Economy of Telecommunications Trade and Investment Policy." In *Telecommunications and Socio-Economic Development,* edited by S. Macdonald and G. Madden. Amsterdam: Elsevier.

———. 1999a. "The Application of the Frequency Approach to Trade in Telecommunications Services." In *Identifying the Roadblocks to International Services Business,* edited by Christopher Findlay and Tony Warren. Sydney: Routledge (forthcoming).

———. 1999b. "Quantity Impacts of Trade and Investment Restrictions in Telecommunications." In *Identifying the Roadblocks to International Services Business,* edited by Christopher Findlay and Tony Warren. Sydney: Routledge (forthcoming).

Warren, Tony, Alexis Hardin, and Malcolm Bosworth. 1997. "International Telecommunications Reform in Australia." Staff Information Paper. Canberra: Industry Commission.

Warren, Tony, Vanessa Tamms, and Christopher Findlay. 1999. "Beyond the Bilateral System: Competition Policy and Trade in International Aviation Services." Paper presented at the American Economic Association Annual Meeting and meeting of the Transportation and Public Utilities Group, New York (January 3).

Williamson, John, ed. 1994. *The Political Economy of Policy Reform.* Washington, D.C.: Institute for International Economics.

[15]

Measuring the Cost of Barriers to Trade in Services

Philippa Dee, Kevin Hanslow, and Tien Phamduc

To what extent can the traditional tools of trade policy analysis be used to analyse the economic costs of barriers to trade in services?

Traditional analysis of trade barriers has focused primarily on the effects of tariffs. These are discriminatory taxes levied on foreign-produced goods at the border of a country.

The Heckscher-Ohlin (HO) framework is a standard framework in which tariffs have been analyzed (Heckscher [1919] 1949; Ohlin 1933). This framework assumes perfect substitutability between domestically produced and foreign goods of the same type, fixed endowments of primary factors of production, and perfect mobility of those factors between sectors within an economy. The framework has been extended to consider more than two goods and factors (Jones and Scheinkman 1977), the presence of a sector-specific factor of production (Mayer 1974; Mussa 1974), imperfect competition (Markusen 1981), increasing returns to scale (Melvin 1969) and product differentiation (Krugman 1979; Helpman 1981).

However, barriers to trade in services are unlike tariffs. They are typically regulatory barriers, rather than explicit taxes. They need not discriminate against foreigners. Indeed, barriers to market access are often designed to protect incumbent firms from *any* new entry, be it by domestic or foreign firms. And barriers to services trade are not restricted to affecting the *out-*

Philippa Dee is assistant commissioner, and Kevin Hanslow is director, at the Productivity Commission, Australia. Tien Phamduc is at the International Business School at Griffith University.

The views expressed in this paper are those of the authors and do not necessarily reflect those of the Productivity Commission. The authors are grateful for early discussions with Anne O. Krueger and comments from Kym Anderson, Chang-Tai Hsieh, Fukunari Kimura, and Will Martin.

put of services firms. One particularly important category of barriers to services trade—restrictions on foreign direct investment by service firms—affects the use of primary factors. These restrictions are recognized in the General Agreement on Trade in Services (GATS) under the World Trade Organization (WTO), since this agreement recognizes commercial presence as one of the modes by which services are traded.

To date, few papers of either a theoretical or an empirical nature have reviewed all these aspects of barriers to services trade. Some early papers largely dismissed concerns that the determinants of comparative advantage in services might differ from those in goods (Hindley and Smith 1984; Deardorff 1985). A few theoretical papers in the late 1980s examined some of the important characteristics of services, including knowledge intensity (e.g., Markusen 1989; Melvin 1989). This characteristic also featured in subsequent analysis of goods trade under imperfect competition (e.g., Grossman and Helpman 1991). However, those early theoretical papers did not look at the nature of barriers to services trade. Recently, a few empirical papers have examined the effects of removing barriers to trade in services. Many of these have failed to take account of barriers to commercial presence as an important category of barriers to trade in services (Brown et al. 1995; Brown, Deardorff, and Stern 1996; Hertel 1999; Nagarajan 1999). One seminal paper by Petri (1997) introduced a treatment of barriers to foreign direct investment in the services sector, but it failed to take into account barriers on the other modes of service delivery. Moreover, all empirical papers have suffered from a dearth of convincing empirical estimates of the incidence and economic significance of barriers to services trade.

A recent empirical paper by Dee and Hanslow (2000) sought to analyze the effects of removing barriers to services trade in a more comprehensive fashion.[1] The barriers included nondiscriminatory barriers to market access as well as discriminatory restrictions on national treatment. They included barriers to commercial presence as well as barriers to the other modes of service delivery. The focus of that paper was to compare the gains from liberalizing services trade with the gains from removing all post-Uruguay barriers to trade in agriculture and manufacturing. The paper also compared the gains from the total removal of barriers to services trade with the gains from several alternative approaches to partial liberalization. It identified significant second-best problems with some approaches to partial liberalization.

The purpose of this paper is to look more deeply at that analysis of services trade liberalization in order to assess the extent to which the traditional Stolper and Samuelson (1941) and Rybczynski (1955) results from the HO framework are still relevant in a more realistic model of services

---

1. Brown and Stern (2001) contains a services model that was developed independently and shares a number of conceptual and data features with the model presented here.

trade liberalization. In the process, the analysis examines whether and how the benefits of services trade liberalization are passed on to other sectors in the economy. Thus, the analysis tries to open up the "black box" of what is a rather complex general equilibrium model of services trade in order to gain insights into the sectoral results from that model in terms of more simple textbook treatments of trade policy analysis.

The structure of the paper is as follows. It first describes the model used—a multisector, multiregional computable general equilibrium model of world trade and investment. The theoretical structure of the model covers both foreign direct investment (FDI) and portfolio investment. The model's database contains estimates of FDI stocks and the activities of FDI firms, each on a bilateral basis. Thus, the model recognizes that both goods and services can be delivered via FDI as well as by conventional trade. The paper then looks at the size of the barriers to trade in services and the cost impost they impose on other sectors of the economy. This analysis uses the first of a comprehensive new set of estimates of barriers to services trade. To understand the general equilibrium effects of removing these barriers, the effects on each sector in selected economies are built up from a more restricted, partial equilibrium multicountry model. To this partial model are gradually added the resource constraints and income linkages associated with general equilibrium. It is as the resource constraints are added that the relevance of Stolper-Samuelson and Rybczynski effects can be analysed. The paper then briefly summarizes the implications of services trade liberalization for regional incomes. Finally, the paper identifies areas for further research.

1.1 The FTAP Model

The model is a version of the Global Trade Analysis Project model (GTAP; Hertel 1997) with foreign direct investment, known as FTAP. The treatment of FDI follows closely the pioneering work of Petri (1997). The FTAP model also incorporates increasing returns to scale and large-group monopolistic competition in all sectors. This follows Francois, McDonald, and Nordstrom (1995), among others, who adopted this treatment for manufacturing and resource sectors, and Brown et al. (1995) and Markusen, Rutherford, and Tarr (1999), who used similar treatments for services. Finally, FTAP makes provision for capital accumulation and international borrowing and lending. This uses a treatment of international (portfolio) capital mobility developed by McDougall (1993) and recently incorporated into GTAP by Verikios and Hanslow (1999). FTAP is implemented using the GEMPACK software suite (Harrison and Pearson 1996). Its structure is documented fully in Hanslow, Phamduc, and Verikios (1999). The model and its documentation are available at the Productivity Commission website at [http://www.pc.gov.au].

14   **Philippa Dee, Kevin Hanslow, and Tien Phamduc**

1.1.1   Theoretical Structure

The FTAP model takes the standard GTAP framework as a description of the *location* of economic activity and then disaggregates this by *ownership*. For example, each industry located in Korea comprises Korean-owned firms, along with U.S., Japanese, and other multinationals. Each of these firm ownership *types* is modeled as making its own independent choice of inputs to production, according to standard GTAP theory, and each firm type has its own sales structure.

On the purchasing side, agents in each economy make choices among the products or services of each firm type, distinguished by both ownership and location, and then among the individual (and symmetric) firms of a given type. Thus, the model recognizes the firm-level product differentiation associated with monopolistic competition. Firms choose among intermediate inputs and investment goods, whereas households and governments choose among final goods and services.

Agents are assumed to choose first among products or services from domestic or foreign locations, with a constant elasticity of substitution (CES) of 5. They then choose among particular foreign locations and among ownership categories in a particular location, both with a CES elasticity of substitution of 10. Finally, they choose among the individual firms of a particular ownership and location, with a CES elasticity of substitution of 15. With firm-level product differentiation, agents benefit from having more firms to choose among, because it is more likely that they can find a product or service suited to their particular needs. Capitalizing on this, Francois, McDonald, and Nordstrom (1995) show that the choice among individual firms can be modeled in a conventional model of firm types (not firms) by allowing a productivity improvement whenever the output of a particular firm type (and hence the number of individual firms in it) expands. However, because the substitutability among individual firms is assumed here to be very high, the incremental gain from greater variety is not very great, and this productivity-enhancing effect is not particularly strong (the elasticity of productivity with respect to output is $1/15 = 0.0667$).[2]

The first two choices, among domestic and foreign locations, are identical to the choices in the original GTAP model. They have been parameterized using values, 5 and 10, that are roughly twice the standard GTAP Armington elasticities. Two reasons can be given for doubling the standard elasticities. One is that only with such elasticities can GTAP successfully reproduce historical changes in trade patterns (Gehlhar 1997). The other is

2. The equivalent elasticity of productivity with respect to *inputs* is $0.0667/(1 - 0.0667) = 0.0714$, where this latter concept is used by Francois, McDonald, and Nordstrom (1995). The elasticities of productivity with respect to output and inputs are not equal because of the assumption of increasing returns to scale. Another reason that scale effects are not strong is that, with this nested structure, the economies of scale are regional rather than global.

that higher elasticities accord better with notions of firm-level product differentiation. Further calibration of the model to historical data using methods of maximum entropy (e.g., Liu, Arndt, and Hertel 2000) may provide a feasible means of refining the above estimates of firm-level substitution possibilities in the future.

The order of the first three choices, among locations and then among ownership categories, is the opposite of the order adopted by Petri (1997). The current treatment assumes that from a Korean perspective, for example, a U.S. multinational located in Korea is a closer substitute for a Korea-owned firm than it is for a U.S. firm located in the United States. Petri's treatment assumes that United States–owned firms are closer substitutes for each other than for Korean firms, irrespective of location.

There are two reasons for preferring the current treatment.

The first is that Petri's treatment produces a model in which multilateral liberalization of tariffs on manufactured goods produces large economic welfare losses, for most individual economies and for the world as a whole—an uncomfortable result at odds with conventional trade theory. The reason for the result is spelled out in more detail in Dee and Hanslow (2000).

The second reason for preferring the current treatment is that, in many instances, it accords better with reality. One of the distinguishing characteristics of services is that they are tailored each time to meet the needs of the individual consumer. Another characteristic is that they are often delivered face-to-face, sometimes making commercial presence (through FDI) the only viable means of trade. These characteristics taken together mean that service firms in a given location, irrespective of ownership, will tailor their services to meet local tastes and requirements and, thus, appear to be close substitutes, as in the current treatment.

Whereas the demand for the output of firms distinguished by ownership and location is determined as above, the supply of FDI is determined by the same imperfect transformation among types of wealth as in Petri (1997). Investors in each economy first divide their wealth between "bonds" (which can be thought of as any instrument of portfolio investment), real physical capital, and land and natural resources in their country of residence. This choice is governed by a constant elasticity of transformation (CET) semielasticity of 1, meaning that a 1 percentage point increase in the rate of return on real physical capital, for example, would increase the ratio of real physical capital to bond holdings by 1 percent. A bond is a bond, irrespective of who issues it, implying perfect international arbitrage of rates of return on bonds. However, capital in different locations is seen as different things. Investors next choose the industry sector in which they invest (with a CET semi-elasticity of 1.2). They next choose whether to invest at home or overseas in their chosen sector (with a CET semi-elasticity of 1.3). Finally, they choose a particular overseas region in which to invest (with a CET semi-elasticity of 1.4).

The less-than-perfect transformation among different forms of wealth can be justified as reflecting some combination of risk aversion and less-than-perfect information. It is important to note, however, that although the measure of economic welfare in FTAP currently recognizes the positive income contribution that FDI can make, it does not discount that for any costs associated with risk taking, given risk aversion. This is an important qualification to the current results and will be the subject of further research.

Although the chosen CET parameters at each "node" of the nesting structure may appear low, the number of nests means that choices at the final level (across destinations of FDI) are actually very flexible. For example, it can be shown that, holding total wealth fixed but allowing all other adjustments across asset types and locations to take place, the implied semi-elasticity of transformation between foreign destinations can easily reach 20 and can be as high as 60. The variation across regions in these implied elasticities comes about because of the different initial shares of assets in various regional portfolios.

The choice of CET parameters at each node was determined partly by this consideration of what they implied for the final elasticities, holding only total wealth constant. They were also chosen so that this version of FTAP gave results that were broadly comparable to an earlier version of GTAP with imperfect international (portfolio) capital mobility, for experiments involving the complete liberalization of agricultural and manufacturing protection (Verikios and Hanslow 1999). Imperfect capital mobility was also a feature of the GTAP-based examination of Asia-Pacific Economic Cooperation (APEC) liberalization by Dee, Geisler, and Watts (1996) and Dee, Hardin, and Schuele (1998). These parameters thus provide a familiar starting point from which refinements could be made in the future, possibly based on methods of maximum entropy.

In one respect, however, the current version of FTAP does differ from previous versions of GTAP with imperfect capital mobility. The GTAP variants assumed that capital was perfectly mobile across sectors, whereas FTAP has less-than-perfect sectoral mobility. Furthermore, the choice of sector is relatively early in the nesting structure, so that the implied elasticities guiding choice of sector, holding only total wealth constant, are relatively low (e.g., 1.2 in the United States). As a result, FTAP tends to exhibit the behavior that resources move less readily between sectors in a given region but more readily across regions in a given sector, although the differences are not dramatic. The current treatment is consistent with the idea that the knowledge capital often required to succeed in FDI, despite the difficulties of language and distance, is likely to be sector specific.

Petri's model assumed that total wealth in each region was fixed. In FTAP, although regional endowments of land and natural resources are fixed (and held solely by each region's residents), regional capital stocks can accumulate over time, and net bond holdings of each region can adjust to help finance the accumulation of domestic and foreign capital by each region's investors. The treatment of capital accumulation follows the original treatment of McDougall (1993) and was also used by Verikios and Hanslow (1999); Dee, Geisler, and Watts (1996); and Dee, Hardin, and Schuele (1998).

With this treatment of capital accumulation, FTAP provides a long-run snapshot view of the impact of trade liberalization, ten years after it has occurred. To the extent that liberalization leads to changes in regional incomes and saving, this will be reflected in changes to the capital stocks that investors in each region will have been able to accumulate. As noted, investors in each region are not restricted to their own saving pool in order to finance capital investment. They may also issue bonds to help with that investment, but only according to their own preferences about capital versus bond holding, and only according to the willingness of others to accept the additional bonds.

1.1.2 Model Database

The starting point for FTAP's database was not the standard GTAP database, because this includes measures of trade and investment barriers that are still to be eliminated under the Uruguay Round agreement. Instead, the starting point was an updated version of the GTAP database, following a simulation in which the barriers yet to be eliminated under the Uruguay Round had been removed. Such a database was provided by the work of Verikios and Hanslow (1999), under their assumption of less-than-perfect capital mobility.

Foreign Direct Investment Data

The Petri treatment of FDI requires the addition of data on bilateral FDI stocks and on the activity levels and cost and sales structures of FDI firms. The methods used to estimate such data were similar to those of Petri. Both APEC (1995) and United Nations (1994) provided limited data on FDI stocks by source, destination, and sector. These data were fleshed out to provide a full bilateral matrix of FDI stocks by source, destination, and sector, using RAS methods (Welsh and Strzelecki 2000). Thus, the individual bilateral estimates may be unreliable, although the more aggregate data match published totals. The resulting estimates are summarized in Dee and Hanslow (2000). The data were collected (and the model implemented) for nineteen regions and three broad sectors. The three sectors—primary (agriculture, resources, and processed food), secondary (other manufacturing), and tertiary (services)—correspond broadly to the three areas of potential trade negotiation in a new trade round. The intention is to use similar methods to produce a model with greater sectoral detail in the future.

One problem with such FDI data is that they distinguish FDI from portfolio investment according to whether the investor (or investing firm) has an

equity interest of 10 percent or more. This *ownership* share may not be sufficient to ensure *control* of an enterprise.[3] For some purposes, researchers
have instead considered affiliates that are majority owned—in which the
combined ownership of those persons individually owning 10 percent or
more from a particular country exceeds 50 percent. In the current context,
a better approach in the future may be to recognize explicitly the size of the
equity stake that different countries (including the local host) have in an enterprise, especially since some barriers to services trade are explicitly designed to control the extent of foreign ownership. This is an area for further
research.

The FDI stock data were used in turn to generate estimates of the output
levels of FDI firms. To do this, we estimated capital income flows by multiplying the FDI stocks by rates of return. These capital rentals were then
grossed up to get an output estimate for FDI firms, using ratios of capital
rentals to output from the GTAP database. Again, the resulting estimates
are similar to those in Petri (1997) and are summarized in Dee and Hanslow
(2000). A possible future refinement would be to use additional information
on the ratio of value added to output from U.S. and Japanese data on the
activities of offshore affiliates (e.g., Baldwin and Kimura 1998; Kimura and
Baldwin 1998). Petri (1997) shows how estimates obtained using different
methods can differ, sometimes widely. Nevertheless, experience shows that
models such as these are more sensitive to estimates of the extent of barriers to services trade than they are to estimates of the underlying services
trade and FDI flows.

The detailed cost and sales structures of FDI firms were assumed to be
the same as for locally owned firms and were obtained by prorating the
GTAP database. A subject for future research would be to make use of information on the true cost and sales structures of FDI firms, again using
available U.S. and Japanese data on the activities of offshore affiliates.

Estimates of Barriers to Services Trade

Estimates of existing barriers to services trade were injected into the
model's database, using the techniques of Malcolm (1998). The process is
documented in Hanslow et al. (2000).

The estimates of barriers to services trade were the first of a comprehensive new set of estimates, documented in Findlay and Warren (2000). The
general methodology of these studies is as follows.

- Qualitative information on barriers to services trade is converted to a
  quantitative index measure of trade restrictiveness, based on coverage

---

3. Another potential problem is that two or more countries can treat that same firm as a foreign affiliate. Although in some contexts this can lead to double counting, in the current context it does not because the FDI stock data have not been "grossed up" to account for other
owners (which could also include local joint venture partners).

and some initial judgments about the relative restrictiveness of the different sorts of restrictions.

- An econometric model is developed to measure the determinants of the economic performance (e.g., price, profit margin, cost, or quantity) of service firms in a given sector in different countries, taking account of all the factors that economic theory would suggest are relevant, including the index measure of trade restrictiveness.
- The economic model is used to estimate the determinants of economic performance. Wherever possible, the components of the trade restrictiveness index are entered separately so that the econometrics can reveal something about the relative weights attached to the separate components.[4]
- The results of the econometrics are used to calculate the effect of trade restrictions on performance. Where necessary, quantity or profit effects are converted to price or cost effects.

Estimates of barriers to trade in banking services along these lines were taken from Kaleeswaran et al. (2000), and estimates of barriers to trade in telecommunications services were taken from Warren (2000). The rates can be taken as indicative of post-Uruguay rates, because although the Uruguay Round established the architecture for services trade negotiations, it did not achieve much in the way of services trade liberalization (Hoekman 1995).

For modelling purposes, the barrier estimates were decomposed according to a two-by-two classification.

- The GATS framework distinguishes four modes of service delivery: via commercial presence, cross-border supply, consumption abroad, and the presence of natural persons. Accordingly, the FTAP model distinguishes barriers to establishment from barriers to ongoing operation. This is similar to the distinction between commercial presence and other modes of delivery, because barriers to establishment are a component of the barriers to commercial presence. Barriers to establishment are modeled as taxes on the movement of capital. Barriers to ongoing operation are modeled as taxes on the output of the service-providing firms.
- The GATS framework also distinguishes restrictions on market access from restrictions on national treatment. As noted above, the former are restrictions on entry, be it by locally owned or foreign-owned firms. In the FTAP model, they are treated as nondiscriminatory. Restrictions on national treatment mean that foreign-owned firms are treated less favorably than domestic firms. These restrictions are treated as discriminatory.

---

4. This is not possible where there is high multicollinearity between the various components, or where there is a lack of in-sample variation in some of the components.

20   **Philippa Dee, Kevin Hanslow, and Tien Phamduc**

Table 1.1   Classifying Barriers to Trade in Banking and Telecommunications Services

	Nondiscriminatory Barriers to Market Access	Discriminatory Derogations from National Treatment
	Barriers to Establishment	
Banking	Are there restrictions on the number of bank licenses?	Are there restrictions on the number of foreign bank licenses? Are there restrictions on foreign equity investment or requirements for foreigners to enter through a joint venture with a domestic bank? Are there restrictions on the permanent movement of people?
Telecommunications	One measure of restriction is actual number of competitors in fixed and mobile markets. Is there an enforced monopoly, partial competition or full competition in various fixed line markets and mobile market? What percentage of the incumbent fixed or mobile operator is privatised?	What percentage of foreign investment is allowed in competitive carriers?
	Barriers to Ongoing Operation	
Banking	Are there general restrictions on raising funds, lending, providing other lines of business, or expanding the number of banking outlets?	Are foreign banks restricted in raising funds, lending, providing other lines of business, or expanding the number of banking outlets? Are there restrictions on the proportion of foreigners on the board of directors? Are there restrictions on the temporary movement of people?
Telecommunications	Are there restrictions on leased lines or private networks? Are there restrictions on third party resale? Are there restrictions on connection of leased lines and private networks to the public switched telephone network?	Are there restrictions on callback services?

Source: McGuire and Schuele (2000) and Warren (2000).

The decomposition of trade barriers into this two-by-two classification follows the classifications used by Kaleeswaran et al. (2000) and Warren (2000). Table 1.1 shows how they classify barriers to trade in banking and telecommunications services. Note that in the banking sector, prudential regulations were not counted as trade barriers or included in the restrictiveness index. This was based on the recognition that they are designed to address a genuine market failure and the judgment that they are generally implemented in an appropriate fashion to that end. It is also consistent with the so-called "prudential carve-out" allowed for in the GATS.

Note also that in the banking study, horizontal (i.e., not sector-specific) restrictions on the permanent movement of people were counted as a barrier to establishment, and hence they were modeled as a barrier to the movement of capital. More properly, these restrictions should be modeled as a barrier to the movement of labor, but so far FTAP does not allow for international labor mobility. Similarly, horizontal restrictions on the temporary movement of people were counted as a barrier to ongoing operation, affecting both offshore affiliates and services delivered via "cross-border" trade, where the latter is broadly defined to include services delivered via the temporary movement of the consumer or the producer. In reality, the barriers affecting true cross-border trade are sufficiently different from those affecting trade involving temporary movement to warrant modeling them separately. These are areas for further research.

A simple average of the estimated price effects of barriers to trade in banking and telecommunications was taken as being typical of most services—all of the GTAP service categories of trade and transport; finance, business, and recreational services; and half of public administration, defense, education, and health. The remainder of public administration, defense, education, and health, along with electricity, water and gas, construction, and ownership of dwellings were assumed to be strictly non-traded (note that engineering services are part of business services, not construction). The resulting average estimates of barriers to trade in the tertiary sector would have been about 50 to 100 percent bigger had the banking and telecommunications estimates been taken as indicative of the whole of the services sector. A procedure for future research is to use the next version of the GTAP database, which will have more services-sector detail, to model barriers to each service separately, thus overcoming the extreme arbitrariness of these assumptions. In the meantime, the computational results should be treated as preliminary and interpreted with appropriate caution.

The resulting structure of post-Uruguay barriers to trade in services is summarized in table 1.2. Barriers to trade in primary (agricultural, resource, and processed food) and secondary (manufacturing) products are also shown for comparison purposes. Barriers to primary products are represented via a combination of taxes on imports, and subsidies (shown in table 1.2 as negative taxes) on exports and output. Unfortunately, at FTAP's three-sector level of aggregation, the actual taxes on primary exports and output are a combination of subsidies used for protective purposes, and taxes (e.g., excises on alcohol and tobacco) used for revenue raising. (Although the average taxes on primary output are not shown in table 1.2, they are all relatively small and mostly positive.) In future, using a database with greater sectoral detail will reduce the problems associated with "aggregation bias."

In the services sector, as noted above, barriers to establishment have been

Table 1.2   Tax Equivalents of Post-Uruguay Barriers to Trade and Investment (%)

	Imports		Exports		Domestic Output (tertiary)	Foreign Affiliates' Output (tertiary)	Domestic Capital (tertiary)	Foreign Affiliates' Capital (tertiary)
	Primary	Secondary	Primary	Tertiary				
Australia	1.69	7.30	0.65	4.81	0.00	0.69	0.62	14.79
New Zealand	1.16	4.51	-3.25	3.78	0.00	0.67	0.41	4.18
Japan	16.19	1.81	-8.12	4.41	3.59	4.75	0.33	3.01
Korea	12.95	6.61	-1.22	4.57	5.11	6.78	1.91	22.01
Indonesia	4.40	6.71	0.00	4.68	13.23	28.11	22.69	68.06
Malaysia	21.18	5.97	6.68	4.50	3.58	10.20	15.35	37.58
The Philippines	16.16	18.51	-0.10	4.80	8.38	22.65	7.40	54.28
Singapore	3.22	0.56	0.01	4.70	3.40	8.32	2.42	24.50
Thailand	12.12	14.81	-16.98	4.14	4.69	13.36	12.16	36.49
China	8.92	28.45	5.13	4.08	18.75	36.40	123.46	250.66
Hong Kong	0.00	0.00	0.00	9.91	1.39	2.36	1.35	5.41
Taiwan	27.31	5.63	-1.82	4.35	2.88	4.90	1.90	19.19
Canada	3.57	1.40	-0.43	3.54	0.25	1.67	0.53	6.11
United States	1.29	2.24	-0.02	4.26	0.07	1.08	0.00	3.83
Mexico	-1.50	2.99	1.89	5.23	2.17	5.59	0.68	12.99
Chile	6.76	10.26	0.02	4.36	2.97	4.11	14.15	20.36
Rest of Cairns[a]	3.82	13.39	6.30	4.49	0.98	5.55	7.19	19.45
European Union	3.17	1.13	-2.33	4.72	0.10	1.31	1.33	6.49
Rest of world	15.94	13.67	0.59	4.95	4.89	13.92	39.07	86.97

Source: FTAP model database.

[a]Rest of Cairns group: Brazil, Argentina, Colombia, and Uruguay.

modeled as taxes on capital. Barriers to ongoing operation may affect either FDI firms or those supplying via the other modes and have been modeled as taxes on the output of locally based firms (either domestic or foreign owned) and taxes of the same size on the exports of firms supplying via the other modes, respectively. The estimates of export taxes on services in the fourth column of table 1.2 are trade-weighted averages of the taxes on exports to particular destinations, where these are equal in turn to the taxes on foreign affiliates' output in the destination region, shown in the sixth column. These are modeled as taxes in the exporting region, rather than as tariffs in the importing region, to allow the rents created by the barriers to be retained in the exporting region. The issue of rents is addressed in more detail shortly.

The model also distinguishes restrictions on market access from restrictions on national treatment. The taxes on domestic capital and domestic output in table 1.2 represent the effects of restrictions on market access (affecting establishment and ongoing operation, respectively). The taxes on the capital and output of foreign affiliates are higher than the corresponding taxes on domestic firms, because they represent the effects of restrictions on both market access and national treatment.

The estimates in table 1.2 indicate that barriers to trade in services are generally at least as large as those on agricultural and manufactured products. Most economies have at least some significant barriers to trade in services. The only regions where barriers are low across the board are New Zealand, Japan, Hong Kong, Canada, the United States, and the European Union. However, this statement should be heavily qualified, because it is based only on estimates of barriers to banking and telecommunications. In the same vein, the estimates of overall barriers to services trade for China are very high, because the estimates of barriers to telecommunications services in China are particularly high, as they are in a number of other low-income developing economies. Estimates based on a broader set of services sectors are likely to produce less variation in overall estimates of services trade barriers across economies.

Barriers to trade in services have been modeled as tax equivalents that generate rents—a markup of price over cost—rather than as things that raise costs above what they might otherwise have been (e.g., Hertel 1999; Brown and Stern 2001). This decision was based on the way in which the price impacts of barriers to trade in banking and telecommunications services were measured. Kaleeswaran et al. (2000) measured the effects of trade restrictions on the net interest margins of banks, a direct measure of banks' markup of price over cost.[5] Warren (2000) measured the effects

5. Net interest margins—a measure of the difference between borrowing and lending rates of interest—can also be thought of as the "price" of financial intermediation services. The econometric model used to test the significance of barriers to trade in banking services was developed from an economic model of financial intermediation.

24   Philippa Dee, Kevin Hanslow, and Tien Phamduc

of trade restrictions on the quantities of telecommunications services delivered, and these were converted to price impacts using an estimate of the elasticity of demand for telecommunications services. Thus, Warren's estimates did not provide direct evidence of a markup of price over cost, but the relative profitability of telecommunications companies in many countries suggests that some element of rent may exist. By contrast, there is evidence that trade restrictions in sectors such as aviation raise costs (Johnson et al. 2000). As estimates of the effects of trade barriers in these sectors are incorporated into the model, it will be appropriate to treat some restrictions as cost-raising rather than as rent-creating.

One important implication of the current treatment is that welfare gains from liberalizing trade in services are likely to be understated, perhaps significantly. If trade restrictions create rents, then the allocative efficiency gains from trade liberalization are the "triangle" gains associated with putting a given quantum of resources to more efficient use. By contrast, if trade restrictions raise costs, the gains from trade liberalization include "rectangle" gains (qualified by general-equilibrium effects) from lower costs, equivalent to a larger effective quantum of resources for productive use.

Because barriers to services trade appear to be significant, and because they have been modeled as taxes, the rents they generate will be significant. A key issue is whether those rents should be modeled as being retained by incumbent firms, appropriated by governments via taxation, or passed from one country to another by transfer pricing or other mechanisms. In FTAP, the rents on exports have been modeled as accruing to the selling region, and those on FDI have been modeled as accruing to the region of ownership, after the government in the region of location has taxed them at its general property income tax rate. Despite this, the asset choices of investors are modeled as being driven by pretax rates of return. This is because many economies, in the developed world at least, have primarily destination-based tax systems. For example, if tax credits are granted for taxes paid overseas, investors are ultimately taxed on *all* income at the owning region's tax rate. Although such tax credits have not been modeled explicitly, their effect has been captured by having investors respond to relative pretax rates of return. Nevertheless, investor choices are also assumed to be determined by rates of return excluding any abnormal rent component. Investors would like to supply an amount of capital consistent with rates of return including abnormal rents, but they are prevented from doing so by barriers to investment. The amount of capital actually supplied is, therefore, that amount that investors would like to supply at rates of return excluding abnormal rents.

Thus, a portion of the rent associated with barriers to services trade is assumed to remain in the region of location in the form of property income tax revenue, whereas the remainder accrues to the region of ownership. Thus, liberalization of services trade could have significant income effects in both home and host regions as these rents are gradually eliminated. Dee and Hanslow (2000) show in detail how significant these effects are, relative to the allocative efficiency effects and other effects normally associated with trade liberalization.

A final point to note is that the model's database does not contain estimates of barriers to investment in agriculture and manufacturing, even though they are likely to be significant. It is unlikely that a new trade round would include negotiations on them. Nevertheless, their omission will affect the model's estimates of the effects of liberalization elsewhere, and the results need to be qualified accordingly.

1.2 The Cost Impact of Barriers to Trade in Services

Table 1.2 shows that the direct "tax equivalents" of barriers to trade in services are often significant, compared with the trade barriers expected to remain in agriculture and manufacturing after full implementation of the Uruguay Round. It also shows that barriers to services trade tend to be much higher in developing than in developed economies.

A priori, this does not mean that the services sectors in developing economies would suffer most from services trade liberalization. Because barriers to services trade are unlike tariffs, there are two key mechanisms by which the services sectors in developing countries could expand following services trade liberalization.

- Not all services trade barriers discriminate against foreign services suppliers, so the services sector could expand because of new domestic entry.
- Some services trade barriers restrict inward FDI, so the services sector could expand because of new foreign entry.

These mechanisms could be sufficient to offset the traditional mechanisms by which a protected sector can be harmed by removal of protection.

- Some services barriers discriminate against foreign services delivered cross-border, so the services sector could contract in the face of additional import competition.
- Services trade liberalization may benefit downstream using industries, and the services sector may lose out in the competition for domestic resources (e.g., labor).

Figure 1.1 examines the extent to which downstream using industries are likely to benefit from services trade liberalization. It shows the direct and indirect cost impost of domestic barriers to trade in services on all sectors in selected model regions, as calculated from the FTAP model database.

In general terms, the figure shows the direct and indirect input requirements needed to produce a unit of final demand in each sector. For example,

26   **Philippa Dee, Kevin Hanslow, and Tien Phamduc**

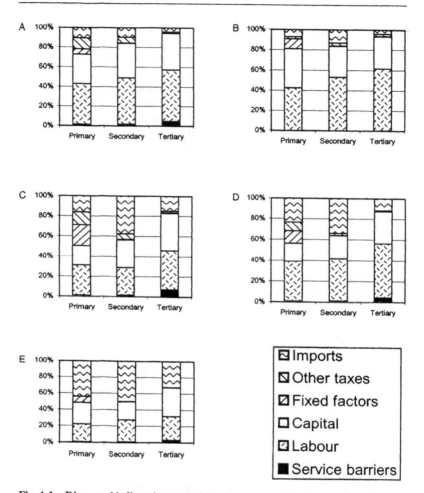

Fig. 1.1   Direct and indirect input requirements per unit of final demand: *A*, Japan; *B*, the United States; *C*, Korea; *D*, Taiwan; *E*, Hong Kong; *F*, Indonesia; *G*, Malaysia; *H*, the Philippines; *I*, Singapore; *J*, Thailand; *K*, China

a unit of processed food (a primary activity) sold to households might require inputs of unprocessed food (another primary activity), as well as
packaging materials from the secondary sector. The packaging materials
might again require inputs from forestry (a primary activity), along with
electricity from the tertiary sector. Each of these direct and indirect inputs
would have its own requirements for labor, capital, fixed factors (land and
natural resources), and imported inputs, and these can be added up. Where

Measuring the Cost of Barriers to Trade in Services   **27**

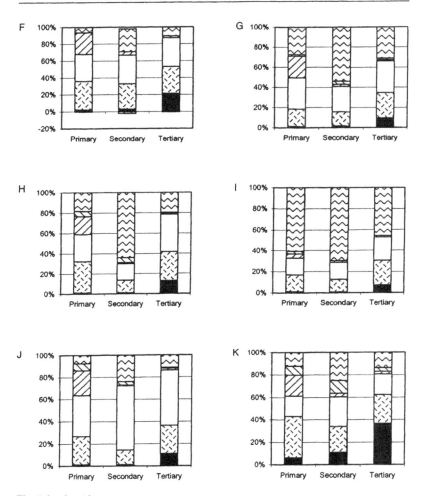

Fig. 1.1 (cont.)

the cost of the direct and indirect inputs is inflated by taxes, the direct and indirect tax contributions can also be calculated.

Thus, the direct and indirect cost impost of domestic barriers to services trade has been calculated by adding together the following:

- the output and capital taxes on direct and indirect services inputs, where those taxes represent the effects of domestic barriers to commercial presence (both establishment and ongoing operation); and
- the export taxes in the source region falling on direct and indirect im-

ported inputs, where these export taxes represent the effects of domestic barriers to cross-border services trade (where the term *cross-border* is interpreted loosely to include services traded via the temporary movement of the producer or consumer).

All other domestic taxes are collected in the contribution of "Other taxes," and all other taxes on imports (primarily tariffs) are included with the contribution of "Imports."

Figure 1.1 shows that, in every region shown, the greatest unit cost impost from services trade barriers falls on the services sector itself. This reflects two factors. First, the services sector experiences a direct taxing effect, whereas in other sectors the burden is indirect, through the higher cost of service inputs. Second, this effect is reinforced by the fact that in both developed and developing economies, the services sector itself tends to have a higher direct services input requirement than any other sector. Although other sectors may need service inputs, the greatest intensity of use of services is within the services sector itself. Thus, as will be seen, the benefits of services trade liberalization in many economies are concentrated within the services sector. This result is contrary to the normal effects of tariff removal, where the benefits are typically concentrated in other sectors.

Another feature of figure 1.1 is that in the economies with the highest per capita incomes (Japan, the United States, Korea, Taiwan, and Hong Kong), the cost impost of domestic services trade barriers on other sectors is minimal. Although these economies tend to be more service dependent, in terms of having higher direct service input requirements, their domestic barriers to services trade are also relatively low.

Somewhat surprisingly, in the economies with the lowest per capita incomes (Indonesia, Malaysia, the Philippines, Singapore, Thailand, and China), the cost impost of domestic services trade barriers on other sectors is not much greater. Only in China, where services trade barriers are particularly high, does the cost impost on other sectors approach 10 percent.[6]

By showing the cost impost of only domestic barriers to trade in services, figure 1.1 understates the potential first-round impact of multilateral liberalization of services trade. When barriers are removed globally, not only will domestic goods and services be cheaper, but so too will goods and services available in other economies. This benefit is likely to be significant in the highly import-intensive economies such as Korea, Taiwan, Hong Kong, Malaysia, the Philippines, and Singapore. Moreover, because the trade and transport services used to ship goods internationally will also be

6. The cost impost is estimated to be particularly high in China because its telecommunications market is particularly restrictive. When estimates of services barriers are incorporated for a broader range of services than banking and telecommunications, the overall cost imposts could differ from those shown here. Not only could the overall impost in China be lower, but the impost in developed countries could also be higher (since banking and telecommunications happen to be sectors in which developed countries are particularly liberal).

cheaper, there will be an additional cost reduction effect not captured in figure 1.1.

1.3 The Sectoral Effects of Removing Barriers to Trade in Services

1.3.1 Partial Equilibrium Effects on Sectoral Output

A useful way to understand the sectoral effects of removing barriers to trade in services is to start with a partial equilibrium framework and to gradually add the economy-wide constraints that distinguish a general from a partial equilibrium approach. This is a very useful technique of analysis, developed by Hertel (1997).

An initial partial equilibrium model is obtained by "turning off" the following parts of FTAP:

- *Factor supply constraints.* Each sector in each region can get all the labor and capital it needs at the going wage or rental price. Thus, the secondary and tertiary sectors in each region have horizontal supply curves (which nevertheless move downward as services barriers are removed). The primary sector continues to have an upward-sloping supply curve because fixed factors (land and natural resources) are still treated as being in fixed supply in each economy.
- *Income linkages.* Irrespective of what is projected to happen to factor prices and other variables, the model's measure of welfare is held fixed in each region. This "equivalent variation" is essentially a measure of net national product, or the real income accruing to the residents of each economy. In general equilibrium, it is affected not just by the amount of activity generated within a region, but also by net foreign interest and dividend payments associated with foreign borrowing and lending and with FDI.
- *The endogenous productivity and taste changes* associated with a love of variety. (In the full FTAP model, firms benefit from a wider choice of intermediate inputs in the same way that consumers benefit from a wider choice of final goods.)

In partial equilibrium, all the demand-side substitution possibilities of the full FTAP model are still in operation. Thus, for example, the demand for the output of the secondary sector in a region will depend on the following factors:

- how the cost (and hence price) of its output changes relative to the cost (and price) of output of secondary sectors in other economies, and how consumers and users in each region substitute between domestic and various imported sources of secondary output as a result of those relative price changes;

30   **Philippa Dee, Kevin Hanslow, and Tien Phamduc**

Table 1.3   **Partial Equilibrium Effects on Selected Regions of Removing Global Barriers to Trade in Services, by sector (%)**

	Primary			Secondary			Tertiary		
	Q	Pd	Pm	Q	Pd	Pm	Q	Pd	Pm
Japan	**-0.3**	-2.4	-0.9	**-1.4**	-2.6	-3.9	**-3.4**	-2.1	-21.9
United States	**-1.3**	-0.7	-1.3	**-7.3**	-0.6	-3.3	**-4.3**	-0.4	-13.6
Korea	**-0.1**	-1.9	-1.0	**2.3**	-2.9	-3.1	**-2.3**	-3.5	-16.3
Taiwan	**1.2**	-1.2	-0.9	**2.9**	-2.3	-2.9	**-4.5**	-2.5	-14.7
Hong Kong	**6.9**	-1.1	0.1	**15.2**	-3.8	-3.9	**-14.5**	-5.2	-23.1
Indonesia	**2.7**	-0.5	-0.9	**8.8**	-3.6	-3.1	**13.4**	-12.1	-30.6
Malaysia	**4.2**	0.5	-0.9	**6.9**	-3.3	-2.9	**0.3**	-8.2	-21.3
The Philippines	**1.2**	-1.1	-0.9	**2.9**	-2.9	-2.9	**8.1**	-7.5	-27.9
Singapore	**18.2**	-1.6	-0.9	**8.9**	-3.5	-3.0	**1.9**	-6.7	-19.6
Thailand	**3.1**	0.6	-1.3	**-5.3**	-1.9	-3.0	**0.3**	-7.6	-21.9
China	**36.6**	18.1	-1.2	**132.0**	-10.2	-2.6	**245.2**	-27.9	-31.9

Source: FTAP model projections, partial equilibrium closure.
Notes: Q = domestic output quantity; Pd = domestic price; Pm = import price.

- how the cost (and hence price) of its output changes relative to the average price (across sources) of primary and tertiary output, and how domestic consumers and government substitute between the outputs of these different sectors as a result of these relative price changes;[7] and
- what the secondary input requirements are per unit of output in other sectors, and whether those other sectors are expanding or contracting.

Thus, even in the partial equilibrium model, the richness of substitution possibilities and interindustry linkages on the demand side make for a rather complicated story.

Because real incomes in each economy are assumed to be fixed, it would be expected that unless substitution effects dominate, the demand for, and hence output of, a commodity or service should increase whenever services trade liberalization reduces its price. And the only sector in which services trade liberalization would conceivably *not* reduce the price is the primary sector, where the return to the fixed factor could conceivably be bid up. Thus, the presumption is that services trade liberalization should reduce prices and increase output. Where this does not occur, it must be as a result of substitution effects.

Within the services sector itself, prices fall and output rises in the ASEAN economies and China (table 1.3). Note that although the prices of domestic services fall in these economies, the prices of imported services

7. In FTAP, as in GTAP, consumers and government are the only agents to substitute directly among different commodities. For intermediate and investment usage, different commodities (aggregated across sources) are used in fixed proportions.

fall by significantly more. Thus, substitution toward imports in these economies might suggest that services output should fall. Offsetting this, however, is an increase in exports of services from these economies. In the services sector, the price of a service import in the destination country can fall by significantly more than its output price in the exporting country. This is primarily because services trade liberalization involves removing the "export tax" equivalent of barriers to cross-border trade imposed by the destination country. Thus, although domestic services in the ASEAN region and China are disadvantaged relative to imports at home, when the same services are exported, their prices compare favorably with service exports from most other regions. (This is indicated indirectly by the fact that the domestic output price of services falls by more in ASEAN and China than in the other regions.) Thus, the services output expansion in ASEAN and China is primarily an export story.

In the higher per capita income economies, services output falls, despite a reduction in the domestic price, because of substitution toward imports. This is in accordance with the relative price movements shown in table 1.3.

The declines in the output of the secondary sector in Japan and the United States are because of substitution toward imports, especially in intermediate usage. For the other higher-income economies (Korea, Taiwan, and Hong Kong), the prices of domestic secondary output do not change greatly relative to secondary import prices, so the secondary-output expansions in these economies are primarily an export story. In ASEAN and China, the secondary-output expansions are because of both increased exports and substitution away from imports.

Although in the secondary and tertiary sectors the results are driven primarily by substitution among different sources of each commodity, in the primary sector it is possible to see the effects of each region's households' substituting among different commodities. This explains the slight falls in the output of the primary sector in Japan and Korea. In these economies, the prices of imported services fall significantly more than the prices of any other final commodity. Households tend to substitute toward imported services and away from everything else. Thus, primary output in these economies falls, despite the fact that the price of domestic primary output falls by more than its import price.

In the United States, the effect on primary-sector output of households' switching away from the primary sector in general is reinforced by substitution (in relative terms) toward primary imports.

In Taiwan, Hong Kong, Singapore, and Thailand, the expansion of the primary sector is primarily an export story. (The landed cost plus insurance and freight [c.i.f.] price of Thai primary exports falls, despite a slight increase in the domestic output price, because of cheaper international trade and transport services.) This can be confirmed by looking at more detailed model results not shown in table 1.3.

In Indonesia, Malaysia, the Philippines, and China, the switch by households away from the primary sector in general is offset by increased intermediate input demand, and some increase in export demand, for primary-sector output. The increased intermediate demand occurs despite an adverse relative price movement against imports (in all but the Philippines), because of interindustry linkages between the primary sector and the downstream secondary and tertiary sectors.

In summary, multilateral liberalization of services trade reduces domestic costs and prices across all economies, and the partial equilibrium sectoral effects are of three types.

- In economies such as those of Japan and the United States, where initial domestic services barriers are particularly low, domestic prices do not fall by much, and substitution toward cheaper imports leads to a reduction in output in all sectors of the economy. Real income can remain constant, however, because of the cheaper imports.
- At the other extreme, in the economies of the ASEAN region and China, where initial domestic services barriers are relatively high, domestic prices tend to fall significantly, and output in (almost) all sectors of these economies expands.
- In between are the economies of Korea, Taiwan, and Hong Kong, where initial domestic services barriers are moderate, but where all sectors are more trade exposed than in Japan and the United States. Thus, although the services sectors in these economies may not benefit from services trade liberalization, at least some of their other sectors benefit from cheaper domestic and imported inputs and thus gain an advantage on export markets.

1.3.2   General Equilibrium Effects on Sectoral Output

The partial equilibrium results of table 1.3 assumed that each sector in each economy could get any additional labor and capital at the going wage or rental price. The results also ignored the income implications of services trade liberalization.

In table 1.4, these effects are gradually reintroduced into the model. The first column reproduces the partial equilibrium results from table 1.3. In the second column, primary factor supply constraints are imposed. As in textbook models, aggregate supplies of capital and labor are assumed to be fixed, and these factors are treated as being perfectly mobile within each sector of the economy. In the third column, sectoral capital stocks are assumed to take the values they would in the full general equilibrium model. Thus, not only do aggregate capital stocks change in each economy, but capital is no longer perfectly mobile across sectors. Finally, the full general equilibrium results are presented. These incorporate not only the primary factor behavior of the full general equilibrium model, but also the associ-

Table 1.4	Partial and General Equilibrium Effects on Sectoral Output in Selected Regions of Removing Global Barriers to Trade in Services (%)			
	Full Partial Equilibrium	Fixed Factors	Capital as in General Equilibrium	Full General Equilibrium
Japan				
Primary	−0.3	0.2	−0.3	−0.4
Secondary	−1.4	0.9	−0.5	−0.3
Tertiary	−3.4	−0.3	0.2	0.1
United States				
Primary	−1.3	2.4	0.4	0.6
Secondary	−7.3	1.9	0.2	0.6
Tertiary	−4.3	−0.7	−0.2	−0.4
Korea[a]				
Primary	−0.1	−0.5	−0.7	−0.8
Secondary	2.3	−0.4	−1.4	−1.6
Tertiary	−2.3	0.3	1.0	1.1
Taiwan[a]				
Primary	1.2	0.4	−0.1	0.1
Secondary	2.9	2.5	0.2	1.0
Tertiary	−4.5	−1.1	0.1	−0.2
Hong Kong[a]				
Primary	6.9	3.7	0.0	0.2
Secondary	15.2	9.0	−1.2	−2.2
Tertiary	−14.5	−2.1	0.4	0.6
Indonesia[a]				
Primary	2.7	−3.4	0.3	0.3
Secondary	8.8	−9.7	2.5	2.6
Tertiary	13.4	8.9	8.5	9.2
Malaysia[a]				
Primary	4.2	−1.1	0.0	0.1
Secondary	6.9	−1.8	0.2	0.1
Tertiary	0.3	3.3	1.5	1.5
The Philippines[a]				
Primary	1.2	−3.0	−1.9	−1.9
Secondary	2.9	−6.6	−2.6	−3.6
Tertiary	8.1	5.6	2.3	2.5
Singapore				
Primary	18.2	3.2	−4.0	−4.0
Secondary	8.9	−4.2	−5.6	−6.6
Tertiary	1.9	4.5	0.6	1.0
Thailand[a]				
Primary	3.1	0.7	−0.2	−0.1
Secondary	−5.3	−8.0	−0.7	−0.8
Tertiary	0.3	8.1	1.3	1.3
China[a]				
Primary	36.6	−6.5	−1.1	−0.2
Secondary	132.0	−16.7	4.5	2.5
Tertiary	245.2	43.7	28.7	32.5

Source: FTAP model projections, partial and general equilibrium closures.

[a]Aggregate capital stock projected to increase in general equilibrium closure.

ated income effects (including the net foreign income flows associated with FDI).

In broad terms, the imposition of factor supply constraints is the single most important step in taking the partial equilibrium sectoral results toward their general equilibrium values.

Even with factor supply constraints, the results for the tertiary sector in each region are qualitatively quite close to the partial equilibrium results:

- the services sectors in Japan and the United States are still smaller than in the absence of services trade liberalization;
- the services sectors in most other high-income economies are also projected to decline (Korea is the exception); and
- the services sectors in the ASEAN region and China still gain from services trade liberalization.

Now, however, the wage-rental ratios in each economy adjust to ensure that the induced output changes in other sectors do not lead to a violation of the overall primary factor supply constraints. Thus, the output of the primary and secondary sectors in Japan, the United States, Taiwan, and Hong Kong is now projected to rise to counteract the decline in their services sectors. In the ASEAN region, China, and Korea, output in many of the primary and secondary sectors is now projected to decline to offset the expansion of their services sectors.

One question is whether the changes in wage-rental ratios in the "fixed factors" version of the model are consistent with those predicted by the Stolper-Samuelson theorem. That theorem would predict that in the face of a decline in the relative price of services (induced by services trade liberalization) there would be a decline in the real return to the factor of production used relatively intensively in the services sector. In most economies, that factor is labor (see figure 1.1). Although the assumption of fixed factor supplies and perfect factor mobility is consistent with the assumptions of the Stolper-Samuelson theorem, there are many other assumptions in the "fixed factors" model that do not match the textbook Stolper-Samuelson assumptions exactly. It is nevertheless useful to see if the "fixed factors" model retains a Stolper-Samuelson flavor in the context of services trade liberalization.

Broadly speaking, the Stolper-Samuelson theorem would predict a decline in the wage-rental ratio in most economies; by contrast, the wage-rental ratio faced by producers in all economies in the "fixed factors" model is projected to rise. The reason is simple. Services trade liberalization includes liberalization of FDI in the services sector. The removal of taxes on service-sector capital leads to a direct and significant decline in capital rentals, relative to wages, because, with fixed capital supplies, the loss of rents from barriers to capital are borne directly by capital owners.[8]

8. The implication of this for regional incomes is not yet incorporated.

Thus, the nature of barriers to services trade leads to a significant departure from one of the standard textbook trade theorems.[9]

The results in the third column hint at the complexity of the capital supply story in the full FTAP model. Even though services trade liberalization involves removing taxes on service-sector capital, it is not always the case that cautious investors would invest more in those service sectors than they would if they viewed investment in any sector as being equally desirable (consistent with perfect sectoral capital mobility). In Japan, the United States, Korea, Taiwan, and Hong Kong, service-sector capital stocks are larger than in the "fixed factors" case, but in the other economies they are smaller. This demonstrates how the capital supply behavior in the FTAP model plays an important role in relocating capital across regions within a sector, as opposed to the textbook treatment of capital allocation across sectors within a region.

One question is whether the sectoral output responses associated with a change in aggregate capital stocks are consistent with those predicted by the Rybczynski theorem. That theorem states that if product prices are fixed (say, by "world prices"), an expansion in capital would lead to an expansion in the output of the product that uses capital relatively intensively and a contraction of the other product. Leamer and Levinsohn (1994, 7) give an insightful reinterpretation of the Rybczynski theorem:

> What is really at stake here is not the Rybczynski Theorem but rather its traveling companion, the Factor Price Equalization Theorem. These results together imply that factor supply changes ... do not have much affect [*sic*] on factor prices because the potential affect [*sic*] on factor prices is dissipated by product mix changes in favor of the products that use the accumulating factor intensively.

Clearly, critical assumptions of the Rybczynski Theorem do not hold in the FTAP model. Products are imperfect substitutes, so that product prices are not "given" to any single region. As a result, relative factor prices can also change to absorb the impact of an increase in capital, so that it does not have to be absorbed by changes in product composition.

However, one would expect the FTAP model to display the same underlying economic forces that lead to the Rybczynski result under its special set of assumptions. This can be demonstrated in an intermediate simulation in which aggregate capital in each region moves as it does in general equilibrium but is still perfectly mobile between sectors (thus, each region still has a unique economy-wide wage-rental ratio). In this intermediate simulation,

9. The particular result depends on the assumption that barriers to trade in services create rents rather than raising costs. If barriers to services trade raise costs and hence move the production possibility frontier toward the origin, then services trade liberalization could raise the real returns to all factors of production, although the effects on relative factor returns could still be unclear a priori. Brown, Deardorff, and Stern (2000) also show how real returns to both factors can be raised by the additional gains from trade arising from increasing returns to scale, competition, and product variety, even when barriers are treated as tariff equivalents.

there is the expected relationship between the direction of movement of the capital stock and whether the wage-rental ratio is higher or lower than in the "fixed factors" version of the model. When the capital stock rises, the wage-rental ratio is higher than in the "fixed factors" case, and when the capital stock falls, the wage-rental ratio is lower.

The final column of table 1.4 incorporates the FTAP model's income linkages: real income in each region is no longer constant but reflects the induced changes in factor prices and international capital movements. Dee and Hanslow (2000) demonstrate that such income effects are crucial to the welfare implications of liberalizing trade in services, as will be seen shortly. However, table 1.4 shows that these income effects do not have strong additional effects on the sectoral distribution of gains from services trade liberalization.

General equilibrium models are often regarded as "black boxes," offering little chance of understanding what is inside. The above analysis suggests that because the structure of barriers to services trade is complex, the hardest part about understanding the effects of multilateral liberalization of services trade is understanding what happens in partial equilibrium.

The partial equilibrium results help to demonstrate how liberalization of services trade can differ from tariff removal. Barriers to services trade affect domestic new entrants as well as foreign suppliers, and the sector to benefit most in output terms from liberalization can often be the services sector itself.

The transition from partial to general equilibrium analysis also demonstrates how some of the standard textbook results fail to hold in the context of services trade liberalization. In particular, because services trade barriers affect the price of service-sector capital as well as service-sector output, the Stolper-Samuelson theorem fails to hold: the movement of relative factor prices is dominated by the removal of the barriers to capital movement. The Rybczynski theorem also fails to hold in its textbook form, but the underlying economic forces that lead to its result are still relevant.

1.3.3   General Equilibrium Welfare Effects

The first column of table 1.5 summarizes the effects of full liberalization of services trade on economic well-being in selected model regions (Dee and Hanslow [2000] present results for all model regions). As in GTAP, the measure of economic well-being is the equivalent variation—essentially a measure of the change in real income in each region, where the deflator is an index of the prices of household consumption, government consumption, and national saving. For FTAP, however, the relevant measure of national income is net national product—the income accruing to the residents of a region—rather than net domestic product—the income generated within the borders of a region. Thus, net domestic product is adjusted for the income earned on outward FDI, net of the income repatriated overseas from inward FDI, plus the income from net bond holdings.

Table 1.5   Welfare Effects of Full Multilateral Liberalisation of Services Trade (absolute change in US$ millions)

	Equivalent Variation	Contribution of Endowment Change to Equilibrium Variation	Contribution of Change in Real FDI Stocks to Equilibrium Variation	Contribution of Change in Real Bond Holding to Equilibrium Variation	Contribution of Change in Rents on FDI Capital and Output
Japan	4,130	-1,030	3,120	-2,978	-8,730
United States	-1,809	-5,713	2,665	1,708	-6,716
Korea	1,886	438	-5	39	123
Taiwan	-142	312	378	-583	-423
Hong Kong	5,896	102	7,829	-621	-8,211
Indonesia	2,470	7,158	-541	-4,519	530
Malaysia	1,015	367	-103	-168	585
The Philippines	1,236	164	-91	47	214
Singapore	-247	-1,071	-198	-108	1,049
Thailand	1,698	305	-24	-393	486
China	90,869	52,164	-12,649	-5,776	12,849

Source: FTAP model projections, general equilibrium closure.

Three of the selected economies are projected to have incomes lower than otherwise as a result of full multilateral liberalization of services trade—the United States, Taiwan, and Singapore. Dee and Hanslow (2000) show that in each case, the losses from multilateral liberalization of services trade would be more than offset by income gains accruing from multilateral liberalization of trade in agriculture and manufacturing. Nevertheless, the source of the income losses from multilateral liberalization of services trade warrants further investigation, especially for the United States, where the losses are projected to be significant.

Dee and Hanslow show that for agricultural and manufacturing liberalization, the welfare results are dominated by two things: the contribution of improvements in allocative efficiency, and the contribution of induced changes in the terms of trade. The model's regions are projected to experience positive income gains, or in a few cases small losses, as a result of these effects.

For services liberalization, changes in FDI patterns contribute several additional effects. First, FDI can lead to an expansion or contraction in the capital stock located within a region, leading to a positive or negative contribution to income generated within a region from this change in national endowments. Second, it can lead to changes in net FDI and net lending positions, with consequent changes in net foreign income flows accruing to residents. Third, it can induce changes in the returns earned on those net foreign asset holdings. An important example here is changes in the rents earned on FDI.

The second column of table 1.5 shows the contribution to real income from changes in real capital endowments. Generally, if capital endowments are higher than otherwise, real GDP will be higher than otherwise, and vice versa.[10] A major reason that Singapore is projected to lose slightly from services trade liberalization is that its capital stock is projected to be lower than otherwise.

However, a lower capital stock located domestically need not always lead to lower incomes for domestic residents. Earnings from higher outward FDI and higher lending abroad could offset it. The third column of table 1.5 shows the contribution to residents' real income from changes in real FDI stocks. The fourth column shows the contribution from changes in real bond holdings. Both also help to indicate the way in which changes in capital endowments are financed.

For example, Japan's capital stock is lower than otherwise, but it has a big increase in outward FDI. In fact, it also borrows (a negative change in bond holding) in order to finance its outward FDI. By contrast, China's increase in capital endowments comes partly from a large increase in inward FDI

---

10. For a few regions, real GDP can be higher than otherwise, even if endowments are lower than otherwise, because the endowments are used more efficiently.

and partly from additional foreign borrowing. Thus, the large projected increase in China's service-sector output and exports, noted above, comes as much from an expansion in foreign-owned service firms located in China as it does from an expansion in Chinese-owned service firms. The United States is projected to have a smaller capital endowment than otherwise, but this is offset to some extent by an increase in outward FDI and increased lending to other regions.

For a few regions, real incomes are affected not so much by changes in net asset positions, but by changes in returns on those assets. Although the details are not shown in table 1.5, Taiwan is projected to lose slightly from services trade liberalization, primarily because in the FTAP database it is a net creditor economy and is adversely affected by a small induced fall in real interest rates.[11]

A further source of change in asset returns is the change in rents generated by barriers to services trade. The last column of table 1.5 shows the income contribution to recipient countries of changes in the rents accruing to FDI, as barriers to services trade are eliminated. What is striking is the loss of rents to the main providers of outward FDI—Japan, Hong Kong, and the United States. In fact, the loss of rents to U.S. incumbent multinationals is more than sufficient to explain its overall projected income loss from multilateral liberalization of services trade. Note, however, that this result is sensitive to the assumption that all barriers to services trade are rent-creating rather than cost-raising.[12]

Generally, although induced changes in capital stocks—both those located domestically and those owned abroad—do not appear to play a major role in explaining the effects of multilateral services trade liberalization on sectoral output, they play a major role in explaining the effects on real regional incomes. Barriers to services trade affect capital movements as well as the output of services firms, so services trade liberalization can have a significant effect on the regional location and ownership of capital. The flow-on effects to regional incomes demonstrate another way in which liberalization of services trade can differ from tariff removal.

1.4 Agenda for Further Research

Much of the research agenda for further development of the FTAP model has been outlined already. It involves continuing to obtain estimates of the price impacts of barriers to services trade along the lines outlined in

---

11. Interest rates fall primarily because of an assumption that government saving *rates* are held constant. Growing revenues and saving *levels*, therefore, allow some government debt retirement.

12. Brown, Deardorff, and Stern (2000) show that if barriers are cost-escalating, then welfare effects are dominated by the movement of real physical capital. However, they have a more simple treatment of profit repatriation and debt service payments than here.

40   Philippa Dee, Kevin Hanslow, and Tien Phamduc

Findlay and Warren (2000), both for additional sectors and for additional modes of service delivery within a sector. The methodologies should in the process reveal whether the barriers are rent-creating or cost-raising. Such methods could also be used to estimate the price impact of barriers to FDI in agriculture and manufacturing. More sectoral detail needs to be incorporated into FTAP, to model the barriers to each service separately. More research is required to obtain more realistic output estimates and cost and sales structures for FDI firms and, if possible, a realistic initial allocation of rents. Additionally, the welfare measure in FTAP needs to be amended to take account of the costs of risk taking, given risk aversion.

In addition, some of the simplifying assumptions made during the original development of FTAP could now be relaxed, and the sensitivity of the results to these assumptions tested. One such assumption was the uniformity of behavioral parameters across sectors and regions. Although this reflected a deliberate research strategy, its importance could be tested using systematic sensitivity analysis (Arndt and Pearson 1996). The importance of data issues (e.g., the initial distribution of rents) and theoretical issues (e.g., investor behavior) could also be explored.

However, there is also scope for much more work using simple analytical models of services trade that better incorporate the features of services and the nature of the barriers to their trade. Insights of the sort available in Markusen, Rutherford, and Hunter (1995), for example, provide invaluable guidance to those attempting to build better empirical models of FDI and services trade.

References

Arndt, C., and K. Pearson. 1996. *How to carry out systematic sensitivity analysis via Gaussian Quadrature and GEMPACK.* GTAP Technical Paper no. 3. Purdue University: Center for Global Trade Analysis.
Asia-Pacific Economic Cooperation (APEC). 1995. *Foreign direct investment and APEC economic integration.* Singapore: APEC Economic Committee.
Baldwin, R. E., and F. Kimura. 1998. Measuring U.S. international goods and services transactions. In *Geography and ownership as bases for economic accounting,* ed. R. E. Baldwin, R. Lipsey, and J. D. Richardson, 9–48. Chicago: University of Chicago Press.
Brown, D. K., A. V. Deardorff, A. K. Fox, and R. M. Stern. 1995. Computational analysis of goods and services liberalization in the Uruguay Round. In *The Uruguay Round and the developing economies,* ed. W. Martin and L. A. Winters, 365–80. Washington, D.C.: World Bank.
Brown, D., A. Deardorff, and R. Stern. 1996. Modeling multilateral trade liberalization in services. *Asia Pacific Economic Review* 2 (1): 21–34.
———. 2000. CGE modeling and analysis of multilateral and regional negotiating options. Paper presented at conference on Issues and Options for the Multilat-

eral, Regional, and Bilateral Trade Policies of the United States and Japan. 5–6 October, University of Michigan.

Brown, D., and R. Stern. 2001. Measurement and modeling of the economic effects of trade and investment barriers in services. *Review of International Economics* 9 (2): 262–86.

Deardorff, A. 1985. Comparative advantage and international trade and investment in services. In *Trade and investment in services: Canada/U.S. Perspectives*, ed. R. Stern, 39–71. Toronto, Canada: Ontario Economic Council.

Dee, P., C. Geisler, and G. Watts. 1996. *The impact of APEC's free trade commitment.* Industry Commission Staff Information Paper. Canberra, Australia: Australian Government Publishing Service, February.

Dee, P., and K. Hanslow. 2000. *Multilateral liberalization of services trade.* Productivity Commission Staff Research Paper. Canberra, Australia: Ausinfo.

Dee, P., A. Hardin, and M. Schuele. 1998. *APEC early voluntary sectoral liberalization.* Productivity Commission Staff Research Paper. Canberra, Australia: Ausinfo.

Findlay, C., and T. Warren, eds. 2000. *Impediments to trade in services: Measurement and policy implications.* London: Routledge.

Francois, J. F., B. McDonald, and H. Nordstrom. 1995. Assessing the Uruguay Round. In *The Uruguay Round and the developing economies*, ed. W. Martin and L. A. Winters, 117–214. Washington, D.C.: World Bank.

Gehlhar, M. 1997. Historical analysis of growth and trade patterns in the Pacific Rim: An evaluation of the GTAP framework. In *Global Trade Analysis: Modelling and Applications*, ed. T. Hertel, 349–63. Cambridge: Cambridge University Press.

Grossman, G., and E. Helpman. 1991. *Innovation and growth in the global economy.* Cambridge: Massachusetts Institute of Technology Press.

Hanslow, K., T. Phamduc, and G. Verikios. 1999. The structure of the FTAP model. Productivity Commission, Canberra. Research Memorandum, December.

Hanslow, K., T. Phamduc, G. Verikios, and A. Welsh. 2000. Incorporating barriers to FDI into the FTAP database. Productivity Commission, Canberra. Research Memorandum.

Harrison, J. W., and K. R. Pearson. 1996. Computing solutions for large general equilibrium models using GEMPACK. *Computational Economics* 9 (2): 83–127.

Heckscher, E. [1919] 1949. The effect of foreign trade on the distribution of income. Reprinted in *Readings in the theory of international trade*, ed. American Economic Association. Philadelphia, Blakiston.

Helpman, E. 1981. International trade in the presence of product differentiation, economies of scale, and monopolistic competition: A Chamberlinian-Heckscher-Ohlin approach. *Journal of International Economics* 11:304–40.

Hertel, T. 1997. *Global trade analysis: Modeling and applications.* Cambridge: Cambridge University Press.

Hertel, T. 1999. Potential gains from reducing trade barriers in manufacturing, services, and agriculture. Paper presented at the 24th Annual Economic Policy Conference, Federal Reserve Bank of St. Louis. 21–22 October, St. Louis, Miss.

Hindley, B., and A. Smith. 1984. Comparative advantage and trade in services. *World Economy* 7:369–90.

Hoekman, B. 1995. Assessing the general agreement on trade in services. In *The Uruguay round and the developing economies*, ed. W. Martin and L. A. Winters, 327–64. Washington, D.C.: World Bank.

Johnson, M., T. Gregan, G. Gentle, and P. Belin. 2000. Modeling the benefits of increasing competition in international air services. In *Impediments to trade in services: Measurement and policy implications*, ed. C. Findlay and T. Warren, 119–51. London: Routledge.

Jones, R., and J. Scheinkman. 1977. The relevance of the two-sector production model in trade theory. *Journal of Political Economy* 85 (5): 909–35.

Kaleeswaran, K., G. McGuire, D. Nguyen-Hong, and M. Schuele. 2000. The price impact of restrictions on banking services. In *Impediments to trade in services: Measurement and policy implications*, ed. C. Findlay and T. Warren, 215–30. London: Routledge.

Kimura, F., and R. E. Baldwin. 1998. Application of a nationality-adjusted net sales and value-added framework: The case of Japan. In *Geography and ownership as bases for economic accounting*, ed. R. E. Baldwin, R. Lipsey, and J. D. Richardson, 49–82. Chicago: University of Chicago Press.

Krugman, P. 1979. Increasing returns, monopolistic competition, and international trade. *Journal of International Economics* 9:469–79.

Leamer, E., and J. Levinsohn. 1994. International trade theory: The evidence. NBER Working Paper no. 4940. Cambridge, Mass.: National Bureau of Economic Research, November.

Liu, J., C. Arndt, and T. Hertel. 2000. Estimating trade elasticities for GTAP: A maximum entropy approach. Paper presented at the Third Annual Conference in Global Economic Analysis. 26–29 June, Melbourne, Australia.

Malcolm, G. 1998. Adjusting tax rates in the GTAP data base. GTAP Technical Paper no. 12. Purdue University, Center for Global Trade Analysis.

Markusen, J. 1981. Trade and the gains from trade with imperfect competition. *Journal of International Economics* 11:531–51.

———. 1989. Trade in producer services and in other specialized intermediate inputs. *American Economic Review* 79 (1): 85–95.

Markusen, J., T. Rutherford, and L. Hunter. 1995. Trade liberalization in a multinational dominated industry. *Journal of International Economics* 38 (1–2): 95–117.

Markusen, J., T. F. Rutherford, and D. Tarr. 1999. Foreign direct investment in services and the domestic market for expertise. Paper presented at the Second Annual Conference on Global Economic Analysis. 20–22 June, Denmark.

Mayer, W. 1974. Short-run and long-run equilibrium for a small open economy. *Journal of Political Economy* 82:955–68.

McDougall, R. 1993. Incorporating international capital mobility into SALTER. SALTER Working Paper no. 21. Industry Commission, Canberra, Australia.

Melvin, J. 1969. Increasing returns to scale as a determinant of trade. *Canadian Journal of Economics* 2:389–402.

———. 1989. Trade in producer services: A Heckscher-Ohlin approach. *Journal of Political Economy* 97 (5): 1180–96.

Mussa, M. 1974. Tariffs and the distribution of income: The importance of factor specificity, substitutability, and intensity in the short and long run. *Journal of Political Economy* 82:1191–204.

Nagarajan, N. 1999. The millennium round: An economic appraisal. Economic Papers no. 139. Directorate General for Economic and Financial Affairs, European Commission, November.

Ohlin, B. 1933. *Interregional and international trade*. Cambridge, Mass.: Harvard University Press.

Petri, P. A. 1997. Foreign direct investment in a computable general equilibrium framework. Paper prepared for the conference on Making APEC Work: Economic Challenges and Policy Alternatives. 13–14 March, Keio University, Tokyo, Japan.

Rybczynski, T. 1955. Factor endowment and relative commodity prices. *Economica* 22:336–41.

Stolper, W., and P. Samuelson. 1941. Protection and real wages. *Review of Economic Studies* 9:58–73.

United Nations. 1994. *World investment directory: Latin America and the Caribbean.* New York: United Nations.

Verikios, G., and K. Hanslow. 1999. Modeling the effects of implementing the Uruguay Round: A comparison using the GTAP model under alternative treatments of international capital mobility. Paper presented at the Second Annual Conference on Global Economic Analysis. 20–22 June, Denmark.

Warren, T. 2000. The impact on output of impediments to trade and investment in telecommunications services. In *Impediments to trade in services: Measurement and policy implications*, ed. C. Findlay and T. Warren, 85–100. London: Routledge.

Welsh, A., and A. Strzelecki. 2000. Estimating domestic and foreign returns to capital for the FTAP model. Productivity Commission, Melbourne, Australia. Research Memorandum, May.

Comment   Fukunari Kimura

The research group of the Productivity Commission of Australia has conducted a series of great effort in quantifying the economic effects of liberalizing trade in services and has contributed to constructive discussion in a number of international academic and semi-academic forums. Admittedly, it is not at all easy to measure the magnitude of barriers to services trade as well as formulating a reasonable policy simulation model with rigorous theoretical framework. Nevertheless, it is crucially important to quantify possible effects of trade liberalization in order for policy makers to carry on a constructive discussion resisting various politico-economic pressures. The current paper presents a step forward in taking care of some of the features unique to trade in services vis-à-vis trade in goods.

Modes of Services Transactions

One of the novel features of this paper is the introduction of explicit treatment for modes of services transactions. The General Agreement on Trade in Services (GATS) of the Marrakesh Agreement defines four modes of services transactions: cross-border, consumption abroad, commercial presence, and natural persons. The past literature has tried to construct simulation models with a structure analogous to that for merchandise trade, but those models could only deal with the first mode, cross-border. The other three modes of services transactions require more sophisticated formulations in terms of factor movements across the national border, the place where factor services are inputted, and the nature of corresponding trade barriers.

Fukunari Kimura is professor of economics at Keio University.

The paper particularly puts emphasis on the most important mode of services transactions, that is, commercial presence. Service provision in this mode is initiated from the establishment of a local affiliate or a local branch through international capital movement (typically foreign direct investment [FDI]), and then services are produced in combination with local resources such as labor. The model traces the service supply structure by introducing international capital movement. Furthermore, the model distinguishes two types of barriers to services trade: barriers to establishing commercial presence and barriers to ongoing operation. These two roughly correspond to the concept of market access and national treatment in the table of concession of GATS. The former is modeled as taxes on the movement of capital, and the latter is formalized as taxes on the output of the service-providing firms.

Of course, the statistical measurement of such barriers, as well as the quantification of international capital movement, is not at all easy, and thus simulation results must be regarded as provisionary. However, the pioneering treatment of mode-3 service transactions will surely become a starting point to formalize services trade in future research.

Handling Capital

The authors call their model FTAP as a special version of GTAP with FDI. Foreign direct investment is different from simple international capital movements such as portfolio investment in an important way: it is accompanied by the movements of firm-specific assets such as technology and managerial know-how. Particularly in less developed economies, affiliates of foreign firms behave quite differently from local indigenous firms in terms of technology, managerial know-how, the pattern of purchases and sales, and the degree of exposure to foreign markets. Therefore, to seriously model FDI, we prefer to distinguish capital by the owner's nationality in addition to the location where capital services are used.[1]

Such expansion of dimension in policy simulation models raises a number of issues to be solved. One issue is the availability of statistical data. The pioneering work by Petri (1997) as well as that of Dee, Hanslow, and Phamduc basically relies on FDI flow data in estimating the magnitude of activities of affiliates of multinational enterprises (MNEs). However, we have a number of problems in this approach to data construction. First of all, we are not sure whether FDI data properly include reinvestment from retained earnings by affiliates abroad. The treatment of joint ventures is another problem. Moreover, the available figures are for investment flows, and thus we need uneasy transformation from flow to stock. After all, we have only capital stock estimates, which may not be a good proxy for the magnitude

---

1. See Baldwin and Kimura (1998) on the more detailed discussion on ownership, control, and location when considering FDI.

of activities of affiliates. We actually have some fragmental but direct information on activities of affiliates of MNEs. The Department of Commerce of the U.S. Government and the Ministry of International Trade and Industry (renamed the Ministry of Economy, Trade, and Industry in January 2001) of the Japanese Government, for example, compile ample activity data on U.S. and Japanese affiliates abroad. Some hosting countries such as Singapore and Malaysia include firm-nationality information in manufacturing censuses. Such information must be utilized to improve the quality of activity data in future research.

Another fundamental issue is the conceptual framework with which to introduce firm-specific assets in theoretically consistent models.[2] This paper makes an important contribution to the literature on this matter. In the model, investors first divide their wealth between "bonds" and "real physical capital," and then the former go to foreign portfolio investment with perfect arbitrage while the latter proceed to domestic physical investment and FDI with imperfect substitution. This treatment allows the introduction of firm-nationality-specific physical capital.

The paper includes an interesting discussion on the nesting structure of commodity demand. Petri (1997) sets the ownership of producers as a higher nest and then goes down to the location of producers as a lower-rank nest. In contrast, the present paper works with the opposite order. The former formulation is attractive if we think much of the existence of firm-specific assets. For instance, VCRs produced in a Sony plant located in Malaysia are closer substitutes for Japanese-made VCRs in Japan than they are for VCRs produced in a local indigenous plant located in Malaysia. Dee, Hanslow, and Phamduc, however, claim that services must meet local tastes and requirements and thus the location of production should come earlier than the nationality of producers. We obviously need more discussion on how to formulate the nationality of firms and the location of production.

Welfare Effects

The paper displays the simulation results of removing barriers to trade in services in a step-by-step, intuitive manner by starting from partial equilibrium effects and then explaining general equilibrium effects. The partial equilibrium results in which factor prices as well as domestic factor supplies are fixed look reasonable; with the removal of barriers to trade in services, countries originally with high barriers will gain the most, and those with low barriers will get hurt. Then factor prices are endogenously adjusted, and international capital movements are allowed in the general equilibrium, where the welfare gains are spread out to most of the countries.

---

2. Kimura and Tsutsumi (1998) list a number of conceptual issues to introduce firm-nationality-specific capital in computable general equilibrium (CGE) models.

Some uneasy results, particularly the negative welfare effects on the U.S. economy in the general equilibrium setting, should not be worried about too much. Rather, we must realize that the setting for FDI is crucially important in estimating the liberalization effects. If, for example, the U.S. service providers are more competitive than Japanese ones, the pattern of FDI may drastically change, resulting in different welfare impacts across countries. Firm-specific or firm-nationality-specific assets can also be a source of market power, which the symmetric constant elasticity of substitution (CES) nesting of product differentiation may not properly capture. Again, the key issue is how to formulate MNEs in simulation models.

Concluding Remarks

In summary, this paper makes a big step forward toward quantifying the cost of barriers to trade in services, which is crucially important in setting up a constructive policy discussion. The simulation results, however, have not reached the level of attracting very serious consideration from the nonacademic circle. A major task will be determining how to formulate MNEs in theoretically rigorous models. Although the paper makes a significant contribution to this subject, we have a number of things to settle in the future from both theoretical and empirical points of view. Another important task for us is to make primary statistical data collection of good quality. As for the FDI-related data, the best way to capture the activities of affiliates of MNEs is to collect information in the framework of host countries' establishment or firm censuses. Physical activities are, after all, much easier to capture than flows of financial transactions. As for service transactions, the balance-of-payments statistics cover only a small portion of trade in services. We must develop a statistical framework to capture various aspects of services trade covering four modes and possibly service contents in merchandise trade.

References

Baldwin, Robert E., and Fukunari Kimura. 1998. Measuring U.S. international goods and services transactions. In *Geography and ownership as bases for economic accounting*, ed. R. E. Baldwin, R. E. Lipsey, and J. D. Richardson, 9–36. Chicago: University of Chicago Press.
Kimura, Fukunari, and Masahiko Tsutsumi. 1998. The CGE modeling strategies with the nationalities of firms. Paper prepared for the conference Making APEC Work: Economic Challenges and Policy Alternatives. 13–14 March, Keio University, Tokyo, Japan.
Petri, P. A. 1997. Foreign direct investment in a computable general equilibrium framework. Paper prepared for the conference Making APEC Work: Economic Challenges and Policy Alternatives. 13–14 March, Keio University, Tokyo, Japan.

[16]

J. BRADFORD JENSEN
Institute for International Economics

LORI G. KLETZER
University of California–Santa Cruz and Institute for International Economics

Tradable Services: Understanding the Scope and Impact of Services Offshoring

Globalization, particularly globalized production, is evolving and broadening from manufacturing into services. Services activities now account for a larger share of global trade than in the past. Services trade has almost doubled over the past decade: in the period 1992 to 2002, exports increased from $163 billion to $279 billion, and imports increased from $102 billion to $205 billion. These changes, and their implications for American firms and workers, have attracted widespread attention.

Coincident with the broadening of global economic integration from manufacturing to services, the face of job displacement in the United States is changing. While manufacturing workers have historically accounted for more than half of displaced workers, over the period 2001–03, nonmanufacturing workers accounted for 70 percent of displaced workers.[1] The share of job loss accounted for by workers displaced from information, financial services, and professional and business services nearly tripled, from 15 percent during the 1979–82 recession to 43 percent over the 2001–03 period. The industrial and occupational shift

---

We appreciate the comments and suggestions of our Brookings Trade Forum discussants, Jared Bernstein and Robert Feenstra, as well as those of Andrew Bernard, Catherine Mann, Michael Mussa, Dave Richardson, Peter Schott, and seminar participants at the Institute for International Economics; the University of California, Santa Cruz; and the 2004 Empirical Investigations in International Trade conference. We gratefully acknowledge the support of the Alfred P. Sloan Foundation.

1. The shift in job loss from manufacturing and production workers toward service and white-collar (nonproduction) workers has been in evidence since the recession of the early 1990s. At that time, concerns about downsizing and reengineering were coincident with a rise in the share of white-collar and service sector job loss. See Podgursky (1992); Farber (1993); Gardner (1993); and Kletzer (1995, 1998).

in job loss has been associated with a rise in the probability of job loss for more-educated workers.[2]

Bringing these two trends together, the changing mix of industries exposed to international trade in services may have deep implications for the structure of U.S. industry and labor markets in the future. Currently, there is little clear understanding of the role of services globalization in domestic employment change and job loss. More fundamentally, there is little clear understanding of the size and extent of services offshoring, how large it is likely to become in the near-term future, or what impact it is having on the U.S. economy.

Fueled by the 2004 presidential race and continued slack in the labor market, the services offshoring debate became headline material. The literature on services offshoring is expanding rapidly. A nonexhaustive list of recent contributors includes: Amiti and Wei (2004); Arora and Gambardella (2004); Bardhan and Kroll (2003): Bhagwati, Panagariya, and Srinivasan (2004); Brainard and Litan (2004); Bronfenbrenner and Luce (2004); Dossani and Kenney (2003, 2004); Kirkegaard (2004); Mann (2003); Samuelson (2004); and Schultze (2004). Despite the attention, relatively little is known about how many jobs may be at risk of relocation or how much job loss is associated with the business decisions to offshore and outsource.

There are a few prominent projections, advanced mostly by consulting firms. The dominant and most widely quoted projection of future job losses due to movement of jobs offshore is Forrester Research's estimate of 3.3 million.[3] Others include: Deloitte Research's estimate that by 2008 the world's largest financial service companies will have relocated up to 2 million jobs to low-cost countries offshore; Gartner Research's prediction that by the end of 2004 10 percent of IT jobs at U.S. IT companies and 5 percent of IT jobs at non-IT companies will have moved offshore; and Goldman Sachs's estimate that 300,000 to 400,000 services jobs have moved offshore in the past three years, and that 15,000 to 30,000 jobs a month, in manufacturing and services combined, will be subject to offshoring in the future.[4]

It is clear that changes in technology are enabling more activities to be traded internationally. What is unclear is how large these trends are likely to become,

---

2. It is still the case that less-educated workers have the highest rates of job loss overall. Over the 2001–03 period, the rate of job loss for workers with a high school diploma or less was .141; for workers with at least some college experience, the rate of job loss was .096 (estimates from the 2004 Displaced Worker Survey). See Farber (2005) for a more detailed examination of worker characteristics and the risk of job loss.

3. See McCarthy (2002). The Forrester projection was updated in 2004 to 3.4 million.

4. See, in order, Gentle (2003); Gartner Research (2004); and Tilton (2003).

the sectors and occupations affected to date and going forward, and the impact on workers of the resulting dislocations. Without understanding the nature and scope of the changes, it is difficult to formulate effective public policy to address emerging needs.

This paper develops a new empirical approach to identifying, at a detailed level, service activities that are potentially exposed to international trade. We use the geographic concentration of service activities within the United States to identify which service activities are traded domestically. We classify activities that are traded domestically as *potentially* tradable internationally. Using the identified industries and occupations, we develop estimates of the number of workers who are in tradable activities for all sectors of the economy. We compare the demographic characteristics of workers in tradable and nontradable activities and employment growth in traded and nontraded service activities. We also examine the risk of job loss and other employment outcomes for workers in tradable activities.

To preview the results, we find considerable employment shares in tradable service industries and occupations. Based on our estimates, there are more workers in tradable professional and business service industries than in tradable manufacturing industries. We also examine the characteristics of workers in tradable and nontradable activities and find that workers in tradable sectors have higher skills and significantly higher wages. Within specific sectors like professional services, the earnings differentials are even larger, approaching 20 percent.

When we examine employment growth trends across traded and nontraded activities, tradable activities have lower growth rates, due primarily to employment losses in manufacturing. Within services, tradable and nontradable activities have similar growth rates except at the lowest end of the skill distribution. Low-skill tradable industries and occupations have negative average employment growth, whereas employment growth in nontraded, low-skill services is positive (though low).

We also examine worker displacement rates in tradable and nontradable service activities. We see some evidence that displacement rates are higher from tradable service industries than from nontradable. We also find higher displacement rates from tradable white-collar occupations than from nontradable. Consistent with the characteristics of employed workers, we find that workers displaced from tradable service activities are more educated, with higher earnings, than workers displaced from nontradable activities. Job loss from tradable and nontradable service activities is costly to workers in terms of earnings losses (comparing new job earnings to old job earnings). Taken together, the results are consistent with the view that economic activity within the United

States is moving toward a U.S. comparative advantage in services, similar to manufacturing.

In the next section we describe our empirical approach to identifying tradable activities. The following sections describe the tradable and nontradable categories for both manufacturing and services activities; compare worker characteristics in tradable and nontradable services; explore the employment trends in tradable and nontradable services; and consider the most recent evidence on job displacement from tradable activities.

Empirical Approach

Historically, services have been considered nontradable, with a paucity of empirical work examining trade in services relative to empirical work on manufacturing. To examine the potential impact of trade in services on the U.S. economy, we wanted to identify the size and scope of services trade at as detailed a level as possible. As many observers and researchers have noted, gathering detailed data on the extent of services offshoring is quite difficult. While the Bureau of Economic Analysis (BEA) provides data on international trade in services, the data on international trade in services that BEA publishes do not provide particularly detailed industry-level data. Table 1 shows the level of industry detail available from BEA.

Our interest in examining trade in services in more detail than what is available through the BEA services trade data necessitated an alternative empirical approach to identifying tradable service activities. Our approach to identifying service activities that are potentially tradable is novel: we use the geographic concentration of service activities in the United States to identify industries and occupations that appear to be traded domestically. From this domestic information, we infer that service activities that can be traded within the United States are also potentially tradable internationally.

Framework

The economic intuition we rely on to develop our baseline measure of tradable services is that nontraded services will not exhibit geographic concentration in production. We observe that goods that are traded tend to be geographically concentrated (to capitalize on increasing returns to scale, access to inputs such as natural resources, etc.), while goods that are not traded tend to be more ubiquitously distributed. We apply this same intuition to service production.

J. Bradford Jensen and Lori G. Kletzer   79

Helpman and Krugman (1985) present a model that demonstrates this intuition. They model a world with two goods, two countries, and three industries, where the first industry is assumed to be a nontradable constant-returns sector, the second industry is an industry with differentiated varieties that are assumed to be costlessly traded, and the third industry is a tradable constant-returns sector. Helpman and Krugman derive the input vectors V(1), V(2), and V(3) for the integrated world equilibrium. With homothetic and identical tastes, if country *j* has a share s^j of world income, it must allocate resources s^j V(1) to the nontradable industry; that is, the production of the nontraded good must be allocated between countries in proportion to their shares of world income. Nontraded goods are distributed uniformly according to population and income.

This intuition is revealed more descriptively by Paul Krugman, who notes, "In the late twentieth century the great bulk of our labor force makes services rather than goods. Many of these services are nontradable and simply follow the geographical distribution of the goods-producing population—fast-food outlets, day-care providers, divorce lawyers surely have locational Ginis pretty close to zero. Some services, however, especially in the financial sector, can be traded. Hartford is an insurance city; Chicago the center of futures trading; Los Angeles the entertainment capital; and so on. . . . The most spectacular examples of localization in today's world are, in fact, services rather than manufacturing. . . . Transportation of goods has not gotten much cheaper in the past eighty years. . . . But the ability to transmit *information* has grown spectacularly, with telecommunications, computers, fiber optics, etc."[5] The idea is that when something is traded the production of the activity is concentrated in a particular region to take advantage of some economies in production. As a result, not all regions will support local production of the good, and some regions will devote a disproportionate share of productive activity to a good and then trade it.[6] We use the geographic concentration of service activity within the United States as an indicator that the service is traded within the United States and thus *potentially* tradable internationally.

The "locational Gini" referred to by Krugman is one of several ways to measure geographic concentration.[7] The measures compare a region's share of

5. Krugman (1991, p. 65).

6. The relationship between geographic concentration of production and trade, particularly exports, has a long tradition in both economic geography (where the measure used is the location quotient) and trade analysis (where the measure used is revealed comparative advantage). The measures of economic concentration used in this paper are different from the location quotient and revealed comparative advantage measures, but all the measures have a similar flavor in that they compare the share of production (or exports) in a particular region to an "expected" baseline.

7. Among the different empirical approaches to measuring geographic concentration and agglomeration are Duranton and Overman (2004).

Table 1. Private Services Trade by Type, 2002

Millions of dollars

Trade type	Exports, 2002	Imports, 2002
Travel	66,547	58,044
Overseas	54,772	44,494
Canada	6,268	6,489
Mexico	5,507	7,061
Passenger fares	17,046	19,969
Other transportation	29,166	38,527
Freight	12,330	25,973
Port services	16,836	12,554
Royalties and license fees	44,142	19,258
Affiliated	32,218	15,132
U.S. parents' transactions	29,066	2,958
U.S. affiliates' transactions	3,152	12,174
Unaffiliated	11,924	4,126
Industrial processes	3,900	1,935
Other	8,024	2,192
Other private services	122,594	69,436
Affiliated services	43,500	32,367
U.S. parents' transactions	25,194	17,529
U.S. affiliates' transactions	18,306	14,838
Unaffiliated services	79,094	37,069
Education	12,759	2,466
Financial services	15,859	3,665
Insurance services	2,839	15,348
Telecommunications	4,137	4,180
Business, professional, and technical services	28,799	10,732
Accounting, auditing, and bookkeeping services	360	716
Advertising	633	1,360

(continued)

employment in or output of an activity with the region's share of overall economic activity. We make use of two common measures of geographic concentration; but before turning to those measures we address one more conceptual issue.

Demand-Induced Agglomeration and Intermediate Services

Measures of geographic concentration are a way to implement the intuition described above. Most measures of concentration use the region's share of employment in an industry relative to the region's share of total employment. The measures of concentration do not differentiate the reasons activity is concentrated. It does not matter whether production is concentrated because of the

J. Bradford Jensen and Lori G. Kletzer   81

Table 1. Private Services Trade by Type, 1992–2002 *(Continued)*
Millions of dollars

Trade type	Exports, 2002	Imports, 2002
Agricultural, mining, and on-site processing services	366	273
Agricultural and mining services	346	259
Waste treatment and depollution services	20	14
Architectural, engineering, and other technical services	1,916	312
Computer and data processing services	3,004	1,057
Construction, architectural, engineering, and		
mining services	n.a.	n.a.
Construction	654	226
Data base and other information services	2,426	236
Industrial engineering	749	185
Installation, maintenance, and repair of equipment	4,992	812
Legal services	3,270	768
Management, consulting, and public relations services	1,696	1,188
Medical services	1,901	n.a.
Miscellaneous disbursements	623	1,522
Operational leasing	3,573	190
Research, development, and testing services	1,086	1,040
Sports and performing arts	175	110
Trade-related services	353	95
Training services	501	361
Other business, professional, and technical services	430	283
Other unaffiliated services	14,700	679

Source: Bureau of Economic Analysis.
n.a. = not available.

location of natural resources, increasing returns in production, or spillovers due to the agglomeration of workers; the concentration of production indicates that the good or service is produced in a location different from where it is consumed. So, in general, the reason for the concentration does not matter to us, except in one instance. If a service is nontradable and demand for the service is concentrated (that is, if industries that use the nontraded service are geographically concentrated), the service industry will be geographically concentrated and we would incorrectly infer that the service is tradable.

To incorporate this case into our approach, we extend the intuition from the framework. If a nontradable industry provides intermediate inputs to a downstream industry, we would expect the geographic distribution of the nontraded intermediate industry to follow the distribution of the downstream industry. Instead of being distributed with income, the nontraded good is distributed in proportion to the geographic distribution of demand for that industry.

We construct region-specific measures of demand for each industry using the 1999 input-output use tables produced by the Bureau of Economic Analysis.[8] This measure of industry demand share ($IDS_{i,p}$) represents how much geographic concentration there is in demand for a good or service i in a particular region p. We construct the demand for industry i in Place of Work Metro Area p by:

$$IDS_{i,p} = \Sigma_j \, (Y_{i,j}/Y_i * InEMP_{j,p}/InEMP_j), \qquad (1)$$

where

$Y_{i,j}$ = the output of industry i used by industry j (including government and private households as "industries");
Y_i = total output of industry i;
$InEMP_{j,p}$ = industry j employment in region p;
$InEMP_j$ = total employment in industry j.

We include both direct use and investment in the "use" of industry i output by industry j.

To construct the region-specific measures of demand for each occupation, we use the industry-region-specific demand measures described above and weight those by the share of occupation employment in an industry.

$$ODS_{o,p} = \Sigma_j \, (IDS_{j,p} * OcEMP_{o,j}/OcEMP_o), \qquad (2)$$

where

$IDS_{j,p}$ = industry demand share for industry j in region p;
$OcEMP_{o,j}$ = occupation o employment in industry j; and
$OcEMP_o$ = total employment in occupation o.

These adjustments take account of the concentration of downstream industry concentration and adjust the "denominator" in the geographic concentration measures that follow.

Measuring Geographic Concentration

The first measure of economic concentration, as described in Ellison and Glaeser (1997), is:

$$EC_i = \Sigma_p \, (s_{i,p} - x_p)^2. \qquad (3)$$

8. For more information, see www.bea.doc.gov/bea/dn2/i-o.htm. We aggregate some BEA input-output (IO) industries to a level consistent with the industry classification used by the Census Bureau on the 2000 Decennial PUMS (Public Use Micro Sample).

J. Bradford Jensen and Lori G. Kletzer   83

The measure is an index for comparing a region's share of industry employment $(s_{i,p})$ with the area's share of aggregate activity/employment (x_p). When an area's employment share in an activity is significantly greater than the area's share of aggregate employment, this is interpreted as indicating a concentration, or specialization, in the given activity. The index *EC* provides a national index for each industry, and measures of *EC* indicating geographic concentration are interpreted as indicative of trade in that activity, in the sense that "local" employment exceeds "local" demand in some areas and the difference is traded outside the area. We modify the *EC* measure to look at the difference between the region's share of industry employment and the region's share of industry demand, as noted above:

$$EC_i = \Sigma_p \, (s_{i,p} - IDS_{i,p})^2. \tag{4}$$

The new measure of *EC* is an index for comparing a region's share of an industry's employment (s_i) with the region's share of demand for that industry $(IDS_{i,p})$.

We do not make the Herfindahl adjustment that Ellison and Glaeser (1999) use in their index of agglomeration because we are not interested in agglomeration (the co-location of different firms in the same industry), but are interested in pure geographic concentration (whether the concentration is due to one firm or a number of firms). If economic activity is concentrated because significant scale economies are captured within a firm, we do not want to discount this concentration.

The second measure of geographic concentration we use is the Gini coefficient. The Gini coefficient (G) for the concentration of industry activity is given by:

$$G_i = |\, 1 - \Sigma_p \, (\sigma Y_{i,p-1} + \sigma Y_p) * (\, \sigma X_{i,p-1} - \sigma X_p) \,|, \tag{5}$$

where p's index regions (sorted by the region's share of industry employment), $\sigma Y_{i,p}$ is the cumulative share of industry i employment in region p, $\sigma Y_{i,p-1}$ is the cumulative share of industry i employment in the region $(p-1)$ with the next lowest share of industry employment, σX_p is the cumulative share of total employment in region p, and σX_{p-1} is the cumulative share of total employment in region $p-1$. We modify the Gini measure to:

$$G_i = |\, 1 - \Sigma_p \, (\sigma Y_{i,p-1} + \sigma Y_{i,p}) \cdot (\sigma IDS_{i,p-1} - \sigma IDS_{i,p}) \,|, \tag{6}$$

where $IDS_{i,p}$ is the region's share of demand for industry i.

84 *Brookings Trade Forum: 2005*

Implementation

We implement these measures using employment information from the 2000 Decennial Census of Population Public Use Micro Sample (PUMS) files. We use as our geographic entity the Consolidated Metropolitan Statistical Area or the Metropolitan Statistical Area where an individual reports working.[9] We construct the measures of geographic concentration for each industry. Industries that are geographically concentrated are considered tradable.

We recognize that the use of worker-level data to investigate economic concentration is somewhat unusual. We pursue this strategy because we are interested in both industrial concentration and *occupational* concentration. The ability to identify both industries and occupations that are tradable is an important feature of the empirical strategy because many of the service activities that are reportedly being globally sourced are tasks within the service "production" process (for example, a bank's customer service/call center component may be moved offshore, but not the banking relationship); occupations correspond more closely to these types of activities than industries do.

We construct the adjusted G and EC measures for both industries and occupations. The correlation between the EC measure and the G measure is quite high, .713 for industries and .732 for occupations. For the remainder of this paper, we focus on the G results.

Classifying Industries and Occupations as Tradable or Nontradable

An important task in our empirical approach is to identify the level of geographic concentration that indicates that an industry or occupation is "tradable."[10] We started exploring where to impose the tradable/nontradable threshold with industries because we have a much better sense of which industries are

9. For regions, we use the Place of Work Consolidated Metropolitan Area (POWCMA5) field on the Decennial PUMS. When POWCMA is coded as a nonmetropolitan area or a mixed metro/nonmetro area, we concatenate the Place of Work state code with the POWCMA5 code. For more information on the 5 percent sample PUMS, see www.census.gov/Press-Release/www/2003/PUMS5.html.

10. While choosing the threshold for nontradable and tradable is inherently arbitrary, we ran a number of robustness checks on the results reported in the paper. With the exception of the share of employment in the tradable sector (which decreases as the threshold rises), the results are robust to the choice of threshold.

Figure 1. Geographic Concentration of Industries

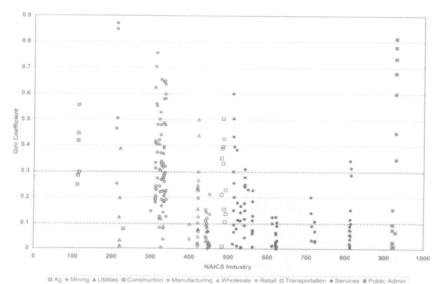

tradable, particularly goods-producing industries. We initially placed industries into three roughly equal groups: Gini class 1 (least geographically concentrated) when the industry Gini was less than .1; Gini class 2 when the industry Gini was between .1 and .3; Gini class 3 (most geographically concentrated) when the Gini coefficient was greater than or equal to .3. Approximately 36 percent of industries are in Gini class 1, about 37 percent are in Gini class 2, and 27 percent are in Gini class 3.

Figure 1 plots the Gini coefficients for all industries by two-digit NAICS code. The pattern exhibited in figure 1 is generally consistent with our priors that tradable industries will be geographically concentrated. For example, industries in the goods-producing sectors of Agriculture, Mining, and Manufacturing are typically in the top two Gini classes. Only five of the ninety-two industries in these sectors are in Gini class 1: Cement and Concrete; Machine Shops; Miscellaneous Manufacturing n.e.c.; Structural Metals and Tanks; and Printing and Related Activities. All of these industries seem to be either nontraded because of a high weight-to-value ratio (such as Cement and Concrete), or they are categories that include a range of potentially dissimilar activities (Miscellaneous Manufacturing n.e.c.) that make them appear to be broadly geographically distributed. Most agriculture, mining, and manufacturing products are considered tradable; so as a first-order approximation, classifying the lowest geographic concentration category (Gini class 1) as nontradable seems appropriate for these sectors.[11]

Using a Gini coefficient of .1 as the threshold for tradable seems to make sense in other sectors as well. Industries in the retail trade sector are primarily classified as nontradable. Industries in the Transportation sector are mostly classified as tradable. In Public Administration, most activities are nontradable; Public Finance and the military are exceptions. In the Service sector, industries are balanced between nontradable and tradable. Table 2 provides a complete list of service industries by 2-digit NAICS sector and the industry's Gini class.[12]

Table 3 shows the share of employment classified in tradable industries by major NAICS group. Again, the employment shares across categories and industries conform to our priors. All employment in the Agriculture and Mining sectors is classified as tradable (in one of the top two Gini classes). In Manufacturing, most employment is in the tradable sector.[13] Utilities are mostly nontradable and Construction is entirely nontraded. For the remainder of the paper, we categorize industries with a Gini coefficient below .1 as nontradable and industries with a Gini coefficient greater than or equal to .1 as tradable.

Size and Scope of Tradable Service Industries

We use the categorization of industries as tradable and nontradable to develop estimates of the employment potentially affected by trade in services. Table 4 shows the share of total employment in tradable and nontradable industries by major NAICS group. In contrast to traditional characterizations of services as predominantly nontradable, our categorization suggests that a significant share of

11. Another check on the industry classification is to examine the correlation of geographic concentration of manufacturing industries with the level of trade intensity in those industries. The mean industry trade share [(imports + exports)/domestic production] for Gini class 1 = .40, Gini class 2 = .57, Gini class 3 = .71. If Manufacturing Machinery n.e.c. is removed from Gini class 1 (by virtue of its not being a consistent industry), the mean trade share for that class falls to .35. The pattern revealed is one of a positive correlation between Gini class and mean trade share, with some notable variation within class.

12. Higher education may appear to stand out in table 2 as a nontradable service industry. U.S. colleges and universities, particularly research institutions, have an acknowledged global comparative advantage and attract many foreign students. The sector also includes community colleges that are, by design, geographically dispersed. The types of specialized scientific occupations associated with research institutions (the most likely to "export" educational services) are geographically concentrated and thus considered tradable.

13. Alternatively, if we modify the cutoff and use .2 as the break between tradable and nontradable, 28 percent of manufacturing employment would be in the nontradable sector.

J. Bradford Jensen and Lori G. Kletzer 87

Table 2. Service Industries, Gini Coefficient Class

2-digit NAICS	Industry description	Gini coefficient class
	Information	
51	Newspaper publishers	1
51	Radio and television broadcasting and cable	1
51	Libraries and archives	1
51	Wired telecommunications carriers	2
51	Data processing services	2
51	Other telecommunication services	2
51	Publishing, except newspapers and software	2
51	Other information services	3
51	Motion pictures and video industries	3
51	Sound recording industries	3
51	Software publishing	3
	Finance and insurance	
52	Savings institutions, including credit unions	1
52	Banking and related activities	1
52	Insurance carriers and related activities	2
52	Nondepository credit and related activities	2
52	Securities, commodities, funds, trusts, and other financial investment	3
	Real estate and rental and leasing	
53	Video tape and disk rental	1
53	Other consumer goods rental	1
53	Commercial, industrial, and other intangible assets rental and leasing	2
53	Real estate	2
53	Automotive equipment rental and leasing	2
	Professional, scientific, and technical services	
54	Veterinary services	1
54	Accounting, tax preparation, bookkeeping and payroll services	1
54	Architectural, engineering, and related services	2
54	Other professional, scientific, and technical services	2
54	Legal services	2
54	Specialized design services	2
54	Computer systems design and related services	2
54	Advertising and related services	2
54	Management, scientific, and technical consulting services	2
54	Scientific research and development services	3
	Management	
55	Management of companies and enterprises	2
	Administrative support	
56	Waste management and remediation services	1
56	Business support services	1
56	Services to buildings and dwellings	1
56	Landscaping services	1
56	Employment services	2

(continued)

Table 2. Service Industries, Gini Coefficient Class *(Continued)*

2-digit NAICS	Industry description	Gini coefficient class
56	Other administrative and other support services	2
56	Investigation and security services	2
56	Travel arrangement and reservation services	2
	Education	
61	Elementary and secondary schools	1
61	Colleges and universities, including junior colleges	1
61	Other schools, instruction, and educational services	1
61	Business, technical, and trade schools and training	2
	Health care and social services	
62	Hospitals	1
62	Nursing care facilities	1
62	Vocational rehabilitation services	1
62	Offices of physicians	1
62	Outpatient care centers	1
62	Offices of dentists	1
62	Offices of optometrists	1
62	Residential care facilities, without nursing	1
62	Child day care services	1
62	Home health care services	1
62	Other health care services	1
62	Office of chiropractors	1
62	Individual and family services	1
62	Community food and housing, and emergency services	2
62	Offices of other health practitioners	2
	Arts, entertainment, and recreation	
71	Bowling centers	1
71	Other amusement, gambling, and recreation industries	1
71	Museums, art galleries, historical sites, and similar institutions	2
71	Independent artists, performing arts, spectator sports, and related industries	2
	Accommodation	
72	Drinking places, alcoholic beverages	1
72	Restaurants and other food services	1
72	Recreational vehicle parks and camps, and rooming and boarding houses	1
72	Traveler accommodation	2

(continued)

total employment is in tradable service industries. For example, more workers are in tradable industries in the services sector than in the manufacturing sector. The sum of the share of total employment in industries that are tradable in professional services (NAICS 51–56) is 13.7 percent and larger than the share of employment in tradable manufacturing industries (12.4 percent). There are sizable service sec-

J. Bradford Jensen and Lori G. Kletzer   89

Table 2. Service Industries, Gini Coefficient Class *(Continued)*

2-digit NAICS	Industry description	Gini coefficient class
	Other services	
81	Beauty salons	1
81	Funeral homes, cemeteries, and crematories	1
81	Personal and household goods repair and maintenance	1
81	Automotive repair and maintenance	1
81	Barber shops	1
81	Religious organizations	1
81	Commercial and industrial machinery and equipment repair and maintenance	1
81	Dry cleaning and laundry services	1
81	Car washes	1
81	Electronic and precision equipment repair and maintenance	1
81	Civic, social, advocacy organizations, and grant-making and giving	1
81	Nail salons and other personal care services	2
81	Other personal services	2
81	Business, professional, political, and similar organizations	2
81	Labor unions	3
81	Footwear and leather goods repair	3
	Public administration	
92	Justice, public order, and safety activities	1
92	Administration of human resource programs	1
92	Other general government and support	1
92	Executive offices and legislative bodies	1
92	Military Reserves or National Guard	1
92	Administration of economic programs and space research	1
92	Administration of environmental quality and housing programs	1
92	Public finance activities	2
92	National security and international affairs	3
92	U.S. Armed Forces, branch not specified	3
92	U.S. Coast Guard	3
92	U.S. Air Force	3
92	U.S. Army	3
92	U.S. Navy	3
92	U.S. Marines	3

tors correctly characterized as having low shares of employment in tradable industries (education, health care, personal services, and public administration). However, because the service sector is much larger than the manufacturing sector, the number of workers potentially exposed to international trade in services is actually larger than the number of exposed workers in manufacturing.

90

Table 3. Share of Sector Employment by Gini Coefficient by NAICS Sector
Percent

NAICS sector	Description	Gini class 1	Gini class 2	Gini class 3
11	Agriculture	0	87.95	12.05
21	Mining	0	24.24	75.76
22	Utilities	80.89	15.31	3.80
23	Construction	100.00	0	0
31	Manufacturing	0	40.39	59.61
32	Manufacturing	21.99	44.88	33.13
33	Manufacturing	14.44	65.36	20.21
3M	Manufacturing	0	100.00	0
42	Wholesale trade	45.82	50.62	3.57
44	Retail trade	81.72	18.28	0
45	Retail trade	88.65	11.35	0
4M	Retail trade	100.00	0	0
48	Transportation and warehousing	42.81	22.03	35.17
49	Transportation and warehousing	0	100.00	0
51	Information	33.25	50.37	16.38
52	Finance and insurance	32.05	50.98	16.97
53	Real estate and rental and leasing	9.06	90.94	0
54	Professional, scientific, technical services	13.95	79.87	6.18
55	Management	0	100.00	0
56	Administrative support	59.53	40.47	0
61	Education	98.89	1.11	0
62	Health care/social services	97.80	2.20	0
71	Arts, entertainment, recreation	67.35	32.65	0
72	Accommodation	81.92	18.08	0
81	Other services	79.77	9.86	10.37
92	Public administration	71.68	4.63	23.69
	All Industries	60.82	29.75	9.43

Occupation Results

We are also interested in categorizing occupations as tradable and nontradable. We are interested in identifying tradable occupations because, at least based on anecdotal reports in the press, some intermediate inputs into service production might be tradable even though the service industry is not (think computer programming for the banking industry). We use a similar methodology to classify occupations into tradable and nontradable categories. We construct a demand-weighted Gini coefficient for each occupation as described above and use the same Gini = .1 threshold for the nontradable/tradable categorization. Table 5 shows the share of employment by Major Standard Occu-

J. Bradford Jensen and Lori G. Kletzer   91

Table 4. Share of Total Employment in Tradable and Nontradable Industries by NAICS Sector

Percent

NAICS sector	Description	Nontradable	Tradable
11	Agriculture	0	1.36
21	Mining	0	0.39
22	Utilities	0.76	0.18
23	Construction	6.86	0
31	Manufacturing	0	2.17
32	Manufacturing	0.81	2.86
33	Manufacturing	1.16	6.86
3M	Manufacturing	0	0.53
42	Wholesale trade	1.66	1.96
44	Retail trade	5.90	1.32
45	Retail trade	2.91	0.37
4M	Retail trade	0.62	0
48	Transportation and warehousing	1.32	1.76
49	Transportation and warehousing	0	1.27
51	Information	1.04	2.08
52	Finance and insurance	1.64	3.47
53	Real estate and rental and leasing	0.16	1.63
54	Professional, scientific, technical services	0.82	5.08
55	Management	0	0.06
56	Administrative support	1.99	1.35
61	Education	8.75	0.10
62	Health care/social services	10.90	0.25
71	Arts, entertainment, recreation	1.12	0.54
72	Accommodation	4.52	1.00
81	Other services	3.76	0.95
92	Public administration	4.14	1.63
	All industries	60.82	39.18

pational Classification group by Gini class. The groupings are largely consistent with our priors. The occupational groups with large shares of employment classified as tradable include: Business and Financial Operations (68 percent); Computer and Mathematical Occupations (100 percent); Architecture and Engineering (63 percent), Legal (96 percent), and Life, Physical and Social Sciences (83 percent).[14] The notable nontradable occupational groups include

14. Van Welsum and Reif (this volume) offer a list of U.S. occupations (at the 3-digit level) identified as "potentially affected by offshoring" in table A-2. As explained in the chapter, their method relies on occupations having "offshorability attributes" that rely on the use of information and communication technologies, highly codifiable knowledge, and no face-to-face contact. There is overlap

Table 5. Share of Occupation Employment by Gini Coefficient by Major Occupation Category

Percent

SOC 2-digit code	Description	Gini class 1	Gini class 2	Gini class 3
11	Management	34.48	61.15	4.37
13	Business/financial operations	31.73	65.96	2.32
15	Computer/mathematical	0	73.07	26.93
17	Architecture/engineering	36.04	58.31	5.65
19	Life, physical, social sciences	16.32	58.61	25.08
21	Community/social services	100.00	0	0
23	Legal	3.78	96.22	0
25	Education and library	99.54	0.46	0
27	Arts, design, entertainment	17.13	75.02	7.85
29	Health care practitioners/technicians	86.56	13.10	0.34
31	Health care support	96.73	3.27	0
33	Protective service	59.83	40.17	0
35	Food preparation/serving	95.68	4.32	0
37	Building maintenance	98.54	1.46	0
39	Personal care service	82.64	7.22	10.13
41	Sales and related	75.41	21.82	2.77
43	Office/administrative support	93.14	6.66	0.20
45	Farm, fish, forestry	0	81.01	18.99
47	Construction/extraction	61.37	36.18	2.45
49	Installation, maintenance, repair	90.00	8.89	1.11
51	Production	80.30	17.15	2.55
53	Transportation/material moving	89.20	5.86	4.95
55	Military specific	0	0	100.00
	All occupations	71.66	24.86	3.47

Education and Library (99 percent nontradable); Health Care Practitioners (86 percent); Health Care Support (97 percent), Food Preparation (96 percent). On the blue-collar side, 90 percent of employment in Installation, Maintenance, and Repair is classified as nontradable, as is 80 percent of Production and 89 percent of Transportation and Material Moving.[15]

---

between the two lists of occupations, although our method identifies a larger set of tradable occupations. Van Welsum and Vickery (2005) offer a list of U.S. industries potentially affected by off-shoring, in table 6. Our detailed industry list shares similarities with theirs, but our list excludes a number of retail industries (dairy stores, liquor stores, and others) included in their list.

15. The geographic concentration results are at first counterintuitive for production occupations given the manufacturing industry results. Production occupations are typically not industry-specific but instead are functional activities and are thus distributed more broadly.

J. Bradford Jensen and Lori G. Kletzer   93

Table 6. Share of Employment in Tradable and Nontradable Occupations and Industries

Percent

Occupation category (SOC 2-digit code)	Nontradable occupations	Tradable occupations
Management occupations (11)		
Non-tradable industries	23.97	26.58
Tradable industries	10.51	38.94
Business and financial operations occupations (13)		
Nontradable industries	14.11	27.72
Tradable industries	17.61	40.56
Computer and mathematical occupations (15)		
Nontradable industries	0	24.22
Tradable industries	0	75.78
Architecture and engineering occupations (17)		
Nontradable industries	8.46	13.30
Tradable industries	27.59	50.66
Life, physical, and social science occupations (19)		
Nontradable industries	7.28	36.49
Tradable industries	9.03	47.20
Legal occupations (23)		
Nontradable industries	3.54	18.89
Tradable industries	0.24	77.33
All occupations		
Total nontradable industries	50.03	10.79
Total tradable industries	21.64	17.54

The last two rows of table 6 show for all occupations how many workers are in occupations classified as tradable in industries classified as nontradable. In the aggregate, the share of workers in tradable occupations and nontradable industries is not large, about 10 percent. However, for business and professional occupations, the share of workers in tradable occupations in nontradable industries is much larger. The typical professional occupation has about 25 percent of employment in tradable occupations in nontradable industries. To the extent that firms can vertically "disintegrate" the provision of these intermediate service inputs, workers in these tradable occupations are potentially vulnerable to trade even though their industry is not tradable. This suggests that for service activities the share of workers potentially vulnerable to trade is probably understated. Outside of education and health care occupations, the typical white-collar occupation involves a potentially tradable activity.

Table 7. Mean Earnings and Demographic Characteristics for Selected and All Industries

Percent, unless otherwise noted

Industry (NAICS code)	Nontradable	Tradable
Manufacturing (3x)		
Employment income (dollars)	36,974	39,901
Male	75.1	67.8
African American	6.1	9.7
Hispanic	9.7	11.7
With advanced degree	2.6	6.0
With bachelor's degree	13.8	20.4
With high school diploma	85.3	82.9
Age	40.0	40.2
Information (51)		
Employment income (dollars)	35,472	49,510
Male	50.9	55.9
African American	10.4	11.5
Hispanic	7.8	7.3
With advanced degree	9.4	10.6
With bachelor's degree	37.4	41.3
With high school diploma	94.2	96.2
Age	38.7	37.6
Finance and insurance (52)		
Employment income (dollars)	38,170	54,460
Male	29.0	42.7
African American	11.5	9.2
Hispanic	7.8	6.4
With advanced degree	7.1	10.2
With bachelor's degree	30.5	43.8
With high school diploma	97.1	97.4
Age	38.1	39.1
		(continued)

Worker Characteristics

Beyond mere employment counts, we also examine demographic characteristics such as education, age, gender, and earnings to identify whether there are differences between workers in tradable service activities and those in nontradable industries and occupations. These characteristics are available from the 2000 Decennial Census of Population Public Use Micro Sample (PUMS) 5 percent sample.[16]

Table 7 shows the demographic characteristics of workers in tradable industries and nontradable industries in aggregate. Workers in tradable industries have

16. For more information on the 5 percent sample PUMS see www.census.gov/Press-Release/www/2003/PUMS5.html.

J. Bradford Jensen and Lori G. Kletzer

95

Table 7. Mean Earnings and Demographic Characteristics for Selected and All Industries *(Continued)*

Percent, unless otherwise noted

Industry (NAICS code)	Nontradable	Tradable
Real estate and rental and leasing (53)		
Employment income (dollars)	23,056	42,915
Male	58.1	51.1
African American	9.1	8.6
Hispanic	10.8	9.7
With advanced degree	1.9	6.7
With bachelor's degree	13.3	29.7
With high school diploma	84.7	90.6
Age	31.1	42.4
Professional, scientific, technical services (54)		
Employment income (dollars)	42,246	57,959
Male	35.3	57.1
African American	5.1	5.5
Hispanic	5.0	5.6
With advanced degree	16.6	25.7
With bachelor's degree	52.5	59.5
With high school diploma	97.1	97.8
Age	39.5	39.3
Management (55)		
Employment income (dollars)	...	61,285
Male	...	45.5
African American	...	5.4
Hispanic	...	4.9
With advanced degree	...	14.3
With bachelor's degree	...	49.7
With high school diploma	...	97.8
Age	...	40.5
Administrative support (56)		
Employment income (dollars)	24,039	28,742
Male	64.1	48.5
African American	11.9	17.6
Hispanic	22.2	12.2
With advanced degree	2.0	5.0
With bachelor's degree	10.7	23.4
With high school diploma	72.3	88.0
	37.2	36.1
All industries		
Employment income	30,966	41,836
Male	49.6	60.1
African American	10.2	9.9
Hispanic	10.4	10.3
With advanced degree	10.2	9.2
With bachelor's degree	26.6	30.2
With high school diploma	87.0	88.7
Age	38.8	39.4

higher incomes, are more likely to be male, and are more likely to have a college
degree (though not an advanced degree). The table also breaks out these same
characteristics for selected service industries classified as tradable and nontradable. We present the results for the manufacturing sector as a benchmark for
demographic characteristics typically associated with trade-affected workers.
Workers in tradable service industries are higher paid and more skilled than
workers in tradable manufacturing. Within services, the most striking feature of
the service industry results is the difference in annual earnings. Across all major
service sector groups, the differential in earnings between tradable and nontradable industries is large, with tradable services having appreciably higher wages.
Service workers in tradable industries also tend to have attained a higher level of
education and are more likely to be male and white.

Table 8 shows the results for all occupations divided into tradable and nontradable groups. Individuals in occupations identified as tradable tend to have
higher earnings, are more likely to be male and have more years of schooling.
The table also shows the same characteristics for selected occupations. Again, as
in the industry results, workers in tradable occupations earn more and are more
highly educated than workers in nontradable service occupations.

In tables 9–12, we estimate a number of regressions to examine whether the
earnings differentials in tradable industries and occupations are the result of higher
educational attainment. Table 9 shows regression results for all industries and
NAICS 51–56 industries. Across all industries, controlling for observable demographic characteristics and industry (2-digit NAICS) and regional (POWCMA)
fixed effects, workers in tradable industries have 6 percent higher wages. For
workers in professional and business service industries, the differential associated
with being in a tradable industry is even larger. Again controlling for observable
demographic characteristics, in the professional service sector, workers in tradable
industries have almost 15 percent higher wages than workers in nontradable industries in the same sector.

Table 10 shows a similar specification for occupations. The first column
reports the results for all occupations, and the second column reports the results
for "high-end" service occupations.[17] Across all occupations, workers in tradable
occupations receive 9 percent higher wages than workers in nontradable occupations. For high-end service occupations, workers in the tradable sector receive
almost 13 percent higher wages, even after controlling for demographic characteristics and occupation group (2-digit SOC) and region.

17. High-end service occupations include SOC major groups 11, 13, 15, 17, 19, 23, and 29.
See table 8 for the names of the SOC major groups.

J. Bradford Jensen and Lori G. Kletzer   97

Table 8. Mean Earnings and Demographic Characteristics for Occupations
Percent, unless otherwise noted

Industry (NAICS code)	Nontradable	Tradable
Management (11)		
Employment income (dollars)	51,399	69,029
Male	56.2	67.3
African American	8.3	4.7
Hispanic	6.8	5.0
With advanced degree	19.9	15.7
With bachelor's degree	46.5	49.6
With high school diploma	95.2	95.8
Age	41.8	42.6
Business and financial operations (13)		
Employment income (dollars)	42,813	51,998
Male	41.3	48.0
African American	10.3	8.3
Hispanic	6.9	5.4
With advanced degree	10.5	16.2
With bachelor's degree	44.0	61.6
With high school diploma	97.6	98.6
Age	40.4	40.2
Computer and mathematical occupations (15)		
Employment income (dollars)	...	54,297
Male	...	70.3
African American	...	6.8
Hispanic	...	4.5
With advanced degree	...	17.8
With bachelor's degree	...	59.9
With high school diploma	...	99.1
Age	...	37.3
Architecture and engineering occupations (17)		
Employment income (dollars)	40,505	62,115
Male	82.5	89.0
African American	5.7	3.9
Hispanic	6.4	4.1
With advanced degree	5.3	25.5
With bachelor's degree	26.2	76.2
With high school diploma	96.2	99.9
Age	39.4	40.6
Life, Physical, and Social Science Occupations (19)		
Employment income (dollars)	29,339	50,000
Male	57.4	59.2
Percent African American	7.0	4.6
Percent Hispanic	7.2	4.0
With advanced degree	11.6	54.4
With bachelor's degree	40.0	85.3
With high school diploma	96.4	99.2
Age	36.0	40.3

(continued)

Table 8. Mean Earnings and Demographic Characteristics for Occupations

Percent, unless otherwise noted

Industry (NAICS code)	Nontradable	Tradable
Legal Occupations (23)		
Employment income (dollars)	71,304	80,265
Male	60.6	51.4
Percent African American	9.1	5.6
Percent Hispanic	4.5	5.1
With advanced degree	58.2	64.1
With bachelor's degree	78.8	76.9
With high school diploma	99.2	99.3
Age	47.7	40.9
Healthcare Practitioners and Technical Occupations (29)		
Employment income (dollars)	39,922	139,375
Male	19.5	70.6
Percent African American	9.8	4.6
Percent Hispanic	4.5	4.8
With advanced degree	17.8	93.4
With bachelor's degree	47.3	97.8
With high school diploma	98.8	99.7
Age	40.5	42.8
Healthcare Support Occupations (31)		
Employment income (dollars)	18,423	18,751
Male	11.9	17.6
African American	24.0	3.7
Hispanic	10.6	5.6
With advanced degree	2.2	9.9
With bachelor's degree	7.9	30.9
With high school diploma	83.8	97.3
Age	37.8	39.0
All Occupations		
Employment income (dollars)	28,789	51,503
Male	48.5	66.7
African American	11.1	7.5
Hispanic	10.9	8.8
With advanced degree	7.4	16.1
With bachelor's degree	21.8	43.9
With high school diploma	86.3	91.0
Age	38.8	39.9

Table 11 examines whether the effects of being in a tradable industry and occupation are independent. Workers in tradable industries *and* tradable occupations are the omitted category. For all industries and occupations, workers in nontradable industries and nontradable occupations have 10 percent lower wages than workers in both tradable industries and occupations. Interestingly, the effect seems to be additive. Workers in either *only* a tradable industry or *only*

J. Bradford Jensen and Lori G. Kletzer   99

Table 9. OLS Regression Results, Tradable Industry Wage Differentials[a]

	All industries	NAICS 50s
Dependent variable: log (employment income)		
Tradable industry	0.060	0.147
	(0.0008)	(0.0016)
Male	0.214	0.225
	(0.0006)	(0.0014)
African American	−0.096	−0.145
	(0.0010)	(0.0024)
Hispanic	−0.215	−0.218
	(0.0010)	(0.0026)
Hours	0.026	0.029
	(0.0000)	(0.0001)
Weeks	0.040	0.039
	(0.0000)	(0.0001)
Advanced degree	0.262	0.224
	(0.0011)	(0.0023)
Bachelor's degree	0.380	0.325
	(0.0008)	(0.0017)
Industry controls (2-digit NAICS)	Yes	Yes
POWCMA[b] controls	Yes	Yes
Summary statistics		
R^2	0.538	0.519
N	5,836,360	1,074,271
Weighted N	122,155,903	23,609,616

a. Standard error in parentheses.
b. Place of Work Consolidated Metropolitan Area.

a tradable occupation receive wages about 5 percent lower than workers in *both* a tradable industry and a tradable occupation. In both professional service industries and "high-end" service occupations, the effect of being in a tradable industry and a tradable occupation is quite large. Workers in tradable industries and occupations in NAICS 50 sector receive wages 17 percent higher than workers in a nontradable industry and nontradable occupation *within the same sector*. For high-end service occupations, the differential is almost as large: workers in tradable industries and occupations make almost 16 percent more than workers in nontradable industries and occupations.

These results demonstrate that tradable industries and occupations pay higher wages, even after controlling for observable characteristics. These effects appear to be independent: being in both a tradable industry and a tradable occupation is associated with a larger (almost double) income differential than being in either a tradable industry or occupation alone.

The comparison of worker characteristics in tradable service activities suggests that tradable services are consistent with U.S. comparative advantage; they

Table 10. OLS Regression Results, Tradable Occupation Wage Differentials[a]

	All occupations	*High-end service occupations*[b]
Dependent variable: log (employment income)		
Tradable occupation	0.091	0.127
	(0.0008)	(0.0014)
Male	0.215	0.245
	(0.0006)	(0.0013)
African American	−0.061	−0.112
	(0.0010)	(0.0023)
Hispanic	−0.187	−0.168
	(0.0010)	(0.0027)
Hours	0.026	0.020
	(0.0000)	(0.0001)
Weeks	0.039	0.038
	(0.0000)	(0.0001)
Advanced degree	0.216	0.227
	(0.0011)	(0.0016)
Bachelor's degree	0.303	0.297
	(0.0008)	(0.0013)
Occupation controls (2-digit SOC)	Yes	Yes
POWCMA[c] controls	Yes	Yes
Summary statistics		
R^2	0.545	0.396
N	5,836,630	1,446,158
Weighted N	122,155,903	30,803,183

a. Standard error in parentheses.
b. High-end service occupations are occupations in SOC major groups 11, 13, 15, 17, 19, 23, and 29.
c. Place of Work Consolidated Metropolitan Area.

are high-skill and high-wage activities (relative to both manufacturing and non-tradable service activities).

Changes in Aggregate Employment Growth

Much of the recent attention to services offshoring has emphasized job losses in specific occupational categories. We examine recent employment growth trends using both aggregate industry data from the Census Bureau's County Business Patterns program and aggregate occupation data from the Bureau of Labor Statistics' Occupational Employment Statistics program.[18] We present the

18. The County Business Patterns program is an establishment-based data collection program that uses primarily administrative data and thus has nearly universal coverage of in-scope estab-

J. Bradford Jensen and Lori G. Kletzer 101

Table 11. OLS Regression Results, Tradable Industry and Occupation Wage Differentials[a]

	All industries and occupations	NAICS 50s	High-end service occupations[b]
Dependent variable: Log (employment income)			
Nontradable industry and nontradable occupation	−0.098 (0.0011)	−0.174 (0.0026)	−0.159 (0.0022)
Nontradable industry and tradable occupation	−0.055 (0.0012)	−0.072 (0.0026)	−0.050 (0.0019)
Tradable industry and nontradable occupation	−0.055 (0.0010)	−0.045 (0.0022)	−0.087 (0.0021)
Tradable industry and tradable occupation	—Omitted category—		
Male	0.205 (0.0007)	0.205 (0.0015)	0.244 (0.0013)
African American	−0.064 (0.0010)	−0.111 (0.0024)	−0.111 (0.0022)
Hispanic	−0.173 (0.0010)	−0.169 (0.0026)	−0.158 (0.0026)
Hours	0.025 (0.0000)	0.027 (0.0001)	0.020 (0.0001)
Weeks	0.039 (0.0000)	0.038 (0.0001)	0.036 (0.0001)
Advanced degree	0.223 (0.0011)	0.197 (0.0024)	0.232 (0.0016)
Bachelor's degree	0.279 (0.0008)	0.245 (0.0017)	0.276 (0.0013)
Industry controls (2-digit NAICS)	Yes	Yes	Yes
Occupation controls (2-digit SOC)	Yes	Yes	Yes
POWCMA[c] controls	Yes	Yes	Yes
Summary statistics			
R^2	0.545	0.540	0.419
N	5,836,630	1,074,271	1,446,158
Weighted N	122,155,903	23,609,616	30,803,183

a. Standard error in parentheses.
b. High-end service occupations are occupations in SOC major groups 11, 13, 15, 17, 19, 23, and 29.
c. Place of Work Consolidated Metropolitan Area.

data broken out as tradable/nontradable and by sector. The results in the previous section indicate that tradable activities in general and tradable services in particular require higher skills than other activities. High-skill activities are consistent with U.S. comparative advantage, and we would expect that as trade

lishments. For more information on County Business Patterns see www.census.gov/epcd/cbp/view/cbpview.html. The Occupational Employment Statistics program is also an establishment-based program, but it is collected through a survey instrument. For more information on the Occupational Employment Statistics see www.bls.gov/oes/home.htm.

Figure 2. Industry Employment Growth, 1998–2002

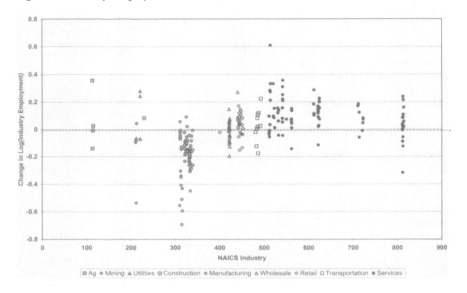

increases, economic activity would shift to activities consistent with U.S. comparative advantage. Thus, we would expect higher-skill industries and occupations to have higher rates of employment growth. We also break out the employment growth rates by industry and occupation skill quartile.[19]

Figure 2 shows the change in industry employment (log) for the period 1998–2002 by NAICS code.[20] Overall, employment in manufacturing industries shrank, and employment in service industries grew. Table 12 presents mean industry employment growth by tradable and nontradable sectors. In the aggregate, the mean tradable industry experienced an employment loss of almost 6 percent, while the mean nontradable industry experienced an employment gain of 5.6 percent. The lower panels of table 12 break out industries by sector, tradable category, and skill quartile. The lower panels of table 12 show that the

19. Industry and occupation skill quartiles are created by placing industries and occupations into skill quartiles based on the share of employees within the industry with a bachelor's degree.

20. We are constrained to use 1998 as our starting point because it is the first year that County Business Patterns was produced on a NAICS basis; 2002 is the most recent year available. Public Administration is not in scope for the County Business Patterns program, so employment change figures are not available for this sector.

J. Bradford Jensen and Lori G. Kletzer   103

Table 12. Industry-Level Employment Change, by Industry Characteristics, 1998–2002

Industry classification	Tradable v. nontradable	Skill quartile	Number of industries	Mean	Standard deviation
Nontradable			88	0.056	0.114
Tradable			149	−0.059	0.198
Ag, Min, Mfg[a]	Nontradable		5	−0.116	0.099
	Tradable		83	−0.173	0.161
Services	Nontradable		91	0.067	0.107
	Tradable		85	0.076	0.145
Ag, Min, Mfg	Nontradable	Skill Q1	3	−0.067	0.102
		Skill Q2	2	−0.190	0.015
	Tradable	Skill Q1	32	−0.191	0.169
		Skill Q2	24	−0.203	0.148
		Skill Q3	16	−0.114	0.103
		Skill Q4	11	−0.147	0.216
Services	Nontradable	Skill Q1	24	0.016	0.080
		Skill Q2	23	0.084	0.098
		Skill Q3	20	0.015	0.106
		Skill Q4	24	0.156	0.088
	Tradable	Skill Q1	7	−0.006	0.233
		Skill Q2	16	0.112	0.104
		Skill Q3	31	−0.007	0.095
		Skill Q4	31	0.139	0.148

a. Agriculture, Mining, Manufacturing.

employment losses are, on average, concentrated in the goods-producing sector (and in the lower portion of the skills distribution).[21] In the service sector, the average nontradable industry experienced 6.7 percent growth, and the average tradable service industry experienced 7.6 percent growth. In general, industries in the lower-skill quartiles have a lower rate of employment growth. Tradable industries do not seem to have dramatically different employment outcomes than nontradable industries, though at the low end of the skill distribution tradable industries had, on average, employment losses.[22]

21. These results are consistent with Bernard, Jensen, and Schott (forthcoming 2006). Bernard, Jensen, and Schott use detailed, plant-level data to examine the impact of imports from low-wage countries on U.S. manufacturing. The results show that activity in U.S. manufacturing is shifting to industries consistent with U.S. comparative advantage.

22. Using a t test to compare the lowest-skill quartile with the highest-skill quartile in the tradable services industry group, we cannot reject the null hypothesis that the means are the same at the 10 percent level.

Table 13. Occupation-Level Employment Change, by Occupation Characteristics, 1999–2003

Occupation classification	Tradable v. nontradable	Skill quartile	Number of industries	Mean	Standard deviation
Nontradable			197	0.022	0.160
Tradable			228	−0.004	0.247
Ag, Prod, Ext, Con[a]	Nontradable		38	−0.044	0.143
	Tradable		77	−0.141	0.228
Services	Nontradable		180	0.036	0.161
	Tradable		180	0.059	0.230
Ag, Prod, Ext, Con	Nontradable	Skill Q1	23	−0.070	0.145
		Skill Q2	12	−0.026	0.140
		Skill Q3	3	0.056	0.125
	Tradable	Skill Q1	56	−0.148	0.235
		Skill Q2	18	−0.150	0.196
		Skill Q3	3	0.014	0.272
Services	Nontradable	Skill Q1	30	0.005	0.114
		Skill Q2	57	0.037	0.173
		Skill Q3	54	0.021	0.165
		Skill Q4	39	0.078	0.164
	Tradable	Skill Q1	10	−0.065	0.111
		Skill Q2	32	0.086	0.210
		Skill Q3	59	0.032	0.181
		Skill Q4	79	0.083	0.269

a. Agricultural, Production, Extractive, Construction
b. Skill Q is Skill Quartile

Table 13 shows similar employment growth rates for 1999–2003 for occupation categories.[23] Similar to industries, tradable occupations in aggregate have lower employment growth rates than nontradable industries on average. Also similar to industries, this is explained primarily by differences between production-related occupations and service activities. Tradable service occupations have, on average, higher employment growth rates than nontradable service occupations. It is interesting to note that, as in tradable industries, at the low end of the skill distribution tradable service occupations have negative employment growth. In comparison, the highest skill category has positive employment growth.[24]

23. We use 1999 as our starting year because it is the first year the Occupational Employment Survey was published on a Standard Occupational Classification basis. We use 2003 as the end point to have a four-year period consistent with the industry data.
24. Using a *t* test to compare the lowest-skill quartile with the highest-skill quartile in the tradable services occupation group, we can reject the null hypothesis that the means are the same.

J. Bradford Jensen and Lori G. Kletzer   105

The employment growth results are consistent with the comparative advantage framework. Employment is shifting toward activities that are consistent with U.S. comparative advantage. Industries and occupations that require higher skills are growing relative to low skill industries and occupations. In both tradable service industries and occupations, those in the lowest skill classes experience negative employment growth on average.

Evidence on the Risk of Job Loss and Characteristics of Displaced Workers

The Displaced Worker Surveys (DWS) provide basic information on the scope and cost of involuntary job loss. The DWSs offer large sample sizes, are nationally representative, and allow several key elements to be investigated, including the incidence of job loss; the characteristics of workers affected; likelihood of reemployment; reemployment industry and occupation; and earnings changes.[25] These surveys have been used extensively to study manufacturing job loss (see Kletzer 2001).

The 2000 census provides the most up-to-date industry and occupational classifications of the services and white-collar jobs of primary interest. The need for updated detail on industry and occupation (currently) limits our use of the Displaced Worker Surveys to the most recent administration, in January 2004. Although we lose the ability to observe services and white-collar job loss over time, we gain the industry and occupational detail necessary for studying services offshoring.

Job displacement from services

Job loss rates by industry are reported in table 14, focusing on the 2001–03 period covered by the January 2004 Displaced Worker Survey. Remembering that this time period covered the dot.com bust and the most recent recession, the Information sector (NAICS 51) had a notably high rate of job loss (.232). Overall, the risk of job loss was lower in services than in manufacturing.

As a reference point, table 14 includes job loss rates by industry for the period 1999–2001, from the 2002 Displaced Worker Survey. The industry classifications are different, reflecting the use of 1990 census codes for the 2002 survey. What is clear is that job loss rates increased from 1999–2001 to 2001–03, most

---

25. See the appendix for more information on the Displaced Worker Surveys.

Table 14. Job Loss Rates, by Industry

Mean

Industry	From the 2004 Displaced Worker Survey (2001–03)			Industry	From the 2002 and 2004 Displaced Worker Surveys	
	Total 2001–03	Tradable	Nontradable		1999–2001	2001–03
Agriculture	0.049	...	...	Agriculture	0.042	0.065
Mining	0.127	...	...	Mining	0.173	0.127
Construction	0.131	...	...	Construction	0.107	0.131
Manufacturing	0.209	...	...	Manufacturing, durables	0.177	0.236
Wholesale and retail trade	0.113	...	...	Manufacturing, nondurables	0.133	0.157
Transport and utilities	0.089	0.077	0.091	Transportation	0.096	0.103
Information	0.232	0.317	0.075	Communications	0.159	0.305
Financial	0.081	0.08	0.081	Utilities and sanitary service	0.054	0.052
Professional and business services	0.144	0.158	0.113	Wholesale trade	0.111	0.123
Education and health services	0.040	0.071	0.039	Retail trade	0.099	0.107
Leisure and hospitality	0.105	0.083	0.113	Finance, insurance, and real estate	0.079	0.080
Other services	0.051	0.03	0.057	Private household	0.044	0.016
Public administration	0.020	...	...	Business and repair services	0.181	0.172
				Personal services	0.080	0.057
				Entertainment and recreation	0.071	0.098
				Hospitals	0.026	0.030
				Other medical	0.052	0.055
				Educational services	0.020	0.030
				Social services	0.033	0.060
				Other professional services	0.071	0.078
				Forestry and fisheries	0.008	0.070
				Public administration	0.017	0.020
Total	0.103	0.153	0.076	Total	0.090	0.106
Manufacturing, tradable	0.213					
Manufacturing, nontradable	0.192					
Nonmanufacturing, tradable	0.128					
Nonmanufacturing, nontradable	0.073					
Dropping agriculture, mining, and construction						
Manufacturing, tradable	0.213					
Manufacturing, nontradable	0.192					
Nonmanufacturing, tradable	0.106					
Nonmanufacturing, nontradable	0.054					
Total		0.126	0.058			

Source: Authors' calculations from the 2002 and 2004 Displaced Worker Surveys, using sampling weights.

notably in Communications (the former name of the sector for some of Information) and Manufacturing.

When we apply our tradable/nontradable distinction to the overall economy, the rate of job loss is notably higher in tradable industries (.153) than in nontradable industries (.076). Within the broad sectors of manufacturing and nonmanufacturing, tradable industries also had higher rates of job loss. The tradable/nontradable distinction is small in manufacturing, with tradable industries having a job loss rate of .213, and nontradable (of which there are few) a rate of .192. Outside of manufacturing, the tradable distinction is large. Tradable nonmanufacturing industries have a rate of job loss of .128, and nontradable industries, .073. This difference is most notable in the Information sector, where the rate of job loss from tradable (3-digit) industries was .317 and the nontradable job loss rate was .075.

Job loss rates by occupation are reported in table 15. The blue-collar occupations faced a higher rate of job loss (about .12) than the white-collar occupations (about .09). Workers in all occupational categories faced a higher rate of job loss in 2001–03 than in 1999–2001. Production workers faced the highest rate of job loss, .206 (the cross-occupation average was .106). Some of the white-collar occupational categories forecast to be at risk of services offshoring had high job loss rates (but lower than Production workers), including Business Operations Specialists (.143), Computer and Math (.177), and Architecture and Engineering (.128).

In the overall economy, tradable occupations had a higher rate of job loss than nontradable occupations, with the greatest difference in white-collar occupations. White-collar workers in tradable occupations faced a job loss rate of .094, and workers in nontradable occupations faced a rate of .065. For blue-collar workers, the tradable job loss rate was .128 and the nontradable rate was .122. There is no clear pattern of exposure to the risk of job loss by tradability within detailed occupations.

Parallel to our discussion of worker characteristics from the 2000 PUMS, table 16 reports demographic and educational characteristics for workers displaced from tradable and nontradable nonmanufacturing industries, with (tradable) manufacturing industries offered as a reference group. As noted by Kletzer (2001), workers displaced from nonmanufacturing industries are slightly younger, less tenured, less likely to be male, and considerably more educated than workers displaced from manufacturing. In tradable nonmanufacturing, 75 percent of displaced workers had at least some college experience. In manufacturing, the share of displaced workers with some college was 46 percent.

Table 15. Job Loss Rates, by Occupation[a]
Mean

	From the 2004 Displaced Worker Survey (2001–03)			From the 2002 and 2004 Displaced Worker Surveys		
Industry	Total 2001–03	Tradable	Nontradable	Industry	1999–2001	2001–03
Management business, financial (white collar)	0.089	0.077	0.091	Executive, administrative, managerial	0.086	0.094
Business operations specialists	0.143	0.121	0.171	Professional specialty	0.059	0.066
Financial specialists	0.054	0.057	0.044	Technician and related	0.088	0.110
Professional and related (white collar)	0.070	0.109	0.033	Sales	0.094	0.109
Computer and math	0.177	0.177	n.a.	Administrative support	0.097	0.106
Architecture and engineering	0.128	0.113	0.158	Private household	0.047	
Life, physical, and social science	0.059	0.057	0.066	Protective services	0.045	0.059
Service (white collar)	0.073	0.072	0.056	Food, health, cleaning, personal	0.069	0.075
Sales (white collar)	0.106	0.123	0.079	Precision production, craft, repair	0.111	0.151
Office and administrative support (white collar)	0.109	0.067	0.092	Operators, assemblers, inspectors	0.181	0.219
Farming, forestry, fishery (blue collar)	0.110	...	...	Transportation and material moving equipment	0.103	0.112

Construction and extractive (blue collar)	0.149	…	…
Installation, maintenance, repair (blue collar)	0.112	0.117	0.083
Production (blue collar)	0.206	0.163	0.169
Transportation and material moving (blue collar)	0.117	0.057	0.096
Handlers, cleaners, helpers		0.139	0.151
Farming, forestry, fishery		0.044	0.067
Armed forces			
Total	0.102	0.101	0.078
Total		0.090	0.103
Blue collar, tradable	0.128	…	…
Blue collar, nontradable	0.122	…	…
White collar, tradable	0.094	…	…
White collar, nontradable	0.065	…	…
Full sample			
Blue collar, tradable	0.175	…	…
Blue collar, nontradable	0.150	…	…
White collar, tradable	0.104	…	…
White collar, nontradable	0.078	…	…
Full sample total	…	0.122	0.087

Source: Authors' calculations from the 2002 and 2004 Displaced Worker Surveys.
a. Agriculture, Mining, and Construction omitted.
n.a. Not available.

Table 16 also shows that in tradable nonmanufacturing industries, displaced workers were more educated, more likely to have health insurance, more likely to lose full-time jobs, and more likely to have higher predisplacement earnings than workers displaced from nontradable industries. The educational attainment differences are stark: 42 percent of workers displaced from nontradable non-manufacturing industries, but 24 percent of workers displaced from tradable nonmanufacturing industries, had a high school diploma or less. The educational differences show up in predisplacement weekly earnings.

Postdisplacement, reemployment rates (also reported in table 16) are higher for displaced nonmanufacturing workers than for manufacturing workers. Reemployment rates are .75 and .77 for nontradable and tradable nonmanufac-turing workers, respectively, .64 for manufacturing workers.

The earnings cost of job displacement, well established for manufacturing workers, also affected nonmanufacturing workers. For the 2001–03 period, with the weak job recovery from the recession, we see large earnings losses. Median earnings losses are smaller for nonmanufacturing than for manufacturing, and a larger share of nonmanufacturing workers experience no earnings loss. Consis-tent with lower predisplacement earnings, workers displaced from nontradable nonmanufacturing industries experienced smaller earnings losses than workers displaced from tradable nonmanufacturing industries.

Table 17 reports worker characteristics and reemployment outcomes for three services sectors: Information; Financial, Insurance and Real Estate; and Profes-sional and Business Services. For the most part, workers in tradable industries in these sectors have higher levels of educational attainment. In Information and Professional and Business Services, predisplacement weekly earnings were higher in tradable industries than in nontradable industries. Consistent with higher earnings, more workers displaced from tradable industries reported that they had health insurance coverage than workers displaced from nontradable industries. Reemployment outcomes (reemployment rates or average earnings losses) are similar within sector, across the tradability of the detailed industries.

Table 18 reports a similar breakdown, by occupation, for sectors: Manage-ment, Business and Financial; Professional and Related; Office and Administra-tive Support. Workers from tradable occupations have higher levels of education, within occupational group, than workers from nontradable occupations. Their predisplacement earnings were higher, as was the availability of health insurance coverage. Men are more highly represented in the tradable occupations. Again, there is no clear pattern of reemployment outcomes by tradability. Earnings losses range from 3 percent to 16 percent, with 40 to 50 percent of reemployed workers reporting no earnings loss.

J. Bradford Jensen and Lori G. Kletzer   111

Table 16. Characteristics of Displaced Workers, by Industrial Sector and Tradability

Worker characteristics	Manufacturing, tradable	Nonmanufacturing, tradable	Nonmanufacturing, nontradable
Age (mean in years)	41.60	39.60	38.10
Standard deviation	11.20	11.10	11.70
Job tenure (mean in years)	7.11	4.40	4.26
Standard deviation	8.43	5.60	5.61
Job tenure > ten years	0.23	0.12	0.14
Educational attainment (share)			
High school dropout	0.14	0.05	0.11
High school graduate	0.40	0.19	0.31
Some college	0.24	0.30	0.33
College +	0.22	0.45	0.25
Male	0.61	0.54	0.45
In predisplacement job			
Share with health insurance	0.75	0.66	0.47
Full-time	0.96	0.90	0.82
If full-time, real weekly earnings (dollars)	342.70	443.18	294.91
Standard deviation (dollars)	300.54	383.08	271.21
Share reemployed	0.64	0.77	0.75
Of reemployed, share full-time	0.80	0.78	0.72
All reemployed			
Change in ln earnings (mean)	−0.32	−0.30	−0.14
Standard deviation	0.89	0.98	1.02
Median change	−0.15	−0.11	−0.03
Share with no loss in earnings	0.42	0.45	0.51
Full-time to full-time			
Change in ln earnings (mean)	−0.21	−0.21	−0.12
Standard deviation	0.76	0.69	0.97
Median change	−0.10	−0.07	−0.03
Share with no loss in earnings	0.42	0.46	0.52

Source: Authors' calculations from the 2004 Displaced Worker Survey, using sampling weights. Agriculture, Mining, and Construction omitted.

Conclusions

This paper develops a new empirical approach to identifying, at a detailed level for the entire economy, industries and occupations that are tradable. Using the methodology, we find substantial employment in tradable service industries and occupations. Workers in these industries and occupations are more highly skilled and have higher earnings than workers in the manufacturing sector and nontradable service activities. The higher earnings are not solely a result of higher skill levels: in regressions controlling for observable characteristics,

Table 17. Characteristics of Selected Service Sector Displaced Workers, by Industry and Tradability

	Information		Financial, insurance, real estate		Professional and business services	
	Tradable	Nontradable	Tradable	Nontradable	Tradable	Nontradable
Job tenure (mean in years)	5.80	4.51	5.82	8.28	3.55	3.24
Standard deviation	7.37	7.25	7.00	9.14	3.98	4.68
Job tenure > ten years	0.192	0.16	0.167	0.259	0.066	0.109
Educational attainment (share)						
High school dropout	0.032	0.00	0.04	0.046	0.047	0.173
High school graduate	0.207	0.038	0.179	0.243	0.157	0.446
Some college	0.262	0.45	0.389	0.354	0.261	0.196
College +	0.499	0.512	0.392	0.357	0.535	0.186
Male	0.559	0.668	0.47	0.479	0.527	0.527
In predisplacement job						
Share with health insurance	0.82	0.62	0.62	0.73	0.66	0.36
Full-time	0.93	0.87	0.91	0.94	0.91	0.83
If full-time, real weekly earnings (dollars)	530.82	387.98	409.88	542.51	504.61	273.95
Standard deviation (dollars)	409.45	350.69	380.43	454.14	415.82	251.57
Share reemployed	0.72	0.81	0.61	0.68	0.71	0.62
Of reemployed, share full-time	0.76	0.87	0.80	0.82	0.80	0.73
All reemployed						
Change in ln earnings (mean)	-0.57	-0.72	-0.16	0.013	-0.34	-0.18
Standard deviation	1.07	2.97	1.09	0.499	0.96	0.93
Median change	-0.34	-0.024	-0.08	0.03	-0.08	-0.03
Share with no loss in earnings	0.346	0.469	0.456	0.531	0.457	0.468
Full-time to full-time						
Change in ln earnings (mean)	-0.40	-1.003	-0.15	0.018	-0.185	-0.162
Standard deviation	0.82	3.328	0.51	0.36	0.737	0.999
Median change	-0.25	-0.07	-0.047	-0.007	-0.034	-0.029
Share with no loss in earnings	0.36	0.344	0.457	0.508	0.49	0.489

Source: Authors' calculations from the 2004 Displaced Worker Survey, using sampling weights.

Table 18. Characteristics of Displaced Workers in Selected Service Occupations, by Occupation and Tradability

Worker characteristics	Management, business, and financial		Professional and related		Office and administrative support	
	Tradable	Nontradable	Tradable	Nontradable	Tradable	Nontradable
Job tenure (mean in years)	6.72	5.03	4.82	4.30	5.31	4.57
Standard deviation	8.04	4.99	6.09	5.25	6.69	5.74
Job tenure > ten years	0.204	0.143	0.111	0.109	0.176	0.136
Educational attainment (share)						
High school dropout	0.008	0.012	0.003	0.026	0.051	0.05
High school graduate	0.132	0.272	0.092	0.115	0.331	0.339
Some college	0.269	0.28	0.198	0.328	0.438	0.406
College +	0.591	0.436	0.708	0.53	0.18	0.204
Male	0.466	0.633	0.717	0.248	0.306	0.241
In pre-displacement job						
Share with health insurance	0.775	0.588	0.794	0.632	0.616	0.577
Full-time	0.965	0.927	0.93	0.791	0.896	0.865
If full-time, real weekly earnings (dollars)	554.78	426.02	523.24	323.60	299.45	261.96
Standard deviation (dollars)	434.23	336.05	369.44	226.58	254.48	198.07
Share reemployed	0.786	0.72	0.80	0.801	0.691	0.755
Of reemployed, share full-time	0.791	0.726	0.805	0.707	0.758	0.763
All reemployed						
Change in ln earnings (mean)	-0.374	-0.364	-0.34	-0.14	-0.227	-0.093
Standard deviation	1.08	1.144	1.155	0.811	0.677	1.063
Median change	-0.127	-0.165	-0.084	-0.037	-0.15	-0.045
Share with no loss in earnings	0.492	0.389	0.455	0.507	0.443	0.512
Full-time to full-time						
Change in ln earnings (mean)	-0.205	-0.357	-0.318	-0.128	-0.113	0.012
Standard deviation	0.852	1.165	1.176	0.343	0.455	0.704
Median change	-0.045	-0.109	-0.068	-0.029	-0.068	-0.025
Share with no loss in earnings	0.528	0.351	0.462	0.515	0.471	0.542

Source: Authors' calculations from the 2004 Displaced Worker Survey, using sampling weights.

workers in selected tradable service activities earn 16–17 percent higher incomes than similar workers in nontradable activities in the same sector.

Examining employment growth across industries and occupations, there is little evidence that tradable service industries or occupations grow more slowly than nontradable industries or occupations overall, though at the low end of the skill distribution employment growth is negative for tradable services. High-skill service activities have the highest employment growth rates.

There is job insecurity associated with employment in tradable activities, including service activities. We find a higher rate of job loss from tradable industries than from nontradable industries, with the greatest difference outside of manufacturing. In comparison with an overall rate of job loss of .103 for 2001–03, tradable nonmanufacturing industries have a rate of job loss of .128 and nontradable industries .073 (though we note the possibility that these differences are driven by the tech bubble). Also within occupations, workers in tradable jobs faced a higher rate of job loss than workers in nontradable jobs, with the greatest difference within white-collar occupations.

These results have several implications. First, it seems inappropriate to consider all service activities as inherently nontradable. The geographic concentration of some service activities within the United States is as great as in manufacturing and is consistent with the view that a number of service industries and occupations are tradable. The share of employment in tradable services is large enough that a better understanding of the forces shaping trade in services warrants our attention. At a minimum, more resources should be devoted to collecting and publishing considerably more detail on international service flows. Continuing to increase the amount of information collected on the use of intermediate service inputs within the United States would also increase our ability to track and understand developments in this large and growing sector.

Second, the results presented in this paper suggest that tradable services are consistent with U.S. comparative advantage. While professional and business services jobs require higher skills and pay higher wages than manufacturing jobs in general, tradable services jobs in these sectors require even higher skills and are more highly paid than nontradable service activities. We would expect that as technological and organizational change increases the potential for trade in services, economic activity in the United States will shift to activities consistent with U.S. comparative advantage.[26] It is therefore possible that further liberalization in international services trade would directly benefit workers and firms in

26. The United States maintains a positive trade balance in service activities; see table 1.

J. Bradford Jensen and Lori G. Kletzer   115

the United States. The policy community should devote more attention to understanding the impediments to services trade.

Third, although tradable services have relatively high employment growth rates overall, at the low end of the skill distribution tradable service activities have negative employment growth. The potential for reallocation across activities in response to shifting trade patterns in services is real. Policymakers should prepare for additional reallocation among this group of workers.

The process of adjustment to job displacement might be eased by service worker characteristics. For the most part, workers displaced from tradable services are different, in terms of job tenure and educational attainment, from workers displaced from (tradable) manufacturing industries. Generalizing from what we know from studies of manufacturing worker job loss, lower levels of job tenure and higher levels of educational attainment may be advantages in seeking reemployment. Given the current availability of data, it is too early to tell. We need data beyond the time period of the "jobless recovery." We also need more information to discern whether workers in tradable activities face different reemployment outcomes than workers in nontradable activities. The evidence we do have tells us that job loss for services workers is costly. These costs underscore the need to have a less porous safety net (for example, by extending Trade Adjustment Assistance [TAA] to services workers and extending wage insurance beyond TAA). Lower rates of employment growth at the lower end of the skill distribution in tradable service activities may have implications for the retraining strategies and opportunities for displaced low-skill workers in both manufacturing and services.

Appendix: Displaced Worker Survey

The Displaced Worker Survey is administered biennially as a supplement to the Current Population Survey (CPS). The first survey was administered in January 1984 and the most recent in January 2004. In each survey, adults (aged 20 years and older) in the regular monthly CPS were asked if they had lost a job in the preceding three- or five-year period due to "a plant closing, an employer going out of business, a layoff from which he/she was not recalled, or other similar reasons."[27] If the answer was yes, a series of questions followed concerning

27. For the 1984–92 surveys, the recall period was five years. Starting in 1994, the recall period was shortened to three years.

the lost job and the period of joblessness. Other causes of job loss, such as quitting and firing, are not considered displacements.[28] This categorization is consistent with our common understanding of job displacement: it occurs without personal prejudice in that terminations are related to the operating decisions of the employer and are independent of individual job performance. This operational definition is not without ambiguity: the displacements are "job" displacements, in the sense that an individual displaced from a job and rehired into a different job with the same employer is considered displaced.

A key advantage of the DWS is its large-scale representative nature. As part of the CPS, it draws on a random sample of 60,000 households, which is weighted to be representative of the U.S. workforce. As a result, the surveys yield responses from large numbers of displaced workers in a wide set of industries. In exchange for breadth of coverage, the DWSs have two weaknesses relevant to any study of the costs of job loss. The first is the relatively short-term horizon. Individuals are surveyed just once, providing information about one postdisplacement point in time, rather than about their experiences over time. The second weakness is the lack of a readily available comparison group of nondisplaced workers. Without such a comparison group, we cannot investigate what would have happened to these workers if they had not been displaced. The lack of a comparison group leads to some unavoidable errors in measuring outcomes such as postdisplacement reemployment and earnings losses. The rate of job loss reported in the tables is calculated as in Farber (1993, 2003, 2005): it is the ratio of the (weighted) number of reported displacements divided by the (weighted) number of workers who were either employed at the survey date or reported a job loss but were not employed at the survey date. See Kletzer (2001) for more discussion of the issues that arise when using the DWSs to measure the incidence of job loss.

---

28. Individuals who respond that their job loss was due to the end of a seasonal job or the failure of a self-employed business are also not included.

J. Bradford Jensen and Lori G. Kletzer   131

References

Amiti, Mary, and Shang-Jin Wei. 2004. "Fear of Service Outsourcing: Is It Justified?" Working Paper WP/04/186. Washington: International Monetary Fund.

Arora, Ashish, and Alfonso Gambardella. 2004. "The Globalization of the Software Industry: Perspectives and Opportunities for Developed and Developing Countries." Working Paper 10538. Cambridge, Mass.: National Bureau of Economic Research.

Bardhan, Ashok Deo, and Cynthia A. Kroll. 2003. "The New Wave of Outsourcing." Working Paper 1103. University of California, Berkeley: Fisher Center for Real Estate and Urban Economics.

Bernard, Andrew B., J. Bradford Jensen, and Peter K. Schott. Forthcoming 2006. "Survival of the Best Fit: Exposure to Low Wage Countries and the (Uneven) Growth of U.S. Manufacturing Plants." *Journal of International Economics* 68 (1): 219–37.

Bhagwati, Jagdish, Arvind Panagariya, and T. N. Srinivasan. 2004. "The Muddles over Outsourcing." *Journal of Economic Perspectives* 18 (Fall): 93–114.

Blum, Bernardo S. 2004. "Trade, Technology and the Rise of the Service Sector: An Empirical Assessment of the Effects on U.S. Wage Inequality." University of Toronto (September).

Brainard, Lael, and Robert E. Litan. 2004. "Offshoring Service Jobs: Bane or Boon—and What To Do?" Brookings Policy Brief 132 (April).

Bronfenbrenner, Kate, and Stephanie Luce. 2004. "The Changing Nature of Corporate Global Restructuring: The Impact of Production Shifts on Jobs in the U.S., China, and around the Globe." U.S.–China Economic and Security Review Commission. October.

Dossani, Rafiq, and Martin Kenney. 2004. "The Next Wave of Globalization? Exploring the Relocation of Service Provision to India." Working Paper 156. Stanford University: Asia Pacific Research Center.

———. 2003. "Went for Cost, Stayed for Quality? Moving the Back Office to India." Stanford University: Asia-Pacific Research Center.

Duranton, Gilles, and Henry G. Overman. 2004. "Testing for Localisation Using Micro-Geographic Data." London School of Economics.

Ellison, Glenn and Edward L. Glaeser. 1999. "The Geographic Concentration of Industry: Does Natural Advantage Explain Agglomeration?" *American Economic Review, Papers and Proceedings* 89 (May): 311–16.

———. 1997. "Geographic Concentration of U.S. Manufacturing Industries: A Dartboard Approach." *Journal of Political Economy* 105 (October): 889–927.

Farber, Henry S. 2005. "What Do We Know about Job Loss in the United States? Evidence from the Displaced Worker Survey, 1984–2004." Working Paper 498. Princeton University: Industrial Relations Section.

———. 2003. "Job Loss in the United States, 1981–2001." Working Paper 471. Princeton University: Industrial Relations Section.

———. 1993. "The Incidence and Costs of Job Loss: 1982–1991." *BPEA*, no. 1: 73–132.

Fernandez, Raquel, 1989. Comment on "Industrial Wage Differential, International Competition and Trade Policy," by Lawrence F. Katz and Lawrence H. Summers. In

Trade Policies for International Competitiveness, edited by Robert Feenstra, pp. 117–22. University of Chicago Press.

Gardner, Jennifer M. 1993 "Recession Swells Count of Displaced Workers." *Monthly Labor Review* 116 (June): 14–23.

Gartner Research. 2004. "Worldwide IT Services Market Forecast, 2002–2007" (January 12).

Gentle, Chris. 2003. "The Cusp of a Revolution: How Offshoring Will Transform the Financial Services Industry." Deloitte Research.

Harrigan, James, and Rita A. Balaban. 1999. "U.S. Wages in General Equilibrium: The Effects of Prices, Technology, and Factor Supplies, 1963–1991." Working Paper 6981. Cambridge, Mass.: National Bureau of Economic Research.

Helpman, Elhanan, and Paul R. Krugman. 1985. *Market Structure and Foreign Trade: Increasing Returns, Imperfect Competition, and the International Economy.* Cambridge, Mass.: MIT Press.

Imbs, Jean, and Romain Wacziarg. 2003. "Stages of Diversification." *American Economic Review* 93 (March): 63–86.

Katz, Lawrence F., and Lawrence H. Summers. 1989a. "Can Interindustry Wage Differentials Justify Strategic Trade Policy?" In *Trade Policies for International Competitiveness*, edited by Robert Feenstra, pp. 85–116. University of Chicago Press.

———. 1989b. "Industry Rents: Evidence and Implications." In *Brookings Papers on Economic Activity: Microeconomics 1989*, edited by Martin N. Baily and Clifford Winston, pp. 209–75. Brookings.

Kirkegaard, Jacob F. 2004. "Outsourcing—Stains on the White Collar?" Washington: Institute for International Economics (February).

Kletzer, Lori G. 2001. *Job Loss from Imports: Measuring the Costs.* Washington: Institute for International Economics.

———. 1998. "Job Displacement." *Journal of Economic Perspectives* 12 (Winter): 115–36.

———. 1995. "White Collar Job Displacement, 1983–91." In *Proceedings of the 47th Annual Meeting*, pp. 98–107. Madison, Wis.: Industrial Relations Research Association.

Krugman, Paul R. 1991. *Geography and Trade.* Cambridge, Mass.: MIT Press.

Landy, Stephen D. 1999. "Mapping the Universe." *Scientific American* 280 (June): 38–45.

Mann, Catherine L. 2003. "Globalization of IT Services and White Collar Jobs: The Next Wave of Productivity Growth." Policy Brief 03-11. Washington: Institute for International Economics.

McCarthy, John C. 2002. "3.3 Million U.S. Services Jobs To Go Offshore." San Francisco: TechStrategy™ Research, Forrester Research (November).

Naughton, Barry J. 2003. "How Much Can Regional Integration Do to Unify China's Markets?" In *How Far across the River? Chinese Policy Reform at the Millennium*, edited by Nicholas Hope, Dennis Tao Yang, and Mu Yang Li, pp. 204–32. Stanford University Press.

Podgursky, Michael. 1992. "The Industrial Structure of Job Displacement 1979–89." *Monthly Labor Review* 115 (September): 17–25.

Poncet, Sandra. 2003. "Measuring Chinese Domestic and International Integration." *China Economic Review* 14 (1): 1–21.

Sachs, Jeffrey D., and Howard J. Shatz. 1998. "International Trade and Wage Inequality: Some New Results." In *Imports, Exports, and the American Worker*, edited by Susan M. Collins, pp. 215–40. Brookings.

Samuelson, Paul A. 2004. "Where Ricardo and Mill Rebut and Confirm Arguments of Mainstream Economists Supporting Globalization." *Journal of Economic Perspectives* 18 (Summer): 135–46.

Schultze, Charles L. 2004. "Offshoring, Import Competition, and the Jobless Recovery." Brookings Policy Brief 136 (August).

Tilton, Andrew. 2003. "Offshoring: Where Have All the Jobs Gone?" *U.S. Economic Analyst* 03/38 (September 19). Goldman Sachs & Co.

Van Welsum, Desirée, and Graham Vickery. 2005. "Potential Offshoring of ICT-Intensive Using Occupations." DSTI Information Economy Working Paper DSTI/ICCP/IE(2004)19/FINAL. Paris: Organization for Economic Cooperation and Development.

Young, Alwyn. 2000. "The Razor's Edge: Distortions and Incremental Reform in the People's Republic of China." *Quarterly Journal of Economics* 115 (November): 1091–35.

[17]

ELSEVIER

Journal of Development Economics 81 (2006) 142–162

JOURNAL OF
Development
ECONOMICS

www.elsevier.com/locate/econbase

Quantifying the impact of services liberalization in a developing country

Denise Eby Konan [a,*], Keith E. Maskus [b,1]

[a]*Department of Economics, University of Hawaii, Honolulu, HI 96822, USA*
[b]*Department of Economics, Box 256, University of Colorado, Boulder, CO 80309, USA*

Received 1 June 2002; accepted 1 May 2005

Abstract

We compare goods versus services liberalization in terms of welfare, outputs, and factor prices in Tunisia using a CGE model with multiple products, services and trading partners. Restraints on services trade involve both cross-border supply (tariff-equivalent price wedges) and on foreign ownership (monopoly-rent distortions and inefficiency costs). Goods-trade liberalization yields a modest gain in aggregate welfare. Reducing service barriers generate relatively large welfare gains and low adjustment costs. Services liberalization increases economic activity in all sectors and raise the real returns to both capital and labor. The results point to the potential importance of deregulating services provision for economic development.
© 2005 Elsevier B.V. All rights reserved.

JEL classification: C68; F13; F14; F23; L8
Keywords: Liberalization; Services; Regulation; Computational economics; Tunisia

1. Introduction

Many developing countries sharply lowered manufacturing tariffs and other impediments to goods trade in the 1990s, both through unilateral trade liberalization and agreements reached in the World Trade Organization (WTO) and regional trade accords. Nevertheless, as Rodrik (2001) has pointed out, traditional trade liberalization seems not to have fully delivered on its promise for prosperity. In this paper we suggest that part of the explanation rests in the continued

---

* Corresponding author. Tel.: +1 808 956 6310; fax: +1 808 956 4347.
 E-mail addresses: konan@hawaii.edu (D.E. Konan), maskus@colorado.edu (K.E. Maskus).
[1] Tel.: +1 303 492 7588; fax: +1 303 492 8960.

0304-3878/$ - see front matter © 2005 Elsevier B.V. All rights reserved.
doi:10.1016/j.jdeveco.2005.05.009

insulation, and resulting poor condition, of the domestic service sectors in many developing countries. These service sectors tend to deliver high-cost and unproductive input services, thereby limiting economic efficiency gains from trade reform. We explore this claim in a computational general equilibrium model of the Tunisian economy.

The mechanisms by which services trade liberalization might improve welfare differ from those of goods trade. Producers respond to a lowering of border barriers in products by reorienting production towards goods in which an economy possesses a comparative advantage. Tariff cuts thus involve a restructuring of the economy. Liberalization of merchandise trade also tends to redistribute income, with abundant factors benefiting disproportionately in the long run.

In contrast, trade in services is not solely a cross-border phenomenon. As the paper by Markusen et al. (in press) points out, many foreign services are best transferred through foreign direct investment (FDI) due to the personal contact required between the service provider and client. Restrictions on FDI or the movement of professional personnel may reduce services trade far more than tariffs or other border barriers limit trade in goods. Indeed, in many developing countries, Tunisia included, laws and regulatory agencies erect entry barriers that essentially rule out FDI in key service sectors.

Foreign direct investment involves inflows of capital and personnel, but more importantly for developing countries it also tends to embody transfers of technology that can upgrade productivity in the domestic economy. Because financial, communications, and professional services are key intermediate inputs into production in all sectors, cost reductions in these sectors could have the effect of upgrading overall productivity (Lipsey, 2001; Markusen, 1989). Thus, whereas liberalizing goods trade moves an economy toward specialization, liberalizing services trade through permitting foreign establishments could lead to more balanced output expansion.[2]

In Tunisia there is a large state presence in many key service sectors. Regulatory agencies limit competition by restricting markets available to producers. Foreign participation is highly restricted and often limited to the services of non-resident Tunisian suppliers. As we discuss below, anecdotal evidence indicates that Tunisia's communication, financial, insurance, distribution, and professional services are expensive, of poor quality, and often inaccessible. Thus, the economy might particularly gain from more openness in the service sector.

In some respects, Tunisia has pursued a strategy of liberalization and alignment with the global economy (World Bank, 2004). For example, Tunisia concluded an Association Agreement with the European Union in 1995. Under this Agreement, border restrictions on industrial-goods imports from the EU were to be phased out over 12 years and the participants agreed to work toward greater financial and technical cooperation. However, the trade opening was confined largely to merchandise, excluding services.

Indeed, Tunisia's 1995 commitments under the General Agreement on Trade in Services (GATS) were few and generally represented a preservation of status quo policies.[3] Reluctance to open services markets to foreign suppliers, which would also involve privatization and

---

[2] Similar comments pertain to trade in intermediate and capital goods. One interesting difference, which we find in our simulations, is that liberalization of goods trade may have sharply stronger impacts on relative factor prices than liberalization of services, because the former generates stronger production reallocation effects favoring the abundant factor.

[3] Of the twelve service sectors defined under the GATS classification scheme Tunisia made commitments in only three: financial services, tourism, and telecommunications. These commitments reflected little more than a codification of Tunisia's existing legal system and have not been expanded.

144   *D.E. Konan, K.E. Maskus / Journal of Development Economics 81 (2006) 142–162*

deregulation, reflects concerns of policymakers about whether the economic benefits would justify the adjustment costs involved. Moreover, Tunisian services are supplied by important domestic interests and this fact makes liberalization difficult to undertake without some indication of the potential for gains and their likely distribution. Hoekman and Djankov (1996) in particular note the potentially large gains in well-being for Tunisian citizens of liberalization in services.

Unfortunately, as discussed in Section 2, empirical studies of the effects through FDI of services liberalization are scarce, in part due to a variety of measurement problems. It is against this backdrop that we conduct the present study. We develop a computable general equilibrium (CGE) model to compare the impacts of services liberalization to that of trade liberalization. A significant innovation is to implement GATS definitions and consider, separately, liberalization of both cross-border services trade and the establishment of domestic presence by FDI. For this purpose we develop estimates of the distortions that the present, relatively closed, environment in Tunisia imposes on the price of services. By simulating the removal of these distortions, we are able to quantify the impacts of liberalization. The potential efficiency gains would be large, on the order of 4% to 5% of initial consumption, while output in all merchandise sectors would rise. Furthermore, the real prices of both capital and labor would increase.

2. Conceptual issues

Trade in services is distinguished from trade in goods by the intangible nature of many transactions. Unlike physical goods, which must cross borders and thus are subject to customs procedures and tariffs, services often involve direct transactions between the consumer and producer. This fact complicates measurement of both service flows and their corresponding impediments. The founders of GATS recognized the importance of the various channels by which services are transacted. GATS identifies four modes of supply: cross-border supply (mode 1), consumption abroad (mode 2), commercial presence (mode 3), and the presence of natural persons (mode 4). Thus GATS extends traditional trade law to include both foreign direct investment (mode 3) and movements of labor (mode 4).

Unfortunately, these legal definitions do not accord well with present international balance of payments accounting practices, as discussed in detail by Karsenty (2000), making difficult the measurement of service trade and its components. Equally problematic is the measurement of impediments to services trade.[4] For example, Hoekman (1995) developed a frequency indicator as an initial attempt to quantify the presence of barriers based on the GATS schedule of commitments by country. While this index provides some indication of the extent of commitments, it is not designed to measure the level of service barriers. Francois (1999) estimated a gravity model of service trade, adopting Singapore and Hong Kong as free-trade benchmarks. Discrepancies in predicted trade patterns were used to indicate the severity of policy barriers. Warren and Findlay (2000) described an ongoing Australian services research project attempting to measure the wedge between price and marginal cost in service sectors in order to get an indication of the impact that impediments might have on prices. The project also seeks to develop quantity impact measures by comparing domestic output to international standards. Unfortunately, the study is incomplete and may not provide information that could be applied to developing economies.

---

[4] Warren and Findlay (2000) and Hoekman (2000) provide excellent surveys of these measurement issues. See also Brown and Stern (2001) and Stern (2002) for discussion of measurement and modeling in services.

D.E. Konan, K.E. Maskus / Journal of Development Economics 81 (2006) 142–162   145

Given severe data limitations, econometric studies on services trade and their barriers are rare. In contrast, a CGE model can provide quantifiable insights with relatively sparse datasets.[5] An early model by Brown et al. (1996) converted Hoekman's frequency indices into an approximation of cross-border barriers to services trade and simulated liberalization in the multi-country Michigan model. Several studies of services barriers exist using the multi-country database established in the Global Trade Analysis Project (GTAP).[6] Hertel (2000) approximated cross-border barriers with the gravity-equation estimates of Francois and treated liberalization as an elimination of resource-using barriers. Robinson et al. (2002) focused on enhancements in total factor productivity arising from imported producer services in a ten-region, eleven-sector CGE model.

A significant limitation of these models is that they do not capture the potential benefit of FDI liberalization in services. Recently, however, FDI has been incorporated into multi-country CGE models. Two examples are Dee and Hanslow (2001) and Brown and Stern (2001). Their approaches to measuring services were somewhat different, with the latter authors using price–cost margins for a number of countries. Both studies assumed imperfect competition in manufactures and services. Typically, FDI was treated as a capital flow and barriers to the right of establishment were modeled as a tax on both the existing investment flow and local sales. Liberalization (removal of the tax) resulted in a global reallocation of capital as sector-level rates of return adjust to a new equilibrium. This approach represents a significant improvement over earlier work, which focused only on cross-border service trade (mode 1). These models are informative about the potential global impacts of the GATS approach.

A contribution of particular note is Brown et al. (1997), who analyzed the potential impacts of the Tunisia–EU Association Agreement in a model with monopolistic competition in non-agricultural sectors. They permitted an exogenous increase in FDI equal to 10% of the initial Tunisian capital stock in response to the Agreement, with the incoming capital allocated according to sectoral returns with industry-specific capital. They do not contemplate liberalization of services, however. Their findings suggest that the EU Agreement would have a modest impact on Tunisian GDP, ranging from −0.1% to +3.3% depending on the scenario.

Unfortunately, the models available to date fall short of capturing domestic effects of services liberalization in such highly regulated developing economies as Tunisia for two reasons. First, service sectors that experienced no FDI in the benchmark economy were assumed to be non-tradable and could not, therefore, be recipients of FDI in counterfactual scenarios. Yet in Tunisia, we might reasonably expect that FDI would occur in several important sectors (such as telecommunications or insurance) in which, under current policy, foreign suppliers are simply not permitted to serve Tunisian residents. Prior methodologies do not offer a reasonable way to predict how responsive FDI flows would be in such sectors in a liberalized environment. Second, the market structure in most service sectors in Tunisia is highly regulated and imperfectly competitive, perhaps best characterized as cartels. As Francois and Wooton (2001) discussed, shallow liberalization without deregulation could essentially be an invitation to foreign firms to join the cartel. Deeper liberalization, involving also deregulation permitting new entry, should bring about a more competitive market structure.

An additional point of departure for our work is to consider the impact of services liberalization on the structure of Tunisia's economy relative to that of commodities trade

---

[5] Whalley (2003) and Dee et al. (2000) survey the computational literature in services.
[6] GTAP is explained in Hertel (1997).

liberalization. The Tunisian input–output table allows us to disaggregate services into 15 sectors. We consider the regulatory environment at a disaggregated level and are able to compare the relative impact of liberalization in individual service sectors. With data on services as intermediate inputs, our simulations indicate how services liberalization may restructure the domestic economy.

As discussed in the following section, our model is designed to capture several static effects of services and goods trade liberalization, including efficiencies from production reallocation, pro-competitive gains from reducing cartel power, and efficiencies from adopting best-practiced technologies. Analysis of pro-competitive impacts in the CGE context stems from the pioneering work of Harris (1984). However, we do not compute gains from increasing returns to scale, as emphasized by Harris (1984), Brown et al. (1997), and others. Nor do we consider the potential for product variety gains from liberalizing services trade, an element introduced by Romer (2004) and introduced into dynamic CGE models by Rutherford and Tarr (2002).

3. Tunisia: services and impediments

Services play a significant role in the Tunisian economy, as is evident from Table 1. Nearly half of all output (excluding tourism) was comprised of services in 1995, according to the input–output table for that year (Institute National de la Statistique, 1998). Services made up one-third of household consumption and 18% of intermediate demand. Tourism was the largest of the tradable services, representing over 15% of imports and more than 19% of all exports. Tourism export services are considered to be rather open.[7]

There is no statistical information on the importance of FDI in Tunisian services trade, as the earnings and sales of foreign-owned subsidiaries are not reported separately from those of domestic firms. However, foreign participation clearly is minimal in the main service activities due to a variety of investment measures, exchange controls and limits on movement of foreign personnel. The most important restriction is the Foreign Commercial Activities Law of 1961 (Decree Law Number 61-14), by which non-Tunisians are required to obtain a trader's permit, *carte de commercant*, to engage in any form of commercial activity. This permit, granted on a discretionary basis, has effectively precluded foreign participation in most wholesale and retail markets. The Investment Code of 1993 is also an important barrier to majority foreign equity projects, with foreign entry requiring approval by regulatory councils. Such approvals are rare and FDI is strictly controlled.[8]

Domestically, the level of competition varies across service sectors. Certain sectors, including computer services, real estate, construction, restaurants, and some distribution activities, are characterized by many participants, even though licensing requirements and other regulations impose burdensome costs on domestic entry and production. In several important sectors, such as automobiles and electronics, exclusive-distributor laws require that foreign suppliers appoint only Tunisian citizens as local agents and also ban parallel imports (Maskus and Lahouel, 2000).

---

[7] Tourism may be exported without being produced because tourists are treated as "foreign consumers" in the input–output table and enter as a component of final demand. The production of tourism services exists in the other service sectors, such as transportation, hotels, and restaurants.

[8] Despite some movements toward liberalization of FDI in 2001, foreign equity participation in Tunisian services other than hotels remains "negligible" according to the World Bank (2004). The essential reasons include reservations from FDI of 225 activities, prior approval requirements in other activities, and cumbersome entry requirements. It is evident that the market was not more open to FDI in 1995, our benchmark year.

D.E. Konan, K.E. Maskus / Journal of Development Economics 81 (2006) 142–162 147

Table 1
Sectoral output and factor shares (%)

	Production	Imports	Household consumption	Intermediate consumption	Exports
Aggregate sectors (% of total)					
Agriculture and fishing	17.5	10.2	32.4	20.1	6.6
Manufacturing	30.0	63.2	29.7	51.3	55.3
Utilities, mining, petroleum	5.8	5.8	4.0	10.9	6.8
Services	46.7	20.8	33.8	17.7	31.2
Service sectors (% of total)					
Construction	8.2	0.0	0.3	0.4	0.0
Distribution/commerce	6.9	0.0	0.0	0.0	0.0
Transportation	5.6	2.7	5.7	4.3	8.7
Communication	1.0	0.1	0.3	1.7	0.4
Hotel	1.5	0.0	3.9	0.1	0.0
Restaurant	4.1	0.0	10.9	0.0	0.0
Finance	2.5	0.2	0.1	4.8	0.3
Insurance	0.3	0.2	0.3	0.6	0.0
Business	1.4	2.1	0.1	2.5	2.5
Real estate	2.6	0.0	5.0	1.3	0.0
Repair	1.3	0.0	1.1	1.8	0.0
Health and education	2.0	0.0	4.9	0.2	0.0
Public	9.0	0.0	0.6	0.0	0.0
Other services	0.2	0.0	0.6	0.0	0.0
Tourism	–	15.4	–	–	19.3

Institute National de la Statistique, 1998, Les Comptes de la Nation Base 1983, agregats et tableaux d'ensemble 1993–1997.

This situation grants effective monopoly power to local agents and substantially raises consumer prices.

In other areas, such as financial and banking services, insurance, and many professional services, entry is tightly controlled by regulatory boards that limit the ability of providers to offer a full range of services and also limit market access. That such restrictions increase costs and limit market size is particularly evident in the insurance industry. Tunisia's 1997 expenditures on insurance premiums were only 1.58% of GDP, a penetration rate far behind those of nearly all middle-income countries and even behind that of several African nations, with an average rate of 5.7% (Swiss, 1999). The insurance market is highly concentrated and dominated by state-owned enterprises, which accounted for roughly half of total insurance premiums (Vittas, 1995). Foreign involvement remains strictly limited. According to the Insurance Code (Article 44) Tunisian residents, and risks situated solely in Tunisia, may only be insured directly by polices from Tunisian-owned companies. Foreign subsidiaries are permitted as a public limited or mutual company and may only serve non-residents.

As Bahlous and Nabli (2000) discussed, the government is also heavily involved in the banking system. Five of the twelve commercial banks in the mid-1990s were public.[9] They initiated 68% of loans and tended to favor state-owned enterprises, which are heavily indebted. Many small and medium-sized enterprises reported difficulties in gaining access to credit (World Bank, 2000, 2004). The ratio of non-performing loans to total assets was 36% and 72% in 1993

---

[9] This situation is still evident in that in the year 2000 there were only 14 commercial banks and these held 2/3 of the economy's financial assets (World Bank, 2004). The government controls the three largest banks.

for the two largest public banks. Goaied (1999) estimated the cost frontier of Tunisian deposit commercial banks with panel data for 1980 to 1995 and found that the mean cost inefficiency of private banks was 28.5% and of public banks was 50.5%.

By standard measures the Tunisian banking system also seems to engage in less monetary intermediation than would be anticipated for a country of its development level. In general, the ratio of domestic credit to GDP rises as countries become richer. The ratio in Tunisia in 1995 was 0.57, which was markedly lower then those in Egypt (0.77) and Jordan (0.88), Arab League countries with even lower income levels.[10] Thus, as a rough indication, monetary intermediation through the Tunisian banking sector is perhaps 30% less than might be expected.

Finally, several service sectors have traditionally been provided by the government and are only now being slowly liberalized to allow limited private participation. These industries include telecommunications, postal services, air transport, health, and education. For example, Tunisie Telecom remains the sole provider of nearly all telecommunications services and regulation is the domain of the Ministry of Telecommunications. As shown in Table 1, communications services comprise only 1% of production in the economy, whereas they make up 4% of GDP in Morocco (Varoudakis and Rossotto, 2001). Tunisian prices are likewise four times those of Morocco (World Bank, 2001). Recent investments in infrastructure have reduced the waiting time for fixed-line installation and the rate of service disruption. The telephone network is fully digitized. Yet Tunisian teledensity falls short of that of other middle-income countries, particularly in rural areas. Internet service accounts are expanding rapidly in response to the granting of two licenses to provide residential and commercial Internet services but monthly access rates are double those in Morocco and much higher than those observed in most liberalized markets.[11]

4. The model and benchmark data

In this section we present the model structure and describe the database used, the details of which are in a technical appendix. We employ what is, in most respects, a standard CGE model of a small open economy. Our contribution is in the explicit treatment of services production and investment. In the benchmark, production decisions in the service sector are distorted by regulations that raise entry costs and limit the rights of foreign enterprises to establish facilities in Tunisia. Counterfactual experiments involve the removal of regulatory investment barriers. As new firms are now permitted to enter, the market structure becomes competitive (eliminating rents) and more efficient (introducing lower cost firms).

Benchmark regulation distorts prices and quantities through two primary channels. One is the *cartel effect* whereby barriers to FDI and excessive regulation limit both domestic and foreign participants in certain service sectors, thus hampering competition and supporting market power on behalf of local firms. This market power creates the opportunity in sector i to charge price markups v_i over marginal cost c_i.

$$c_i(1 + v_i) = p_i \tag{1}$$

The markup depends on the number of firms, price elasticity of demand, and conjectures about reactions of rival firms. We assume that the rents generated by markups accrue to the representative agent.

---

[10] The source for these data is International Monetary Fund, *International Financial Statistics Yearbook 1997*.

[11] Modernization of this sector seems to have improved technical efficiency considerably by 2003 (World Bank, 2004), though entry remains tightly controlled.

D.E. Konan, K.E. Maskus / Journal of Development Economics 81 (2006) 142–162   149

Second is a *cost inefficiency effect*. Marginal costs in a regulated environment may be excessively high as low-cost foreign suppliers are excluded from the market. Additionally, domestic suppliers may be forced to absorb into their costs various regulations on provision and bureaucratic procedures. These activities do not contribute to output and generate pure economic waste (Hoekman and Konan, 2000). Thus, resource-using service barriers λ_i raise marginal costs above 'best-practiced' marginal costs c_i^* that would prevail in a liberalized environment.

$$c_i^*(1 + \lambda_i) = c_i \qquad\qquad (2)$$

Combining Eqs. (1) and (2) shows that the wedge between price and true marginal costs depends on the product of an ad valorem markup and a proportionate waste factor.

Ultimately it would be preferable and interesting to locate empirical information on these two wedges in each sector in order to simulate the effects of their separate and joint removal. Unfortunately, we only have estimates of the entire price–cost wedge and cannot perform this decomposition except on assumed shares. Thus, our counterfactual scenarios make two assumptions. First, we assume that barriers to FDI generate wedges consisting of half rents and half waste. Second, based on the discussion in the prior section we distinguish three types of service sectors: (i) competitive with inefficient technologies, or "low rent, high cost" (construction, distribution, hotels, restaurants, real estate, and repair); (ii) monopolized with efficient technologies, or "high rent, low cost" (communication); and (iii) monopolized with inefficient technologies, or "high rent, high cost" (transport, finance, insurance, and business services).

Services liberalization involves confronting a domestic cartel with the possibility of competitive markets with foreign entry. It is important to note that liberalization does not, in our model, generate endogenous changes in FDI flows. Rather, the scenarios involve changes in ownership and market structure in ways that improve efficiency and alter the distribution of rents. This assumption reflects the fact that in several service sectors there is no foreign participation (that is, FDI) in the benchmark equilibrium. In that context it is impossible to determine what the impact of liberalization would be on "marginal" FDI flows, which would not be meaningful. It also permits us to retain a fixed aggregate capital stock in the model, rather than engaging in dynamic simulations of endogenous investment and capital allocation. In this context, the estimates of welfare changes from liberalization of establishment rules are likely to be understated relative to full long-run gains.

Model equations are presented in the Appendix and the model is depicted in Fig. 1. We assume that production of agricultural, mineral, and manufacturing goods is characterized by constant returns to scale and perfect competition, implying that prices equal marginal costs of output.[12] Services production is subject to constant returns as well, though in the initial benchmark it is monopolized as discussed above. It should be stressed that a number of services, such as telecommunications, transport, and finance, likely are subject to increasing returns and, to the extent that trade liberalization expands output in those sectors, additional gains would accrue to the economy that we do not capture here. Note also that we engage solely in static simulations, without permitting endogenous increases in product differentiation and variety. For these reasons, in addition to our conservative estimates of price–cost wedges, computed welfare gains are liable to be underestimated.

In all sectors, production functions are approximated with Leontief technologies using composite intermediate inputs and real value added. A constant elasticity of substitution (CES)

---

[12] See, for example, Konan and Maskus (2000).

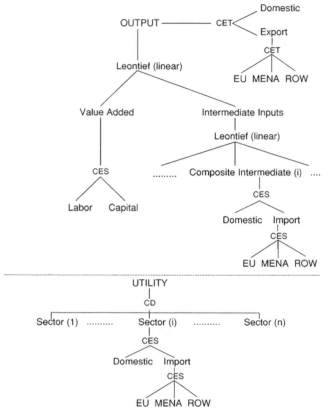

Fig. 1. Model structure.

production function describes the substitutability between labor and capital inputs in producing real value added. Intermediate inputs and final goods are differentiated by country of origin according to the Armington assumption, so that export and import prices differ across regions.[13] The three trading regions are the European Union (EU), the Arab League countries,[14] and the rest of the world (ROW).

In each sector, demand for domestically produced and imported goods is represented by a CES function, and intermediate imports are also differentiated across regional sources of supply in a CES structure. Similarly, Tunisian industries supply regionally differentiated goods to both domestic and foreign markets (exports). Production follows a nested two-stage constant

---

[13] In some contexts the Armington assumption can be problematic for it may generate large terms-of-trade effects that dominate welfare calculations. However, De Melo and Robinson (1989) showed that models allowing product differentiation are well behaved under a small open economy assumption; in effect the economy is a price taker at the level of aggregate trade flows and each region's aggregation is sufficiently distinctive to support the Armington assumption. In any event, we consider here only Tunisian import (FDI) liberalization, which would be expected to worsen the country's terms of trade. The fact that we find large welfare increases suggests that the issue is not important.

[14] These countries are designated MENA, for Middle-East North-African nations.

elasticity of transformation (CET) function. Total output is first calculated as the sum of domestic supply and total exports, with the latter then being allocated across the same destination regions according to a sub-CET function. Capital and labor are assumed to be freely mobile across sectors, whereas the stock of factor endowments are exogenous, implying that our simulations pertain to long-run outcomes of liberalization.

A representative consumer maximizes a nested CES utility function with a corresponding multi-staged budget constraint. In the first stage, the consumer decides how much to spend on goods from each sector, given the budget constraint. Income elasticities across sectors are set at unity as given by a Cobb–Douglas (CD) utility nest. In the second nest, the consumer determines domestic and aggregate import expenditures in each sector according to a CES function. Then given a budget for imports, the consumer selects purchases of imports from each region. These latter functions also characterize the split between government consumption and investment spending on domestic and imported goods and services. The representative consumer receives income from primary factors (labor and capital), net transfers from the government, the current-account deficit, and any net economic rents from the operation of restrictions on services trade.

Two standard closure rules are imposed: the savings–investment balance and a fixed current-account balance. The savings–investment balance is based on the assumption that the capital stock is exogenously fixed at the benchmark level. This stock is financed through forced consumer savings that act as a direct (lump-sum) tax. The interest rate (an index price of the composite capital stock) is endogenous and determined by factor-demand conditions. The current-account balance is the sum of the merchandise trade balance, the services balance, net foreign worker remittances, and (negative) net payments on foreign capital.[15] We assume that foreign reserves will be held constant so that the current account will be just offset by (the negative of) the capital account. The current-account balance itself is held constant in real terms throughout the simulations. Income from foreign remittances less foreign capital payments enters as an exogenous addition to the representative agent's income. To hold the current-account balance fixed while international prices are constant requires a balancing item. This is accomplished by means of a change in the home "real exchange rate," which refers implicitly to a change in the home price index (generated by changes in price of home-produced goods) sufficient to sustain a constant current-account balance as import and export volumes change.[16]

The government budget deficit is a deduction in available income for the representative agent, constituting a transfer to government consumption. The deficit is held fixed during our simulations. Thus, if a policy reform causes prices to fall, thereby reducing the tax revenues required to finance government expenditures, this tax saving is transferred to the representative agent. At the same time, if trade liberalization results in lost tariff revenues, the revenues are recouped by means of allowing household lump-sum taxes to vary endogenously.

The data for the model consist of a Social Accounting Matrix (SAM) and other parameters, such as import and export trade flows by region, sectoral tax and tariff rates, and elasticities of substitution and transformation. Because there is little empirical evidence on relevant elasticities

---

[15] In the 1995 benchmark year, foreign remittances were approximately 650 million Dinars while net capital income totaled negative 680 million Dinars according to the IMF *Balance of Payments Statistics Yearbook*.

[16] Tunisia has maintained a managed floating exchange rate system. The system has become more flexible, and the real exchange rate has depreciated somewhat leading up to implementation of the EU free-trade agreement, World Bank (2004).

for the Tunisian market, we make standard assumptions about their values. In particular, labor–capital substitution is set at unity in a Cobb–Douglas value-added production function. Benchmark trade elasticities are drawn from Rutherford et al. (1995) and Konan and Maskus (2000). The various trade elasticities are 2.0 for substitution between domestic and imported goods, 5.0 for substitution among regional imports and for transformation between domestic output and exports, and 8.0 for transformation among regional export destinations. These data are assembled into a consistent set of relationships between intermediate demand, final demand, and value-added transactions using the 1995 input–output table for Tunisia on a diskette provided by the Institut National De La Statistique (INS) along with the 1998 INS *Les Comptes de la Nation* report.

Trade and tariff data, provided in Table 2, were aggregated to the input–output sectoral basis using import weights consistent with the concordance between the input–output table and the tariff classification. Tariff rates were determined by collections data for 1995 and vary across regions due to duty drawback provisions as well as preferential treatment of the EU and the Arab League. There are no data on tariff collections on services, reflecting the absence of formal trade taxes, and we take their tariff rates to be zero. This treatment is the same as that in Chatti (2000), while Brown et al. (1997) assume there are no barriers to trade in Tunisian services.

Table 3 lists our estimated price wedges due to service barriers, which are the key parameters to be altered in the simulations. Mode 1 restrictions on cross-border trade are treated as ad valorem tariff-equivalent non-tariff barriers. These are simply set to zero in the liberalization exercises. Sectors listed as non-traded (indicated by nt) remain non-traded post-liberalization. In terms of mode 3, we would ideally like to estimate the impact that services barriers have on both price markups and on resource costs to distinguish between the pro-competitive effects and the

Table 2
Benchmark trade shares and tariffs

Sectors	EU trade share (%)		Trade-weighted import tariff	
	Imports	Exports	EU	Rest of world
Agriculture	38.7	68.7	13.5	13.0
Process foods	55.3	71.9	17.6	18.5
Chemicals and glass	48.8	24.0	21.1	23.6
Non-ferrous metals	57.7	70.4	15.3	21.2
Metalwork	67.8	58.8	15.3	17.5
Machinery	77.0	86.0	6.5	8.5
Automobiles and trucks	87.6	40.8	6.3	10.8
Automobile parts	57.1	71.0	0.1	1.7
Electrical parts	66.4	50.4	4.3	7.8
Electronics	66.4	50.4	4.3	7.8
Household appliances	66.4	50.4	4.3	7.8
Chemicals	75.7	39.2	9.0	10.3
Clothing and textiles	92.3	94.8	17.7	21.6
Leather	93.3	96.6	25.1	28.3
Wood	41.1	66.7	16.4	16.6
Paper	74.4	20.6	11.1	5.3
Plastics	72.9	28.0	14.5	18.7
Other manufacturing	72.9	76.2	8.1	15.8
Mining	30.6	86.0	17.4	2.5
Petroleum	63.3	38.7	12.2	20.2
Services	70.0	76.0		

Table 3
Barriers to trade in services (NTB ad valorem price equivalent %)

	Mode 1	Mode 3
	Cross-border trade	Foreign presence
Construction	*nt*	3
Distribution	*nt*	5
Transportation	50	3
Communications	200	30
Hotel	*nt*	3
Restaurant	*nt*	3
Finance	30	30
Insurance	50	50
Business, insurance and leasing	10	10
Real estate	10	10
Repair	nt	3
Health and education	nt	nt
Public	nt	nt
Other services	nt	nt

nt—non-traded modes of supply.

cost-reduction effects. Warren and Findlay (2000) suggested computing the pro-competitive impacts using price–cost margins (or "net interest margins"). We would also like to capture the cost-reduction effects by comparing actual costs to a constructed estimate of costs if services were provided according to a 'world's best-practiced' cost function. Unfortunately, none of these measurements are attainable for Tunisia, as is the case for most countries.

The services barriers given in Table 3 are based on industry studies in Tunisia, extensive discussions with Tunisian industry experts, country economists and government officials, and Zarrouk (2000). The financial services barriers estimates are taken from our observation that the level of monetary intermediation in the banking system is about 30% lower than in comparable countries (Bahlous and Nabli, 2000) and on the estimation of Goaied (1999) of the cost inefficiencies in the financial sector. This is in line with the estimates of Kalirajan et al. (2000) for the banking sectors in Chile, Singapore, South Korea, and Thailand. The price wedges in insurance, communications, and transportation reflect the high level of benchmark regulation in those sectors and comparisons with markets in similar countries (Vittas, 1995; World Bank, 2000). The distribution and retail sectors show large inefficiencies and are very fragmented, making our 5% inefficiency measure conservative. Many professional services are subject to a nationality requirement, thus restricting foreign participation, and it is likely that our 10% estimated price wedge is low. While the construction, hotel, and restaurant sectors are viewed here as already substantially liberalized and subject to a small price-cost wedge, foreign participation remains subject to the investment code and projects are granted upon approval of a *Cahier des Charges*. Remaining sectors (health and education, public services, and other services) are taken to be exempt from potential liberalization.

It is important to note that these price wedges, while not constituting formal tariffs, do serve to restrict cross-border trade (mode 1) in services. Further, they increase costs of producing and trading other goods through the input–output structure. Thus, for example, the high costs in telecommunications make it relatively difficult for Tunisian exporters to sell textiles and carpets abroad through Internet services and telephone contacts. In this regard, our approach captures the cost impacts that would arise from modeling service tariffs.

154   *D.E. Konan, K.E. Maskus / Journal of Development Economics 81 (2006) 142–162*

5. Results

The liberalization scenarios considered can be broken down in several ways. First, liberalization of investment barriers in services is considered. Sensitivity analysis demonstrates the importance of the decomposition of the price wedge into resource-using versus rent-generating barriers. The second step is to distinguish between liberalization of border barriers and investment barriers, broadly. Next, the impacts of liberalization are broken down on a sectoral basis. The final set of scenarios compares the impact of services liberalization to that of traditional liberalization of trade in goods.

Note that we do not consider any reciprocal liberalization in exporting regions. It is possible that Tunisia will experience efficiency gains from the EU Association Agreement, its membership in the WTO, and any FDI preferences that may exist in the Arab League. In particular, we could expect large benefits from a decision by the European Union to permit greater temporary movement of service providers (mode 4), given that in 1995 approximately 480,000 Tunisian migrant workers lived there and contributed remittances constituting 34% of Tunisian GDP (Jbili and Enders, 1996). However, our focus is to isolate the potential gains from unilateral services liberalization associated with competition and efficiency.

Thus, Table 4 presents potential impacts of lifting barriers to foreign investment in services (mode 3 delivery). As discussed in the previous section, investment barriers are assumed to drive an observable wedge between price and marginal cost. Unobserved is the decomposition of the wedge into two sources of distortion: rent-generating (cartel effect) and resource-using (inefficiency effect). Four benchmark possibilities are considered in Table 4. First (column one), assume that barriers to foreign investment solely preserve a domestic cartel and generate pure economic rents for Tunisian interests. That is, Tunisian service producers use world-class technologies and face costs equivalent to those of the low-cost world producer. Upon liberalization, foreign entry is assumed to eliminate the price-wedge as markets become competitive. Domestic rents are completely dissipated to the benefit of Tunisian services consumers. The result is a modest gain in welfare of the representative household of one-third of 1%, measured as equivalent variation in the representative agent's real income.

Table 4
Liberalization of foreign direct investment in services under alternative assumptions on benchmark investment barriers

	Rent scenario (1)	Baseline scenario (2)	Mixed scenario (3)	Inefficiency scenario(4)
Macroeconomic variables (% change)				
Welfare, household income (EV)	0.33	4.00	4.31	7.68
Consumer price index (CPI)	−7.09	−7.11	−7.11	−7.13
Real returns to labor	4.39	3.20	3.24	2.04
Real returns to capital	6.55	6.99	6.97	7.43
Labor turnover	3.44	3.42	3.40	3.79
Capital turnover	4.87	4.90	4.92	5.06
Production (share of GDP)				
Agriculture (bench=19.5%)	21.1	21.2	21.2	21.3
Manufacturing (32.8%)	28.5	28.7	28.7	28.9
Mining and utilities (7.0%)	6.8	6.8	6.8	6.7
Services (40.7%)	43.6	43.3	43.3	43.1

D.E. Konan, K.E. Maskus / Journal of Development Economics 81 (2006) 142–162   155

At the other extreme (column four), assume services markets are perfectly competitive in the benchmark, but that Tunisian firms do not employ world-class production techniques and are thus inefficient. Entry by foreign firms introduces cost-saving innovations and services prices fall. Welfare increases dramatically, by nearly 8%. This large difference from the initial benchmark case reflects the fact that elimination of a pure rent wedge generates a small net gain in efficiency from resource reallocation, but most of the gross gains are transfers from the prior rent stream earned by the representative agent.[17] In both cases consumer prices fall about 7%. Note that while both scenarios increase returns to both labor and capital (non-labor value added), labor gains relatively more in the pure rent-wedge case. This suggests that one effect of the protected cartel is to restrain wages in relation to what they would be under full efficiency. Capital gains are relatively larger when the pure cost wedge is removed.

Two additional scenarios involve combinations of rent-generating distortions and benchmark inefficiencies within services sectors. In the "baseline scenario," it is assumed that the price-wedge is an equal combination of the rent-generating and resource-using distortions (column 2 of Table 4). Welfare impacts mix efficiency gains with rent losses for the representative agent. The result is a 4% increase in welfare and a 7% fall in the consumer price index. Gains from liberalization are skewed toward capital, the price of which increases 7%. Five percent of the capital stock changes sector of employment. Real returns to labor increase by 3% and 3% of the labor force changes sector of employment.

The 'mixed' scenario, considers an environment where the composition of the price–cost wedge varies across sectors (column 3 of Table 4). The margin attributed to rents is assumed to be 33% in relatively competitive sectors, including construction, distribution, hotels, restaurants, real estate, and repair services. The remaining 67% is consumed in cost inefficiencies. Rents account for 67% of the wedge in communications. The margin in remaining sectors, transportation, finance, insurance and business, is assumed to be evenly distributed between rents and inefficiency costs. Foreign ownership liberalization improves welfare by 4.3% increase in equivalent variation and lowers the CPI by 7.11%. Real returns to labor and capital improve by 3.24% and 6.99%, respectively. Interestingly, the macroeconomic outcome closely resembles that of the 'baseline scenario,' which provides support for taking baseline conditions as a reasonable approximation for further analysis.

The bottom part of Table 4 indicates impacts on major sectoral production shares. The figures in parentheses in the left-most part indicate benchmark output shares before any liberalization. Liberalization itself tends to favor relative output expansion in agriculture and services, while restraining the manufacturing and mining shares. Thus, the initial structure of protection for services actually restrains domestic output in that sector. The remaining columns compare these shares across FDI-liberalization cases. While these shares are essentially stable across benchmark assumptions, moving from the rent-wedge case to the efficiency-wedge case slightly favors agriculture and manufacturing, while reducing the share of services.

Table 5 provides liberalization scenarios by the two modes of service delivery considered, assuming an equal split of price markups between rents and costs (baseline scenario) in the benchmark. Assume that Tunisia eliminates all border barriers (mode 1 barriers) on tradable services, and does so on a non-discriminatory or most-favored-nation (MFN) basis. This would raise welfare, as measured by equivalent variation in the representative agent's real income, by about 1.2%. While both factors would gain in terms of real returns, the benefits would be larger

---

[17] As discussed in Anderson and van Wincoop (2001), liberalization of trade costs that generate rents for home agents have smaller welfare impacts than liberalization of "real" trade costs that absorb resources.

Table 5
Baseline services liberalization scenarios

	Border liberalization (mode 1)	Investment liberalization (mode 3)	Full services liberalization (mode 1 and 3)
Macroeconomic variables (% change)			
Welfare, household income (EV)	1.22	4.00	5.30
Consumer price index	−1.02	−7.11	−8.04
Real returns to labor	0.57	3.19	4.23
Real returns to capital	1.32	6.99	8.23
Labor turnover	0.78	3.42	3.73
Capital turnover	0.98	4.90	5.35
Production (share of GDP)			
Agriculture (bench= 19.5%)	19.9	21.2	21.4
Manufacturing (32.8%)	31.7	28.7	28.2
Mining and utilities (7.0%)	7.1	6.8	6.8
Services (40.7%)	41.3	43.3	43.6

for capital (a 1.32% increase in price), with the real wage increasing by less than 1%. In terms of factor adjustment, 0.8% of the labor force and 1% of capital would turn over industry of employment.

The investment liberalization (mode 3) scenario shown in column 2 of Table 5 is the same as that discussed above (column 2 of Table 4). Finally, the aggregate impact of liberalizing both investment barriers and border barriers (modes one and three) is slightly more than additive as shown in column 3, raising welfare by 5.3%. Note that roughly 75.5% of estimated welfare gains may be attributed to investment liberalization, while 23.0% are due to border liberalization. This leaves a small positive residual gain of 1.5% reflecting the fact that both types of barriers together interact to generate a larger income loss than they would separately. It is interesting that this interaction process affects labor and capital differently. The individual liberalization impacts on the real wage sum to less than the joint impact of full liberalization, suggesting that the barriers interact to restrain wages. The opposite is true for the real price of capital. Finally, note in the bottom panel that any policy reform expands the share of services compared to the initial benchmark. However, mode 1 liberalization favors manufacturing and mining over full liberalization in mode 1 and mode 3, which favors agriculture and services. Indeed, full services liberalization would increase the services share of GDP from 40.7% to 43.6%, a large shift in relative output.

It is possible also to consider the gains from liberalizing individual service sectors, as reported in Table 6.[18] For this purpose we compute the impacts of liberalizing both mode 1 and mode 3 delivery options in six of the 11 tradable service sectors. About 41% of the welfare gains of full liberalization may be attributed to reforms in financial and transportation sectors. The impact of liberalization in business services, distribution, and communications are also substantial. Note that these individual trade reforms are not neutral with respect to factor prices. Opening up the construction sector would actually reduce the real wage moderately.

---

[18] Note that sector-level reforms are assumed to occur in isolation while full liberalization entails the simultaneous liberalization of all modeled service sectors. The aggregate impact does not equal the sum of the sectoral impacts due to interactions between sectors with joint liberalization.

Table 6
Baseline services liberalization (Mode 1 and Mode 3), by sector

	Communications	Construction	Transportation	Business, insurance, and leasing	Distribution	Finance	All service sectors
Welfare (EV)	0.46	0.32	1.09	0.60	0.44	1.08	5.30
Real returns to labor	0.90	−0.13	0.62	0.66	1.23	0.60	4.23
Real returns to capital	0.46	0.10	1.44	1.69	0.54	2.29	8.23
Labor turnover	0.35	0.15	1.03	1.34	0.68	1.84	3.73
Capital turnover	0.40	0.11	1.23	1.89	0.89	2.62	5.35

Capital income would gain significantly from liberalization of transportation, business services, and finance.

The final set of scenarios compares liberalization of goods and services. Goods-trade liberalization is modeled as a non-discriminatory and unilateral elimination of the commodity tariffs given in Table 2. Results are shown in Table 7. Household welfare is estimated to increase by 1.5%, in contrast to the 5.3% gain from full services liberalization. As Stolper–Samuelson theory would predict, the gains are largely experienced by the abundant factor, labor, while there is relatively little change in the real returns to other value added. The real wage increases nearly 19% while returns to capital increase 3.5%. Goods trade involves a shift of production to sectors in which Tunisia demonstrates a comparative advantage. Thus, factor turnover is relatively high at 10% for both workers and capital. There is a significant increase in the manufacturing share of total output from 32.8% in the benchmark to 42.8% in the free goods-trade environment. Agriculture declines substantially as a relative component of output, as do services.

Liberalizing service barriers and goods tariffs simultaneously yield a potential gain in welfare of 6.7%. These gains are less than the sum available under the isolated liberalization packages, indicating that there is a slightly offsetting interaction between the two commitments. Gains from joint liberalization, however, are more evenly distributed across labor and capital than they are in either individual reform. Thus, removal of goods tariffs strongly favors labor while

Table 7
Comparing goods and services liberalization (baseline case)

	Goods liberalization (eliminate tariffs)	Services liberalization (mode 1 and 3)	Goods and services liberalization
Macroeconomic variables (% change)			
Welfare, household income (EV)	1.52	5.30	6.67
Consumer price index	−1.07	−8.04	−9.07
Real returns to labor	18.93	4.23	17.67
Real returns to capital	3.46	8.23	13.61
Labor turnover	9.83	3.73	3.40
Capital turnover	10.38	5.35	5.89
Production (share of GDP)			
Agriculture (bench = 19.5%)	15.3	21.4	19.1
Manufacturing (32.8%)	42.8	28.2	33.6
Mining and utilities (7.0%)	5.2	6.8	5.6
Services (40.7%)	36.7	43.6	41.7

removal of service barriers favors capital. Both factors experience significant real price increases with joint liberalization.

That the blended goods and services liberalization package does not generate gains for the abundant factor (labor) at the expense of the scarce factor (capital), as Stolper–Samuelson trade theory would predict, is remarkable. It is also notable that the structure of output is closer to that with an isolated services liberalization than to one with solely goods tariff elimination, as noted in the bottom panel. The productivity gains associated with lower service costs raise real returns for both factors and make service-intensive sectors relatively more globally competitive. Thus, in an important sense, removing commodity tariffs without services liberalization tends to "over-adjust" the economy toward manufacturing and away from agriculture and services. Freeing up services moves the structure back toward the fully efficient outcome in the final column. Indeed, a pure goods-trade liberalization results in a much greater movement of labor and more dramatic changes in the composition of production.

6. Conclusions

This paper considers how services liberalization differs from that of goods liberalization using an applied general equilibrium model of the Tunisian economy. Not surprisingly, goods-trade liberalization reorients production towards manufacturing (especially in textile and electronics) in line with Tunisia's benchmark comparative advantage. In contrast, the overall composition of production with services liberalization remains fairly stable, with only slight increases in manufacturing and service provision and a small decrease in agriculture and mining. The gains under services liberalization are more evenly distributed across factors than are those under goods liberalization, where gains are strongly concentrated in the hands of workers (the abundant factor). Fewer workers are required to change positions to accommodate services liberalization, implying less impact on frictional unemployment. Thus, we might expect less political resistance to services liberalization relative to goods liberalization.

Interestingly, combining goods and services liberalization appears to offer the best of both worlds. The gains from jointly freeing up goods and services are nearly additive in the two independent reforms. Yet the overall structure of the economy remains similar to that of the benchmark, with relatively small changes in the employment location of workers. Services liberalization therefore eases the adjustment costs involved in the liberalization of goods trade as the expansion of economic activity would no longer be restrained by the lagging competitiveness of Tunisia's service sector.

The potential welfare implications of services liberalization are clearly positive and substantial. Even given modest assumptions about the current environment for trade in services, welfare (measured as equivalent variation) and GDP are both estimated to increase more than 7%. These gains are more than three times the magnitude of the estimated gains from goods-trade liberalization alone. Further, perhaps 75% of services liberalization gains may be achieved from the liberalization of foreign investment barriers that impede mode 3 delivery of services. Granting the right of establishment to foreign firms stands to increase real household income by 4%. In contrast, liberalization of cross-border trade in services (mode 1) results in a roughly one-percent gain in household income.

The finding that Tunisia would gain from unilateral services liberalization, with balanced gains to factors, but has failed to do so clearly suggests that political-economy constraints are important. It is likely that significant rents accrue to incumbent service providers, which are able to block market deregulation. In this context, the government may be faced with the prospect of compensating these incumbents in some fashion to effect true change. One means might be to pursue reciprocal services liberalization in major export markets while supporting efficiency-enhancing investments in Tunisian services. The GATS approach has yet to effect significant opening of important services in the EU or the Arab League countries that would benefit Tunisian exporters. One obvious approach would be to encourage the EU to provide greater opportunities for temporary workers from Tunisia through mode 4 negotiations. While this change would benefit Tunisian laborers it would not directly compensate existing domestic service providers. Thus, some of the income gains to workers might need to be transferred to service incumbents to buy out their resistance to reforms.

We stress that the uncertainties surrounding estimated price wedges and the allocation of those wedges between rent and production inefficiency deserve further exploration. Improved estimates of service barriers are critical for a more accurate determination of the magnitude of the potential impacts of liberalization. Still, recall that conservative assumptions were made here about the existing distortions and the potential competitive effects and efficiency improvements with liberalization. It is likely that a liberalizing reform would bring even greater gains than those reported here.

Acknowledgements

We gratefully acknowledge Sherry Stephenson, Bernard Hoekman, Mohamed Goaied, Ari Van Assche, and Dominique van der Mensbrugghe for valuable discussions throughout the writing of this paper. We also thank Robert Lipsey, participants at the European Trade Study Group in Nottingham, UK, and two anonymous referees for constructive comments.

Appendix A. Model equations and notation

A. Production

1. Value added function	$V_i = [a_{Li}L_i^{(\sigma i - 1)/\sigma i} + a_{Ki}K_i^{(\sigma i - 1)/\sigma i}]^{\sigma i/(\sigma i - 1)}$
2. Imported intermediates	$M_{iN} = [\Sigma_r \delta_{ri}m_{riN}^{(\eta i - 1)/\eta i}]^{\eta i/(\eta i - 1)}$
3. Composite intermediate	$z_{ji} = [\gamma_{di}d_{ji}^{(\eta j - 1)/\eta j} + \gamma_{mi}m_{ji}^{(\eta j - 1)/\eta j}]^{\eta j/(\eta j - 1)}$
4. Final goods technology	$Y_i = \min[z_{1i}/a_{1i}, .. z_{ni}/a_{ni}, V_i/a_{VA}]$
5. Domestic and foreign sales	$Y_i = [\alpha_{Di}D_i^{(ei-1)/ei} + \alpha_{Xi}X_i^{(ei-1)/ei}]^{ei/(ei-1)}$
6. Export allocation	$X_i = [\Sigma_r \beta_{ri}X_{ri}^{(ei-1)/ei}]^{ei/(ei-1)}$
7. Marginal cost condition	$(1+\lambda_i)c_iY_i = \Sigma_j(1+v_j)p_jd_{ji} + \Sigma_j\Sigma_r(1+u_j+t_{rj})p_{rj}^m m_{rji} + (w_KK_i + w_LL_{1i})$

B. Utility

8. Utility function	$U = \Pi_iC_i^{bi}; \Sigma_ib_i = 1$
9. Domestic and import consumption (applies also to G_i and I_i^F)	$C_i = [\phi_{Di}D_{iC}^{(\psi i - 1)/\psi i} + \phi_{MiC}M_{iC}^{(\psi i - 1)/\psi i}]^{\psi i/\psi i - i}$
10. Import allocation (applies also to M_{iG} and M_{i1}^F)	$M_{iC} = [\Sigma_r\delta_{ri}M_{riC}^{(\eta i - 1)/\eta i}]^{\eta i/\eta i - 1}$

C. Constraints and balancing items

11. Agent's budget constraint	$\Sigma_i\tilde{p}_i^CC_i = w_K\bar{E}_K + w_L\Sigma_iL_i + - \Sigma_i\tilde{p}_i^{IF}I_i^F - \Sigma_ip_iI_i^1 - r^FK^F - D + \Sigma_i v_iY_i$
12. Government budget constraint	$\Sigma_i\tilde{p}_i^GG_i = D + \Sigma_i\tau_{Vi}\tilde{p}_i^CV_i + \Sigma_i\Sigma_rtp_{ri}^m(M_{riC} + M_{ril}^F)$
13. Current-account balance	$0 = \Sigma_r\Sigma_i(1/e)(p_{ri}^mM_{ri} - p_{ri}^xX_{ri} - w_{LL}^FL^F + r^FK^F)$
14. Product market clearance	$S_i = \Sigma_ja_{ij}Y_j + G_i + I_i^F + I_i^1 + C_i$
15. Factor market clearance	$\Sigma_iK_i = \bar{E}_K; \Sigma_iL_i = \bar{E}_{1L}$
16. Zero profits	$p_i D_i + \Sigma_rp_{ri}^xX_{ri} = c_iY_i$
17. Supply value balance	$\tilde{p}_iS_i = \tilde{p}_i^z\Sigma_ja_{ij}(1+v_i)Y_j + \tilde{p}_i^CD_{iC} + \tilde{p}_i^CD_{i1}^F + \tilde{p}_i^GD_{iG} + \tilde{p}_i^{IF}I_i^I + \Sigma_r(1+u_i+t_{ri})p_{ri}^m(M_{riC}+M_{riG}+M_{ri1}^F)$

(continued on next page)

Appendix A (*continued*)

D. Price relationships and identities

18. Components of domestic sales	$D_i = D_{iC} + D_{iI}^F + I_i^1 + D_{iG}$
19. Components of import sales	$M_i = M_{iN} + M_{iC} + M_{iI}^F + M_{iG}$
20. Domestic price of intermediate imports (holds also for imports for G)	$p_{ri}^N = (1 + u_i + t_{ri}) p_{ri}^m$
21. Domestic price of imports for C (holds also for imports for I^F)	$p_{ri}^C = (1 + u_i + t_{ri}) p_{ri}^m$
22. Consumer price of domestic goods (holds also for purchases for I^F)	$p_i^C = (1 + v_i) p_i$
23. Capital-market equilibrium	$\tau_{K1} + w_{K1} = \ldots = \tau_{Kn} + w_{Kn}$ (mobile capital sectors)

List of variables

L_I	Domestic labor inputs, sector i ($i = 1, .., 34$)
K_I	Capital (other value added) inputs, both mobile and immobile
V_I	Value added
M_I	Total imports
M_{ri}	Imports from region r (r = EU, MENA, ROW)
M_{iN}	Imports of commodity i for intermediate use
m_{riN}	Imports for intermediate use from region r (r = EU, MENA, ROW)
z_{ji}	Composite intermediate input of j into i ($j = 1, .., 34$)
d_{ji}, m_{ji}	Intermediate usages of domestic and imported goods
Y_I	Output of good i
D_i, X_i	Output for domestic sales and exports
D_{iC}, D_{iG}, D_{iI}^F	Domestic sales: private and public consumption, capital formation
X_{ri}	Exports of good i to region r
c_i	Index of marginal cost of production
p_i	Domestic producer price index
$\tilde{p}_i^Z, \tilde{p}_i^C, \tilde{p}_i^{IF}, \tilde{p}_i^G$	Domestic price indexes (home and imported prices)
w_K, w_L	Factor price indexes
U	Utility
$\tilde{p}_I$	Composite price index for total domestic supply
C_i, G_i	Private and public consumption
I_i^F, I_i^1	Fixed capital formation and inventory investment
M_{iC}, M_{iG}	Imports for private and public consumption
M_{iI}^F	Imports for fixed capital formation
M_{riC}, M_{riG}	Imports for private and public consumption from region r
M_{riI}^F	Imports for fixed capital formation from region r
K^F	Net payments on foreign capital holdings
e	Real exchange rate (price index for foreign exchange)
B	Current-account balance
D	Government budget deficit (held fixed)
S_I	Supply on domestic market ($D_i + M_i$)
p_{ri}^N	Domestic price index for intermediate imports
p_{ri}^C, p_{ri}^G	Domestic price indexes for imports of private and public consumption
p_{riI}^F	Domestic price index for imports for gross capital formation
p_i^C, p_{iI}^F	Price index for private consumption/fixed capital of domestic goods
p_{ri}	Producer price index for goods exported to region r

List of parameters

σ_i	Substitution elasticity between capital and labor
η_a	Substitution elasticity between intermediates and value added
η_i	Armington elasticity on imports between regions
η_j	Substitution elasticity between domestic and imported intermediates
ε_i	Transformation elasticity between domestic and exported output
e_i	Transformation elasticity on exports between regions
ψ_i	Substitution elasticity between domestic and imported consumption
t_{ri}	Tariff rate on imports from region r ($t_{ri}=0$ for service sectors)
u_i	Resource-using services border barriers ($u_i=0$ for non-service sectors)
v_i	Service rents on output ($v_i=0$ for non-service sectors)
λ_i	Service resource-using barriers on output ($\lambda_i=0$ for non-service sectors)
$\bar{E}_K, \bar{E}_{1L}$	Endowment of capital and labor
p_{ri}^m	Price of imports from region r
p_{ri}^x	Price of exports in region r
r^F	Price of foreign capital payments

References

Anderson, James E., van Wincoop, Eric, 2001. Borders, trade, and welfare. In: Collins, Susan, Rodrik, Dani (Eds.), Brookings Trade Forum, pp. 207–243.

Bahlous, Mejda, Nabli, Mustapha K., 2000. Financial Liberalization and Financing Constraints on the Corporate Sector in Tunisia, Working Paper No 2005, Economic Research Forum for the Arab Countries.

Brown, Drusilla K., Stern, Robert M., 2001. Measurement and modeling of the economic effects of trade and investment barriers in services. Review of International Economics 9, 262–286.

Brown, Drusilla K., Deardorft, Alan V., Stern, Robert M., 1996. The liberalization of services trade: potential impacts in the aftermath of the Uruguay round. In: Martin, Will, Winters, Alan (Eds.), The Uruguay Round and the Developing Countries. Cambridge University Press, Cambridge.

Brown, Drusilla K., Deardorff, Alan V., Stern, Robert M., 1997. Some economic effects of the free trade agreement between Tunisia and the European Union. In: Galal, Ahmed, Hoekman, Bernard (Eds.), Regional Partners in Global Markets: Limits and Possibilities of the Euro–Med Agreements. Centre for Economic Policy Research, London.

Chatti, Rim, 2000. General Equilibrium Assessment of Trade Liberalization Effects under Cournot Oligopoly Market Structures: The Case of Tunisia, Economic Research Forum for the Arab Countries, Iran, and Turkey. Working Paper, vol. 2009.

Dee, Philippa, Hanslow, Kevin, 2001. Multilateral liberalization of services trade. In: Stern, Robert M. (Ed.), Services in the International Economy. University of Michigan Press, Ann Arbor.

Dee, Philippa, Hardin, Alexis, Holmes, Leanne, 2000. Issues in the application of CGE models to services trade liberalization. In: Findlay, Christopher, Warren, Tony (Eds.), Impediments to Trade in Services: Measurement and Policy Implications. Routledge, London.

De Melo, Jaime, Robinson, Sherman, 1989. Product differentiation and the treatment of foreign trade in computable general equilibrium models of small economies. Journal of International Economics 27, 47–67.

Francois, Joseph, 1999. A Gravity Approach to Measuring Services Protection (Manuscript). Erasmus University.

Francois, Joseph, Wooton, Ian, 2001. Market structure, trade liberalization, and the GATS. European Journal of Political Economics 17, 389–402.

Goaied, Mohamed, 1999. Cost-Frontier Analysis of Tunisian Commercial Banking Sectors (manuscript).

Harris, Richard G., 1984. Applied general equilibrium analysis of small open economies with scale economies and imperfect competition. American Economic Review 74, 1016–1032.

Hertel, Thomas W., 1997. Global Trade Analysis: Modeling and Applications. Cambridge University Press, New York.

Hertel, Thomas W., 2000. Potential gains from reducing trade barriers in manufacturing, services and agriculture. Multilateral Trade Negotiations: Issues for the Millenium Round. Federal Reserve Bank of St. Louis, St. Louis.

Hoekman, Bernard, 1995. Tentative First Steps: An Assessment of the Uruguay Round Agreement on Services. Policy Research Working Paper, vol. 1455. World Bank, Washington DC.

Hoekman, Bernard, 2000. The next round of services negotiations: identifying priorities and options. Multilateral Trade Negotiations: Issues for the Millenium Round. Federal Reserve Bank of St. Louis, St. Louis.

Hoekman, Bernard, Djankov, Simeon, 1996. Catching Up with Eastern Europe? The European Union's Mediterranean Free Trade Initiative. Policy Research Working Paper, vol. 1562. World Bank, Washington DC.

Hoekman, Bernard, Konan, Denise Eby, 2000. Rents, red tape, and regionalism: economic effects of deeper Integration. In: Hoekman, Bernard, Zarrouk, Jamel (Eds.), Catching Up with the Competition: Trade Policy Challenges and Options for the Middle East and North Africa. University of Michigan Press, Ann Arbor.

Institute National De La Statistique (INS), 1998. Les Comptes de la Nation, agregats et tableaux d'ensemble 1993–1997. INS Press, Tunis.

Jbili, Abdelali, Enders, Klaus, 1996. The Association Agreement between Tunisia and the European Union (available at). www.worldbank.org/fandd/english/0996/articles/040996.htm.

Kalirajan, Kaleeswaran, McGuire, Greg, Nguyen-Hong, Duc, Schuele, Michael, 2000. The price impact of restrictions on banking services. In: Findlay, Christopher, Warren, Tony (Eds.), Impediments to Trade in Services: Measurement and Policy Implications. Routledge, London.

Karsenty, Guy, 2000. Assessing trade in services by mode of supply. In: Sauve, Pierre, Stern, Robert M. (Eds.), GATS 2000: New Directions in Services Trade Liberalization. Brookings Institution Press, Washington DC.

Konan, Denise Eby, Maskus, Keith E., 2000. Joint trade liberalization and tax reform in a small open economy: the case of Egypt. Journal of Development Economics 61, 365–392.

Lipsey, Robert, 2001. The new economy: theory and measurement. Paper for 27th Annual PAFTAD Conference: The New Economy: Challenges for East Asia and the Pacific, Canberra, Australia.

Markusen, James R., 1989. Trade in producer services and in other specialized intermediate inputs. American Economic Review 79, 85–95.

Markusen, James R., Rutherford, Thomas F., Tarr, David, in press. Trade and Direct Investment in Producer Services and the Domestic Market for Expertise, Canadian Journal of Economics.

Maskus, Keith E., Lahouel, Mohamed, 2000. Competition policy and intellectual property rights in developing countries. The World Economy 23, 595–611.

Robinson, Sherman, Wang, Zhi, Martin, Will, 2002. Capturing the implications of services trade liberalization. Economic Systems Research 14, 3–33.

Rodrik, Dani, 2001. Trading in Illusions. Foreign Policy, 54–62 (March/April).

Romer, Paul M., 2004. New goods, old theory, and the welfare costs of trade restrictions. Journal of Development Economics 43, 5–38.

Rutherford, Thomas, Tarr, David, 2002. Trade liberalization, product variety and growth in a small open economy: a quantitative assessment. Journal of International Economics 56, 247–272.

Rutherford, Thomas, Rutstrom, E.E., Tarr, David, 1995. The Free Trade Agreement Between Tunisia and the European Union (manuscript). World Bank.

Stern, Robert M., 2002. Quantifying barriers to trade in services. In: Hoekman, Bernard, Mattoo, Aaditya, English, Philip (Eds.), Development, Trade and the WTO: A Handbook. World Bank, Washington DC.

Swiss, Re, 1999. World Insurance in 1997: Booming Life Business, but Stagnant Non-Life Business. Sigma, vol. 3/99.

Varoudakis, Aristomene, Rossotto, Carlo Maria, 2001. Regulatory Reform and Performance in Telecommunications: Unrealized Potential in the MENA Countries. World Bank. (manuscript).

Vittas, Dimitri, 1995. The Insurance Sector in Tunisia. Working Paper. Financial Sector Development Department, World Bank. (March).

Warren, Tony, Findlay, Christopher, 2000. Measuring impediments to trade in services. In: Sauve, Pierre, Stern, Robert M. (Eds.), GATS 2000: New Directions in Services Trade Liberalization. Brookings Institution Press, Washington DC.

Whalley, John, 2003. Liberalization of China's Key Service Sectors Following WTO Accession: Some Scenarios and Issues of Measurement. Industry Canada. (manuscript).

World Bank, 2000. Tunisia: Social and Structural Review 2000: Integrating into the World Economy and Sustaining Economic and Social Progress. World Bank, Washington, DC.

World Bank, 2001. Republic of Tunisia: Information and Communications Technology Strategy Report, Washington D.C.

World Bank, 2004. Republic of Tunisia: Development Policy Review: Making Deeper Trade Integration Work for Growth and Jobs, Washington DC.

Zarrouk, Jamel, 2000. Regulatory regimes and trade costs. In: Hoekman, Bernard, Zarrouk, Jamel (Eds.), Catching Up with the Competition: Trade Opportunities and Challenges for Arab Countries. University of Michigan Press, Ann Arbor.

[18]

THE IMPACT ON RUSSIA OF WTO ACCESSION AND THE DDA: THE IMPORTANCE OF LIBERALIZATION OF BARRIERS AGAINST FDI IN SERVICES FOR GROWTH AND POVERTY REDUCTION

Thomas Rutherford, David Tarr,
and Oleksandr Shepotylo

Summary

Taking price changes from the GTAP model of world trade, this chapter uses a small, open economy computable general equilibrium (CGE) comparative static model of the Russian economy to assess the impact of free trade in the rest of the world (ROW) and a successful completion of the Doha Development Agenda (DDA) on the Russian economy and especially on the poor. Those results are compared with the impact of Russian accession to the WTO on income distribution and the poor. The model incorporates all 55,000 households from the Russian *Household Budget Survey* (HBS) as "real" households in the model. Crucially, given the importance of FDI liberalization as part of Russian WTO accession, FDI and Dixit-Stiglitz endogenous productivity effects from liberalization of import barriers against goods and FDI in services are also included.

468   Poverty and the WTO: Impacts of the Doha Development Agenda

It is estimated that Russian WTO accession in the medium run will result in gains averaged over all Russian households equal to 7.3 percent of Russian consumption (with a standard deviation of 2.2 percent of consumption), with virtually all households gaining. The analysis finds that ROW free trade would result in a weighted average gain to households in Russia of 0.2 percent of consumption, with a standard deviation of 0.2 percent of consumption; a successful completion of the DDA would result in a weighted average loss to households of -0.3 percent of consumption (with a standard deviation of 0.2 percent of consumption). Russia, as a net food importer, loses from subsidy elimination, and the gains to Russia from tariff cuts in other countries are too small to offset these losses. These results strongly support the view that Russia's own liberalization is more important than improvements in market access as a result of reforms in tariffs or subsidies in ROW. Foremost among the Russian reforms is liberalization of barriers against FDI in business services.

These reasons for these results are (a) barriers to FDI in services are high relative to Russian barriers to imports of goods, so liberalization of services is crucial to the realization of large gains from WTO accession; (b) Russian exports are dominated by energy products, on which ROW tariffs are low, so there is little new market access provided to Russia from the ROW liberalization of these products; (c) Russia imports a lot of food products, which are subsidized on world markets and whose prices will rise in the DDA; and (d) FDI in services and endogenous productivity effects in imperfectly competitive goods and services sectors are crucial, because this chapter shows that a constant returns to scale (CRS) model would produce much smaller gains.

Introduction

There are two potentially quite important events on the horizon for Russia with respect to the WTO. First, Russia is negotiating accession to the WTO and, as of late 2004, had signed bilateral agreements on its accession with at least 12 WTO members, including the EU, China, and the Republic of Kórea. At the same time, the members of the WTO are negotiating tariff and subsidy cuts under the DDA. As a result of WTO member countries' changes in tariffs and subsidies agreed under the DDA, Russia will face a new set of prices for its exports and imports on world markets. This chapter evaluates the impact of the likely changes in world prices as a result of a conclusion of the DDA (and of ROW free trade) on Russia and on poverty in Russia. These effects are also compared with the impact on Russia of Russian WTO accession.

Russian WTO accession is primarily a set of commitments by Russia to liberalize its own trade and, crucially, open up its FDI regime in business services. The comparison of Russian WTO accession with the impact of the DDA on Russia then devolves fundamentally to a question of whether Russia can gain more from trade and subsidy reform in ROW or from its own liberalization.

This chapter uses the model that the authors have developed through two earlier papers. Jensen, Rutherford, and Tarr (forthcoming) developed a small, open economy model of Russia that incorporated FDI in business services with Dixit-Stiglitz, love-of-variety, endogenous productivity effects from investment and trade liberalization in business services and imperfectly competitive goods sectors. Substantial gains for Russia were found from its WTO accession, deriving primarily from the liberalization of barriers against FDI in services. This chapter shows that a CRS model without FDI in business services (which the authors believe is an inappropriate model specification, given the importance of FDI commitments in Russian WTO negotiations) would produce estimated gains that are dramatically smaller. In Rutherford, Tarr, and Shepotylo (2004) (RT&S), the Jensen, Rutherford, and Tarr model is extended by incorporating all the 55,000 households of the Russian HBS as agents in the general equilibrium model. That is, the chapter utilizes a "real household" model of the Russian economy with endogenous productivity effects. RT&S show that WTO accession could be expected to benefit virtually all the poor, but an inappropriately specified CRS model, without liberalization of barriers against FDI in services, and endogenous productivity effects would produce much smaller average welfare gains and the wrong sign for about 7 percent of the Russian population.

This chapter uses the same model and dataset as that used in RT&S to examine the impact on poverty in Russia of the DDA and as a result of ROW free trade. Crucially, these impacts are compared with the impact on Russia of its own liberalization through the commitments it will make as part of its WTO accession. This process enables assessment of the relative benefits to Russia of liberalization of countries in ROW of their tariffs or subsidies with liberalization in Russia of its barriers against FDI and goods imports. The impacts on Russia overall are examined at the decile level, as well as on the entire distribution of Russian households through the real household model of Russia.

As with the other country case studies in this volume, the starting point for the analysis of the DDA and ROW free trade impacts is the vectors of percentage changes in the price of exports and imports for Russia as a result of the completion of the DDA or ROW free trade. These vectors are derived from simulations of the Global Trade Analysis Project (GTAP) model presented in chapter 3. These new price vectors are taken as exogenous shifts in the terms of trade (TOT) facing Russia.

The mean welfare gain to Russia from its WTO accession, averaged over all households, is 7.3 percent of Russian consumption (with a standard deviation of 2.2 percent of consumption) in the medium run. It is found that virtually all households obtain at least some increase in their income. Nearly all the household gains fall between 2.0 percent and 25 percent of consumption. Poor households do slightly better than rich households because the wage rate of unskilled labor rises more than the return on capital. If an inappropriately specified CRS model were used, the gains from WTO accession would be only about 1.2 percent of consumption, with about 7 percent of households expected to lose—that is, the WTO accession estimates are decisively affected by liberalization of barriers against FDI in business services sectors and endogenous productivity effects in business services and goods.

Regarding the impact on Russia of cuts in the tariffs and subsidies of other countries, it is found that ROW free trade (which encompasses free trade in goods outside Russia and the elimination of export subsidies, with domestic support for agriculture retained) would result in a weighted average gain to households in Russia of 0.2 percent of consumption, with a standard deviation of 0.2 percent of consumption. The analysis suggests that a successful completion of the DDA (which is modeled as the elimination of export subsidies, substantial cuts in tariffs outside Russia,[1] and reduction in domestic support for agriculture) would result in a weighted average loss to households of -0.3 percent of consumption. Russia, as a net food importer, loses from subsidy elimination, and the gains to Russia from tariff cuts in other countries are too small to offset these losses (in part because Russian exports are dominated by energy products, which face low tariffs in ROW). The impacts on Russia from these TOT changes tend to favor neither the rich nor the poor.

Thus, in the medium term, what other countries in the WTO do in terms of their tariff changes or changes in export subsidies or domestic support will have a very small effect on Russian households and poverty. However, it is estimated that virtually all households will gain from Russian WTO accession; these gains are substantial, and they are very slightly progressive.[2] The distribution of gains across the 55,000 households is decisively affected by the inclusion of liberalization of barriers against FDI in business services sectors and endogenous productivity effects in business services and goods. These results strongly support the view that Russia has by far the most to gain from its own liberalization, especially in business services, rather than from improvements in market access as a result of reforms in tariffs or subsidies in ROW. Foremost among the gains from its own liberalization is the gains from liberalization of barriers against FDI in business services. The broader implications here are that developing countries might experience larger gains in poverty reduction if the WTO could more effectively negotiate cuts in barriers against FDI in services.

Despite the significant gains estimated from WTO accession, during a transition period, it is likely that many households with displaced workers will lose as they are forced to seek new employment. This work suggests that there will be a decline in employment in light industry, the food industry, mechanical engineering and metal working, and construction materials. Workers in these sectors will suffer losses from transitional unemployment and will likely incur expenses related to retraining or relocation. Some of the poorest members of the population are ill equipped to handle these transition costs. Thus, despite a likely substantial improvement in the standard of living for almost all Russians after adjustment to the WTO, government safety nets are very important to help with the transition—especially for the poorest members of society.

The model and data are briefly described in the next section. The focus in this chapter is on the evidence for endogenous productivity effects from liberalization of barriers against imports and FDI in services. Results are presented in section 2. Brief conclusions are in the final section.

The Model

A small, open economy CGE model of the Russian economy with 55,000 households is used. As noted, this chapter builds on two earlier papers where the model and data are documented. Jensen, Rutherford, and Tarr (forthcoming) describe the structure of the single representative agent model, disaggregation of the official Russian input-output table, and calculation of the Russian tariff and export tax rates. RT&S extend the model to incorporate the entire 55,098 households of the Russian HBS.[3] The reader is referred to those papers for more detailed documentation of the model. Given its importance to this chapter, it is worthwhile to briefly summarize some of the important evidence on the liberalization of barriers against FDI in services, productivity impacts of greater variety of imported goods, and the approach to estimating barriers to FDI in Russian business services sectors.

The key modeling features that distinguish this chapter from previous applied general equilibrium (AGE) modeling exercises linking trade and poverty is that FDI in business services and additional varieties of business services are permitted to endogenously increase the productivity of sectors using that service through the Dixit-Stiglitz variety effect (see Markusen, Rutherford, and Tarr [forthcoming] for elaboration). The approach also allows for Dixit-Stiglitz productivity effects in goods, for both final consumers and intermediate use, as explained in Ethier (1982). These features have a fundamental effect on the results for the estimated impact of WTO accession on poverty in Russia.

Competitive Sectors

There are 35 sectors in the model listed in table 16.1. These sectors fall into three categories: competitive sectors producing goods and services, imperfectly competitive goods sectors, and imperfectly competitive services sectors. The structure of production is depicted in figure 16.1. In competitive sectors, price equals marginal costs and imports and domestic goods are differentiated (the Armington assumption). See de Melo and Tarr (1992) for a description of the details of how these sectors are modeled. Protection rates are reported in table 16.2 and will be further discussed below.

Table 16.1.   Structure of Value Added, Factor Shares, Imports, and Exports in Russia [a]

Sectors	Imports[a]		Exports[b]		Value Added (%)	Factor shares as percent of value added[c]		
	Share	Intensity	Share	Intensity		Unskilled Labor (%)	Skilled Labor (%)	Capital (%)
Sectors					100.0	21	63	16
Business services								
Railway transportation	0	1	0	1	3.3	11	85	5
Truck transportation	1	4	0	1	1.5	8	88	4
Pipelines transportation	1	2	0	0	3.6	11	58	31
Maritime transportation	2	52	1	56	0.3	14	81	5
Air transportation	0	8	2	39	0.6	14	84	2
Other transportation	0	2	0	3	1.1	9	85	6
Telecommunications	1	11	0	5	1.2	16	79	5
Financial services	0	3	0	2	1.5	10	86	4
Science and science servicing	0	5	0	6	0.8	35	61	4
Subtotal	5		3		13.9			
Differentiated Goods								
Ferrous metallurgy	4	18	10	37	1.9	9	85	7
Nonferrous metallurgy	2	16	17	55	2.3	12	81	7
Chemical and oil-chemical industry	7	29	8	33	1.8	20	74	7
Mechanical engineering and metal working	27	36	9	17	5.2	30	66	4
Timber and woodworking and pulp and paper industry	2	17	5	31	1.4	17	79	5
Construction materials industry	1	8	0	2	1.6	19	75	5
Light industry	17	69	1	13	0.7	63	32	5
Food industry	21	30	3	6	3.3	17	76	7
Other industries	1	13	0	5	0.6	22	76	3
Subtotal	82		53		18.8			

Table 16.1. (Continued)

	Imports[a]		Exports[b]		Value Added (%)	Factor Shares as Percent of value added[c]		
	Share	Intensity	Share	Intensity		Unskilled Labor (%)	Skilled Labor (%)	Capital (%)
Extractive industries								
Oil extraction	1	8	18	70	2.9	1	12	87
Gas	0	1	15	26	0.9	1	10	89
Coal mining	0	5	1	10	1.1	2	52	47
Subtotal	1		34		4.9			
Constant returns industries								
Electric industry	0	0	0	1	3.6	9	84	6
Oil processing	1	7	6	18	0.8	3	89	8
Other fuel industries	2	3	0	3	0.0	49	33	18
Construction	3	4	0	0	8.6	10	86	4
Agriculture and forestry	0	4	0	1	7.6	47	31	22
Post	2	2	1	9	0.3	15	78	7
Trade	0	1	0	1	22.9	20	53	27
Public catering	1	16	0	2	0.1	19	81	1
Other goods-producing sectors	0	0	0	0	0.8	23	76	1
Communal and consumer services				0	5.6	19	72	9
Public health, sports, and social security	0	0	0	0	3.1	44	52	4
Education, culture, and art	0	1	0	0	4.0	56	40	4
Geology and hydrometeorology	0	0	0	0	0.2	45	52	3
Administration and public associations	0		0	0	4.8	22	76	1
Subtotal	9		7		62.3			

Source: Author's calculations.

Note: Because of rounding, the sum of shares as a percentage does not always equal 100.

a. Share is sector imports as a percentage of economywide imports. Intensity is sector imports as a percentage of sector consumption.

b. Share is defined analogous to imports. Intensity is sector exports as a percentage of sector output.

c. After reconciliation with the HBS.

474 Poverty and the WTO: Impacts of the Doha Development Agenda

Table 16.2. Tariff Rates, Export Tax Rates, Estimated Ad Valorem Equivalence of Barriers to FDI in Services Sectors and Estimated Improved Market Access from WTO Accession (ad valorem in percent by sector)

Sectors		Tariff rates	Export tax rates	Estimated change in export prices from WTO accession	Equivalent % barriers to FDI	
					Base year	Post-WTO accession
ELE	Electric industry	4.5	0.0	0.0		
OLE	Oil Extraction	0.0	7.9	0.0		
OLP	Oil processing	3.8	4.6	0.0		
GAS	Gas	0.5	18.8	0.0		
COA	Coal mining	0.0	0.0	0.0		
OFU	Other fuel industries	2.6	2.6	0.0		
FME	Ferrous metallurgy	2.9	0.4	1.5		
NFM	Nonferrous metallurgy	7.4	5.3	1.5		
CHM	Chemical and oil-chemical industry	7.1	1.6	1.5		
MWO	Mechanical engineering and metalworking	7.2	0.0	0.0		
TPP	Timber and woodworking and pulp and paper industry	9.9	6.9	0.0		
CNM	Construction materials industry	10.6	1.6	0.0		
CLO	Light industry	11.8	4.1	0.5		
FOO	Food industry	11.3	3.1	0.5		
OTH	Other industries	6.4	0.0	0.5		
AGF	Agriculture and forestry	8.2	0.6	0.0		
OIN	Other goods-producing sectors	0.0	0.0	0.5		
TMS	Telecommunications				33	0
SCS	Science and engineering servicing				33	0
FIN	Financial services				36	0
RLW	Railway transportation				33	0
TRK	Truck transportation				33	0
PIP	Pipelines transportation				33	0
MAR	Maritime transportation				95	80
AIR	Air transportation				90	75
TRO	Other transportation				33	0

Source: Authors' estimates.

Figure 16.1.   Production and Allocation of Output

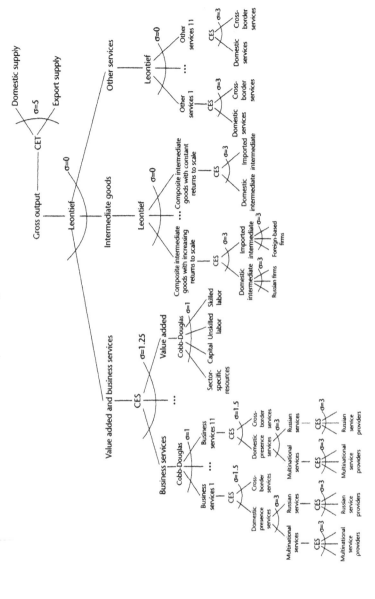

Source: Authors.

476   Poverty and the WTO: Impacts of the Doha Development Agenda

Imperfectly Competitive Sectors

In imperfectly competitive goods sectors, goods are produced with a fixed cost and constant marginal costs. Foreign firms supply the Russian market with production facilities abroad. Symmetry is assumed among domestic firms as well as among foreign firms, but costs differ between domestic and foreign firms. This model has firm-level competition with pricing decisions based on large-group monopolistic competition. The ratio of marginal costs to average costs is assumed fixed, which with the pricing assumption implies that output per firm is fixed. Both final and intermediate users of the output of imperfectly competitive sectors obtain a variety-adjusted unit more cheaply when there are additional varieties on offer via the Dixit-Stiglitz effect. Entry and exit are determined by a zero profit condition.

Business Services Sectors

Business services are supplied both by competitive firms on a cross-border basis and, because many services are more effectively supplied with a domestic presence, by imperfectly competitive firms (both multinational and Russian) that have a domestic presence in Russia. For imperfectly competitive firms, the cost and pricing structure is similar to that of imperfectly competitive goods producers, except that production of services by multinational service providers is done in Russia. Multinational service providers will import some of their technology or management expertise when they decide to establish a domestic presence in Russia. Thus, their cost structure differs from that of Russian service providers. They incur costs related to both imported inputs and Russian primary factors, in addition to intermediate factor inputs. These services are characterized by firm-level product differentiation. Restrictions on FDI, right of establishment, the movement of business personnel, lack of intellectual property protection, and contract enforcement have major, direct impacts on multinational firms providing services to the market.

The number of multinational and Russian firms that are present in the Russian market depends on profitability in that market. For multinational firms, the barriers to FDI affect profitability. Reduction in the constraints on FDI will typically lead to productivity gains from the Dixit-Stiglitz variety effect because when more varieties of services are available, buyers can obtain varieties that more closely fit their needs.

Primary Factors

Primary factors of production are capital and skilled and unskilled labor. There are five types of capital in the model: (1) mobile capital that can be used in any sector without adjustment costs (46 percent of the total capital stock); (2) sector-specific capital in the energy sectors, namely ownership of the mineral resources in oil extraction, gas, and coal mining (representing 15 percent of total capital); (3) sector-specific capital required for expansion of output in imperfectly competitive domestic firms producing either goods or services (representing 32 percent of the capital in the benchmark); (4) sector-specific capital required for expansion of output in imperfectly competitive foreign firms producing either goods or services (representing 5 percent of the capital in the benchmark); and (5) ownership of licenses for monopoly rents in services sectors (representing 2 percent of capital in the benchmark). There are no data that would allow association of specific capital holdings in given sectors with particular households. Thus, it is assumed that all households that hold capital also hold the different types of capital in the same proportions.

Household Consumer Demand

It is assumed that each household maximizes a Cobb-Douglas utility function of the aggregate 35 goods in the model subject to its budget constraint (which is factor income net of transfers). Factor income shares, aggregated to the decile level, are reported in table 16.3.[4] Each of the 35 aggregate commodities is a CES (Armington) aggregate of imported goods or services and goods or services produced in Russia. In imperfectly competitive goods sectors, imported and Russian produced goods are Dixit-Stiglitz aggregates of the outputs of foreign or Russian firms. The structure of consumer demand in imperfectly competitive services sectors (equivalent to business services in this model) is depicted on the left side of figure 16.1 under "Business services." Competitively supplied cross-border services and imperfectly competitive services produced in Russia are a constant elasticity of substitution (CES) (Armington) aggregate as well. Services produced in Russia are a Dixit-Stiglitz aggregate of services provided by multinational service providers and Russian service providers. Given the elasticity assumptions in this chapter, there is pure firm-level product differentiation (no preference biases for varieties according to country of origin) for all Dixit-Stiglitz goods and services.

Consumer demand, as well as firm-level demand, exhibits love of variety in imperfectly competitive goods. Given that there are weak separability and homothetic functions at all levels of consumer demand, the conditions for two-stage (or multistage) budgeting are satisfied. Given the initial data on each of the households and the assumptions on the structure of demand, the approach involves solving for the parameter values in each of the 55,000 household utility functions that are consistent with optimization by the households. Thus, the demand functions of all households are dependent on their initial choices and, in general, differ from one another.[5]

Table 16.3. Factor Income Shares and Their Standard Deviations by Consumption Decile

	All households			Rural households			Urban households		
	Unskilled labor (%)	Skilled labor (%)	Capital %	Unskilled labor (%)	Skilled labor (%)	Capital (%)	Unskilled labor (%)	Skilled labor (%)	Capital (%)
Decile 1 (0–10%)	40.9 (39.5)	56.8 (39.8)	2.3 (5.3)	45.8 (39.5)	50.8 (39.6)	3.4 (6.2)	35.6 (38.6)	63.2 (38.8)	1.2 (3.8)
Decile 2 (11–20%)	37.6 (37.6)	58.5 (38.0)	3.9 (8.8)	42.8 (38.2)	51.5 (38.2)	5.8 (11.3)	34.1 (36.7)	63.4 (37.0)	2.6 (6.1)
Decile 3 (21–30%)	32.2 (37.1)	62.3 (37.6)	5.4 (10.1)	40.0 (37.9)	52.5 (38.2)	7.5 (12.8)	28.5 (36.2)	67.0 (36.5)	4.5 (8.4)
Decile 4 (31–40%)	30.1 (36.2)	62.9 (36.5)	7.0 (10.8)	36.8 (39.3)	54.2 (38.6)	9.1 (13.3)	27.3 (34.5)	66.5 (34.9)	6.2 (9.4)
Decile 5 (41–50%)	27.5 (35.4)	62.5 (35.2)	10.0 (12.3)	34.7 (38.3)	53.7 (36.0)	11.6 (13.9)	25.0 (34.0)	65.5 (34.4)	9.5 (11.7)
Decile 6 (51–60%)	25.3 (34.7)	60.9 (34.1)	13.8 (14.6)	35.4 (40.0)	49.3 (36.8)	15.3 (16.4)	22.1 (32.1)	64.5 (32.3)	13.3 (13.9)
Decile 7 (61–70%)	20.7 (30.9)	61.4 (31.9)	17.9 (16.0)	33.2 (38.3)	50.4 (35.9)	16.4 (16.9)	17.6 (27.8)	64.1 (30.1)	18.3 (15.7)
Decile 8 (71–80%)	16.8 (28.5)	62.1 (29.7)	21.1 (16.2)	31.2 (36.8)	48.0 (34.6)	20.8 (19.1)	13.9 (25.4)	65.0 (27.6)	21.1 (15.5)
Decile 9 (81–90%)	16.1 (27.2)	55.2 (28.4)	28.7 (17.3)	28.0 (37.3)	46.6 (32.9)	25.4 (19.3)	14.4 (24.7)	56.5 (27.4)	29.2 (16.9)
Decile 10 (91–100%)	11.2 (24.9)	47.2 (27.0)	41.7 (22.1)	23.3 (33.9)	39.9 (27.7)	36.8 (21.1)	10.5 (23.9)	47.6 (26.9)	41.9 (22.2)

Source: Authors' calculations.

Note: Numbers in parentheses are the standard deviations of the decile factor share.

Evidence on the Productivity Impact of Services Liberalization

A growing body of evidence and economic theory suggests that the close availability of a diverse set of business services is important for economic growth. The key idea is that a diverse set (or higher-quality set) of business services allows users to purchase a quality-adjusted unit of business services at lower cost. As early as the 1960s, the urban and regional economics literature argued that nontradeable intermediate goods (primarily producer services produced under conditions of increasing returns to scale) are an important source of agglomeration externalities that account for the formation of cities and industrial complexes, as well as differences in economic performance across regions. The more recent economic geography literature (for example, Fujita, Krugman, and Venables [1999]) has also focused on the fact that related economic activity is economically concentrated as a result of agglomeration externalities (for example, computer businesses in Silicon Valley, ceramic tiles in Sassuolo, Italy).

Evidence comes from a variety of sources. Ciccone and Hall (1996) show that firms operating in economically dense areas are more productive than firms operating in relative isolation. Hummels (1995) shows that most of the richest countries in the world are clustered in relatively small regions of Europe, North America, and East Asia, and the poor countries are spread around the rest of the world. He argues this is partly explained by transportation costs for inputs, because it is more expensive to buy specialized inputs in countries that are far away than it is for the countries where a large variety of such inputs are located. Marshall (1988) shows that in three regions in the United Kingdom (Birmingham, Leeds, and Manchester) almost 80 percent of the services purchased by manufacturers were bought from suppliers within the same region. He cites studies that show that firm performance is enhanced by the local availability of producer services. In developing countries, McKee (1988) argues that the local availability of producer services is very important for the development of leading industrial sectors.

As Romer (1994) has argued, product variety is a crucial and often overlooked source of gains to the economy from trade liberalization. In this chapter's model, greater availability of varieties is the engine of productivity growth, but it appears that there are also other mechanisms through which trade may increase productivity.[6] Consequently, variety is taken as a metaphor for the various ways increased trade can increase productivity. Winters, McCulloch, and McKay (2004) summarize the empirical literature by concluding that "the recent empirical evidence seems to suggest that openness and trade liberalization have a strong influence on productivity and its rate of change." There are several key articles regarding product variety. Broda and Weinstein (2004) find that increased product variety contributes to a fall of 1.2 percent per year in the "true" import price index. Hummels and Klenow (2002) and Schott (forthcoming) have shown that product variety and quality are important in explaining trade between nations. Feenstra and others (1999) show that increased variety of *exports* in a sector increase total factor productivity in most manufacturing sectors in Taiwan, China, and the Republic of Korea, and they have some evidence that increased input variety also increases total factor productivity. Finally, Feenstra and Kee (2004) show that the export variety and productivity of a country are positively correlated.

Barriers to FDI in Services Sectors

In Russia, it is relatively easy to find a number of prominent examples of barriers in the services sectors. For example, in telecommunications, Rostelekom has a monopoly on long-distance, fixed-line telephone service. In its bilateral agreement on WTO accession with the EU, Russia has agreed to end the Rostelekom monopoly. In banking, although Russia allows multinationals to invest in new banks in Russia, there is a prohibition on multinationals opening branches in Russia. This distinction has been a significant point of contention in the accession negotiations. There are also limits on how much of the insurance market can be controlled by foreign banks. Also, maritime transportation *within* Russia is limited to Russian ships. Commitments within the context of WTO accession should provide significantly greater access to multinational service providers in these key sectors.[7]

To estimate the ad valorem equivalence of barriers to FDI, this work began by commissioning surveys in telecommunications; banking, insurance, and securities; and maritime and air transportation services by Russian research institutes that specialize in these sectors. Using these surveys as well as supplementary data, Kimura, Ando, and Fujii (2004a, 2004b, 2004c) used the methodology explained in the volume by Findlay and Warren (2000) to estimate the barriers to FDI in the Russian services sector.

For each of these service sectors, authors in the Findlay and Warren volume evaluated the regulatory environment across many countries; the same regulatory criteria were assessed for all countries in a particular service sector. The price of services was then regressed against the regulatory barriers to determine the impact of any of the regulatory barriers on the price of services. Assuming that the international regression is valid for Russia and using their survey-based assessment of the regulatory environment, Kimura, Ando, and Fujii estimated the ad valorem equivalent impact of a reduction in barriers to FDI in these services sectors. The results are reported in table 16.2.

Estimated Impacts of Russian WTO Accession

Specification of the Counterfactuals

This chapter examines and compares the potential impact on Russia of the DDA as well as the impact on Russia of the changes it will make as a result of commitments it will take on as part of its WTO accession. First, results are produced for Russian WTO accession. These results are based on the integrated "real" 55,000-household model explained in RT&S (2004). In the WTO scenario, it is assumed that (1) barriers against FDI in business services are reduced as indicated in table 16.2; (2) seven sectors subject to antidumping actions in export markets receive slightly improved prices in their market access (this is implemented as an exogenous increase in their export price as shown in table 16.2); and (3) the tariff rates of all sectors are reduced by 50 percent. In all scenarios, unless otherwise stated, it is assumed that the government taxes households in equal percentages of household income so that government revenue remains unchanged. The macroeconomic impacts of this scenario are presented in column 1 of table 16.5. In Jensen, Rutherford and Tarr (forthcoming), it is shown that the most important impact of WTO accession on Russia is the liberalization of barriers against FDI in business services.[8] Column 2 presents results where only these barriers are liberalized (by the amount shown in table 16.2). In column 3, the barriers against FDI in services are reduced by 50 percent of the cuts shown in table 16.2. Column 4 presents results of a scenario in which tariff barriers are reduced by cutting them by 50 percent across the board.

Columns 5 and 6 present results of the impact of changes in world prices deriving from reforms undertaken at the global level. The changes in world prices derived from the GTAP model are taken as exogenous changes in the export and import prices facing Russia and are reported in detail in table 16.4. Then the 55,000-household model is run to examine the impact of these price changes on sector output, exports, imports, household welfare, and other economic variables. Column 5 considers full elimination of tariffs outside Russia and full elimination of export subsidies outside Russia, with cuts in domestic agricultural support. Column 6 evaluates the impact on Russia of the likely impact of the DDA without Russian participation in the cuts in tariffs and subsidies beyond its WTO accession commitments. This is defined as full elimination of export subsidies and cuts in domestic agricultural support and tariffs in industrial countries, with developing countries making lesser cuts, as detailed in chapter 2.

Table 16.4. Changes in Export and Import Prices Facing Russia on World Markets as a Result of the Doha Round or Rest of the World Free Trade[a] (ad valorem in percent by sector)

Sectors		Doha SDT[a]		ROW Free Trade	
		Export prices	Import prices	Export prices	Import prices
ELE	Electric industry	0.2	-0.1	0.7	0.0
OLE	Oil Extraction	0.2	0.1	1.0	0.3
OLP	Oil processing	0.2	0.1	1.0	0.3
GAS	Gas	0.1	-0.1	0.5	0.2
COA	Coal mining	0.2	0.9	0.9	1.1
OFU	Other fuel industries	0.2	0.1	0.9	0.3
FME	Ferrous metallurgy	0.2	-0.1	0.8	-0.3
NFM	Nonferrous metallurgy	0.2	-0.1	0.7	-0.7
CHM	Chemical and oil-chemical industry	0.2	-0.2	0.7	-0.3
MWO	Mechanical engineering and metal working	0.2	-0.2	0.7	-0.2
TPP	Timber and woodworking and pulp and paper industry	0.2	-0.2	0.8	-0.2
CNM	Construction materials industry	0.2	0.0	0.8	0.2
CLO	Light industry	0.3	0.1	1.5	-0.3
FOO	Food industry	0.5	2.3	1.5	2.7
OTH	Other industries	0.2	-0.1	0.8	-0.3
AGF	Agriculture forestry	0.1	0.4	0.7	0.9
OIN	Other goods-producing sectors	0.3	0.0	0.9	-0.2

Source: GTAP model estimates.

a. Doha SDT assumes expected Doha Round reductions in tariffs and domestic support subsidized with smaller cuts for developing countries and no cuts for the LDCs, without participation of Russia.

Aggregate Results in the Full, 55,000-Household Model

Aggregate results are summarized in table 16.5. Welfare results in this table are obtained by aggregating the equivalent variation (EV) gains (as a percent of consumption) of the 55,000 consumers.[9]

WTO Accession Scenarios

For the general WTO scenario (column 1 in table 16.5), rather substantial aggregate gains are obtained for a comparative state trade model, equal to 7.3 percent of aggregate consumption, with a standard deviation in the welfare gains among

Table 16.5. Impact of Russian WTO Accession and the DDA on Economywide Variables in Russia[a]

Commodity	WTO accession (1)	Reform of FDI barriers only (2)	WTO accession w/partial reform of FDI barriers (3)	50% Reduction of tariff barriers in Russia only (4)	Rest of the world free trade full removal of domestic support (5)	Doha (6)
Aggregate welfare						
Welfare (EV as % of consumption)	7.3	5.3	4.1	1.3	0.2	-0.3
	(2.2)[a]	(1.5)	(1.3)	(0.8)	(0.2)	(0.2)
Welfare (EV as % of GDP)	3.4	2.4	1.9	0.6	0.1	-0.1
Government budget						
Tariff revenue (% of GDP)	0.9	1.4	0.8	0.8	1.3	1.3
Tariff revenue (% of change)	-33.2	10.9	-35.2	-38.3	3.9	2.6
Aggregate trade						
Real exchange rate (% of change)	2.6	1.1	1.8	2.0	-0.9	-0.5
Aggregate exports (% of change)	14.4	3.7	11.9	8.1	0.5	-0.6
Returns to mobile factors						
Unskilled labor (% of change)	3.7	2.9	1.7	0.6	0.2	-0.1
Skilled labor (% of change)	5.3	2.8	3.2	1.7	0.0	-0.3
Capital (% of change)	1.8	1.4	2.2	1.0	-0.2	-0.3
Percent of factors that must adjust						
Unskilled labor	1.2	0.4	1.3	1.2	0.3	0.4
Skilled labor	1.4	0.7	1.0	0.6	0.2	0.3
Capital	0.5	0.1	0.4	0.3	0.3	0.4

Source: Authors' estimates.

Note: Results are percentage of change from initial equilibrium.

a. Numbers in parentheses are the standard deviations.

households of 2.2 percent of consumption.[10] Column 2 shows that the main driving force for this result is the reduction of Russian barriers against FDI in the services sectors. Liberalization of barriers to FDI is responsible for an estimated welfare gain of 5.3 percent of consumption (with a standard deviation in the welfare results among households of 1.5 percent of consumption), more than 70 percent of the total welfare gain from Russian WTO accession. Given that these estimates indicate that barriers against FDI in services are much higher than tariff barriers, and that there will be only small gains in market access, the relative importance of liberalization of barriers to FDI is not surprising. Column 3 also shows the results of estimates of the impact of only a 50 percent reduction in the barriers to FDI, along with the same improved market access and tariff reduction that would be implemented in the WTO scenario. The gains are reduced to 4.1 percent of consumption, with a standard deviation in the welfare gain of 1.3 percent of consumption; the gains remain substantial, but significantly reduced as a result of a less significant reduction in FDI barriers. A 50 percent reduction in tariff barriers yields a welfare gain of 1.3 percent of consumption (with a standard deviation of 0.8 percent). Although the gains are significantly less than the gains from services liberalization, this is a large gain for a country whose tariffs are not very high. The significant size of the gain is due to the endogenous productivity effects of goods liberalization.[11]

The intuition for these results is the following: Reduction of barriers against multinational service providers or foreign goods producers increases the (tariff-ridden) demand curve for multinational services or foreign goods. In imperfectly competitive sectors, this induces entry of new multinational service providers or new varieties of foreign goods until zero profit is restored. Despite the reduction in domestic varieties, there is a net increase in varieties overall. This serves to lower the quality-adjusted cost of purchasing the services or goods in downstream industries, and this acts like an externality that increases total factor productivity in the downstream using sectors.[12]

Because households cannot change their factor endowments among unskilled labor, skilled labor, and capital, but they can substitute among commodities consumed, impacts on factor incomes through changes in factor prices tend to dominate the welfare impacts in this type of model.[13] In the WTO scenario, the wage rate of skilled labor increases by 5.3 percent, the wage rate of unskilled labor increases by 3.7 percent, and the return on capital increases by 1.8 percent. Although the return to capital rises relative to a basket of consumption goods, it does not rise as much as wages. The return to capital increases less than wages because owners of "specific capital" in imperfectly competitive sectors that are subject to increased competition from imports or from FDI will see a reduction in the value of their returns. Returns to mobile capital increase by more than

6 percent, even faster than returns to skilled labor, because the economy shifts resources into the more capital-intensive sectors and away from more unskilled labor-intensive sectors, such as light industry and mechanical engineering and metal working. But the return on sector-specific capital in the imperfectly competitive sectors falls so that the total return on capital rises less than wages. The ratio of skilled to unskilled labor in the expanding sectors is greater than that in the contracting sectors. As a result, the wage rate of skilled labor rises faster than the wage rate of unskilled labor.[14]

Changes in the World Trading Environment: Impacts on Russia

Columns 5 and 6 of table 16.5 examine the impact on Russia as a result of changes in the world trading environment. Column 5 examines the impact of ROW free trade (without Russian participation),[15] the removal of all export subsidies in agriculture, and the removal of domestic support in agriculture. Russia's estimated welfare gain will be 0.2 percent of consumption, with a standard deviation among households of 0.2 percent of consumption.

Although the impact on Russia of ROW free trade outside Russia and the removal of export subsidies alone are positive, the most noticeable aspect of these estimates is how small they are in relation to the 7.3 percent estimated gain that Russia will obtain from its commitments as part of its WTO accession. This result follows a common strand in the literature, suggesting that the largest gains from trade liberalization come from own-liberalization and not from the actions of other countries. In this case, the liberalization of Russian barriers against FDI with endogenous productivity effects from liberalization of trade and FDI barriers are also incorporated as part of the WTO accession scenario.[16]

Column 6 examines possible outcomes of the DDA without any reforms in Russia. It is estimated that, on average, Russia will lose about -0.3 percent of consumption, with a standard deviation across households of 0.2 percent of consumption. These losses are due to the TOT loss to Russia from paying higher prices for food imports as a result of export subsidy removal. Without very substantial tariff cuts in ROW to offset the losses from removal of export subsidies in agriculture, Russia loses from the adverse TOT effects of higher prices for food imports.

To verify this intuition, the impact of the elimination of export subsidies, without any change in tariffs or domestic support, is evaluated separately. It is estimated that Russia will lose -0.4 percent of consumption from the removal of export subsidies. These results are explained by the fact that Russia is a net food importer. Elimination of export subsidies in agriculture results in higher prices for food and agricultural products on world markets. Thus, the TOT shift against Russia as a result of the elimination of these subsidies.

486   Poverty and the WTO: Impacts of the Doha Development Agenda

Results Aggregated to the Decile Level

To ascertain the impact of the DDA and WTO accession on the poor, the 55,000 households are separated into ten deciles, with 10 percent of the households in each. Households are ranked according to per capita income, with decile 1 made up of the poorest 10 percent of the households, decile 10 made up of the richest 10 percent, and so on. The model is run with all 55,000 households. The results of the aggregated EV gains (as a percent of consumption) of the households in each decile are presented in table 16.6. The aggregated results for rural and urban households in each decile are also presented in this table. In addition, the standard deviation of the disaggregated EV results within each decile is shown.

WTO Accession and FDI Liberalization

Columns 1 and 2 of table 16.6 present the results for Russian WTO accession and Russian reduction of barriers against FDI in services where the gains of the households within each decile are weighted to obtain weighted average mean gains for the households. All 10 representative households gain significantly, but the richest households gain slightly less in percentage terms than the poorest. This is because the return on capital increases less than the wage rate of unskilled labor. Table 16.4 shows that the rich depend more on earnings from capital than the rest of the population, so the impact on their income is affected more by the relatively lower increase in the returns to capital.[17] Skilled labor is more evenly distributed across income deciles, reflecting the fact that government employees, such as researchers and teachers, often receive very low wages and retirees living on a pension were often skilled workers.[18]

Rural households typically gain less than urban households. This occurs because rural households have less education and are therefore classified as less skilled than urban workers in the same income group, and unskilled wages do not increase as much as skilled worker wages.

ROW Free Trade and the DDA Scenarios

The results in column 4 of table 16.6 show that the impact of ROW free trade, removal of export subsidies, and reduction in domestic support yields very little difference in the results across deciles. Household welfare in all deciles increases by an amount between 0.1 percent and 0.3 percent of consumption. That is, the results for all deciles fall within 0.1 percent of the weighted average for the entire population (also shown in table 16.5) of 0.2 percent welfare increase as a percent of consumption. Similar results apply to the Doha scenario shown in column 5—the weighted average estimated welfare gains for virtually all deciles is within 0.1 percent of the estimated weighted average for the entire population in the respective

between 2 percent and 25 percent of consumption.[19] The distribution of gains for the poorest decile of the population is close to the distribution for the entire population, although the mean of the gains is slightly larger, and the richest decile gains slightly less than the average of the population—that is, WTO accession produces slightly progressive effects for the reasons already mentioned.[20]

Figures 16.3 and 16.4 plot the comparable distributions across the 55,000 households based on ROW free trade and the Doha scenario. For ROW free trade, it is estimated that 98 percent of the households will experience a change in welfare of between -0.3 percent and 0.7 percent of consumption. For the Doha scenario, it is estimated that 98 percent of the households will experience a change in welfare of between -0.8 percent and 0.2 percent of consumption. As was evident in the results at the decile level, the impact on the rich and the poor does not differ significantly: the impacts of ROW free trade or Doha on Russian households are neither progressive nor regressive.

Figure 16.5 compares the distributions of gains for all Russian households from the WTO accession, ROW free trade, and Doha scenarios. The figure makes it evident that WTO accession results in dramatically larger gains for Russian

Figure 16.3.   Distributions of Estimated Welfare Gains for Russian Households from ROW Free Trade for the Entire Sample, the Poorest Decile, and the Richest Decile

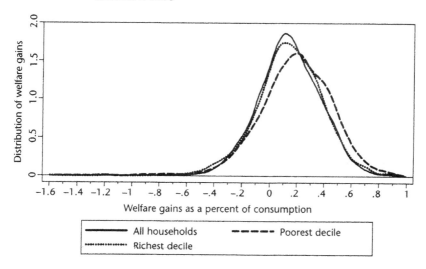

Source: Authors' calculations.
Note: Graph is truncated in a range from -1.6 to 1.

492   Poverty and the WTO: Impacts of the Doha Development Agenda

**Figure 16.4.   Distributions of Estimated Welfare Gains for
                 Russian Households from Doha for the Entire
                 Sample, the Poorest Decile, and the Richest Decile**

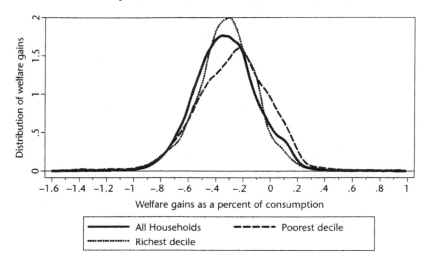

Welfare gains as a percent of consumption

———— All Households   ━ ━ ━ ━ Poorest decile
⋯⋯⋯⋯⋯ Richest decile

Source: Author's calculations.
Note: Graph is truncated in a range from -1.6 to 1.

households than the impact on Russia of either ROW free trade or Doha. ROW
free trade is more beneficial than Doha for Russian households. However, the distributions of gains from ROW free trade and the Doha scenario significantly overlap with each other, so that a large part of the distribution from Doha is obscured
by the ROW free trade distribution. The difference in impact on Russia between
ROW free trade and Doha is rather small compared with the estimated gains that
Russia could reap from its own reforms as embodied in its WTO accession commitments.

Policy Implications

Although this analysis has not accounted for the transition costs associated with
such trade reforms, it is clear that the process of adjustment to this new trade and
investment climate is likely to result in losses for many households. As discussed at
length in Jensen, Rutherford, and Tarr (forthcoming), a decline in employment in
light industry, the food industry, mechanical engineering and metal working, and
construction materials is expected. These displaced workers will have to find new

The Impact on Russia of WTO Accession and the DDA   **493**

Figure 16.5.   Distributions of Estimated Welfare Gains: WTO Accession, Doha, and ROW Free Trade Model Results Compared (55,098 households sampled)

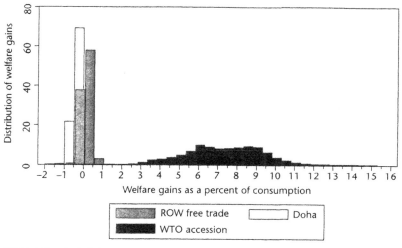

Source: Authors' calculations.

employment. They will suffer losses from transitional unemployment and will likely incur expenses related to retraining or relocation. Thus, despite a likely substantial improvement in the standard of living for almost all Russians after adjustment to a new equilibrium after accession to the WTO, government safety nets are very important to help with the transition—especially for the poorest members of society, who can ill afford a harsh transition.

The central finding in this chapter is that Russia will gain more from WTO accession commitments than from a prospective Doha scenario, and this is primarily due to its own services liberalization. The findings suggest that, in the medium term, what other countries in the WTO do in terms of their tariff changes or changes in export subsidies or domestic support will have a very small effect on Russian households and poverty. However, virtually all households will gain from Russian WTO accession in the medium term: these gains are substantial and they are very slightly progressive. These findings suggest that the gains to other developing countries from participation in the WTO might be considerably enhanced if reductions in barriers against FDI in services were included in the negotiations. By deepening reforms to include the services sector, the prospects for enhanced economic growth and sustained poverty reduction are much improved.

494   Poverty and the WTO: Impacts of the Doha Development Agenda

Notes

1. This analysis does not assume any Russian tariff cuts as part of the DDA to sharply contrast own liberalization versus ROW liberalization regarding impacts on Russia.

2. A small, open economy model of Russia is used. In a small, open economy model, there are no adverse TOT effects. That is, the optimal tariff for Russia in this model is zero. Unilateral tariff cuts increase welfare in this model all the way to a zero tariff. However, the GTAP model is a multiregion model with an Armington structure that implies that all countries, as unique suppliers of their differentiated goods, have market power on their exports and an optimal tariff. Given the elasticities assumed in the GTAP model, the optimal tariff is about 15 percent, so unilateral tariff cuts below 15 percent are typically welfare reducing.

3. The development of a new algorithm was key to solving a CGE model with such a large number of household-agents in the model. In RT&S we explain the intuition for that algorithm and provide a graphical interpretation. With the Internet version of this chapter, the General Algebraic Modeling System (GAMS) code for that algorithm is provided.

4. Households are modeled endogenously based on the 55,000 households of the Russian HBS. The HBS, which is representative at the regional level, has very detailed information on household consumption expenditures and information about age, gender, education, and occupation of each member of the household. It also has information about expenditures and savings and, by implication, household income. The major shortcoming of the HBS for the purposes here is that it does not contain information on the sources of income of the households. For sources of household income, a different source of information is required. Here the authors turn to the Russian Longitudinal Monitoring Survey, which has less than 5,000 observations and is not representative of the population on the regional level. However, it has extensive information on individual and household sources of income: wages and profits from first, second, and third jobs; pensions and unemployment benefits; and profits and dividends from accumulated assets.

Both small area estimation and matching techniques are used to generate sources of income data for all 55.000-plus households in the HBS. The procedures are described in RT&S. Results from both techniques yield similar results.

5. The model is solved using GAMS–MPSGE (Rutherford 1999) and the algorithm developed for this problem to solve general equilibrium models with a large number of agents.

6. Trade liberalization may induce firms to move down their average cost curves, import higher-quality products, or shift production to more efficient firms within an industry. Tybout and Westbrook (1995) find evidence of this latter type of rationalization for Mexican manufacturing firms.

7. Estimates of barriers in air and maritime transportation are higher than in other sectors because of strong barriers to operation within Russia in these sectors. But because there is less international pressure in these sectors for cuts in these barriers, the authors believe that WTO accession will not have as significant an effect in these sectors.

8. Barriers against business services are liberalized only in the WTO accession scenario. Given that business services represent only 14 percent of value added, this is a strong result. The intuition is explained in section 4.2 below.

9. The EV of each household is weighted by its share of base-year expenditures.

10. CGE evaluations of trade policy changes typically estimate gains of less than 1 percent of GDP. See Rutherford and Tarr (2002) for a discussion and several examples.

11. The large gains are achieved although the Russian capital stock is held constant in this model.

12. It has been shown (RT&S 2004) that if constant returns to scale are assumed in all sectors of the economy, the estimated welfare gains from Russian WTO accession are reduced to 1.2 percent of consumption. These results show that incorporating liberalization of barriers to FDI in the analysis as well as the Dixit-Stiglitz-Ethier formulation for endogenous productivity effects are both crucial in explaining the rather substantial estimated gains from Russian WTO accession.

13. See, for example, Harrison, Rutherford, and Tarr (2003).

14. The data do not allow us to distinguish capital holdings at the household level among the various types of capital. Thus, all households are assumed to hold the five kinds of capital in the model in equal proportions. Households that depend disproportionately on specific capital that falls in return would be expected to lose from WTO accession.

15. It is assumed that any commitments for tariff reduction as part of the DDA will not apply to Russia, because Russia is not yet a member of the WTO and the terms of its accession agreement will define its tariff regime within the time frame of the DDA. Thus, it is assumed that Russia does not participate in these global liberalization scenarios. However, Russia is assumed to benefit from improved market access as a result of liberalization in other countries—presuming that WTO membership will be in place by the time the Doha scenario is implemented.

16. To put these numbers in perspective, Rutherford and Tarr (2002) have analytically derived the relationship between a permanent increase in the steady-state growth rate and EV. A welfare gain of 10 percent of consumption corresponds to a permanent increase in the growth rate of about 0.4 percent. Although cross-country assessments of the impact of trade liberalization on growth have been criticized, several authors have estimated that trade liberalization could increase the growth rate by between 1 percent and 2.5 percent. One criticism of these regressions is that trade liberalization is often accompanied by macro stabilization, institutional reforms, and other market reforms, and the trade liberalization variable in the cross-country regressions may be picking up these other effects. But WTO accession involves a range of reforms, including institutional reforms necessary to accompany FDI liberalization, and trade liberalization may be a sine qua non of the overall reform process, because other interventions such as state subsidies often are unsustainable in an open economy.

17. Household income in Russia exceeds household consumption for almost all households because Russia has a large current account surplus. Consistency between the macro balances and the household data in construction of the SAM implies that household factor income must be larger than household consumption for most households to allow for the transfer of capital to foreigners as well as to pay for investment. It follows that the change in factor income as a percent of consumption will be larger than the change in factor income as a percent of household income.

18. An individual is classified as skilled if he or she has any education post–high school. In this study, skills are defined at the individual level. Labor and capital shares are defined individually, as are aggregated factor shares within the household.

19. For the scenario in which barriers to FDI are cut by only 50 percent of the cuts in the WTO accession scenario, 98 percent of the households experience a gain of between 0.9 percent and 6.3 percent of consumption.

20. Although households that are heavily endowed with specific capital in declining sectors will lose on average from WTO accession, those who can form joint ventures with foreign investors will likely see the value of their specific capital holdings increase.

References

Broda, Christian, and David Weinstein. 2004. "Globalization and the Gains from Variety." NBER Working Paper 10314. National Bureau of Economic Research, Cambridge, MA. http://www.nber.org/papers/w10314

Ciccone, A., and R. Hall. 1996. "Productivity and the Density of Economic Activity." *American Economic Review* 86 (1): 54–70.

de Melo, Jaime, and David G. Tarr. 1992. *A General Equilibrium Analysis of US Foreign Trade Policy.* Cambridge, MA: MIT Press.

Ethier, W. J. 1982. "National and International Returns to Scale in the Modern Theory of International Trade." *American Economic Review* 72 (2): 389–405.

Feenstra, R., D. Madani, T. H. Yang, and C. Y. Liang. 1999. "Testing Endogenous Growth in South Korea and Taiwan." *Journal of Development Economics* 60: 317–41.

Feenstra, Robert C., and Hiau Looi Kee. 2004. "On the Measurement of Product Variety in Trade." *American Economic Review* 94 (2): 145–49.

Findlay, Christopher, and Tony Warren, eds. 2000. *Impediments to Trade in Services: Measurement and Policy Implications.* London: Routledge.

Fujita, Masahisa, Paul Krugman, and Anthony J. Venables, 1999. *The Spatial Economy: Cities, Regions, and International Trade.* Cambridge, MA: MIT Press.

Harrison, Glenn W., Thomas F. Rutherford, and David G. Tarr. 2003. "Trade Liberalization, Poverty and Efficient Equity." *Journal of Development Economics* 71 (June): 97–128.

Hummels, David. 1995. "Global Income Clustering and Trade in Intermediate Goods." Ph.D. dissertation, University of Michigan.

Hummels, David, and Peter Klenow. 2002. "The Variety and Quality of a Nation's Trade." NBER Working Paper 8712. National Bureau of Economic Research, Cambridge, MA.

Jensen, Jesper, Thomas F. Rutherford, and David G. Tarr. Forthcoming. "The Impact of Liberalizing Barriers to Foreign Direct Investment in Services: The Case of Russian Accession to the World Trade Organization." *Review of Development Economics.* http://www.worldbank.org/trade/russia-wto

Kimura, Fukunari, Mitsuyo Ando and Takamune Fujii. 2004a. "Estimating the Ad Valorem Equivalent of Barriers to Foreign Direct Investment in the Telecommunications Services Sectors in Russia.?" http://www.worldbank.org/trade/russia-wto.

Kimura, Fukunari, Mitsuyo Ando and Takamune Fujii. 2004b. "Estimating the Ad Valorem Equivalent of Barriers to Foreign Direct Investment in the Maritime and Air Transportation Service Sectors in Russia." http://www.worldbank.org/trade/russia-wto.

Kimura, Fukunari, Mitsuyo Ando and Takamune Fujii. 2004c. "Estimating the Ad Valorem Equivalent of Barriers to Foreign Direct Investment in Financial Services Sectors in Russia," http://www.worldbank.org/trade/russia-wto.

Markusen, James, Thomas Rutherford, and David Tarr. Forthcoming. "Foreign Direct Investment in Services and the Domestic Market for Expertise." *Canadian Journal of Economics.* Available as Policy Research Working Paper 2143, World Bank. http://www.worldbank.org/trade.

Marshall, J. N. 1988. *Services and Uneven Development.* London: Oxford University Press.

McKee, D. L. 1988. *Growth, Development, and the Service Economy in the Third World.* New York: Praeger.

Romer, Paul. 1994. "New Goods, Old Theory and the Welfare Costs of Trade Restrictions." *Journal of Development Economics* 43 (1): 5–38.

Rutherford, Thomas F. 1999. "Applied General Equilibrium Modeling with MPSGE as a GAMS Subsystem: An Overview of the Modeling Framework and Syntax." *Computational Economics* 14 (1/2): 1–46.

Rutherford, Thomas F., and David G. Tarr. 2002. "Trade Liberalization, Product Variety and Growth in a Small Open Economy: A Quantitative Assessment." *Journal of International Economics* 56 (2): 247–72.

Rutherford, Thomas F., David G. Tarr, and Oleksandr Shepotylo. 2004. "Poverty Effects of Russia's WTO Accession: Modeling "Real" Households and Endogenous Productivity Effects." http://www.worldbank.org/trade/russia-wto

Schott, Peter. Forthcoming. "Across-Product versus Within-Product Specialization in International Trade" *Quarterly Journal of Economics.*

Tybout, James, and Daniel Westbrook. 1995. "Trade Liberalization and the Dimensions of Efficiency Change in Mexican Manufacturing Industries." *Journal of International Economics* 39 (1): 53–78.

Winters, L. Alan, Neil McCulloch, and Andrew McKay. 2004. "Trade Liberalization and Poverty: The Evidence So Far." *Journal of Economic Literature* 42 (March): 72–115.

[19]

The Effects of the Services Directive
on Intra-EU Trade and FDI

Henk Kox
Arjan Lejour*

International policy heterogeneity creates trade and investment costs for service firms doing business in other countries. Service providers have to comply with different rules in each foreign market where they operate. Complying with these regulations causes fixed market-entry costs, specific for each export market. We develop a new indicator for bilateral policy heterogeneity that is used as a proxy for the costs of policy heterogeneity. We explain bilateral services trade and services FDI in the European Union using a gravity model augmented with the heterogeneity indicator. We find a robust and strong negative impact of policy heterogeneity costs on services trade and FDI. The empirical results are used for assessing the potential impacts of the Services Directive proposed in 2004 by the European Commission. Several elements in the proposals would effectively reduce policy-related market-entry costs for services providers. We project that the 2004 Services Directive could increase intra-EU services trade by 30% to 62% and direct investment in services by 18% to 36%.

LES EFFETS DE LA DIRECTIVE SUR LES SERVICES

L'hétérogénéité des politiques menées à l'échelle internationale crée des coûts additionnels pour les firmes de services réalisant des échanges ou des investissements dans d'autres pays. Les fournisseurs de services doivent en effet se conformer à divers types de règles sur chaque marché où ils opèrent. Ces réglementations engendrent des coûts fixes d'entrée, spécifiques à chaque marché à l'export. Dans ce cadre, nous développons un nouvel indicateur d'hétérogénéité bilatérale afin de l'utiliser comme proxy dans l'évaluation de ces coûts. Nous tentons ainsi d'expliquer le commerce bilatéral de services et les IDE dans le secteur des services en utilisant un modèle de gravité intégrant cet indicateur. Nous dégageons un impact négatif, hautement significatif, de ces coûts d'hétérogénéité sur ce type de commerce et d'IDE. Ces estimations sont ensuite utilisées pour évaluer l'impact potentiel de la Directive sur les services proposée en 2004 par la Commission. Plusieurs volets de cette Directive pourraient effectivement réduire les coûts d'entrée pour les fournisseurs de services. Dans nos projections, cette Directive sur les services pourrait ainsi accroître le commerce de services intra-européen de 30 à 62%, et l'investissement direct dans les services de 18 à 36%.

JEL Classification: F13, F15, F17, F23, L5, L8

* Corresponding author a.m.lejour@cpb.nl. Both authors are affiliated to CPB Netherlands Bureau for Economic Policy Analysis, P.O. Box 80510, 2508 GM The Hague, the Netherlands (www.cpb.nl).

Revue économique

INTRODUCTION

In 2004 the European Commission launched a *Proposal for a Directive of the European Parliament and of the Council on Services in the Internal Market* (EC [2004]). Its aim is to boost the EU's Internal Market in Services by reducing regulation-based impediments to trade and direct investment in the services market. The proposals are motivated by the idea that differences in regulation hamper trade and direct investment in services. Anecdotic evidence underpins this idea, but systematic analyses are lacking so far. This paper conducts such a systematic analysis, assessing the trade and direct-investment effects of the proposed directive.

A cornerstone of the European Union (EU) is the principle that goods, services, capital and labour can move freely between the member states. The internal market for goods seems to function well after the implementation of the Single Market programme in 1992. That is however not the case for the internal market in services. Service providers often experience obstacles if they want to export their services to other EU member states, or when they want to start a subsidiary company in other EU member states. The EC [2002] found that these impediments are to a considerable degree caused by national regulations for service exporters, foreign investors in services, and for the service product itself. Such regulations are mostly made for domestic purposes without much regard for the interests of foreign service providers.

A key element of the 2004 European Commission proposals for the services market is the "country of origin" principle. A service firm has to meet the standards set by regulation of the country of origin, but may –except for some specified exceptions– no longer be confronted by additional regulation in the EU country where the service is delivered. Moreover the establishment of foreign subsidiaries will be facilitated by introducing a single point of contact where foreign firms can fulfil all their administrative and regulatory obligations. The directive also aims to eliminate unnecessary discriminatory elements in national regulations (*e.g.* nationality and residence requirements).

Our study investigates the potential effects of the proposals on trade and FDI in services. OECD researchers had already investigated what impact the relative strictness of national regulation has on trade and investment.[1] An innovation that we introduce is that we do not just look to the relative strictness of regulations, but also to the inter-country heterogeneity in form and contents of the regulations, because it is at this level that the market-entry costs arise for individual firms. We develop a new quantitative indicator to measure bilateral differences in regulation, based on some 200 specific items in product-market regulation. The new indicator is tested econometrically in a gravity model for explaining bilateral trade and FDI in commercial services between the EU countries. Policy heterogeneity turns out to have a significantly negative impact on the level of

---

1. They assess the relative strictness of national product-market regulation on a scale from 0 to 6 (*cf.* Golub and Nicoletti [2004], and Nicoletti *et al.* [2003b]). They conclude that a reduction in national regulation to that of the least-regulated country (the United Kingdom) could increase bilateral trade in services in the OECD by about 20%, whereas foreign investment in services stock could increase by 10-20%.

Revue économique — vol. 57, N° 4, juillet 2006, p. 747-770

Henk Kox, Arjan Lejour

bilateral trade and FDI. The estimated parameters are used for simulating the potential effects of the proposed EU Services Directive. After assessing at a detailed level how the proposed measures will affect the degree of policy heterogeneity in the EU, we calculate the effects of the measures on bilateral trade and investment. We find quite substantial effects of reducing policy heterogeneity. Commercial service trade may increase between 30 and 62 per cent, while foreign direct investment may increase between 18 and 36 per cent.

REGULATION HETEROGENEITY
AS A MAJOR BARRIER TO INTRA-EU SERVICE TRADE

Service markets have a long history of regulation. Partly, this is due to the externalities that the production of some services may cause for third parties, such as environmental effects of transport, the impact of bank reliability on the overall financial system, or the safety aspects of building design. But there is also a more innate cause for government intervention associated with the very nature of the service product. The production and consumption of the service products often cannot be separated in place and time, making it difficult to standardise a service product. The quality of the product is *a priori* uncertain for the consumer –more than holds for commodities. In the case of a simple service product such as a haircut, this uncertainty problem is generally manageable. The information problem for the individual service buyer is however more serious in the case of more complex professional and medical services that require the input of specialist knowledge. The buyer of such service products is confronted with a structural information asymmetry as to the quality of the service product, sometimes even after the transaction took place. To repair such structural asymmetries public authorities have since ages applied regulations for certain professional services.

Partly because of this long historic tradition, each authority uses its own system of quality safeguards for domestic consumers and service buyers. That was fine perhaps in an autarkic system, but it is certainly a great nuisance in a situation with increasing international trade. Service exporters are confronted with different regulations and requirements in each destination country. Before being able to sell one single service, they first incur the fixed costs of complying with the qualification demands and further regulatory requirements in the destination country (*cf.* EC [2002]). Such up-front costs can be a prohibitive barrier for entering export markets, in particular for small and medium-sized enterprises.

The real trade barriers is not caused by regulation as such, but by the heterogeneity of regulations in EU countries. This can be illustrated by a small thought experiment. Suppose that all EU member states have an identical qualification requirement for firms that sell a particular service. Complying with this requirement is a one-off effort for the firm. Once having incurred these fixed costs, it could allow the firm to reap economies of scale by expanding into other EU member states. Hence, a harmonised regulation can even be an incentive for internationalisation.

The picture changes when each EU member state has its own qualification criteria, causing different and additional compliance effort for the firms that want to operate across the borders. Now there are fixed costs for each specific country

749

Revue économique

market. Moreover, due to the fact that the qualification requirements are –in form and content– specific for that national market, the costs cannot be spread out over production that is destined for other EU markets. It means that the qualification costs are sunk costs for each national market; they cannot be recovered when market entry is not succesful. Figure 1 pictures these effects for a service provider who subsequently enters a number of EU export markets.[1] The implication is that not regulation as such forms a trade barrier, but the fact that regulatory requirements differ by country. It restricts the scope for intra-European economies of scale in complying with regulations.[2]

Figure 1. *Cost effect of regulation heterogeneity
in EU internal market (perspective of exporting firm)*

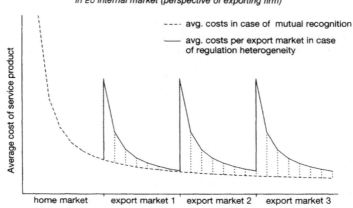

---- avg. costs in case of mutual recognition

—— avg. costs per export market in case of regulation heterogeneity

Average cost of service product

home market   export market 1   export market 2   export market 3

market size (home market plus exports)

Qualification requirements and associated costs for legal and other assistance are mostly independent of firm size. The entry-deterring effect will therefore be strongest for small and medium-sized firms. They form the large majority of service providers. Even if member states have different preferences for services regulation, they might still adopt a common architecture in service regulation, or make more use of mutual recognition of national qualifications of services firms. Implicitly, the shaded area in Figure 1 shows the firm-level cost and efficiency gains that can be attained by a system that allows firms to achieve more economies of scale in dealing with regulation requirements, for instance under mutual recognition.

Not only service providers are hampered by the heterogeneity in regulatory regimes. The higher level of average costs will push up the price level of the ser-

---

1. We assume that exporters sequentially enter other EU markets, after exploiting the local demand potential of each market.
2. Kox and Lejour [2005] prove this in a theoretical model using Dixt-Stiglitz type of preferences and fixed, country-specific qualification costs.

Revue économique — vol. 57, N° 4, juillet 2006, p. 747-770

Henk Kox, Arjan Lejour

vice, to the detriment of individual consumers and firms purchasing the service. Moreover it restricts the choice possibilities for consumers because it makes foreign service providers refraining from entering the market. Regulation heterogeneity results in a lower level of foreign competition, and it suppresses the influx of foreign service providers with new products and innovative working methods. The result is an upward effect on domestic service prices.[1] In the case of producer services, it leads to higher input prices for EU-based firms.

EU SERVICES DIRECTIVE

In 2004 the EC has proposed a directive to reduce policy-related impediments for trade in commercial services. The proposed directive has a "horizontal" approach: it applies the same principles to a large part of the EU service sector.[2] It is intended to become effective from 2010 onwards, and may have large impacts on the European service economy.

A key element of the directive is the "country of origin" principle. A service has to fulfil the regulation of the country of origin, and may not be hindered by (additional) regulation in the destination country. The introduction of the country-of-origin principle (COOP) implies that EU member states apply mutual recognition with regard to domestic regulations of the service exporting country. The COOP mean that firms no longer have to comply with qualitatively different rules in the destination countries; they can more or less (with specified exceptions) work according to the regulations in their country of origin. In practice this means mutual recognition of national regulatory regimes. With the CoOP the European Commission hoped to avoid the tedious and time-consuming case-by-case procedures (at European Court of Justice) against discriminatory treatment of foreign firms by individual member states. To strengthen the basis for mutual recognition, the proposed EU directive includes a number of measures that will stimulate inter-governmental exchange of information on regulation in services. Another element of the directive is a ban on discriminative nationality and residence restrictions for the management of foreign service firms.

Since production and consumption of a service often cannot easily be split in time and place, service providers often have to move abroad for delivering the service. The most important channel for providing a service in another country is through setting up a foreign subsidiary (cf. Karsenty [2002]). Some elements of the proposed EU directive target directly at removing barriers for direct investment in the service sector, like the obligation for EU member states to create a single point of contact for foreign firms. A single point of contact will be the place where the foreign service providers can fulfil all their administrative and regulatory obligations.

---

1. Ghellinck *et al.* [1996] found that intra-EU sectoral price differences were largest for services sector; they attributed this to the existence of non-tariff barriers for intra-European service trade.
2. Including the commercial service sectors Trade and Distribution, Business Services, Hotels and Restaurants, Personal Services, Construction. Not covered by the proposed Directive are: Banking, Insurance, Transport, and Medical Services.

751

Revue économique

QUANTIFYING POLICY HETEROGENEITY

Policy heterogeneity has many dimensions, and does not easily lend itself for a quantitative analysis, let alone in an internationally comparative context. In order to estimate the effect of differences in regulation on international trade and direct investment in services, we had to develop an index for bilateral policy heterogeneity for product-market regulation. As basic data source we use the OECD International Regulation database, fed by official inputs from governments of OECD member states. It is by far the most detailed and structured dataset on national differences in product-market regulation: it gives information on over 1100 economic policy comparison items for the benchmark year 1998 (Nicoletti, Scarpetta and Boylaud [2000]). We made a selection by removing all items that were either too industry-specific, too general or irrelevant for service markets. In the end we preserved 183 detailed aspects of product market regulation for assessing heterogeneity in economic policies. Most of the remaining items are of a more or less general nature, or at least they can be considered as representative for a country's overall product market regulation approach in commercial services.[1]

Our index for bilateral regulatory heterogeneity builds upon detailed pairwise comparisons between individual countries for specific aspects of product market regulation, both regarding the form and the contents of the regulation. For each item in the cleaned-up database we assess whether two countries are identical or not. It yields information of a binary nature: when the two countries differ in that particular regulation item we assign a value of *1*, and when there is no difference we assign the value of *0* to the regulation heterogeneity index. The results per item are aggregated for all relevant items per country pair. The value of the composite indicator ranges between *1* in case of complete dissimilarity and *0* in case of identical product-market regulations. Table 1 reports the average bilateral policy heterogeneity. It is lowest between Denmark and Ireland (0.26) and highest between the UK and Poland (0.70).

The impact of regulatory heterogeneity on trade may differ by policy area. We have therefore decomposed the overall heterogeneity index into five specific policy areas, identified in the OECD regulation database. The five sub-domains of product-market regulation are: *barriers to competition; administrative barriers for start-ups; regulatory and administrative opacity; explicit barriers to trade and investment;* and *state control.*

Disaggregation allows us to test in which policy areas the international regulatory heterogeneity has its largest trade impact on services. The decomposition was done on basis of additional information from the OECD regulation database. Table 2 shows the relative weights. It also indicates how we expect that heterogeneity in policy sub-domains affect bilateral trade (expected sign of coefficient). These expectations take into account that exports and foreign direct investment (setting up a local production unit) can be substitutes as a form of international service supply.

---

1. The data selection procedure is described in Kox, Lejour and Montizaan (2004, Annex I). The list of selected regulatory items is available upon request.

Revue économique — vol. 57, N° 4, juillet 2006, p. 747-770

Henk Kox, Arjan Lejour

Table 1. *Heterogeneity of product market regulation among EU member states, year 1997/1998*

	Denmark	Greece	Sweden	UK	Austria	Belg.-Luxem	Finland	France	Germany	Ireland	Italy	Netherlands	Portugal	Spain	Czech Rep.	Poland	Hungary
Denmark	0.00	0.46	0.40	0.36	0.45	0.39	0.43	0.46	0.38	0.26	0.46	0.40	0.46	0.42	0.53	0.63	0.62
Greece		0.00	0.42	0.44	0.43	0.36	0.44	0.43	0.41	0.48	0.47	0.39	0.38	0.41	0.43	0.39	0.34
Sweden			0.00	0.34	0.48	0.39	0.47	0.43	0.39	0.32	0.49	0.32	0.51	0.45	0.48	0.54	0.43
UK				0.00	0.50	0.40	0.43	0.46	0.37	0.30	0.50	0.40	0.49	0.37	0.57	0.70	0.46
Austria					0.00	0.50	0.43	0.43	0.46	0.46	0.37	0.40	0.42	0.45	0.45	0.36	0.46
Belgium-Lux						0.00	0.38	0.35	0.39	0.43	0.45	0.34	0.42	0.37	0.52	0.50	0.44
Finland							0.00	0.41	0.41	0.45	0.44	0.32	0.42	0.43	0.45	0.45	0.41
France								0.00	0.43	0.43	0.37	0.34	0.42	0.48	0.46	0.45	0.45
Germany									0.00	0.32	0.43	0.37	0.39	0.40	0.48	0.57	0.48
Ireland										0.00	0.49	0.44	0.42	0.40	0.52	0.62	0.55
Italy											0.00	0.41	0.44	0.43	0.51	0.40	0.49
Netherlands												0.00	0.35	0.41	0.38	0.46	0.35
Portugal													0.00	0.44	0.44	0.43	0.39
Spain														0.00	0.53	0.53	0.43
Czech Republic															0.00	0.36	0.46
Poland																0.00	0.38
Hungary																	0.00

Country data are corrected for non-response or missing data.

753

Revue économique

Explicit barriers to trade and direct investment includes for instance quantity restrictions, measures that can be expected to have a strong and directly negative impact on bilateral trade. However, heterogeneity with regard to this sub-domain may also imply high costs for complying with regulatory requirements in investment. If direct investment is hampered, firms could decide to serve the foreign market through exports. Therefore, the overall effect is difficult to predict *a priori*.

More heterogeneity in *administrative burdens for start-ups* could stimulate trade. The reason is that administrative burdens make it more difficult for foreign service firms to set up a local subsidiary in the other country. The latter increases the relative attractiveness of exporting as a way of delivering services to these markets. Hence, a positive impact on bilateral service trade might result.

State control is most important in services that use fixed infrastructures (rail, communication, distribution of electricity, water and gas), although there is still little international trade in most of these services.

Regulatory *Barriers to competition* is an area that is close to the operational functioning of service firms, so that we expect a negative impact of heterogeneity in this sub-domain. This also applies for *Regulatory and administrative opacity*.

Table 2. *Detailed indicators*
of regulation heterogeneity by sub-domain of product-market regulation

Components of heterogeneity indicator and covered policy domains	Number of items in the dataset	Weight as % of total number of items for overall PMR heterogeneity indicator	Expected impact of sub-domain heterogeneity on bilateral trade
Regulatory and administrative opacity	13	7.1	negative
Explicit barriers to trade and investment	14	7.7	not clear
Other outward barriers[a]	5	2.7	a)
Administrative burdens on start-ups	45	24.6	positive
Barriers to competition	61	33.3	negative
State control	45	24.6	negative
Overall PMR heterogeneity indicator	183	100	negative

a) The policy heterogeneity index for this sub-domain is not used in the regressions because it is only based on five reported items.

REGULATION IMPACT ON BILATERAL SERVICE TRADE

The impact of international regulatory heterogeneity on international service trade is investigated in the context of a gravity model. Helpman and Krugman [1985], and Bergstrand [1989] have shown that the model can be derived from a trade model with differentiated goods and monopolistic competition. Deardorff [1998] demonstrated that it can also be consistent with the Heckscher-Ohlin trade theory. Recently, Anderson and Van Wincoop [2004] have shown that the gravity model can be derived from any theoretical trade model obeying some

754

Henk Kox, Arjan Lejour

After correcting for period effects (time dummies) and country effects (dummies for origin and destination country), there is still the possibility that unobserved country-pair effects affect the results. An excessive loss of degrees of freedom prevents us from including dummies for all country-partner pairs. We solve this by transforming variables as deviations from their mean (hence: DM).[1] For each destination country it focuses on the differences between origin countries, and for each origin country it assesses the differences between destination countries. In this way two equations for bilateral exports are obtained: an "origin" equation; and a "destination" equation. The "origin" equation expresses all variables as deviations from their values for the average origin (=export) country. If variable Z_{kj} is a bilateral variable of equation (1) the variables of the "origin" equation read as:

$$\Delta_k Z_{kj} = Z_{kj} - \frac{1}{I} \sum_{i=1}^{I} Z_{ij} \qquad (2)$$

in which I and J represent the number of countries for origin and destination. If Z represents exports from country k to j the transformed variable $\Delta_k Z_{kj}$ indicates the exports of country k to country j in deviation of the average exports to country j. Similarly, the "destination" equation expresses bilateral imports and all explanatory variables as deviations from their values for the average destination (=import) country:

$$\Delta_m Z_{im} = Z_{im} - \frac{1}{J} \sum_{j=1}^{J} Z_{ij}. \qquad (3)$$

After transforming all bilateral variables in this way, we estimate the two equations simultaneously by the full-information maximum likelihood (FIML) procedure. The advantage of the transformed variables is that the origin-specific unobserved effects are accounted for in the origin equation. At the same time we can add explicit country-dummies to take account of the unobserved effects for the destination countries. Similarly, in the destination equations the destination-specific unobserved effects are accounted for by the transformation, and the origin-specific unobserved effects are evaluated by adding explicit country-dummies. Additional degrees of freedom are gained by assuming that in each of the two equations the incremental information provided by the unobserved country-pair effect over the "pure" origin (or destination) effect is random, and can be included in the error term.[2] In the origin and destination equation we impose identical coefficients for the year dummies, and for those variables that express bilateral differences: physical distance, language distance, and regulatory heterogeneity.

The two last columns of Table 3 show the FIML regression results with the transformed (DM) variables. The coefficients of most variables are comparable to the ones found for OLS with fixed effects. The coefficient for physical distance

---

1. It is a "within" fixed-effect estimator (*cf.* Verbeek [2004]). In many cases the within estimator gives identical results as for estimating the non-transformed equation with dummies. In this case not, because of the bilateral variables. The method is introduced for bilateral trade by Erkel-Rousse and Mirza [2002].

2. Thus assuming that the deviations of bilateral fixed effects from their means are i.i.d. random terms.

is higher now. The coefficient for policy heterogeneity in *Regulatory and administrative opacity* is no longer significant; apparently it picked up specific country-pair effects in the OLS regressions. The estimated parameters for regulation heterogeneity with respect to the areas *Barriers to competition* and *Explicit barriers to trade and direct investment* remain invariably negative and significant. The year dummy for 2001 is no longer significant in the FIML estimates.

Summing up, the regression results for bilateral trade in *other commercial services* are fairly stable over various specifications and estimation procedures.[1] A robust result is that inter-country differences with regard to product-market regulation in the areas of *Barriers to competition* and *Explicit barriers to trade and direct investment* have a significant negative impact on bilateral service trade. Finally, another firm result is that we consistently find empirical support for the Porter hypothesis that a high level of home-market regulation negatively affects the international competitiveness of exporters from that country.

REGULATION IMPACT ON BILATERAL DIRECT INVESTMENT

Intuition tells us that direct investment is also affected by gravitational factors like market size and distance. The knowledge-capital model of the multinational enterprise –most articulately formulated in Markusen [2002]– provides a theoretical basis for this. The knowledge-capital framework explicitly deals with the firm's choice between exporting and setting up foreign affiliates, thereby distinguishing between resource-seeking (vertical) and market-seeking (horizontal) multinationals. It analyses the direct-investment decision by taking into account the role of factors like market size, firm-level scale economies derived from knowledge capital, plant-level scale economies, and trade costs. Some of these elements are typical gravity factors, and it is no coincidence that the knowledge–capital model has stimulated econometric work in a gravity type framework (*e.g.* Brainard [1997]; Barrios *et al.* [2001]; Carr *et al.* [2001]). All find support for gravity variables driving cross-border investment.

We apply a gravity analysis to bilateral FDI stocks in order to investigate whether direct investment is affected by policy heterogeneity. On the basis of these results we subsequently analyse the potential FDI impacts caused by the 2004 EU Services Directive. As variables for the knowledge-assets model we included a technology variable: the labour productivity in the service sector of the origin country. For estimating the effect of heterogeneity in regulation on FDI stocks we apply the following reduced-form regression equation:

$$\ln(FDI_{ij}) = \beta_0 + \beta_1 \ln(GDP_i) + \beta_2 \ln(GDP_j) + \beta_3 \ln(DIS_{ij})$$

$$+ \beta_4 Lan_{ij} + \beta_5 PMR_i + \beta_6 \ln(H_i) + \beta_7 \sum_k HET_{ijk} \qquad (4)$$

$$+ \beta_8 BEN_j + \beta_9 RFD_j + \varepsilon_{ij}$$

---

1. Using the seemingly unrelated regression (SUR) method instead of the FIML method does not affect the results significantly.

Henk Kox, Arjan Lejour

in which FDI_{ij} represents the FDI stock from country i in the reporting county j. This FDI stock is explained by the GDP in the origin country and the destination country, by the physical distance (DIS_{ij}) between the two countries, and the language distance, $Lan \cdot H_i$ is the labour productivity in the service sector of the country of origin. Regulation heterogeneity between origin and destination country for domain k of product market regulation is expressed by HET_{ijk}. The variable PMR_i represents the level of product-market regulation in the origin country, while BEN_j and RFD_j respectively represent *Barriers to entrepreneurship* and FDI restrictions[1] in the destination country. We further add country dummies for origin and/or destination country.

No authorised international data set is available for bilateral FDI stocks in the services sector.[2] Sectoral data on FDI are available on a country basis, but not on a bilateral basis with countries of origin and destination specified. We therefore use bilateral total FDI stock data, covering all sectors. Data are from the OECD for the year 1999. More recent bilateral FDI stock data and bilateral data by sector are not available. In order to prevent that using total FDI stock data creates a bias in estimating the impact of the EU directive on investment, we apply a weighting procedure to exclude effects on sectors that are not affected by the proposed EU directive. Bilateral FDI stocks are used rather than annual FDI flows, for three reasons. The first reason is a very practical one: to our knowledge there is no authorised international dataset available for bilateral FDI flows. The second reason is that stock data are closer to the level of actual production by foreign affiliates than annual flow data. Thirdly, bilateral FDI flows are very volatile from one year to another; a few large transactions like mergers may cause large swings in the annual data, sometimes causing negative flows.

We test the hypotheses for a slightly larger country group than we did for bilateral service trade because for more country pairs bilateral data in FDI are available than in services. We include data for three EU accession countries (Poland, Hungary and the Czech Republic) and the USA, as the EU's largest outside direct investment partner in the sample.[3] We have used OLS with fixed effects and the SUR method with the transformed variables (DM) as estimation methods. The latter method is used to test for possible unobserved variables in the bilateral relations between FDI partner countries.

RESULTS FOR BILATERAL FDI

The empirical results are presented in Table 4. All estimated coefficients for the typical gravity variables are significant and have the expected sign. In general, the coefficients for the market size proxy (GDP) are similar for the destination

---

1. For the relative intensity of restrictions with regard to FDI we use an index developed by the OECD (Golub [2003]).

2. We used OECD data on bilateral FDI stocks on which we applied a consistency check, similar to the one applied for bilateral services trade, for identifying the most reliable reporting country, see Kox *et al.* [2004].

3. We have also included a country dummy for the USA and for the EU's accession countries in our country set. These dummies are not significant. The regression results with country dummies are available upon request.

Revue économique

Table 4. *Regression results: explaining bilateral foreign direct investment (inward), 1999*

	Estimation Method[a]			
	OLS, fixed effects origin	OLS, fixed effects destination	SUR[b] DM origin + Fixed effects	SUR[b] DM destination + fixed effects
Variables augmented gravity model				
Ln GDP Origin		0.92*** (0.10)	0.95*** (0.09)	
Ln GDP Destination	0.91*** (0.08)			0.74*** (0.06)
Language	− 0.69 (0.46)	− 0.46 (0.52)	− 0.1 (0.14)	− 0.15 (0.14)
Ln Distance	− 0.74*** (0.15)	− 1.08*** (0.16)	− 1.08*** (0.13)	− 1.08*** (0.13)
Ln (service sector productivity origin country)		2.13*** (0.30)	0.05*** (0.01)	
Regulation variables				
Heterogeneity, administrative barriers for start-ups	0.19 (0.53)	− 0.38 (0.68)	0.48 (0.44)	0.48 (0.44)
Heterogeneity, barriers to competition	− 2.77*** (0.96)	− 3.71*** (1.21)	− 3.28*** (0.84)	− 3.28*** (0.84)
Heterogeneity, regulatory and administrative opacity	− 0.94 (0.64)	− 1.20 (0.77)	− 0.89 (0.56)	− 0.89 (0.56)
Heterogeneity, state control	− 1.32 (0.89)	− 1.47 (1.04)	− 1.42* (0.77)	− 1.42* (0.77)
Heterogeneity, explicit barriers to trade and investment	0.58 (0.48)	1.48* (0.81)	0.30 (0.54)	0.30 (0.54)
Level product-market regulation, origin country		− 0.78*** (0.20)	− 0.87*** (0.18)	
Barriers to entrepreneurship, destination country	− 0.45*** (0.15)			− 0.21 (0.13)
FDI regulation indicator, destination country	− 4.91*** (1.78)			− 8.27*** (1.42)
Country dummies	Origin, significant	Destination, significant	Destination, significant	Origin, significant
Number of observations	261	196	195	260
Adjusted R-squared	0.80	0.77	0.66	0.47

a) Absolute value of standard error in brackets. Code: *** = coefficient significant at 1% confidence level; ** = coefficient significant at 5% confidence level; * = coefficient significant at 10% confidence level. Standard errors are white heteroskedasticity consistent.
b) Seemingly Unrelated Regression (SUR), applying simultaneous estimation of equations for origin and destination countries. All bilateral variables are transformed as deviations from their individual country-wise mean (DM). *Cf.* main text.
Data source for OECD regulation data: OECD [2003]; Nicoletti, Scarpetta and Boylaud [2000]; and Golub [2003] for FDI restriction indicators.

country and the origin country. The coefficient for distance is about minus 1, which is close to its theoretical value. It is however much lower for OLS with fixed effects of the country of origin. The bilateral linguistic distance variable is not significant in explaining the variation of bilateral FDI stocks: it may be explained by the fact that service multinationals typically use local personnel in their affiliates. The productivity of services in the origin country –used as a proxy for knowledge-related assets that provide firm-level scale economies for foreign affiliates– is significant in all specifications has the predicted sign. This result therefore is consistent with the prediction of the knowledge-capital model.[1]

Now we get to the policy variables. Heterogeneity in *Barriers to competition* and in S*tate control* (only for the preferred SUR method) have a significant negative impact on bilateral FDI. The effect of heterogeneity in *Regulatory and administrative opacity* is also negative, but not significant. Heterogeneity in *Barriers to start ups* has a small positive effect, but this is not statistically significant. Heterogeneity in *Explicit barriers to trade and direct investment* has a positive effect, but it is not significant at the 5% level. Interestingly less heterogeneity in these barriers increases bilateral trade but lowers investment. This resembles the "tariff jumping" effect: firms serve the foreign market by exports if trade barriers are low, but serve this market by foreign direct investment if the barriers are high. The estimation result confirms the hypothesis that a high level of product market regulation in the origin country reduces outward investment, because more regulation hampers competitiveness. The same holds for the hypothesis that the level of regulation (*Barriers to entrepreneurship*, FDI *restrictions*) in the destination country has a negative impact on direct investment.

THE IMPACT OF THE EU SERVICES DIRECTIVE

The regression results in Tables 3 and 4 confirm the hypothesis that regulatory heterogeneity hampers trade and direct investment in services. We use these results to calculate the potential effects of the proposed EU measures. First, we assess how the EU proposals would affect the five heterogeneity sub-indicators, assuming that the proposals would be fully implemented.

The implication of the country-of-origin principle (COOP) is that the wide diversity of national rules and standards would cease to be a major obstacle to services suppliers trading in other member states. The COOP respects that individual EU member states have different preferences for the level of regulation of their service industries. However, for imported services they are asked to apply mutual recognition of regulatory regimes in other member states. Kox *et al.* [2004] estimate for each of the 183 policy items used for calculating policy heterogeneity indices, to what extent (heavily, moderately, not affected) the effective policy heterogeneity on this item is affected by the proposed EU directive.[2] The results are subsequently aggregated according to the the five heterogeneity indicators by sub-domain. Table 5 gives the results, showing the expected reduction

---

1. In some specifications we have also included R&D intensities. The coefficients of these variables are not significant.

2. Detailed information is on request available from the authors.

Revue économique

by sub-domain of product-market regulation. Because of the uncertain impact of the EU directive on some regulatory comparison items –in particular for those items that are partially affected– we use a bandwidth indicating minimum and maximum effect.

Table 5. *Expected impacts of proposed EU measures*
on intra-EU policy heterogeneity, by policy domain

Components of heterogeneity indicator and covered policy domains	Average bilateral heterogeneity between 14 EU member states in 1998[a]	Reduction of the components of indicator due to implementation EU directive[b]
Regulatory and administrative opacity	0.38	66-77%
Explicit barriers to trade and investment	0.21	73-78%
Administrative burdens for start-ups	0.55	34-46%
Barriers to competition	0.32	29-37%
State control	0.42	3-6%
Overall PMR heterogeneity indicator	0.39	31-38%

a) Excluding Luxembourg due to insufficient data. Zero represents no heterogeneity, and one maximum heterogeneity.
b) Based on detailed item-wise consideration of the match between the proposed EU directive and the 183 specific regulation items selected from the OECD database as basis for calculating the heterogeneity indicators. If all items for a sub-domain would be fully affected by the EU directive, the expected impact would 100%. If no items are affected, the expected impact is 0%. Because of the uncertain impact of the EU directive on some regulatory comparison items –in particular for those items that are partially affected– we use a bandwidth indicating a minimum and maximum effect.

Source: Kox *et al.* [2004].

Table 5 shows that the heterogeneity components *Regulatory and administrative opacity* and *Explicit barriers to trade and direct investment* are heavily affected by the EU directive. The heterogeneity components *Administrative burdens for start-ups* and *Barriers to competition* are moderately affected by the EU directive and the component *State control* is hardly affected. The *State control* regulation items mainly relate to network sectors. The latter are not covered by the proposed EU services directive. We combine the heterogeneity-reduction effects reported in Table 5 with the parameter estimates for the policy variables, taking results based on the FIML and SUR estimation of the transformed variables with fixed effects for the country of origin (last column in Tables 3 and 4) as our preferred results. For every EU-country pair separately we calculate how their bilateral trade and FDI might be changed due to the EU proposals. The effect differs by each country pair, because the initial heterogeneity in regulation also varies for each country pair.[1]

---

1. Note that exports and FDI stocks are estimated in logs. So the new export or (FDI stock) level equals the old level times the exponent of the product of the change in heterogeneity and the estimated coefficient. We have calculated this for each country-pair and averaged these results to derive the total EU-effect, using the size of bilateral services trade and FDI stocks, respectively, as weights.

Henk Kox, Arjan Lejour

We account for uncertainties by combining the uncertainty effects of the parameter estimates –using a spread between plus and minus one standard deviation around the estimated coefficients– with the bandwidth of the heterogeneity effects in Table 5. For direct investment, our scenario includes the effect of a lower *level* of national FDI restrictions in the destination countries.[1] We did not account for different implementation stages, but instead we quantified the effects of full implementation of the EU directive, indicating the bandwidth of the resulting maximal effects on service trade and direct investment.

Table 6 shows the results. Full implementation of the proposed Services Directive could increase intra-EU trade in commercial services by 30 to 62 per cent, while the percentage increase of foreign direct investment in services in the EU is between 18 and 36 per cent. The increase in trade and FDI is mainly caused by a reduction in the heterogeneity of the *Barriers to competition*. For FDI, also the reduced intensity of FDI restriction is of importance.

Table 6. *Potential impacts of 2004 EU Services Directive on trade and FDI in (commercial) services*

	Minimum effects	Central effects	Maximum effects
Total intra EU trade increase	**30**	**44**	**62**
of which:			
• due to reduced heterogeneity in *Barriers to competition*	25	36	51
• due to less heterogeneity in *Explicit barriers to trade and direct investment*	5	8	11
Total intra EU FDI increase (incl. rounding differences)	**18**	**26**	**36**
of which:			
• due to reduced heterogeneity in *Barriers to competition*	7	12	18
• due to less FDI restrictions (level effect)[a]	11	13	16
• due to reduced heterogeneity in *State control*	0	1	2

a) In the scenarios we assume that investors from other EU countries will experience a 30% reduction in the level of FDI restriction of the destination country.

Table 6 presents average results for the EU as a whole. Below this surface we find substantial variation for individual countries. In Table 7 we show that at country-level the effects of the proposed measures may differ substantially. We give the expected changes in intra-EU exports and imports (other commercial services), and in the incoming and outgoing FDI stocks, for the central-effect variant.[2]

---

1. For the level effect we assume a 30% reduction for investors from other EU member states. This is a conservative estimate, since the directive aims at abandoning discriminatory regulation.

2. Our FDI analysis concentrated on cumulative direct investment *stocks*, and since the adaptation of FDI stocks occurs mainly through annual FDI flows, the effect on annual direct investment flows will be much higher. To what extent this is the case depends on the length of the adaptation period.

Revue économique — vol. 57, N° 4, juillet 2006, p. 747-770

Revue économique

Exports of commercial services by Greece and Portugal could grow by more than 70 per cent. Four countries may gain between 50 and 60 per cent (Austria, Italy and Spain, and Denmark). Five countries, among which the largest EU countries, may gain between 40 and 50 per cent on intra-EU services exports: Germany, the UK, France, Sweden, Finland, Ireland. Finally, Belgium-Luxemburg and the Netherlands are expected to increase trade by 30 to 40 per cent. Likewise, Table 7 presents the simulated changes in imports. All EU member states will see their service exports and imports grow as a result of the measures. The EU service markets will become more open, so that intra-EU price and cost differences become more important, giving rise to further reallocations.

Table 7. *Relative increase in services trade and FDI stocks due to the 2004 EU Service Directive[b]*

Impact by EU-member state	Trade		Foreign direct investment[a]	
	Exports	Imports	Outgoing stock	Incoming stocks
Austria	58	56	36	65
Belgium-Luxembourg	38	37	25	23
Czech Republic	–	–	33	43
Denmark	60	58	33	29
Finland	47	44	29	41
France	42	45	24	25
Germany	48	47	31	25
Greece	72	68	27	36
Hungary	–	–	47	45
Ireland	45	37	23	22
Italy	53	53	31	39
Netherlands	37	37	24	21
Poland	–	–	36	53
Portugal	72	67	42	39
Spain	52	45	33	41
Sweden	44	41	25	31
United Kingdom	41	41	24	21
EU14	44	44	–	–
EU17	–	–	26	26

a) In the simulations, we account for the effects of the EU measures on the level of FDI restrictions in destination countries, and for the decreased heterogeneity in product-market regulation within the EU.
b) The reported effects are for the Central-Effects variant.

The projected growth in outward FDI stocks may vary from 47 per cent for Hungary to 23 per cent for Ireland. For inward FDI stocks, the variation in relative growth between countries is even wider: from 65 per cent in Austria to 21 per cent in the Netherlands. Like in the case of service trade, the dispersion in growth rates between individual countries is determined by the initial characteristics of each country's FDI destination countries and FDI origin countries. Countries, from which most FDI initially went to countries with strong bilateral heterogeneity in

Revue économique — vol. 57, N° 4, juillet 2006, p. 747-770

Henk Kox, Arjan Lejour

product-market regulations and/or high levels of FDI restrictions, will experience the strongest effect from the EU measures. Conversely, member states whose direct investment partners had similar product-market regulations and low levels of FDI restrictions will experience relatively few effects of the proposed directive.

These country effects are calculated using the gravity equations for trade and FDI. These take only account of the effect to which extent trade or FDI will change in response to less heterogeneity in regulation induced by the Services Directive ignoring trade and direct investment effect between other country pairs. Due to more integrated markets some member states will specialise in providing *other commercial services* while others will not. This does not necessarily imply that these other member states will lose from implementing the Services Directive. They can benefit from lower prices in *other commercial services* and they can expand their specialisation in other sectors, because some of their resources are shifted from other commercial services. De Bruijn *et al.* [2006] assess these effects using a general equilibrium model. They find that the Services Directive will also cause shifts in country specialisation patterns. Some original EU member states increase their relative specialisation in commercial services due to the more open borders. The new Member States, however, will see relatively the largest imports in commercial services, while they will reallocate more resources to their manufacturing activity, because it is in the latter sector that they have the largest comparative advantage vis-à-vis the "old" EU member states.

CONCLUSIONS

We derive firm indications that the EU service sector might benefit from the proposed EU directive through a substantial increase in international trade and investment. Assuming full implementation of the proposals, we estimate that bilateral commercial service trade could increase by about 30% to 62%. Expressed in terms of total intra-EU trade (goods and services) the increase ranges between 2 and 5 per cent. FDI in services could also increase by about 18% to 36%. These effects will materialise over several years after the implementation of the proposals.

Our results indicate an order of magnitude of the trade and direct-investment effects following from the proposed Services Directive. We do not give a welfare analysis. Domestic (and European) welfare effects may likely result from price and income effects of the measures, and the effects on innovation and productivity. Moreover, EU member states may for several reasons prefer to have their own product-market regulations in place. This is a matter of national and EU-level policy trade-offs. This analysis only assesses the missed opportunities for intra-EU trade and FDI in services when countries prefer a continuation of different national product-market policies.

Finally, with our findings on the importance of policy heterogeneity as a trade barriers we may also look beyond the intra-EU services market. The results are potentially important for a next round in the GATS/WTO negotiations on the liberalisation of international service trade. Most of the GATS negotiations now centre around market-access issues. WTO members should perhaps put more emphasis on mutual recognition as an important and effective area for boosting international trade in services.

Revue économique

REFERENCES

ANDERSON J. and VAN WINCOOP E. [2004], "Trade costs", *Journal of Economic Literature*, vol. XLII (September), pp. 691-751.

BARRIOS S., GÖRG H. and STROBL E. [2001], "Multinational enterprises and new trade theory: Evidence for the convergence hypothesis", *CEPR Discussion Paper* 2827, London.

BELOT M. and EDERVEEN S. [2005], "Indicators of Cultural and Institutional Barriers in OECD Countries", *CPB Memorandum*, The Hague.

BERGSTRAND J. [1989], "The generalized gravity equation, monopolistic competition, and the factor-proportions theory of international trade", *Review of Economics and Statistics*, 23.

BRAINARD S. [1997], "An empirical assessment of the proximity-concentration trade-off between multinational sales and trade", *American Economic Review*, 87 (4).

CARR D.L., MARKUSEN J.R. and MASKUS K.E. [2001], "Estimating the knowledge capital model of the multinational enterprise", *American Economic Review*, 91.

DEARDORFF A.V. [1998], "Determinants of Bilateral Trade: does Gravity Work in a Neoclassical World?", in J.A. FRANKEL (ed.), *The Regionalization of the World Economy*, University of Chicago Press.

DE BRUIJN R., KOX H. and LEJOUR A. [2006], "The trade-induced effects of the Services Directive and the country of origin principle", *CPB document* 108, The Hague.

EC [2002], "Report from the Commission to the Council and the European Parliament on the State of the Internal Market for Services", Brussels.

EC [2004], "Proposal for a Directive of the European Parliament and of the Council on Services in the Internal Market", SEC (2004) 21, Brussels.

ERKEL-ROUSSE H. and MIRZA D. [2002], "Import price elasticities: reconsidering the evidence", *Canadian Journal of Economics* 35, pp. 282-306.

GAULIER G., MAYER T. and ZIGNAGO S. [2003], Notes on CEPII's distances measures, Paris www.cepii.fr.

GHELLINCK E. de *et al.* [1996], "Price competition and price convergence, The Single Market Review Series, Impact on Competition and Scale Effects", DRI/European Commission, Brussels 1996.

GOLUB S.S. [2003], "Measures of restrictions on inward foreign direct investment for OECD countries, OECD Economic", *Department Working Paper* no. 357, Paris.

GRÜNFELD L.A and MOXNES A. [2003], "The Intangible Globalization: Explaining the Patterns of International Trade and Foreign Direct Investment in Services", Norwegian Institute of International Affairs, *Mimeo*.

HELPMAN E. and KRUGMAN P. [1985], *Market Structure and Foreign Trade*, Cambridge (Mass.), The MIT Press.

KARSENTY G. [2002], "Trends in Services Trade under GATS Recent Developments", paper at symposium on Assessment of Trade in Services, 14-15 March 2002, WTO, Geneva.

KIMURA F. and LEE H. [2004], "The gravity equation in international trade in services, paper presented in ETSG conference", University of Nottingham.

KOX H., LEJOUR A. and MONTIZAAN R. [2004], "The free movement of services within the EU", *CPB Document* 69, The Hague (revised version of September 2005).

KOX H. and LEJOUR A. [2005], "Regulatory heterogeneity as obstacle for international services trade", *CPB Discussion Paper* 49, The Hague.

LEJOUR A. and DE PAIVA VERHEIJDEN J.-W. [2007] (forthcoming), "Services trade within Canada and the European Union: what do they have in common?", *Services Industries Journal*.

MARKUSEN J.R. [2002], *Multinational firms and the theory of international trade*, Cambridge (Mass.), MIT Press, Cambridge.

NICOLETTI G., SCARPETTA S. and BOYLAUD O. [2000], "Summary indicators of product market regulation with an extension to employment protection legislation", *OECD Economic Department Working Paper* no. 226, Paris.

Henk Kox, Arjan Lejour

NICOLETTI G. [2001], "Regulation in Services: OECD Patterns and Economic Implications", *OECD Economic Department Working Paper* no. 287, Paris.

NICOLETTI G. and SCARPETTA S. [2003a], "Regulation, Productivity and growth: OECD evidence", *OECD Economic Department Working Paper* no. 347, Paris.

NICOLETTI G., GOLUB S., HAJKOVA D., MIRZA D. and YOO K.-Y. [2003], "Policies and international integration: influences on trade and foreign direct investment", *OECD Economic Department Working Paper* no. 359, Paris.

OECD [2003], "OECD Statistics on International Trade in Services; Partner Country Data and Summary Analysis", Paris.

PORTER M. [1990], *The competitive advantage of nations*, London, MacMillan Press.

VERBEEK M. [2004], *A guide to modern econometrics*, Chichester, J. Wiley & Sons.

Revue économique — vol. 57, N° 4, juillet 2006, p. 747-770

[20]

Services Policy Reform and Economic Growth in Transition Economies

Felix Eschenbach and Bernard Hoekman

Groupe d'Economie Mondiale, Science Po, Paris;
World Bank, Washington, D.C., and CEPR, London

Abstract: Major changes have occurred in the structure of former centrally planned economies, including a sharp rise in the share of services in GDP, employment, and international transactions. However, large differences exist across transition economies with respect to services intensity and services policy reforms. We find that reforms in policies toward financial and infrastructure services, including telecommunications, power, and transport, are highly correlated with inward FDI. Controlling for regressors commonly used in the growth literature, we find that measures of services policy reform are statistically significant explanatory variables for the post-1990 economic performance of transition economies. These findings suggest services policies should be considered more generally in empirical analyses of economic growth. JEL no. F14, F43, O14, O40
Keywords: Services; economic growth; transition economies

1 Introduction

One of the stylized facts of economic development is that the share of services in GDP and employment rises as per capita incomes increase (Francois and Reinert 1996). This reflects increasing specialization and exchange of services through the market ("outsourcing")—with an associated increase in variety and quality that may raise productivity of firms and welfare of final consumers, in turn increasing demand for services. It also reflects the limited scope for (labor) productivity in provision of some services, implying that over time the (real) costs of these services will rise relative to

Remark: This paper was written while Hoekman was visiting the Groupe d'Economie Mondiale, Institut d'Etudes Politiques, Paris. We are grateful to a referee, Harmen Lehment, Aaditya Mattoo, Joe Francois, Beata Smarzynska Javorcik, Robert M. Stern and Alan Winters for comments and suggestions on earlier drafts, and to Joe Francois, Francis Ng and Julia Woertz for assistance with data. The views expressed are personal and should not be attributed to the World Bank. Please address correspondence to Felix Eschenbach, Groupe d'Economie Mondiale, Science Po, 197 Bld. St. Germain, 75007 Paris, France; e-mail: felixeschenbach@yahoo.com

© 2006 The Kiel Institute   DOI: 10.1007/s10290-006-0091-7

merchandize, as will their share of employment (Baumol 1967; Fuchs 1968). Services are increasingly becoming tradable as a result of the greater mobility of people and technological change. This further increases the scope for specialization in production and trade. The competitiveness of firms—both domestic enterprises operating on the local market and exporters on international markets—depends importantly on the availability, cost, and quality of producer services such as finance, transport, and telecommunications.

Services industries were generally neglected under central planning. Marxist thinking emphasized the importance of tangible (material) inputs as determinants of economic development, and classified employment in the services sector as unproductive. The lack of producer services was reflected in transport bottlenecks, queuing for and low quality of telecommunications, the absence of efficient financial intermediation, and much lower employment in services than was the case in OECD countries (e.g., less than 1 percent of the labor force was employed in finance and insurance) (Bićanić and Škreb 1991). Many of the services that are critical to the functioning of a market economy simply did not exist—not just a financial sector that could allocate investment funds efficiently, but also design, advertising, packaging, distribution, logistics, management, after sales services, etc.

In this paper we analyze the impact of service sector policy reforms on the growth performance of 24 transition economies. There are large differences in economic performance across these transition economies. Our primary objective is to explore to what extent services-related policies help explain these differences. We start with a brief discussion of shifts in the structure of these economies and developments in trade and inward FDI in services (Section 2). Section 3 turns to the role of the service sector as an engine of economic growth. We first present a snapshot of prevailing policies toward trade and investment in services and the changes that have occurred since the early 1990s, focusing in particular on so-called backbone service industries: finance, telecommunications, and infrastructure (including utilities). We then investigate the impacts of services policies and reforms on growth, controlling for standard explanatory variables commonly used in the literature. We find that services policies are an important determinant of growth performance. Section 4 concludes.

748 Review of World Economics 2006, Vol. 142 (4)

2 Shifts in the Structure of Services in Transition Economies

The share of services in GDP and employment has grown significantly since 1990 in almost all transition economies. Compared to the high income OECD average in 1990—when the share of services in employment and GDP was around 63 percent—transition countries in Europe and Central Asia (ECA) lagged far behind: services accounted for 30–40 percent of GDP and employment. As of 2003, services shares had increased substantially. The greatest growth is observed in the Baltic States, which have almost converged on the OECD average of 68 percent in terms of GDP shares, although employment shares remain lower (Figure 1). The Central and Eastern European (CEE) countries that acceded to the EU in 2004 have also converged to a large extent. Much less progress has been made by the Central Asian countries, where natural resource-based activities continue to constitute a major share of GDP.[1]

There is also a distinct pattern in labor productivity performance. The CEE, South-East European (SEE) and Baltic states register an increase in productivity, both overall and within services (broadly defined to include government).[2] Conversely, for those other countries where data is available, there has been a decline in the measured value of services output per employee. These countries also have not increased their overall labor productivity performance in the last decade. Noteworthy is the performance of the Baltic countries, where labor productivity in services outpaced the productivity increase in other sectors of the economy. Convergence with respect to high-income OECD countries in terms of productivity levels is still far from being achieved, however.

Input-output tables for the year 2001, the latest available year for many ECA countries, provide information on differences in economic structure and the extent to which ECA countries have converged to comparators in the rest of world as regards both intermediate services use and final demand, as well as on the service intensity of exports. Table 1 reports information on the sectoral intensity of exports: the direct contribution of agriculture, mining, manufactures, and services to total exports, expressed as a share of total exports of goods and services.[3] Albania, Croatia, and the Baltic States are the most services-intensive in exports. The first column in Table 2

---

[1] See Figure 1 for the definition of country groups used in this paper.
[2] Output data are measured in constant 1995 US dollars, as reported in the World Development Indicators.
[3] We are grateful to Joe Francois for sharing these data.

Eschenbach/Hoekman: Services Policy Reform and Economic Growth   749

Figure 1: *Changes in the Share of Services in GDP and Employment and Labor Productivity*

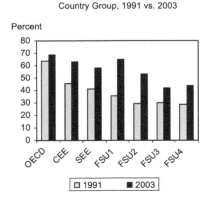

Share of Services Sector in GDP by
Country Group, 1991 vs. 2003

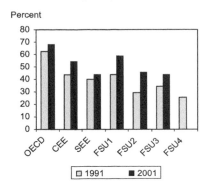

Employment Share of Service Sector by
Country Group, 1991 vs. 2001

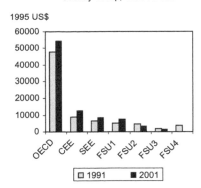

Labor Productivity of Service Sector by
Country Group, 1991 vs. 2001

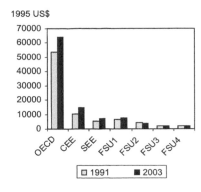

Labor Productivity of All Sectors by
Country Group, 1991 vs. 2003

Note: CEE = Central and Eastern European countries (Poland, Hungary, Czech and Slovak Republics, Slovenia); SEE = Albania, Bosnia and Herzegovina, Bulgaria, Croatia, FYR Macedonia, Romania, and Serbia and Montenegro; FSU1 = Estonia, Latvia, and Lithuania; FSU2 = Russia, Ukraine, Belarus, Moldova; FSU3 = Armenia, Azerbaijan, Georgia; FSU4 = Kazakhstan, Kyrgyzstan, Tajikistan, Turkmenistan, Uzbekistan.
Source: World Bank, *World Development Indicators.*

reports the sum of the direct and indirect linkage effects generated by a unit of export revenue—the total activity generated by (going into) one unit of foreign exchange (exports). The average "multiplier" is 3.6, i.e., every US dollar of exports generates $3.6 in economic activity. On average a little

Table 1: *Sectoral Share of Total Export Revenue (Selected Transition Economies)*

	Agriculture/food/mining	Manufactures	Services
Albania	19	35	46
Croatia	9	49	42
Czech Rep.	5	80	15
Hungary	7	76	17
Poland	10	73	17
Romania	4	85	10
Slovakia	4	86	10
Slovenia	4	81	15
Estonia	11	66	22
Latvia	13	64	24
Lithuania	13	63	24
Russia	40	52	8

Source: GTAP Input-Output data derived from Social Accounting Matrices for 2001.

Table 2: *Total Export Related Activity (Direct Plus Indirect Linkages), 2001*

	Total "multiplier"	Shares			
		Agriculture/food	Mining	Manufactures	Services
Albania	4.8	20	4	24	52
Croatia	2.9	18	1	36	45
Czech Rep.	3.0	10	2	61	27
Hungary	2.8	10	2	51	37
Poland	4.2	17	3	43	38
Romania	6.6	27	3	39	30
Slovakia	2.9	12	3	57	28
Slovenia	2.9	10	1	58	31
Estonia	2.5	15	2	49	35
Latvia	3.0	17	1	36	47
Lithuania	3.5	17	4	36	42
Russia	3.6	14	17	30	39
Memo:					
Cyprus	2.5	10	7	30	52
Turkey	3.7	17	2	40	41
China	3.7	18	3	62	17
Malaysia	2.1	8	3	64	25
Germany	3.3	7	1	49	43

Source: GTAP Input-Output data derived from Social Accounting Matrices for 2001.

over one third of this total activity is services-related, ranging from a high of 52 percent (Albania) to a low of 27 percent (Czech Republic). Many transition countries are more services oriented than developing countries such as China or Malaysia.

Although technology is making it easier to trade services, often a commercial presence remains required to sell services, i.e., FDI. Given the lack of a service sector under central planning, FDI can be expected to play a particularly important role, more so than in countries where incumbent competition confronts foreign providers. FDI is an important channel for foreign providers to contest infrastructure service markets. FDI sometimes takes the form of greenfield investment, but has mostly occurred through privatization. The extent of privatization varies substantially by country and sector, with Central European and Baltic countries the leaders in attracting FDI in infrastructure. The SEE countries have attracted the least. On average, services account for some 62 percent of the stock of FDI in the reporting countries (Table 3).[4] Finance, transport, communications and distribution services account for the largest share of this FDI. The service intensity of FDI is highest in the Baltic states, presumably reflecting their relatively small size and limited manufacturing base, and lowest in Romania and the Ukraine. Services FDI is also very high as a ratio of GDP in the Baltic States. It is lowest in Romania, Russia and the Ukraine.

3 Services Reforms and Growth Performance

The forgoing snapshot of trends in the share of services in GDP, employment, output per worker, trade, and FDI reveal both substantial convergence toward European countries, but also a distinct difference between Central European/Baltic states and Central Asian and CIS (Commonwealth of Independent States) economies. Given that trade and FDI in services can be expected to be associated with the acquisition of new technologies, higher service standards and more effective delivery, these differences should help explain the observed higher labor productivity performance in services in the former. The question explored in the rest of this paper is whether these services developments are determinants of the aggregate growth perform-

---

[4] Aggregate data on FDI inflows are available for a wider set of countries, but these are not broken down across services sectors.

Table 3: *Inward FDI Stock by Sector (End 2003 Unless Indicated Otherwise; Shares in Total (percent))*

	CZ	HU	PL	SK	SI	EE	LV	LT	BG	CR	RO	RU flow	UK
	2002	2002	2002		2002							00–02	2002
Agriculture, forestry, fishing	0.1	1.3	0.4	0.2	0.0	0.4	1.5	0.8	0.3	0.3	0.7	0.4	2.1
Mining and quarrying	1.4	0.3	0.3	0.8	0.0	0.4	0.6	0.8	1.1	3.1		45[a]	2.4
Manufacturing	35.5	45.8	35.8	37.5	43.3	18.2	15.5	31.1	33.4	30.6	54.3		46.4
Electricity, gas, water supply	6.9	4.6	2.6	11.7	1.0	2.4	3.4	4.4	1.0	1.1			1.6
Construction	1.9	1.1	2.6	0.7	0.1	2.5	1.0	1.2	2.7	0.9	2.4	2.2	2.9
Distribution and repair services	11.9	11.1	17.1	11.2	14.5	15.9	18.0	17.9	18.0	6.9	16.4	22[b]	18.5
Hotels and restaurants	1.2	1.1	0.6	0.5	0.4	1.7	1.3	1.6	1.7	4.0	2.4		2.3
Transport, storage & comm.	13.6	10.1	10.4	10.0	4.4	17.7	11.9	17.1	15.7	25.0	7.8	9.5	7.2
Financial intermediation	15.9	10.3	21.3	23.5	18.8	28.1	15.0	15.7	17.7	24.6		1.8	8.1
Real estate, rental & business act.	9.3	11.7	7.5	3.2	15.2	11.4	24.5	7.3	3.9	3.1		8.2	4.7
Education, health, social work	0.2	.	.	0.4	0.1	0.1	0.1	0.2	0.3	0.0			2.3
Other community & personal ser.	2.4	.	.	0.3	0.5	0.8	1.1	1.5	0.8	0.5		0.2	1.5
Other not classified activities	0.0	1.0	1.4	.	1.7	0.4	6.0	0.3	3.2	.	16[c]	11.0	
Real estate purchases by foreigners	.	1.5	.										
Total services share [d]	56.2	47.9	60.9	49.8	55.7	78.6	78.9	62.8	65.2	64.9	45	54.6	47.5
Value of services FDI stock ($ bn)	26.7	22.9	36.8	5.6	2.8	5.1	2.6	3.1	3.3	7.4	5.7	35.5	3.6
Services FDI stock as % of GDP	31.6	27.7	17.6	17.6	7.7	60.7	26.8	37.8	16.6	26.1	9.4	8.2	7.3

[a] Covers all industry, including mining/energy. – [b] Includes hotels and restaurants. – [c] Includes finance and business services. – [d] Not including utilities.

Source: WIIW-Wifo Database on FDI, July 2004 edition.

ance of countries. The services outcome variables are of course endogenous, influenced by the policy stances of governments, so that the focus is on the impact of services policy reforms.

Service sector reform involves a mix of deregulation (the dismantlement of barriers to entry and promotion of competition) and improved regulation (putting in place an appropriate legal environment, strengthening regulatory agencies, increasing their independence, etc.). The policy challenge is to achieve a balance between effective regulation and increasing the contestability of markets. Much has been done by transition countries to reform and adapt policies and regulatory regimes for service industries. Figure 2 plots three indicators of the extent of policy reform in banking, non-bank financial services, and infrastructure. These indices, constructed by the European Bank for Reconstruction and Development (EBRD), range from 0 to 4.3, and span the period 1990–2004.[5] The value of the indices is set at zero for 1989, so that the 2004 value provides a measure of the progress that has been made by countries in converging to "best practice" standards—measured by a maximum value of 4.3. Data are available annually for the 1990–2004 period.

Figure 2: *Services Reform Index, 2004*

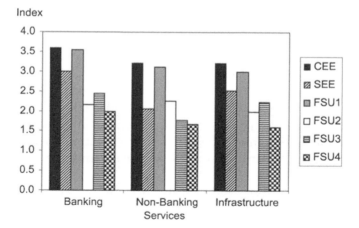

Source: EBRD (2004).

---

[5] See Appendix for more detailed information on the construction of the EBRD reform indices.

Central and East European (CEE) and Baltic states (FSU1) have made the most progress in all three services policy areas. For the other transition countries there is significant variation across indices. SEE have advanced the most on reforms in banking and infrastructure, followed by the Caucasus (FSU3), while European CIS countries (FSU2) have done the most in the non-bank financial area, followed by SEE. The Central Asian republics have made the least progress in all three areas, with one country—Turkmenistan—not advancing at all in any area.[6]

While significant progress has been made by many transition economies in services reforms, there is also substantial cross-country heterogeneity in terms of liberalization and the quality of the regulatory framework for key "backbone" services. Differences in policy reforms are reflected by differences in FDI in services. This is confirmed by the correlation coefficients in the Appendix Table A1 relating investment climate and the combined service sector reform variables to the stock of FDI as a share of GDP.[7] The higher coefficient for the services reform variable relative to the investment climate indicator is suggestive of the important role service-related policies may play in attracting FDI.

The goal of this paper is to investigate whether reforms have had a positive effect on output growth for the countries under consideration. Standard economic growth theory postulates that growth is a function of capital and labor inputs. It accords no special role to services. Services play a more prominent role in the literature on financial sector development (see Levine 1997 for a survey), which recognizes that financial intermediaries do not simply passively convert savings into physical investment. Instead, temporary or permanent growth effects of capital accumulation and productivity improvement are supported by financial intermediaries (banks, capital markets) that actively mobilize savings and channel these toward profit-maximizing investment opportunities. Another strand of the growth literature that (implicitly) emphasizes a services dimension stresses the importance of human capital and R&D in generating growth (e.g., Lucas 1988; Romer 1990).

The role of producer services of the type captured by the infrastructure services reform index in the growth process has not attracted much

---

[6] For a more detailed discussion of the evolution of services policies in transition economies, see Eschenbach (2006) and World Bank (2005).

[7] As discussed in the Appendix, the investment climate reform variable measures progress in terms of privatization, price liberalization (including the foreign exchange regime), and corporate governance.

attention in the theoretical or empirical growth literature. Francois (1990) develops a model that points to the importance of such producer services for economic growth, although his model is not dynamic. He argues that the increasing importance of producer services in modern economies reflects economies of scale and specialization. As firm size increases and labor specializes, more activity needs to be devoted to coordinating and organizing the core businesses of a company. This additional activity is partly outsourced to external service providers. The associated organizational innovations and expansion of "logistics" (network) services yields productivity gains that in turn should affect the economy-wide growth performance by enhancing the efficiency of production in all sectors. The associated cost reductions can have the effect of upgrading overall productivity, and are likely to be enhanced by, if not conditional on, increased FDI in services (Konan and Maskus 2006; Markusen et al. 2005).[8]

In what follows we explore the impact of financial and infrastructure services policy reforms on growth using time-series data for a panel of 24 transition economies covering the 1990–2004 period.[9] Tables A1 and A2 describe the data sources and provide pair-wise correlation coefficients, respectively. We exclude three countries for which the coverage of macroeconomic data over time is poor (Turkmenistan, Serbia/Montenegro, Bosnia/Herzegovina). We start with simple OLS country fixed effects regressions[10] (Table 4). The dependent variable is the growth rate of per capita GDP. In most of the literature, the main factor driving growth is assumed to be investment (e.g., Levine and Renelt 1992). Transition economies experienced large swings in investment in the first half of the 1990s, with the collapse of central planning and the initial lack of market institutions leading to sharp reductions in investment (Roland 2000; Falcetti et al. 2002). Subsequently, a gradual buildup of a domestically and externally financed private capital stock occurred. This well-known U-shaped pattern of output and investment collapse and recovery suggests that the *change* in the investment ratio may be used as an alternative to the investment-GDP ratio as a measure of investment.[11]

---

[8] Most of the quantitative analyses of the impact of services policy reforms has used static applied general equilibrium models. These find that services policies are important for welfare—e.g., Konan and Maskus (2006).

[9] See Mattoo et al. (2006) for a complementary, cross-sectional analysis of the effects of service sector policies on growth.

[10] The fixed effects model allows to some extent for heterogeneity across countries.

[11] In the empirical analysis we do not use several variables that are often used in growth regressions. These include measures of human capital, trade openness and initial per capita

Table 4: *Per Capita GDP Growth and Service Sector Policies in a Panel of 24 Transition Economies*

	OLS fixed effects							Two-stage least squares fixed effects			
	(1)	(2)	(3)	(4)	(5)	(6)	(7)	(8)	(9)	(10)	(11)
Independent variables											
(a) Investment/GDP	0.67 (0.74)										
(b) Δ Investment/GDP		0.56 (5.97)***	0.39 (4.73)***	0.28 (3.80)***	0.32 (4.21)***	0.28 (3.93)***	0.21 (3.06)***	0.61 (4.26)***	0.69 (4.73)***	0.69 (4.53)***	0.82 (5.31)***
(c) Inflation			−0.002 (−4.50)***	−0.0011 (−2.68)***	−0.0012 (−3.06)***	−0.001 (−2.66)***	−0.0006 (−1.49)	−0.001 (−2.69)***	−0.001 (−3.00)***	−0.0004 (−0.75)	−0.0007 (−1.54)
(d) Crisis			−16.36 (−8.29)***	−12.1 (−6.90)***	−13.23 (−7.36)***	−12.23 (−7.00)***	−9.13 (−5.44)***	−10.9 (−5.85)***	−11.73 (−6.06)***	−8.74 (−3.98)***	−10.09 (−4.75)***
(f) Finance				8.29 (10.26)***				7.71 (8.93)***		13.32 (7.11)***	
(g) Infrastructure					6.8 (8.81)***				6.3 (7.75)***		10.35 (6.54)***
(f) Service						8.47 (10.28)***					
(g) Invclim							8.87 (13.01)***				
Instruments								exogenous variables= (c), (d), (f) plus: first lag of (a)	exogenous variables= (c), (d), (g) plus: first lag of (a)	exogenous variables= (c), (d) plus: first lag of (a), first lag of growth, Gastil	exogenous variables= (c), (d) plus: first lag of (a), first lag of growth, Gastil
R-squared	0.01	0.09	0.29	0.37	0.37	0.38	0.44	0.38	0.37	0.34	0.34
No. of obs.	348	332	329	329	329	329	329	329	329	322	322

t-values in parentheses. *** denote significance at the 1 percent level.

The reduced form models (1) and (2) test the alternative hypotheses of a linear vs. non-linear relationship between investment and growth. Investment/GDP is statistically insignificant (model 1), while the change in the ratio is significant. Thus, the initial collapse and the subsequent recovery in GDP growth was associated with changes in the rate of change in investment at a fast pace: first falling and subsequently rapidly growing investment ratios. We therefore use the change in investment in the regressions. In model (3) we account for inflation and crisis. Inflation, a measure of macroeconomic stability, is expected to have a negative impact on growth. Crisis is a dummy variable that equals one in years when countries experienced armed conflict or a major financial crisis. It captures conflicts affecting Georgia, Armenia, Azerbaijan, and Tajikistan and the financial crises in Russia and Albania. These events will be captured in part by other variables, but not completely, and we want to control for them explicitly in any event. Both variables have the predicted sign and are statistically significant at the 1 percent level.

In models (4) and (5) we add the annual EBRD reform indices that were discussed previously, the premise being that service sector policy reform affects growth indirectly by supporting FDI inflows as well as the efficiency of domestic investment. The indices are constructed to reflect finance and infrastructure policy frameworks in a relatively broad sense (see Appendix 1 for details). Both indicators are significant at the one percent level. The coefficients suggest, ceteris paribus, that a one point increase in the reform index (scaled from no reform=1 to 4.3) is associated with an increase in the per capita growth rate of 6.8 (Infrastructure) and 8.5 (Finance) percentage points. Given the huge differentials in growth rates during the observed period this is not as large as it appears, but still amounts to a sizeable impact. The analysis of the model fit suggests that the reform indices add substantial explanatory power (the R^2 increases from 0.29 in model (3) to 0.37 in models (4) and (5)). The banking sector reform measure has a slightly larger effect in explaining observed growth than does the infrastructure policy reform variable. In those transition economies where financial intermediation existed during the 1990s, the output col-

---

income. The reason is that our country sample is quite specific in the sense that all experienced a sharp fall in output in the first half of the 1990s, notwithstanding relatively high levels of human capital. Also, trade volumes during the early transition do not reflect integration with world markets but rather traditional COMECON barter trade relations. As a result of these factors, conditional convergence is not observed in the data, and including these variables, yields rather counterproductive results.

lapse was much less pronounced and the subsequent recovery occurred at a faster pace.[12] Strengthening the financial sector and bolstering confidence in the private commercial banking sector by improving the policy framework therefore is of great importance.[13] Indeed in many of the countries in question, potential depositors still shy away from banks and credit remains influenced by or subject to direct or indirect government control. As discussed above, the policy reform agenda in infrastructure spans many dimensions, including pro-competitive regulation of public providers—tariffs that reflect costs and provide incentives for providers to pursue efficiency improvements, ensuring access to networks and interconnection on reasonable terms, and the development of effective, independent regulatory bodies.

In models (6) and (7) we alternatively use the service sector reform and the investment climate indices (introducing these variables jointly gives rise multicollinearity, see Table A1). They both cover a broader spectrum of economic activities and therefore turn out to have slightly more explanatory power than Finance and Infrastructure alone. The investment climate in particular relates to industrial and other sectors as well, and not just to services.

In models (8) through (11) we repeat the exercise of models (4) and (5) using two-stage least squares regression analysis so as to take into account the potential simultaneity bias in the relationship between growth and investment (models (8) and (9)), and, in addition, between growth and the reform stance (models (10) and (11)). The lag of the investment/GDP ratio is highly correlated with the current change in the investment/GDP ratio, but exogenous to current GDP growth, making it a useful instrument. The results are similar, with the coefficient estimate of the investment variable being somewhat higher on average than in the OLS regressions. The reform indices, however, lose very little, if any, explanatory power.

In models (10) and (11) we take account of the fact that reform and economic performance are to some extent simultaneously determined. We hypothesize that the sectoral regulatory policy reforms will be more effective if the economy is already on a stable growth path and if the political framework has been changed so as to have generated (allow for) greater

---

[12] Campos and Coricelli (2002: 29ff) and Roland (2000) discuss the importance of missing and underdeveloped credit markets in the early transition period.

[13] This spans adoption of and compliance with good practice standards defined by organizations such as the IMF, BIS, and IOSCO, including credible and effective implementation-cum-enforcement by regulatory authorities.

accountability for outcomes. We therefore use the lag of per capita GDP growth and the Gastil index as instruments for our two reform indices.[14] The coefficients of our reform indices are much higher now, and remain statistically significant. The result suggests there may be a "virtuous circle" in which recent economic performance and progress toward political freedom make current reform measures more effective in stimulating growth.[15]

4 Conclusions

Controlling for a number of standard explanatory variables used in the growth literature (investment, crises, inflation), we find a statistically significant positive association between per capita GDP growth and measures of service sector policy reforms. Two-stage estimates hint at a "virtuous circle" in which growth and political reform foster the efficiency of reform, which in turn stimulates growth. Although the sample of countries was limited to transition economies—annual policy reform indicators of the type compiled by the EBRD do not exist for developing countries—the findings indicate that services policies should be considered more generally in empirical analyses of economic growth. Services such as finance, telecommunications, and transport are major inputs into the production of goods and services—including agriculture as well as manufacturing. The costs of these inputs can account for a major share of the total cost of production, and are thus important factors affecting the competitiveness of firms. Services are also important determinants of the productivity of workers in all sectors—education, training, and health services are key "inputs" into the formation and maintenance of human capital. Thus, service sector reforms potentially can do much to enhance economic growth and efficiency.

---

[14] The Gastil index is a measure of the extent of democratic accountability and political freedoms in a country. It is reported by Freedom House. It is based on responses to an annual survey involving 10 political rights questions (grouped into three subcategories) and 15 civil liberties questions (grouped into four subcategories). The index ranges from 1 (most free) to 7 (least free). See http://www.freedomhouse.org/template.cfm?page=35& year=2005. See also Table A1.

[15] The first stage regressions, not reported here, clearly show a positive association between the degree of political freedom/civil liberties as reflected in the Gastil index and lagged per capita GDP growth on the one, and the reform measures on the other hand.

Appendix

The EBRD Services Reform Indices

The index ranges from 1 (little progress) to 4.3 (most advanced implementation of reform agenda) and has been compiled on an annual basis for the 1990–2004 period.

1. *Finance* = average of the following two banking and non-banking reform indicators:

- *Banking and interest rate liberalization:* A 4.3 means full convergence of banking laws and regulations with BIS standards, provision of full set of competitive banking services.
- *Securities markets and non-bank financial institutions:* 4.3 means full convergence of securities laws and regulations with IOSCO standards, fully developed non-bank intermediation.

2. *Infrastructure* = average of the following five infrastructure reform indicators:

- *Electric power:* 4.3 means tariffs cost-reflective and provide adequate incentive for efficiency improvements. Large-scale private sector involvement in the unbundled and well-regulated sector. Fully liberalized sector with well-functioning arrangements for network access and full competition in generation.
- *Railways:* 4.3 means separation of infrastructure from operations and freight from passenger operations. Full divestment and transfer of asset ownership implemented or planned, including infrastructure and rolling stock. Rail regulator established and access pricing implemented.
- *Roads:* 4.3 means fully decentralized road administration. Commercialized road maintenance operations competitively awarded to private companies. Road user charges reflect the full costs of road use and associated factors, such as congestion, accidents, and pollution. Widespread private sector participation in all aspects of road provision. Full public consultation on new road projects.
- *Telecommunications:* 4.3 means effective regulation through and independent entity. Coherent regulatory and institutional framework to deal with tariffs, interconnection rules, licensing, concession fees, and spectrum allocation. Consumer ombudsman function.
- *Water and waste water:* 4.3 means water utilities fully decentralized and commercialized. Fully autonomous regulator exists with complete authority to review and enforce tariff levels and quality standards. Widespread private sector participation via service/management/lease contracts. High-powered incentives, full concessions and/or divestiture of water and waste-water services in major urban areas.

3. *Service* = average of Infrastructure and Finance

Eschenbach/Hoekman: Services Policy Reform and Economic Growth   761

4. *Invclim* = investment climate measure, the average six EBRD reform indicators:

- *Large-scale privatization:* 4.3 means standards and performance typical of advanced industrial economies; more than 75 percent of enterprise assets in private ownership and significant progress on corporate governance of these enterprises
- *Small-scale privatization:* 4.3 means standards and performance typical of advanced industrial economies; no state ownership of small enterprises; effective tradability of land.
- *Governance and enterprise restructuring:* 4.3 means standards and performance typical of advanced industrial economies; effective corporate control exercised through domestic financial institutions and markets, fostering market-driven restructuring.
- *Price liberalization:* 4.3 means standards and performance typical of advanced industrial economies; complete price liberalization with no price control outside housing, transport and natural monopolies.
- *Trade and foreign exchange system:* 4.3 means standards and performance typical of advanced industrial economies; removal of most tariff barriers; membership in WTO.
- *Competition policy:* 4.3 means standards and performance typical of advanced industrial economies; effective enforcement of competition; unrestricted entry to most markets.

Source: EBRD (2004).

Table A1: *Pair-Wise Correlation Coefficients of Variables Used in Panel Analysis*

	No.	1	2	3	4	5
Growth	1	1				
Investment/GDP	2	0.10	1			
Δ investment/GDP	3	0.30	0.35	1		
Inflation	4	−0.30	−0.13	−0.05	1	
Crisis	5	−0.42	−0.03	−0.17	0.20	1
FDI/GDP	6	0.35	0.31	−0.01	−0.24	−0.12
Finance	7	0.51	0.16	0.17	−0.27	−0.32
Infrastructure	8	0.48	0.14	0.15	−0.23	−0.26
Service	9	0.51	0.16	0.16	−0.26	−0.30
Invclim	10	0.59	0.03	0.23	−0.28	−0.31
Gastil	11	−0.17	−0.15	−0.07	0.15	0.28

Table A1: *continued*

	No.	6	7	8	9	10	11
Growth	1						
Investment/GDP	2						
Δ investment/GDP	3						
Inflation	4						
Crisis	5						
FDI/GDP	6	1					
Finance	7	0.72	1				
Infrastructure	8	0.78	0.88	1			
Service	9	0.78	0.97	0.97	1		
Invclim	10	0.68	0.89	0.82	0.88	1	
Gastil	11	−0.44	−0.65	−0.63	−0.67	−0.56	1

Table A2: *Documentation of Data Used in Panel Analysis*

Variable	Definition	Source
Growth	Per capita GDP growth	World Bank, WDI
Investment/GDP	Gross fixed capital formation in percent of GDP	IMF WEO
Δ Investment/GDP	Change in investment/GDP ratio	IMF WEO
Inflation	Consumer price inflation	IMF WEO
Crisis	Dummy for financial crisis/armed conflict	n.a.
FDI/GDP	Stock of FDI as percent of GDP	WIIW[a]
Finance	Average of EBRD reform indices on banking and non-banking financial sector, see Appendix for details	EBRD Transition Report
Infrastructure	Average of EBRD reform indices on infrastructure (telecom, rail, road, water, power), see Appendix for details	EBRD Transition Report
Invclim	Average of EBRD reform indices on privatisation and liberalization, see Appendix for details	EBRD Transition Report
Service	Average of Invclim and Infrastructure, see Appendix for details	EBRD Transition Report
Gastil	Average of Civil Liberties and Political Rights indices	Freedom House

Sample countries

Albania	Czech Republic	Latvia	Russia
Armenia	Estonia	Lithuania	Slovak Republic
Azerbaijan	Georgia	Macedonia	Slovenia
Belarus	Hungary	Moldova	Tajikistan
Bulgaria	Kazakhstan	Poland	Ukraine
Croatia	Kyrgyz Republic	Romania	Uzbekistan

[a] Wiener Institut für Internationale Wirtschaftsvergleiche.

References

Baumol, W. (1967). Macroeconomics of Unbalanced Growth. *American Economic Review* 57(3): 415–426.

Bićanić, I., and M. Škreb (1991). The Service Sector in East European Economies: What Role Can It Play in Future Development. *Communist Economies and Economic Transformation* 3 (1): 221–233.

Campos, N., and F. Coricelli (2002). Growth in Transition: What We Know, What We Don't, and What We Should. *Journal of Economic Literature* 40 (3): 793–836.

EBRD (European Bank for Reconstruction and Development) (2004). *Transition Report 2004.* London: EBRD.

Eschenbach, F. (2006). Reform of Services Policy and Commitments in Trade Agreements. In S. Evenett and B. Hoekman (eds.), *Economic Development and Multilateral Cooperation.* London: Palgrave-MacMillan and World Bank.

Falcetti, E., M. Raiser, and P. Sanfey (2002). Defying the Odds: Initial Conditions, Reforms, and Growth in the First Decade of Transition. *Journal of Comparative Economics* 30 (2): 229–250.

Francois, J. F. (1990). Producer Services, Scale, and the Division of Labor. *Oxford Economic Papers* 42 (4): 715–729.

Francois, J. F., and K. Reinert (1996). The Role of Services in the Structure of Production and Trade: Stylized Facts from a Cross-Country Analysis. *Asia-Pacific Economic Review* 2 (1): 35–43.

Fuchs, V. (1968). *The Service Economy.* New York: Columbia University Press.

Konan, D., and K. Maskus (2006). Quantifying the Impact of Services Liberalization in a Developing Country. *Journal of Development Economics* 81 (1): 142–162.

Levine, R., and D. Renelt (1992). A Sensitivity Analysis of Cross-Country Growth Regressions. *American Economic Review* 82 (4): 942–963.

Levine, R. (1997). Financial Development and Economic Growth: Views and Agenda. *Journal of Economic Literature* 35 (2): 688–726.

Lucas, R. E. Jr. (1988). On the Mechanics of Economic Development. *Journal of Monetary Economics* 22 (1): 3–42.

Markusen, J., T. Rutherford, and D. Tarr (2005). Trade and Direct Investment in Producer Services and the Domestic Market for Expertise. *Canadian Journal of Economic* 38 (3): 758–777.

Mattoo, A., R. Rathindran, and A. Subramanian (2006). Measuring Services Trade Liberalization and Its Impact on Economic Growth: An Illustration. *Journal of Economic Integration* 21 (1): 64–98.

Roland, G. (2000). *Transition and Economics: Politics, Markets and Firms.* Cambridge, Mass.: MIT Press.

Romer, Paul M. (1990). Endogenous Technological Change. *Journal of Political Economy* 98 (5): 71–102.

World Bank. (2005). *From Disintegration to Reintegration: Eastern Europe and the Former Soviet Union in International Trade.* Washington, D.C.: World Bank.

[21]

Review of International Economics, 9(2), 233–248, 2001

International Provision of Trade Services, Trade, and Fragmentation

*Alan V. Deardorff**

Abstract

This paper examines the special role that trade liberalization in service industries can play in stimulating not only trade in services but also in goods. International trade in goods requires inputs from several services industries (trade services, such as transportation, insurance, and finance) in order to complete and facilitate international transactions. Restriction on the ability of national service providers to provide these services across borders and within foreign countries creates additional costs and barriers to international trade above those that would arise in otherwise comparable intranational exchange. As a result, trade liberalization in services can yield benefits, by facilitating trade in goods, that are larger than one might expect from analysis of the services trade alone. This paper explores this idea using simple theoretical models to specify the relationships between services trade and goods trade. The paper also notes the role of services trade in a model of international industrial fragmentation, where production processes can be separated across locations but at some cost in terms of additional service inputs. The incentives for such fragmentation can be larger across countries than within countries, owing to the greater differences in factor prices and technologies available. However, the service costs of international fragmentation can also be larger, especially if regulations and restrictions impede the international provision of services. As a result, trade liberalization in services can also stimulate fragmentation of production of both goods and services, thus increasing international trade and the gains from trade even further.

1. Introduction

A signal accomplishment of the Uruguay Round of multilateral trade negotiations was the incorporation of trade in services into a GATT-like framework within the World Trade Organization. The incentive to acknowledge even the existence of trade in services came primarily from US private-sector service providers who chafed under restrictions that limited their ability to operate in foreign markets. They were understandably envious of the institutional facilities made available to goods traders by the General Agreement on Tariffs and Trade (GATT) for limiting barriers to market access. These service providers succeeded in making the case, first in the United States and then in the GATT negotiations, that similar rules should apply to international service transactions. The result was the General Agreement on Trade in Services, GATS, which is now one of three rather unequal pillars of the WTO.[1] The GATS has so far not accomplished very much in the way of actual liberalization. But the framework for negotiation that it provides for the next round of trade negotiations promises to foster a process that many hope will eventually do for trade in services what fifty years of GATT negotiations did for trade in goods.

The motive for liberalizing trade in services, coming as it did from the service industries themselves, was to permit rationalization of service activities along the lines of comparative advantage. It was also, not incidentally, intended to expand the sales and profits of those service providers who were operating from the base of such a comparative advantage. In this sense, the benefits from trade liberalization in services, as

*Deardorff: Department of Economics, University of Michigan, Ann Arbor, MI 48109-1220, USA. E-mail: alandear@umich.ed. The author acknowledges beneficial discussions with Bernard Hoekman, Bob Stern, Kathleen Trask, and Jaume Ventura.

well as the costs to those without comparative advantage, are the same as those that trade theory has long attributed to liberalization of trade in goods. Indeed, many have argued that the fundamentals of trade in services are really no different from trade in goods, and only the difficulties of measuring and monitoring trade in services make it distinctive, from a practical policy perspective (see, e.g., Deardorff, 1985).

However, for many services the benefits from liberalization extend, in a sense, beyond this, and that is what I will focus on in this paper. Many services play a critical facilitating role in the international trade of products other than themselves, including both goods and other services. This is most obviously true of transportation services, which are necessary for all international trade in goods. But it is also true, perhaps to a lesser extent, of other services such as finance, insurance, and communication, as well as some professional services that are often needed in order to complete the international exchange of goods. And this is equally if not more true of international exchange of services themselves. Tourism, for example, depends critically on international provision of passenger transportation.

It follows, therefore, that liberalization of trade in services can generate benefits beyond the service sectors themselves by reducing the real barriers to trade in other sectors. This is not entirely unique to services, of course. Much trade in goods is of intermediate products,[2] and liberalization of goods trade yields many of its benefits not to consumers directly, but by reducing the costs of other goods. But the mechanism by which service trade can stimulate goods trade is somewhat different, and it bears examination in its own right. That will be the main purpose of this paper: to illustrate, with simple trade theory, how liberalization of trade in services can enhance the gains from trade in goods.

I will do this first, in section 2, by using the standard partial-equilibrium trade model to compare the benefits of trade liberalization in goods with those from reduced costs of trading that might arise from liberalization of trade in services. In section 3, I add the role of trade services to the discussion; and then, in section 4, I write down a more specific framework for determining and decomposing their costs. This decomposition allows me to identify and focus on the several ways that these costs can be reduced by permitting service providers to operate across national borders. The gains here include the gains from exploiting comparative advantage, of course, but they also go beyond this by permitting providers to avoid duplication of certain fixed costs, and perhaps by allowing them to operate over shorter distances. In section 5, I provide a brief discussion of several specific types of trade services, and the extent to which they conform to the more general description of my model.

The benefits from services liberalization become larger if we also add another phenomenon that has been attracting increasing attention recently among trade economists: fragmentation. Suppose that technologies permit production of goods to be fragmented across countries—split into parts that can be done in different locations—and suppose also that fragmentation, like trade, requires additional inputs of internationally provided services. If those services are unavailable or prohibitively expensive, fragmentation will not occur. But as technology and/or trade liberalization in services make them available or bring down their costs, fragmentation will become viable after all. Thus liberalization of services trade can yield even further benefits by permitting greater fragmentation-based trade. This is not fundamentally any different from other gains from trade. But I will argue, in section 6, that it has the potential to be quantitatively more important.

The importance of all of this, as I mention in my concluding section 7, is increasing as negotiations within the WTO continue to reduce barriers to trade and as resistance to globalization also mounts. When this paper was first commissioned and drafted, a new round of WTO negotiations seemed imminent. That is no longer the case, after the events in Seattle in late 1999.[3] However, more limited negotiations within the WTO continue, and there is nonetheless scope for extending the liberalization that has already begun, especially in services. The arguments of this paper suggest that the payoffs may be particularly great for expanding the coverage and effectiveness of the GATS.

2. Gains from Reductions in Trade Barriers

To start, let us look at the conventional benefits from trade liberalization. That is, consider a good that is imported from a large world market subject to a tariff. Figure 1 shows in two panels what the effects of lowering that tariff will be, under two different assumptions. Panel A shows what happens if the initial tariff is not prohibitive, while panel B shows the prohibitive case. In both, the new tariff is positive and permits trade. The downward-sloping line in each panel shows the demand for imports of a good within the importing country, while p_w is the given world price.

In panel A, the initial tariff, t_1, raises the price of imports to $p_w + t_1$, which is below the intercept of the demand curve and therefore permits a quantity of the good, q_1, to be imported. When the tariff drops to t_2, the price falls to $p_w + t_2$, and the quantity of imports rises to q_2. The welfare effects of this are well known: consumer surplus (net of producer surplus for competing domestic producers) rises from area a to area $a + b + c$, while tariff revenue changes from $b + d$ to $d + e$. The net effect is that the country's welfare rises by the shaded area, $c + e$. It is perhaps worth noting that if the tariff had fallen to zero, then the net gain would also include area f.

In panel B, the initial tariff is high enough to drive imports to zero, and the domestic price is elevated by less than the tariff, just to the intercept of the demand curve. Here there is no tariff revenue to be lost from tariff reduction, and the country gains the entire shaded area $a + b$, composed of the increase in consumer surplus a and tariff revenue b. The gain in welfare appears to be much larger here, but note that the tariff reduction is also much larger. A tariff cut comparable to that in panel A would have

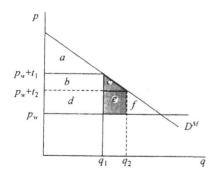

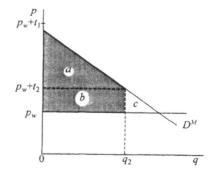

A. Reduction of a non-prohibitive tariff   B. Reduction of a prohibitive tariff

Figure 1. Tariff Reduction

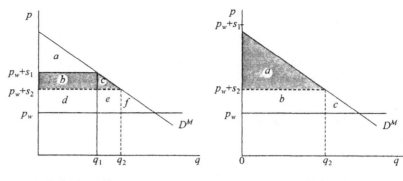

A. Reduction of a non-prohibitive   B. Reduction of a prohibitive
transport cost   transport cost

Figure 2. Reduction in Transport Cost

yielded less; but since it would include the revenue from the higher new tariff, it might still be larger than the gain in panel A. In contrast, if the new tariff were zero in this case, then again area *c* would be added to the country's net gain.

Now suppose that trade is not costless, as so far assumed, but rather that to get goods to the domestic market from the world market, where they are bought at price p_w, requires that traders purchase certain trade services, such as transportation. In some ways such service costs would seem to be analogous to tariffs, in that they add to the domestic cost of the imported good. Therefore it may seem that the analysis just done for a tariff cut would also suffice for analyzing the effects of services liberalization, once we establish that this will reduce their costs. This is not quite right, however, because service costs of trade are real costs, not just transfers to the government. A separate analysis is needed.

Figure 2 repeats Figure 1, but for the most obvious example of a service cost of trade: transportation. The difference from Figure 1 is that t_1 and t_2 are replaced by identical real costs of shipping, s_1 and s_2. These are not transfers to the domestic government, but real resource costs. That is, they are paid to the transportation providers to cover the increased cost of resources that are required for the additional transportation services. This could increase the profits or other incomes of the service providers themselves, but I will simplify by assuming that their costs are constant and that service markets are competitive. It follows that the price of the service remains constant and equal to average cost, therefore yielding no profit or other increase in producer surplus in the service market itself.

The welfare effects of this fall in shipping cost are somewhat different from the fall in the tariff. In panel A, the new gain for the country is the shaded area *b* + *c*, all of which is a gain in net consumer surplus. There is no tariff revenue for the government to lose, but on the other hand area *e* is now an increase in real resource costs, not just a transfer to government. Clearly the gain from a drop in shipping costs can be larger or smaller than the gain from an equal drop in a tariff, depending on whether area *b* is greater than or smaller than area *e*. If shipping costs were to fall to zero, on the other hand, then the gain would necessarily be larger than an equal drop in a tariff.

INTERNATIONAL PROVISION OF TRADE SERVICES 237

If transport costs are initially prohibitive, however, as in panel B, then the gain from their decline is necessarily smaller than from an equal drop in a prohibitive tariff, unless both of them drop to zero. The reason is simply that the new shipping cost is a real cost, while the new tariff is not.

3. Gains from Reductions in Barriers to Services Trade

The simplest way to think about trade liberalization in services generally is within the same framework of Figure 1. For example, suppose we are interested in construction services, which can potentially be provided by work crews from a foreign company, so long as they are permitted to operate within the domestic country and are not taxed too heavily. Figure 1 will apply exactly to this case, panel A for a case in which imports of construction services are subject to additional taxes or other fees paid to the local government, panel B to the case where foreign providers are simply excluded. Similarly, suppose that foreign construction companies are allowed to operate within the country but subject to requirements that they jump through various real hoops not required of domestic companies. Then the case is that of Figure 2, which of course could also include the actual transport costs of getting their crews and equipment to the country's borders.

In general, then, the gains from trade liberalization in services may be very much analogous to liberalization of tariff and nontariff barriers to trade in goods, and this trade may be analyzed in the same ways. This is a point that I and others made when trade in services first began to be discussed, as in Deardorff (1985).

However, there is one category of services that has some special features worth noting: trade services. By these I mean any services the demands for which arise directly from trade itself, presumably from trade in other industries. Perhaps these services can also be analyzed with the tools above, but their special features make them worth looking at specifically.

The prototypical trade service is transportation. I will focus mostly on that, and my terminology will reflect that, but there are certainly other services that have these features as well, as I will discuss later.

The key is that since trade by definition crosses national borders, any services that cater to that trade are likely to be needed on both sides of the border as well. But if trade in services is not permitted—that is, if service providers are not allowed to operate across these borders—then trade itself is likely to be more costly, if it is possible at all.

An example comes easily to mind in the case of transportation. As I understand it, prior to the North American Free Trade Agreement (NAFTA), Mexican truckers were not allowed to operate within the United States, nor US truckers inside Mexico. If a good was to be shipped by truck between the two countries, then it had to be carried on one country's trucks to the border, unloaded, and then reloaded onto the other country's trucks at the border, and finally shipped the rest of the way.

The costs of this awkward arrangement are obvious, and surely large. Even assuming that the countries allowed the trucks far enough inside their borders to permit them to unload and reload on the same lot, so that they did not have to hand-carry goods across the border, this restriction of trucking added to the transportation process a wholly unnecessary step of unloading and reloading.

In addition, it must surely be true that trucking firms incur a portion of other fixed costs that do not vary with distance shipped,[4] and that had to be duplicated by firms from both countries every time a good was traded in this way. Adding any other sources

238   *Alan V. Deardorff*

of increasing returns to scale and distance that might be present in transportation technology, and one can easily imagine that trade costs were greatly enhanced by this prohibition on (literally) cross-border provision of transportation.

This trucking example will provide the template for my rudimentary model of cross-border provision of trade services. But before I embark on the modeling, however, let me stress the importance of all this, for which the model itself is unnecessary. The point will be that trade in trade services brings down the real cost of trade. The benefits from this may be represented by movement along a demand curve for the service itself, like those of Figures 1 and 2 applied to the service industries, but that misses what is so important about these services. Rather, by allowing cross-border provision of trade services we bring down the costs of trade in other things, not just for those services but for everything else. Thus, while a reduced barrier to trade in construction services will increase net consumer surplus of demanders of buildings, a reduced barrier to trade in transportation or another trade service will increase net consumer surplus in *every* industry where trade in the product can avail itself of those services. We're talkin' big bucks here, or at least big utils.

4. A Model of Trade Services

Consider any service, such as transportation, that provides an input that is useful for accomplishing the trade in a good or goods. Output of the trade service is measured in some appropriate units, such as units of the good transported, value of the good insured, etc. Output may also be characterized by one or more other dimensions that are important for determining the usefulness of the service to traders, such as distance or speed, although I will initially allow for neither of these and later, in this paper, will incorporate only distance. In all cases I will focus on the service associated with a particular shipment of a good, S, from a foreign country, F, to the home country, H. I am interested in determining what gives rise to the portion of the cost of shipping the good that arises from input of a some arbitrary trade service, and how this trade-service cost may change as we liberalize trade in the service industry. This cost may be thought of as one component of the shipping cost examined in Figure 2.

To start with, suppose that the per unit cost of the trade service—what I will now call the shipping cost, s—is simply constant, at a rate c that varies across countries where the service providers may be based, in response to the usual determinants of comparative advantage. That is, service providers from country I will have a constant cost $c^I(A^I, w^I)$, where A^I is the technology available in country I for providing this trade service, and w^I is a vector of factor prices, including wages, in country I. Together, these two arguments embody the usual Ricardian and Heckscher–Ohlin determinants of comparative advantage, the latter entering through relative factor endowments that determine factor prices in general equilibrium. In general these may themselves depend on the openness of trade in services, although that is not something I will allow for here.

Suppose that initially there is no trade in services, and that the home country permits this particular trade service to be provided only by domestic firms with costs $c^H(A^H, w^H)$. Liberalization of trade in services would presumably permit these services to be supplied by a provider based in the foreign country, F, from which the good is being imported. Its costs are $c^F(A^F, w^F)$. Or the service might come from a provider based in some third country, I, with costs $c^I(A^I, w^I)$. If either of these is lower than $c^H(A^H, w^H)$, then we have the usual gains from trade arising from comparative advantage. However,

INTERNATIONAL PROVISION OF TRADE SERVICES 239

as noted above, these gains will manifest themselves in lower trade costs of other industries.

Following the trucking example mentioned above, however, I will now complicate the service technology, allowing its unit cost per amount shipped to depend on both quantity shipped and distance. Consider again a shipment S of a good from an arbitrary location A to another location B. The quantity shipped is Q^S. Then, using a service provider from country I, the total cost of the service for the shipment is assumed to take the following form:

$$C^I = c_0 + c_1 Q^S + c_2 D_{AB} + c_3 Q^S D_{AB}, \tag{1}$$

where the parameters c_i, like c above, depend on technology and factor prices in country I:

$$c = (c_0, \dots, c_3) = (c_0(A^I, w^I), \dots, c_3(A^I, w^I)). \tag{2}$$

The first of these parameters, c_0, is a fixed cost per shipment that does not depend on the quantity shipped, nor on the distance shipped. Its presence does not imply the existence of increasing returns to scale, in the usual sense, since it will be repeated for every shipment that the service firm administers. However, it does imply that the cost per unit shipped, $s^I = C^I/Q^S$, declines with the quantity shipped. An example would be the bureaucratic requirements for getting permission for a shipment. The c_1 parameter is simply cost per unit shipped, analogous to the only cost allowed above, such as the cost of loading and unloading. Parameters c_2 and c_3, on the other hand, involve distance. c_2 is a cost per unit of distance, but note that it does not depend on quantity shipped, and therefore should be thought of as another fixed cost. It too will cause s to decline with quantity shipped. In the trucking example, this would include much of the variable cost of transportation, such as the driver's wage, which depends on time spent on the road but not on how much is in the truck. Finally, c_3 is a cost that depends on both distance and quantity, such as part of the fuel cost in transportation that depends on both distance and load.

In general, then, the service cost of a shipment depends on both the quantity shipped and distance, through parameters that in turn depend on technology and factor prices of the country providing the service:

$$C^I = C(Q^S, D; A^I, w^I). \tag{3}$$

The service cost per unit shipped, s, is this divided by Q^S, which I will abbreviate as $s^I(D)$, since I will not be varying Q^S:

$$s^I = C^I/Q^S = C(Q^S, D; A^I, w^I)/Q^S = s^I(D). \tag{4}$$

That is the technology, and some notation to represent it. Now I make a critical assumption about policy: I assume that, in the absence of trade in services, service providers are permitted to operate *only* in their own countries. What this means, for the services needed to accomplish a shipment from foreign country F to home country H, is that only a foreign service provider can service the shipment up to the border, and only a home-country provider can service it from there on. Thus I will represent the origin of the shipment as location F, within country F, and the destination a location in H called H. But no service provider is permitted to service it the whole way. Instead, there is a location B on the border between the countries (or perhaps in international waters), where one provider stops and the other takes over.

With this assumption, the total service cost for the shipment in service autarky becomes:

$$C^{Aut} = C^F(Q^S, D_{FB}; A^F, w^F) + C^H(Q^S, D_{BH}; A^H, w^H)$$
$$= (c_0^F + c_0^H) + (c_1^F + c_1^H)Q^S$$
$$+ c_2^F D_{FB} + c_2^H D_{BH} + c_3^F Q^S D_{FB} + c_3^H Q^S D_{BH}, \tag{5}$$

and the service cost per unit shipped—again in service autarky—is:

$$s^{Aut} = [C^F(Q^S, D_{FB}; A^F, w^F) + C^H(Q^S, D_{BH}; A^H, w^H)]/Q^S$$
$$= \frac{(c_0^F + c_0^H)}{Q^S} + (c_1^F + c_1^H)$$
$$+ \frac{c_2^F D_{FB} + c_2^H D_{BH}}{Q^S} + (c_3^F D_{FB} + c_3^H D_{BH}). \tag{6}$$

If trade in services is now permitted, service for the entire shipment will be provided by a single provider, and in general it may or may not be a provider from one of the two countries who are trading the good. Let country L, which may be H or F, have the lowest cost of providing the service for this particular route from point F to point H, not necessarily passing through point B. This then is the cost if free cross-border provision of services is permitted:

$$s^{Free} = s^L(D_{FH}) = \frac{c_0^L}{Q^S} + c_1^L + \frac{c_2^L D_{FH}}{Q^S} + c_3^L D_{FH}$$
$$\leq \min_{H,F}[s^F(D_{FH}), s^H(D_{FH})]. \tag{7}$$

This cost is evidently lower than the cost in autarky, s^{Aut}. To see the several ways that cross-border provision of services can reduce these costs, I now decompose the cost reduction into three parts, numbered 1, 2, and 3, as follows:

$$s^{Aut} - s^{Free} = s^F(D_{FB}) + s^H(D_{BH}) - s^L(D_{FH})$$
$$1 := [s^F(D_{FB}) - s^L(D_{FB})] + [s^H(D_{BH}) - s^L(D_{BH})]$$
$$2 : + \left(\frac{c_2^L}{Q^S} + c_3^L\right)[(D_{FB} + D_{BH}) - D_{FH}]$$
$$3 : + \left\{\frac{c_0^L}{Q^S} + c_1^L\right\}(2 - 1). \tag{8}$$

1. Comparative advantage. The first line of the decomposition in (8) is the conventional gains from trade due to comparative advantage. It includes the cost reduction that is possible if a different producer, operating from a different base of comparative advantage, does essentially what was being done before. That is, continuing to service the shipment in two parts within each country, we replace the service providers in both with the low-cost provider that may operate from a different country and that therefore, with better technology and/or different factor prices, may be able to provide the service for lower cost. Of course it is possible that the low-cost provider is from one of these two countries themselves, in which case one of the bracketed terms in line 1 is zero. These gains may be large or small depending on the importance of comparative advantage in this context. They may even be negative, if the low-cost provider's advantage derives mainly from servicing longer distances than these internal ones.

INTERNATIONAL PROVISION OF TRADE SERVICES   241

2. Reduced distance.   It is possible that the border location, through which trade must pass if service trade is not permitted, happens to lie exactly on the least-cost trade route between the two countries, in which case the second effect identified above will be zero. But in general this will not be the case, and a more direct route will exist that bypasses that particular border location. In general, therefore, there will be some cost savings simply from traversing and servicing a shorter distance, as $D_{FH} < D_{FB} + D_{BH}$.

3. Elimination of fixed costs.   The most important cost savings, however, are likely to be found in line 3 of the decomposition. By switching from two service providers to a single one, even if they both have the same technology (as they do in line 3), the need is eliminated to incur two sets of fixed costs. That is, those costs that do not vary with distance, but instead are incurred for each shipment regardless of distance and perhaps in proportion to output, are needlessly duplicated when two providers share the task. One whole set of these fixed costs is therefore saved when the task is unified. To stress this, I have included the arithmetically unnecessary expression "(2–1)" in line 3 of the decomposition, to remind us that fixed costs are being reduced from twice the curly-bracketed expression to only one times it. Of course, whether this is in fact a large source of cost savings depends on the size of these fixed costs, which could for some technologies be negligible. But casual observation suggests that it is often large.

This is all that my model has to say directly about the cost savings from cross-border provision of trade services. However, realistically, there are several more such sources of savings that may enter, and these should be mentioned even though they do not appear explicitly in the model.

4. Economies of distance.   This one is in the model, at least partially, but it is hard to separate from the other effects. Different service technologies may be more or less well suited to serving shipments over longer distances, and often those suited for longer distances will not be commercially viable for the short distances that lie only inside of countries. The specification of technology used above incorporates this feature, to an extent, through the cost parameters that do and do not vary with distance. Thus the least-cost provider may achieve that low cost, once trade is free, primarily because its costs that vary with distance are small compared with its fixed costs that do not. As mentioned above, either or both bracketed expressions in line 1 of (8) could be small or even negative if the low-cost provider is inefficient over short distances, and the cost savings from the more appropriate technology would then be merged into the savings from reduced fixed costs in line 3. Perhaps more importantly, the formulation here has not allowed for any choice of techniques, except across providers. But in fact such choices do exist, and even a domestic provider that currently services only short routes may substitute more appropriate techniques once service trade makes them useful. This substitution, if it occurred, could only reduce costs further.

5. Economies of scale.   As I stressed above, the formulation here, despite appearance, does not include any economies of scale. That is, a service provider saves nothing in costs by serving multiple shipments of the same size and distance. Yet such economies of scale undoubtedly exist as well, in some trade-service industries just as in many other industries. As cross-border provision of services permits more efficient providers to displace those less efficient, the surviving firms will become larger and may therefore have lower costs. There is nothing new about this effect, but once again it should be remembered that this cost saving too, if it happens, will stimulate trade and the gains from trade in the industries whose trade relies on it.

242   *Alan V. Deardorff*

6. Border frictions. In the model here, the worst that happens when a trade route is arbitrarily divided across service providers from the two countries is that they simply do their work back to back. In fact, when impediments to cross-border provision of services exist, it is likely that the costs of interfacing between the two providers will be higher. In the US–Mexican trucking example that motivated my model, one can easily imagine that the costs of transferring a cargo from a Mexican truck to an American one will exceed just the costs of unloading and then reloading. If the equipment used by both trucking companies are not compatible, it may be necessary to repack a load or transfer it also to another shipping container. If procedures used by the two work crews are not the same, additional inefficiencies may arise from the effort to make them conform. At a minimum, one may simply need a roof over the heads of the workers and their cargo, something that would have been provided naturally at the origin and destination of the shipment. These additional costs could have been included in the model here, at the cost of a bit more notation, but it seems enough merely to point them out separately.

7. Time. I mentioned earlier that an important dimension of service provision is time, but I did not include it explicitly in the model here. No doubt the time cost associated with different modes of trade servicing could mostly be included implicitly in the parameters of this model. But it is worth mentioning separately as well, since reduced time costs seem likely to be one of the important benefits of cross-border service provision. When services must be provided by separate institutional entities, it is almost inevitable that time will be wasted in coordinating them. This is time that could easily have been saved if a single provider were permitted to handle the whole job. In a world where timely provision of inputs and outputs has become one of the most critical elements of competitive success, these time benefits must be far from trivial.

8. Regulatory costs. Many services are regulated by governments. To the extent that these regulations exclude foreign services providers completely, then of course liberalization of services trade means changing these regulations. In some cases, however, foreign service providers are permitted to operate within a country, but the regulations that apply to them increase their costs compared with domestic firms. For example, trucking companies may be permitted to carry cargo into a country but not out, forcing them to bear the cost of returning the trucks to their home market empty. Regulations may also require that certain categories of demanders—especially government agencies themselves—use domestic providers. Like nontariff barriers in goods, these asymmetric regulations undermine competition and efficiency, and their removal will be beneficial. In addition, applying the same regulations to both foreign and domestic service providers may facilitate the use of a single provider for an entire transaction, permitting the sort of cost reduction that has been the subject of this paper.

9. Red tape costs. Even if the same regulations apply to both foreign and domestic providers in an industry, it may still be necessary to bear the costs of satisfying these regulations in both countries in order to service a complete international transaction. This was mentioned above as one of the sources of the fixed cost, c_0, in the model, but the duplication of this cost will not be eliminated merely by permitting providers to operate in both countries subject to their domestic regulations. They will still have to fill out forms in both countries, undergo inspections in both, etc. Services trade liberalization therefore needs to include provisions for either harmonizing the regulations themselves across countries, so that a single set of procedures will satisfy regulators in both, or it should include mutual recognition agreements whereby firms need only be certified in one country in order to operate in both. Of course, this raises difficult issues when countries disagree on what levels of regulation are needed to protect their citizens' health and safety. But only if this problem is resolved can the full benefits of cross-border service trade be enjoyed.

5. Specific Trade Services

The discussion so far has attempted to be general, saying things that may apply to any and all trade services. In this section I say a few words about each of several specific and familiar trade services, primarily to address whether they seem to fit well or poorly into the mold of this model. In addition, in some cases, I will acknowledge special characteristics of these specific trade services that may make them particularly important for enhancing trade in goods.[5]

Transport Services

The model was largely motivated, as said above, by the example of trucking services between Mexico and the United States. It therefore seems to fit best the circumstances of transport services more generally. Certainly, transportation services of all sorts are characterized by costs that vary with both quantity shipped and distance. In addition, there routinely exist fixed costs per shipment that are independent of quantity, distance, or both, such as take-off and landing costs of aircraft, maintenance of railway tracks, and the pay of stevedores in ocean shipping.

Policies regulating the cross-border provision of transport services are apparently as widely varied as the services themselves, but they are notoriously encumbered by restrictions favoring national suppliers. These range from restrictions on domestic flights by international carriers to the notorious Jones Act restrictions on ocean shipping within US territorial waters. Some of these restrictions are meant less to protect domestic suppliers than to protect favored categories of labor, often at the suppliers' expense, and thus seem to operate more directly on the cost parameters of an industry than on who can operate. But either way, one can expect liberalization of trade in transport services to greatly lower the costs of trade.

Insurance

International trade is inevitably more risky than domestic trade, because of the broader range of unpredictable shocks to which it is subject from climate, culture, and government interference, not to mention the financial uncertainty of different national currencies and markets. Insurance to protect against these uncertainties is therefore an essential input to international trade, even more so than to domestic commerce. For many of these uncertainties, it is not strictly necessary for the insurance provider to operate physically in a foreign territory, and therefore much of the required insurance can be provided completely by a domestic carrier within, say, the exporter's country of origin. The principal gain from trade in insurance services may therefore be the availability of lower-cost insurance from a foreign carrier—the gain attributed to comparative advantage above.

However, there are surely some risks associated with trade within a foreign country that are not well covered by a domestic carrier. Indeed, some risks may not even be recognized as requiring insurance, leaving a trader exposed to risks that they are not aware of, but that they could have known if they had hired the services of a local provider as well. As a result, the prudent international trading company is likely to require the services of several insurance companies specializing in their several countries of operation. And as in the transport case, the cost of this more complete coverage is likely to be reduced if a single provider, operating routinely in all relevant markets, can provide the coverage.

In other words, while the terminology of the model here was largely taken from the transport industry, it seems likely that it fits the market for insurance as well, although perhaps to a lesser extent.

Communication

Increasingly in the modern world, international trade requires rapid and effective communication to specify the details of a transaction and tailor them to the needs of all concerned. It would be hard to overestimate the importance of modern communication technologies for the growth of world trade in recent decades. And yet to a surprising extent, communications are still encumbered by different national standards and restrictions on who can use them, forcing international businesses to work around these restrictions by patching together pieces from different companies and different technologies. The rise of the internet is changing much of that, and perhaps such national restrictions on communications will lose their bite as this occurs. But greater freedom for communication firms to operate worldwide will nonetheless still serve a purpose of facilitating trade.

Travel Services

Much of the travel industry—both passenger transportation and other services such as hotels, restaurants, and local transportation—is geared to tourists and therefore not directly relevant here except as a category of trade itself that relies heavily on trade services. However, these same services are also used by those who travel on business, and these are an essential input to international trade. In spite of advances in long-distance communication, the on-site presence of people in face-to-face contact and engaged in direct oversight of activities continues to be essential for international commerce. Travel services are therefore a nontrivial input to international trade, even in goods.

Like the other categories of trade services considered here, travel services can be provided more efficiently if done by single, or at least allied, providers that span national borders, so as to coordinate reservations and other aspects of their service. Much of this has already been facilitated in recent years by the formation of international networks of airlines and hotel chains, but these are seldom as efficient as a single larger or merged firm operating across borders.

Professional Services

International transactions, no less than domestic ones, require the services of all manner of professionals. Lawyers are needed to vet contracts with both domestic and foreign suppliers and customers. Accountants must keep the books in a manner compatible with different national requirements. Expansion of a company's operations is likely to require the services in different countries of architects, contractors, real estate agents, and the like. In each case, the service must be tailored to the local market, so that it may seem that separate providers are necessarily called for. However, the services must also be integrated and compatible with what is being done by the same firm

INTERNATIONAL PROVISION OF TRADE SERVICES 245

in other countries, and this requires effective communication among them. This is most easily accomplished if the national-based providers work together regularly, as they would if they were part of a single multinational service company. Looked at in this way, the costs of professional services may not be all that different from others discussed here. And for many such services, such as law, professionals from one jurisdiction are prohibited from practicing in another.

Financial Services

The final service category I will consider is financial services. This includes a wide variety of services that are necessary for international trade, ranging from export financing to foreign exchange. However, this is the one category where it is not obvious, to me at least, that international provision of the services is really necessary. Most of a trading firm's financial needs can be met, I suppose, within a national firm that knows the client well, and, except for minor transactions like providing currency to the firm's overseas travelers, the national firm need not have a presence abroad.

However, this does not in any way diminish the importance of the financial services themselves, or mean that well-functioning world financial markets are not critically necessary for international trade. In Deardorff (2000), I examine the disruption that can be caused for trade by a financial crisis that undermines confidence in a nation's currency and its financial institutions. To the extent that more integrated world financial markets can lessen the likelihood of such disruptions, trade and the gains from trade will be among the beneficiaries.

6. Fragmentation

The focus here has been on various ways in which liberalization of trade in services may reduce the costs of trade, and thereby lead to gains from trade as discussed in section 2. The potential for such gains has arguably expanded in recent years as production processes have become more and more fragmented into smaller pieces done in different locations. This process of fragmentation has appeared in the literature of international trade in several forms and under several names—such as international specialization, outsourcing, and even globalization.[6] A common theme has been that fragmentation permits countries to specialize ever more finely in the bits of production processes in which they have the greatest comparative advantage, and that by locating these different bits in different countries and coordinating them internationally, the world economy can achieve ever greater gains in productive efficiency.

The process of fragmentation is not at all new, but it has been newly extended in recent decades in part by technological changes that have made the international coordination of fragmented production increasingly feasible. These technologies have primarily appeared in service industries, where more rapid and effective transportation and communication across countries has been a precondition for reducing the costs of final products by producing them in stages in different countries. As a result, the international provision of many services has come to play a larger and larger role in international trade, even beyond what it was when products were more typically produced in one place.

This expanded role of services due to fragmentation also gives rise to additional potential gains from further reductions in the costs of services, such as have been the focus of this paper. In one sense, one can simply think of the effects of reduced trade

246   *Alan V. Deardorff*

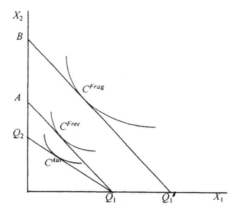

Figure 3. Gains from Trade and Fragmentation

costs depicted in Figure 2 as being repeated over an ever larger number of traded fragments, and thus multiplying the gains from trade.

Another approach is shown in Figure 3, which is adapted from Deardorff (1998).
There, the gains from trade in a simple Ricardian trade model are contrasted with the
gains from fragmentation in the same model. The Ricardian straight-line transformation curve for two goods without fragmentation is shown as the line $Q_1 Q_2$, and the level
of consumption in autarky as point C^{Aut}. Conventional trade allows the country to
specialize in good 1, producing at Q_1 and trading at world prices given by the slope of
line $Q_1 A$ to achieve consumption at point C^{Free}. If the technology for good 1 becomes
fragmented, however, then the country can specialize in just one fragment—whichever
one it produces relatively most cheaply—and trade the fragment on the world market
for a larger quantity of good 1 than it could have produced itself without fragmentation, Q_1'. The country's budget line trading on the world market is therefore shifted
out by fragmentation, and it can achieve the higher consumption level C^{Frag}. The
message here is that fragmentation expands a country's consumption possibility set,
not just by improving its terms of trade of one final good for another, but by expanding the maximum attainable amount of all final goods, almost as though by an improvement in productivity.[7]

But fragmentation also involves much greater inputs of services than would be
needed for trade in final goods only, in order to coordinate the fragments. Therefore,
these gains are conditional upon the availability of such services at low cost. The recent
emergence of fragmentation as an increasingly important phenomenon in the global
economy owes its existence to technological improvements that have brought these
costs down to historically low levels. The additional benefits from even greater fragmentation will depend on lowering these costs still further through the sorts of
liberalization of trade in services that have been examined in this paper.

7. Conclusion

The message of this paper is that there is tremendous scope for the world to benefit
by liberalizing trade in services. This is especially true for trade in what I have called

trade services—those that facilitate trade in goods and in other services. By bringing down the costs of trade services, liberalization can generate benefits that are not confined only to the services markets themselves, but that will appear in the markets for every other kind of trade that they facilitate.

The paper has examined a variety of ways in which removing barriers to the cross-border provision of trade services can lower their costs. These include the gains that conventionally arise from comparative advantage, but in the framework presented here there are additional gains as well that are plausibly larger. These arise especially when restrictions in services markets require that the services needed to facilitate a single trade must be provided by two different national service providers. When that is the case, removal of such restrictions has the added benefit of eliminating duplicated fixed costs.

Regardless of the size of any cost reduction in trade services, the benefits for trade are arguably enhanced by the phenomenon of fragmentation. The more that production processes become split across locations, with the fragments tied together and coordinated by various trade services, the greater are the gains from reductions in service costs. Since fragmentation seems to characterize an increasing portion of world specialization and trade, the importance of service liberalization is growing apace.

All of this is particularly timely right now, as the world hesitates in its forward movement toward more liberal trade. The creation of the World Trade Organization and the GATS provided a framework for making real progress in reducing barriers to trade in services. Had a new trade round been inaugurated at the Seattle 1999 ministerial meeting, as expected, then the arguments made in this paper could have buttressed the case for intensive negotiations in services, where the payoffs can be so great. As it is, however, the timing and perhaps even the likelihood of a new round is in doubt. A backlash against many aspects of globalization now questions the benefits and the equity of reducing trade barriers and constraining trade policies. How these issues will be resolved is not yet clear, but it does seem evident that the benefits from services liberalization are immune to many of these objections. I would hope that the members of the WTO will be able to move ahead in services liberalization even as other aspects of the WTO agenda may be stalled.

References

Arndt, Sven W., "Globalization and the Open Economy," *North American Journal of Economics and Finance* 8 (1997):71–9.

Deardorff, Alan V., "Comparative Advantage and International Trade and Investment in Services," in Robert M. Stern (ed.), *Trade and Investment in Services: Canada/US Perspectives*, Toronto: Ontario Economic Council (1985):39–71.

————, "An Economist's Overview of the World Trade Organization," in *The Emerging WTO System and Perspectives from Asia*, Joint US–Korea Economic Studies 7 (1997).

————, "Fragmentation in Simple Trade Models," Discussion Paper 422, Research Seminar in International Economics, University of Michigan (1998).

————, "Financial Crisis, Trade, and Fragmentation," Discussion Paper 458, Research Seminar in International Economics, University of Michigan (2000).

Deardorff, Alan V. and Robert M. Stern, "What the Public Should Know about Globalization and the World Trade Organization," Discussion Paper 460, Research Seminar on International Economics, University of Michigan (2000).

Dixit, Avinash K. and Gene M. Grossman, "Trade and Protection with Multistage Production," *Review of Economic Studies* 59 (1982):583–94.

Feenstra, Robert C., "Integration of Trade and Disintegration of Production in the Global Economy," *Journal of Economic Perspectives* 12 (Fall) (1998):31–50.

Feenstra, Robert C. and Gordon H. Hanson, "Globalization, Outsourcing, and Wage Inequality," *American Economic Review* 86 (1996):240–5.

Grossman, Gene M. and Elhanan Helpman, "The Internationalization of Economic Acitivity," National Science Foundation grant, July (1999).

Hoekman, Bernard and Carlos A. Primo Braga, "Protection and Trade in Services," Policy Research Working Paper 1747, Washington, DC: World Bank (1997).

Hummels, David, Dana Rapoport, and Kei-Mu Yi, "Vertical Specialization and the Changing Nature of World Trade," *FRBNY Economic Policy Review*, June (1998):79–99.

Jones, Ronald W. and Henryk Kierzkowski, "The Role of Services in Production and International Trade: A Theoretical Framework," in Jones, R. W. and Anne O. Krueger (eds.), *The Political Economy of International Trade: Essays in Honor of Robert E. Baldwin*, Cambridge, MA: Blackwell (1990):31–48.

Sanyal, Kalyan K. and Ronald W. Jones, "The Theory of Trade in Middle Products," *American Economic Review* 72 (1982):16–31.

Notes

1. The other two are the GATT itself and the agreement on trade related intellectual property rights (TRIPS). See Deardorff (1997) for a more complete discussion of the World Trade Organization.

2. Sanyal and Jones (1982), in fact, argued that *all* trade is of intermediate products, what they called "middle products."

3. See Deardorff and Stern (2000) for some discussion of those events.

4. Loading and unloading are themselves such fixed costs.

5. See Hoekman and Primo Braga (1997) for a useful discussion of many actual barriers to trade in services.

6. Although there may be slight differences in what various authors mean by the terms they use, this list of variations on the theme of fragmentation includes "disintegration" (Feenstra, 1998), "internationalization" (Grossman and Helpman, 1999), "intra-product specialization" (Arndt, 1997), "multistage production" (Dixit and Grossman, 1982), and "vertical specialization" (Hummels et al., 1998). Others have used standard terms such as "subcontracting" and "outsourcing" (Feenstra and Hanson, 1996) to address what are certainly important aspects of the phenomenon. I follow Jones and Kierzkowski (1990) in using the term "fragmentation."

7. It is not literally that production possibilities are necessarily expanded by fragmentation, as explained more fully in Deardorff (1998), where production possibilities are viewed in three dimensions including both an intermediate input and the final product, as well as the other good that both may be traded for.

Journal of Economic Perspectives—Volume 21, Number 3—Summer 2007—Pages 131–154

Transportation Costs and International Trade in the Second Era of Globalization

David Hummels

From 1950–2004, world trade grew at a rapid average rate of 5.9 percent per annum. The annual growth rate of manufacturing trade was even faster, at 7.2 percent. For the world as a whole, the ratio of trade relative to output more than tripled over the last five decades (World Trade Organization, International Trade Statistics, 2005). Similarly, the sum of U.S. imports and exports rose from 6.5 percent of GDP in 1960 to about 20 percent of GDP in the early 2000s (based on data at ⟨http://www.bea.gov⟩).

One prominent possible explanation for the rise in international trade is a decline in international transportation costs. Economic historians have documented how technological change led to substantial reductions in shipping costs from 1850–1913 (Harley, 1980, Harley, 1989; North, 1958, 1968; Mohammed and Williamson, 2004). Econometric evidence has subsequently linked shipping cost declines to rapid growth in trade during that first era of globalization (Estevadeordal, Frantz, and Taylor, 2003). The decades since World War II have also witnessed significant technological change in shipping, including the development of jet aircraft engines and the use of containerization in ocean shipping. However, documentation of the actual decline in shipping costs in recent decades has been lacking. This paper will draw on an eclectic mix of data to characterize the patterns of international ocean and air transportation costs in the last few decades.

Understanding modern changes in transportation costs turns out to be unexpectedly complex. Shifts in the types of products traded, the intensity with which they use transportation services, and whether these goods are shipped by ocean or air freight all affect measured costs. At various times, improvements in transportation technology have been partially offset by significant changes in input costs and

■ *David Hummels is Associate Professor of Economics, Purdue University, West Lafayette, Indiana. His e-mail address is* ⟨*hummelsd@purdue.edu*⟩.

in the nature of what is traded. Moreover, the economic effects of improved transportation are apparent not only in *how much* trade has grown, but also in *how* trade has grown. Improvements in the quality of transportation services—like greater speed and reliability—allow corresponding reorganizations of global networks of production and new ways of coping with uncertainty in foreign markets.

I begin with an overview of how goods are transported across international borders, with an emphasis on ocean and air transport. I discuss different ways of placing transportation costs in economic context and then discuss patterns of technological changes and price indexes for international air and ocean shipping. I employ regression analysis to sort out the role of cost shocks and technological and compositional change in shaping the time series in transportation costs and then draw out implications of these trends for the changing nature of trade and integration. Much of the data employed here can be difficult to find, but of great use to researchers going forward. An appendix at the end of the paper describes where to find data and offers links to a website that provides all of the data underlying this paper's tables and figures.

How Goods Move

Roughly 23 percent of world trade by value occurs between countries that share a land border. This proportion has been nearly constant over recent decades, though it varies significantly across continents. For Africa, the Middle East, and Asia, between 1 and 5 percent of trade by value is with land-neighboring countries; for Latin America, trade with land neighbors is 10 to 20 percent of the whole, and for Europe and North America it is 25–35 percent of trade. Detailed data on the value of trade by different modes of transportation are sparse, but U.S. and Latin American data suggest that trade with land neighbors is dominated by surface modes like truck, rail, and pipeline, with perhaps 10 percent of trade going via air or ocean, based on my calculations using data from United Nations Commodity Trade Statistics Database (UN Comtrade), the U.S. Census Bureau's *U.S. Exports/ Imports of Merchandise,* and the Economic Commission for Latin America and the Caribbean's International Transport Database (Base de datos de Transporte Internacional), or the ECLAC BTI, all discussed in more detail in the appendix.

For trade with nonadjacent partners, nearly all merchandise trade moves via ocean and air modes. Bulk commodities like oil and petroleum products, iron ore, coal, and grains are shipped almost exclusively via ocean cargo. Bulk cargoes constitute the majority of international trade when measured in terms of weight, but are a much smaller and shrinking share of trade when measured in value terms.

Manufactured goods are the largest and most rapidly growing portion of world trade. To illustrate how they are transported, Table 1 reports worldwide data on ocean and air shipping of non-bulk-traded goods. Air shipments represent less than 1 percent of total tons and ton-miles shipped, but are growing rapidly. Between 1975 and 2004, air tonnages grew at 7.4 percent per annum, much faster than both

Table 1A
World Trade

Year	World trade			World trade			
	All goods		Manufactures	Quantities of nonbulk cargoes			
	(2000 US$bn)	Million tons	(2000 US$bn)	Million tons		Billion ton-miles	
				Ocean	Air	Ocean	Air
1951			179				0.2
1955	505	880	222				0.3
1960	623	1080	301	307			0.7
1965	844	1640	453	434		1537	1.8
1970	1152	2605	684	717		2118	4.3
1975	2341	3072	1307	793	3.0	2810	7.7
1980	3718	3704	2009	1037	4.8	3720	13.9
1985	2759	3382	1683	1066	6.5	3750	19.8
1990	4189	4008	2947	1285	9.6	4440	31.7
1995	5442	4651	4041	1520	14.0	5395	47.8
2000	6270	5983	4688	2533	20.7	6790	69.2
2004	8164	6758	6022	2855	23.4	8335	79.2
Annualized growth rates							
Whole sample	7.40	5.37	7.04	5.20		4.43	11.72
1975–2004	4.40	2.76	5.41	4.52	7.37	3.82	8.35

Table 1B
U.S. Air Trade

Year	U.S.: Air share of trade value (excluding North America)	
	Imports	Exports
1951		
1955		
1960		
1965	8.1	11.9
1970	12.1	19.5
1975	12.0	19.3
1980	13.9	27.6
1985	19.8	36.3
1990	24.6	42.3
1995	33.1	44.3
2000	36.0	57.6
2004	31.5	52.8
Annualized growth rates		
Whole sample	3.55	3.89
1975–2004	3.40	3.53

Sources: World trade data from the World Trade Organization's "International Trade Statistics, 2005," and authors calculations. World air shipments from the International Air Transport Association's (IATA's) *World Air Transport Statistics.* World ocean shipments from United Nations Conference on Trade and Development's *Review of Maritime Transport.* U.S. data from the U.S. Census Bureau's *Statistical Abstract of the United States, U.S. Imports of Merchandise,* and *U.S. Exports of Merchandise.*

ocean tonnage and the value of world trade in manufactures in this period. The relative growth of air shipping is even more apparent in looking at ton-miles shipped, with 11.7 per annum growth rates going back to 1951.

Because the heaviest goods travel via ocean, weight-based data on international trade significantly understate the economic importance of air shipping. Table 1B reports the value share of air shipments in U.S. trade with nonadjacent partners. In the past 40 years, air shipments have grown to represent a third of the value of U.S. imports and more than half of U.S. exports with countries outside North America. Data on mode of transport for international trade are not broadly available for other countries, but the increased U.S. reliance on air shipping does not appear to be an anomaly. Excluding land neighbors, the air share of import value in 2000 exceeded 30 percent for Argentina, Brazil, Colombia, Mexico, Paraguay, and Uruguay (based on author's calculations using data from *U.S. Exports/Imports of Merchandise* and ECLAC BTI).

Why has air transport grown so rapidly? As the next sections show, a major factor has been a sharp decline in the relative cost of air shipping. Less obviously, but perhaps as important, Table 1 shows that a dollar of traded merchandise weighs much less today than in previous years. From 1960–2004, the real value of trade in manufactures grew about 1.5 percent per year faster than the weight of nonbulk cargoes. If bulk commodities are included in the calculation, the real value of all trade grew 1.8 percent faster per year than the weight of all trade.

A fall in the weight/value ratio of trade leads to more air transport for two reasons. First, the marginal fuel cost of lifting a 100 kilogram package into the air is considerably higher than the cost of floating it on water. Second, consumers are sensitive to changes in the delivered price of merchandise, not to changes in the transportation price. If transportation is but a small fraction of the delivered price, then when choosing transport mode, the explicit costs of transportation may be trumped by implicit costs such as timeliness or reliability.

Consider this example. I want to import a $16 bottle of wine from France. Air shipping costs of $8 are twice ocean shipping costs of $4. Going from ocean to air increases the delivered cost by $4 or 25 percent of the original price. Now I want to import a $160 bottle of wine from France. The shipping costs are the same, but the $4 cost to upgrade to air shipping represents just a 2.5 percent increase in the delivered price. The consumer is much more likely to use the faster but more expensive shipping option when the percentage effect on delivered price is smaller.

Similarly, the gains from employing air rather than surface shipping are more pronounced on longer routes. Choosing air transport from the United Kingdom to France might save a shipper five hours, while choosing air transport from China to France might save five weeks. Further, as I show below, the marginal cost of air shipping cargo an additional mile is falling rapidly. These insights help explain a final interesting pattern in the Table 1 data: over time, the average air shipment is getting longer and the average ocean shipment is getting shorter. Combining the tons and ton-miles data (for example 8,335 billion ton-miles/2855 million tons in 2004), ocean-shipped cargo traveled an average of 2,919 miles in 2004, down from

3,543 miles in 1975. In contrast, air-shipped cargo traveled 3,383 miles on average in 2004, up from 2,600 miles in 1975.

Transportation Costs in Perspective

There are three ways to put the economic importance of transportation costs in perspective: by examining 1) transportation costs relative to the value of the goods being moved; 2) transportation costs relative to other known barriers to trade, like tariffs; and 3) the extent to which transportation costs alter relative prices.

Ad Valorem Measures of Transportation Costs

International trade economists typically express transportation costs in ad valorem terms, that is, the cost of shipping relative to the value of the good. This is equivalent to the percentage change in the delivered price as a result of paying for transportation.[1]

The best data for evaluating the ad valorem impact of transportation costs over time comes from a few importers such as New Zealand and the United States that collect freight expenditures as part of their import customs declarations.[2] These data enable us to examine ad valorem transportation costs for an individual good, or to calculate aggregate expenditures on transportation divided by aggregate import value. This aggregate measure is equivalent to an average of ad valorem transport costs for each good, after weighting each good by its share of value in trade.[3]

The New Zealand data cover 1963–1997, a period in which aggregate transportation expenditures fluctuated between a low of 7 percent of import value (in 1970) and a high of 11 percent (in 1974) but exhibited no clear trend. The U.S. data cover 1974–2004, a period in which aggregate expenditures on freight

---

[1] Transportation costs drive a wedge between the price at the place of origin and the price at the destination. Denoting the origin price as p, destination price as p^*, and per unit shipping costs as f, $p^* = p + f$. Then the ad valorem percentage change in prices induced by transportation is $p^*/p = 1 + f/p$. A common but inaccurate approach is to model the f term as a constant percentage τ of value shipped, in which case the ad valorem cost is $p^*/p = 1 + \tau p/p = 1 + \tau$ and is independent of the goods price.

[2] Several authors investigating trade growth have employed indirect measures of transportation costs constructed using a "matched partner" technique. In principle, exporting countries report trade flows exclusive of freight and insurance and importing countries report flows inclusive of freight and insurance. If measured without error, comparing the valuation of the same flow reported by both the importer and exporter yields a difference equal to transport costs. However, Hummels and Lugovskyy (2006) show that the "matched partner" technique is subject to enormous measurement error and in fact produces time series variation that is orthogonal to actual variation in shipping costs.

[3] F^k represents transportation expenditures for a single good k. Summing F^k over goods and dividing by the total value of imports gives aggregate expenditures, τ^{agg}, on transportation as a share of trade, $\tau^{agg} = \Sigma_k F^k / \Sigma_k (pq)^k = \Sigma_k \tau^k s^k$. This is the same as averaging the ad valorem transportation expenditure for each good, $\tau^k = F^k/(pq)^k$, after weighting each good by its share in trade, $s^k = (pq)^k / \Sigma_k (pq)^k$.

declined steadily from about 8 percent of the value of total imports in 1974 down to about 4 percent in 1997 before leveling off. However, the apparent downward trend in the U.S. data may be misleading. The contrast with the New Zealand data and evidence in the next section makes clear that much of the apparent decline in aggregate U.S. transport expenditures in this period is an artifact of the 1974 starting point and the large effect of the oil shock on prices in that year.

Aggregate freight expenditures can paint an incomplete picture of transportation costs. Since the share of trade in a particular product or from a particular exporter tends to be low when shipping costs are high, goods with high transportation costs tend to receive low weights when aggregating. A switch toward more proximate trading partners, or toward more transportable goods, can lower the aggregate value of expenditures on transportation even if true shipping costs are unchanged. Similarly, an increase in transport service quality can raise aggregate expenditures considerably. In the sections below, I provide measures that control for these important compositional shifts.

Transportation Costs vs. Tariffs

Studies examining customs data consistently find that transportation costs pose a barrier to trade at least as large as, and frequently larger than, tariffs. Trade negotiations have steadily reduced tariff rates, with average U.S. import tariffs dropping from 6.0 to 1.5 percent since 1950 (U.S. International Trade Commission) and worldwide average import tariffs dropping from 8.6 to 3.2 percent between 1960 and 1995 (Clemens and Williamson, 2002). As tariffs become a less important barrier to trade, the contribution of transportation to total trade costs—shipping plus tariffs—is rising.

Transport expenditures on the median good were half as much as tariff duties for U.S. imports in 1958 (Waters, 1970) and equal to tariff duties in 1965 (Finger and Yeats, 1976). By 2004, aggregate expenditures on shipping for total imports were three times higher than aggregate tariff duties paid. For the median individual shipment in U.S. imports in 2004, exporters paid $9 in transportation costs for every $1 they paid in tariff duties. Moreover, the United States is actually a notable outlier in that it pays *much less* for transportation than other countries. In 2000, aggregate transportation expenditures for major Latin America countries were 1.5 to 2.5 times higher than for the United States (based on author's calculations using *U.S. Imports of Merchandise* and ECLAC BTI data).

Transportation Costs and the Relative Prices of Goods

Ad-valorem transportation costs for a particular product depend on how far the good is shipped, the quality of the transport service offered, and the weight/value ratio of the good. Because all three factors vary considerably across shipments, transportation costs significantly alter relative prices and patterns of trade.

Transportation costs play an especially large role in altering relative prices across exporters and determining bilateral variation in trade. This pattern can be seen by calculating ad-valorem transportation costs for each product in U.S. imports in 2004 and sorting exporters from most to least expensive. For a typical product, exporters in the 90th percentile of costs faced shipping charges that were 11 times greater than those faced by exporters in the 10th percentile. This bilateral variation is considerably more than is found in tariff rates.

Fixing origin and destination, transportation costs also change the relative prices of different goods in the export bundle. The weight/value ratio of a good is a useful summary statistic both for the intensity of transportation services it consumes, and of the impact that transportation costs will have on its delivered price. Compare the cost of shipping $100 of coal (weighing a metric ton) to $100 of computer microchips (weighing a few ounces). The greater weight and bulk of the equivalent value of coal requires greater stowage space and fuel expenditures to move, which means that transportation increases the delivered price of coal relative to microchips. Similarly, compare the impact of transportation costs on the delivered price of a $10 wristwatch and a $1,000 wristwatch of similar weight and size. The $1,000 watch will typically require higher quality transportation services such as more insurance, greater care in handling, and more rapid delivery, but these services are not 100 times more expensive than those demanded for the $10 watch. Hummels and Skiba (2004) estimate that a 10 percent increase in product price leads to an 8.6 percent fall in the ad-valorem transport cost. That is, transportation lowers the delivered price of high-quality relative to low-quality goods.

Air Transport

Commercial aviation has undergone rapid technological change, including improvements in avionics, wing design, materials, and most importantly the adoption of jet engines. Jet engines are faster, more fuel efficient and reliable, and require much less maintenance compared to the piston engines they replaced. Gordon (1990) calculates price indices for aircraft that adjust for these quality changes and finds dramatic declines in real prices of aircraft after jet engines were introduced. From 1957–1972, the period in which jet engine usage became widespread, quality-adjusted real prices for aircraft fell at a rate of 12.8 to 16.6 percent per year, depending on the method of calculation. Quality change in commercial aviation slowed considerably after 1972, but quality-adjusted aircraft prices were still dropping by 2.2 to 3.8 percent per year from 1972–1983.

Air Transportation Prices

Data on international air transportation prices are sparsely reported. However, the limited data do paint a clear portrait of decline over time in air shipping prices.

The International Air Transportation Association surveys international air carriers and reports worldwide data on revenues and quantities shipped in their annual *World Air Transport Statistics* (WATS). Figure 1 shows average revenue per ton-kilometer shipped for all air traffic worldwide, indexed to 100 in 2000. Over this 50-year period, this measure of costs per ton fell more than ten times that much.

138   Journal of Economic Perspectives

Figure 1
Worldwide Air Revenue per Ton-Kilometer

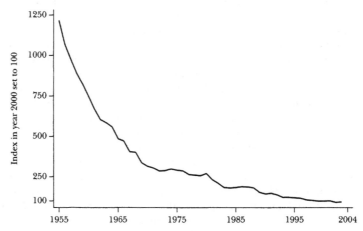

Source: International Air Transport Association, *World Air Transport Statistics,* various years.

Expressed in 2000 U.S. dollars, the price fell from $3.87 per ton-kilometer in 1955 to under $0.30 from 1955–2004. As with Gordon's (1990) measure of quality-adjusted aircraft prices, declines in air transport prices are especially rapid early in the period. Average revenue per ton-kilometer declined 8.1 percent per year from 1955–1972, and 3.5 percent per year from 1972–2003.

The period from 1970 onward is of particular interest, as it corresponds to an era when air transport grew to become a significant portion of world trade, as shown in Table 1. In this period, more detailed data are available. The U.S. Bureau of Labor Statistics reports air freight price indices for cargoes inbound to and outbound from the United States for 1991–2005 at ⟨http://www.bls.gov/mxp⟩. The International Civil Aviation Organization (ICAO) published a "Survey of International Air Transport Fares and Rates" annually between 1973 and 1993. These surveys contain rich overviews of air cargo freight rates (price per kilogram) for thousands of city-pairs in air travel markets around the world. The "Survey" does not report the underlying data, but it provides information on mean fares and distance traveled for many regions as well as simple regression evidence to characterize the fare structure. Using this data, I construct predicted cargo rates in each year for worldwide air cargo and for various geographic route groups.

I deflate both the International Civil Aviation Organization and Bureau of Labor Statistics series using the U.S. GDP deflator to provide the price of air shipping measured in real U.S. dollars per kilogram, and normalize the series to equal 100 in 1992. The light dashed lines in Figure 2 report the ICAO time series on worldwide air cargo prices from 1973–1993 (with detailed data on annual rates of change for each ICAO route group reported in the accompanying note).

Transportation Costs and International Trade in the Second Era of Globalization   *139*

Figure 2
Air Transport Price Indices

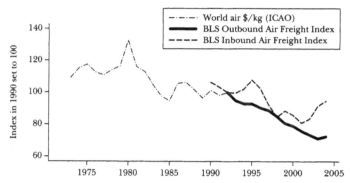

Source: International Civil Aviation Organization (ICAO), "Survey of Air Fares and Rates," various years; U.S. Department of Labor Bureau of Labor Statistics (BLS) import/export price indices, http://www.bls.gov/mxp/.

Notes: ICAO Data on Route Groups:

Annualized growth rates for 1973–80 of shipping price per kg (in year 2000 dollars): All routes 2.87; North Atlantic 1.03; Mid Atlantic 3.45; South Atlantic 3.98; North and Mid Pacific −3.43; South Pacific −2.49; North to Central America 3.63; North and Central America to South America 2.34; Europe to Middle East 4.80; Europe and Middle East to Africa 1.84; Europe/Middle East/Africa to Asia/Pacific 3.32; Local Asia/Pacific 0.97; Local North America 1.63; Local Europe 4.51; Local South America 2.53; Local Middle East 1.92; Local Africa 4.94.

Annualized growth rates for 1980–93 of shipping price per kg (in year 2000 dollars): All routes −2.52; North Atlantic −3.59; Mid Atlantic −3.36; South Atlantic −3.92; North and Mid Pacific −1.48; South Pacific −0.98; North to Central America −0.72; North and Central America to South America −1.34; Europe to Middle East −3.02; Europe and Middle East to Africa −2.34; Europe/Middle East/Africa to Asia/Pacific −2.78; Local Asia/Pacific −1.52; Local North America −1.73; Local Europe −2.63; Local Central America 0.97; Local South America −2.25; Local Middle East −1.46; Local Africa −2.43.

Pooling data from all routes, prices increase 2.87 percent annually from 1973 to 1980 and then decline 2.52 percent annually from 1980 to 1993. The increases in the first period largely reflect oil price increases. The timing of the rate reduction also coincides well with the WATS data, which show little price change in the 1970s and more rapid declines in the 1980s. The post-1980 price declines vary substantially over routes, with longer routes and those involving North America showing the largest drops.

Bureau of Labor Statistics data on air freight outbound from the United States for 1992–2004 are plotted with the solid line in Figure 2, while inbound data to the United States for 1991–2004 are plotted with the thick dashed line. The real price of outbound air freight fell consistently at a rate of 2.1 percent per year in this period. The real price of inbound air freight fell 2.5 percent per year from 1990–2001 and then rose sharply (4.8 percent per year) thereafter, perhaps reflecting greater security costs after September 11, 2001.

Whether looking at quality-adjusted prices for aircraft, simple average revenue measures of air transportation prices, or more carefully constructed air freight price indices, one sees a clear picture. Prices drop precipitously after the introduction of jet engines, and at a slow, steady pace in the three decades thereafter.

Ocean Transport

Ocean transport of dry (non-oil) cargo consists of two distinct markets: tramp and liner shipping. Tramps have traditionally been used for shipping large quantities of bulk commodities on a charter basis, with shipping prices set in spot markets. In recent years, a small fraction of containerized tramps have been employed to lift general cargoes. Liners are used for "general" cargoes—that is, all but large quantity bulk cargoes—and ply fixed trade routes in accordance with a predetermined timetable. The liner trade is organized into cartels, or conferences, which discuss, and perhaps collude in, the setting of prices and market shares. The extent to which these cartels are able to charge monopoly markups is an open question in the literature. Davies (1986) argues that, despite apparent collusive behavior by the liner conferences, the general cargo market is contestable and that this prevents incumbent firms from colluding to raise rates. Sjostrom (1992) reviews an older empirical literature that links shipping prices to product prices as evidence for market power. More recently, Hummels, Lugovskyy, and Skiba (2007) show that liners charge shipping prices that are much higher for goods whose import demand is relatively inelastic, which is precisely what one would expect if shipping firms were exercising market power.

Ocean shipping has undergone several important technological and institutional changes in the postwar era: the growth of open registry shipping, scale effects from increased trade volumes, and the introduction of containerization. Open registry shipping is the practice of registering ships under flags of convenience—for example, Liberia or Panama—to circumvent higher regulatory and manning costs imposed by wealthier nations. Open registry fleets comprised 5 percent of world shipping tonnage in 1950, 31.1 percent in 1980, and 48.5 percent in 2000 (OECD, *Maritime Transport*, for 1950; UNCTAD, *Review of Maritime Transport*, various years). Tolofari (1986) estimates that vessel operating costs for open registry ships are from 12 to 27 percent lower than traditional registry fleets, with most of the estimated savings coming from manning expenses.

The rise in world trade may have had significant impacts on shipping prices through scale effects. In periods of rapidly rising demand, shipping capacity becomes scarce and spot shipping prices rise quickly. Over longer periods however, rising demand for shipping may actually lower shipping prices. The reason is that the capacity of a modern ocean-going liner vessel is large relative to the quantities shipped by smaller exporting nations. As a consequence, vessels may stop in a dozen ports and in many different countries to reach capacity. As trade quantities increase, it is possible to realize gains from several sources more effectively. First, trade growth along a route promotes entry with rival liner companies competing away transportation markups. This effect is not trivial; in 2006, one in six importer-exporter pairs was served by a single liner service, and over half were served by three or fewer (Hummels, Lugovskyy, and Skiba, 2007). Service also becomes more frequent, with days rather than weeks elapsing between vessel calls in port. Second, a densely traded route allows for effective use of hub-and-spoke shipping econo-mies—small container vessels move cargo into a hub where containers are aggre-gated into much larger and faster containerships for longer hauls. Examples include the European hub of Rotterdam, as well as Asian hubs in Singapore and Hong Kong. Third, the movement of some goods, like bulk commodities, crude oil, refrigerated produce, and automobiles requires specialized vessels. Increased quan-tities of trade allow introduction of these specialized ships along a route. Similarly, larger ships will be introduced on heavily traded routes, and these ships enjoy substantial cost savings relative to older smaller models still in use.

An example of these effects in combination can be seen in the introduction of containerized shipping. Containerized shipping is thought by many specialists to be one of the most important transportation revolutions in the twentieth century; Levinson (2006) provides an excellent and accessible popular history of contain-erization and its effects. The use of standardized containers provides cost savings by allowing goods to be packed once and moved over long distances via a variety of transport modes—truck, rail, ocean liner, rail, then truck again—without being unpacked and repacked. In this way, containerization reduces direct port costs such as storage and stevedoring (port labor) as well as indirect costs incurred during lengthy port stops (the rental rate on unused capital while a ship sits idle in port). The indirect costs are critical: estimates place break-bulk (noncontainer) cargo ships' time in port at one-half to two-thirds of the ship's life (UNCTAD, *Unitization of Cargo,* 1970). Containerization also creates savings on the ocean leg. Larger and faster ships substantially reduce the price per ton-mile while the ship is steaming, but they incur higher indirect port costs (idle time) in proportion to their in-creased capital expense (Gilman, 1983). Because containerships spend more time steaming, investments in larger, faster ships become feasible.

Containerized shipping was first introduced in the United States in the 1960s, then on U.S.–Europe and U.S.–Japan routes in the late 1960s and into the 1970s, then to developing countries from the late 1970s onward. The reason behind this seemingly slow pattern of diffusion lies in the large fixed costs of adoption, and the differential cost savings that containers yield. To make full use of containerization requires container-ready ocean liners and ports adapted to container use, which require specialized cranes, storage areas, and rail-heads. As a result, containeriza-tion was first adopted on the most heavily traded routes. Developing nations were especially slow to adopt, both because of lower scale and because of factor prices. In countries where capital is scarce and labor abundant, the capital cost of building container ports is higher, and the port labor cost savings of containers much lower.

Price Indices

Have technological and institutional changes resulted in lower ocean shipping prices? To answer this I examine price indices, based on U.S. dollars per quantity shipped, for tramp and liner shipping. Many such indices exist, but two stand out for their length of coverage.

For the price of tramp trip charters, I will focus on the index originally constructed by the *Norwegian Shipping News (NSN)* and later continued by *Lloyd's Shipping Economist.* A trip charter is a contract to ship a large quantity of a dry bulk commodity between specific ports, and may include some minimal loading and/or unloading expenses. The trip charter price index represents a weighted bundle of spot market prices, measured in U.S. dollars per ton, for shipping major bulk commodities on several important routes worldwide.

For the price of liner shipping, I will focus on an index constructed by the German Ministry of Transport. The liner index emphasizes general cargoes, including containerized shipping and manufactured merchandise of all sorts, and so is more representative of the commodity composition of the majority of world trade. It also covers loading and unloading expenses, which are particularly relevant since reductions in cargo handling costs are thought to be a major source of gains from containerization. This index does not offer comprehensive geographic coverage, focusing only on liners loading and unloading in Germany and the Netherlands.

To evaluate the real costs of shipping over time, an appropriate deflator must be chosen. Tramp prices are set in competitive markets and quoted in U.S. dollars. I deflate these indices using the U.S. GDP deflator, and also using a price index for bulk commodities typically shipped via tramps. This commodity index includes the price of iron ore and various grains, based on the price series taken from *International Financial Statistics* published by the IMF. Using the U.S. GDP deflator provides a constant dollar value for the unit price of tramp shipping a given quantity of merchandise. Using the bulk commodity price index yields the price of shipping a bundle of goods relative to the price of that bundle, a crude measure of the ad valorem barrier posed by shipping costs. The liner index is deflated using the German GDP deflator, and a composite traded goods price index for Germany.

Figure 3 displays the price series for trip charters and shows several price spikes. The price spikes in the 1970s are clearly attributable to oil price shocks, and the price spike in the 1954–1957 period is probably due to a combination of high demand from unexpectedly large U.S. grain exports to Europe and the Suez Canal Crisis. The latter led to sharply increased war premiums and expensive rerouting of ships on Asia–Europe trade routes when the Suez Canal was closed. Setting aside these spikes, we can see two clear trends. The price of bulk shipping measured in real dollars per ton (the solid line) has declined steadily over time so that it is now half as much as in 1960 and a third the price in 1952. However, when measured relative to the commodity price deflator (the dashed line), there are large fluctuations but no downward trend. While the cost of shipping a ton of wheat or iron ore

Transportation Costs and International Trade in the Second Era of Globalization 143

Figure 3

Tramp Price Index

(with U.S. GDP deflator and with commodity price deflator)

Source: United Nations Conference on Trade and Development, *Review of Maritime Transport,* various years.
Note: Tramp prices deflated by a U.S. GDP deflator and tramp prices deflated by commodity price deflator.

has steadily declined, the cost of shipping a dollar value of wheat or iron ore has not.

Figure 4 displays the liner price time series. Measured relative to traded goods prices, liner prices rise steadily against German import prices before peaking in 1985. Measured relative to the German GDP deflator (solid line), liner prices decline until the early 1970s, rise sharply in 1974 and throughout the late 1970s, spike in the 1983–1985 period, then decline rapidly thereafter.

The very sharp increases in the German cost of shipping from 1983–1985 is likely due to the rapid real depreciation of the German deutschmark in this period, which made German purchases of all international goods and services more expensive. Accordingly, the 1983–85 spike is probably not representative of what happened worldwide in this short period.

However, the rapid liner price increases facing Germany in the 1970s did occur more broadly. Throughout the 1970s, UNCTAD's annual *Review of Maritime Transport* reported in some detail price changes announced by shipping conferences, with annual nominal increases of 10–15 percent being common across nearly all routes. The same publication also reports the ad valorem shipping rates for a small number of specific commodities and routes from 1963–2004. Examples include rubber shipped from Malaysia to Europe, cocoa beans shipped from either Ghana or Brazil to Europe, and tea shipped from Sri Lanka to Europe. Converted to real dollars per quantity shipped, these liner prices increased by 67 percent in the 1970s.

Figure 4
Liner Price Index
(with German GDP deflator and with German traded goods price deflator)

Source: United Nations Conference on Trade and Development *Review of Maritime Transport,* various years.
Note: Liner prices deflated by a German GDP deflator and liner prices deflated by a German traded-goods price deflator.

Why Didn't Containerization Reduce Measured Ocean Shipping Rates?

These liner rate increases reported in Figure 4 are especially surprising given that they occurred shortly after the introduction of containerization to European liner trades. If containerization and the associated productivity gains led to lower shipping prices, as is widely believed and as Levinson (2006) qualitatively argues, the effect should appear in the liner series. Yet liner prices exhibit considerable increases, both in absolute terms and relative to tramp prices after containers are introduced. Further, data series that span the introduction of containerization, such as the New Zealand imports data and the UNCTAD *Review of Maritime Transport* series measuring costs for specific goods and routes, show no clear decline either.

One possible explanation for this puzzling finding is that the real gains from containerization might come from unmeasured quality change in transportation services. Containerships are faster than their predecessors, and for loading and unloading are much quicker than with break bulk cargo. In addition, containers allow cargo tracking, so that firms know precisely where goods are en route and when they will arrive. As I describe in more detail below, speed improvements are of substantial and growing value to international trade. To the extent that these quality improvements do not show up in measured price indices, the indices understate the value of the technological advance.

Still, many of the purported improvements of container shipping should have lowered explicitly measured ocean shipping costs, and apparently did not. Why?

Levinson (2006) argues that the historical data series are inadequate for capturing the true cost savings of containerization. Measuring the true impact of containers requires data on freight prices for similar goods and routes, with some shipments using containers while others do not. The U.S. Waterborne Trade Database has such data for 1991–2003. Blonigen and Wilson (2006) use these data to estimate the dependence of shipping costs on container usage in the cross-section. They show that, at a point in time, increasing the share of trade that is containerized by 1 percent lowers shipping costs by only .05 percent. If these cost estimates apply equally well to the introduction of containerization in the longer time series, the quantitative impact of containers on reducing shipping costs may have been modest, even if all else were held equal.

But all else was not equal. In the period during which containerization was spreading, input costs, including fuel, ship prices, and port costs, were skyrocketing. Sletmo and Williams (1981) report that liner operating costs rose 14–18 percent per annum in the 1970s as a result of the oil price shocks, with an especially large impact for more fuel-hungry containerships. They further report that while shipbuilding prices increased fleetwide, they rose twice as fast for containerships as for conventional freighters, attributing the difference to a more intensive use of steel and labor in containerships. A UNCTAD (1977) study, "Port Problems," revealed port cost increases in the 1970s ranging from 10 to 40 percent per annum, resulting in an overall increase in liner conference costs of as much as 7.5 percent per annum.

The Role of Technology, Composition, and Cost Shocks: Evidence from U.S. Customs Data

My discussion to this point has told a number of plausible stories about the causes of the changing costs of international transportation over time, but given the fragmented and partial international evidence on these transportation costs, it has not tested these hypotheses. In this section, I offer some regression evidence on how changes in technology, composition of trade, and cost shocks affect international transportation costs. I will rely here on *U.S. Imports of Merchandise* data for 1974–2004, which report value of imports from each exporter with commodities disaggregated to the five-digit SITC level. These data provide extremely detailed shipment characteristics including transport mode (air, ocean, land); weight; value; freight and insurance charges; and duties.

The first step is to construct data series on ad valorem transportation costs for air shipping and ocean shipping. The dashed line in Figure 5 reports an unadjusted measure of ad valorem air shipping costs: that is, aggregate expenditures on air shipping divided by the value of airborne imports. This line trends down slowly, dropping only 2 percentage points over 30 years.

As discussed earlier, measures of aggregate transportation expenditures calcu-

Figure 5
Ad Valorem Air Freight

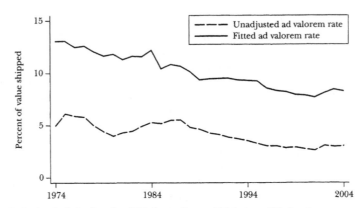

Source: Author's calculation based on U.S. Census Bureau *U.S. Imports of Merchandise.*
Note: The unadjusted ad valorem rate is simply expenditure/import value. The fitted ad valorem rate is derived from a regression and controls for changes in the mix of trade partners and products traded.

lated in this way do not take into account changes in the mix of trade partners or products traded. Thus, the next step is to construct a value for ad valorem air shipping costs that controls for these changes in composition. I use a regression in which the dependent variable is the ad valorem air freight cost in logs for commodity k shipped from exporter j at time t. The independent variables include a separate intercept for each exporter-commodity shipped, the weight/value ratio in logs for each shipment, and year dummy variables. The exporter-commodity intercepts control for the fact that iron-ore from Brazil has higher transportation costs in every period than shoes from Taiwan, and the weight/value ratio controls for compositional change over time within an exporter-commodity, for instance, Taiwan shipping higher quality shoes.

The resulting fitted trend (the solid line) in Figure 5, is the value of the dummy variable for each year and is equivalent to ad valorem transportation expenditures after controlling for compositional change. Once changes in the trade partner and product mix have been taken into account, the fitted ad valorem cost exhibits a greater absolute decline in air transportation costs.

Figure 6 provides a parallel picture for ocean shipping. Again, the dashed line shows aggregate expenditures on ocean shipping divided by total value of ocean shipping in each year. It shows an initially rapid decline in transportation expenditures, followed by a 25-year period in which rates fluctuate but do not otherwise decline. To control for compositional change, I use the same regression as with air shipping only now the dependent variable is the ad valorem ocean freight cost in logs for commodity k shipped from exporter j at time t. The solid line shows the

Transportation Costs and International Trade in the Second Era of Globalization   147

Figure 6
Ad Valorem Ocean Freight

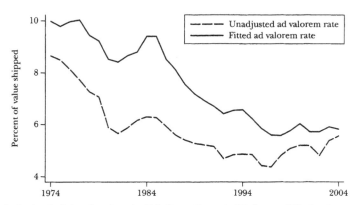

Source: Author's calculations based on the U.S. Census Bureau's *U.S. Imports of Merchandise.*
Note: The unadjusted ad valorem rate is simply expenditure/import value. The fitted ad valorem rate is derived from a regression and controls for changes in the mix of trade partners and products traded.

coefficient on the dummy variables by year, which represents ad valorem ocean shipping costs after controlling for exporter-commodity composition and changing weight/value ratios. The fitted rates decline initially, then increase through the mid-1980s, then decline for the subsequent 20 years.

Figures 5 and 6 reveal a seeming paradox in the data. Even though the aggregate weight/value ratio of trade is falling, the weight/value ratio for both air and ocean shipping is increasing. How can this be? If we arrange goods along a continuum from heaviest to lightest, goods at the heaviest part of the continuum tend to be ocean shipped, and those at the lightest part tend to be air shipped. This pattern can be seen in the level of the ad valorem freight expenditures (dashed lines) in Figures 5 and 6, where ocean shipping appears to be more expensive than air shipping. It is not: the higher costs incurred for ocean shipping are due to the fact that the average ocean-shipped manufactured good is 25 times heavier than the average air-shipped manufactured good. As the relative price of air/ocean shipping falls, goods at the margin shift from ocean to air shipping (Harrigan, 2005, provides a formal model of this process). Relative to the set of air-shipped goods, these marginal goods are heavy, and the average weight of air-shipped goods rises. But relative to the set of ocean-shipped goods, these marginal goods are light, and by losing them the average weight of ocean-shipped goods rises as well. The difference between the unadjusted and the fitted lines in Figures 5 and 6 show this compositional shift in effect. Fitted costs for air and ocean shipping that control for this shift exhibit larger declines for both ocean and air shipping than aggregate expenditures, which fail to control for the shift.

The U.S. import data can also be used to examine what determines the level

Table 2

Determinants of Transportation Costs over Time
(*dependent variable is the ad valorem freight cost in logs for commodity* k *shipped from exporter* j *at time* t)

Elasticity of ad-valorem freight costs with respect to:	Air shipments		Ocean shipments	
	(1)	(2)	(3)	(4)
Weight/Value	0.492*	0.494*	0.410*	0.374*
Fuel costs	0.263*	0.055*	0.327*	0.232*
Distance	0.269*	0.436*	0.151*	
Distance × Trend		−0.009*		
Trend		0.060*		
Containerized share of trade			−0.029*	−0.134*
N	777966	777966	763997	787418
R^2	0.51	0.52	0.37	0.33

Source: Authors' calculations based on data from the U.S. Census Bureau's *U.S. Imports of Merchandise.*
Note: The dependent variable is the ad valorem air freight cost in logs for commodity *k* shipped from exporter *j* at time *t*. In column one, the independent variables (all in logs) are the weight/value ratio of each shipment, fuel costs in each year, and the distance shipped between the exporter and the U.S. entry port. Column two adds a yearly trend, and an interaction between distance shipped and the yearly trend. Regressions for columns 1, 2, and 3 include commodity (SITC 5 digit) fixed effects. Regressions for Column 4 includes exporter-commodity fixed effects.
* Significant at 1% confidence level.

of shipping costs and what causes shifts in transportation costs over time. For the first two columns of Table 2, the dependent variable is the ad valorem air freight cost in logs for commodity *k* shipped from exporter *j* at time *t*. In column one, the independent variables (all in logs) are the weight/value ratio of each shipment, fuel costs in each year, and the distance shipped between the exporter and the U.S. entry port. Column two adds a yearly trend as well as an interaction between distance shipped and the yearly trend. In both columns, I include separate intercepts for each commodity to control for differences in shipping expenses across goods that do not change over time.

Ad-valorem air transportation costs are increasing in the weight/value ratio of the good, jet fuel expenses, and the distance shipped. Interestingly, the effect of distance is steadily eroding over time. In 1974 the elasticity of air transportation costs with respect to distance was 0.43, but had dropped to 0.16 by 2004. To better understand the impact of this change, we can calculate the air shipping price paid by an exporter 14,000 kilometers from the United States compared to an exporter 2,000 kilometers away. The distant exporter would have paid air shipping prices that were 2.3 times that of the proximate exporter in 1974, but only 1.3 times that of the proximate exporter in 2004.

If we measure prices in units of price/kilogram, we can use the coefficient on weight/value to calculate the freight charges faced by high- and low-priced goods.

For example, a volume of shoes that is worth $100 per kilogram will face much lower ad valorem costs of air shipping than shoes worth $10 per kilogram:

$$f^{\$100}/f^{\$10} = \left(\frac{\$100/kg}{\$10/kg}\right)^{0.494-1} = .31.$$

As Schott (2003) notes, the variance of U.S. import prices within a particular product category has grown over time. As the spread between high-priced and low-priced goods in each product category widens, the cost advantage enjoyed by high-end goods is growing over time.

In column three of Table 2, the dependent variable is the ad valorem ocean freight cost in logs for commodity k shipped from exporter j at time t. As before, the independent variables include the weight/value ratio of the shipment, fuel costs, distance shipped, and a separate intercept for each commodity. To this, I add the exporter's share of trade that is containerized in that year. This regression allows me to see whether exporters who containerize their trade enjoy lower shipping expenses after we control for the composition of trade and fuel costs in each year. Finally, some exporters may have systematically higher transportation costs in all years. If this is related to the prices (value/weight) of goods they trade, or the likelihood that they will adopt containerized cargoes, it will lead to biased estimates of these coefficients. In column four, I include separate intercepts for each exporter-commodity so that the regression only uses time series changes to identify each effect.

Ocean shipping costs are increasing in the shipment's weight/value ratio, fuel costs, and distance shipped. The measured effect of container usage is quite a bit different when comparing columns three and four. When using cross-country information in column three, we find a very small effect—doubling the share of trade that is containerized lowers shipping costs by only 2.9 percent. But when controlling for cross-country differences and looking at growth in container usage over time in column four, we find that doubling container usage lowers shipping costs by 13.4 percent.

Figures 5 and 6 show steady downward trends in U.S. ocean and air shipping prices. However, part of this apparent decline may be due to the fact that the U.S. data series starts in 1974 when oil prices—a critical transportation input—were unusually high. The elasticity of transportation costs with respect to fuel prices reported in Table 2 is especially useful as it enables us to approximate what costs might have been prior to the 1974 oil shock. Ocean bunker fuel prices rose four-fold in real terms between 1973 and 1974. Combining this with the measured elasticity of 0.232 in the fourth column of Table 2 implies a 92 percent increase in ocean shipping costs in this year. That estimate matches very closely the estimates of fuel-related cost increases constructed from shipping fleet microdata (Sletmo and Williams, 1981). Taking the average fitted value of ocean shipping costs in 1974 from Figure 6 (9.9 percent ad valorem) and using this implied cost shock gives 1973 ad valorem ocean costs of 5.2 percent—a level comparable to rates in 2000.

Taken together, the evidence from Table 2 supports the qualitative and anecdotal evidence on ocean transportation described above. Containerization significantly reduced ocean shipping costs, but evidence of this effect in aggregate data was originally overshadowed by the dramatic increases in input costs in the 1970s. As Figures 4 and 6 clearly show, it was only when crude oil prices began to drop in the mid 1980s that ocean shipping costs really began to fall.

Implications: Transportation and the Changing Nature of Trade

Transportation Quality and Speed of Delivery

To this point, I have focused on the cost of shipping a good while taking the quality of the transportation service as fixed. However, the quality of international transport has improved over the past 30 years, with the most notable gain being shorter transportation time. Ocean liner service itself has become much faster than in years past, both because the ships are larger and faster, and because their loading and unloading time is dramatically lowered by containerization. But even after these improvements, ocean shipping is still a slow process. Shipping containers from Europe to the U.S. Midwest requires 2–3 weeks; from Europe to Asia requires five weeks. In contrast, air shipping requires a day or less to most destinations. Consequently, the ten-fold decline in air shipping prices since the late 1950s means that the cost of speed has fallen dramatically.

The economic effect of the declining cost of speed depends on how valuable timeliness is in trade. In Hummels (2001), I estimate a demand for timeliness by examining the premium that shippers are willing to pay for speedy air shipping relative to slow ocean shipping. There are two effects. First, every day in ocean travel time that a country is distant from the importer reduces the probability of sourcing manufactured goods from that country by 1 percent. Second, conditional on exporting manufactures, firms are willing to pay just under 1 percent of the value of the good per day to avoid travel delays associated with ocean shipping. Falling air transportation costs can then help explain trade growth: those goods with the highest estimated time sensitivity have exhibited the most rapid growth in trade.

Time in transit doesn't matter much for bulk commodities and simple manufactures. But for goods like fresh produce and cut flowers, lengthy travel times lead to spoilage. More generally, if there is uncertainty in demand plus lags between production and final sales, firms may face a mismatch between what consumers want and what the firm has available to sell. In the case of apparel, for example, firms are unable to predict in advance which fashions will be especially popular, making the ability to respond quickly to revelation of market information an important advantage. Evans and Harrigan (2005) show that clothing lines with high restocking rates are more likely to be obtained from exporters closest to the U.S. market. Aizenman (2004) argues theoretically and Schaur (2006) shows empirically that the use of airplanes is an alternative solution to the timeliness problem when foreign demand is uncertain. By using a mix of ocean and air shipping, firms can respond rapidly to demand shocks, essentially using airplanes as a real hedge for market volatility.

There are several factors that may explain increases in time sensitivity in the past decades. As the composition of trade has shifted from commodities to more complex manufactures, time sensitivity grows. Also, as consumer incomes rise, their willingness to pay for precise product characteristics grows. That in turn puts pressure on manufacturers to produce to those specifications and to be rapidly adaptable. Finally, Harrigan and Venables (2004) examine a model of location choice with industrial demand for inputs and the presence of uncertainty (in demand, in production costs, and in the timing of delivery). Their model shows that the need to respond to uncertainty in a timely way creates an important force for agglomeration—for locating firms producing industrial inputs near the down-stream firms that will use those inputs. However, as an empirical matter, recent decades have seen rapid growth in international vertical specialization, a process by which firms separate the stages of production (R&D, component production, assembly) across countries according to comparative advantage (Hummels, Ishii, and Yi, 2001). How can a growing need for timeliness in industrial demands coincide with a growing dispersal of operations around the globe? Faster transport provides an answer.

Distance and Trade

Transportation costs co-vary with distance and are larger and exhibit much greater variability across exporters than do tariffs. This provides a plausible expla-nation for one of the most robust facts about trade: countries trade primarily with neighbors. Roughly a quarter of world trade takes place between countries sharing a common border, and half of world trade occurs between partners less than 3,000 kilometers apart (Berthelon and Freund, 2004). Even after controlling for other plausible correlates such as country size, income, and tariff barriers, the distance between partners explains much of bilateral trade volumes.

Recent changes in transportation would seem to suggest that the grip of distance should be weakening. Air transport tends to be preferred to ocean transport on especially long-distance shipments (Harrigan, 2005). As the level of air transport costs drop relative to the level of ocean transport, long distance trade becomes relatively more attractive. Further, as Table 2 shows, the marginal cost of an additional mile of air transport is dropping rapidly. Strangely then, the distance profile of world trade is little changed over the past 40 years (Berthelon and Freund, 2004; Disdier and Head, 2004). This pattern presents a significant puzzle for future research.

Conclusions

Changes in international transportation in the second half of the twentieth century are more than just a story of declining costs. For air shipping, to be sure, advances in technology have propelled a sharp decline in costs: average revenue per ton-kilometer shipped dropped by 92 percent between 1955 and 2004. As a result, air shipping grew in this period from an insignificant share of trade to a third of U.S. imports by value and half of U.S. exports outside of North America.

Ocean shipping, which constitutes 99 percent of world trade by weight and a majority of world trade by value, also experienced a technological revolution in the form of container shipping, but dramatic price declines are not in evidence. Instead, prices for ocean shipping exhibit little change from 1952–1970, substantial increases from 1970 through the mid-1980s, followed by a steady 20-year decline. That is not to say that the container revolution is unimportant; after all, estimates in this paper show that increasing the share of trade that is containerized lowers shipping costs from 3 to 13 percent. However, these savings were trumped in the 1970s by sharp increases in fuel and port costs. Indeed, ocean freight costs in recent years have again begun to increase with the cost of crude, and port congestion has become an especially severe problem in those countries with rapidly growing trade volumes (Bajpai, Carruthers, and Hummels, 2003).

Economic historians have argued that technological change in ocean shipping was the critical input to growing trade in the first era of globalization during the latter half of the nineteenth century. I would argue that technological change in air shipping and the declining cost of rapid transportation has been a critical input into a second era of globalization during the latter half of the twentieth century. There is perhaps a third era in cross-border trade unfolding even now, again driven by rapid improvements in a technology for connecting people across great distances. Clearly, the telecommunication and Internet revolution has already affected international integration, leading to growing trade in information and technology, in services outsourcing, and in migration of highly skilled professionals. The impact of these changes and the extent to which they displace older forms of integration bear close watching in the years to come.

Appendix
Notes on Data Sources

Much of the data used in this paper, including the New Zealand customs data, some transportation-focused extracts of the U.S. customs data, and data series collected from various issues of paper publications of the International Civil Aviation Organization's *Survey of International Air Transport Fares and Rates*, the International Air Transport Association's (IATA's) *World Air Transport Statistics*, and United Nations Conference on Trade and Development's (UNCTAD's) *Review of Maritime Transport*, can be most easily obtained directly from the author's website at ⟨http://www.mgmt.purdue.edu/faculty/hummelsd/research/jep/data.html⟩. Going forward, the IATA and UNCTAD publications are updated annually and an excellent source of ongoing information.

The best source of customs data that includes transportation costs is *US Imports of Merchandise*, available on CDs for 1990–2006. These can be obtained directly from the U.S. Census Bureau, and many university libraries have monthly and/or annual data CDs back to 1990. Rob Feenstra has posted annual extracts of these data (including freight expenditures, but lacking transportation mode or entry port detail) from 1974 to 2001 at ⟨http://www.nber.org/data/⟩. Similar data have been collected for the last 10 years for many Latin American countries by the Economic Commission for Latin America and the Caribbean ECLAC in the form of the International Transport Database (Base de datos de Transporte Internacional), or BTI (see ⟨http://www.eclac.cl/transporte/perfil/index.htm⟩). The U.S. Maritime Administration provides a great deal of useful data at its website ⟨http://www.marad.dot.gov⟩, including the U.S. Waterborne Trade Database. It contains much of the same detail as the *U.S. Imports of Merchandise* data, but with more information on port usage, whether cargo is containerized, and whether it is shipped by liner or tramp.

Finally, several private and public organizations provide detailed data on international trade and transportation issues. Among the best are the U.S. Bureau of Transportation Statistics at ⟨http://www.bts.gov⟩ and the Air Transport Association at ⟨http://www.airlines.org/economics⟩.

■ *The author thanks Robert Feenstra, Jan Hoffman, Gordon Wilmsmeier, Christine Mc-Daniel, and Jeffrey Williamson for providing data; Bruce Blonigen, Alan Deardorff, James Harrigan, Pete Klenow, and Scott Taylor for comments and suggestions. Adina Ardelean, Georg Schaur, Yong Kim, Julia Grebelsky, and Dawn Conner provided outstanding research assistance.*

References

Aizenman, Joshua. 2004. "Endogenous Pricing to Market and Financing Cost." *Journal of Monetary Economics*, 51(4): 691–712.

Bajpai, Jitendra, Robin Carruthers, and David Hummels. 2003. "Trade and Logistics: An East Asian Perspective." In *East Asia Integrates*, ed. Kathie Krumm and Homi Kharas, 117–139. Washington, DC: World Bank.

Berthelon, Matias, and Caroline L. Freund. 2004. "On the Conservation of Distance in International Trade." World Bank Policy Research Working Paper 3293.

Blonigen, Bruce, and Wesley Wilson. 2006. "New Measures of Port Efficiency Using International Trade Data." National Bureau of Economic Research Working Paper 12052.

Clemens, Michael, and Jeffrey Williamson. 2002. "Why Did the Tariff–Growth Correlation Reverse after 1950?" National Bureau of Economic Research Working Paper 9181.

Davies, John E. 1986. *The Theory of Contestable Markets and its Application to the Liner Shipping Industry.* Canadian Transport Commission.

Disdier, Anne-Celia, and Keith Head. 2004. "The Puzzling Persistence of the Distance Effect on Bilateral Trade." Centro Studi Luca D'Agliano Development Studies Working Paper 186.

Estevadeordal, A, B. Frantz, and A. Taylor. 2003. "The Rise and Fall of World Trade, 1870–1939." *Quarterly Journal of Economics*, 118(2): 359–407

Evans, Carolyn, and James Harrigan. 2005. "Distance, Time, and Specialization" *American Economic Review*, 95(1): 292–313.

Finger, J.M., and Alexander Yeats. 1976. "Effective Protection by Transportation Costs and Tariffs: A Comparison of Magnitudes." *Quarterly Journal of Economics*, 90(1): 169–76.

Gilman, Sidney. 1983. *The Competitive Dynamics of Container Shipping*. University of Liverpool Marine Transport Center.

Gordon, Robert. 1990. *The Measurement of Durable Goods Prices*. University of Chicago Press.

Harley, C. Knick. 1980. "Transportation, the World Wheat Trade, and the Kuznets Cycle, 1850–1913." *Explorations in Economic History*, 17(3): 218–50.

Harley, C. Knick. 1988. "Ocean Freight Rates and Productivity, 1740–1913: The Primacy of Mechanical Invention Reaffirmed." *Journal of Economic History*, 48(December): 851–76.

Harley, C. Knick, (1989) "Coal Exports and British Shipping, 1850–1913." *Explorations in Economic History*, 26(3): 311–38.

Harrigan, James. 2005. "Airplanes and Comparative Advantage." National Bureau of Economic Research Working Paper 11688.

Harrigan, James, and Venables, Anthony. 2004. "Timeliness, Trade and Agglomeration." National Bureau of Economic Research Working Paper 10404.

Hummels, David. 2001. "Time as a Trade Barrier." Unpublished paper, Purdue University.

Hummels, David, Ishii, Jun, and Yi, Kei-Mu. 2001. "The Nature and Growth of Vertical Specialization in World Trade." *Journal of International Economics*, 54(1): 75–96.

Hummels, David, and Volodymyr Lugovskyy. 2006. "Are Matched Partner Trade Statistics a Usable Measure of Transportation Costs?" *Review of International Economics*, 14(1): 69–86.

Hummels, David, Volodymyr Lugovskyy, and Alesandre Skiba. 2007. "The Trade Reducing Effects of Market Power in International Shipping." National Bureau of Economic Research Working Paper 12914.

Hummels, David, and Alexandre Skiba. 2004. "Shipping the Good Apples Out: An Empirical Confirmation of the Alchian–Allen Conjecture." *Journal of Political Economy*, 112(6): 1384–1402.

International Air Transport Association. Various years. *World Air Transport Statistics*.

International Civil Aviation Organization (ICAO). Various years. "Survey of International Air Transport Fares and Rates."

Levinson, Mark. 2006. *The Box: How the Shipping Container Made the World Smaller and the World Economy Bigger*. Princeton University Press.

Mohammed, Saif I., and Jeffrey G. Williamson. 2004. "Freight Rates and Productivity Gains In British Tramp Shipping 1869–1950." *Explorations in Economic History*, 41(2): 172–203.

North, Douglass. 1958. "Ocean Freight Rates and Economic Development 1750–1913." *Journal of Economic History*, 18(4): 537–55.

North, Douglass. 1968. "Sources of Productivity Change in Ocean Shipping, 1600–1850." *Journal of Political Economy*, 76(5): 953–70.

OECD. Various years. *Maritime Transport*.

Schaur, Georg. 2006. "Hedging Price Volatility Using Fast Transport." Unpublished paper, Purdue University.

Schott, Peter K. 2004. "Across-Product versus Within-Product Specialization in International Trade." *Quarterly Journal of Economics*, 119(2): 647–78.

Sjostrom, William. 1992. "Price Discrimination by Shipping Conferences." *Logistics and Transportation Review*, June, 28(2): 207.

Sletmo, Gunnar, and Ernest Williams. 1981. *Liner Conferences in the Container Age*. MacMillan.

Tolofari, S. R. 1986. *Open Registry Shipping: A Comparative Study of Costs and Freight Rates*. Gordon and Breach Science Publishers

United Nations Conference on Trade and Development. Various years. *Review of Maritime Transport*.

United Nations Conference on Trade and Development. 1970. *Unitization of Cargo: Report*.

United Nations Conference on Trade and Development. 1977. *Port Problems: Causes of Increases in Port Costs and their Impact*.

U.S. Census Bureau. (Various years.) *Statistical Abstract of the United States*. http://www.census.gov/compendia/statab/.

U.S. Census Bureau. (Various years.) *U.S. Exports of Merchandise*. http://www.census.gov/foreign-trade/reference/products/catalog/expDVD.html.

U.S. Census Bureau. (Various years.) *U.S. Imports of Merchandise*. http://www.census.gov/foreign-trade/reference/products/catalog/impDVD.html.

U.S. International Trade Commission. 2004. "Value of U.S. Imports for Consumption, Duties Collected, and Ratio of Duties to Values, 1891–2003." Internal memo/set of tables. Produced by Statistical Services Division, Office of Investigations, Office of Operations, U.S. ICT.

Waters, W. G. (1970), "Transport Costs, Tariffs, and the Patterns of Industrial Protection." *American Economic Review*, 60(5): 1013–20.

World Trade Organization. 2005. International Trade Statistics (from the WTO website). (2006 statistics available at http://www.wto.org/english/res_e/statis_e/its2006_e/its06_toc_e.htm.)

[23]

ELSEVIER

European Journal of Political Economy
Vol. 17 (2001) 389–402

European Journal of
POLITICAL
ECONOMY

Market structure, trade liberalization and the GATS

Joseph Francois [a,b,*], Ian Wooton [b,c]

[a] *Tinbergen Institute and Faculty of Economics, Erasmus University, 3000 DR Rotterdam, Netherlands*
[b] *Centre for Economic Policy Research, 90–98 Goswell Road, London EC1 7RR, UK*
[c] *Department of Economics, Adam Smith Building, University of Glasgow, Glasgow G12 8RT, UK*

Received 1 October 1999; received in revised form 1 September 2000; accepted 1 September 2000

Abstract

In this paper, we examine the interaction between the different modes of market access commitments in services (cross-border and establishment), market structure, and regulation. In this context, we focus on the impact of improved domestic market access for a foreign-service provider on a domestic service market. We work with a model where the domestic industry is assumed to be imperfectly competitive and, as a result of domestic regulation, able to act as a cartel. We also examine the incentives for the domestic firms to accommodate the entry of the foreign firm by inviting it to join the cartel. © 2001 Published by Elsevier Science B.V.

JEL classification: F12; F13; F23
Keywords: Services trade; Trade liberalization; Market access; Imperfect competition

1. Overview

From its inception, the multilateral trading system has been focused on trade in goods. Hence, from 1947 through the Tokyo Round, services were not covered in successive rounds of trade negotiations. The Uruguay Round, and the subsequent launch of the WTO, changed this. They brought an incorporation of services into the multilateral trading system under the General Agreement on Trade in Services (GATS). However, the actual degree of liberalization has been relatively limited,

---

* Corresponding author. Faculty of Economics, Erasmus University Rotterdam, Burg Oudlaan 50-H8-18, 3000DR Rotterdam, Netherlands. Tel.: +31-10-408-1256; fax: +31-10-408-9146.
E-mail address: francois@few.eur.nl (J. Francois).

0176-2680/01/$ - see front matter © 2001 Published by Elsevier Science B.V.
PII: S0176-2680(01)00033-7

390   *J. Francois, I. Wooton / European Journal of Political Economy 17 (2001) 389–402*

with many of the GATS schedules involving simple stand still commitments (or less). It is generally recognized that there still remains significant scope for liberalization in the service sectors.

This paper is concerned with the analytical implications of service-sector liberalization, and in particular the role of market structure. The trade theory literature has traditionally focused on trade in goods, with the literature on international trade in services being a relatively limited and recent addition. (See, for example, Francois, 1990a; Francois and Schuknecht, 1999; Hoekman, 1994; Markusen, 1988, 1989; Sampson and Snape, 1985; Stern and Hoekman, 1988; Deardorff, 1985). In addition, while there is a sizable empirical literature on service sector policy and deregulation, this is largely focused on domestic deregulation.[1] In contrast, we focus here explicitly on cross-border trade in services, and the interaction of international trade with market structure and public regulation.[2]

Of course, in many ways, the insights from the theoretical literature on international trade apply equally to goods and services. This is particularly true for cross-border trade. There are, however, some important differences. One is the role of proximity (see Francois, 1990b; Sampson and Snape, 1985), which has important analytical implications. The significance of proximity for service transactions means that "trade" in the case of services often requires a mix of cross-border transactions and local establishment (i.e., FDI). The importance of trade through affiliates is illustrated, for the case of the US, in Table 1. The US is the leading service exporter, with US$245.7 billion in 1998. The level of US service sales through affiliates (establishment trade) is comparable. Establishment sales amounted to US$258 billion in 1997, which compares to US$240 billion in direct exports.

The empirical and operational importance of establishment leads to a second important difference between goods and services. This is an institutional difference. While the GATT emphasizes barriers at the border (tariffs, quotas, etc.), the GATS has a different focus. From the outset, it has emphasized both cross-border barriers and barriers to local establishment. Consequently, the GATS blurs trade and investment restrictions, and covers both trade and investment rules to the extent that they limit market access in service sectors.

Given the structure of the GATS, negotiations involve parallel commitments on cross-border trade and local establishment by foreign service providers. We argue in this paper that these two modes (a simplification of the four modes actually listed in the GATS) can carry different implications for national welfare, market structure, profits, and related metrics tied to trade liberalization. In particular, given imperfect competition in services (often in conjunction with domestic

---

[1] A thorough overview is provided by WTO (1998).

[2] An exception is Cho (1988), who discusses Korean–US negotiations on insurance and the implications of the Korean insurance cartel for the gains from trade in insurance services.

J. Francois, I. Wooton / European Journal of Political Economy 17 (2001) 389–402   391

Table 1
US cross-border and affiliate trade in services

Year	US cross-border exports	US cross-border imports	US foreign sales through affiliates	Foreign sales in US through affiliates
	Billions of dollars			
1987	86.0	73.9	72.3	62.6
1988	100.1	81.0	83.8	73.2
1989	117.1	85.3	99.2	94.2
1990	136.2	98.2	121.3	109.2
1991	151.2	99.9	131.6	119.5
1992	162.3	100.4	140.6	128.0
1993	170.6	107.9	142.6	134.7
1994	186.0	119.1	159.1	145.4
1995	202.2	128.2	190.1	149.7
1996	221.1	137.1	223.2	168.4
1997	240.4	152.4	258.3	205.0
1998	245.7	165.3		

Source: Bureau of Economic Analysis, 1999.

regulation), realization of gains from trade liberalization is tied closely to issues of market regulation and market structure.[3] This, in turn, means that assessment of services commitments should take into account market structure and regulatory issues that affect the degree of competition.

The remainder of the paper is organized as follows. In Section 2, we provide some background and motivation. In Section 3, we develop a stylized model of trade in services, involving alternatively establishment or cross-border trade. In Section 4, we then examine liberalization of trade and establishment restrictions. Finally, our results are summarized in Section 5.

2. Background

As noted by Hill (1977), a critical distinction between goods and services is that services are consumed as they are produced. As a result of the flow nature of the transaction, service transactions involve an interaction between user and provider. Using this characteristic, Sampson and Snape (1985) differentiate between services that require physical proximity, and those that do not. Thus, a distinction is made between cross-border and local supply of services. The GATS

---

[3] Competition in service sectors can also have important implications for trade in goods. For example, cartels in the international transportation sector can pose a significant barrier to trade in goods (Francois and Wooton, 2001). In addition, the presence of transport costs typically means prices are not fully transmitted across markets (i.e., markets are segmented). This has important implications for trade and competition linkages.

392   *J. Francois, I. Wooton / European Journal of Political Economy 17 (2001) 389–402*

also recognizes this distinction, in that it covers service trade that requires no direct proximity (the cross-border mode) and trade which involves proximity (the remaining three modes: movement of providers, movement of consumers, and foreign establishment).

While GATS commitments relate to these four modes, there are also overlapping commitments in other areas under the WTO umbrella. For example, the code on government procurement provides scope for government commitments on market access to domestic service markets, to the extent that they supply the procurement market. In addition, the rules on trade-related investment measures (TRIMs), to the extent that they touch on service operations, also provide scope for overlapping commitments.

Critically, while competition policy is not formally a part of the WTO structure, competition also has an important role to play in market access. WTO members have recognized that competition policy can be relevant to the extent that it impinges on commitments made within the WTO. Hence, the recent US–Japan dispute over photographic film hinged on the degree of competition in the distribution sector, while threatened US action in the 1990s on Japanese auto imports also emphasized competition in the domestic distribution and sales network. Though these touch indirectly on market access in services, there are also more direct links between competition and market access in services.

Traditionally, many of the service sectors, such as banking, telecommunications, air transport, and insurance, have been heavily regulated. This regulation has sometimes, as in the case of PTTs, been undertaken in conjunction with state-sanctioned monopoly or outright state ownership. More recently, there has been a move toward deregulation and divestment of state ownership. While the most visible example may be telecommunications, similar moves are occurring in the banking and other sectors. For this reason, GATS-related negotiations on services have taken and will take place in the context of domestic regulatory changes, and in a climate of imperfect competition.

3. The model

To explore some of these issues, we start with a simple model of a domestic service sector that is imperfectly competitive. In addition to the domestic oligopoly, there is a foreign cross-border firm, but there are barriers protecting the domestic firms from the foreign competition. Within this framework, we examine the implications of lowering these barriers and giving the foreign firm open access to consumers through granting the firm the right of establishment in the domestic country.

3.1. Basic structure

Formally, consider the market for a homogeneous service S in the home (h) country. This service is provided by n identical domestic firms within a regulated

J. Francois, I. Wooton / European Journal of Political Economy 17 (2001) 389–402 393

industry, as well as by a single foreign (f) firm based overseas and facing barriers to serving the domestic consumers. The inverse demand for the service relates the market price to the total quantity supplied to the market (the sum of the outputs of the home firms and the foreign firm)

$$p = x - y(nq_h + q_f). \tag{1}$$

The revenues of the two types of firm are derived directly from the demand curve (1)

$$R_i = [x - y(nq_h + q_f)]q_i, \quad \text{for } i = \text{h,f}. \tag{2}$$

Home firms face a constant marginal cost c, while the foreign firm additionally has to pay t to provide the service to home consumers. This cost may reflect cross-border taxes, but is better viewed as a result of regulatory and other barriers to foreign operations in the home market. The foreign firm may, of course, also sell services in a third market. We are effectively assuming market segmentation here which, combined with the constant-marginal-cost assumption, lets us proceed with the model developed in this section. Consequently, total costs and marginal costs of the two types of firms are, respectively,

$$C_h = cq_h \quad MC_h = c \tag{3}$$
$$C_f = (c + t)q_f \quad MC_f = c + t.$$

The marginal revenue of the foreign firm is determined by the partial differentiation of Eq. (2), imposing the Cournot assumption that firms set quantity strategically, while assuming no subsequent reaction by competing forms (that is, $\partial q_h / \partial q_f = 0$). The firm's perceived marginal revenue is

$$MR_f = x - y(nq_h + 2q_f). \tag{4}$$

Equating marginal revenue to marginal cost for the foreign firm yields the reaction function

$$q_f(q_h) = \frac{x - (c + t) - ynq_h}{2y}. \tag{5}$$

The marginal revenues of the home firms will depend on the assumed structure of the home market. Home firms are assumed to be regulated and the nature of this regulation is crucial to the firms' behavior. To bind the range of effects, we adopt two polar assumptions about regulation. The first is that the regulator ensures that the home firms behave independently, engaging in pure Cournot competition with both their domestic and foreign rivals. The other extreme is to assume that the domestic regulator promotes collusion on the part of home firms, such that they act as a cartel. In either situation, the foreign firm is at first assumed to be a Cournot competitor.[4] We shall consider, below, the implications of the foreign firm being welcomed as a new member in the cartel.

---

[4] We assume Cournot competition rather than Bertrand, as the latter would result in the competition between the foreign and home firms driving the price to the competitive level.

394   J. Francois, I. Wooton / European Journal of Political Economy 17 (2001) 389–402

Consider firstly the perceived marginal revenue for a representative, non-cooperative home firm (labeled hn), whose Cournot assumption is that its domestic and foreign rivals will not change their outputs in response to its output change ($\partial q_{hk}/\partial q_{hj} = \partial q_f/\partial q_{hj} = 0$, for $k \neq j$)

$$MR_{hn} = x - y[(n+1)q_h + q_f],$$ (6)

where, using symmetry, it is assumed that all home firms choose the same level of output. The corresponding reaction function for a non-cooperative individual home firm is

$$q_{hn}(q_f) = \frac{x - c - yq_f}{(n+1)y}.$$ (7)

This can be contrasted with the behavior of the representative firm (labeled hc) that is part of a regulated cartel. This firm acts in collaboration with the other home firms, each adjusting output by the same anticipated amount. Consequently, the perceived marginal revenue of a representative cooperative home firm is

$$MR_{hc} = x - (2nq_h + q_f).$$ (8)

The corresponding reaction function is

$$q_{hc}(q_f) = \frac{x - c - yq_f}{2ny}.$$ (9)

3.2. Output equilibria

The foreign firm's reaction function (5) can be interacted with each of the home country's two possible reaction functions, Eqs. (7) and (9), to solve for the market equilibrium in the non-cooperative and cartel cases, respectively. When the home firms compete with both domestic and foreign firms, the equilibrium output levels are

$$q_{hn}^* = \frac{x - c + t}{(n+2)y}$$ (10)

$$q_{fn}^* = \frac{x - c - (n+1)t}{(n+2)y}$$

In the case of cartel behavior on the part of the home firms, the firms' equilibrium levels of output are

$$q_{hc}^* = \frac{x - c + t}{3ny}$$ (11)

$$q_{fc}^* = \frac{x - c - 2t}{3y}.$$

The reaction functions and the corresponding production equilibria are illustrated in Fig. 1. As should be expected, home firms supply more when they act

J. Francois, I. Wooton / European Journal of Political Economy 17 (2001) 389–402   395

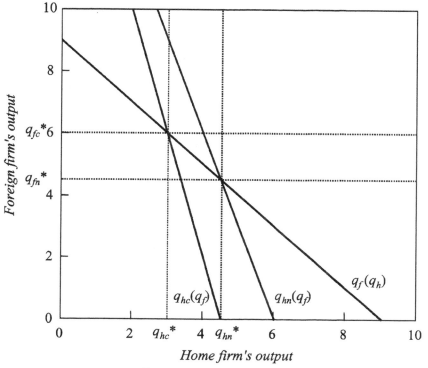

Fig. 1. Equilibrium output levels.

non-cooperatively. The foreign firm is able to free ride on the restrictive behavior of the cartel, selling a greater equilibrium quantity than when the home firms behave non-cooperatively.

4. Industry structure and market access

We now consider the implications for consumer welfare and the profitability of firms when the competitive structure of the service industry is changed as a result of commitments to liberalize market-access conditions. This change can arise either through giving the foreign firm better market access or through forcing home firms to act more competitively.

4.1. Improving cross-border access

Market access for the foreign firm is improved by reducing t, the impediment the firm faces in servicing the home market from abroad. The foreign firm would

396   *J. Francois, I. Wooton / European Journal of Political Economy 17 (2001) 389–402*

be accorded national treatment if $t = 0$, equivalent to the firm having the right of establishment in the home market and consequently being able to compete on an equal footing with the domestic firms. We shall, later, discuss the potential implications for the foreign firm being admitted to the domestic cartel.

We can solve for the price of the service when the domestic firms in the home country behave non-cooperatively by substituting the equilibrium outputs (Eq. (10)) into the inverse demand function (1), yielding

$$p_n^* = \frac{x - (n+1)c + t}{n+2}. \tag{12}$$

Profits of a firm are the difference between its revenues (Eq. (2)) and its costs (Eq. (3))

$$\pi_i = R_i - C_i, \qquad \text{for } i = \text{h,f}. \tag{13}$$

Thus, equilibrium profits are calculated by substituting Eq. (10) into Eq. (13)

$$\pi_{hn}^* = \frac{(x - c + t)^2}{(n+2)^2 y} \tag{14}$$

$$\pi_{fn}^* = \frac{[x - c(n+1)t]^2}{(n+2)^2 y}.$$

Fig. 2a illustrates the effects of reducing the trade barrier t on price p_n^*, profits of the foreign firm π_{fn}^*, and profits of the home industry Π_{hn}^* (n times the profits of an individual firm π_{fn}^*, where $n = 2$ in these simulations). The higher the barrier to the foreign firm, the smaller its market share and its profits, while the domestic firms enjoy a higher level of profitability. The market price rises with the barrier as home firms face progressively less competition from abroad resulting in a less competitive price. When the trade barrier is eliminated, all firms compete on an equal basis and receive the same level of profits (so that the profits of the home industry are n times those of the foreign firm).

Similar calculations can be made for the equilibrium price and profit levels when the regulated home firms behave as a cartel, by substituting the equilibrium output levels (Eq. (11)) into Eq. (1) for the price

$$p_c^* = \frac{x + 2c + t}{3}, \tag{15}$$

and into Eq. (13) for firms' profit levels

$$\pi_{hc}^* = \frac{(x - c + t)^2}{9ny} \tag{16}$$

$$\pi_{fc}^* = \frac{(x - c - 2t)^2}{9y}.$$

J. Francois, I. Wooton / European Journal of Political Economy 17 (2001) 389–402 397

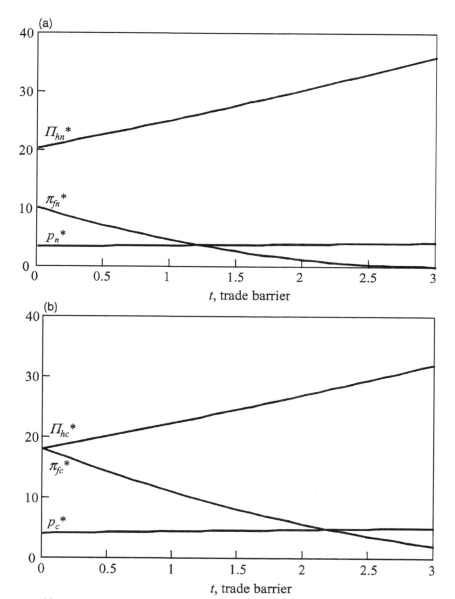

Fig. 2. (a) Improving cross-border access (non-cooperative home firms). (b) Improving cross-border access (home cartel).

398   *J. Francois, I. Wooton / European Journal of Political Economy 17 (2001) 389–402*

Fig. 2b shows the impact of trade-barrier reduction on the price p_c^*, foreign firm's profits π_{fc}^*, and the profits of the cartelized home industry $\Pi_{hc}^* = n\pi_{hc}^*$ (where n is once again assumed to be equal to 2). In large respect, the lines are the same as those for the non-cooperative home industry, illustrated in Fig. 2a. The principal difference is that, when all barriers are eliminated (giving the foreign firm equal access to the market) the foreign firm and the home industry have equal market shares. This is because the domestic firms behave as if they were a single firm.

4.2. Domestic competition policy

We turn next to competition policy. Within our analytical framework, a natural instrument for simulating the effects of domestic regulation is n, the number of home firms. Calculating the equilibria for the cases of a domestic cartel and of a competitive single home firm (that is $n = 1$), yields the same outcome. Consequently, we can determine the impact of forcing a cartelized home industry to behave more competitively by calculating the non-cooperative equilibrium outcome for increasing values of n, between 1 and the actual number of firms in the industry.[5]

We illustrate the results of this exercise in Fig. 3. In the figure, the equilibrium price p_n^* and the profits of the foreign firm π_{fn}^* and the home industry Π_{hn}^* are shown as a function of n, the number of firms in the home industry. The foreign firm faces a barrier to trade and hence will always have a lower level of profitability than its home counterpart in the domestic market. However, it will have higher profits, the fewer home firms with which it has to compete. Profits of the home industry are not monotonic in the number of home firms. Two home firms grab a larger share of the market than does a cartel so that, even though the overall market is more competitive, the home industry in total is better off with the increased competition. Larger numbers of non-cooperative home firms will, however, drive down overall profits in the market and lower the total profits of the home firms, despite their increased share of sales.

4.3. The camel's nose under the tent (admitting the foreigner into the cartel)

Given that the foreign firm has been given the right of establishment, is it in the interests of any party to have it join the domestic firms in the cartel? This is a solution that has been followed in practice, with examples including the Korean and Swiss insurance industries' responses to pressure from the US (see, for example, Cho, 1988 on Korea). Within our framework, whether or not the foreign

---

[5] This technique was used by the authors in Francois and Wooton (2001) in their discussion of shipping conferences and maritime trade. Also, see Francois and Horn (1998).

J. Francois, I. Wooton / European Journal of Political Economy 17 (2001) 389–402   399

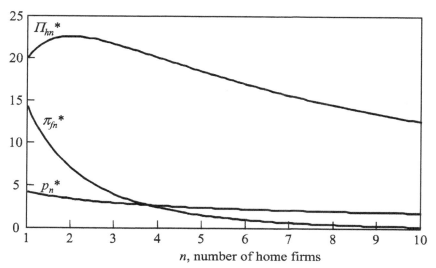

Fig. 3. Encouraging domestic competition.

firm would agree to such an arrangement proves to hinge on the size of trading costs. We consider the earnings of firms at various trade costs, both when the foreign firm is in competition with the cartel (subscripted, as before, by c) and when it has been admitted as a full participant in the restrictive agreement (subscripted by a). The results are illustrated in Fig. 4, where the number of home firms is again set at 2.

It is clear that in the case illustrated when the trade costs $(t > t_2)$ are high the cartel wants to keep the foreign firm out, while the foreign firm would like to have the right of establishment, even as part of the cartel. At middle trade costs $(t_1 < t < t_2)$, the home cartel is feeling heightened pressure on its profits from the increasingly competitive foreign firm. The cartel would therefore like to admit the foreign firm to the cartel, an option that the foreign firm also prefers. At low trade costs $(t < t_1)$ the foreign firm would rather compete with the home cartel than be a part of it. The consumer always appears to lose from the formation of the cartel, even if it avoids trade costs in the process of admitting the foreign firm.

The interest of a domestic industry, in terms of favoring or opposing a foreign right of establishment, will depend on the conditions for cross-border access. The industry's position can be reversed as cross-border restrictions are negotiated down. This is because, given the erosion of its market power through increasing trade, the domestic industry may find it advantageous to co-opt the foreign sector by inviting it into the cartel and sharing rents. Once cross-border barriers are sufficiently low, however, the foreign view of establishment is that it would prefer

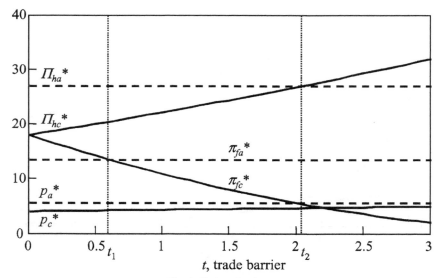

Fig. 4. Choice of regime.

to play against, rather than with, the cartel. The effect of establishment on competition therefore depends on cross-border access. With high trading costs, establishment may reduce welfare through profit shifting.

5. Summary

The GATS places emphasis on two broad modes of trade: cross-border (i.e., international) trade, and trade through local establishments. Cross-border trade includes movement of service providers, movement of consumers, and cross-border sales. Hence, in contrast to trade in goods, GATS-based negotiations take place on the dual margins of trade and investment concessions. Our approach in this paper has been to work with a formal model of oligopoly to examine the effects of market-access concessions on domestic and foreign firms and on domestic consumers. We have argued that the relative benefits of cross-border and establishment-related market-access concessions hinge critically on underlying issues of regulation and market structure. In particular, the interests of the domestic and foreign industry will depend, in part, on the impact that trade has made on the market power of domestic firms.

We summarize our analytical results in three groupings: rather obvious, somewhat less obvious, and even less obvious. The last set of results constitutes the substantive contribution of the paper. On the rather obvious front, given an

J. Francois, I. Wooton / European Journal of Political Economy 17 (2001) 389–402 401

imperfectly competitive industry (whether Cournot competition or perfect collusion), less market access (i.e., greater restrictions) results in the foreign service provider having a smaller market share and profits; domestic service providers becoming increasingly profitable, and a higher home-market price.

Our less obvious results arise from our consideration of the effects of less competition within a regulatory environment that tolerates collusion among a small number of domestic firms. We showed that the foreign firm will have higher profits the less competitive the domestic industry, profits of the home industry are not monotonic in the number of home firms, and initial moves away from monopoly can actually boost the market share and profits of the entire domestic industry.

Even less obvious (and the main lesson to carry away from our analysis) is the incentive for bringing a foreign firm into a domestic cartel. This involves establishment, and yields the following three results. When the trade costs are high, a domestic cartel wants to keep the foreign firm out (i.e., it opposes establishment), while the foreign firm would like to have the right of establishment, even as part of the cartel. At more moderate trade costs, both the home and foreign firms favor bringing the foreign firm into the domestic cartel. At low trade costs, the foreign firm would rather compete with the home cartel than be a part of it.

Collectively, this last set of results points to linkages between the degree of competition, the mode and degree of market access, and the pro-competitive effects of liberalization. When we introduce establishment in conjunction with low cross-border barriers, we find that the foreign-service provider takes on the domestic cartel. This is clearly a pro-competitive result. At higher levels of cross-border trade barriers, establishment may instead lead to an equilibrium where the foreign sector is simply co-opted into the domestic cartel. This has well known negative consequences related to profit shifting. The impact of establishment on the degree of competition, and on potential gains or losses from liberalization, hinges on the underlying degree of competition (a regulatory issue), but also on barriers to cross-border trade.

Acknowledgements

This paper was prepared for the World Services Congress, Atlanta, GA, November 1999. We thank Bob Stern and the participants in our WSC session.

References

Cho, Y.J., 1988. Some policy lessons from the opening of the Korean insurance market. World Bank Economic Review, 241–254.

Deardorff, A.V., 1985. Comparative advantage and international trade and investment in services. In: Stern, R.M. (Ed.), Trade and Investment in Services: Canada/US Perspectives. Ontario Economic Council, Toronto.

Francois, J.F., 1990a. Increasing returns due to specialization, monopolistic competition, and trade in producer services. Canadian Journal of Economics 23, 109–124.

Francois, J.F., 1990b. Trade in nontradables: proximity requirements and the pattern of trade in services. Journal of International Economic Integration (now the Journal of Economic Integration) 5, 31–46.

Francois, J.F., Horn, H., 1998. Competition policy and trade in an open economy. Tinbergen Institute discussion paper.

Francois, J.F., Schuknecht, L., 1999. International trade in financial services, competition, and growth performance. Centre for Economic Policy Research discussion paper no. 2144.

Francois, J.F., Wooton, I., 2001. Trade in international transport services: the role of competition. Centre for Economic Policy Research discussion paper no. 2377.

Hill, T.P., 1977. On goods and services. Review of Income and Wealth 23, 315–338.

Hoekman, B., 1994. Conceptual and political economy issues in liberalizing international transactions in services. In: Deardorff, A.V., Stern, R.M. (Eds.), Analytical and Negotiating Issues in the Global Trading System. Studies in International Trade Policy. University of Michigan Press, Ann Arbor, MI, pp. 501–538.

Markusen, J.R., 1988. Production, trade, and migration with differentiated, skilled workers. Canadian Journal of Economics 21, 492–506.

Markusen, J.R., 1989. Trade in producer services and in other specialized intermediate inputs. American Economic Review 79, 85–95.

Sampson, G.P., Snape, R.H., 1985. Identifying the issues in trade in services. The World Economy 8, 171–181.

Stern, R.M., Hoekman, B.M., 1988. Conceptual issues relating to services in the international economy. In: Lee, C.-H., Naha, S. (Eds.), Trade and Investment in Services in the Asia-Pacific Region. Pacific and World Studies, vol. 1. Inha University, Inchon, Korea, pp. 7–25.

WTO, 1998. Economic effects of services liberalization: overview of empirical studies. WTO document S/C/26/Add. 1, May 29.

[24]

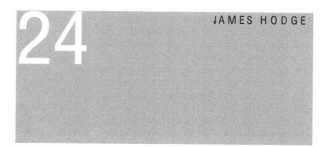

JAMES HODGE

LIBERALIZATION OF TRADE IN SERVICES IN DEVELOPING COUNTRIES

The term "services" covers a broad range of industries that typically dominate absolute output and employment in most countries. It encompasses both intermediate services (communications, transport, financial intermediation, electricity and gas, distribution, construction, and business services) and final demand services (tourism and travel, recreation, education, health, and environmental services).

Services have only recently been added to the agenda of multilateral trade talks, and the first agreement concerning them, the General Agreement on Trade in Services (GATS), was concluded in the Uruguay Round. Services have also come to prominence in a number of regional agreements, including the European Union (EU), the North American Free Trade Agreement (NAFTA), and the Common Market of the South (MERCOSUR). The reason for this interest is the growing volume of services trade made possible by developments in information and communications technology, and the greater market access resulting from the widespread deregulation of public utilities. For the past decade, growth of trade in services has outstripped that in manufacturing. Services trade now makes up a quarter of all cross-border trade and more than half of all sales by affiliates of multinationals (Hoekman and Mattoo 2000).

What Does Liberalization Mean for Trade in Services?

Trade liberalization involves providing greater market access to foreign firms by lowering the barriers to trade. This is a relatively straightforward concept for goods trade, where liberalization involves the reduction of tariffs. It is infinitely more complex for services, where the nature of trade and the types of barriers encountered are very different. There are four modes of supplying services trade, reflecting the greater need for at least some interaction between the consumer and the producer of services:

- *Cross-border trade*—electronic or physical transactions across borders, such as air or maritime transport and financial trading (mode 1)
- *Consumption abroad*—movement of the consumer to a foreign country for reasons such as tourism or education (mode 2)
- *Commercial presence*—direct investment for the purpose of delivering services such as local telecommunications or electricity (mode 3)
- *Presence of natural persons*—temporary movement of a producer to provide services such as business consulting or construction (mode 4).

The choice of mode of supply by producers is determined by technical feasibility and the various

221

barriers to trade that exist across each mode (Hoek-man and Mattoo 2000). Commercial presence tends to be the dominant mode of supply for all but transport and tourism services; cross-border trade is the next most important. Trade through the presence of natural persons is typically small for all sectors, and consumption abroad is only significant for tourism. Barriers to trade are typically regulatory in nature. They include measures that restrict market access by foreign firms (for example, by reserving supply for a public monopoly or through nonrecognition of professional qualifications) or that discriminate against them once they are in the market through, for example, different tax treatment or local borrowing limitations for foreign firms (UNCTAD 1995c).

Liberalization of trade in services therefore involves the reduction of regulatory barriers to market access and discriminatory national treatment across all four modes of supply. This is not to be confused with the process of deregulation that many countries are pursuing. The focus of deregulation is to reduce the total amount of state regulation in a sector, while that of trade liberalization is to ensure that existing regulation does not discriminate against foreign participation in the market. Trade liberalization is consistent with countries' continuing to regulate industries for the purposes of consumer protection, prudential management of the economy, control of natural monopolies, or the achievement of social goals.

Moving to a nondiscriminatory regulatory regime, however, can require significant changes in how some sectors, in particular, public utilities, are currently regulated. Network-based utilities such as electricity, transport, and telecommunications have typically been operated as public monopolies because of the natural monopoly aspects of their production and in order to pursue universal service through cross-subsidization. Changes in technology, increases in demand, and the ability to subdivide the production chain have led to a decline in the importance of the natural monopoly argument in many of these sectors. In this case, continued monopolization for the sake of universal service, when alternative regulatory means of fulfilling these social objectives are available, would clearly fall foul of attempts to give market access to foreign firms.[1] Procompetitive regulatory reform would have to precede liberalization of services.

Another key policy area that comes under the spotlight in services trade liberalization is the treatment of foreign direct investment (FDI). Commercial presence is a key mode of supply for services, and developing countries have historically placed significant restrictions on FDI in order to encourage domestic ownership of capital, limit repatriation of profits, and increase the linkages of the multinational firm with upstream suppliers. Full liberalization of the commercial presence mode of supply would outlaw most of these measures in the services sectors. There is, however, a developmental aspect to the GATS that allows low-income countries to impose limited conditions on FDI, such as training and technology transfer (UNCTAD 2000c).

Gains from Liberalization

The traditionally low tradability of services may create the impression that the gains from services liberalization are small. Because, however, services have a strong intermediate role, the gains from trade include both the direct effect on the sector itself and the indirect effect on all the other sectors in the economy that make use of the service (see Box 24.1). For this reason, Markusen (1989) finds that the potential gains from trade in intermediate services are significantly higher than the gains from trade in final goods. A further reason for the potentially large gains from trade in services is that this trade currently faces very high barriers to trade in comparison with trade in goods. Dee and Hanslow (2001) used a computable general equilibrium (CGE) model to generate rough estimates of the current worldwide gains from services liberalization.[2] They found that the gains are approximately the same as for full liberalization of trade in both agricultural and manufacturing goods.

Standard Gains from Trade

Many developing countries are concerned that most of the gains from trade liberalization will accrue to industrial countries. This perception is based on the observation that many services sectors are human capital–intensive, physical capital–intensive, or both—which means that industrial countries will have a comparative advantage and will dominate any trade after liberalization. This argument, however, ignores the facts that all countries have comparative advantage in *some* area, that services have a key intermediate role in the economy, and that services are largely traded through FDI (Hodge and Nordas 1999).

BOX 24.1 REALIZING THE GAINS FROM FINANCIAL LIBERALIZATION

Argentina. A study of the liberalization of the Argentine banking sector found improved performance in the areas in which foreign banks specialized (Clarke and others 1999). Foreign entry lowered net margins and profits in lending to manufacturing, while margins and profits in consumer lending remained high, as foreign banks had not penetrated that segment. The ratio of operational costs to total assets declined from 1.3 percent in 1990 to 0.5 percent in 1997. Foreign banks also played a role in revitalizing the undercapitalized banking sector with a new infusion of capital.

Colombia. Barajas, Steiner, and Salazar (1999) chronicle the Colombian experience with foreign entry. Colombia followed highly restrictive policies and banned FDI in banking in 1975. In 1991, however, there was a reversal of the restrictive FDI policy, and the rules of entry and exit were significantly liberalized. The deregulation lowered intermediation spreads, reduced administrative costs, and increased loan quality. Intermediation spreads declined almost 8 percentage points between 1991 and 1998 for domestic and foreign banks. Nonperforming loans as a percentage of total loans fell from 7 percent in 1991 to 3 percent in 1998 for foreign banks and stood steady at 6 percent for domestic banks during that period.

Turkey. Denizer (1999) looks at foreign bank entry into the Turkish banking sector, which had been highly regulated and concentrated, dominated by a few large banks with extensive branch networks. Liberalization began in 1980 with a marked decrease in directed credit programs and the elimination of interest rate controls. Commercial presence was liberalized, and large numbers of new foreign banks entered. The number of foreign banks increased from 4 in 1980 to 23 in 1990, and in 1997, after mergers, the number stood at 17. Foreign bank entry had the effect of reducing net interest margins, returns on assets, and overhead expenses of domestic banks. It qualitatively changed Turkish banking by introducing financial and operations planning and improving the credit evaluation and marketing system. Foreign banks also took the lead in

spreading electronic banking and introduced new technologies. The number of ATMs increased rapidly (to 6,500 locations by 1997), and in 1997 Turkey led Europe in new credit card issues.

Africa. The institutional and regulatory framework plays a critical role in realizing the gains from financial liberalization. For example, financial reforms were introduced in many African countries in the 1990s, but they have been less successful than expected (World Bank 2000a). Some of the reasons for the disappointing results are directly related to the financial system, while others pertain to the general economic environment. The restructuring of state-owned banks was not sufficient to change the behavior of the financial institutions; public authorities still pressured these institutions to lend money to loss-making public enterprises; liberalization failed to trigger competition in the banking sector; and governments were mostly reluctant to close down distressed state banks. Liberalization of interest rates in the presence of uncontrolled fiscal deficits had a pernicious effect on domestic public debt, which in turn led to larger deficits. Finally, a crucial shortcoming was the lack of adequate regulatory and supervision mechanisms to monitor the functioning of the financial system.

Republic of Korea. The collapse of the Korean economy in 1997 is another case that reveals the precariousness of financial liberalization in an imperfect policy environment. Korea did liberalize its financial markets substantially, but it encouraged the development of a highly fragile financial structure.* By liberalizing short-term (but not long-term) foreign borrowing, the Korean authorities made it possible for the larger and better-known banks and *chaebols* to assume heavy indebtedness in short-term foreign currency debt. Meanwhile, large *chaebols* in the second tier greatly increased their short-term indebtedness in domestic financial markets (funded indirectly through foreign borrowing by the banks), and the funds borrowed were invested in overexpansion of productive capacity. Financial regulation and supervision were fragmented, with responsibilities

(continued)

DEVELOPING COUNTRIES AND NEGOTIATIONS ON TRADE IN SERVICES

BOX 24.1 (CONTINUED)

spread in an unclear way between the Bank of Korea and several parts of the Ministry of Finance. In addition, Korea had a restrictive regime regarding foreign bank entry. Until the 1997 crisis, the Korean banking system was virtually closed to foreign banks, in contrast to some other East Asian economies such as Hong Kong (China), which was almost completely open for all financial services. Korea's restrictive regime impeded the development of local institutions and may have contributed to large capital outflows as foreign creditors refused to roll over their loans.

* The financial structure was fragile with respect to the financial instruments employed (too much reliance on short-term bills), the financial intermediaries that were unwittingly encouraged (lightly regulated trust subsidiaries of the banks and other newly established near-bank financial intermediaries), and market infrastructure development (failure to develop the institutions of the long-term capital market). See, for instance, Claessens and Glaessner (1999).
Source: Prepared by the volume editors, based on Claessens and Glaessner (1999); World Bank (2000a, 2001a).

Developing countries have already shown that they do have some comparative advantage in services and are able to export a broad range of services effectively. The most significant export is tourism, which accounts for a large proportion of total export revenues among poorer countries (Karsenty 2000). Other natural resource–based exports include water and electric power.[3] Labor-intensive sectors such as construction have clear comparative advantages for developing countries, but trade has been limited by trade barriers, including the reluctance of most countries to extend to the less-skilled occupations the permissible temporary movement of people to deliver a service (UNCTAD 2000b). Developing countries are, however, also active in sectors that are more intensive users of human capital or of physical capital. The best-known example is software services exports by India, which is now a multibillion dollar industry. Other examples of information technology–related services include back-office processing and call centers. Part of the reason for developing countries' entry into these activities is that firms in communications and transport services are able to carve up the production chain, allowing developing countries to operate in the labor-intensive parts of the chain. Another reason is that some developing countries are exploiting their comparative advantage in these sectors relative to their less-developed neighbors. For instance, South Africa exports a full range of financial and business services to the southern African region, allowing it to maintain a positive trade bal-

ance on its services account (Hodge and Nordas 1999).

The initial benefit from this specialization and trade is the increased output and consumption that become possible as resources are reallocated to their most productive use in the economy. This expands output in the sector of comparative advantage while lowering the cost of both domestically produced and imported goods. The fact that trade expands the scale of the market is important if there are economies of scale in production: it makes possible further benefits from trade, as firms are able to reduce unit costs. It also permits a far greater number of differentiated services to exist simultaneously, adding value for consumers (Krugman 1996).

Because of economies of scale in research and development (R&D), an expanding market may increase the incentive for those activities, enhancing long-run growth rates (Grossman and Helpman 1991). Furthermore, learning is enhanced through technological spillovers in exporting. Trade also increases the extent of competition in the market, which lowers the market power of existing firms and brings down their price-cost markups. This is particularly important in services, where, typically, large-scale economies exist, severely limiting competition in small economies.

Finally, trade liberalization across a broad range of services can also lower inflationary pressure within an economy as prices fall for a significant share of total output. This can provide an important stimulus to investment and economic growth (OECD 1997d).

Gains from Services as Intermediate Inputs

Even in the extreme case in which developing countries have no comparative advantage in services, they could still gain from trade in services because it enables them to concentrate on nonservice sectors in which they have a comparative advantage (agri-

culture, mining, and some manufacturing). This, of course, assumes that their liberalization in services is matched by liberalization in these other sectors by their trading partners, so that specialization is possible. The argument is strengthened in the case of services because of the prominent intermediate role of that sector (see Boxes 24.2 and 24.3).

BOX 24.2 CONTRIBUTION OF INEFFICIENT INTERNAL TRANSPORT SYSTEMS TO THE CONCENTRATION OF CHINA'S EXPORT INDUSTRIES IN COASTAL REGIONS

A remarkable feature of China's dramatic expansion in international trade over the past two decades has been the concentration of export-oriented industries in coastal regions. The four most important coastal provinces, Guangdong, Jiangsu, Fujian, and Shanghai, have been the main recipients of outward-oriented foreign investment, with the remaining share going either to other coastal provinces or to regions adjoining coastal areas. The provinces in the central core—usually referred to as lagging provinces—have barely benefited from the incoming investment. Although dispersion of export-oriented units has narrowed the disparities in coastal incomes as the southern coast regions catch up with the affluent eastern coast, the export boom has exacerbated the coastal-inland gap. Thus, while China's economic reforms have been successful in raising living standards for a considerable share of the population, a large number of the people in inland provinces still live below the poverty line.

A contributing factor to coastal agglomeration has been inefficiencies in China's internal transport systems. Disparities in transport infrastructure between the coastal and inland provinces have narrowed considerably since 1990 as a result of policies aimed at promoting more regionally balanced economic development. Nevertheless, evidence of increasing interprovincial trade between inland regions, and between inland and coastal regions, suggests that it is not the lack of transport infrastructure per se that has hindered inland provinces from actively participating in foreign trade; rather, inadequacies in transport *services* constitute the more binding

constraint on the better integration of China's hinterland economy.

The compositional shift of exports from low-value raw materials to high-value manufactured goods has made transport increasingly suitable for containerization. Although the volume of container traffic in China has increased significantly since 1990, this traffic is largely confined to coastal regions and is associated with the ocean-going leg of travel. There is much less container traffic in inland areas, and no significant change in the percentage of seaborne containers traveling beyond port cities and coastal provinces. Trucking rates for moving a container 500 kilometers inland are estimated to be about three times more, and the trip time five times longer, than would be the case in Europe or the United States. China's railways still charge what is in effect a penalty rate for moving containers. Priority on the congested rail network is given to low-value bulk freight (mostly coal) rather than to high-value freight such as containers.

Surveys of major foreign shippers, shipping lines, and freight forwarders based in the United States, Japan, and Hong Kong (China) indicate that China's transport systems, particularly for inland transport, are well below international standards. Respondents pointed to the lack of container freight stations, yards, and trucks in inland regions. Border procedures were perceived as cumbersome and time-consuming due to the many certification requirements and the duplication of documents—in part, a consequence of the lack of coordination between the different government agencies involved in the various modes of transport. Container tracking capability was

(continued)

225

DEVELOPING COUNTRIES AND NEGOTIATIONS ON TRADE IN SERVICES

particularly poor, with shippers often unaware of their containers' whereabouts. Shippers attributed this problem to poorly trained staff, the lack of a reliable recovery system, and the inadequate accountability system in government agencies. Finally, the intermodal transport system was seen as poorly integrated, with no streamlined procedures to support the continuous movement of containers between the coast and inland areas.

Another source of inefficiencies is the dominance of state-owned enterprises and the lack of competition in transport services markets. Since pricing in many of the intermediate transport services activities is controlled, the companies have little incentive for aggressively pursuing cost-cutting methods, and, due to lack of competition,

intermediate services providers represent the interests of transport operators. The outcome is that value-added service and reliability, which are essential for winning business confidence in a modern economy, are not priorities for most participants. Investment by foreign enterprises and joint ventures between foreign and domestic enterprises in intermediate transport services are limited in inland regions. Although foreign investment is not prohibited, there are restrictions on their activities, such as requirements that firms carry only the parent companies' products.

Sources: Prepared by the volume editors based on World Bank (1996a); Atinc (1997); Naughton (2001); Graham and Wada (forthcoming).

Services are used intensively in the production and trade of all goods and services in the economy, including in agriculture and mining. Typically, services make up 10–20 percent of production costs and all the costs of trading—communications, transport, trade finance and insurance, and distribution services (Hodge and Nordas 1999). The price and quality of services are therefore crucial in determining the cost of all other products in the economy. The reduction in tariffs on goods to historically low levels and the emergence of global production networks have made services even more important in determining the competitiveness of goods producers. In countries where tariffs are low and the price of services is high, manufacturers may well face negative effective rates of protection. In fact, Limão and Venables (1999) conclude that Africa's poor trade performance is almost exclusively attributable to poor infrastructure-based services. (They find that a 10 percent decrease in transport costs increases trade by 25 percent.) Another consideration is that entry into global production networks requires efficient and timely delivery. Low-quality services that delay production or transport effectively exclude producers from such networks.

The effects extend beyond any one-time gains and may have an impact on the growth rates of countries. Poor-quality, high-priced services not only

affect the current operations of manufacturers but also discourage future investment by locals and foreigners by lowering the profitability of such investment. This partly explains why FDI is limited in the poorest countries despite access to cheap labor. Honglin Zang and Markusen (1999) argue that FDI is unlikely to materialize outside extractive industries if multinationals do not have access to skilled local workers, social infrastructure, utilities, and legal institutions of the necessary quality, at a reasonable price. The result is not just a static loss from poor service delivery but a dynamic growth loss.[4] One reason for low-quality and high-priced services in developing countries is the narrow downstream market for these services. Rodriguez-Clare (1996) argues that small economies may get caught in a development trap because the narrow downstream market constrains the extent of specialization and the exploitation of scale economies in the services sector. This leads to lower-quality and higher-priced services, which in turn limit the ability of the downstream industry to expand.

By expanding the market for intermediate services and by lowering the price and improving the quality of services, trade liberalization should enable poorer countries to better exploit the comparative advantages they do have. Producers of primary and manufacturing goods in developing

BOX 24.3 LESSONS FROM REFORMING ARGENTINA'S PORTS

As part of its overall program of macroeconomic stabilization, liberalization, and public sector reform, the government of Argentina initiated in the 1990s a comprehensive reform of the port sector. The reform was a major success in that it greatly improved the performance of Argentina's largest seaports, facilitating a rapid, more than fourfold expansion in the volume of seaborne trade between 1990 and 2000, from 249,000 TEUs (20-foot-equivalent units) to 1,070 million TEUs.

Before 1990, Argentinean ports were characterized by institutional inadequacies (including a major corruption problem), inefficient cross-subsidization, and insufficient investment in the modernization of the sector. Tariffs charged by the publicly operated ports were reportedly among the highest in the world. Total cargo moved in the ports fell by 10 percent between 1970 and 1989, with the port of Buenos Aires alone experiencing a 52 percent reduction in traffic.

The overall reform program consisted of a combination of devolution of most port responsibilities to the provinces, private sector participation, and promotion of service competition. Provinces were given the freedom to operate, concession, or close ports, with the exception of large ports, for which the creation of independent autonomous companies was foreseen. In the case of the port of Buenos Aires, six terminals were competitively concessioned to the private sector, with payment of a leasing fee to the government for use of infrastructure assets, following the landlord port model. To improve the contestability of port operations, the government established free entry into the sector by allowing any operator to build, manage, and operate a port for public or private use. A new regulatory agency, Autoridad Portuaria

Nacional, was created under the Ministry of the Economy. Finally, the restructuring process included a significant labor reform that eliminated restrictive work regulations and softened the social impact of labor reductions.

The main economic effect of the overall reforms was to transform Argentina's ports from the most expensive ones in Latin America into the cheapest ones. Private investment picked up in the second half of the 1990s, leading to a substantial expansion in capacity. Productivity has grown sharply, significantly reducing operational costs and duration of stay in ports. Combined with more intense competition between port services providers, this has resulted in a reduction in overall container terminal handling prices, as shown in the table.

Despite these impressive achievements, unresolved issues from the first wave of port reforms and from changes in the competitive environment in the sector, although not pressing, demand solutions in the long run. Intraport competition is working effectively, but the likelihood of future mergers between terminal operators at the port of Buenos Aires raises the risk of collusion. Improved monitoring and benchmarking mechanisms, as well as the fine-tuning of price regulations, may be necessary to ensure that services continue to be provided cost-efficiently. Inefficient customs operations are a key constraint on further productivity gains in the sector and represent a priority for future reform. Finally, some aspects of Argentina's port policy, such as restrictions on the circulation of containers, are reported to restrain intermodal integration. Addressing this issue in the context of the wider policy framework on multimodal transport would contribute to better performance of the transport system nationwide.

Improved Performance in the Port of Buenos Aires

Indicator	1991	1997
Cargo (thousands of tons)	4,000	8,500
Containers (thousands of TEUs)	300	1,023
Capacity (thousands of TEUs)	400	1,300
Cranes (number)	3	13
Productivity (tons per employee)	800	3,100
Average container time at port (days)	2.5	1.3
Charges per container (US$/TEU)	450	120

Note: TEU, 20-foot-equivalent unit.

Source: Prepared by the volume editors, based on Trujillo and Nombela (1999) and Trujillo and Estache (2001).

DEVELOPING COUNTRIES AND NEGOTIATIONS ON TRADE IN SERVICES

countries should become more competitive, and the countries should become more attractive as investment locations for industries relocated from industrial countries. In fact, services liberalization may actually lead to greater industrialization in developing countries (Hodge and Nordas 1999).

Gains from FDI as a Means of Trade

The use of FDI as the preferred means of delivery makes services liberalization unique in terms of the additional gains it provides to developing countries. Imports of services through FDI bring with them inflows of physical capital, human capital, and technology—factors important for overcoming some of the main development constraints that poor countries face. Foreign capital inflows make possible a higher savings rate and thus the potential for a higher investment rate because domestic funds can be diverted to other opportunities. Inflows of foreign capital also lower the balance of payments constraint on growth and permit lower real interest rates. This and the boost to short-term growth rates should crowd in greater domestic investment.

Because foreign entrants will employ significant numbers of the local work force, this process should result in a period of sustained development of the human capital of the local labor force involved. Technology transfer may well be enhanced via spillovers from use of local suppliers and employee turnover. The demonstration effect of using new technology and management techniques could also improve their adoption by domestic firms. Finally, many services make use of common inputs. Thus, a reform package that liberalizes a few sectors at once may well see the emergence of a sufficient critical mass to develop an intermediate industry. Of particular interest in this respect is the information technology industry, which is a crucial input to all services and is fundamental in bringing about productivity improvements and new product development.

Adjustment Costs

Although liberalization of trade in services may yield overall gains for developing countries, the benefits will be unevenly distributed among different groups in society. The clear winners in this process are all the downstream users of any service that is liberalized and the owners of capital and labor in the services sectors of comparative advan-

tage. These groups are likely to realize growth in profits and employment. The potential losers from trade are firms and labor working in services with no comparative advantage. The effects of the mix of various modes of supply, including FDI, are more difficult to assess (see Box 24.4).

Firms in the import-competing sectors are likely to see their abnormal profits eroded by entry of foreign firms, but they may not exit the market even if they are less efficient. If the firms have considerable market power and large sunk investments, they should be able to survive entry and continue to produce. For instance, most incumbent public utilities tend to survive entry relatively easily and remain dominant years after procompetitive reform. Underperformance is likely, however, to lead to change in ownership (possibly to foreign ownership) and to a push for efficiency. This efficiency drive will lead to significant adjustment costs on the part of labor, particularly in public utilities, which have been a source of social employment in developing countries. Once these firms are privatized and opened to competition, the quickest source of efficiency gains is to shed labor. For example, in Argentina the electricity distribution companies shed up to 40 percent of employment over 30 months (Alexander and Estache 1999).

The loss of employment from productivity improvements will be offset to some extent by output expansion, but this is rarely sufficient to maintain employment in highly inefficient public utilities in the short run. If foreign entry also expands the market through increases in the variety of services available, the job losses may well be offset completely in the same sector. Nevertheless, certain categories of labor may still lose out. The drive for productivity improvements will shift demand toward higher-skilled workers, leaving lower-skilled workers to bear the brunt of job losses.[5] It is important, however, to place any sectoral job losses in a general equilibrium context alongside employment gains in downstream industries and sectors of comparative advantage.

The other means through which labor benefits from regulatory protection is through the wage premium (Rose 1985). Full trade liberalization is likely to reduce this premium, resulting in a drop in real wages. Opening up the presence of natural persons mode of supply will put direct pressure on wages for both skilled and unskilled labor, with little effect on owners of capital.

BOX 24.4 WELFARE GAINS FROM SERVICES LIBERALIZATION: THE CASE OF TUNISIA

Konan and Maskus (2000) have studied the implications of services liberalization for the Tunisian economy, using a computable general equilibrium (CGE) model. Taking actual data as the foundation, they analyze the effect of liberalizing six services sectors: communications, construction, transport, business and insurance, distribution, and finance. The model is developed so as to consider three different modes of liberalization: "import" liberalization of cross-border trade; the right of establishment by foreign investors; and increased "exports" through cross-border movement of natural persons. The Tunisian economy is relatively closed and also faces constraints imposed by other countries on its exports through the movement of individuals.

The main finding is that services liberalization could yield significant gains for Tunisia, with welfare gains equivalent to 7 percent of GDP. These gains are nearly twice as large as those the model predicts for Tunisia from its preferential agreement with the European Union (EU). The largest benefits, as shown in the figure, come from the liberalization of foreign investment in financial services, communications, and transport. Liberaliza-

tion vitalizes the economy by eliminating inefficiency, through increased international competition. Services are available not only at lower prices but also in greater variety through an increase in the number of firms operating in the country. More efficient financial, communications, and transport sectors are also likely to attract foreign firms to Tunisian industries, leading to an increase in the variety of goods and services available to consumers and producers and improving welfare. If Tunisia were to obtain a 20 percent increase in overseas permits for its guest workers in foreign markets, the additional gain in welfare would be equivalent to 0.4 percent of GDP.

The estimated costs of restructuring the economy turn out to be small. For example, it is predicted that a mere 3 percent of the work force would have to change sectors—a much lower figure than the 6.6 percent adjustment the model predicts as a consequence of the Tunisia-EU free trade agreement on goods trade. The gentler impact on the labor market is a consequence of the fact that services liberalization induces foreign investment, so that workers simply change employers within the same sector.

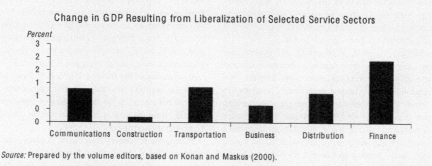

Change in GDP Resulting from Liberalization of Selected Service Sectors

Source: Prepared by the volume editors, based on Konan and Maskus (2000).

A further concern for many countries is the potential social loss from reform. This may arise as low-income households lose access to necessary services once cross-subsidization is removed and commercial concerns focus on profitable segments of the market. Subsidization of such groups can still

occur under a reformed regulatory regime but through different mechanisms, such as a nondiscriminatory levy on all providers in the industry, proceeds from which are distributed directly to the households requiring assistance (Bergman and others 1998). Regulatory reform provides the additional benefit of facilitating price reductions that allow larger numbers of low-income households to demand such services and that raise the real income of those households that are already making use of the services (Hodge 2000).

Undertaking Trade Liberalization in Services

In undertaking liberalization in services, it is necessary to lay the institutional foundations for reform, identify a coherent strategy that maximizes the gains while minimizing the adjustment costs, and manage the political consequences of reform to keep the process on track.

Preparing the Institutional Foundations for Liberalization

The institutional foundations for liberalization can include understanding the current trade stance, establishing the governmental process for trade negotiations, and creating the institutions to manage liberalization. The regulatory nature of trade barriers in services makes it difficult to identify the current trade stance in each sector. Instead of merely referring to a tariff schedule, as with goods, policymakers need to examine each piece of regulation in each sector to establish whether it in any way denies market access or discriminates against foreign firms. This is time consuming and is unlikely to result in a clear and quantifiable estimate of the size of the current barriers in each sector.

Putting together a governmental process for devising trade policy is equally problematic. In most countries each services sector has had its own supervisory government department, primarily to oversee the implementation of social goals through public utilities. Although a trade and industry department usually has a mandate to undertake trade negotiations, other departments clearly have a stake in the process and need to be included in the work of devising and implementing a trade liberalization strategy. These other line departments may be "captured" by the industry itself through historical joint planning and may frustrate the reform process. Furthermore, because liberalization is likely to raise revenues from privatization, the process is often captured by the state treasury, which delays the liberalization process to maximize the revenues from the sale of public enterprises. South Africa's

policy on public asset restructuring, which identifies revenue maximization as an explicit goal, has been part of the reason for delays in the privatization process.

In the case of public utilities that are currently state monopolies, there needs to be an initial process of preparing the ground for any future liberalization. At a bare minimum, these state enterprises need to be corporatized, an independent regulatory body has to be established for the industry, and effective antitrust legislation and institutions have to be put in place. Pinheiro (2000) notes that poor sequencing was to blame for some of the unsatisfactory results of regulatory reform in Latin America. Often, regulatory reform was concluded only after firms were privatized. Corporatization entails establishing the enterprise as a distinct business entity with a consolidated asset and liability register that makes it possible to pursue partial or full privatization and competition at a later date. The sector regulator and antitrust authorities are needed to manage competition in a liberalized services sector.

The effectiveness of regulation and competition will, to a large extent, determine the size of the gains from trade and how different groups in society share them (Alexander and Estache 1999).[6] Ineffective regulation and competition will result not in lower prices but in higher profits, benefiting the owners of capital rather than labor or consumers. Furthermore, in a more liberal environment in low-income countries, these owners of capital may well be foreign firms. This applies with equal force to the sector itself and to the downstream producers who will benefit from lower input prices. Sartar (2000) notes that one of the failings of reform in India has been the inability to create effective competition. African countries have found that lack of regulatory capacity is an important barrier to further liberalization in the continent (WTO 2000a).

Putting the regulatory framework in place entails a determination of how the industry will be regulated in a more competitive environment, including how social goals will be met in a competitively neutral manner once monopoly cross-subsidization is prohibited. Much of the focus of trade negotiations in services has been on laying this foundation by establishing clear regulatory principles for opening up network industries in a nondiscriminatory and competitive fashion.[7] Because supply in a liberalized environment will mostly take the form of FDI, it is important that the regulatory framework and process be considered fair and credible to potential investors. This is especially true for telecommunications, electricity, and transport, which involve large sunk investments. Any lack of credibility will result either in lack of entry and competition or in demands by investors for higher returns to cover regulatory risk. Either way, the gains from trade are lowered. Creating a suitable environment for foreign investment extends beyond regulatory certainty; it may include strengthening the legal system, stabilizing the macroeconomic environment, and permitting the repatriation of profits.

Preparing the ground for liberalization is not a public utilities issue alone. For instance, it is widely accepted that liberalization of trade in financial services requires careful preparation so that liberalization will not cause a financial crisis. Such crises can impose significant costs on the economy, from bailing out banks to disruption of real economic activity; they are estimated to cost countries anywhere from 2 to 40 percent of GDP (WTO 1997a). The prerequisites for a successful liberalization are considered to be macroeconomic stability, structural reforms in how banks are regulated, and implementation of effective prudential regulation (WTO 1997a).[8]

Sequencing and Timing of Liberalization

Once the foundation for liberalization has been laid, the next step is to devise a trade liberalization strategy aimed at maximizing the gains and minimizing the adjustment costs. The strategy needs to set out in detail the sequence and timing of liberalization across the different sectors, the modes of supply, and the two groups of barriers (market access and national treatment). It also needs to focus on what concessions are desired from trading partners across these various dimensions. A degree of caution should be observed when designing the liberalization process, as some of the key sectors have a profound impact on the workings of the economy. For example, a rash liberalization of the financial services sector could spark bank failure and might plunge the country into a recession. Once reforms have been carried out, it is difficult to reverse them temporarily to safeguard domestic industries (UNCTAD 2000b). For instance, once a foreign firm has invested infrastructure in services delivery, it is not possible to remove the firm's oper-

ating license without imposing severe costs on the firm and losing policy credibility.

The sequencing and timing of liberalization in different services sectors will depend in part on progress in laying the institutional foundations for reform. Complications at this stage may affect the feasibility of going ahead with reform. (For instance, reform of the transport sector in South Africa has been delayed by many years in order to restructure and reduce the excessive debt of the transport public utility.) Ideally, reform should initially be targeted at those sectors that are likely to bring about the most significant gains for the country. These would consist of services that provide important intermediate inputs to the rest of the economy or to specific sectors that the country wishes to promote, or sectors in which protection has resulted in a considerable inefficiency cost to society. (The two are often the same—specifically, in the case of public utilities). The reason for targeting intermediate inputs is that most of the gains from services liberalization are from the downstream effects. Sectors that have an economywide downstream effect, such as communications, transport, finance, and electricity, yield the most gains for liberalization effort. They also serve as inputs into other services sectors whose successful liberalization may well depend on prior liberalization of the intermediate services. For example, success in the tourism sector depends to a large extent on a cheap and efficient transport system (both domestic and international), adequate communications, and widespread foreign exchange trading. Similarly, attraction of foreign FDI and domestic expansion of information technology services will depend on adequate and inexpensive communications services.

The next choice is which modes of supply to open and which barriers to remove. This process can be simplified by eliminating any technically infeasible modes. If liberalization is to have a significant effect on the sector, the dominant mode of supply should be opened up. In most cases this is the commercial presence mode, which is in any case popular as a target for liberalization because of the potentially greater gains and lower adjustment costs. Governments feel they have greater control over the impact of liberalization if the foreign firms are operating within their borders. This is especially true of financial services, where it is feared that consumers cannot be protected when transactions are cross-border. Merely opening a sector to commercial presence

DEVELOPING COUNTRIES AND NEGOTIATIONS ON TRADE IN SERVICES

may, however, not be the most effective route in all cases. If the domestic market is limited in size, and if scale economies are site-specific, then opening up only to commercial presence may severely restrict the extent of possible competition and product differentiation, thereby limiting the gains from trade. In this case, opening cross-border supply may be necessary in order to realize the potential gains. Inadequacies in the country's stock of human capital may also limit the gains from opening up commercial presence only. For example, liberalization of the financial sector in South Africa created additional demand for skilled labor, pushing up wages and increasing staff turnover in the sector. Because of wage inflation, many of the efficiency gains from liberalization accrued to skilled workers, at the expense of lower prices (Hodge 2001). In this instance, simultaneous liberalization of the movement of persons mode of supply would have allowed entry of foreign professionals, possibly preventing excessive wage inflation.

The move toward full trade liberalization can be made in stages, with the extent of competition and foreign ownership being two of the crucial variables. It is common for developing countries, in liberalizing their public utilities, to begin by offering an equity stake to a foreign partner while restricting competition. The logic behind such an approach is that the foreign partner injects capital and technology to raise the level of efficiency and prepare the enterprise to survive competition. Exclusivity also increases the price of the initial equity sale, and competitive upgrading raises the price of the subsequent equity sale. Although this approach yields revenue rewards for the state and provides gains from reducing the level of technical inefficiency in the firm, it provides no incentives for sharing these gains. It is likely that any efficiency gains will be fed into higher profits, not lower prices, thus denying any downstream benefits to industrial users and consumers. But introducing competition alone without allowing foreign entry may also severely limit the gains from reform. This is especially true of sectors with high rates of technological change, where domestic producers are likely to lag significantly. In these sectors, the potential efficiency gains are considerable. Foreign entrants often introduce new products that not only expand the market, offsetting any potential employment and market share losses, but also offer the most benefits to downstream final goods producers.

It is also common to introduce competition while the state still has an equity stake in the incumbent producer (see Box 24.5). This can be problematic; the independence of the regulatory process is brought into question when one of the competitors has the power to dictate the rules. This situation may discourage investment and effective competition.

The final component of a liberalization strategy is to place demands on trading partners for market opening. In previous rounds of negotiations in the GATS, developing countries have opened up without making many demands on other countries. The obvious place to begin such an exercise is with an investigation of the comparative advantages of the country in services. Because of the high incidence of trade barriers in the past, a country needs to examine both current and potential comparative advantages. For instance, many developing countries have huge potential in health tourism, but the portability of health insurance in other countries limits the ability of foreign consumers to take advantage of these services (UNCTAD and WHO 1998).

Countries should also consider their role in both the regional and international trading systems. For many services, the extent of feasible cross-border trade is limited to a region because of the need to be close to the consumer. This is true for electricity because the farther power is transmitted, the more is lost. It is also the case with most business and financial services, where local knowledge and short travel times are important. In this case a country may offer some comparative advantage in the region despite suffering from a comparative disadvantage internationally. Opening trade in these services may attract international interest through commercial presence and may strengthen the domestic industry so that it can exploit regional cross-border trade. Thus, both Mauritius and Botswana have liberalized their financial services market in the hope of becoming regional financial hubs. This type of strategy would require placing demands on regional neighbors to open up their economies to such trade.

Managing the Liberalization Process

As has been noted, liberalization will create losers even if there are overall gains to society. For this reason, it is important to manage the reform process so as to avoid having interest groups derail the process. Some of these interest groups may well

BOX 24.5 ACHIEVING EFFECTIVE COMPETITION IN TELECOMMUNICATIONS: THE ASIAN EXPERIENCE

A number of country case studies have concluded that larger welfare gains arise from the introduction of effective competition than from a mere change in ownership (see, for example, Wellenius 1997). But how can effective competition be achieved? Experience has shown that even though there is no necessary link between the pattern of ownership and the degree of competition, the presence of a publicly owned incumbent operator can inhibit the emergence of competitive forces. Governments often shield public incumbents by limiting competition to small market segments or geographic areas. Another critical ingredient in effective competition is procompetitive regulation. New entrants often find it difficult to compete if interconnection prices favor incumbents or if telephone numbers are not portable.

The experience with telecommunications reform in India bears testimony to these forces. India initiated reforms in the mid-1990s and decided to open its market for local services to competition while retaining the public monopoly on long-distance and international services. The licensing of competitive operators by the sector ministry, which is also the main incumbent operator in India, was poorly managed. Moreover, conflicts between the ministry and the newly created regulatory agency concerning interconnection and licensing terms have delayed network expansion and have adversely affected the confidence of private investors. By contrast, China maintained its state monopoly, but an ambitious public investment program led to a more than 10-fold expansion of the fixed network in the 1990s, from 8 million mainlines in 1992 to 109 million in 1999.

Taking the experience from the world's two most populous countries at its face value, can we conclude that no policy reform is better than some reform, especially in countries where institutions are weak? Not necessarily. One has to keep in mind that in the 1990s China, which already had a higher GDP per capita than India, experienced dramatic economic growth that in turn fueled investment in telecommunications.

Moreover, network growth has also picked up recently in India, after the government succeeded in resolving some of the institutional constraints facing the sector. Nonetheless, this experience suggests that countries are more likely to achieve effective competition if state ownership is divested and procompetitive regulatory mechanisms are introduced.

These insights are borne out by a recent study on telecommunications performance in 12 developing Asian economies over the period 1985–99. The Asian region has seen markedly different approaches to sector reform and varying degrees of progress in achieving reform targets. Some countries, such as India, the Republic of Korea, and, recently, China, have introduced competition in selected fixed-line market segments while the incumbent operator was under full public ownership. Others, including Indonesia, Malaysia, and Pakistan, privatized their state-owned monopolies first and deferred the introduction of competition to a future date—sometimes through explicit exclusivity periods granted to private investors. Some, such as Sri Lanka, introduced competition and privatized more or less at the same time, while others (for example, Thailand) have made limited, if any, progress toward private, more competitive market structures.

Countries also differed in their choice of the fixed-market segment that was first opened to competition. The region was among the first in the world to open up local markets to competition. Hong Kong (China), India, and Singapore liberalized this market segment first. Korea, Malaysia, and the Philippines began with competition in international services, while China started liberalization by introducing a second domestic long-distance carrier.

The approach to regulation has also differed across countries. It is striking that in a large number of major economies, including China, Indonesia, Japan, Korea, Malaysia, Taiwan (China), and Thailand, regulatory functions are still exercised by the sector ministry or other government bodies. In several of the economies that do have a separate regulator—Hong Kong

(continued)

DEVELOPING COUNTRIES AND NEGOTIATIONS ON TRADE IN SERVICES

BOX 24.5 (CONTINUED)

(China), Pakistan, and the Philippines—the responsibility for establishing interconnection rates lies with the dominant operator, although the regulator is responsible for arbitration of disputes.

Controlling for several economic factors, the study's econometric investigation found that, by themselves, competition for local services, regulation, and privatization of the incumbent operator did not exert any significant influence on main-

line penetration but that the interaction of the three had a significant positive impact on telephone availability. Arguably, the three policy variables used capture only imperfectly a multidimensional reform process. The results do, however, indicate that successful liberalization depends on a combination of privatization, competition, and effective regulation.

Source: Fink, Mattoo, and Rathindran (2001).

be within the government—for example, a supervisory government department having strong links with incumbents that may well lose from the process. To maintain the momentum of reform, it is important to make common cause with the winners from reform in order to counter political pressures from the losers. This is invariably difficult, since the losers are concentrated and organized firms, while the winners are generally dispersed and unorganized downstream users. To create a balance internally, the government should broaden the decisionmaking process to include the trade and industry department, which represents industrial users, and any other line departments whose users are affected—for instance, the tourism and agriculture departments. Outside the government, industry associations and consumer groups can provide vocal support for reform. Choosing sectors that offer rapid delivery of benefits from liberalization is a means of quickly building widespread support. Finally, the GATS may be used to lock the government into liberalization and prevent future backtracking under political pressure.

Notes

1 Such regulatory measures include a nondiscriminatory universal service tax and direct subsidy to the consumer; equal universal service obligations for new entrants; and competitive bidding for fulfilling universal service orders subsidized by the state.

2 The estimate included only OECD and Asian countries.

3 Water and electricity exports to South Africa form the basis of most of Lesotho's exports (Mochebelele 1998).

4 King and Levine (1993) find that development of the financial sector precedes faster economic growth.

5 Liberalization of financial services in South Africa led to a growing demand for higher-skilled workers, increasing employment and raising the wage premium (Hodge 2001).

6 The reason for the influence of regulation and competition on gains from trade is that many of the gains are concentrated in the category of procompetitive effects.

7 The Reference Paper of the WTO Agreement on Basic Telecommunications is the first to provide regulatory guidelines to signatories of the agreement

8 Structural reforms in bank regulation mainly include ensuring that social policy is not implemented through the banking system by such means as political lending or repression of interest rates on government debt.

References

Alexander, Ian, and Antonio Estache. 1999. "The Role of Regulatory Reform and Growth: Lessons from Latin America." Prepared for TIPS Annual Forum. Johannesburg, September 19–22. Processed.

Atinc, Tamar Manuelyan. 1997. "Sharing Rising Incomes: Disparities in China." World Bank, Washington, D.C.

Barajas, Adolfo, Roberto Steiner, and Natalia Salazar. 1999. "Foreign Investment in Colombia's Financial Sector." IMF Working Paper WP/99/150. Washington, D.C.

Claessens, Stijn, and Thomas Glaessner. 1999. "Internationalization of Financial Services in Asia." Paper presented at the conference "Investment Liberalization and Financial Reform in the Asia-Pacific Region," Sydney, Australia, August.

Denizer, Cevdet. 1999. "Foreign Entry in Turkey's Banking Sector, 1980–1997." Prepared for World Trade Organization–World Bank Conference on Liberalization and Internationalization of Financial Services, Geneva, May.

Graham, Edward, and E. Wada. Forthcoming. "Foreign Direct Investment in China: Effects on Growth and Economic Performance." In Peter Drusdale, ed., *Achieving High Growth: Experience of Transitional Economies in East Asia*. Oxford, U.K.: Oxford University Press.

Grossman, Gene M., and Elhanan Helpman. 1991. *Innovation and Growth in the World Economy*. Cambridge, Mass.: MIT Press.

Hodge, J. 2000. "Liberalising Communications Services in South Africa." *Development Southern Africa* 17 (3, September): 373–87.

Hodge, J., and H. Nordas. 1999. "Trade in Services: The Impact on Developing Countries." Report to Norwegian Foreign Ministry. Processed.

Hoekman, Bernard, and Aaditya Mattoo. 2000. "Services, Economic Development and the Next Round of Negotiations on Services." *Journal of International Development* 12 (2, March): 283–96.

Honglin Zang, K., and J. Markusen. 1999. "Vertical Multinationals and Host-Country Characteristics." *Journal of Development Economics* 59: 233–52.

Karsenty, Guy. 2000. "Just How Big Are the Stakes? An Assessment of Trade in Services by Mode of Supply." In Pierre Sauvé and Robert M. Stern, eds., GATS 2000: *New Directions in Services Trade Liberalization*. Washington, D.C.:Brookings Institution Press and Harvard University.

Limão, Nuno, and Anthony J. Venables. 1999. "Infrastructure, Geographical Disadvantage and Transport Costs." Policy Research Working Paper Series 2257. World Bank, Trade, Development Research Group, Washington, D.C.

Markusen, James R. 1989. "Trade in Producer Services and in Other Specialized Intermediate Inputs." *American Economic Review* 79 (1): 85–95.

Naughton, Barry. 2001. "Problems of Lagging Regions in China." Background paper submitted to the World Bank Resident Mission, Beijing.

Pinheiro A. 2000. "The Brazilian Privatisation Experience: What's Next?" Prepared for the Global Development Network Conference, Tokyo, December 10–13.

Rodriguez-Clare, A. 1996. "The Division of Labour and Economic Development." *Journal of Development Economics* 49: 3–32.

Rose-Ackerman, Susan. 1999. *Corruption and Government*. Cambridge, U.K.: Cambridge University Press.

Trujillo, Lourdes, and Antonio Estache. 2001. "Surfing a Wave of Fine Tuning Reforms in Argentina's Ports." World Bank, Washington, D.C. Processed.

Trujillo, Lourdes, and Gustavo Nombela. 1999. "Privatization and Regulation of the Seaport Industry." Policy Research Working Paper Series 2181. World Bank, Washington, D.C.

UNCTAD. 1995c. *World Investment Report 1995: Transnational Corporations and Competitiveness*. UN sales no. E.95.II.A.9. New York and Geneva.

———. 2000b. *Positive Agenda and Future Trade Negotiations*. New York.

———. 2000c. *World Investment Report 2000*. New York and Geneva.

Wellenius, Bjorn. 1997. "Telecommunications Reform: How to Succeed." Public Policy for the Private Sector Note 130. World Bank Group, Finance, Private Sector, and Infrastructure Network, Washington, D.C.

World Bank. 1996a. "Container Transport Services and Trade: Framework for an Efficient Container Transport System." Report 15303-CHA. Washington, D.C.

———. 2000a. *Can Africa Claim the 20th Century?* Washington, D.C.

———. 2001a. *Finance for Growth: Policy Choices in a Volatile World*. World Bank Policy Research Report. New York: Oxford University Press.

WTO. 2000a. "Communication from Mauritius on Behalf of the African Group." Doc. Ref. S/CSS/W/7. Geneva.

[25]

ELSEVIER

Journal of Banking & Finance 25 (2001) 891–911

Journal of
BANKING &
FINANCE

www.elsevier.com/locate/econbase

How does foreign entry affect domestic banking markets? [☆]

Stijn Claessens [a,*], Aslı Demirgüç-Kunt [b], Harry Huizinga [c]

[a] *Financial Sector Strategy and Policy, The World Bank, 1818 H Street N.W., Washington, DC 20433, USA*
[b] *Development Research Group, The World Bank, Washington, DC, USA*
[c] *CentER and Department of Economics, Tilburg University, Tilburg, Netherlands*

Received 25 March 1999; accepted 26 February 2000

Abstract

Using 7900 bank observations from 80 countries for the 1988–1995 period, this paper examines the extent and effect of foreign presence in domestic banking markets. We investigate how net interest margins, overhead, taxes paid, and profitability differ between foreign and domestic banks. We find that foreign banks have higher profits than domestic banks in developing countries, but the opposite is the case for developed countries. Estimation results suggest that an increased presence of foreign banks is associated with a reduction in profitability and margins for domestic banks. © 2001 Elsevier Science B.V. All rights reserved.

JEL classification: E44; G21

Keywords: Foreign entry; Domestic banking

[☆] The findings, interpretations, and conclusions expressed in this paper are entirely those of the authors. They do not necessarily represent the views of the World Bank, its Executive Directors, or the countries they represent.
[*] Corresponding author. Tel.: +1-202-473-7212; fax: +1-202-522-2031.
E-mail address: cclaessens@worldbank.org (S. Claessens).

892 *S. Claessens et al. / Journal of Banking & Finance 25 (2001) 891–911*

1. Introduction

In recent decades, international trade in goods and financial services has become increasingly important. To facilitate such trade, many banking institutions have also become international.[1] Banks have expanded internationally by establishing foreign subsidiaries and branches or by taking over established foreign banks. The internationalization of the banking sector has been spurred by the liberalization of financial markets worldwide. Developed and developing countries alike now increasingly allow banks to be foreign-owned and allow foreign entry on a national treatment basis.

Financial liberalization of this kind proceeds, among other reasons, on the premise that the gains from foreign entry to the domestic banking system outweigh any losses. Several authors have addressed the potential benefits of foreign bank entry for the domestic economy in terms of better resource allocation and higher efficiency (see Levine, 1996; Walter and Gray, 1983; Goldberg and Saunders, 1981; Gelb and Sagari, 1990). Levine (1996) specifically mentions that foreign banks may (i) improve the quality and availability of financial services in the domestic financial market by increasing bank competition, and enabling the greater application of more modern banking skills and technology, (ii) serve to stimulate the development of the underlying bank supervisory and legal framework, and (iii) enhance a country's access to international capital.

There may also be costs to opening financial markets to foreign competition. Stiglitz (1993), for instance, discusses the potential costs to domestic banks, local entrepreneurs, and the government resulting from foreign bank entry. Domestic banks may incur costs since they have to compete with large international banks with better reputation; local entrepreneurs may receive less access to financial services since foreign banks generally concentrate on multinational firms; and governments may find their control of the economy diminished since foreign banks tend to be less sensitive to their wishes.

As yet, little evidence exists of the effects of an internationalization of the banking sector other than several case studies of foreign bank entry. McFadden (1994) reviews foreign bank entry in Australia, and finds that this has led to improved domestic bank operations. Bhattacharaya (1993) reports on specific cases in Pakistan, Turkey, and Korea, where foreign banks facilitated access to foreign capital for domestic projects. Pigott (1986) describes the policies that have made increased foreign bank activity possible in nine Pacific Basin countries, and provides some aggregate statistics on the size and scope of

---

[1] See Aliber (1984) for an early survey of the literature on the internationalization of banking.

foreign banking activities in these markets. [2] Using aggregate accounting data, Terrell (1986, Table 20-2) compares the banking markets of 14 developed countries (8 of which allow foreign bank entry) for 1976 and 1977. Interestingly, in this sample, countries that allowed foreign bank entry on average experience lower gross interest margins, lower pre-tax profits, and lower operating costs (all scaled by the volume of business). Terrell (1986), however, does not control for influences on domestic banking other than whether or not foreign banks are permitted to enter.

This paper aims to provide a systematic study of how foreign bank presence has affected domestic banking markets in 80 countries. To do this, we use bank-level accounting data and macroeconomic data for the 1988–1995 period. We first examine the scale of foreign bank operations in each of the 80 countries. We define a bank to be foreign if at least 50% of its shares is foreign-owned, i.e., when there is foreign control of a bank's operations. As measures of foreign bank presence, we consider the importance of foreign banks both in terms of numbers and in terms of assets.

We then extend the work on the accounting decomposition of interest margins by Hanson and Rocha (1986) and, more recently, Demirgüç-Kunt and Huizinga (1999). Specifically, we use the data to investigate how foreign banks differ from domestic banks in terms of interest margins, taxes paid, overhead expenses, loan loss provisioning, and profitability. We find that, while foreign banks have lower interest margins, overhead expenses, and profitability than domestic banks in developed countries (consistent with Terrell's (1986) findings), the opposite is true in developing countries. This suggests that the reasons for foreign entry, as well as the competitive and regulatory conditions found abroad, differ significantly between developed and developing countries.

Next, we estimate empirically how increased foreign bank presence, measured as the change in the ratio of the number of foreign banks to the total number of banks, affects the operation of domestic banks. We find that increased presence of foreign banks is associated with reductions in profitability, lower non-interest income, and overall expenses of domestic banks.

The remainder of this paper is organized as follows. Section 2 presents data on the relevance of foreign banks in 80 national banking markets. Section 3 presents the empirical results, while Section 4 concludes.

---

[2] Cho and Khatkhate (1989) provide in-depth case studies of financial liberalization in five Asian countries, however with no particular emphasis on foreign bank entry. Liberalization, though, is shown to lead to faster growth of the financial system and to increased competitiveness of the banking system, even if there is no conclusive evidence that financial liberalization leads to lower intermediation margins. In their comparative study, Frankel and Montgomery (1991) also bypass the issue of internationalization.

894 *S. Claessens et al. / Journal of Banking & Finance 25 (2001) 891–911*

2. The data

We use information from the financial statements of domestic and foreign commercial banks. The data come from the BankScope data base provided by IBCA (for a complete list of data sources and variable definitions, see Appendix A). Coverage by IBCA is comprehensive, with banks included roughly accounting for 90% of the assets of banks in each country. The data are compiled by IBCA mostly from the balance sheet, income statement and applicable notes found in audited annual reports. Each country has its own data template which allows for differences in reporting and accounting conventions. These are converted to a "global format" which is a globally standardized template derived from the country-specific templates. The global format contains 36 standard ratios which can be compared across banks and between countries. To our knowledge, this is the most comprehensive data base that allows cross-country comparisons. While the underlying data reflects international accounting standards as much as possible, and IBCA makes an effort to standardize individual bank data while converting to the global format, some differences in accounting conventions regarding the valuation of assets, loan loss provisioning, hidden reserves, etc., no doubt remain. [3] We try to capture some of these remaining differences by using country-dummies in our regressions.

We start with the entire universe of commercial banks, with the exception that for France, Germany and the US only several hundred commercial banks listed as 'large' are included. To ensure reasonable coverage for individual countries, we include only countries where there are data for at least three banks – domestic and/or foreign – in a country for a given year. This yields a data set covering 80 countries during the years 1988–1995, with about 7900 individual commercial bank observations. This data set includes all OECD countries, as well as many developing countries and economies in transition.

While comprehensive, this data set does not allow us to distinguish between wholesale versus retail banking markets. It can be argued that since foreign bank entry initially commonly takes place in the wholesale banking market, it is more appropriate to study the impact of entry in this market instead of the national geographic market. However, unless various customer markets are completely segmented, foreign bank presence at the wholesale level can be expected to have an impact at the retail level as well. Specifically, as foreign banks expand their operations at the wholesale level, the threat of foreign banks encroaching on retail markets may be also induce greater efficiency and lower costs of domestic banks at the retail level.

---

[3] See Vittas (1991) for an account of the pitfalls in interpreting international bank operating ratios.

S. Claessens et al. / Journal of Banking & Finance 25 (2001) 891–911   895

Another, related distinction concerns de novo foreign entry versus entry through the foreign acquisition of a (sizable) domestic bank. The two types of foreign entry may have different implications for domestic banks. Data available, however, do not allow us to make this distinction either.

We first provide information on the aggregate income statement items for all domestic and foreign banks in each of the 80 countries individually. We then present averages for country groups, by income and geographical location to better illustrate the differences between domestic and foreign banks in developing and developed countries. From the bank's income statement, the following accounting identity follows:

$$\text{net margin/ta} + \text{non-interest income/ta}$$
$$= \text{before tax profits/ta} + \text{overhead/ta} + \text{loan loss provisioning/ta}. \quad (1)$$

The first two ratios are the accounting values of a bank's net interest income over its total assets, or net margin/ta, and its net non-interest income over total assets, non-interest income/ta. The non-interest income/ta captures the fact that many banks also engage in non-lending activities, such as investment banking and brokerage services, which generate income. To measure bank profitability in the accounting identity, we use the bank's before-tax profits over total assets, or before tax profits/ta. This latter variable can subsequently be broken down into the after tax profits/ta and tax/ta variables. The overhead/ta variable represents the bank's entire overhead over total assets, while loan loss provisioning/ta simply measures actual provisioning for bad debts over total assets.

Similar to other studies on the effects of changes in market structures on firm performance, we focus on accounting measures of income and profitability rather than rates of return on stocks. This is for several reasons. For one (risk-adjusted), financial returns on bank stocks are equalized by investors in the absence of prohibitive international investment barriers or other transaction costs. Comparing these returns across different banking systems would thus not allow us to investigate the effects of different degrees of competition and the effects of foreign bank entry. For this reason, Gorton and Rosen (1995) and Schranz (1993) focus on accounting measures of profitability when examining managerial entrenchment and bank takeovers. Also, financial returns data are not available for a similarly large set of banks and countries.

First, we document the extent of foreign bank presence in national banking environments. Table 1 presents two measures of foreign bank presence: the share of the number of banks that are foreign-owned, and the share of foreign bank assets in total bank assets. The number presence measure is an appropriate measure, if the number of domestic and foreign banks determines competitive conditions. This might be the case, if domestic banking firms adjust the pricing of their lending and other activities as soon as foreign entry

Table 1
Share of foreign banks in domestic banking systems: 1988–1995[a]

Country	No. of foreign banks in total	Foreign bank assets in total	Total number of banks	Country	No. of foreign banks in total	Foreign bank assets in total	Total number of banks
Argentina	0.37	0.10	9	Lithuania	0.10	0.09	7
Australia	0.37	0.05	26	Luxembourg	0.89	0.80	107
Austria	0.29	0.31	10	Malaysia	0.09	0.06	47
Bahrain	0.81	0.97	7	Malta	0.00	0.00	7
Belgium	0.29	0.05	47	Mexico	0.04	0.02	19
Bolivia	0.29	0.36	10	Morocco	0.33	0.21	8
Botswana	0.75	0.94	4	Nepal	1.00	1.00	3
Brazil	0.37	0.30	41	Netherlands	0.48	0.10	20
Canada	0.64	0.07	69	New Zealand	0.85	0.91	8
Chile	0.32	0.25	20	Nicaragua	0.17	0.20	12
China	0.13	0.00	5	Nigeria	0.30	0.51	9
Colombia	0.23	0.05	28	Norway	0.12	0.01	19
Costa Rica	0.24	0.05	22	Oman	0.00	0.00	6
Cyprus	0.25	0.11	7	Pakistan	0.30	0.12	15
Czech Rep.	0.54	0.51	15	Panama	0.35	0.39	8
Denmark	0.02	0.00	56	P. New Guinea	0.50	0.34	5
Dom. Rep.	0.08	0.03	12	Paraguay	0.43	0.39	20
Ecuador	0.46	0.52	5	Peru	0.43	0.35	22
Egypt	0.10	0.01	9	Philippines	0.46	0.57	17
El Salvador	0.20	0.28	4	Poland	0.30	0.14	28
Estonia	0.43	0.35	7	Portugal	0.18	0.04	34
Finland	0.00	0.00	11	Qatar	0.00	0.00	3
France	0.24	0.08	95	Romania	0.17	0.01	7
Germany	0.37	0.25	80	Russia	0.08	0.06	14
Greece	0.58	0.77	16	S. Africa	0.22	0.02	14
Guatemala	0.00	0.00	24	Saudi Arabia	0.34	0.43	4
Haiti	0.00	0.00	3	Singapore	0.29	0.62	19
Honduras	0.29	0.23	3	Spain	0.36	0.31	38
Hong Kong	0.60	0.69	28	Sri Lanka	0.14	0.08	7
Hungary	0.61	0.61	19	Swaziland	1.00	1.00	3
India	0.00	0.00	5	Sweden	0.07	0.00	18
Indonesia	0.35	0.16	18	Taiwan	0.14	0.09	24
Ireland	0.42	0.11	12	Thailand	0.08	0.02	12
Israel	0.09	0.02	22	Tunisia	0.39	0.35	7
Italy	0.09	0.01	64	Turkey	0.13	0.01	29
Jamaica	0.50	0.48	10	UK	0.24	0.19	70
Japan	0.09	0.21	73	US	0.04	0.03	370
Jordan	0.43	0.95	7	Venezuela	0.07	0.02	17
Korea	0.23	0.23	40	Yemen	0.00	0.00	3
Lebanon	0.49	0.57	5	Zambia	0.71	0.46	3
Average for 80 countries					0.31	0.26	25

[a] A foreign bank is defined to have at least 50% foreign ownership. Figures reported are ratios of number of foreign banks to total number of banks and foreign bank assets to total bank assets in each country, respectively, averaged over the 1988–1995 period. Total number of banks is for 1995.

S. Claessens et al. / Journal of Banking & Finance 25 (2001) 891–911   897

occurs to prevent the foreign entrants from capturing significant market share. Alternatively, the share presence measure can be appropriate, if foreign banks start to have an impact on the pricing and profitability of domestic banks only after gaining market share. Foreign banks may, for example, have to be sizable for there to be any significant pressure on the spreads of domestic banks. Note that both presence measures capture actual foreign banking presence, and thus do not capture the disciplining effects on domestic banks of potential foreign bank entry. The threat of foreign bank entry is difficult to measure, however, in part as it very difficult to objectively measure the barriers to entry in a banking market, and in any case the absence of barriers may be closely related to actual entry.

From Table 1, we see that for about three-fifths of the countries the number foreign presence measure exceeds the asset presence measure (this is the case for France, Germany, Italy, the UK and the US, but not Japan). This is also the case for a simple average of all the countries. This reflects that foreign banks tend to be smaller than domestic banks. Either presence measure is zero for Finland, Guatemala, Haiti, India, Malta, Oman, and Yemen, reflecting in part regulatory barriers to foreign bank entry. At the other extreme, Nepal and Swaziland only have foreign-owned banks in our sample. Other countries with a large foreign bank presence (with both foreign presence measures exceeding 75%) are Bahrain, Botswana, Luxembourg, and New Zealand. A colonial past or the presence of a large neighboring country might explain some of these high ratios. Among the developed countries, Denmark, Finland, Italy, Sweden and the US have relatively insulated banking markets, with foreign presence measures below 10%.[4] The last column for each country reports the total number of banks in the sample for 1995.

Next, we consider whether there is a systematic link between foreign bank presence and national income. In Table 2, we present average foreign presence shares by national income group.[5] Interestingly, the foreign asset share in the low-income countries in our sample is comparable to that of high-income countries, with somewhat higher presence shares for middle-income countries. This finding suggests that the differences in national foreign presence shares in Table 1 are not necessarily due to differences in levels of national income. Table 2 also provides a breakdown of the average foreign presence share by geographical regions which exhibits quite a bit of variation.[6] While these

---

[4] Previous studies, such as DeYoung and Nolle (1996) report foreign bank presence ratios of almost 50% for the US. However these studies define a bank as foreign if has more than 10% foreign ownership. In addition, these studies include off-shore operations of foreign banks. Data reported in Federal Reserve Bulletins confirm the figures we obtain above.

[5] For country groupings by income, see the World Development Report (1996).

Table 2
Share of foreign banks in domestic banking systems: Aggregates by income group and regions[a]

	No. of foreign banks in total		Foreign bank assets in total		
	Mean	Std. dev.	Mean	Std. dev.	N
Income groups					
Low income	0.26	0.31	0.21	0.30	12
Lower middle income	0.33	0.22	0.31	0.29	28
Upper middle income	0.32	0.25	0.31	0.31	14
High income	0.28	0.24	0.19	0.26	26
Regions					
Africa	0.59	0.33	0.58	0.40	5
Asia	0.31	0.27	0.28	0.31	14
Latin America	0.25	0.16	0.21	0.17	19
Middle East and North Africa	0.27	0.26	0.31	0.37	11
Transitional economies	0.31	0.21	0.25	0.23	7
Industrial economies	0.29	0.25	0.18	0.26	24

[a] A foreign bank is defined to have at least 50% foreign ownership. Figures reported are number of foreign banks to total number of banks and foreign bank assets to total bank assets in each income group or region averaged over the 1988–1995 period. Income and region classifications follow World Bank definitions as published in the World Development Report (1996).

aggregates are interesting, the high dispersion within groups suggests that grouping by income or region may not be very informative.

Next, Table 3 presents the net interest margins and other accounting variables for domestic and foreign banks separately in each of the 80 countries in the 1988–1995 period. An ownership indicator of "D" refers to the group of domestic banks, while an indicator of "F" refers to the foreign banks. As already evident from Table 1, not all countries have both domestic and foreign banks.

In some developing countries (such as Argentina, Costa Rica, and Venezuela), foreign banks realize net interest incomes of around 10% of assets or higher. Also in many developing countries (for example Egypt, Indonesia, Argentina and Venezuela) foreign banks in fact report significantly higher net interest margins than domestic banks. Instead, in most developed countries (for instance, in France, Austria, Australia, Japan, the UK and the US), foreign banks report significantly lower net interest margins than domestic banks.

These differences may reflect the differing market conditions foreign banks find abroad. In developing countries, foreign banks may be able to realize high interest margins because they are exempt from credit allocation regulations and

---

[6] Countries in transition are China, the Czech Republic, Estonia, Hungary, Lithuania, Poland, Romania, Russia, and Slovenia. Neither this group of countries nor the industrial economies are in regions in the strict sense.

S. Claessens et al. / Journal of Banking & Finance 25 (2001) 891–911   899

Table 3
Bank spreads and profitability: Domestic vs. foreign banks 1988–1995[a]

Country	Own- ership	Net margin/ta	Non-int. income/ta	Over- head/ta	Tax/ ta	Loan loss prov./ta	Net profit/ta
Argentina	D	5.8	5.2	7.5	0.4	1.5	1.7
	F	9.9	8.1	12.6	0.4	2.4	2.5
Australia	D	3.4	1.2	3.1	0.4	0.5	0.8
	F	1.0	1.9	1.8	0.0	0.9	0.1
Austria	D	1.9	0.5	1.5	0.1	0.6	0.4
	F	1.4	0.8	1.7	0.0	0.3	0.3
Bahrain	D	2.5	0.8	1.5	0.0	0.9	0.1
	F	1.9	0.8	1.4	0.0	1.0	0.4
Belgium	D	2.2	1.0	2.4	0.2	0.3	0.5
	F	2.1	0.6	2.5	0.1	0.5	0.2
Bolivia	D	1.7	2.1	5.0	0.6	0.5	−2.2
	F	3.8	1.7	3.5	0.5	0.9	0.7
Botswana	F	5.7	2.3	4.1	0.9	0.1	2.1
Brazil	D	9.8	4.9	11.9	1.1	1.4	0.9
	F	6.8	4.1	7.2	1.1	1.1	1.7
Canada	D	2.5	1.2	2.2	0.3	0.6	0.3
	F	1.9	0.7	2.7	0.2	1.1	0.0
Chile	D	4.5	−0.2	3.1	0.1	0.7	0.5
	F	3.9	−0.2	2.8	0.0	0.5	0.4
Colombia	D	5.8	6.0	8.2	0.6	1.0	2.2
	F	6.6	5.1	8.5	0.8	0.7	2.2
Costa Rica	D	9.9	1.6	6.6	0.3	5.2	1.2
	F	17.3	10.5	10.7	1.8	4.5	11.6
Cyprus	D	3.3	3.1	3.1	0.6	0.3	1.1
Czech Rep.	D	2.9	1.4	1.8	0.4	2.2	−0.1
	F	2.9	1.7	2.5	0.6	1.3	0.5
Denmark	D	4.8	1.0	3.7	0.2	1.7	0.3
	F	6.5	1.5	5.0	0.6	1.1	1.2
Dominic. Rep.	D	6.5	3.0	6.1	0.6	0.5	2.3
	F	8.2	3.1	5.2	1.1	0.8	2.6
Ecuador	D	8.1	2.7	8.3	0.3	1.0	1.8
	F	6.3	5.5	8.3	0.3	0.8	2.8
Egypt	D	1.0	2.0	1.4	0.2	1.0	0.9
	F	2.0	2.1	1.7	0.5	1.0	1.0
El Salvador	D	3.1	1.6	2.8	0.0	0.4	1.5
	F	3.8	1.6	2.9	0.2	0.7	1.7
Finland	D	2.0	1.2	2.4	0.2	2.2	−1.4
France	D	2.5	1.4	2.7	0.2	1.1	0.1
	F	1.7	1.6	2.5	0.1	0.8	0.1
Germany	D	2.2	1.2	2.1	0.3	0.6	0.3
	F	1.9	1.1	2.0	0.3	0.7	0.3
Greece	D	3.7	2.0	3.9	0.3	0.4	0.9
	F	2.7	2.4	3.0	0.4	0.6	1.0
Haiti	D	2.7	2.8	3.6	0.4	0.4	1.0
Hong Kong	D	2.7	1.3	1.6	0.3	0.1	2.0
	F	2.5	1.3	1.6	0.3	0.2	1.9

Table 3 (Continued)

Country	Own-ership	Net margin/ta	Non-int. income/ta	Over-head/ta	Tax/ta	Loan loss prov./ta	Net profit/ta
Hungary	D	**5.4**	8.6	**9.2**	0.7	2.0	1.5
	F	**4.4**	4.0	**3.5**	0.6	2.0	2.5
India	D	1.9	1.6	1.0	0.2	0.3	1.1
Indonesia	D	**3.3**	1.1	**2.7**	0.4	0.7	0.9
	F	**4.0**	1.4	**3.4**	0.4	0.7	1.0
Ireland	D	3.3	0.9	2.5	0.3	0.5	0.9
Israel	D	3.3	**1.9**	**3.7**	0.6	0.7	0.3
	F	2.9	**1.5**	**3.3**	0.7	0.6	0.6
Italy	D	3.4	**1.3**	3.3	0.5	0.5	**0.4**
	F	3.5	**1.8**	3.6	0.6	0.5	**0.6**
Jamaica	F	8.8	2.8	6.6	1.4	0.6	3.0
Japan	D	**1.6**	0.2	**1.3**	0.2	0.1	0.2
	F	**1.4**	0.3	**1.1**	0.2	0.2	0.2
Jordan	D	2.3	1.6	**2.7**	0.3	**0.7**	0.6
	F	1.9	1.2	**1.9**	0.2	**0.3**	0.8
Korea	D	2.1	1.5	2.4	**0.3**	0.5	**0.6**
	F	1.9	1.4	2.3	**0.2**	0.5	**0.4**
Lebanon	D	**3.4**	0.9	2.2	0.3	0.7	1.1
	F	**2.6**	1.1	2.0	0.2	0.5	0.9
Lithuania	D	10.0	4.5	7.6	1.6	5.6	0.4
	F	6.4	7.2	7.2	1.7	8.0	−3.3
Luxembourg	D	0.9	1.2	1.0	0.2	**0.5**	0.3
	F	0.8	0.9	1.0	0.2	**0.3**	0.4
Malaysia	D	2.7	0.8	**1.9**	**0.4**	0.4	**0.8**
	F	2.4	0.9	**1.3**	**0.6**	0.3	**1.1**
Malta	D	2.4	1.1	2.1	0.4	0.1	0.9
Mexico	D	4.6	**2.1**	4.5	0.3	1.2	1.0
	F	3.1	**1.3**	4.2	0.1	1.1	−0.9
Morocco	D	3.5	1.3	3.5	0.6	0.0	0.9
	F	3.3	1.1	3.7	0.3	0.0	0.4
Nepal	D	3.6	2.1	2.4	1.0	0.5	1.8
Netherlands	D	**1.8**	**1.5**	**2.3**	**0.2**	0.3	**0.5**
	F	**1.0**	**0.5**	**0.9**	**0.1**	0.3	**0.2**
Nicaragua	D	4.5	3.0	6.8	0.2	1.0	−0.5
	F	4.8	3.1	6.4	0.3	0.6	0.7
Nigeria	D	5.5	6.1	**8.1**	0.8	2.1	2.0
	F	4.4	4.9	**5.7**	0.5	1.7	1.4
Norway	D	**3.2**	1.1	**2.7**	0.1	**1.2**	**0.3**
	F	**2.5**	2.3	**2.0**	0.4	**0.6**	**1.7**
Oman	D	4.2	1.4	3.3	0.2	0.5	1.5
Panama	D	2.2	**1.5**	**2.1**	0.1	0.4	**1.2**
	F	2.4	**0.6**	**1.2**	0.0	1.0	**0.6**
Papua New	D	**4.5**	3.5	**5.4**	**0.1**	1.8	**0.2**
Guinea	F	**2.7**	5.1	**4.5**	**0.5**	0.6	**1.6**
Paraguay	D	6.4	2.2	**5.7**	0.5	**0.8**	2.0
	F	7.2	2.5	**7.3**	0.4	**1.3**	1.7

(continued overleaf)

S. Claessens et al. / Journal of Banking & Finance 25 (2001) 891–911   901

Table 3 (Continued)

Country	Own-ership	Net margin/ta	Non-int. income/ta	Over-head/ta	Tax/ ta	Loan loss prov./ta	Net profit/ta
Peru	D	6.6	5.8	9.6	0.7	1.8	0.8
	F	6.4	5.6	9.5	0.7	1.6	0.9
Philippines	D	3.8	2.9	**3.9**	0.3	0.3	2.0
	F	4.1	3.1	**4.4**	0.3	0.4	2.1
Poland	D	**4.9**	2.1	**3.3**	1.6	1.5	2.2
	F	**6.6**	3.0	**4.3**	1.8	1.1	2.6
Portugal	D	3.4	**1.0**	2.5	**0.2**	**1.1**	**0.6**
	F	3.4	**1.3**	2.3	**0.6**	**0.4**	**1.4**
Qatar	D	1.9	1.1	1.8	0.0	0.4	1.1
Romania	F	9.1	1.9	2.7	2.2	3.5	5.0
Russia	D	6.6	9.3	7.6	2.2	2.8	3.7
Singapore	F	1.7	0.9	1.2	0.4	0.1	1.1
South Africa	D	**4.4**	**2.4**	3.8	0.4	0.7	1.2
	F	**3.2**	**0.9**	3.1	0.3	1.1	0.4
Spain	D	**4.0**	**1.1**	3.1	**0.5**	0.6	**0.9**
	F	**2.9**	**1.4**	3.2	**0.2**	0.6	**0.3**
Sri Lanka	D	4.1	2.2	2.7	0.7	0.4	2.5
Swaziland	F	5.5	2.7	6.0	0.4	0.8	1.1
Sweden	D	2.9	1.5	**2.4**	0.1	**1.8**	0.2
	F	1.9	0.9	**1.2**	0.0	**0.6**	1.0
Taiwan	D	2.1	1.1	1.6	0.2	0.3	1.0
	F	2.1	0.8	1.5	0.2	0.3	0.9
Tunisia	D	2.3	1.9	2.9	0.2	1.1	0.7
Turkey	D	7.5	4.0	6.3	1.1	0.8	3.8
	F	8.0	3.7	7.1	1.0	0.8	3.8
UK	D	**2.6**	**2.5**	**3.0**	**0.4**	0.7	0.8
	F	**1.8**	**1.4**	**1.8**	**0.3**	1.4	0.0
US	D	**3.9**	**1.8**	**3.6**	**0.5**	0.7	**1.0**
	F	**3.3**	**1.2**	**3.0**	**0.3**	0.7	**0.5**
Venezuela	D	**6.7**	2.7	6.3	0.2	**1.1**	**1.9**
	F	**13.7**	3.9	7.2	0.4	**0.4**	**9.7**
Yemen	D	2.8	−0.5	1.6	0.6	0.3	0.9
Zambia	D	−4.7	9.5	0.4	0.3	2.4	1.7

[a] Ownership denotes if a bank is a foreign bank (F) or domestic (D). A foreign bank is defined to have at least 50% foreign ownership. Net margin/ta is defined as net interest income over total assets. Non-interest income/ta is net non-interest income over total assets. Overhead/ta is overhead divided by total assets. Tax/ta is taxes paid over total assets. Loan loss provisions/ta is loan loss provisions over total assets. Net profit/ta is net profits divided by total assets. Ratios are calculated for each bank in each country and then averaged for domestic and foreign banks separately over the country's sample period. All ratios are in percentages. Data are from BankScope data base of the IBCA. Detailed variable definitions and sources are given in Appendix A. Pairs of entries that are significantly different from each other (at a 5% level or less) are in bold.

Country averages for China, Estonia, Guatemala, Honduras, New Zealand, Pakistan, Saudi Arabia and Thailand are not reported due to incomplete income statements.

other restrictions which are a net burden on margins. Where state banks dominate a large share of the banking system, non-commercial criteria may be frequently used to allocate credit, with resulting downward pressure on margins. Furthermore, pervasive market inefficiencies and outmoded banking practices that exist in developing countries should also allow foreign banks to reap higher net interest margins than domestic banks, outweighing the information disadvantages they possibly may face.

Developed country banking markets tend to be more competitive with more sophisticated participants. The low margins of foreign banks in developed countries may in addition be due to the fact that any technical advantages foreign banks may have in these markets are not significant enough to overcome the informational disadvantages they face relative to domestic banks.

The overhead/ta variable reflects the bank's overhead associated with its deposit and loan operations as well as any other activities. Foreign banks might on one hand have high overhead costs if they have to overcome large informational disadvantages, but on the other they may have low overhead expenses if they engage mostly in wholesale transactions. Many developed countries, such as Australia, Japan, the UK and the US have foreign banks with significantly lower overhead costs (as a percentage of assets) than domestic banks. In many developing countries, however, foreign banks tend to have higher overhead than domestic banks, although the difference is not significant most of the time.

Next, the tax/ta variable reflects primarily the corporate income tax in the host country. Differences in this variable between domestic and foreign banks may reflect different de-jure tax treatment, although most countries do not discriminate in this regard. More likely, any tax burden differences reflect differences in the activity mix between foreign and domestic banks and foreign banks' efforts to shift profits worldwide so as to minimize their global tax bill. Prima facie, foreign banks can be expected to have more opportunities to shift taxable income abroad than domestic banks. In any event, banks have an incentive to shift profits out of (into) high-tax (low-tax) jurisdictions. An interesting case is the US, where foreign banks pay taxes as a share of assets at about two-thirds the taxes paid by domestic banks (tax/ta of 0.3% vs. 0.5%). Also in some other developed countries, such as in Australia, Austria, Belgium, Netherlands, Spain, and the UK, foreign banks pay relatively low taxes. This pattern is not as pervasive in developing countries: counter examples include Malaysia and Egypt. An important determinant of actual tax bill is no doubt tax enforcement, which varies from country to country.

The loan loss provisioning/ta variable measures the new provisioning made during the accounting year for any previously contracted credits. Differences between domestic and foreign banks here may reflect a difference in customer

S. Claessens et al. / Journal of Banking & Finance 25 (2001) 891–911   903

mix (with foreign banks concentrating on large corporations rather than mortgage or consumer loans). Alternatively, different provisioning ratios may reflect differences in foreign and domestic banks' ability to screen bad credit risks and willingness to provision for bad risks. Foreign banks have higher provisioning ratios in some countries including Australia, Canada, Germany, Japan, and the UK but most of these differences are not significant. We see significantly lower provisioning ratios in Austria, Denmark, France and Sweden. Also in some developing countries, foreign banks differ statistically significantly from domestic banks in this regard.

Finally, Table 3 provides information on differences in net profits over assets, or net profits/ta, between domestic and foreign banks. As an accounting residual, this variable is affected by each of the foregoing accounting variables in the table. In addition, the required net profits of foreign banks may be influenced by the tax regime of the bank's parent country. A foreign bank that will benefit from a foreign tax credit, for instance, may accept a relatively low net-of-host-country-tax profitability. At the same time, domestic and foreign banks may accept different net profits to the extent that their cost of capital differs. Foreign banks, specifically, may be able to raise equity capital internationally, and therefore accept a lower net profitability. Although the significance levels vary, the data show that foreign banks have lower net profits in most developed countries, whereas they generally have higher net profits in developing countries. This supports DeYoung and Nolle (1996) who argue that foreign banks in the US have been relatively less profitable because they valued growth above profitability.

Table 4 provides a summary of Table 3 by averaging this data for domestic and foreign banks by different country groupings. Considering the breakdown by income, we see that foreign banks, on an average, obtain the lowest interest margins in high-income countries, and their margins are significantly lower than those of domestic banks in upper middle and high income countries. At the same time, foreign banks achieve higher interest margins than domestic banks in low income and lower middle income countries, although this difference is significant only for the lowest income group. Overhead expenses, taxes and net profitability of foreign banks in low-income countries similarly tend to be relatively high (although these results are not significant). In high income countries, however, these ratios are significantly lower for foreign banks. Note that banks in low-income countries have significantly higher overhead expenses than banks in high-income countries, despite generally lower wages in low-income countries. This probably reflects bank overstaffing and possibly difficulties in evaluating loans in low-income countries. Differences in loan loss provisioning ratios vary across income groups. Foreign bank provisioning ratios are significantly lower than those of domestic banks in high income countries, possibly reflecting the fact that foreign banks generally provide relatively little risky consumer credit. The opposite is true in upper

Table 4

Bank spreads and profitability: Domestic vs. foreign banks, selected aggregates 1988–1995[a]

	Net margin/ta	Non-int. income/ta	Overhead/technical assistance	Tax/ta	Loan loss prov./ta	Net profit/ta
Income groups						
Low income						
Domestic	**2.72**	2.64	3.69	0.38	1.15	1.05
Foreign	**3.71**	3.01	4.39	0.54	1.20	1.21
Lower middle income						
Domestic	5.93	3.30	5.73	0.65	1.30	1.89
Foreign	6.09	3.90	5.84	0.67	1.07	2.44
Upper middle income						
Domestic	**4.23**	2.10	**4.31**	0.41	**0.87**	**0.83**
Foreign	**3.78**	2.35	**3.60**	0.44	**1.11**	**1.12**
High income						
Domestic	**3.22**	**1.44**	**2.97**	**0.37**	**0.72**	**0.65**
Foreign	**1.70**	**1.12**	**1.97**	**0.24**	**0.62**	**0.35**
Regions						
Africa						
Domestic	**4.88**	**3.82**	**5.38**	0.55	1.24	**1.49**
Foreign	**3.78**	**1.94**	**4.36**	0.41	1.44	**0.89**
Asia						
Domestic	**2.68**	1.19	**2.34**	0.33	0.41	**1.02**
Foreign	**2.98**	1.70	**2.74**	0.32	0.40	**1.42**
Latin America						
Domestic	6.20	3.12	6.61	**0.43**	1.34	**1.20**
Foreign	6.93	3.93	7.01	**0.62**	1.29	**2.26**
Middle East and North Africa						
Domestic	2.43	**1.72**	**2.69**	**0.39**	0.83	0.63
Foreign	2.18	**1.05**	**1.93**	**0.21**	0.96	0.58
Transitional economies						
Domestic	**5.23**	4.40	**5.06**	1.13	2.30	1.34
Foreign	**4.48**	3.30	**3.43**	0.89	1.68	1.87
Industrial economies						
Domestic	**3.38**	1.49	**3.10**	**0.39**	**0.73**	**0.73**
Foreign	**1.78**	1.19	**2.07**	**0.25**	**0.64**	**0.36**

[a] Net margin/ta is defined as net interest income over total assets. A foreign bank is defined to have more than 50% foreign ownership. Non-interest income/ta is net non-interest income over total assets. Overhead/ta is overhead divided by total assets. Tax/ta is taxes paid over total assets. Loan loss provisions/ta is loan loss provisions over total assets. Net profit/ta is net profits divided by total assets. Ratios are calculated for each bank in each country and then averaged for domestic and foreign banks separately over the country's sample period. All ratios are in percentages. Data are from Bankscope data base of the IBCA. Detailed variable definitions and sources are given in Appendix A. Pairs of entries that are significantly different from each other (at 5% level or less) are in bold. Includes only countries that have both domestic and foreign banks.

middle income countries, however. The reason may be that foreign banks are at an informational disadvantage in identifying good credit risks, or that they have more conservative provisioning policies.

Turning to the breakdown by geographical region, we see that interest margins are highest in Latin America and in the transitional economies. In both cases, high overhead expenses seem to be the driving factor behind the high interest margins. In Asia and Latin America, foreign banks have higher interest margins than domestic banks, but this difference is significant only for the first group. These are the two geographic regions, where foreign banks also have higher non-interest income ratios. In Africa, Middle East and industrial economies domestic banks have significantly higher non-interest income. Turning to taxes paid, the taxation of banking appears to be very high in transition economies. Foreign banks pay higher taxes than domestic banks only in Latin America. Provisioning levels are not significantly different except in industrialized economies where foreign banks provision less. Finally, only in Asia and in Latin America do foreign banks achieve significantly higher net profitability than domestic banks.

3. Empirical estimation

In their previous work, Demirgüç-Kunt and Huizinga (1999) investigate how a variety of bank variables, including ownership, affect banks' net interest income and profitability. [7] Foreign ownership was found to be associated with higher net interest margins and profits in developing countries, while this result was reversed in developed countries. That paper did not investigate, however, how foreign bank entry, i.e., a change in foreign bank presence, might affect the operation of domestic banks. In this paper, we extend the previous work by examining in detail if foreign bank entry is correlated with changes in any of the five variables in the accounting equation (1).

To start, we estimate the following equation in first differences: [8]

$$\Delta I_{ijt} = \alpha_0 + \exists \Delta FS_{jt} + \exists_i \Delta B_{it} + \exists_j \Delta X_{jt} + \varepsilon_{ijt}, \tag{2}$$

where I_{ijt} is the dependent variable (say, before tax profits/ta) for domestic bank i in country j at time t; FS_{jt} is the share of foreign banks in country j at time t (i.e., number of foreign banks divided by the total number of banks); B_{it} are bank variables for domestic bank i at time t; X_{jt} are country variables for country j at time t. Further, α_0 is a constant, and $\exists$, $\exists_i$, and $\exists_j$, are coefficients, while ε_{ijt} is an error term. All regressions include country and time-specific fixed

---

[7] See also Barth et al. (1997) who use bank-level accounting data for 1993 to study the impact of bank powers on the return to equity for a set of 19 countries.

[8] Eq. (2) is a reduced form equation that relates endogenous banking variables, such a profitability to banking 'inputs' such as bank equity and non-interest earning assets and a set of controls, including the foreign bank share. DeYoung and Nolle (1996), among others, more explicitly derive a profit function that relates profitability to bank inputs and various controls.

effects. The estimation uses weighted least squares, with the weights being the inverse of the number of domestic banks in a country in a given year (to correct for varying numbers of banks across countries). We report heteroskedasticity-corrected standard errors.

The estimation results, Table 5, indicate that foreign bank entry is significantly associated with a reduction in domestic bank profitability (column 3), and also a reduction in non-interest income and overhead expenses (columns 2 and 4), although these results are less significant. We do not see a significant association of net interest margins or loan loss provisioning with foreign entry. We interpret these results to mean that foreign bank entry is associated with greater efficiency in the domestic banking system. Holding other factors constant, high profits reflect an absence of competition, while high overhead costs may reflect less efficient management and inferior organizational structures. Foreign bank entry may enable domestic banks to reduce costs as they assimilate any superior banking techniques and practices of foreign entrants. Alternatively, or complementary, foreign bank entry may force domestic bank managers to give up their sheltered 'quiet life' and to exert greater effort to reach cost efficiency. [9]

Turning to control variables, we see that inflation and real interest rate variables are positively related to the net interest margin, before tax profits, and overheads. [10] These results are consistent with the notion that a higher interest rate and a higher inflation lead to higher bank margins and profits, but also to higher operating costs. Increases in overhead/ta are also associated with relatively higher interest and non-interest income and lower profits. [11] The first difference of per capital income, or Gdp/cap, interestingly is associated with reduced costs as well as lower loan loss provisioning. Perhaps banks can more easily reduce costly employment when incomes are growing.

As an alternative definition of the foreign bank share, we use the ratio of foreign bank assets to total bank assets. After substituting for the foreign bank share, we find this variable enters all five (unreported) regressions as in Table 5 with the same, negative sign, but with an insignificant coefficient. This suggests that the number of foreign banks rather than their size is associated with competitive conditions in national banking markets. One possible explanation is that domestic banks already change their competitive behavior upon the

---

[9] Berger and Hannan (1998) estimates that the efficiency costs related to market power as explained by the 'quiet life' hypothesis are substantial.

[10] Throughout the paper excluding variables with insignificant coefficients from regressions does not change the results in any significant way. Insignificant coefficients are reported to facilitate comparisons across different specifications.

[11] This is consistent with the findings of Demirgüç-Kunt and Huizinga (1999) that some portion of overhead costs is passed on to bank depositors and other lenders. Nevertheless, since the cost are not passed on completely, bank profits do suffer from higher overhead.

S. Claessens et al. / Journal of Banking & Finance 25 (2001) 891–911   907

Table 5
Change in foreign bank presence and change in domestic bank performance[a]

	(1) ΔNet margin/ta	(2) ΔNon-int. income/ta	(3) ΔBefore tax profits/ta	(4) ΔOver-head/ta	(5) ΔLoan loss prov./ta
ΔForeign bank share	−0.001	−0.023*	−0.028**	−0.015*	−0.009
	(0.012)	(0.013)	(0.014)	(0.009)	(0.012)
ΔEquity/ta	0.017	0.040	−0.002	0.060	0.085
	(0.033)	(0.085)	(0.138)	(0.040)	(0.110)
ΔNon-int. assets/ta	−0.000	0.032	−0.014	0.061***	0.071
	(0.016)	(0.027)	(0.048)	(0.018)	(0.056)
ΔCust & short-term funding/ta	−0.008	0.044	0.026***	−0.023*	−0.005
	(0.015)	(0.033)	(0.028)	(0.014)	(0.014)
ΔOverhead/ta	0.408***	0.411***	−0.597**		0.482*
	(0.147)	(0.125)	(0.279)		(0.265)
ΔGdp/cap	−0.002*	−0.001	0.001	−0.002**	−0.003***
	(0.001)	(0.001)	(0.002)	(0.001)	(0.001)
ΔGrowth	0.018***	−0.024**	0.006	0.016***	−0.006
	(0.007)	(0.010)	(0.008)	(0.005)	(0.008)
ΔInflation	0.019***	−0.009	0.013**	0.016***	−0.002
	(0.007)	(0.006)	(0.007)	(0.005)	(0.006)
ΔReal interest	0.025***	−0.013**	0.016*	0.015***	−0.004
	(0.008)	(0.006)	(0.009)	(0.005)	(0.009)
Adj. R^2	0.19	0.12	0.15	0.12	0.22
No. of obs.	4592	3904	4592	4592	3993

[a] Regressions are estimated using weighted least-squares pooling bank level data across 80 countries for the 1988–1995 time period. Only domestic bank observations were used. Number of banks in each period is used to weight the observations. Regressions also include country and time dummy variables that are not reported. In column (1) the dependent variable is the one period change in net margin/ta defined as interest income minus interest expense over total assets. In column (2) it is the one period change in net non-interest income/ta. In column (3) it is the change in before tax profits over total assets (before tax profits/ta). In column (4) one period change in overhead/ta is the dependent variable defined as personnel expenses and other non-interest expenses over total assets. In column (5) the dependent variable is the change in loan loss provisions divided by total assets. Foreign bank share is the ratio of number of foreign banks to total number of banks. All independent variables are in first differences. Detailed variable definitions and data sources are given in Appendix A. Heteroskedasticity-corrected standard errors (White, 1980) are given in parentheses.
* Significant at 10% level.
** Significant at 5% level.
*** Significant at 1% level.

entry of foreign banks before these banks have gained their long-run market share. It may also reflect that a contestable and competitive banking system depends more on the number of banks, rather than their asset shares. Even in the long run, the number of foreign competitors may be related to, say, domestic banking profits, even if their lending market share (as proxied by relative asset size) does not. [12]

4. Conclusion

Banking markets are becoming increasingly international on account of financial liberalization and overall economic and financial integration. This paper presents evidence on the scale of foreign participation in national banking markets in 80 countries. Also, it provides some evidence on how foreign banks' financial conditions differ from those of domestic banks. These differences can reflect a different customer base, different bank procedures as well as different relevant regulatory and tax regimes. A main finding is that foreign banks tend to have higher interest margins, profitability, and tax payments than domestic banks in developing countries, while the opposite is true in developed countries.

In the literature on foreign banking, it is frequently asserted that foreign bank entry can render national banking markets more competitive, and thereby can force domestic banks to start operating more efficiently. This paper provides empirical evidence that for most countries, a larger foreign ownership share of banks is associated with a reduction in the profitability and margins of domestically owned banks.

Overall, these results are consistent with a hypothesis that in the long run, foreign bank entry may improve the functioning of national banking markets, with positive welfare implications for banking customers.

Another interesting finding of the paper is that the number of entrants matters rather than their market share. This indicates that the impact of for-

---

[12] This can be illustrated by a simple Cournot model of competition between n domestic banks and n^* foreign banks. Let domestic and foreign banks offer a homogeneous product ('loans'). Marginal cost of production is constant at c and c^* for domestic and foreign banks, respectively. Demand is negatively related to price, as $a - bp$, while total supply is $nq + n^*q^*$, with the q's being loan supply of a domestic and a foreign bank. By number, the relative foreign bank share is n^*/n. By asset size, relative foreign bank share is $s^* = (n^*q^*)/(nq)$. In the Cournot–Nash equilibrium, we find that $s^* = 1 + [(n^* - n)(a - bc) + bn^*(c - c^*)(2n + 1)]/N$ with $N = n[a - b(n^* + 1)c + bn^*c^*]$. Let fixed costs of entry be such that one or more foreign banks can enter, i.e., n^* increases. To assess the impact on s^*, we can differentiate this variable w.r.t. n^* (not ignoring the integer constraint on n^*). Unreported calculations show that $\mathrm{d}s^*/\mathrm{d}n^*$ has the same sign as $a - bc + b(c - c^*)[(2n + 1)(a - bc) - n]$ which is ambiguous. Hence, it is possible to change the ratio n^*/n (and profits of domestic banks), while not changing s^*. Therefore, the foreign number share may be correlated with profits, even if the foreign asset share is not. It is then possible that a change in n^* affects the profits of each domestic bank without affecting the relative market share of foreign banks.

eign bank entry on local bank competition is felt immediately upon entry rather than after they have gained substantial market share.

The relaxation of restrictions on foreign bank entry can have risks, however. In particular, by increasing competition and thereby lowering the profits of domestic banks, foreign entry may reduce charter values of domestic banks, making them more vulnerable. This may have a destabilizing effect on the financial system especially if the domestic prudential regulations and supervision are not strong. To reap the benefits of foreign bank entry and minimize its potential costs, policy-makers need to pay attention to the timing of the liberalization process and ensure adequate regulation and supervision.

Acknowledgements

We thank two referees for valuable comments and Anqing Shi and Luc Laeven for excellent research assistance.

Appendix A. Variable definitions and sources

Net margin/ta – interest income minus interest expense over total assets.

Before tax profits/ta – before tax profits over total assets.

Equity/ta – book value of equity (assets minus liabilities) over total assets.

Non-interest earning assets/ta – cash, non-interest earning deposits at other banks, and other non-interest earning assets over total assets.

Customer & short term funding/ta – all short term and long term deposits plus other non-deposit short term funding over total assets.

Overhead/ta – personnel expenses and other non-interest expenses over total assets.

Foreign bank share – Foreign bank share is the number of foreign banks to total number of banks. A bank is defined to be a foreign bank if it has at least 50% foreign ownership.

All individual bank level variables are obtained from BankScope data base of IBCA.

Gdp/cap – real GDP per capita in thousands of US$.

Growth – annual growth rate in real GDP.

Inflation – the annual inflation of the GDP deflator.

Real interest – the nominal interest rate minus rate of inflation. Where available, nominal rate is the rate on short term government securities. Otherwise, a rate changed by the Central Bank to domestic banks such as the discount rate is used. If that is not available, then the commercial bank deposit interest rate is used.

Openness – exports plus imports divided by GDP.

Interest rate data are from the IMF, International Financial Statistics. Other macro data are from World Bank National Accounts.

References

Aliber, R.Z., 1984. International banking, a survey. Journal of Money, Credit and Banking 16, 661–712.

Barth, J.R., Nolle, D.E., Rice, T.N., 1997. Commercial banking structure, regulation, and performance, an international comparison. Comptroller of the Currency Economics Working Paper 97-6.

Berger, A.N., Hannan, T.H., 1998. The efficiency cost of market power in the banking industry; a test of the "quiet life" and related hypotheses. Review of Economics and Statistics 80, 454–465.

Bhattacharaya, J., 1993. The role of foreign banks in developing countries: A survey of evidence. Cornell University, Mimeo.

Cho, Y.J., Khatkhate, D., 1989. Lessons of financial liberalization in Asia, a comparative study. World Bank Discussion Paper 50, World Bank.

Demirgüç-Kunt, A., Huizinga, H., 1999. Determinants of commercial bank interest margins and profitability: Some international evidence. World Bank Economic Review 13 (2), 379–408.

DeYoung, R., Nolle, D.E., 1996. Foreign-owned banks in the US: Earning market share or buying it. Journal of Money, Credit and Banking 28, 622–636.

Frankel, A.B., Montgomery, J.D., 1991. Financial structure: An international perspective. Brookings Papers on Economic Activity, 1, 257–310.

Gelb, A., Sagari, S., 1990. Banking. In: Messerlin, P., Sanvant, K. (Eds.), The Uruguay Round: Services in the World Economy. The World Bank and UN Centre on Transnational Corporations, Washington, DC.

Goldberg, L.G., Saunders, A., 1981. The determinants of foreign banking activity in the US. Journal of Banking and Finance 5, 17–32.

Gorton, G., Rosen, R., 1995. Corporate control, portfolio choice, and the decline of banking. Journal of Banking 50, 1377–1420.

Hanson, J.A., Rocha, R., 1986. High interest rates, spreads, and the cost of intermediation, two studies. Industry and Finance Series 18, World Bank.

Levine, R., 1996. Foreign banks, financial development, and economic growth. In: Claude, E.B. (Ed.), International Financial Markets. AEI Press, Washington, DC.

McFadden, C., 1994. Foreign banks in Australia. The World Bank, Mimeo.

Pigott, C.A., 1986. Financial reform and the role of foreign banks in Pacific Basin. In: Cheng, H. (Ed.), Financial Policy and Reform in Pacific-Basin Countries. Lexington Books, Lexington, MA.

Schranz, M.S., 1993. Takeovers improve firm performance: Evidence from the banking industry. Journal of Political Economy 101, 299–326.

Stiglitz, J.E., 1993. The role of the state in financial markets. In: Proceedings of the World Bank Annual Conference on Development Economics, pp. 19–52.

Terrell, H.S., 1986. The role of foreign banks in domestic banking markets. In: Cheng, H. (Ed.), Financial Policy and Reform in Pacific-Rim Countries. Lexington Books, Lexington, MA.

Vittas, D., 1991. Measuring commercial bank efficiency, use and misuse of bank operating ratios. Policy Research Working Paper 806, World Bank.

Walter, I., Gray, H.P., 1983. Protectionism, and international banking, sectoral efficiency, competitive structure and national policy. Journal of Banking and Finance 7, 597–609.

White, H., 1980. A heteroskedasticity-consistent covariance matrix estimator and a direct test for heteroskedasticty. Econometrica 48, 817–838.

World Development Report, 1996. World Bank.

[26]

Review of International Economics, 9(2), 249–261, 2001

Trade in International Transport Services: The Role of Competition

Joseph F. Francois and Ian Wooton*

Abstract

The paper is concerned with trade in transport services (not cabotage but rather international shipping, transport, and related logistical services) and the importance of competition and market structure in the sector. It examines implications of liberalization for profits, trade, and national gains from trade. Though past GATS (General Agreement on Trade in Services) maritime negotiations involved the maritime nations, this paper also flags interests of consuming nations (particularly poorer developing countries). Issues raised in the analytical section are illustrated through a computational example, to provide a rough sense of orders of magnitude and the importance of the issues raised for basic gains from improved market access.

1. Introduction

The conclusion of the Uruguay Round in 1993 and the subsequent launching of the World Trade Organization marked an important shift in the multilateral trading system. The post-World War II trading regime (commonly referred to as GATT 1947) was focused on the rules governing merchandise trade between industrial countries. In contrast, while the new WTO system includes a revamped GATT (now called GATT 1994), it also includes a parallel institutional framework devoted to services trade—the General Agreement on Trade in Services (GATS). It also appears to include a deeper commitment by the developing countries to participate in the multilateral trading system.

While the Uruguay Round included negotiations on market access in several service sectors, these negotiations proved problematic, even by Uruguay Round standards.[1] In the end, the negotiators declared victory and went home, agreeing to reschedule (i.e., extend) service negotiations for some time after the victory parties. With service negotiations decoupled from simultaneous negotiations in other sectors, the negotiating game changed.[2] In the end, some of these negotiations (like financial services) did conclude successfully. The same cannot be said for maritime services.

Sticking points in the maritime negotiations included cabotage restrictions and national preference schemes. In retrospect, given that the industry is largely protected from competition on domestic routes (cabotage) and exempted from antitrust rules for international routes, it is not surprising that the industry and its negotiating representatives resisted liberalization.[3] The US delegation, for example, was backed by a very vocal domestic industry, and stood strongly opposed to making market access commitments in the sector, especially with regard to cabotage.[4] While the extended negotiations on maritime services lasted two years beyond the end of the Uruguay

* Francois: Tinbergen Institute, Erasmus University, Burg Oudlaan 50, 3062 PA Rotterdam, The Netherlands. E-mail: francois@few.eur.nl. Wooton: Department of Economics, University of Glasgow, Glasgow G12 8RT, UK. E-mail: i.wooton@socsci.gla.ac.uk. This paper was prepared for the CEPR/NBER International Seminar in International Trade, Cambridge, MA, June 1999. We are grateful for the helpful comments of participants, especially those of our discussant, Drusilla Brown. We are also indebted to Leonard Cheng, Gregg Huff, and Siri Pettersen Strandenes for their suggestions. This paper was revised while Wooton was visiting the Economic Policy Research Unit, University of Copenhagen, and he wishes to thank them for their hospitality.

Round, they were finally laid to rest on 28 June 1996 when WTO member delegations agreed to suspend negotiations. They deferred them again, this time until the next round of comprehensive service negotiations, scheduled to begin in the year 2000.

This paper is concerned with trade in international transport, logistics, and related services. While our discussion will often be couched in terms of the maritime sector, the basic analytics apply to the full chain of services required to complete the trans- actions that turn exports into imports at the dock. The paper itself is divided into three parts. The first offers a brief overview of the structure of the maritime industry. This includes some discussion of patterns of ownership and demand, discussion of the insti- tutionalized cartels that dominate the industry, and the (limited) available evidence on the effect of these cartels on price. Armed with stylized facts, we then develop an ana- lytical model that illustrates some of the basic issues at stake with liberalization of mar- itime services trade. This involves not only the implications for the profits of the industry (one issue that has certainly been well represented in past negotiations), but also the implications for levels of trade and national gains from trade. Since the past negotiations involved the maritime nations themselves, we think it also appropriate to flag the interests of the consumer (i.e., nonmaritime) nations. These include the poorer developing countries. Finally, we supplement the analytics with a numeric example. The numerics serve two functions. One is to illustrate the issues raised in the analytical section of the paper through example. The other is to place this example in the context of actual numbers, to provide a crude gauge of the relative magnitudes of the effects discussed.

2. The International Shipping Industry

Market Structure

In the maritime world, the oceans are populated with shipping conferences. Con- ferences meet regularly to set rates, analyze market conditions, and assess other developments like fuel prices and port charges. A recent development has been supplementation of conferences with "talking agreements" and similar arrangements. As of the end of 1998, one of these agreements, the Transpacific Stabilization Agree- ment, controlled about 86% of US waterborne trade with Asia.[5] Another cartel, the Trans-Atlantic Conference Agreement (TACA), controls a comparable share of North Atlantic trade. The shipping press characterizes the Pacific as a region where individ- ual shipping lines are prone to "break ranks" on prices (apparently a bad thing) unless held in check by the cartel rules adopted by conference lines (apparently a good thing).

In the case of US routes (a nontrivial share of world trade), the job of policing the cartels is carried out by the US government Individual shipping lines are subject to punitive fines, imposed by the Federal Maritime Commission (FMC), if they break ranks with the published schedule of rates. To promote their activities, conferences are given exemptions from antitrust laws.[6] Transparency of pricing is enforced (including required internet publication of rates) to ensure that price fixing is adhered to. "The FMC's role in enforcing filed rates implies that conference agreements are policed by an outside agency at no cost to the conference. Thus, the tariff filing and enforcement requirements potentially facilitate the exercise of conference market power" (Clyde and Reitzes, 1995).

Different institutional arrangements stand as monuments to multilateral and regional efforts to regulate shipper arrangements. Notable is the UNCTAD Code of Conduct for Liner Conferences (UNCTAD, 1975, TD/CODE/13). The United

TRADE IN INTERNATIONAL TRANSPORT SERVICES   251

States never ratified the code, while European countries demanded exemptions (known as the Brussels package) from crucial parts of the code. The consensus is that, at best, "the UNCTAD Code of Conduct occupies a very limited part in the regulatory framework of liner shipping." At a regional level, the United States has allowed the TACA to extend its antitrust exemption up/downstream to include intermodal rate fixing, while the EU has not yet set policy on intermodal rate fixing (Veenstra, 1999, ch. 3).

Despite the fact that this sector is literally at the center of world trade, the economic impact of these arrangements on the gains from trade and their interaction with trade policy has not been emphasized in the limited literature.[7] Rather the literature, starting with Koopmans (1939) and Tinbergen (1959), is more narrowly focused on the determination of shipping rates and the role of market structure. This includes Deakin and Seward (1973), Heaver (1973), and Talley and Pope (1985). Sjostrom (1992) argues that much of this recent literature on shipping rates is actually inconclusive, because of incorrect model specification.

Clyde and Reitzes (1995) examine shipping rates filed by ocean liner conferences with the FMC between 1985 and 1988. They look for evidence as to whether the rate structure in ocean shipping markets is based on costs, the exercise of market power by conferences, or the exercise of market power by firms in a manner unrelated to the conference system. They conclude that "some aspects of the conference system may contribute to higher shipping rates, particularly when the conference has a sizable market share." They also find that "conferences do not act as perfect cartels maximizing the joint profits of their members." This last finding is consistent with the tone of the maritime press, which has described constant efforts (aided and abetted by national maritime administrations) to introduce or restore price discipline in the face of the temptation for individual members to cheat.[8]

Sjostrom (1989) suggests that these shipping conferences may exist, not as monopolizing cartels, but to ensure that shipping services are provided in a market in which there is no competitive equilibrium. In a market with avoidable fixed costs, the core may be empty and he argues that collusion imposes an equilibrium where otherwise none would exist. He tests this hypothesis against that of the conference being a cartel and finds some support for the theory of the core.

Shipping Margins Versus Import Tariffs

In terms of relative costs to trade, shipping margins are now far more important to many countries than are tariff barriers. Successive rounds of trade liberalization under the auspices of the GATT/WTO have made dramatic reductions in average tariffs, while regional arrangements, such as the EU and NAFTA, have reduced trade barriers further still.

This contrasts with shipping margins of over 8% (see Ajmadi et al., 1996, for more on this point). Many countries would gain far more, in terms of market access, from squeezing shipping margins than from a further reduction in OECD tariff rates. We will return to this point in the computational section of the paper.

3. A Theoretical Model

We now turn to an analytical model of trade with transport costs. The framework we develop has interesting policy implications. For example, we show that it is possible to use shipping cartels as a second-best instrument for manipulating the terms of trade.

252   *J. F. Francois and Ian Wooton*

Hence, with European preference schemes, one can easily imagine a situation where shipping cartels to Africa would allow the partial recapture of market-access concessions made under preferential trading schemes. The rents would be split with the cartels. If the cartels are themselves European, the recapture is complete. In a more general sense, the combination of high shipping margins and concentrated ownership (see UNCTAD, 1992) suggests a strong consumer (i.e., nonmaritime) country interest in an effective, pro-competitive maritime agreement under the GATS.

The message about competition actually covers the whole logistics chain. Any choke point, in terms of competition, in the chain of services that facilitates trade can lead to the type of result developed here. If not resulting from the shipping operations themselves, it may arise due to corrupt port management or a monopoly on handling and loading.

The Basic Model

Much of the literature on trade and transportation has been focused on general-equilibrium patterns of trade and on the uniqueness of equilibrium (see, e.g., Wegge, 1993). As we are concerned instead with market structure, we buy ourselves a great deal of analytical simplicity by working with a reduced-form, dual structure. The formal model that emerges provides a framework for both our analytical discussion of equilibrium given market power in the transport sector and for the calculation of welfare effects in the numerical section of the paper.

We start by defining the general equilibrium for a small country in terms of dual expenditure and revenue functions. As will become evident, for individual product markets (more generally for standard two-good models and alternatively for the stylized representation of exports and imports of composite goods), this approach allows us to illustrate general-equilibrium results through the familiar geometric tools normally associated with partial-equilibrium models (Martin, 1997; Francois and Hall, 1997). The value of output is defined by the function $g(p, v)$ and the expenditure function by $e(p, u)$:

$$g(p,v) = \max_{h} (p \cdot h | (h,v) \text{ feasible}), \tag{1}$$

$$e(p,u) = \max_{c} (p \cdot c | f(c) \geq u). \tag{2}$$

In equations (1) and (2), $e(p, u)$ is the expenditure required to achieve the level of utility u from consumption of c at the vector of domestic prices p; while $g(p, v)$ is the GDP function indicating the maximum revenue from production (of h) that can be generated with resource endowments v at domestic prices p. For notational simplicity, it is convenient to combine equations (1) and (2) into a net revenue function:

$$z(p,u,v) = e(p,u) - g(p,v). \tag{3}$$

The vector of domestic demands for output is given by e_p, the first derivative of $e(p, u)$ with respect to p, while domestic supplies are represented by g_p. The trade matrix (net imports M) is then the first derivative of the net revenue function with respect to price:

$$M(p) = z_p(p,u,v) = e_p - g_p. \tag{4}$$

The gap between the domestic and border prices, $(p - p^*)$, is the tax on trade, so that trade-tax revenues are given by $(e_p - g_p)(p - p^*)$. In discussing the impact of changes in

TRADE IN INTERNATIONAL TRANSPORT SERVICES 253

the trade regime, we work with a second-order Taylor-series expansion of this system. This amounts to focusing exclusively on the first and second derivatives of z and leads to our assuming that import demand and export supply are (approximately) linear.

Within this framework, we emphasize the trade in an export commodity that is produced in the *export* market and then shipped, at some cost, to the *import* market where it is sold (i.e., exchanged for imports). Let the quantity of the export commodity traded be q. Producers of the good are assumed to be small, perfectly competitive firms located in one or several countries. The industry supply curve for exports is linear in producer prices p_p:

$$p_p = a + bq. \tag{5}$$

The shipping industry provides the service of transforming exports into imports at the dock.[9] This service is provided at a price σ (the *shipping margin*, essentially the difference between the f.o.b. and c.i.f. prices) that depends on competitive conditions in the shipping industry.[10] We assume that the shipping industry is imperfectly competitive, with n identical, profit-maximizing firms in competition with rival shipping firms. The shippers have large fleets that can be used on many different global shipping routes. From this stock, they choose to allocate a certain quantity to service this particular trade. Thus the shipping firms compete in quantities.

Consumers in the foreign market have a linear inverse-demand function for imports, relating the price they are charged, p_c, to the quantity traded, q, as follows:

$$p_c = x - yq. \tag{6}$$

We assume that the good faces an import barrier in the form of an *ad valorem* tariff of t.[11] The price paid by consumers in the destination consequently exceeds the price received by producers as a result of both the shipping margin and the tariff $p_c = (1 + t)(p_p + \sigma)$. Rewriting this as an expression for the shipping margin, we get:

$$\sigma = p_c / (1+t) - p_p. \tag{7}$$

The total revenue of a representative firm i, producing quantity q_i, is σq_i. We assume that the shipping firms are identical and behave as Cournot competitors. Substituting (5), (6), and (7) into total revenue yields an expression for the perceived marginal revenue of a firm:

$$MR_i = \frac{x}{1+t} - a - \frac{(1+s)[(1+t)b + y]}{s(1+t)} q_i, \tag{8}$$

where $s \equiv 1/n$ is the market share enjoyed by each of the shipping firms. We assume that the real costs of shipping (insurance and freight) are constant, and the marginal cost of transport is:[12]

$$MC = c. \tag{9}$$

Solving (8) and (9) provides the equilibrium quantity of the good supplied:

$$q = \frac{x - (a+c)(1+t)}{[b(1+t) + y](1+s)}, \tag{10}$$

while the equilibrium shipping margin is:[13]

$$\sigma = \frac{xs + (1+t)(c - as)}{(1+t)(1+s)}. \tag{11}$$

254   *J. F. Francois and Ian Wooton*

The associated prices of the good for consumers and producers, respectively, are:

$$p_c = \frac{x[b(1+t)(1+s)+ys]+y(a+c)(1+t)}{[b(1+t)+y](1+s)},$$

$$p_p = \frac{b[(as-c)(1+t)+x]+ay(1+s)}{[b(1+t)+y](1+s)}. \tag{12}$$

If $s = 1$, the shipping industry is monopolised. As s becomes smaller, the firms' perceived demand for the good becomes more elastic and they lose market power. With s close to zero, each firm has an infinitesimal share of the market and behaves competitively. There are two elements to the market power of a firm. Firstly, they charge consumers a price that exceeds the shippers' marginal costs. In addition, the shippers exploit their monopsony power with producers. The producers have increasing marginal costs and, consequently, the shippers restrict their purchases.

Effects of Increased Competition

We simulate the effects of increasing the level of competition through a change in the number of firms in the shipping industry, n. (Such increased competition may follow from GATS-related liberalization of the shipping route itself, or from related liberalization somewhere else in the logistics chain.) If n rises, the market share s of each incumbent firm declines. They will perceive their market demand to be more elastic and will consequently behave more competitively. If, however, the number of firms were to fall, the industry will become more concentrated and the remaining firms will exercise the increased power from a growing market share.

Of course, there need not actually be a change in the number of firms. Rather, s can instead be viewed as an indicator of the degree of competitiveness in the shipping market. In this interpretation, a fall in s reflects a more competitive environment (as n becomes larger, market shares decline and the shippers' margin gets closer to marginal cost). This could occur if the shipping conference's influence in maintaining common rates were to decline or if its activities became subject to antitrust rules. An increase in s would indicate that the conference was exerting greater influence in the market, resulting in more collusion.

Figure 1 shows the effects of changing s on prices, quantities, and profits. As the shipping industry shifts from behaving as perfect competitors to acting as a monopolist, the consumers pay an increasing price and the volume shipped declines. Given that less of the product is being demanded, the price received by the producers falls. The (shaded) growing gap between the producer and consumer price is σ, the margin captured by the shippers, and this rises monotonically as the industry becomes increasingly concentrated. Thus, when the industry behaves competitively, the shipping margin equals c, the marginal cost of shipping. The margin reaches its highest level when there is complete collusion and the shippers fully exploit their monopoly power with both producers and consumers.

Benefits of Trade Liberalization

How does the tariff affect the trading situation? With a competitive shipping industry, the beneficiaries of trade liberalization would be the consumers in the importing country and the exporting producers. With a less-than-perfectly-competitive shipping industry, the benefits of the more liberal trade regime are partially captured by the

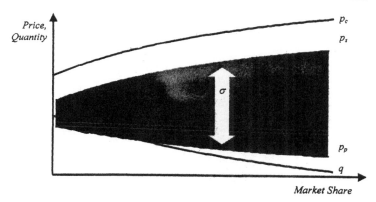

Figure 1. Effects of Market Share

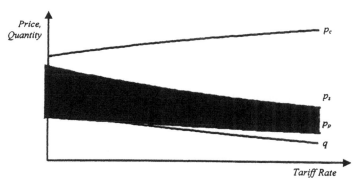

Figure 2. Effects of Trade Liberalization

shipping firms. Figure 2 illustrates the equilibria that arise with a duopolized shipping industry for various levels of tariff.[14]

As the tariff is reduced, the quantity traded rises, as the consumer price has declined. This rise in demand results in a higher price being received by the producers. However, the benefits of the trade liberalization are not fully passed through to producers and consumers. The shippers are able to take advantage of the more liberal trade regime, replacing part of the trade-tax wedge (between consumer and producer price) by one of their own, a greater monopolistic markup. As the tariff continues to fall, the shipping firms receive a larger margin over their marginal costs, resulting in increasingly large profits.

The relationship between the concentration of the shipping industry, the tariff barrier, and the optimal shipping margin is illustrated in a contour plot in Figure 3. The more concentrated the industry (or the stronger the cartel) and the lower the tariff barrier, the greater is the shipping margin.

256   *J. F. Francois and Ian Wooton*

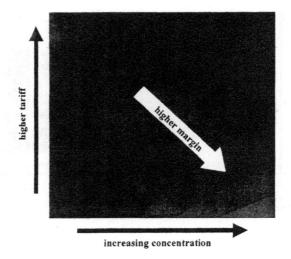

Figure 3. Trade Liberalization, Industry Concentration and the Shipping Margin

4. A Numerical Example

We now turn to a computational example, based on the analytical results derived above. We work directly within our theoretical framework in order to relate welfare changes to trade and the structure of the shipping industry. To do this, recall that from the point of view of exporters the impact of imperfect competition in the shipping sector is realized as a deterioration in the equilibrium terms of trade. A convenient approach to evaluating the welfare impact of such a terms-of-trade shock in general equilibrium is the balance-of-trade function (Lloyd and Schweinberger, 1988; Anderson and Neary, 1992). Under this approach we estimate a money measure of the change in welfare resulting from the shock by evaluating the change in the balance of trade necessary to maintain constant utility (i.e., the net transfer needed to maintain welfare), given the change in realized relative border prices. A shock to the general equilibrium system that reduces domestic utility effectively increases the income needed to achieve a given level of utility, and hence requires a transfer from the rest of the world to maintain that utility level.

The balance of trade, B, is simply the net revenue function defined in equation (3). That is:

$$B = z(p,u,v). \tag{13}$$

We can approximate the impact of our terms-of-trade shock on welfare with a second-order Taylor-series expansion of equation (13), obtaining the following for the producers:

$$\Delta B = q\Delta p_p - \frac{1}{2b}(\Delta p_p)^2. \tag{14}$$

We have implemented the system of equations defined in section 3, supplemented by equation (14), as a simple computational model. We work with three stylized

TRADE IN INTERNATIONAL TRANSPORT SERVICES   257

Table 1. Trade and Income Data for Stylized Regional Developing Economies

	Sub-Saharan and Southern Africa	Latin America	South Asia
Values as percentages of GDP			
GDP	100.0	100.0	100.0
Exports (f.o.b.)	23.6	10.4	12.8
Exports (c.i.f.)	24.9	11.0	13.4
Imports (f.o.b.)	23.7	11.9	14.5
Imports (c.i.f.)	24.6	12.4	15.0
Tariff revenue on exports	1.2	0.6	0.9
Percentages			
Tariff on exports in export markets	4.9	5.2	6.4
Export tax equivalent of shipping margins	9.6	10.1	9.1
Point estimates			
Demand elasticity for exports	−10.0	−10.0	−10.0
Export supply elasticity	3.5	3.5	3.5

Source: Trade and GDP data are taken from the GTAP version 4 dataset.

regional developing economies, based on average macroeconomic data for 1995. These data are presented in Table 1.[15]

Our basic experiment involves a hypothetical full elimination of tariffs in export markets for each of these stylized economies (i.e., full, unconditional market access). We observe the shipping margins on these trades (the sum of the inbound and outbound differences between the c.i.f. and f.o.b. measures), but cannot determine whether the margins reflect the costs of transportation or are an artifact of the degree of market power that the shipping conferences enjoy. (We also miss the additional distribution/shipping margins associated with related costs inside the border.) Consequently, in our empirical exercise we assume a variety of specific market structures for the shipping industry, ranging from competition to perfect collusion (monopoly) and allocate the shipping margin between marginal costs and profits accordingly. The welfare effects of trade liberalization, assessed under these alternative assumptions about market structure, are provided in Table 2.

It can be seen from Table 2, panel A, that the benefits of improved market access depend critically on the degree of competition in the shipping industry. At the one extreme, a competitive shipping sector implies a full passthrough of terms-of-trade improvements to the producers. In contrast, a more collusive industry is able to capture a significant share of the realized gains that follow from these changes in market access conditions. For example, in all cases, approximately one-half of the gains from full and unconditional market access can be lost by producers to the shipping industry when the latter is concentrated and fully exploits its market power, capturing part of these gains for itself. The related effects include smaller increases in trade volumes (panel B), and a sharp rise in shipping prices (panel C).

The message that emerges from these experiments is that, in terms of rough orders of magnitude, the competitive structure of the shipping industry is indeed an important issue. Realized gains from market access concessions depend critically on the pricing structure of the industry that facilitates trade.

258   *J. F. Francois and Ian Wooton*

Table 2. Effects of Trade Liberalization for Stylized Regional Developing Economies

	Perfect competition	Number of firms				Monopoly
		n = 10	n = 5	n = 4	n = 2	
A. *Income effect of trade liberalization (indexed to perfect competition)*						
Sub-Saharan and Southern Africa	100.0	90.8	83.3	80.0	72.6	51.6
Latin America	100.0	90.7	83.2	79.9	75.0	51.4
South Asia	100.0	90.5	82.8	79.5	74.5	50.8
B. *Effect of trade liberalization on exports (percentage change)*						
Sub-Saharan and Southern Africa	31.8	29.2	27.0	26.1	22.2	17.5
Latin America	33.5	30.8	28.5	27.5	26.0	18.4
South Asia	41.4	38.0	35.2	33.9	32.1	22.7
C. *Effect of trade liberalization on shipping prices (percentage change)*						
Sub-Saharan and Southern Africa	0.0	4.6	8.5	10.2	12.7	25.5
Latin America	0.0	4.6	8.5	10.2	12.7	25.5
South Asia	0.0	6.3	11.6	13.9	17.4	34.7

5. Summary and Conclusions

Our goal in this paper has been to examine the importance of market structure in the transport sector for the distribution of gains from trade and the benefits of trade liberalization. We have shown that the presence of an imperfectly competitive intermediary can have a significant effect on trade flows and the allocation of gains from trade. Trade liberalization in the absence of some form of deregulation of the shipping industry will not result in the increased benefits that would otherwise be imagined, as the shipping firms will grab a portion of the gains from trade.

Combining an analytical model with "real data," we have shown that the relative magnitude of these effects can be quite significant. Trade liberalization with the present trading climate can lead to shipping firms capturing a significant proportion of the benefits of multilateral trade concessions. This highlights the important relationship between trade and competition in the shipping sector itself (maritime, air, trucking, and related links in the logistics chain) and the gains from trade in other sectors. GATS negotiations in this area have important implications for multilateral efforts aimed more broadly at trade liberalization.

References

Amjadi, A., U. Reincke, and A. J. Yeats, "Did External Barriers Cause the Marginalization of sub-Saharan Africa in World Trade?" Discussion Paper 348, Washington, DC: World Bank (1996).

Anderson, J. and J. P. Neary, "Trade Reform with Quotas, Partial Rent Retention, and Tariffs," *Econometrica* 60 (1992):57–76.

Brander, J. A. and B. J. Spencer, "Tariff Protection and Imperfect Competition," in H. Kierzkowski (ed.), *Monopolistic Competition and International Trade*, Oxford: Oxford University Press (1984).

TRADE IN INTERNATIONAL TRANSPORT SERVICES 259

Center for Global Trade Analyis, *Global Trade, Assistance, and Protection: The GTAP 4 Data Package*, West Lafayette: Purdue Research Foundation (1999).

Clyde, P. S. and J. D. Reitzes, "The Effectiveness of Collusion under Antitrust Immunity," US Federal Trade Commission, Bureau of Economics Staff Report (1995).

Deakin, B. M., and T. Seward, *Shipping Conferences: A Study of their Origins, Developments, and Economic Practices*, Cambridge: Cambridge University Press (1973).

Finger, J. M., "Policy Research," *Journal of Political Economy* 89 (1983):1270–71.

Francois, J. F. and H. K. Hall, "Partial Equilibrium Modelling," in Francois J. F. and K. A. Reinert (eds.), *Applied Methods for Trade Policy Analysis: A Handbook*, New York: Cambridge University Press (1997).

Francois, J. F. and A. Strutt, "Post-Uruguay Round Tariff Vectors for GTAP Version 4," (mimeo), Rotterdam: Tinbergen Institute (1999).

Francois, J. F. and I. Wooton, "Intermediation Chains and International Trade," in preparation (2001).

Getzler, L., *The Welfare Effects of International Trade Policy: Distance and Transportation Costs Make a Difference*, Dissertation, Madison: University of Wisconsin (1997).

Heaver, T. D., "The Structure of Liner Freight Rates," *Journal of Transport Economics and Policy* 4 (1973):257–65.

Household Goods Forwarders Association, "Maritime/ocean shipping: conferences: still alive and well," *The Portal On-line* (1998a). Available at www.hhgfaa.org/feb_98.

———, "Maritime/ocean shipping: shipping reform and shippers associations," *The Portal On-line* (1998b). Available at www.hhgfaa.org/oct_98.

Hufbauer, G. C. and K.-A. Elliott, *Measuring the Costs of Protection in the United States*, Washington, DC: Institute for International Economics (1994).

Hummels, D., "Transportation Costs and International Integration in Recent History," (mimeo), University of Chicago (1999).

Koopmans, T., *Tanker Freight Rates and Tankship Building: An Analysis of Cyclical Fluctuations*, Netherlands Economic Institute report 27, Haarlem: De Erven F. Bohn NV (1939).

Lloyd, P. J. and A. G. Schweinberger, "Trade Expenditure Functions and the Gains from Trade," *Journal of International Economics* 24 (1988):275–97.

Martin, W., "Measuring Welfare Changes with Distortions," in Francois, J. F. and K. A. Reinert (eds.), *Applied Methods for Trade Policy Analysis: A Handbook*, New York: Cambridge University Press (1997).

Sjostrom, W., "Collusion in Ocean Shipping: A Test of Monopoly and Empty Core Models," *Journal of Political Economy* 97 (1989):1160–79.

———, "Price Discrimination by Shipping Conferences," *Logistics and Transportation Review* 28 (1992):207–16.

Talley, W. K. and J. A. Pope, "Determinants of Liner Conference Rates under Containerization," *International Journal of Transport Economics* 12 (1985):145–55.

Tinbergen, J., "Tonnage and Freight," in Klassen, L. H. et al. (eds.), *Jan Tinbergen Selected Papers*, Amsterdam: North-Holland (1959).

United Nations Conference on Trade and Development, *United Nations Conference of Plenipotentiaries on a Code of Conduct for Liner Conferences*, vol. II, Final Act, TD/CODE/13/Add.1, New York: UN Publications (1975).

———, *Review of Maritime Transport*, Geneva: UNCTAD (1992).

United States Department of Transportation Maritime Administration, *A Report to Congress on US Maritime Policy*, Washington, DC: USDOT (1998).

United States International Trade Commission, *The Economic Effect of Significant US Import Restraints*, Washington, DC: USITC Publication 2699 (1993).

Veenstra, A. W., *Quantitative Analysis of Shipping Markets*, Delft: Delft University Press (1999).

Wegge, L.-L., "International Transportation in the Heckscher–Ohlin Model," in Herberg H. and N. V. Long (eds.), *Trade, Welfare, and Economic Policies: Essays in Honor of Murray C. Kemp*, Ann Arbor: University of Michigan Press (1993):121–42.

260   *J. F. Francois and Ian Wooton*

Notes

1. It is not too far off the mark to characterize initial GATS negotiations as an exercise in defining precisely what was being negotiated. The result is a mix of traditional cross-border "trade" along with establishment issues related to rights of establishment (i.e., "investment"). Together, these imply an extension of the basic GATT concept of market access to cover both trade and investment commitments related to deliverable services.

2. As Finger (1983) would say, the situation changed to one where a positive decision could be taken by a limited group of participants.

3. In the early 1990s a series of studies by the USITC (1993) and also the Institute for International Economics (Hufbauer and Elliot, 1994) came out estimating the cost of US cabotage restrictions. The initial reaction of the US Maritime Administration was to claim that trade economists misunderstood the issue. As argued at USITC hearings, the basic logic was "There is no trade in cabotage services. Hence there can be no cost of trade protection." The logic of the industry when dealing with their regulators is one of "price stability" and quantity management. Even within the United Nations, the UNCTAD reports on maritime transport (see UNCTAD, 1992, for example) devote considerable discussion to the problem of oversupply. Viewed another way, such oversupply makes it difficult for cartels to maintain desired pricing structures.

4. Officially, "the US delegation has taken the position that the United States already maintains a high level of access in its maritime sector—as indicated by the 96 percent of our foreign trade that is carried in foreign-flag vessels—and needs to maintain its support programs, small as they are, to help assure the availability of national flag tonnage for sealift purposes. . . . The decision to suspend the negotiations was strongly supported by the US Maritime Administration and other members of the US delegation" (USDOT, 1998).

5. Once concluded, this particular agreement announced a $300 per 40-foot container rate increase for May 1998 (*The Portal On-line*, January/February 1998).

6. The rationale for such exemptions is that conferences provide price stability and limit uncertainty regarding available tonnage. This includes both US and Canadian law. The US Shipping Act of 1984 eliminated the public-interest standard of antitrust law, reversing a trend toward greater antitrust scrutiny. As a result, conference agreements are not subject to an approval process, but instead can be challenged by the FMC. The FMC has never attempted to stop formation of a conference (Clyde and Reitzes, 1995). There have been some recent initiatives to reform these laws, though the maritime press has argued that these "reforms" may actually strengthen current antitrust exemptions.

7. An exception is Getzler (1997).

8. The maritime press also offers anecdotal evidence on price discrimination. For example, *The Portal On-line* (October 1998) focuses on the example of the cost of moving a container through ports on the US East Coast. In theory, the cost should be the same regardless of destination. However, while it cost $420 in 1998 to move a 40-foot container under Trans-Atlantic Agreement contracts, it estimates that it cost $600 in 1998 to move the same container through the same facilities under Mediterranean conference contracts, and $550 under Inter-American Freight Conference contracts.

9. In this paper, there is only one stage of intermediation (shipping). In our companion paper, Francois and Wooton (2001), we consider the implications of having several intermediaries in moving the good from producer to consumer.

10. Note here that the relevant cost is that of full transformation of exports into imports, which includes the shipping margin on the outbound and inbound journey. Analytically, we solve here for a total value for this margin, though of course it may technically be shared across the inbound and outbound journeys.

11. Brander and Spencer (1984) examine the optimal trade restriction for an importing country when faced with an imperfectly competitive supplier. They show that, dependent upon demand conditions, this policy may take the form of a tariff or a subsidy. When demand is linear (as is the case in our model), Brander and Spencer find that a positive tariff is the appropriate instru-

TRADE IN INTERNATIONAL TRANSPORT SERVICES   261

ment, but this will change with other configurations of demand. Their model has constant marginal costs for the supplier. In contrast, because we assume increasing opportunity costs for exports, our shippers face increasing marginal costs. As a result, a tariff becomes the preferred instrument for a wider range of cases than in the Brander and Spencer model. In any event, our focus is not on rediscovering the optimal strategic interactions between large players. Instead, we choose to consider the implications for the market of exogenous reductions in tariffs resulting from a round of trade liberalization.

12. We do not consider changes in these real costs of transport, our focus being on the additional margin charged by shipping firms as a result of their market power. Hummels (1999) investigates the issue of whether transport costs have declined and concludes that they have not.

13. This shipping margin is essentially the "best response" of the shipping industry to the import tariff. We more closely examine the strategic interplay between agents in Francois and Wooton (2001).

14. The figures for different numbers of shipping firms are qualitatively very similar, except in the case of competition when shipping industry profits are zero at all times and, consequently, all the benefits of trade liberalization accrue to the producers and consumers.

15. The full model, implemented both in Mathcad and as an Excel spreadsheet, is available upon request. Protection data are from Francois and Strutt (1999). Other data are from Center for Global Trade Analysis (1999).

[27]

THE WORLD BANK ECONOMIC REVIEW, VOL. 16, NO. 1 81–108

Trade in International Maritime Services:
How Much Does Policy Matter?

Carsten Fink, Aaditya Mattoo, and Ileana Cristina Neagu

Maritime transport costs significantly impede international trade. This article examines why these costs are so high in some countries and quantifies the importance of two explanations: restrictive trade policies and private anticompetitive practices. It finds that both matter, but the latter have a greater impact. Trade liberalization and the breakup of private carrier agreements would lead to an average of one-third lower liner transport prices and to cost savings of up to US$3 billion on goods carried to the United States alone. The policy implications are clear: there is a need not only for further liberalization of government policy but also for strengthened international disciplines on restrictive business practices. The authors propose an approach to developing such disciplines in the current round of services negotiations at the World Trade Organization.

Maritime transport costs have a profound influence on international trade. In many cases, their trade-inhibiting effect dwarfs that of customs duties.[1] For instance, the average incidence of transport cost exceeds that of tariffs on imports from the majority of U.S. trading partners (figure 1). More generally, economic research highlights the role of transport costs in determining geographical patterns of trade, production, industrial structure, and income (Venables and Limao 1999). Interesting new work even suggests that transport costs (as an element of trade costs) help explain a variety of puzzles in the field of international macroeconomics, such as the well-known home biases in consumption and investment and the excessive volatility of exchange rates (Obstfeld and Rogoff 2000). These observations are interesting from a policy point of view, however, only if something can be done about these costs. Are transport costs exogenously determined by technological developments or can they be influenced by policy?

Carsten Fink, Aaditya Mattoo, and Ileana Cristina Neagu are with the Development Research Group at the World Bank. Their e-mail addresses are cfink@worldbank.org, amattoo@worldbank.org, and ineagu@worldbank.org, respectively. This article is part of the World Bank's research program on trade in services, which is supported in part by the U.K. Department of International Development. The authors thank Marc Juhel and Alexander Yeats for stimulating discussions and Simon Evenett, Bernard Hoekman, Pierre Latrille, Marcelo Olarreaga, Isidro Soloaga, David Tarr, seminar participants at the World Bank, and two anonymous referees for helpful comments.

1. This has been demonstrated in several studies. See Waters (1970), Finger and Yeats (1976), Sampson and Yeats (1977), Conlon (1982), and Amjadi and Yeats (1995).

FIGURE 1. The Relative Importance of Transport Costs and Tariffs for U.S. Imports, 1998

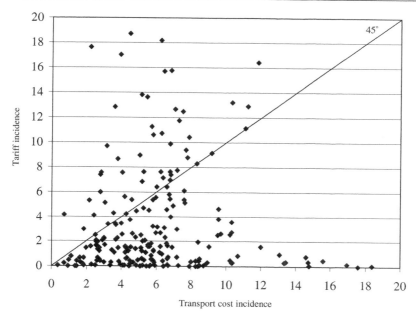

Note: Each dot represents a country. The tariff incidence is calculated as the ratio of actual duties paid over import values. Similarly, the transport cost incidence represents the share of transport charges in import values. Five countries (Benin, Guinea, the Solomon Islands, Togo, and Samoa) exhibit a transport cost incidence greater than 20 percent and are not shown.
Source: U.S. Bureau of the Census.

Some researchers argue that restrictive trade policies keep maritime transport costs high, notably the cargo reservation schemes and monopoly rights granted to providers of port and auxiliary services (Bennathan 1989, Amjadi and Yeats 1995, Francois and others 1996; Hummels 1999). Some also argue that private anticompetitive practices—primarily but not exclusively of the maritime conferences—are responsible for keeping costs high (Francois and Wooton 1999, Hummels 1999). However, most observers also argue that both public and private trade-restrictive policies are becoming less important (White 1988, Franck and Bunel 1991, World Trade Organization [WTO] 1998). Yet the available evidence suggests that transport costs, especially for liner trade, are not falling—despite dramatic improvements in technology, especially in the form of containerization (Hummels 1999).

This article seeks to assess the relative importance of public and private trade-restrictive actions in explaining the price of maritime transport services. To measure these prices, we use newly published data on U.S. waterborne transport from the U.S. Department of Transportation. A major advantage with these data is that they are broken down by type of service—liner, bulk, and tanker. It is more difficult to put together a comprehensive data set on public policies and private practices, a problem that has inhibited meaningful empirical research in this area. The few attempts to measure the restrictive impact of government policies have only limited coverage (McGuire, Schuele, and Smith 2000), and there has not been, as far as we know, an attempt to use existing information on carrier agreements.[2] This article draws on a database, created as part of the World Bank's services project, which contains information on both policy and private rate-fixing arrangements affecting maritime trade with the United States.

These data made it possible to carry out the econometric analysis presented here. Our estimates confirm, first of all, the importance of all the standard determinants of transport prices, ranging from distance to technology. More interesting, we find that both public policy and private practices continue to exercise a significant influence on maritime transport prices. Somewhat surprisingly, private anticompetitive practices seem to have a stronger influence on prices than public restrictions.

What are the implications for policy? The negotiations on maritime transport were the only post–Uruguay Round services negotiations that completely failed. This failure implied an unfortunate loss of political momentum for reform of domestic policies and, less obviously, a lost opportunity to develop procompetitive rules. To some extent, an effort was made to develop rules that would ensure nondiscriminatory access to port services.[3] But these rules, concerned primarily with ensuring market access, did little to protect consumers from the anticompetitive practices of international cartels. An international initiative is needed because these practices cannot be adequately addressed only through national competition policy, given the weak enforcement capacity of small states. A further reason for developing a first-best international response to these practices is to prevent recourse to an inferior national response: recall that the cargo-sharing schemes imposed by many developing countries were primarily a response to the perceived power of conferences. A possible way forward is to strengthen the provision of the General Agreement on Trade in Services (GATS), dealing with anticompetitive business practices to ensure that collusive pricing does not erode the gains from liberalization.

2. Kang (2000) uses the policy indicators developed by McGuire, Schuele, and Smith (2000) to estimate the impact of restrictive maritime policies on bilateral shipping margins, defined as the ratio of cost-insurance-freight import values to free-on-board export values. This approach suffers from well-known data problems (import and export values are not reported by the same statistical entities) and by the undesirable property that shipping margins vary with unit values of shipped goods. The empirical approach adopted here addresses both of these problems.

3. In some respects, the approach to port services, which can be seen as essential facilities often controlled by major or monopoly suppliers, was analogous to the approach to basic telecommunications networks established in the procompetitive regulatory principles.

I. An Overview of International Maritime Transport

Maritime transport services consist of three types of activities: *international maritime transport* (freight and passengers), that is, the actual transportation service performed once the commodity is on board a ship in a country until the moment when the vessel reaches the destination port of a different state;[4] *maritime auxiliary services*, that is, any activities related to cargo manipulation in ports and on ships;[5] and *port services*, that is, activities related solely to ship management in ports.[6] This article uses data pertaining to restrictions affecting each segment of the market.

Due to differences in commodity types as well as to technological improvements in the shipping industry (most importantly, containerization), international maritime freight transport has developed specialized branches. Thus, *liner shipping*—meaning maritime transport of commodities by regular lines that publish in advance their calls in different harbors—is distinct from *tramp shipping*, referring to transport performed irregularly, depending on momentary demand. Typically, liner carriers transport commodities with a higher degree of industrial processing using containers, whereas noncontainerized raw materials (crude and refined oil, iron ore, grain, coal, and bauxite), generically known as bulk, tend to be carried in tramp carriers.[7]

Tramp shipping is generally believed to be a fairly competitive market, mostly free from restrictions (WTO 1998). By contrast, liner shipping has traditionally been subject both to private cartel-like arrangements and government restrictions. This article concentrates on the liner segment of the market.

Cargo Reservation Schemes

Over time, the most important category of barriers applied to international maritime transport has been various cargo reservation schemes. These schemes require that part of the cargo carried in trade with other states must be transported only by ships carrying the national flag or interpreted as national by other criteria. These policies have typically been justified by either security (self-sufficiency in times of war) or economic (infant industry) concerns.

4. International transport as defined by GATS excludes cabotage, which refers to transportation of commodities between ports of the same country.

5. In the GATS classification, maritime auxiliary services include maritime cargo handling, storage and warehousing, customs clearance, container station and depot, maritime agency, and maritime freight forwarding.

6. In the GATS classification, port services include pilotage, towing and tug assistance, provisioning, fueling and watering, garbage collecting and disposal, port captain's services, navigation aids, shore-based operational services, and emergency repair facilities.

7. Bulk traffic is typically divided into two categories: tanker (including crude oil and oil-related products) and dry bulk (including iron ore, grain, coal, bauxite, and phosphates). Note that the distinction between liner and bulk is not watertight. There exists a gray area that includes break-bulk (that is, loose, noncontainerized cargo transported using liners), general cargo (nonbulk commodities transported on liners without using containers), or containerized goods transported by tramp carriers.

Cargo reservation takes various forms. It can be imposed unilaterally, so that ships flying national flags are given the exclusive right to transport a specified share of the cargo passing through the country's ports. An alternative and more common form involves cargo sharing with trade-partner countries on the basis of bilateral or multilateral agreements. A specific form of such a scheme is the U.N. Conference on Trade and Development (UNCTAD) Liner Code of Conduct or the 40-40-20 rule. This legal instrument, which was adopted in 1974 and entered into force in 1983 by its ratification by more than 70 countries, was meant to counteract the anticompetitive actions of liner conferences, which are cartel-like arrangements. In many cases, access of outside shipping companies to a liner conference used to be restricted,[8] so governments applying the Liner Code required these cartels to divide the cargo transported according to the following rule: 40 percent for ships belonging to the exporting country, 40 percent for ships belonging to the importing country, and 20 percent for ships belonging to other countries. These restrictions were intended to encourage the development of the shipping industry of developing countries.

Cargo reservation schemes have declined in significance, as more countries have phased them out formally or chosen not to implement them. For example, in Asia, Indonesia adopted an "open sea" policy in the late 1980s, Thailand abolished all cargo reservations in 1993, and Korea's commitment to phase out its "designated cargo system," made in 1995 on becoming a member of the Organisation for Economic Co-operation and Development (OECD), was fully implemented by 1998. In Africa, Côte d'Ivoire and Senegal are among the countries that have eliminated cargo-sharing schemes. In Latin America, Chile pioneered liberalization in 1979 and Peru phased out most restrictions in the early 1990s. A further indication of the reduced importance of cargo sharing is the spread of "open registries" in many countries and the intensification of the "deflagging" process, that is, the transfer of ships to open registries to enable the ship owners to benefit from more efficient cost conditions (WTO 1998). The UNCTAD Liner Code, which was never applied on a large scale, is even less visible today, being applied mostly on routes between West Africa and Europe.[9]

Nevertheless, the evidence we have obtained on policy suggests that 11 of the countries in our sample, ranging from Benin to India, still have in place reservation policies that at least nominally restrict the scope for trade. Most of these countries subscribed to the UNCTAD Liner Code, whereas others (for example, Brazil, China, and Nigeria) implemented schemes that were similar in spirit.

---

8. The United States banned closed conferences. Cargo sharing and shipping conferences interacted over time, and in many cases authorities tailored their policies by taking into account the presence of carrier agreements. For example, Chile's cargo reservation mechanism, before the liberalization of the past decades, was designed so as to favor access of Chilean shipping companies into conferences and to restrain conference pressures on nonaffiliated carriers (Bennathan 1989).

9. In many countries, national shipping companies that had access to the reserved share, but did not possess sufficient technical means for its transportation, used to sell their preferential right to cargo, a practice that resulted eventually in a higher transport cost.

Nicaragua offers an example of a country that imposes a reciprocity condition, that is, access for foreign ships depends on whether their home countries grant Nicaraguan ships access.

There are few empirical studies of the impact of cargo reservation. The most frequently cited is Bennathan's (1989) analysis of the determinants of freight charges in Chile's export trade with the United States before and after elimination of cargo reservation. The results show that the indicators of cost-based pricing have greater explanatory power after liberalization than the indicators of demand-based pricing. This is seen as evidence of increased competition in the liner shipping industry. In another study, Pálsson (1997) suggests that in the South American market, the abolition of cargo sharing led to a decline in shipping rates to and from Europe by 20–50 percent, and to and from the United States by 25–35 percent. This study also indicates that cargo rates from Europe to Abidjan and Dakar declined by 10–20 percent a year after liberalization in 1995 (Pálsson 1997).[10] None of these studies provide any details on how these estimates were obtained, and to our knowledge there is not any cross-country analysis of the impact of cargo-reservation schemes.

Price Fixing and Other Cooperative Agreements

Maritime carriers enter various types of agreements, which help them enjoy advantages that arise from cooperation on technical or commercial matters. Far from being a recent phenomenon, carriers' collusive habits are deeply rooted in the history of maritime transportation, and the first shipping conferences, covering the routes between the United Kingdom and Calcutta, date back to 1875. By joining carrier agreements, shipping companies retain their juridical independence but consent to common practices with the other members regarding pricing, traffic distribution, and/or vessel capacity utilization. Examples of carrier agreements that were recognized in U.S. regulation by the end of 1998 were conference agreements, cooperative working agreements, joint services agreements, pooling agreements, space charter agreements, and trans-shipment agreements.

Conference agreements are made between two or more ocean common carriers, and provide for the fixing of and adherence to uniform tariff rates and conditions of service.[11] Conferences are the most widespread type of rate-binding agreement. In the United States, conferences are required by law not to restrict the entry and exit of any shipping company. Therefore, shipping conferences in U.S. foreign trade are "open," whereas those covering other routes may be closed

---

10. There are also some studies of the impact of the U.S. Jones Act, which prohibits foreign shipping firms from transporting goods or people from one U.S. location to another. Estimates of the price-increasing effect range from 100 percent (USITC 1991) of the average world price to a high of 300 percent (White 1988). Francois and others (1996) estimate that the welfare costs of this protection (assuming a conservative 100 percent price difference) are at least $3 billion a year.

11. Because conferences are a characteristic of liner shipping, they are also referred to as liner conferences.

to outside carriers.[12] The U.S. Shipping Act of 1984 defines cooperative working agreements as agreements that establish exclusive, preferential, or cooperative working relationships, but that do not fall precisely within the arrangements of any specifically defined agreement. Only some of the carrier agreements have a rate-binding clause, that is, they declare that they engage in unique price setting for transport services provided by all members.

The high incidence of conferences and other types of carrier agreements in maritime transport is due to the fact that the United States, the European Union, and many other countries exempt shipping conferences from antitrust regulation on the ground that they provide price stability and limit uncertainty regarding available tonnage.[13] The exemption from antitrust law is compounded by the Federal Maritime Commission's role in helping police price-fixing arrangements. The 1984 U.S. Shipping Act required all ocean carriers to file their rates with the Federal Maritime Commission and publish their rate and schedule information. Secret discounting on filed rates was considered illegal. Through the imposition of fines, the commission was authorized to ensure that the filed rates were actually charged.[14] However, conferences were required to allow for independent action, meaning that members could post a rate different from the conference rate, provided they notified the conference in advance. Although this provision created some flexibility, there was probably limited incentive to make public preannounced price cuts that were likely to be matched by rivals.

In recent years, the power of conferences has eroded for two reasons. The first is the entrance in the market of strong and efficient outside shipping companies. Containerization and other forms of technological progress have made it possible for outsiders to supply the same services as the conferences at lower costs to consumers. A second development is the change in regulations affecting international shipping, notably the U.S. Ocean Shipping Reform Act of 1998, which amended the Shipping Act of 1984 and went into effect in May 1999. While preserving the antitrust immunity of the rate-setting conference system, the Ocean Shipping Reform Act allows for the confidentiality of key terms (prices are included in this category) in contracts between shippers and carriers. This amendment is bound to create greater scope for price competition.

12. Recently, the European Commission claimed that steps taken by the Trans Atlantic Conference Agreement (TACA) to comply with the "open" conference obligations of U.S. law had constituted an abuse of their dominant position. It was alleged that TACA offered inducements to certain shipping lines to enter trans-Atlantic trade as parties to the conference rather than as independents (Levitt 2000).

13. Francois and Wooton (1999). See also Davies (1986), who states that "generally these cartels have been exempted from domestic legislation on competition, primarily because of jurisdictional problems stemming from the international character of the industry, but also because governments have judged them useful for promoting the health of both international trade and national merchant marines" (p. 300).

14. The rationale for these measures was ostensibly to protect small shippers from being disadvantaged by their inability to extract discounts from shipping companies.

88 THE WORLD BANK ECONOMIC REVIEW, VOL. 16, NO. 1

In response to these developments, two types of arrangements have begun to emerge. First, shipping lines now sometimes enter discussion agreements. These allow conference and nonconference carriers serving a particular trade lane to discuss and share information about rates, costs, capacity, and service. The members may adopt voluntary rate, capacity, and service guidelines. Second, shipping companies and conferences tend to enter more wide-ranging organizations, such as consortia, alliances, and global alliances. There are two interesting questions, only the first of which we address in this article: How much do the traditional conferences still matter? Although these new arrangements are different from conferences from a juridical point of view, how different are they in actual behavior?

Some recent events provide implicit evidence of the continued influence of collusive practices. Although price fixing by conferences is exempted from the scope of competition law, the abuse of a conference's dominant position and the extension of collusion to other areas have provoked the wrath of European competition authorities. In 1992, the European Commission imposed fines against the members of the French/West African Ship Owners Conference.[15] The commission found that the conference had deterred the entry of other operators by a combination of loyalty agreements with shippers and predatory pricing against nonconference lines. Furthermore, competition between lines belonging to different conferences had been prevented by a partitioning of shipping routes: members of one conference were prohibited from operating in the ports served by another conference unless they first obtained membership, through a long, uncertain procedure, of that second conference.

In 1998, the European Commission fined the Trans Atlantic Conference Agreement (TACA) a sum of $314 million. The European Commission concluded that the conference, which controlled more than 60 percent of the traffic crossing the Atlantic at the time, set prices not only for the ocean leg but also for inland transportation by truck or train as well.[16] In May 2000, the European Commission imposed a penalty on 15 liner shipping companies that were members of the Far East Trade Tariff Charges and Surcharges Agreement (FETTCSA)—an agreement abandoned in 1994 following action by the European Commission. Altogether, the companies controlled 80 percent of the traffic between northern Europe and the Far East. Again, the target of action was not price fixing per se, but the FETTCSA members' collective strategy of not offering discounts from published fares.[17] Finally, reports in the maritime press also suggest that despite an

---

15. See p. 13 of the Annex of the Communication from the European Community and its Member States to the WTO Working Group on the Interaction between Trade and Competition Policy, WT/WGTCP/W/140, June 8, 2000.

16. As reported by CNN, the event marked a new record for fines imposed by the European Commission on a cartel. This was the first time that any EU authority had assessed the compatibility of liner conference practices with EU competition law.

17. See "FETTCSA: Commission fines shipping lines for an illegal price agreement on the Europe / Far East trade" (DN: IP/00/486), available from the European Commission's Web page.

increase in entry, the limited reductions in transport costs are attributable to the legal privileges granted to shipping company agreements.[18]

Notwithstanding this evidence, the issue of whether liner conferences were in a position to exercise market power has provoked some debate, primarily over the question of whether liner shipping markets are contestable. One view is that liner shipping markets satisfy a list of a priori conditions of contestability (Davies 1986, Zerby 1988). The entrant and the incumbent lines have access to the same technology and, provided that the market is not affected by any other distortions (such as cargo reservation), all shipping lines are equally placed with respect to access to cargo. Ship mobility and an active secondhand market imply that no significant sunk costs arise in the industry. Furthermore, the incumbent shipping lines are likely to provide a slow price response to the new entrants, especially if the former are organized in conferences, where price decisions require consensus among members. The frequent entry and exit on certain maritime routes has been cited as evidence of the contestability of these markets (Davies 1986).

An alternative view questions each of these assertions (Pearson 1987, Jankowski 1989). First, it argues that building up goodwill represents a substantial sunk cost, and lines cannot enter and exit markets with complete disregard of the effect this has on their reputation. Advertising and agency costs expended to establish regular liner services are also examples of intangible sunk costs.[19] Second, there is evidence that conferences have developed quick price-response mechanisms to respond to entry, including the use of action committees vested with the power to match the rates offered by an outsider. These arguments are in line with the findings of the European Commission cited previously. Finally, the frequency of entry and exit is clearly not convincing evidence of contestability: after all, at least in equilibrium, a contestable market would witness no entry at all.

As far as we know, there has been only one attempt to examine econometrically the influence of conferences. Clyde and Reitzes (1995) find no statistically significant relationship between freight rates and the market share of conferences serving a route. However, they find that the level of freight rates is significantly lower on routes where conference members are free to negotiate service contracts directly with shippers. On this basis, they conclude that the evidence on whether liner conferences are effective cartels is at best mixed. They suggest that there is an alternative interpretation of their results: the industry's antitrust immunity and tariff filing and enforcement requirements potentially facilitate the ability

---

18. See, for example, "Obstacles Lie Ahead," *1999 Year-end Economic Review, Bangkok Post*, 1999.

19. Franck and Bunel (1991) suggest that it may be appropriate to distinguish between two market segments in liner shipping by the type of entry criterion. In the first, entry is easy and competition from occasional outsiders is strong because they adopt a hit-and-run strategy and are not concerned with staying in business. In the second, an outsider is interested in competing on a long-term basis with the conferences and providing as high-quality services as them, so it is more difficult to comply with the entry conditions.

of all carriers to collude, not just those carriers that are conference members. Furthermore, in seeking to determine the influence of the market share of conferences, they consider only the routes on which conferences exist. They do not test a more basic hypothesis that the critical effect is of the existence of a conference on a particular route rather than its precise share of the market.

Restrictions on Port and Auxiliary Services

Both port and auxiliary services, particularly cargo handling, have tended to be monopolized. Liberalization of these services has two aspects. One is to ensure that foreign ships serving the domestic market obtain nondiscriminatory access to such services. The second is to allow competition, domestic and foreign, in the supply of the service itself.

Seaports are typically coordinated by public or, in fewer cases, private organizations called port authorities. Depending on the role assumed by these institutions, seaports can be classified into different categories. With *landlord ports*, the port authority owns and manages port infrastructure and private firms provide the rest of port and maritime auxiliary services; private firms are able to own superstructure and operate assets pertaining to infrastructure by concession or licensing. With *tool ports*, the port authority owns both infrastructure and superstructure, but private firms provide services by renting port assets through concessions or licenses (for example, Antwerp, Belgium). Finally, with *service ports*, the port authority owns assets and supplies services by directly hiring employees.

Trujillo and Nombela (1999) argue that the landlord port is the most desirable category from the efficiency point of view, since it allows private enterprise and market forces to play a role in the supply of services, while preventing monopolization of essential assets by private firms. For instance, in the case of Puerto Nuevo in Buenos Aires, six terminals were competitively commissioned to the private sector, with substantial foreign participation in the case of three.[20] The government also established free entry in the sector by allowing any operator to build, manage and operate a port for public or private use. These reforms transformed Argentine ports from the most expensive in Latin America to among the cheapest. Average charges per container declined from $450 to $120 and container time at port declined from 2.5 to 1.3 days (Trujillo and Estache 2001). Chile also witnessed a significant improvement in port performance after the competitive allocation of the right to operate ports, with five major world operators participating in the bidding consortia (Foxley and Mardones 2000).[21]

20. Terminals 1 and 2 were originally awarded to an international consortia headed by P&O Australia in partnership with Fasce SA, a local stevedore company (Trujillo and Estache 2001). Terminal 5 was awarded to an international consortium headed by the Manila-based international operator International Container Terminal Services, Inc.

21. Hutchinson, P&O, Stevedoring Services of America, HHLA and ICTSI. In fact, World Bank (2000) reports that the top nine international terminal operators account for 40 percent of the world's container liftings.

This anecdotal evidence indicates that international participation in the provision of terminal services is now a reality and that the introduction of competition can make a substantial difference in performance. With this broad benchmark in mind, we seek to capture some of the restrictions in place on port and auxiliary services.

II. THE MODEL

In this section, we develop an econometric model of liner transport prices for U.S. imports. The analysis focuses on the ocean leg of the journey because the data available do not directly capture the price of maritime auxiliary services and port services.[22] Nevertheless, the analysis includes policy restrictions affecting the latter type of services. This is because the restrictions are likely to have an adverse effect on the efficiency with which these services are supplied to liners and hence push up the costs of liner services—for example, because of longer waiting or unloading times.[23]

We do not formally derive our estimation equation from a fully specified structural model of competition or collusion among liner companies, but our approach can be best understood in terms of a simple constant-elasticity pricing formula. This pricing rule relates the U.S. dollar price of shipping product k from foreign port i (which is located in country I) to U.S. port j (which is located in U.S. customs district J), P_{ijk}, to the marginal cost for this service, $MC(i, j, k)$, and a markup term, $\Phi(I, J, k)$:

$$(1) \qquad\qquad P_{ijk} = \Phi(I, J, k)\, MC(i, j, k).$$

The markup term is a function of the elasticity of demand perceived by liner companies serving the routes between country I and customs district J for product k. The pricing formula in equation (1) could, for example, be easily derived from a model of Cournot competition.

Taking natural logs of equation (1) yields

$$(2) \qquad\qquad p_{ijk} = \phi(I, J, k)\, mc(i, j, k),$$

where lowercase letters refer to natural logs of the respective variables.

Unfortunately, we do not have any direct information on the costs of maritime transport operations. We therefore decompose the *marginal cost term, $mc(i, j, k)$,* as follows:

$$(3) \qquad mc_{ijk} = \alpha_J + \lambda_k + \gamma T_{ijk} + \delta d_{iJ} + \eta q_{iJ} + \rho CR_I + \varphi^1 PS^1{}_I + \varphi^2 PS^2{}_I.$$

---

22. More precisely, the data reflect transport charges incurred in bringing the merchandise from alongside the carrier at the port of export and placing it alongside the carrier at the first U.S. port of entry.

23. The possibility of measurement error provides a more mundane reason for considering the impact of restrictions on the port and auxiliary services. Although in principle the liner transport prices do not include the prices of these services, in practice such a clean truncation may not have been possible.

The first term, α_J, reflects an effect specific to each U.S. customs district. It captures differences across customs districts in port services and other auxiliary services, such as cargo handling, and has been included for the reasons noted above. The second variable, λ_k, is a product-specific effect that captures differences in the physical properties of shipped goods, such as weight or size.

The third effect is a technological effect represented by the share of goods shipped in containers, T_{ijk}. Since containerization is likely to reduce the marginal cost of liner services, we expect the coefficient γ to have a negative sign.[24] The fourth cost variable is (the natural log of) the shipping distance between foreign port i and the main port in customs district J, d_{iJ}. There is some evidence that the effect of shipping distance on transport cost becomes less important for longer distances (Hummels 1999), and so we expect $0 < \delta < 1$. Fifth, we include an economies-of-scale effect represented by (the natural logarithm of) the total value of U.S. imports carried by liners (including nontextile goods) between foreign port i and district J, q_{iJ}. If there are economies of scale with regard to traffic originating from the same port, we expect the coefficient η to be negative.

Finally, we add three policy indicators that capture restrictions maintained by I's government affecting the supply of maritime services by foreigners. These restrictions are expected to lead to inefficiencies and the employment of outdated technology. Specifically, CR_I is a dummy that indicates whether exporting countries maintain any form of cargo reservation policy for the domestic shipping fleet affecting trade with the United States. PS^1_I is an index that captures the existence of barriers to the foreign supply of cargo-handling services, considered to be one of the most important auxiliary services. PS^2_I is an index that measures the number of port services (for example, pilotage, towing, navigation aids, and waste disposal) that are mandatory for incoming ships. In the absence of more direct data on the openness of the port services regime, the extent to which the use of such services is mandatory is used as an indicator of the restrictiveness of the port services regime. As noted above, the costs of auxiliary and port services are not directly captured by the maritime price data, but restrictions in both are relevant because they could push up the costs of liner services.

The *markup term*, $\phi(I, J, k)$, is assumed to depend on the following four variables:

$$(4) \qquad \phi(I, J, k) = \mu_k + \tau CR_I + \psi^1\, A^1{}_{IJ} + \psi^2\, A^2{}_{IJ}.$$

The first term, μ_k, reflects a product-specific effect that captures differences in transport demand elasticities across sectors. Note that the transport demand elasticities are derived from the final demand for product k in the United States. The second variable is again the variable that captures the existence of cargo reservation policies, which directly limit the extent of competition from foreign liners and thus may push up markups. The third and fourth effects, $A^1{}_{IJ}$ and $A^2{}_{IJ}$,

---

24. Over 80 percent of U.S. imports are containerized. Noncontainerized shipments are because certain foreign ports, mostly in the developing world, are not yet equipped with container terminals.

are due to the existence of collusive agreements among liner companies on routes between country I and customs district J. We distinguish between two kinds of collusive agreements: price-fixing agreements (which include most conferences) and cooperative working agreements that do not have a binding rate-setting authority. A single agreement typically covers routes between the ports of a foreign country and one or more U.S. coastal districts that each consists of several customs districts. Because collusion between liner companies is likely to push up markups, we expect both coefficients ψ^1 and ψ^2 to show a positive sign. But conference and other price-fixing agreements are likely to be more powerful and to have a greater impact on transport prices than cooperative working agreements, that is, we expect $\psi^1 > \psi^2$.

Substituting equations (4) and (3) into equation (2) and inserting an error term, ε_{ijk}, we obtain

$$(5) \qquad \begin{aligned} p_{ijk} = {} & \alpha_J + \beta_k + \gamma T_{ijk} + \delta d_{iJ} + \eta q_{iJ} + \psi^1 A^1{}_{IJ} + \psi^2 A^2{}_{IJ} \\ & + \omega\, CR_I + \varphi^1\, PS^1_I + \varphi^2\, PS^2_I + \varepsilon_{ijk}, \end{aligned}$$

where $\beta_k \equiv (\lambda_k + \mu_k)$, $\omega \equiv (\rho + \tau)$, and we expect the coefficients on the three policy indicators, ω, φ^1, and φ^2, to have a positive sign.[25]

We calculate the transport price, p_{ijk}, as the share of liner transport charges in import values for good k (at the six-digit HS aggregation) multiplied by the unit value of imports. The U.S. Department of Transportation defines transport charges as all freight, insurance, and other charges (excluding import duties) incurred in bringing the merchandise from alongside the carrier at the port of export and placing it alongside the carrier at the first U.S. port of entry.[26] However, actual data reported may include charges for port services and inland transportation.[27] To reduce the potential bias resulting from differences in inland transportation costs, we exclude observations for which the origin of the import is different from the country of the port of shipment (for example, landlocked countries) as well as all in-transit shipments.[28] The appendix provides additional information on the construction and sources of all variables.

Table 1 presents an overview of our estimation data set. It covers all U.S. imports carried by liners from the 59 countries for which we could find information on maritime policies. Data refer to 1998. Liner imports account for around 65 percent of the total value of maritime imports, the remaining 35 per-

---

25. Because we estimate both product fixed effects and customs district–specific effects, we need to drop one dummy variable (for one customs district) to avoid perfect colinearity among the explanatory variables.

26. If insurance costs are not closely correlated with transport charges, there is the possibility that our transport price variable is distorted. However, this should at least partially be remedied by the inclusion of product fixed effects, because differences in insurance costs are likely to be greatest across products.

27. According to e-mail communication with an official from the U.S. Department of Transportation.

28. Note that we do not exclude the trade originating in third countries and in-transit traffic when calculating total import values q_{iJ}.

TABLE 1. Overview of U.S. Imports Carried by Liners in 1998

Countries	Number of countries	Liner transport charges (million $)	Liner import charges (million $)	Share of liner maritime imports (%)		Share of liner imports in total imports (%)	
				Total	Non-oil[a]	Total	Non-oil[a]
Developing	37	3,940	82,400	64.88	74.82	48.76	53.10
Industrial	22	3,080	104,500	64.20	66.24	50.73	51.23
Total	59	7,020	186,900	64.71	70.04	50.13	52.38

[a]Excluding HS category 27.
Source: U.S. Department of Transportation and U.S. Bureau of Census.

cent being carried by tramp services.[29] About half of all U.S. imports (including all modes of transport—maritime, air and road) from the 59 countries considered are carried by liners.

III. THE ESTIMATES

We begin with ordinary least squares estimation of equation (5) over the entire dataset. The error term ε_{ijk} is assumed to be independently distributed across exporting countries, but we allow for interdependence among observations within each country.[30] The results are presented in table 2.

Although the coefficients mostly accord with our expectations, this empirical approach has a weakness: it ignores competition from alternative modes of transportation, expressly tramp maritime services (bulk and tanker), air transport, and road transport (in the case of Canada and Mexico). For a number of product categories, it is likely that shippers face an explicit tradeoff between the quality and cost of shipping a good by these alternative modes of transport. One approach to remedying this problem is to exclude all products for which competition from tramp maritime and air services is important. Since it is difficult to make a clean separation based on product characteristics alone, we adopt a method relying on the revealed importance of the alternative modes. Specifically, we exclude all observations where either the share of air transport as a percentage of total imports for shipping product k from country I to customs district J is positive, or the share of tramp services for a particular product k on all routes between country I and district J exceeds 15 percent.

29. However, if we exclude U.S. oil imports (HS category 27), this share rises to 70 percent and liner transport becomes relatively more important for developing countries.

30. Instead of using a fixed-effect specification as in equation (5), we also estimated a model with random product effects and maintaining the customs district fixed effects. This model yielded very similar estimation results. Moreover, the Hausman test rejected the null hypothesis that the individual effects are uncorrelated with our regressors in the model, supporting the use of fixed instead of random product effects.

TABLE 2. Full-Sample Fixed-Effects Model

Variable	Estimate	
Distance	0.298**	(4.97)
Containerization	−0.071**	(−2.80)
Total liner imports	−0.017*	(−2.07)
Price-fixing agreements	0.488**	(5.52)
Cooperative agreements	0.050	(1.21)
Cargo reservation	−0.067	(−0.77)
Cargo-handling services	−0.203*	(−2.44)
Mandatory port services	0.357**	(2.52)
Number of products	4,356	
Number of observations	250,237	
F-statistic	65.11**	
Adjusted R^2	0.775	

*Significant at the 5 percent level.
**Significant at the 1 percent level.
Note: The dependent variable (liner transport prices), distance, and total liner imports are expressed in natural logs; all other variables are expressed in actual levels; fixed effects are product-specific and U.S. customs district–specific (see text). The regression assumes an independently distributed error term across exporting countries, but allows for interdependence among observations within each country. t-statistics are in parentheses. The F-statistic tests the joint significance of all independent variables (except the fixed effects).
Source: Authors' calculations.

This reduces our sample size from 250,237 to 98,997 observations. The estimation results with the reduced sample are presented in the first column of table 3.

Although these results are in line with our expectations, it is possible that the exclusion of observations introduces a sample bias in our estimation. We therefore adopt a sample selection model, where we estimate the likelihood of a shipment having no competition from air and tramp services (as defined above) in two separate probit equations. The explanatory variables in these probit equations are (the natural logs of) the unit value and the unit weight of shipments and, in the case of air transport, a dummy variable that captures the existence of an open-skies agreement between country I and the United States.[31] We estimate

31. Because the unit weight is unavailable for selected shipments, the number of observations in the probit regression is somewhat smaller than in the full sample. In the case of tramp services, we also included country fixed effects, except for Benin, for which the share of tramp services was below 15 percent for all observations. As in the liner pricing regression, we assumed that the error term in each probit equation is independently distributed across exporting countries, but allowed for interdependence among observations within each country.

this model using the Heckman two-step estimation procedure, assuming that the error terms in the two probit regressions are uncorrelated.[32]

The results of the sample selection model are presented in the second to fourth columns of table 3. In the "air" probit equation, the estimated coefficient on unit value is significantly negative and the coefficient on unit weight is significantly positive, suggesting that valuable and light products are more likely to be sent by air. By contrast, in the "tramp" probit equation, the coefficient on unit value is significantly positive and the coefficient on unit weight is significantly negative, indicating that tramp services are primarily used for heavy commodities with low unit values.[33]

In the final regression, we exclude Mexican and Canadian imports from our (already reduced) sample. For these two countries, road transport is an alternative mode of transport that may compete with maritime and air services. Table 4 presents the estimation results with both the simple reduced sample and the sample selection approach, which are similar to those presented in table 3.

Estimates of the Model Coefficients

The results from the different estimating methods reveal a reassuring consistency. The estimated coefficient on distance lies between 0.2 and 0.3 and is always significantly different from both zero and one. This confirms that transport cost increases with distance but less than proportionately. As we expected, containerization, as measured by T_{ijk}, works to reduce liner prices, the estimated coefficient being statistically significant. The coefficient on the total value of U.S. imports carried by liners, q_{ij}, takes a small and significant negative value. This suggests that there are economies of scale with regard to traffic originating from the same port, and that small countries or economies with small trading volumes may be relatively disadvantaged.

Consider now the impact of restrictions on trade in maritime services. The most striking finding is the strong positive impact on liner prices of the existence of rate-binding conference and other price-fixing agreements. The existence of cooperative working agreements has a weaker impact that is not always statistically significant. These results confirm our expectation that price-fixing agreements matter and are more important than cooperative working agreements.[34]

---

32. See Maddala (1983, p. 282) for a description of this model. The assumption that the error terms in the two probit regressions are uncorrelated seems reasonable: decisions on whether to ship goods by air or by vessel are likely to be independent of decisions on the mode of maritime transport.

33. Interestingly, the explanatory power is higher in the air probit regression than the tramp probit regression.

34. It is possible, in principle, that the formation of collusive carrier agreements is an endogenous variable—that collusion is more likely on more profitable routes. To account for this possibility, we estimated a treatment-effects model that corrects for the possible selectivity bias of the dummy variable on price-fixing carrier agreements (see Greene 1997, pp. 981–82, and Maddala 1983, p. 6). Similar to the sample selection model, we used the Heckman two-step estimation procedure that first estimates a probit model of the selection process and then the regression model with an additional selectivity correction variable. Our explanatory variables in the probit model were exporter GDP, unit weight, unit

The evidence on policy restrictions is mixed. The coefficient of the variable capturing the existence of cargo reservation policies is close to zero and not statistically significant in any of the regressions. This result gives credence to the claim that cargo reservation policies no longer exert an important influence on liner trade. The estimated coefficient on the restrictiveness index of cargo-handling services is the only one that has a counterintuitive sign and is statistically significant in the first set of estimates (table 2), but with other, arguably more reliable methods (tables 3 and 4), it ceases to be significant. Recall that our dependent variable captures the cost of complementary services not explicitly but only to the extent that they feed through into the ocean-leg liner prices. In this respect, the index on the restrictiveness of port policy probably has a stronger claim to significance. Our estimates would seem to confirm this—the coefficient is consistently positive and statistically significant. This result also seems in line with current wisdom that the biggest policy hurdles to competitive provision of shipping services are to be found at the ports rather than in the ocean leg.[35] However, it must be kept in mind that we are only using an indirect measure of port policy restrictiveness.

Estimates of the Consequences of Policy Changes

The estimated model can be used to calculate hypothetical reductions in transport prices due to both the breakup of private carrier agreements and allowing greater competition in the provision of port services. For this purpose, we take the estimated coefficients from the sample selection model in table 3, which we consider to be the most reliable estimates both from an economic and econometric standpoint. Table 5 presents the simulated price reductions. The breakup of conference and other price-setting agreements would lead to a more dramatic reduction in transport prices (32 percent) than the breakup of cooperative working agreements (18 percent), whereas the liberalization of port services would cause a 35 percent drop in the price of liner services.[36]

If we compute the trade-weighted percentage reductions in transport prices across all observations included in the sample selection model, the average total

---

value, and total liner traffic between the exporting country and the importing coast district. Only exporter gdp made a positive and significant contribution to the likelihood of observing price-fixing agreements. The selectivity correction parameter, however, had a negative sign in the main regression and, accordingly, inflated the coefficient on the price-fixing dummy variable. This result would suggest that rate-binding carrier agreements typically occur on routes with lower prices. This counterintuitive finding may be due to the inadequacies of our explanatory variables in the probit equation. Alternatively, the formation of liner agreements may be less an outcome of market forces and more the result of historical and institutional forces, which are exogenously determined.

35. Of course, savings from the liberalization of port services are likely to be greater when their full impact on aggregate maritime transport costs is taken into account.

36. The policy simulation makes the simplifying assumption that the mandatory use of certain port services, such as pilotage, cannot be justified by safety or related concerns. This assumption does not seem unreasonable, given that safety standards can also be enforced in more liberal policy environments.

TABLE 3. Reduced-Sample and Sample Selection Models

Variable	Reduced-sample model	Sample selection model		
		Air probit	Tramp probit	Liner transport prices
Distance	0.202** (4.58)			0.228** (5.27)
Containerization	-0.132** (-3.89)			-0.116** (-3.00)
Total liner imports	-0.018* (-2.39)			-0.025** (-3.40)
Price-fixing agreements	0.443** (5.78)			0.379** (5.01)
Cooperative agreements	0.132* (2.64)			0.202* (2.53)
Cargo reservation	-1.106 (-1.13)			-0.099 (-1.01)
Cargo-handling services	-0.104 (-1.14)			-0.064 (-0.56)
Mandatory port services	0.307** (2.26)			0.437** (2.83)
Unit value		-0.385** (-18.44)	0.130** (13.12)	
Unit weight		0.448** (17.49)	-0.131** (-11.52)	
Open skies agreement		0.007 (0.07)		
Sample selection correction (air)				0.399** (3.19)
Sample selection correction (tramp)				-0.733* (-2.37)
Number of products	4,214			4,208
Number of observations	98,997	250,159	250,159	98,815
F-statistic	39.43**			42.51**
Adjusted R^2	0.779			0.783
Pseudo R^2		0.130	0.054	

*Significant at the 5 percent level.
**Significant at the 1 percent level.

Note: The dependent variable (liner transport prices), distance, total liner imports, unit value, and unit weight are expressed in natural logs; all other variables are expressed in actual levels; fixed effects are product-specific and U.S. customs district-specific (see text). All regressions assume an independently distributed error term across exporting countries but allow for interdependence among observations within each country. The sample selection correction variables are computed following Heckman's two-step estimation procedure. t-statistics (for liner price regressions) and z-statistics (for probit regressions) are in parentheses. The F-statistic tests the joint significance of all independent variables (except the fixed effects).

Source: Authors' calculations.

TABLE 4. Reduced-Sample and Sample Selection Models without Mexico and Canada

Variable	Reduced-sample model	Sample selection model		
		Air probit	Tramp probit	Liner transport prices
Distance	0.221** (4.12)			0.215** (4.79)
Containerization	-0.147** (-4.49)			-0.142** (-4.13)
Total liner imports	-0.017* (-2.19)			-0.024** (-3.30)
Price-fixing agreements	0.464** (5.65)			0.372** (4.60)
Cooperative agreements	0.124* (2.58)			0.192* (2.46)
Cargo reservation	-0.092 (-0.95)			-0.089 (-0.88)
Cargo-handling services	-0.107 (-1.17)			-0.068 (-0.59)
Mandatory port services	0.298** (2.24)			0.410** (2.69)
Unit value		-0.402** (-27.28)	0.131** (12.84)	
Unit weight		0.469** (27.56)	-0.132** (-11.30)	
Open skies agreement		0.021 (0.22)		
Sample selection correction (air)				0.465** (3.94)
Sample selection correction (tramp)				-0.694* (-2.26)
Number of products	4,190			4,184
Number of observations	97,676	247,673	247,673	97,518
F-statistic	36.74**			50.83**
Adjusted R^2	0.781			0.784
Pseudo R^2		0.136	0.054	

*Significant at the 5 percent level.

**Significant at the 1 percent level.

Note: The dependent variable (liner transport prices), distance, total liner imports, unit value, and unit weight are expressed in natural logs; all other variables are expressed in actual levels; fixed effects are product-specific and U.S. customs district-specific (see text). All regressions assume an independently distributed error term across exporting countries but allow for interdependence among observations within each country. The sample selection correction variables are computed following Heckman's two-step estimation procedure. t-statistics (for liner price regressions) and z-statistics (for probit regressions) are in parentheses. The F-statistic tests the joint significance of all independent variables (except the fixed effects).

Source: Authors' calculations.

TABLE 5. Simulated Reductions in Transport Prices

Simulation	Breakup of cooperative working agreements	Breakup of price-fixing agreements	Cumulative effect of the breakup of private carrier agreements	Liberalization of port services	Cumulative total effect
1. Percentage reductions on restricted routes	18.30	31.56	44.09	35.43	63.90
2. Trade-weighted percentage reductions across all observations in our dataset	7.11	18.71	24.25	8.66	30.76
3. Total savings across all observations in our dataset:					
Absolute value(in million $)	140	371	484	201	637
As a percent of total transport charges[a]	5.59	14.80	19.42	7.99	25.59
4. Projected total savings across all exporting countries and all sectors (in million $)[b]	575.1	1,522.6	1,997.9	822.0	2,632.7

Note: These calculations are based on the estimated coefficients of the sample selection model in table 3. Given the functional form of the regression equation, the individual effects do not sum to the total effect.

[a]The share of total savings in total transport charges is equivalent to the unweighted average percentage reductions in transport prices.

[b]The projected total savings in the last row apply the percentage savings in total transport charges estimated for the reduced sample to total liner transport charges for all U.S. imports.

Source: Authors' calculations.

100

reduction would be 30.8 percent—made up of the cumulative effects of the breakup of carrier agreements (24 percent) and the liberalization of port services (9 percent). Total savings would sum to $637 million of transport charges. To get a sense of the overall magnitudes involved, we can project these savings to total U.S. imports carried by liners across all sectors and all routes. Our simulations reveal that the removal of public restrictions to liner trade would lead to savings of up to $822 million and the breakup of private cartels would bring about additional savings of up to $2 billion.

There are two important qualifications to these estimates. First, the pattern of restrictions in our limited sample may not be representative of the pattern of restrictions in trade of all products across all routes. Second, competition from other modes of transport for some products may limit the ability of carrier agreements to fix prices. But note that our simulation pertains to the savings arising from goods carried to the United States alone. The imports of the United States are only about a fifth of total world merchandise imports. So global gains from the elimination of all forms of restriction are likely to be substantially larger, particularly if we take into account the indirect benefits from reducing impediments to trade.

IV. Conclusion

Our estimates confirm the general belief that cargo reservation policies, which proliferated in the 1970s and 1980s, are no longer an important barrier to trade. However, it emerged that both public policy, specifically in the form of restrictions on the provision of port services, and private practices continue to exercise a significant influence on maritime transport prices. Interestingly, private anticompetitive practices have a stronger influence on prices than public restrictions do.

These results challenge the notion that collusive carrier arrangements have lost their significance over the past decade. In defense, maritime industry sources frequently point to the fact that liner operators hardly break even and, on this basis, argue that there is little scope for price reductions. But it is well known that protection and cartel-like behavior in the presence of fixed costs can lead to inefficient entry and reduced profitability. The benefits of competition typically arise not only from increased allocative efficiency—that is, pricing close to costs—but also from increased internal efficiency—that is, a reduction in costs. There may be scope for increasing this latter type of efficiency in the maritime industry.

Our results need to be qualified. First, we focused only on routes leading to the United States. Although there is need for further research on other routes, the paucity of transport data in other countries is a major constraint. Second, the analysis herein has focused solely on the maritime leg of the transport journey and has not examined distortions on the inland section. Evidence suggests that the ocean leg accounts for a little more than a third of total door-to-door shipping charges (OECD 1968, Livingston 1986). Unfortunately, there are no comprehensive data on such charges. An ambitious future research program would seek to disaggregate the components of door-to-door shipping charges and subject them to an analysis similar to that carried out in here. A critical component of such a program would be to develop better measures of the restrictiveness of port and auxiliary services than have been used here.

Notwithstanding these qualifications, this article has certain implications for policy. The elimination of policy restrictions to trade in maritime transport services is likely to produce substantial gains. Many of these restrictions can be removed unilaterally, and the GATS can be used to bind the openness to reduce uncertainty and the possibility of policy reversals. But it is not enough to eliminate policy restrictions. There is also a need to deal with the private anticompetitive practices of international maritime cartels. Large states can probably tackle such practices unilaterally through their own competition laws, despite the extra-territoriality problems involved. But small states with limited enforcement capacity are at a disadvantage; the problem is accentuated by the fact that major trading countries have diluted the application of competition disciplines to the maritime sector. One positive development described earlier is the elimination by the United States of some of the provisions in its shipping law that helped police price-fixing arrangements. Whether collusion can be sustained in the absence of such facilitating devices is open to question. But we would argue that there is cause for concern as long as the basic rate-setting conference system continues to enjoy antitrust immunity.

An international initiative would seem desirable. One approach would be to deal with the problem by creating sector-specific competition rules, as in the case of basic telecommunications. Or, if such anticompetitive practices also affect other services sectors, there may be a need to strengthen the general GATS disciplines. Currently, Article IX of the GATS (which deals with private anticompetitive practices) has little substance, providing only for an exchange of information and consultations. The current round of services negotiations offers an opportunity to strengthen this provision.

What form could such a strengthening take? We believe that the harmonization of either sector-specific or general competition rules is probably neither feasible nor necessary. Our proposal is much simpler and would involve the creation of two obligations. The first would end the exemption of collusive agreements in the maritime sector from national competition law. The second would create the right of foreign consumers to challenge anticompetitive practices by shipping lines in the national courts of countries whose citizens own or control these shipping lines. The second obligation is necessary to deal with a possible failure to enforce and already has a precedent in the WTO rules on intellectual property and government procurement.[37]

Would it be feasible to create such rules? History does not provide cause for optimism. The procompetitive rules in basic telecommunications, in line with

---

37. See Mattoo and Subramanian (1997) for an elaboration of this argument.

most WTO rules, were designed to protect the market access rights of foreign suppliers, and conventional political-economy forces supported their creation. To establish rules that enable small countries to protect their consumers from foreign oligopolies will be far more difficult. In fact, the negotiating history of the GATS reveals successful opposition to the strengthening of Article IX from some of the countries that exempt maritime conferences from the scope of their antitrust laws. However, the reluctance of many developing countries to make liberalization commitments under the GATS did not strengthen their case. One strategy in the current round of services negotiations would be for a coalition of developing countries to put forward an offer of substantial liberalization conditional on the strengthening of Article IX. By targeting the twin maladies of maritime trade, such a strategy, if successful, would provide substantial global benefits.

APPENDIX: DATA

Data on liner transport charges, import values, the percentage of containerized cargo, total imports carried by liners and the market share of tramp services are from the Waterborne Trade Database compiled by the U.S. Department of Transportation. The containerization variable is measured in terms of the weight of goods shipped. Tramp services are defined as bulk and tanker services. Unit values, unit weights, and the market share of air services are computed from the U.S. Merchandise Imports Database published by the U.S. Department of Commerce. This source does not publish data separately by foreign and U.S. ports; we therefore have to use these variables at the more aggregate level, that is, U.S. trading partners and U.S. customs districts.

Shipping distances were kindly provided from a private service called BP Marine. Some missing ports that are included in the Waterborne Transport Database had to be approximated by the closest neighboring port. Information on private carrier agreements between U.S. coastal districts and individual countries comes from the Federal Maritime Commission (1998). We excluded agreements signed before 1970 and also those with an unspecified regional coverage (for example, the Far East), because the *de facto* coverage of such agreements may only relate to a few particular routes. The potential bias introduced by this exercise is likely to be small because most routes covered by such regional agreements are also covered by country-specific agreements. As mentioned in the text, we construct two dummy variables to account for the presence of carrier agreements on maritime routes. The first refers to conferences and other price-fixing agreements and the second captures cooperative working agreements that do not have a binding rate authority. Data on the existence of open-skies agreements were taken from the Web site of the U.S. Department of Transportation.

The three indicators of trade restrictions are constructed based on information compiled from the following sources: WTO (1994), various WTO Trade Policy Reviews, GATS schedules of commitments (available online at http://gats-info.eu.int/index.html), APEC Individual Action Plan submissions (available

106   THE WORLD BANK ECONOMIC REVIEW, VOL. 16, NO. 1

TABLE A-1. (continued)

Country	Cargo reservation	Cargo-handling services	Mandatory port services	Price-fixing carrier agreements	Cooperative working agreements
Spain	0	0	0.06	1.00	0.00
Sweden	0	0	0.06	1.00	0.00
Taiwan	0	0.5	0.00	0.00	0.00
Thailand	0	0.5	0.63	0.00	0.38
Togo	1	0	0.00	0.00	0.00
Tunisia	0	0.5	0.13	0.00	0.00
Turkey	0	0	0.00	0.43	0.00
United Kingdom	0	0	0.31	1.00	0.00
Uruguay	0	0	0.00	0.00	1.00
Venezuela	1	0	0.00	1.00	1.00
Vietnam	0	0	0.00	0.00	0.50

Note: The indicators on "price-fixing carrier agreements" and "cooperative working agreements" show the average value of the 0-1 dummy variable used in the estimation. This value lies between 0 and 1 if not all U.S. coastal districts are covered by the agreements affecting a particular country.
Source: Authors' calculations.

REFERENCES

Amjadi, Azita, and Alexander Yeats. 1995. "Have Transport Costs Contributed to the Relative Decline of Sub-Saharan African Exports? " Policy Research Working Paper No. 1559, World Bank, Washington, D.C.

Bennathan, Ezra. 1989. "Deregulation of Shipping: What Is to Be Learned from Chile?" World Bank Discussion Papers No. 67, World Bank, Washington, D.C.

Clyde, Paul S., and James D. Reitzes. 1995. "The Effectiveness of Collusion under Antitrust Immunity, the Case of Liner Shipping Conferences." Federal Trade Commission, December.

Conlon, R. M. 1982. "Transport Cost and Tariff Protection of Australian Manufacturing." *Economic Record* 58(160):73–81.

Davies, J. E. 1986. "Competition, Contestability and the Liner Shipping Industry." *Journal of Transport Economics and Policy* 2(3):299–312.

ECLAC (U.N. Economic Commission for Latin America and the Caribbean). 1999. "Inventory of Measures Affecting Trade in Services." Manuscript, United Nations, New York.

Federal Maritime Commission. 1998. "Carrier Agreements in the U.S. Oceanborne Trades." Bureau of Economics and Agreement Analysis, Washington, D.C.

Finger, J. M., and Alexander Yeats. 1976. "Effective Protection by Transportation Costs and Tariffs: A Comparison of Magnitudes." *Quarterly Journal of Economics* 90(1):169–76.

Foxley, Juan, and José Luis Mardones. 2000. "Port Concessions in Chile: Contract Design to Promote Competition and Investment." Viewpoint: Public Policy for the Private Sector, Note No. 223, World Bank, Washington, D.C.

Francois, Joseph, and Ian Wooton. 1999. "Trade in International Transport Service:

The Role of Competition." Centre for Economic Policy Research Discussion Paper No. 2377, Centre for Economic Policy Research, London.

Francois, Joseph, Hugh Arce, Kenneth Reinert, and Joseph Flynn. 1996. "Commercial Policy and the Domestic Carrying Trade: A General Equilibrium Assessment of the Jones Act." *Canadian Journal of Economics* 29(1):181–98.

Franck, Bernard, and Jean-Claude Bunel. 1991. "Contestability, Competition and Regulation, the Case of Liner Shipping." *International Journal of Industrial Organization* 9(1)141–59.

Greene, William H. 1997. *Econometric Analysis*, 3d ed. Upper Saddle River, N.J: Prentice Hall.

Jankowski, W. B. 1989. "Competition, Contestability and the Liner Shipping Industry." *Journal of Transport Economics and Policy* 23(2):199–203.

Hummels, David. 1999. "Have International Transportation Costs Declined?" Manuscript, University of Chicago, Chicago, Ill.

Kang, Jong Soon. 2000. "Price Impact of Restrictions on Maritime Transport Services," in C. Findlay and T. Warren, eds., *Impediments to Trade in Services: Measurement and Policy Implications*. London: Routledge.

Levitt, M. 2000. "The Treatment of Liner Shipping Under EU and US Law: The Transatlantic Conference Agreement," in S. J. Evenett, A. Lehmann, and B. Steil (eds), *Antitrust Goes Global*. Washington, D.C.: Brookings Institution Press.

Livingston, Ian. 1986. *International Transport Costs and Industrial Development in the Least Developed Countries*. UNIDO/IS.616, Vienna: UNIDO.

Maddala, G. S. 1983. *Limited Dependent and Qualitative Variables in Econometrics*. Cambridge, Mass.: Cambridge University Press.

Mattoo, A., and A. Subramanian. 1997. "Multilateral Rules on Competition Policy: A Possible Way Forward." *Journal of World Trade* 31(5):95–115.

McGuire, Greg, Michael Schuele, and Tina Smith. 2000. "Restrictiveness of International Trade in Maritime Services," in C. Findlay and T. Warren, eds., *Impediments to Trade in Services: Measurement and Policy Implications*. London: Routledge.

Obstfeld, M., and K. Rogoff. 2000. "The Six Major Puzzles in International Macroeconomics: Is There a Common Cause?" NBER Working Paper No. 7777, National Bureau for Economic Research, Boston.

OECD. 1968. *Ocean Freight Rates as Part of Total Transport Costs*. Paris: OECD.

Pálsson, Gylfi. 1997. "Containerized Maritime Trade between West-Africa and Europe: Multiple Ports of Call versus Hub-and-Spoke." Mimeo, World Bank, Washington, D.C.

Pearson, Roy. 1987. "Some Doubts on the Contestability of Liner Shipping Markets." *Maritime Policy Management* 1:71–78.

Sampson, G. P., and A. J. Yeats. 1977. "Tariff and Transport Barriers Facing Australian Exports." *Journal of Transport Economics and Policy* 11(2):141–54.

Trujillo, L., and G. Nombela. 1999. "Privatization and Regulation in the Seaport Industry." Policy Research Working Paper No. 2181, World Bank, Washington, D.C.

Trujillo, Lourdes, and Antonio Estache. 2001. "Surfing a Wave of Fine Tuning Reforms in Argentina's Ports." Mimeo, World Bank, Washington, D.C.

U.S. International Trade Commission. 1991. "The Economic Effects of Significant U.S. Import Restraints, Phase III: Services." USITC Publication 2442, Washington, D.C.

Venables, A. J., and N. Limao. 1999. "Geographical Disadvantage: A Heckscher-Ohlin-von Thunen Model of International Specialization." Policy Research Working Paper No. 2256, World Bank, Washington, D.C.

Waters, W. G. 1970. "Transport Costs, Tariffs, and the Patterns of Industrial Protection." *American Economic Review* 60(5):1013–20.

White, Lawrence J. 1988. *International Trade in Ocean Shipping Services*. Cambridge, Mass.: Ballinger Publications.

World Bank. 2000. "Module 2: The Evolution of Ports in a Competitive Worlds, Module 2." From the World Bank Port Reform Tool Kit, World Bank, Washington, D.C.

WTO. 1994. "Questionnaire on Maritime Transport Services." Negotiating Group on Maritime Transport Services (s/NGMTS/w/2), World Trade Organization, Geneva.

———. 1998. "Maritime Transport Services." Background Note by the Secretariat (s/c/w/62). World Trade Organization, Geneva.

Zerby, J. A. 1988. "Clarifying Some Issues Relating to Contestability in Liner Shipping and Perhaps Also Eliminating Some Doubts." *Maritime Policy and Management* 15(1):5–14.

[28]

Some Policy Lessons from the Opening of the Korean Insurance Market

Yoon Je Cho

This article examines the recent dispute between the United States and the Republic of Korea over the opening of Korea's insurance market to U.S. companies. The article assesses the interests and motivations of both countries that lay behind the formal arguments presented during the negotiation process. It also analyzes whether the long-run interests of both developing and industrial countries would be well served by the approach to the opening of the market adopted in this case—sharing the rent while continuing to regulate the insurance market. The analysis suggests that the opening of a developing country's insurance market (or the wider financial services market) would serve the long-run interests of both developing and industrial countries only if it were accomplished in the context of overall domestic liberalization of the finance industry. "Opening" of the market, if this means only the sharing of the rents that were generated by regulation of the market, is unlikely to be beneficial to developing countries.

This examination of the recent United States–Korea trade dispute over the limitations placed on the access of U.S. firms to the Korean insurance market provides an opportunity to investigate the interests and motivations of industrial and developing countries with respect to international transactions in financial services. The article also derives some policy lessons for other developing countries that may face a similar trade negotiation environment.

Section I of the article briefly discusses the policies of the government of the Republic of Korea with respect to the insurance market, describes the structure and size of the market, and suggests some reasons for the strong interest of U.S. firms in entering the market. Section II introduces the trade dispute, and describes the issues between the two countries and their respective positions on these issues during the negotiations pursued under Section 301 of the U.S. Trade Act (see appendix). It also investigates the motivations underlying the formal arguments during negotiations and describes the bargaining counters

The author is an economist in the Technical Department of the Asia Region of the World Bank. This article was prepared for the World Bank Conference on Developing Countries' Interests and International Transactions in Services, Washington, D.C., July 15–16, 1987. The author is grateful to J. Michael Finger and Brian Hindley for their valuable suggestions, to Jagdish Bhagwati and Andrej Olechowski for helpful comments, and to Peter Bocock for editorial assistance.

240 THE WORLD BANK ECONOMIC REVIEW, VOL. 2, NO. 2

used by each party. Section III draws some conclusions from the case and identifies their implications for future negotiations between developing and developed countries on transactions in financial services. Section IV examines the national welfare implications of the relationship between the opening of financial services markets and the regulation of these markets and elaborates on the policy lessons that can be derived for other developing countries facing similar trade negotiations.

I. THE KOREAN INSURANCE MARKET

The Korean insurance industry is young (most insurers in the market date back only to the 1950s), but its growth has been rapid, owing to rapid economic growth and to strong government encouragement of the industry. The government has created various types of compulsory insurance and has authorized life insurance companies to receive a quasi-pension type of savings and to claim tax deductions on premiums.

Although government policy has fostered rapid expansion of the insurance industry, it has also imposed various restrictions on the industry that have inhibited its efficient development in terms of quality of service and international competitiveness. The government regulates asset management, with the objective of channeling funds into the finance of strategic industrial sectors designated by the government. The government also exercises detailed control over the business activities of insurance firms, through formal regulations, administrative guidance, or both. Premium rates are strictly controlled. The government has severely restricted entry into the industry and has tried to limit competition, both domestic and foreign.[1]

More recently, however, in conjunction with the overall economic liberalization policy pursued since 1980, the government has allowed more autonomous management and freer competition among insurance firms. But the pace of liberalization in insurance has been slow.

Life Insurance

At the end of 1986, the life insurance industry was dominated by six companies, all of them Korean.[2] No firm, either domestic or foreign, had been allowed entry to the life insurance market for three decades (except to sell insurance to resident aliens).

Life insurance firms in Korea are primarily savings institutions. About 95 percent of premium income comes from savings, which are in a form similar to time deposits at banks. Only 5 percent of premiums are paid directly for

---

1. Koreans often describe this protective policy as a "fleet policy," which means that the government wants every insurance company to achieve a similar market share and profit. It does not want any company to fail.

2. The insurance industry in Korea is divided strictly into life and nonlife insurance. No company may handle both types of business.

insurance. Thus the rapid growth of life insurance companies has been due
largely to their role as savings institutions rather than to demand for insurance.

To a great extent, this feature of Korea's life insurance business is due to
government policy. In the 1960s, in order to mobilize domestic resources to
finance its ambitious economic growth plans, the Korean government designated life insurance companies as savings institutions, eligible to receive a
quasi-pension type of savings from groups of employees of companies and
associations. The government has also used other measures to encourage the
role of life insurance companies as depositories of savings.

The growth of the life insurance industry, and of other nonbank financial
institutions such as investment and finance companies, has been particularly
rapid in recent years (see table 1). This growth received its impetus from two
main factors: (1) a reduction in inflation, which attracted financial savings to
nonbank financial institutions, especially long-term savings institutions such as
life insurance companies (which also offered higher interest rates than did the
banking sector) and (2) the Korean government's domestic financial liberalization policy, which enhanced the attractiveness of financial savings.

The ratio of life insurance premium income to gross national product (GNP)
provides an indication of the speed and extent of the growth of the life insurance industry. In 1980 this ratio was 1.6 percent, but by 1983 it had reached
4.0 percent, a higher value than in the United States or the United Kingdom
(see table 2). By 1984 it had reached 4.7 percent.

Despite this rapid growth, however, available evidence suggests that Korean
life insurance firms have not reached the levels of efficiency and competitiveness
achieved in most industrial countries. Government regulation of premium rates
and asset management of Korean life insurance firms has led to inefficiency and

Table 1. *Growth of the Korean Insurance Industry, 1976–84*
(in billions of won)

Item	1976	1978	1980	1982	1984
Premium income					
Life insurance	85	243	603	1,685	3,084
		(73.6)	(25.9)	(82.8)	(33.0)
Nonlife insurance	99	202	387	633	874
		(56.6)	(30.3)	(27.9)	(14.2)
Total assets					
Life insurance	145	355	998	2,488	5,314
		(67.5)	(48.1)	(69.5)	(44.2)
Nonlife insurance	141	326	607	918	1,111
		(48.2)	(36.1)	(18.9)	(6.5)
GNP	13,381	24,225	37,205	51,787	65,380
	(37.5)	(33.7)	(17.4)	(12.4)	(12.6)
GNP deflator	46.6	65.7	100.0	124.1	137.5
	(15.7)	(21.2)	(15.9)	(3.0)	(3.5)

Note: Figures in parentheses are annual growth rates in nominal terms.
Sources: Korea Insurance Corporation (1986); Republic of Korea (1986).

242   THE WORLD BANK ECONOMIC REVIEW, VOL. 2, NO. 2

Table 2. *Comparison of the Life Insurance Industry in Selected Economies,
1983*

Item	Korea	United States	Japan	United Kingdom	Taiwan	Malaysia
Per capita GNP (U.S. dollars)	1,884	14,093	9,696	8,144	2,744	1,849
Life insurance premium paid (millions of U.S. dollars)	2,915	80,809	49,106	16,280	684	—
Per capita premium paid (U.S. dollars)	72.9	344.7	411.8	289.0	36.8	—
Premium per GNP (percent)	4.0	2.44	4.15	3.71	1.48	0.85

Sources: Republic of Korea (1986); Swiss Reinsurance (1985).

a sort of cartelized market. One recent study shows that the Korean life insurance companies' management expenses (or their intermediation costs as financial institutions) are much higher than those of commercial banks for the same amount of savings mobilization (Lee, Kim, and Park 1986). The study suggests that if commercial banks were to add an insurance feature to their time deposits, they could fulfill the same function as life insurance companies but at a much lower cost. Another indication that Korean insurance firms have not been wholly efficient in serving buyers of insurance is the prosperity of insurance providers organized outside the mainline insurance industry, such as the Marine Association Mutual Insurance Fund and the Teachers Association Mutual Insurance Fund.

Nonlife Insurance

Total premium income of nonlife insurance companies is currently about 28 percent of that of the life insurance industry, and the share has been shrinking since 1980 because of the rapid growth of the life insurance industry. Thirteen companies are licensed to sell nonlife insurance, including two U.S. firms and three joint ventures between Korean and non-Korean companies.

Until recently, nonlife insurance in Korea has been dominated by the pool system, in which member firms share total premium income according to a preestablished formula. Mortgage insurance, marine insurance, and compulsory fire insurance companies operated as pools from their beginnings, whereas automobile insurance was monopolized by a government-sponsored insurance company. Although the pool system and the monopolies have been gradually phased out during the 1980s, some categories of insurance, such as compulsory fire insurance, still operate under the pool system.[3]

The nonlife insurance industry has few incentives for innovation or improvement of the quality of service or marketing skills. This situation may account for the industry's failure to penetrate the household sector: as of 1985, only 13 percent of nonlife insurance business came from household customers, whereas

3. In seven major cities of Korea, buildings of more than four stories are required by law to have fire insurance, which is operated in the pool system and is referred to as the compulsory fire pool.

Table 3. *Selected Indicators of the Size of the Korean Insurance Industry and Its International Standing, 1980–84*

Indicator	1980	1981	1982	1983	1984
Premium paid (millions of U.S. dollars)					
Total	1,502	2,024	3,096	3,877	4,785
	(23)	(19)	(14)	(12)	(11)
Life	915	1,317	2,250	2,915	3,728
	(17)	(13)	(11)	(10)	(7)
Nonlife	587	707	846	962	1,056
	(24)	(23)	(20)	(19)	(17)
Per capita premium paid (U.S. dollars)					
Total	39.4	52.3	78.7	97.5	117.9
	(31)	(31)	(25)	(24)	(23)
Life	24.0	34.0	57.2	72.9	91.9
Nonlife	15.4	18.3	21.5	24.1	26.0
Premium paid per GNP (percent)	2.89	3.34	4.82	5.28	6.05
	(20)	(20)	(12)	(10)	(7)

Note: Figures in parentheses are Korea's rank in the world insurance business.
Sources: Korea Insurance Corporation (1986); Swiss Reinsurance (1985).

corporate customers accounted for 87 percent (Korea Insurance Corporation 1986).

Interest of U.S. Firms in the Korean Insurance Market

The Korean insurance market is quite large by international standards. In terms of total premiums paid, as of 1984 only ten national markets were larger than that of Korea, which ranked seventh in life insurance and seventeenth in nonlife insurance. In terms of the ratio of premiums paid to GNP, Korea ranked seventh in the world (see table 3).

Because of the large size of the market, its high growth potential in a rapidly growing econony, and the relative inefficiency of the local insurance industry, the market is very attractive to foreign firms. Some U.S. insurers have already obtained limited entry to the market because of the special relationship between the United States and Korea. These firms have recently become more actively interested in expanding their business and therefore in removing the restrictions under which they must operate. In addition, U.S. firms that have not yet entered the market are also more interested in Korea as a potential source of business.

II. THE UNITED STATES–KOREA DISPUTE ON THE OPENING OF THE KOREAN INSURANCE MARKET

Since 1968, several foreign insurers have been licensed to underwrite certain kinds of life and health insurance policies for resident aliens, including U.S. Armed Forces personnel and their families.[4] At present, seven U.S. companies provide such insurance in Korea.

4. This section draws heavily on Cho (1987b).

In 1968, two U.S. insurers, American Home Assurance Company (AHA) and American Foreign Insurance Association (AFIA), received licenses to underwrite other kinds of insurance for resident aliens. Later, in 1977 and 1978, these companies were also licensed to write fire and other casualty policies for Korean nationals.[5]

In September 1985, the U.S. Trade Representative (USTR) initiated an investigation under Section 301 of the U.S. Trade Act into Korea's policy of prohibiting or restricting U.S. firms from providing insurance services.[6] The opening of the life insurance market and the compulsory fire pool was a central issue.

The U.S. government demanded that the compulsory fire pool be dismantled or that the two U.S. firms operating in Korea be given access to the pool, with shares of premium income equal to those of the Korean firms. Because the Korean government had specific reasons for opposing abolition of the pool, including an unwillingness to immediately close down the company that organized and managed the pool, the ensuing negotiations focused on the participation of the U.S. firms and their shares in the fire pool. In addition, the United States demanded that several U.S. firms be licensed to sell life insurance by June 1986 and that three additional nonlife insurance firms be licensed by the end of 1987.

U.S. Position and Motivation

The United States approached the case on legal grounds, based mainly on "national treatment" arguments. The U.S. firms argued in their petition that the Korean government's restrictions on their access to the life insurance and compulsory fire insurance markets denied them the benefits to which they were entitled under the 1956 Treaty of Friendship, Commerce, and Navigation between the United States and Korea.[7] They alleged that the policies of the Korean government violated its treaty obligations and the international legal norms incorporated in Section 301(e). The USTR transmitted these arguments to the Korean government without alteration.

Why did the U.S. firms chose this moment to make their complaints? One

5. In October 1984, AFIA transferred its license to CIGNA, another U.S. insurer.

6. This was not the first U.S. case brought under Section 301. In 1979, AHA filed a petition on the grounds that it was not being treated equally to other firms in the Korean nonlife insurance market. Its complaint was based upon its exclusion from the pools for noncompulsory and compulsory fire insurance. AHA also alleged that it was excluded from the marine insurance market. In 1981, the Korean government responded by licensing AHA and AFIA to write marine insurance. By 1984, the noncompulsory fire pool had been abolished, and the U.S. insurers were given unrestricted licenses to underwrite noncompulsory fire insurance, pursuant to an agreement in connection with the Section 301 petition filed in 1979. Life insurance was not an issue in this petition.

7. The treaty specifies: "Neither party shall take unreasonable nor discriminatory measures that could impair the legally acquired rights or interests within its territories of nationals and companies of the other party in the enterprises which they have established . . . [and that] nationals and companies of either party shall be accorded national treatment with respect to engaging in all types of commercial, industrial, financial and other activities for gain (business activities) within the territories of the other party, whether directly or by agent or through the medium of any form of lawful juridical entity."

plausible explanation lies in the recent explosive expansion of the Korean life insurance industry and projections of strong future growth. These characteristics, combined with the relatively inefficient management of Korean insurance firms and the oligopolistic structure of the market, made entry potentially very profitable. In particular, the fire pool, although accounting for only 3 percent of the fire insurance market, was the most lucrative part of the nonlife insurance market, so U.S. firms had a strong interest in sharing in its profits.

Entry would also enable U.S. firms to invest in the Korean capital market, in which investment by foreign nationals was restricted. Investments in the Korean capital market by foreign bank branches and special funds managed by foreign finance companies (such as the Korea Fund) have been very profitable.

Korea's Position and Motivations

Korea argued that limiting foreign entry did not violate "national treatment" because the policy of protecting the industry from overcompetition and securing its stability also involved restrictions on the entry of domestic firms. For example, the government had limited the number of domestic life insurance firms to six during the last thirty years. Therefore, it argued, U.S. firms were treated no differently than domestic firms that did not succeed in gaining access to the life insurance market.

Behind the formal arguments, however, Korea's restrictions seemed to be motivated largely by three concerns. First, the Korean government believed that the inefficiency of domestic firms relative to U.S. firms would lead to a significant reduction in the market share of domestic firms, resulting in bankruptcies among inefficient firms and serious instability in the financial market. That the increased competition resulting from the entry of U.S. firms would probably improve the quality of service and the efficiency of domestic firms was admitted by the government. It believed, however, that improvements in efficiency and welfare could be obtained through deregulation and by enhancing competition among domestic firms, and that foreign entry was not essential to achieve that goal. Second, the government did not want foreign firms to share in the rent generated by the oligopolistic structure of the insurance industry, which had developed as a result of extensive government regulation and protection. A third concern, given the government's intention to continue to regulate and control the insurance industry,[8] was its belief that foreign firms are harder to control than domestic firms, a belief that was based on its experience in dealing with foreign bank branches in Korea.

The Negotiation and Its Results

Negotiations between the U.S. and Korean governments took place in November 1985 (Washington, D.C.), December 1985 (Seoul), and June 1986 (Seoul). The United States demanded that Korea (1) permit full participation

---

8. A discussion of whether regulation should be relaxed on efficiency grounds is beyond the scope of this article.

of the two U.S. firms in the compulsory fire pool; (2) allocate shares of fire pool premium income equally among the U.S. and Korean firms; (3) allow other U.S. insurers (the number of companies was unspecified) to enter the life insurance market by the end of June 1986; and (4) allow three additional nonlife insurance firms and four life insurance firms to enter the market by the end of 1987.

The initial Korean response was to propose that the issues be discussed in a multilateral forum, through the dispute-settlement procedures of the General Agreement on Tariffs and Trade. The Koreans felt that their trade surplus with the United States and their weak political position vis-à-vis the United States undermined their bargaining position in bilateral negotiations under Section 301. Korea also wanted a multilateral forum because it believed that multilateral negotiations would take more time than bilateral negotiations, thus permitting it to maintain the status quo in the insurance market for a longer period.

The Korean suggestion was not accepted by the United States. The USTR threatened to recommend that the president take action against Korea's exports to the United States if the issues were not resolved by September 1986.

The threat was effective. The United States is a major Korean export market, accounting in 1985 for 35 percent ($10.7 billion; billion is 1,000 million) of total exports and a trade surplus of about $4 billion (Republic of Korea 1987). Moreover, the increasingly protectionist stance of the U.S. Congress put the U.S. negotiators in a strong position. The threat of possible cuts in the Generalized System of Preferences (GSP) and of increased protection against Korea's major exports (such as electronics, textiles, footwear, and steel) provided the United States with effective leverage for obtaining concessions in the insurance market.

Korea, meanwhile, had little leverage. Under these circumstances, the Korean government believed that the best that it could achieve would be to postpone a massive influx of U.S. firms.

On July 21, 1986, the two governments simultaneously announced the results of the negotiations. Most of the U.S. demands were accepted. Specifically, the government of Korea agreed (1) that the two U.S. firms would participate in the fire pool by July 1986; (2) that the member companies would determine the method of sharing pool premium income, with the Korean government ensuring that the distribution would be equitable (in a supplementary announcement immediately following this one, the Korean government agreed that U.S. firms would get the same share as Korean firms);[9] (3) that one U.S.

---

9. The United States had proposed that equal shares of premium income be distributed among companies, whereas Korea had proposed that the income be shared on the basis of company size. The two U.S. firms (which are branches) are much smaller than the Korean firms; their total share in the nonlife insurance market is less than 2 percent.

firm would be licensed to enter the life insurance market by the end of 1986; and (4) that qualified U.S. firms would be permitted to enter both the life and nonlife insurance markets.

III. Conclusions from the Trade Dispute Case

Four conclusions can be drawn from this dispute and its outcome. First, it is probably more realistic to approach insurance transactions (or more broadly, transactions in financial services) between developed and developing countries in the context of international investment rather than international trade. The United States presented its arguments in the dispute strictly in those terms. The U.S. government suggested that multilateral negotiations on trade in services should be restricted to nonfactor services, that is, services that can be traded between countries in the conventional sense, without requiring the relocation of either buyer or seller. Such trade in financial services, however, can be realistically considered only among countries without foreign exchange controls and restrictions on capital account transactions. In other words, a person or firm wishing to buy an insurance policy or to undertake financial transactions with firms (or banks) in a developed country must first be able to convert domestic currency freely into the foreign currency. In most developing countries, however, foreign exchange and capital accounts are strictly controlled.[10] Thus it is necessary to establish a local entity in order to sell financial services in these countries.

A second conclusion is that both governments basically represented the interests of their insurance firms. They entered the negotiations with the perception that the main issue was the sharing of profits (or rents) in Korea's insurance market. Broader considerations—for example, the effect of the outcome of the negotiations on economic efficiency or consumer welfare—seem not to have arisen.

The issues from the beginning were those of "national treatment" and U.S. entry to the market through "establishment." The U.S. government concentrated its efforts specifically on improving access for U.S. firms to Korea's relatively inefficient, highly regulated (and oligopolistic) insurance market. Alternatively, it could have pressed for relaxation of the strong domestic regulation of the Korean insurance industry and for freer general conditions of entry.

Issues such as deregulation of cartelized premium rates did not assume any importance in the negotiations. This fact partly reflects the sensitivity and

---

10. The advisability of liberalizing the capital market in developing countries in which there are still many distortions in the commodity market is a matter of controversy. The experience with liberalization in the Southern Cone countries suggests the importance of the order in which liberalization takes place; premature opening of the capital market in the presence of domestic market distortions can cause serious macroeconomic disruptions and massive capital flight.

difficulty of the issue of domestic policy reform in financial markets and the strong objections of developing country governments to such discussions. However, it also reflected a U.S. interest in obtaining for U.S. firms a share of the profit and rent of Korea's highly protected and oligopolistic market. Whether the repeated application of such an approach in other developing countries would improve welfare in the world economy is highly questionable.

The third conclusion is that, given the strong U.S. pressure for opening up the market and the threat of retaliation against Korea's exports to the United States, the Korean government's decision to open the insurance services market to U.S. firms made economic sense. By accommodating the U.S. demand, Korea chose more trade rather than less. The potential loss in exports as a result of U.S. retaliation would lead to a far greater reduction in GNP than would opening the insurance market to U.S. firms.[11] If, in addition, the cost of protection and the benefits of increased competition (improvements in efficiency and consumer welfare) are included in the calculation, the net cost of refusing U.S. entry would be even greater.[12]

A fourth conclusion relates to the issue of deregulation versus the sharing of rents in a protected, cartelized market. The principal concern of the Korean government during the negotiations was not to lose the domestic firms' market and profit shares to U.S. firms and to protect domestic firms from the shock of foreign competition. Despite the Korean recognition of the positive effects that could result from increased competition, the government gave little consideration to liberalizing the domestic market as an element of its response to U.S. demands. In a sense, the government entered negotiations with the assumption that it would maintain the current level of regulation of insurance firms. From this position stemmed its decision to allow U.S. firms to enter and share equally in the premium income of the compulsory fire pool—rather than to disband the pool and deregulate the market so that rents from the protected and cartelized market would disappear.

Given the current trade negotiation environment, developing countries like Korea may need to consider which approach would better serve their national

11. For example, the United States apparently suggested at one point in the negotiations that if Korea refused to open its insurance market, the United States would cut its GSP grant to Korean exports and increase protection, thus reducing the volume of Korea's major exports. Had there been a 50 percent cut in the GSP grant and a 5 percent reduction in the export volume of Korea's major exports, Korea would have experienced a 1.5 percent reduction in total exports, or roughly a 0.4 percent reduction in annual GNP. The cost to Korea of allowing entry to the U.S. insurers, however, would be less than 0.01 percent of GNP (assuming they received 2/13 of the compulsory fire pool business and a 5 percent share in the rest of the insurance market and had a net profit rate of 2 percent of total premium revenue). A variety of other scenarios under different assumptions are explored in Cho (1987a), all with essentially similar results.

12. There may also be direct and indirect benefits in terms of technological, pecuniary, marketing, or entrepreneurial stimuli that result from the entry of foreign firms. See Lall (1978) and Caves (1974) for a discussion of the effect of foreign investment in host country markets.

interest: to maintain protected and cartelized market structures and share the resulting rents with foreign firms or to deregulate these markets and allow the rents to be redistributed to buyers through competition.

IV. Deregulation of Domestic Markets: An Alternative Strategy for Developing Countries in the Current Trade Negotiation Environment

What is the best strategy for developing countries in the current international trade environment? The effects of different policy options on national welfare can be illustrated with a diagram such as figure 1, which is a simple supply and demand curve for insurance services.[13]

Suppose that in a protected insurance market, the government-regulated premium rate is P_c. Then I_c is the amount of insurance services sold, the combined area of W and X is the rent to insurance companies, and the triangular area Y is the welfare loss. If the country continues its market protection with regulated premium rates while allowing foreign companies to enter and share the market (I_iI_c being their market share), then the total welfare loss to the national economy would be $Y + X$, where X is the rent going to foreign firms, which they may repatriate to their home country.[14] Thus a country's welfare may worsen after allowing foreign firms to enter a domestic market in which prices are regulated.

If, instead, the country deregulates the domestic market and allows more competition, then the rent that insurers received under regulation will go to the buyers, and the increased competition will achieve the further welfare gain Y. In addition, in the competitive market, domestic insurance firms will have a strong incentive to learn from foreign firms, which will in turn lead to advances in technology, innovation, improvement of management skills, and so on. This effect may shift the overall domestic supply curve S (including both domestic and foreign firms) down to S'. If this happens, the welfare gain ($Y + Z$ + part of Z')[15] will be greater than under domestic deregulation without entry of foreign firms (Y).[16]

13. Figure 1 illustrates the effects of different policy options on national welfare. It should be noted, however, that the figure abstracts from various complicated insurance market issues such as adverse selection and the moral hazard effect. In the insurance market, we cannot draw a simple upward sloping supply curve and a downward sloping demand curve, because under conditions of asymmetric information they may be subject to adverse selection and the moral hazard effect. In some cases, the market may even fail to achieve a stable equilibrium point (see Rothschild and Stiglitz 1976).

14. The profit going to foreign firms may be even larger than B because their supply curve may lie below curve S because of their efficiency. But the part larger than B would not be a net cost to the host country in terms of the opportunity cost concept.

15. The welfare gain will be only some part of D' with the remainder being increased profit for foreign firms.

16. This argument is based on partial equilibrium analysis. The welfare gain may be greater in the general equilibrium context.

250   THE WORLD BANK ECONOMIC REVIEW, VOL. 2, NO. 2

Figure 1. *The Welfare Effects of Various Policy Options for the Korean Insurance Market*

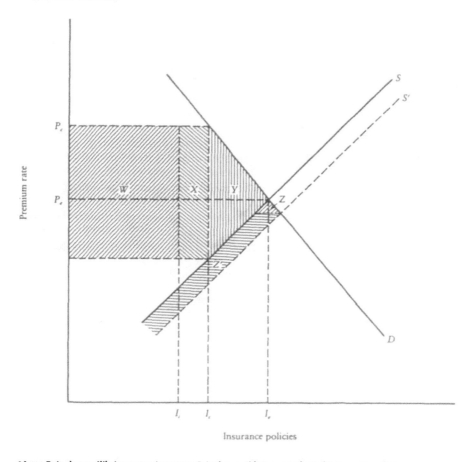

Note: P_e is the equilibrium premium rate; I_e is the equilibrium number of insurance policies.

This analysis suggests that if a country takes the policy option of allowing foreign entry while maintaining regulation, the result may be in a net loss (X) to the economy, whereas if it takes the policy option of allowing foreign entry while deregulating the market, the result would be an increase in the welfare of the economy ($Y + Z$ + part of Z') beyond what could be achieved without foreign transactions (Y.

Despite the teachings of simple economic theory, many developing-country governments intervene to protect cartelized market structures. Advocates of such policies often justify them in terms of externalities of one kind or another or second best arguments (for example, the need to take into account market imperfections or the instability of price equilibrium when markets are thin). It is also true, however, that underlying these arguments is the desire of governments to maintain their political power to distribute rents—or to retain their leverage over the private industrial sector through their power to distribute rents.

For this reason and others, the financial services industry in developing countries is often heavily controlled by the government.[17] It is not the purpose of this article to take a position on the merits of this approach, although it is worth noting that many empirical studies suggest that government intervention only increases distortions and inefficiency.[18]

Rather, the purpose of this article is to suggest, through the example of the United States–Korea trade dispute and the simple market analysis presented above, that developing countries facing strong pressure to open their financial services markets to foreign firms can increase their national welfare by liberalizing the domestic market when (or preferably before) opening it to foreign firms. In other words, *the case for deregulation of domestic financial services markets in developing countries becomes stronger in the current international trade environment.* For a developing country government that insists on maintaining a regulatory and protective regime that generates rents for service suppliers, the current trade environment will increase the cost of this policy. For a developing country that initiates deregulation and develops a competitive domestic market environment, however, the current trade environment offers an opportunity to enhance national welfare.

V. Conclusion

Financial services markets (including banking and insurance) are heavily regulated and protected by the government in many developing countries. Market structures are oligopolistic, and prices are often set by cartels. This heavy government intervention and lack of competition have led to inefficiencies in the financial services industries in these countries.

Restrictive government policies are often justified in terms of externalities and market imperfections. But many developing countries have regulated their financial services industries as an element of industrial policy, in order to promote strategic industries by providing them with preferential access to credit at low cost. In the process, the profitability of financial institutions has been

---

17. Governments in many developing countries control or own the financial services industry as a tool of their industrial policy. Governments set prices which may not reflect market conditions, and then direct asset management in support of strategic industrial sectors.

18. For example, a recent liberalization of banks and nonbank financial intermediaries in Korea has substantially increased the efficiency of credit allocation (see Cho and Cole 1986).

supported by government-determined interest rates, service fees, or premium rates that often do not reflect market conditions.

The international trade environment has recently changed and is less favorable for developing countries. Increasingly, industrial countries are retaliating against the various financial and fiscal subsidies that developing countries provide for their exports by establishing countervailing duties and other protective measures. At the same time, industrial countries (especially the United States) are exerting stronger pressure on developing countries to open their financial services markets to foreign firms.

Economists have made a strong case for financial services market liberalization in developing countries on the grounds of economic efficiency and growth. This argument has not been well received by many developing countries for various reasons, including its variance from their own economic philosophies. This article has argued, however, that the case for liberalization of domestic financial services is *stronger* under the current international trade negotiation environment, notwithstanding the various arguments used by developing countries to justify maintaining their regulatory and protective regimes.

It can also be argued that industrial countries should encourage developing countries to move toward liberalization of their financial services sector. But "liberalization" of financial services may not be beneficial to developing countries if opening the financial services market is considered by both sides to mean sharing the rents generated by regulation of the market—as in the United States–Korea case—rather than opening the domestic market to competition. If this approach becomes widespread, developing countries may become increasingly reluctant to open their markets, while continued government regulation and the inefficiencies resulting from lack of competition will restrict the development of financial services markets. By limiting the markets or the size of the markets that firms from industrial countries can enter, this approach may lead to economic losses in the long term for industrial countries as well. Liberalization of transactions in financial services will be beneficial to both developing and industrial countries in the long run only if market expansion is discussed in the context of overall liberalization of domestic financial services in developing countries.

APPENDIX: SECTION 301 OF THE U.S. TRADE ACT

Section 301 of the U.S. Trade Act authorizes the president of the United States to take action against foreign trade practices that violate international trade agreements or burden or restrict U.S. commerce in an unjustifiable, unreasonable, or discriminatory fashion. Action may be initiated by the U.S. Trade Representative (USTR) directly or at the direction of the president, or following a petition from any interested persons, including business or labor. If a petition is filed, the USTR has forty-five days to determine if an investigation is warranted.

Section 301 directs the USTR to seek advice from public and private groups and to consult with the foreign country involved in the dispute as part of its investigation. Most cases are resolved through negotiations with the country whose practices are being questioned. If the USTR finds that unfair trade practices exist and the dispute cannot be resolved through negotiations or through the General Agreement on Tariffs and Trade dispute-settlement procedures, the USTR makes a recommendation to the president of the United States on what action, if any, he should take.

Under Section 301, the president has the authority to take all appropriate and feasible actions within his power to obtain the elimination of unfair trade practices. Specifically, he may impose duties, fees, or restrictions on products and services of the offending country; these goods do not necessarily have to be related to the goods and services which are the subject of the complaint. The president may also deny licenses issued by U.S. federal regulatory agencies to foreign service suppliers. The degree and duration of these actions is determined by the president. (Adapted from a U.S. presidential press release, September 7, 1985.)

REFERENCES

Bhagwati, Jagdish N. 1987. "Trade in Services and the Multilateral Trade Negotiations." *World Bank Economic Review* 1, no. 4 (September): 539–47.

Caves, Richard E. 1974. "Multinational Firms, Competition, and Productivity in Host-Country Markets." *Economica* 41 (May): 176–93.

Cho, Yoon Je. 1986. "Status of Korea's Financial Liberalization." Draft, International Economic Research Division, World Bank Development Research Department. February.

———. 1987a. "Developing Country Strategy for International Trade in Financial Service—Lessons from the Opening of the Korean Insurance Market." Paper presented at the World Bank Conference on Developing Countries' Interests and International Transactions in Services, Washington, D.C., July.

———. 1987b. "How the United States Broke into Korea's Insurance Market." *World Economy* 10 (December): 483–96.

Cho, Yoon Je, and David Cole. 1986. "The Role of the Financial Sector in Korea's Structural Adjustment." World Bank Development Research Department. Processed. Washington, D.C.

Kim, Kiwhan. 1986. "Trade Negotiations and the Developing Countries of Asia: Possible Benefits and Costs." Occasional Paper 86-02. Seoul, Korea: Ilhae Institute.

Korea Insurance Corporation. 1986. *Insurance Statistics Yearbook*. Seoul.

Lall, Sanjaya. 1978. "Transactionals, Domestic Enterprises, and Industrial Structure in Host LDCs: A Survey." *Oxford Economic Papers* 30 (July):217–48.

Lee, Young Ki, Myung K. Kim, and Jin W. Park. 1986. "An Analysis of the Comparative Advantage and Competitiveness of the Life Insurance Industry." *Hanguk Gaebal Yungu* (Korean Development Institute) 8, no. 2 (June): 104–126.

Republic of Korea. 1986. *Korean Economic Indicators.* Seoul, Korea: Economic Planning Board.

Rothschild, Robert, and J. E. Stiglitz. 1976. "Equilibrium in Competitive Insurance Markets: An Essay on the Economics of Inperfect Information." *Quarterly Journal of Economics* 90 (November): 629–50.

Swiss Reinsurance. *Sigma.* Swiss, 1985.

[29]

Journal of Economic Integration
20(4), December 2005; 688-726

Relaxing the Restrictions on the Temporary Movement of Natural Persons: A Simulation Analysis

Terrie L. Walmsley
Purdue University

L. Alan Winters
World Bank

Abstract

While the liberalisation of trade has been at the forefront of the global agenda for many decades, the movement of natural persons remains heavily guarded. Nevertheless restrictions on the movement of natural persons across regions impose a cost on developing and developed economies that far exceeds that of trade restrictions on goods. This paper uses a global CGE model to investigate the extent of these costs, by examining the effects of an increase in developed countries' quotas on both skilled and unskilled temporary labour equivalent to 3% of their labour forces. The results confirm that restrictions on the movement of natural persons impose significant costs on nearly all countries (over $150 billion in all), and that those on unskilled labour are more burdensome than those on skilled labour.

- **JEL Classifications:** J61, C68
- **Key words:** Applied general equilibrium modeling, Temporary Movement of natural persons, GATS Mode 4, Skill, Welfare

---

*Corresponding address: Terrie L. Walmsley, Agricultural Economics, Purdue University, 403 West State Street, West Lafayette, IN 46637, USA, Tel: +1-765-494-5837, Fax: +1-765-496-1224, E-mail: twalmsle @purdue.edu. L. Alan Winters, World Bank, 1818 H Street, Washington, DC 20433, USA, E-mail: lwinters@worldbank.org

The alterations made to the GTAP model can be divided into six distinct features: productivity, allocation methods, income, welfare, sectoral allocation and balancing equations. We refer to the new model as GMig.

A. Productivity

The differences between the productivities of permanent labour and temporary labour are a significant factor that could potentially affect the expected benefits of relaxing the restrictions on TMNP. In GMig we define both the number of temporary migrants and the equivalent number of average temporary migrants, given their home productivity relative to that of the average temporary migrant.[6] The equivalent number of temporary migrants ($QTM^{*}_{i,r}$) is found by multiplying the number of temporary migrants ($QTM_{i,r}$) by their base-level productivity ($A_{i,r}$: Equation 1), where i is the set of labour types (skilled and unskilled labour) and r is the set of regions (defined in column I of Table 2).

$$QTM^{*}_{i,r} = QTM_{i,r} \times A_{i,r} \tag{1}$$

Estimates of base productivity ($A_{i,r}$) are obtained from the wage data in the GTAP database.[7] We assume that wage differentials in the 1997 database reflect productivity differences between workers from these regions, part of which will arise due to the fact that there are quotas on the movement of labour. The purpose of calculating temporary migrant equivalents is to ensure that remittances sent back to the home region and welfare calculations are adjusted to reflect the fact that these temporary migrants may have higher/lower productivities than the average migrant (prior to moving into the host region) and that their wages and remittances reflect this.

We do not have data on bilateral flows of labour. Hence, when temporary labour is allocated across host regions, it is assumed to have the same productivity as the average temporary migrant (ATM^{Av}_{i}). This average productivity depends on the home regions of the temporary migrants and hence might change with the

---

[6]These productivities are determined relative to the productivity of the average temporary migrant in the initial data. The productivity of an average temporary migrant was set equal to 1 and the productivities of permanent residents from particular regions set relative to this. Thus if wages in the USA were 3 times that of the average temporary migrant then their productivity was 3 times that of the average temporary migrant.

[7]A_{ir} are parameters of the model, not outcomes. Wages and actual productivity, however, are outcomes, linked to the level of employment in any sector.

Table 2. Regions

I All Regions	II Labour Importers	III Labour Exporters	IV European Union	V European Union Part- ners[a]	VI North America[b]	VII North American Partners[c]
USA	∨				∨	
Canada	∨				∨	
Mexico		∨				∨
UK	∨		∨			
Germany	∨		∨			
Rest of EU	∨		∨			
Rest of Europe	∨					
Eastern Europe		∨		∨		
Former Soviet Union		∨		∨		
Australia-New Zealand	∨					
China		∨				∨
Japan	∨					
Rest of East Asia		∨				∨
South East Asia		∨				∨
India		∨		∨		∨
Rest of South Asia		∨		∨		∨
Brazil		∨				∨
Rest of Latin America		∨				∨
Middle East and Northern Africa		∨		∨		
South Africa		∨		∨		
Rest of World		∨				

a. EU Partners are the group of countries/regions where most of the temporary labour in the EU currently comes from.

b. Developed North American countries.

c. North American Partners are the group of countries/regions where most of the temporary labour in North America currently comes from.

composition of temporary flows. For example, if more temporary migrants come from home regions with lower productivities the average productivity of the temporary migrant will decline.[8] Thus

---

[8]This has been occurring in the United States over the last two decades, as more workers from Mexico have entered, replacing the foreign workers from Europe. Since the productivity of a Mexican worker is lower than that of a European worker, the productivity and hence the relative wage of the average migrant worker has fallen (Borjas, 2000).

$$ATM_i^{Av} = \sum_r \left(\frac{QTM_{i,r}}{QTM_i}\right) \times A_{i,r} \tag{2}$$

Once working in the host region, temporary labour will acquire some of the productivity of the host region. For example a worker from the USA, who goes to work temporarily in Mexico cannot be expected to be as productive as she would have been in the USA, so her productivity is adjusted downwards to reflect the productivity of the workers in Mexico. Likewise an Indian worker entering the UK would increase his/her productivity to reflect the higher productivity in the UK. Equation 3 expresses the productivity of the temporary labour ($ATL_{i,r}$) as the average productivity (ATM^{Av}_i) of a temporary migrant plus a proportion (β) of the difference between the host region's productivity ($A_{i,r}$) and the average temporary migrants productivity (ATM^{Av}_i). We fix β as 0.5 for most of our experiments, but do experiment with alternatives.

$$ATL_{i,r} = ATM_i^{Av} + \beta \times (A_{i,r} - ATM_i^{Av}) \tag{3}$$

This productivity is then used to determine the equivalent, productivity weighted, quantity of temporary labour which enters the labour force of the labour importing region (Equation 4). The equivalent quantity of temporary workers ($QTL^*_{i,r}$) is given by the actual quantity ($QTL_{i,r}$) multiplied by the productivity of the temporary labour ($ATL_{i,r}$).

$$QTL_{i,r}^* = QTL_{i,r} \times ATL_{i,r} \tag{4}$$

Two assumptions in this sub-section are uncomfortable, but, we believe unavoidable. First, if we had data on bilateral flows of temporary labour, the productivity effects and remittance behaviour could be flow-specific and more convincing. Unfortunately, however, we can locate no such bilateral-flow-specific data. Second, the catch-up parameter is obviously crude, but in the absence of information we do not have a better estimate. Borjas (2000) reports eventual catch-up of over 100% for permanent migrants (i.e., overtaking local wages), but for temporary workers the catch-up will inevitably be significantly smaller. On the other hand, many environmental and complementary factors in the developed host country will allow even entirely unreconstructed developing country service workers to increase their output when they move. We guess that assuming a value of one-half is fairly conservative, but have no empirical estimates on which to base our work.

B. Allocation Methods

Since data on bilateral flows of guest workers between regions are generally unavailable or of dubious quality, the movement of natural persons has been incorporated into the model in such a way as to minimise the amount of data required. Figure 1 illustrates the method used. The model postulates a global labour pool, which collects temporary migrants from their home region, mixes them together and then allocates them across host regions. The temporary workers are then added to the supply of labour in the host region and allocated across sectors within the region according to labour demand. In the host country temporary workers' wages are related to their productivity. Part of the wage is sent back to the home region via the global pool as remittances (Figure 2), while the remaining income is added to the income of the host population where it is then allocated across consumption, saving and government spending to maximise utility.[9]

Allocation can occur in two ways: across host regions (B in Figure 1) or across home regions (A in Figure 1). In this paper we assume an excess demand for temporary work places in developed countries and examine the case where quotas on such workers are exogenously increased by 3% of those countries' current skilled and unskilled labour forces. Our problem, therefore, is to determine where these additional workers come from, i.e. their home regions (A in Figure 1).

Figure 1. Allocation of Migrant Workers to the Host Region and Sector

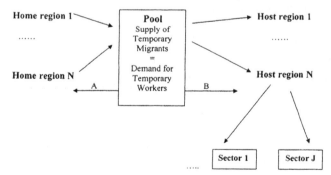

---

[9]Again restrictions on the availability of data preclude us from allocating the income of the temporary worker across consumption, saving and government spending separately. See Walmsley (2002) for an example of how this could be incorporated using a number of simplifying assumptions and an extensive calibration procedure.

Relaxing the Restrictions on the Temporary Movement of Natural Persons   697

Figure 2. Remittances

Figure 3. Income

Temporary workers are allocated across home countries ($QTM_{i,r}$) by labour force shares ($L_{i,r} / L_i$) (Equation 5).

$$QTM_{i,r}/QTM_i = L_{i,r}/L_i \qquad (5)$$

This is clearly not precisely true, but in the absence of information on which to base a more sophisticated allocation it seems the least arbitrary assumption to make. We do vary it below in the sensitivity tests and could easily alter the assumption further to explore allocations of specific policy interest.

C. Income

Separate calculations are made for income earned by permanent labour, temporary labour and temporary migrants (Figure 3). Total income earned in the host region, by permanent and temporary labour, is also calculated for the purposes of allocating income across private and government consumption and saving to maximise utility.

In the standard GTAP model, income includes all factor incomes ($Y_{f,r}$, where f is the source of income: skilled and unskilled labour, land, capital and natural resources) less depreciation (D_r), plus taxes (T_r). In GMig factor incomes include income earned on factors owned by temporary and permanent labour ($Y_{f,r} = YPL_{f,r} + YTL_{f,r}$, where $YPL_{f,r}$ is the income from factor f, earned by permanent labour and $YTL_{f,r}$ is the income from factor f earned by temporary labour[10]). In addition, we must also take account of net remittances ($NR_{i,r}$, where i is the two labour types: skilled and unskilled labour). Net remittances ($NR_{i,r}$) equal remittances received

---

[10]$YTL_{f,r}$ is non-zero only for skilled and unskilled labour. Temporary labour does not earn income from other factors of production.

$(RR_{i,r})$ from temporary migrants less remittances paid $(RP_{i,r})$ by temporary labour.

$$Y_r = \sum_f Y_{f,r} - D_r + T_r + \sum_i NR_{i,r} \qquad (6)$$

Remittances paid are assumed to be a fixed proportion of wages, as observed in the base data. They vary by host country and average 20% across all hosts. Thus remittances paid by temporary workers reflect changes in the number of equivalent temporary workers $(QTL^*_{i,r})$ and the wages they receive. These remittances paid were then summed and allocated across home regions as remittances received (Figure 2). Remittances received from temporary migrants by a home region are assumed to reflect their numbers of temporary migrant equivalents and average remittances.[11] The latter reflect wages and hence productivities, and since productivities vary with both the home and host country composition of temporary movement, so too will average remittances.[12]

Remittance flows hardly affect the global benefits of temporary migration, but they do affect its distribution between countries. It is well understood that temporary migrants tend to remit more heavily than permanent migrants and we could have assumed that marginal remittance rates were higher than average observed rates. In the absence of hard evidence of what the increase should be, however, we chose not to over-ride actual data. An increase in remittance rates would shift welfare from the migrants to the residents back home—having hardly any effect on our welfare estimates by home country but twisting those by host country in favour of developing countries.[13]

As stated previously, regional income is the sum of the incomes earned by temporary and by permanent labour. For the welfare calculations we treat these incomes separately. The income of temporary labour is assumed to include the income from labour $(YTL_{i,r}$: i is skilled and unskilled labour) less remittances sent home $(RP_{i,r}$: Equation 7); all other income, including income on land, capital etc,

---

[11]In the absence of data on bilateral flows of temporary workers we are obliged to assume that all remittances vary proportionately with the average.

[12]The average productivity of migrants reflects their origins, while the extent of productivity catch-up reflects their allocation over host countries.

[13]It has been suggested to us that we should model the responsiveness of remittances to real exchange rates. We choose not to, however: the long-run changes in real exchange rates implied by relatively small changes in temporary migration are too small to be significant, and the short-term fluctuations observed in the real world merely affect timing not the hypothetical steady-state with which we can deal.

Relaxing the Restrictions on the Temporary Movement of Natural Persons   699

Figure 4. Welfare

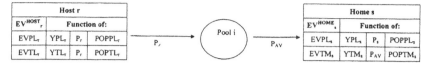

taxes and remittances received are earned by permanent labour.

$$YTL_r = \sum_f (YTL_{i,r} - RP_{i,r}) \tag{7}$$

The income of temporary migrants by home region is discussed in section 2.4 as part of the calculation of welfare of temporary migrants.

D. Welfare

In the standard GTAP model the measure of welfare change used is the Equivalent Variation (EV), which is obtained from the income and utility function of each regional household.[14] In GMig, however, the EV of the host region has to be divided into two components, as with income: the EVs for permanent (EVPL$_r$) and temporary (EVTL$_r$) workers. The calculation of welfare for the various agents is illustrated in Figure 4.

In any situation, the welfare of permanent labour, excluding any temporary migrants that are temporarily working abroad, (EVPL$_r$) is a function of the utility derived from the income of the permanent workers (YPL$_r$), which includes remittances received from workers abroad. The utility of permanent residents is a function of their (total) income, numbers and the prices of goods they purchase with this income (Figure 4). Given this utility with and without the policy changes under analysis, we can then calculate the EV for permanent workers.

The welfare of temporary labour (EVTL$_r$) is found similarly. Their welfare is a function of the utility derived from the income of the temporary residents (YTL$_r$), from which remittances paid have already been subtracted. Their utility is a

---

[14]Note that in GMig, the income of permanent residents and temporary workers is added together (Figure 3) and then allocated across private and government consumption and saving. This means that the utility derived in the standard GTAP model is for a regional household, which is made up of permanent residents and temporary labour. Note that remittances paid are removed from the income of temporary labour and remittances received are included in the income of permanent residents prior to this aggregation. The purpose of this aggregation is to ensure that income is allocated across spending in the region in which it is spent.

function of their (total) income, numbers and the price level in the host region (Figure 4), and from these EVs can be calculated.

The welfare change for a region as host (EV_r^{HOST}), can now be found by summing the parts for permanent and temporary labour (Figure 4). The total EV of all temporary workers (EVTL) is then equal to the sum across regions of the EVs of all the temporary workers (EVTL$_r$, Equation 9).

$$EV_r^{HOST} = EVPL_r + EVTL_r \qquad (8)$$

$$EVTL = \sum_r EVTL_r \qquad (9)$$

The income of the temporary labour by host region and labour type is aggregated across host regions (Equation 10) and distributed across home regions to find the income attributable to temporary migrants from each region (Equation 11: Figure 3). The distribution of total income by all temporary labour (YTM$_i$) across home regions depends on the equivalent quantities of temporary migrants (QTM*$_{i,r}$) from the home region relative to the total (QTM*$_i$).

$$YTM_i = \sum_r (YTL_{i,r} - RP_{i,r}) \qquad (10)$$

$$YTM_r = \frac{QTM_{i,r}^*}{QTM_i^*} \times YTM_i \qquad (11)$$

This income is then used to determine the utility and EV of the temporary migrants (Figure 4). An average price has to be used to determine utility of temporary migrants - the average price for goods paid by temporary labour in their host regions.[15]

Once the EV of temporary migrants is determined, the welfare change by home region (EV_r^{HOME}, Equation 12), regardless of temporary residence (Figure 4), and the world welfare change (WEV, Equation 13) can also be calculated by simply summing the relevant regional figures.

$$EV_r^{HOME} = EVTM_r + EVPL_r \qquad (12)$$

$$WEV = \sum_r EV_r^{home} = \sum_r EV_r^{host} \qquad (13)$$

---

[15]Another method would have been to aggregate the EV of all temporary labour across host regions and then allocate this welfare across home regions according to the shares. This would have avoided the need to determine an average price. However this method would not have allowed us to take into account differences in the supply of skilled and unskilled labour across home regions.

E. Sectoral Allocation

The last issue to be examined relates to what industries the temporary labour will be employed in or what sectors the temporary migrants will come from. In the standard GTAP model, labour moves across sectors to equalise the wage - thus labour moves to the sectors with the highest demand. This is also the standard closure for GMig. On the other hand, since Mode 4 is restricted to services and since particular service sectors in the developed economies, e.g. the computing sector in the USA, are interested in obtaining skilled temporary workers, it is interesting to think what happens if labour is restricted to specific sectors.

This is achieved in the model by dividing the sectors into two groups: one group of sectors which employ temporary labour (A); and a second group of sectors which do not (B). The supply of labour to each group must equal its demand, and labour can flow freely within each group but not between them. All temporary labour flows are supplied to the group of sectors which accept temporary labour (A), while the supply of labour to the other group (B) is held fixed. This approach also has implications for permanent labour. In order that the inflow of temporary labour not just be off-set by outflows of permanent labour, we have to fix supplies of permanent labour in each group. Hence labour is not perfectly mobile, except between sectors of the same group, and wages differ between the two groups. We note that Borjas and Freeman (1992) found that permanent residents do tend, in fact, to move out of geographical areas in which there has been an influx of foreign workers, leaving the total labour force unchanged, so our assumption of the opposite for TMNP should be considered rather carefully.

F. Balancing Equation

Finally, in all our exercises the total number of temporary migrants (QTM_i) from all home regions equals the total number of temporary labour (QTL_i) in all host regions.[16]

$$QTM_i = QTL_i \qquad (14)$$

III. Data

The primary database used to support the GMig model is version 5 of the GTAP

---

[16]The share allocation method ensures this equality holds, although other methods may not.

Database (Dimaranan *et al.*, 2001). Version 5 of the GTAP database contains 66 countries/regions and 57 sectors. The GTAP database was supplemented with additional data on the labour force, numbers of temporary migrants and workers, and their remittances and wages. In this section we provide the sources for this additional data, outlining the assumptions made for filling in any missing data, the calculation of wage data and the calibration procedure used.

The additional data were collected at the country level for 211 countries and then aggregated into the 66 regions identified in version 5 of the GTAP database. The new data include information on population, labour force, numbers of skilled and unskilled labour, the number of temporary workers by skill level located in each region, the number of temporary migrants by skill level from each region and the value of remittances entering and leaving the region. Data were found for as many countries as possible, using the International Labour Organisation's International Labour Migration Database,[17] and missing values were then filled to get estimates for all 211 countries.

The filling process involved using data on the numbers of temporary migrants and of temporary labour to estimate remittances in and out respectively or alternatively using remittance data to obtain estimates of numbers of temporary migrants and/or labour. Where data on neither remittances nor the number of people were available, the values were assumed be zero. This was the case for temporary migrants from the United States, Canada, UK and Germany and for temporary labour working in Mexico.

In a limited number of cases the ILO International Migration database also included estimates of the skill level of the temporary labour. These estimates were used wherever possible to obtain a split between skilled and unskilled workers. In the other regions, the skill levels of migrants were assumed to reflect those of their home labour force, while the skill levels of temporary workers were assumed to reflect the overall skill breakdown of the temporary migrants.

Once the numbers of workers were obtained, these were used to find the wages earned by the temporary workers. A measure of the productivity of a worker, relative to the average migrant worker was estimated based on the wage per

---

[17] A handful of these numbers were altered if other evidence suggested that the number provided by the ILO International Migration Database was a significant underestimate. For example the number of temporary migrants from the Philippines and the number of temporary workers in the USA were revised upwards to reflect other data collected by Walmsley (1999). The revisions to temporary workers in the USA reflect estimates of the number of illegal temporary workers in the USA.

worker in each region. A temporary worker entering the host region was assumed to have the average wage of a temporary migrant plus a portion of the difference between the average wage of a temporary migrant and the wage obtained by a permanent resident of the host region (Related to Equation 3). This reflects the fact that the temporary worker's productivity will partially adjust to reflect the productivity in the host region. For example, the productivity of an African entering the UK will increase relative to his productivity at home as he/she will now have more productive tools. However, it will not increase to the same level as a permanent resident as foreigners do not have all the specific tools required for the UK, e.g. language, UK education etc. Borjas (2000) examined the case of permanent migrants entering the USA and found that they received 80-90% of the wages of a permanent resident initially.[18] This proportion increases as the migrant's time in the country increases and additional USA specific skills were gathered.[19] As our workers are temporary, they do not have time to adapt and a temporary migrant is unlikely to have the same entrepreneurial characteristics as a permanent migrant. Hence we expect that temporary migrants would have a smaller degree of convergence to the permanent residents' wage. In this paper we generally assume that temporary labour acquires 50% of the difference in productivities, but we also experiment with values of 25% and 75% (Equation 3).

Remittances are an important source of income for many labour exporting regions, such as Thailand and the Philippines. The inclusion of remittances in the income of the region means that income is now defined as income earned on land, labour and capital located in the region plus taxes plus net remittances received. The GTAP database (which ignores remittances) must be altered to reflect this new definition and to ensure that this new definition of income is consistent with aggregate spending.

To ensure that income equals spending in GMig, one of the GTAP components of spending must be altered. We choose to reduce saving by the value of the net

---

[18]Whether the average migrant received 80% or 90% depends on the skills of the migrant worker. In the 1970s migrants to the USA earned 90% of the wage of a USA worker, as many of them were from Europe and had higher skills. More recently, with the increase in immigrants from Latin America, skills and hence wages, have declined.

[19]In fact Borjas (2000) found that as time progressed migrants' wages increased to 10% more than the average native wage. He suggested that this may be the result of self-selection, i.e. a migrant who chooses to move permanently may be more entrepreneurial than the average worker in his/her home country.

remittances paid, because:

• In the construction of the GTAP database, Private Consumption and Government consumption are adjusted to ensure that they are consistent with other sources, such as World Bank. Therefore in the GTAP database, it is saving which adjusts to take account of the fact that GTAP takes no account of remittances. Hence if we wish to include remittances, saving should be adjusted back again.
• The use of saving minimises the re-calibration required. The only restriction pertaining to saving in the GTAP database is that global saving equals global investment. Since global remittances received equal global remittances paid, the global saving – investment identity is automatically satisfied when these remittances are added to or subtracted from saving.

Finally the data were aggregated into 21 regions and 22 sectors for undertaking the analysis. A list of the regions and the commodities can be found in column I of Table 2 and the stub of Figure 3, respectively.

IV. Simulations

A number of simulations were undertaken using the GMig model to examine how relaxing the restrictions on the temporary movement of natural persons (TMNP) is likely to affect developed and developing countries. The paper commences by focusing on a single simulation of an increase in developed country quotas on the numbers of skilled and unskilled temporary workers. Following this the effects of other issues, such as sectoral allocation, the size of the shock and the choice of labour importing and exporting regions, are examined.

Quotas on the temporary movement of natural persons are assumed to increase in a number of traditionally labour importing regions, and to be filled by labour from a number of traditionally labour exporting countries according to their labour force shares. Table 2 divides the regions used in this analysis in to labour importing and labour exporting regions (columns II and III respectively).[20] The quotas are increased by an amount which would allow the quantity of both skilled and

---

[20]The decision of whether a region was a labour exporter or importer was based on wage rates (high wages were expected in labour importing countries and low wages in labour exporters), data on the quantities of temporary migrants relative to temporary workers and the level of development.

Table 3A. Changes in the Movement of Skilled Natural Persons ('000s of people)

I Region	II Skilled Temporary Workers prior to increase in quotas 1997	III Skilled Temporary Migrants prior to increase in quotas 1997	IV Skilled Temporary Workers after to increase in quotas	V Skilled Temporary Migrants after to increase in quotas
USA	767	0	3169	0
Canada	41	0	308	0
Mexico	0	204	0	428
UK	183	0	742	0
Germany	804	0	1624	0
Rest of EU	747	3945	3061	3945
Rest of Europe	355	232	471	232
Eastern Europe	5	53	5	413
Former Soviet Union	12	74	12	1122
Australia and New Zealand	33	0	256	0
China	61	38	61	528
Japan	68	324	1374	324
Rest of East Asia	55	30	55	422
South East Asia	647	972	647	1962
India	3	49	3	1265
Rest of South Asia	12	60	12	240
Brazil	108	127	108	497
Rest of Latin America	465	273	465	1050
Middle East and Northern Africa	2603	600	2603	1320
Southern Africa	160	95	160	1036
Rest of World	21	73	21	371
Total	7150	7150	15156	15156

Source: Authors' shocks and simulations

unskilled labour supplied in the host (or labour importing) countries to increase by 3%.[21] Table 3 describes the initial number of temporary workers (by host) and temporary migrants (by home) and their numbers after the change in quotas. For example, in the case of the USA, the number of skilled temporary workers

---

[21]By this we mean the number of workers (actual bodies) increases by 3% of the labour force. Note that since relative productivities differ this may not mean that the labour force increases by 3%, since the labour force increases by the number of equivalent workers. For example the USA may allow in 3% more workers but if their productivity is half that of the typical USA worker, the labour force will increase by much less than 3%.

Table 3B. Changes in the Movement of Unskilled Natural Persons ('000s of people)

I Region	II Unskilled Temporary Workers prior to increase in quotas 1997	III Unskilled Temporary Migrants prior to increase in quotas 1997	IV Unskilled Temporary Workers after to increase in quotas	V Unskilled Temporary Migrants after to increase in quotas
USA	4140	0	6903	0
Canada	222	0	528	0
Mexico	0	2529	0	2681
UK	989	0	1564	0
Germany	4339	0	5184	0
Rest of EU	3526	4060	5925	4060
Rest of Europe	1919	238	2038	238
Eastern Europe	27	474	27	652
Former Soviet Union	65	670	65	1186
Australia and New Zealand	176	0	389	0
China	128	593	128	3019
Japan	366	324	1671	324
Rest of East Asia	299	139	299	257
South East Asia	1696	7100	1696	7819
India	16	1198	16	2826
Rest of South Asia	174	2907	174	3389
Brazil	584	1789	584	2074
Rest of Latin America	1055	3087	1055	3450
Middle East and Northern Africa	13542	7130	13542	7669
Southern Africa	866	1266	866	2136
Rest of World	78	703	78	952
Total	34207	34207	42731	42731

Source: Authors' shocks and simulations

increases from 0.77 million to 3.2 million (table 3A) while unskilled numbers increase from 4.1 million to 6.9 million (table 3B). For China the numbers of skilled temporary migrants increases from 0.038 million to 0.5 million, while that for the unskilled increases from 0.6 million to 3 million.

Because the skills mix of the increased labour flow is proportional to developed countries' endowments, it does not affect their labour proportions (although, of course, it increases their labour/capital ratio). In developing countries, on the other hand, it reduces the skilled/unskilled ratio strongly, with consequential strong effects on the wage gap.

V. The Results

A. Macroeconomic Effects

Table 4 presents the principal results of the main simulation. For each region, it reports changes in the welfare of temporary workers (column II), temporary migrants (III) and permanent residents (IV). The first two refer to the same people, first by their country of work and second by country of origin (permanent residence). These columns refer both to the workers newly mobile as a result of the liberalisation, and to the temporary workers (migrants) already identified in the

Table 4. Welfare of Agents[a]

I Regions	II Welfare of temporary workers	III Welfare of temporary Migrants	IV Welfare of permanent residents	V Welfare by home region III + IV	VI Welfare by host region II + IV
USA	73079	0	-2956	-2956	70123
Canada	5596	0	1050	1050	6646
Mexico	0	5515	-1429	4086	-1429
UK	12641	0	851	851	13492
Germany	15994	0	2454	2454	18448
Rest of EU	36611	53525	34	53559	36645
Rest of Europe	2920	6921	631	7552	3551
Eastern Europe	-7	3745	-1404	2341	-1412
Former Soviet Union	-18	8766	-3587	5180	-3605
Australia-New Zealand	3900	0	376	376	4276
China	-54	9681	-2136	7546	-2190
Japan	25219	8131	4542	12673	29761
Rest of East Asia	-87	11402	-7475	3927	-7563
South East Asia	-621	8564	-2581	5983	-3202
India	-3	2639	16027	18666	16024
Rest of South Asia	-50	1519	350	1869	301
Brazil	-210	13400	-7253	6147	-7463
Rest of Latin America	-508	12065	-3775	8290	-4283
Middle East and Northern Africa	-3236	17296	-7504	9792	-10740
South Africa	-208	4392	82	4474	-126
Rest of World	-25	3143	-923	2220	-948
TOTAL	170932	170704	-14626	156078	156306

a. $US millions

Source: Authors' simulations

base run. The table also presents the results for each region as a "home" country (V) - permanent residents plus temporary migrants (in SNA terms a "national"concept) - and "host" country - permanent resident plus temporary workers (a "domestic" concept).

The increase in the developed countries' quotas of both skilled and unskilled temporary labour increases world welfare by an estimated $US156 billion – about 0.6% of initial income. The gain, which arises from increasing quotas by only 3% of the labour force of the developed economies, is considerable, and is around 1.5 times that expected from the liberalisation of all remaining trade restrictions ($US104 billion).

The labour exporting (or developing) economies gain most from the increase in quotas on the movement of labour (Column V in Table 4). Most of this increase is the result of higher incomes earned by the temporary migrants themselves (Column III). Despite the higher remittances received from temporary workers, the permanent residents of the developing countries generally lose as a result of the outflow of temporary migrants (Column IV): the decrease in labour endowments dramatically raises the wages of skilled workers (Column II of Table 5), but has mixed effects on unskilled wages (Column III). Real GDP (Column V) and the returns to other factors such as capital (Column IV) fall. In the few cases in which the income and welfare of permanent residents rise, India, the rest of South Asia and South Africa, they do so because increased remittances outweigh the declines in capital income. In India, remittances increase strongly by 4% of the initial level of income. This increases the demand for domestic goods because India is relatively closed, reduces the decline in production in the economy, and raises local prices, which, in turn, generates a large terms of trade gain. Real wages for both skilled and unskilled workers rise[22] (Columns II and III in Table 5). With the exception of Brazil, developing economies experience an improvement in their terms of trade (Column VI): shifting factors from developing to developed countries reduces the relative supply of developing country output and hence raises its price relative to that of the developed countries.

---

[22]There may be a case for modelling India to have a pool of unemployed unskilled workers who will become employed in India as a result of the outflow of temporary migrants. While in this case the quantity of unskilled workers would rise, the real wages of unskilled workers would remain fixed. Total earnings would rise as there would be fewer people in the informal or unproductive sectors and so the overall welfare effect would not be very different from that reported with flexible wages. This is examined in section 5.7.

temporary labour may also affect the results somewhat, so we now consider restricting mobility to 'traditional' pairs labour importing and exporting regions. Thus we relax EU and US quotas in turn (by the same amounts as previously), but restrict the sourcing to their 'traditional' labour suppliers – see Table 2.

From the perspective of both North America and the EU, taking temporary migrants only from their traditional partner countries, reduces the welfare benefits of relaxing quotas.[28] The reason is that the partner countries tend to have lower productivities than the average sending countries so that the increment to production is less.[29]

The partner countries, however, generally do better when they are the only suppliers of temporary labour. Although the gains to the temporary migrants as a whole are slightly smaller, due to their lower productivities, there are fewer partner regions to share them. The losses to the permanent residents of the traditional partner regions are greater as more skilled and unskilled labour move abroad to fill the quotas. However, overall, taking both the permanent residents and the temporary migrants into account, the home regions generally gain from the change (Table 9).

In terms of the non-partners, the welfare loses of the permanent residents are smaller than previously as they are no longer losing any labour. However, they are also missing out on the higher incomes and remittances of the temporary labour. In general, the welfare of the non-partner regions is lower than when they supply labour – although the extent of the loss depends on the level of development.

F. Quotas increased as a portion of Current Temporary Workers

So far, the shock to the quantity of temporary labour has been equal to 3% of the labour force of each labour importing region. To test how sensitive the results are

---

[28]Note that when comparing the welfare of the EU as the importing region when all regions supply temporary labour with the case where only the partners supply temporary labour (table 9) it appears as though welfare increases by more in the partner case. This is because the welfare gain in the partner case includes a big gain to temporary migrants from the Rest of Europe. If this is removed the results are consistent with the statement made above.

[29]In the case of North America, this is mainly because the outflow of workers from the EU is included in "all" but excluded from "partners". Likewise, in the case of the EU, North America is included in "all" but excluded from "partners". If these developed economies are not included in "all", productivity is still lower for "partners" in the EU, since East Asia is not a traditional partners. East Asia has very high productivity compared to the other labour exporters. In North America, the results would not be significantly different.

Table 9. Welfare[a] Results for Alternative Labour Importing and Exporting Regions

I Region	II Importing Region: European Union		III Importing Region: North America	
	Exporting Region: Partners	Exporting Region: All	Exporting Region: Partners	Exporting Region: All
Importing Region[b]	26395	17773	-355	129
Partners[c]	20421	10933	28555	17856
Non-Partners[d]	8306	5558	37107	38703
Total	55121	34265	65307	56688

a. $US millions
b. Importing region depends on experiment – In EU simulations it includes UK, Germany. In North American simulations it includes the USA and Canada.
c. Partner regions depend on experiment – EU partner regions are given in Column V of Table 2. North American partners are given in Column VII in Table 2.
d. Non-Partner regions are all regions except the importing and Partner regions – again these differ depending on the simulation.

Source: Authors' simulations

to this allocation across labour importing regions, we now allocate the same total of workers proportionately not to the labour force, but to the number of current temporaries in the database.

Overall the total benefits to the world economy were virtually unchanged, but the distribution changes quite dramatically. Thus, for example, the Rest of Europe receives a much larger increase in the labour supply than previously (1.043 million rather than 0.118 million unskilled and 0.95 million rather than 0.115 million skilled) and gains correspondingly more. Temporary labour and the home regions also appear to gain a little from moving to regions where other temporary labour were already located. Current guest workers go to those regions where wages/ productivity are highest. Hence if new temporaries are allocated pro rata to current temporaries, they have higher productivity than if they allocate according to labour force shares.

G. Endogenous supply of Unskilled labour in the Developing Countries

Finally, we examine the impact of postulating that the developing, labour-exporting, regions have surpluses of unskilled labour, which could be drawn on to replace the loss of workers due to temporary migration with no increase in real wages. The results are as expected. In those developing economies where the loss of unskilled labour formerly caused real wages to rise – e.g. India and South East

Table 10. Endogenous Supply of Unskilled Labour in Developing Countries[a]

I	II	III
Region	Welfare of Permanent Workers	Welfare of Home region
USA	-2924	-2924
Mexico	-1494	4020
UK	862	862
Germany	2490	2490
Rest of EU	110	53626
Eastern Europe	-1792	1952
Former Soviet Union	-6538	2219
China	-2281	7400
Japan	4587	12717
Rest of East Asia	-9485	1910
South East Asia	-2144	6421
India	17140	19783
Rest of South Asia	476	1995
Brazil	-8744	4650
Rest of Latin America	-4691	7370
Southern Africa	260	4653
Rest of World	-1087	2055
Total	-18636	152038

a. $US millions

Source: Authors' simulations

Asia – endogenising the labour supply leads to higher unskilled employment and aggregate incomes. As a result the welfare of permanent workers falls by less (or rises further: Table 10). In the countries where real wages fell in Table 5, the supply of unskilled labour falls further, as permanent workers join the pool of unemployed, and welfare falls. Overall the world welfare increase is slightly smaller in this case than previously.

H. Sensitivity Analysis

Finally we examine how sensitive the results are to changes in the shocks and the parameters. We analyse four cases.

First, if the shock to quotas is doubled to 6% then the gains also approximately double (Row V in Table 11). This assumes, of course, that people will want to move and that the quotas are still binding. Thus within this bound, the model is pretty linear so that scaling the above results is perfectly legitimate to get at different size shocks.

Second, we change the proportion of the wage or productivity gained by the

Table 11. Welfare[a] Results for Sensitivity Analysis

		Labour Import-ing Developed Countries	Labour Export-ing developing countries	Total	% of Standard Simulation (Row I)
I	Standard[b]	75558	80521	156078	100
II	25% of productivity gained	120931	114614	235545	151
III	75% of productivity gained	30128	46237	76365	49
IV	% of current temporaries	85407	72330	157738	101
V	6% shock	138921	168356	307278	197
VI	Trade Liberalisation	45052	59241	104293	67

a. $US millions
b. Shock is equal to 3% of labour and assumes temporary workers gain 50% of host regions productivity.

Source: Authors' simulations

temporary labour (b in Equation 3). Currently we assume that 50% of the difference between the productivity of a host worker and the average productivity of a temporary migrant is made up by the temporary worker when working in the host region. Now we change this to 25% and 75%. An increase in â increases global welfare (Row II in Table 11) because we have higher world output. The increase is felt by both the developed and developing economies. Developed (or labour importing) economies gain because labour is more productive when it enters the region. As a result the effective labour-force and production are higher, and labour costs are lower. The return on capital rises further and the output and welfare of the host region rises. Temporary labour also gains as a result of gaining more productivity and hence receiving higher wages.

The developing (labour exporting) countries can be split into two groups – those with significant skilled-labour intensive production and those which rely more on unskilled workers. The higher incomes in the developed economies due to the higher productivity lead to higher demand for developing countries exports, and the higher remittances cause developing countries' domestic demand to increase as well. However, because developed country output has increased so strongly, these increases in demand are satisfied through increased imports, so output falls and the wages of unskilled and skilled labour rise by less than previously. In the unskilled labour intensive regions, higher remittances off-set the relatively modest production falls and income and welfare are higher. In regions that use skilled labour more intensively, and hence whose output bundles are closer to those of the